Applied Microeconometrics

Damian Clarke

The MIT Press
Cambridge, Massachusetts
London, England

The MIT Press
Massachusetts Institute of Technology
77 Massachusetts Avenue
Cambridge, MA 02139
mitpress.mit.edu

The MIT Press would like to thank the anonymous peer reviewers who provided comments on drafts of this book. The generous work of academic experts is essential for establishing the authority and quality of our publications. We acknowledge with gratitude the contributions of these otherwise uncredited readers.

This book was set in Times New Roman by Westchester Publishing Services. Printed and bound in the United States of America.

Library of Congress Cataloging-in-Publication Data

Names: Clarke, Damian author
Title: Applied microeconometrics / Damian Clarke.
Description: Cambridge, Massachusetts : The MIT Press, [2026] | Includes bibliographical references and index.
Identifiers: LCCN 2025032219 (print) | LCCN 2025032220 (ebook) | ISBN 9780262053648 paperback | ISBN 9780262053655 pdf | ISBN 9780262053662 epub
Subjects: LCSH: Econometrics | Microeconomics—Econometric models
Classification: LCC HB139 .C53 2026 (print) | LCC HB139 (ebook)
LC record available at https://lccn.loc.gov/2025032219
LC ebook record available at https://lccn.loc.gov/2025032220

10 9 8 7 6 5 4 3 2 1

EU Authorised Representative: Easy Access System Europe, Mustamäe tee 50, 10621 Tallinn, Estonia | Email: gpsr.requests@easproject.com

Applied Microeconometrics

To my family: Cristina, Emi, and Oli for bringing me great joy and happiness, and my parents and siblings for their endless support and love.

Contents

Preface

This book discusses the theory and practice of applied microeconometrics. In particular, the book aims to provide an overview of microeconometric methods frequently used for causal inference in applied research. Throughout the book, we will examine the range of tools that an applied microeconometrician, or any social scientist using quantitative methods with micro-level data, needs in their tool kit. This includes experimental methods, as well as observational methods such as difference-in-differences designs, regression discontinuity designs, instrumental variable methods, and machine learning–based causal methods, among other themes.

The book is targeted at a graduate level and assumes some familiarity with econometrics, including tools from statistics and linear algebra. Nevertheless, the book builds up the methods discussed from first principles, laying out key assumptions for causal analysis and a range of considerations that an applied researcher will need to know. In this sense, the book seeks to serve practitioners of microeconometrics and social scientists generally. It thus may suit a range of readers who seek a rigorous treatment of causal methods, including master's (or very advanced undergraduate) students, PhD students, and researchers who may be well out of graduate school and seeking an up-to-date compendium on the practice of applied microeconometrics.

This book can serve as a reference manual, but it can also be structured around a one- or two-semester sequence in applied microeconometrics. While chapters 1 and 2 provide the foundation of later chapters and should be covered in any course, chapters 3–6 could be considered in a different order in a course without losing too much flow. In a one-semester course, covering the entire book may be a stretch, though certain later chapters that cover slightly more advanced themes could be left for further reading. In a two-semester course, readers could delve into this book in a much deeper way, in particular making the most of a range of the applied materials and coding resource discussed below. Throughout this book, there is substantial leeway to work with real data; among questions and the applied coding examples, data from fifty-one papers have been provided in a ready-to-use fashion. These data are based on real studies conducted over the past three decades, including classic empirical papers focused on causal methods, as well as recently published papers from a range of highly visible journals in economics. In a two-course sequence, these materials could be used at length, along with introductions to a chosen computer language among those introduced in the website the accompanies this text.

Using This Book

This book aims to cover the requisite theory while also delving into the applied considerations relevant for research. I believe that the best way to learn this in practice is to explore real papers and data, and for this reason, an accompanying series of examples from real papers is provided as an online resource that can be freely consulted with the book. This website is available here: https://www.damianclarke.net/books/microeconometrics

Apart from applied examples, this site also provides a full discussion of how one can get up and running with the methods discussed in this book in multiple statistical languages. This includes a primer on each language, discussing the necessary elements to implement the estimators and methods explored in this book. At the time of the printing of this book, this site provides a full set of resources in Python, R, and Stata. These languages are covered due to their widespread use in applied microeconometrics, and given that all of the tools discussed in this book are available in each of these languages. These are also languages with active development communities, such that new econometric methods, including many recent methods discussed in this book, are quickly incorporated into the code base.

At times, more elaborate empirical or simulated examples to support the methods discussed in the book are provided on this site. In particular, these are included as highlighted code callouts in each chapter. These are all provided in each of the languages discussed above in the accompanying website.

While the book is a stand-alone text focused on the central elements of applied microeconometrics, it assumes that readers have taken previous econometrics courses and are comfortable with econometric theory typically taught in the first year of a masters program. Thus, this book should not be viewed as a substitute for such foundational econometrics texts. For this reason, at the end of each chapter, a short set of key texts are mentioned that both provide further historical context to the methods discussed in each chapter, as well as further reading on any key points that are likely covered in typical textbooks covering econometric theory.

End-of-chapter exercises typically require the use of data from real papers. All datasets required are available as csv and dta files on the book website. For a discussion of exactly how to download data directly into the language you are using, refer to the data section of the website at https://www.damianclarke.net/books/microeconometrics/data.

Acknowledgments

I have a debt of gratitude to many people who have directly or indirectly helped in the preparation of this book. This book originally began as a series of lecture notes and has gained considerably from iterations over multiple academic years at the University of Oxford, The University of Santiago de Chile, and the University of Chile. I am grateful to the students and teaching assistants who have participated in these courses—in particular, María Fernanda Castillo Faúndez, Nicolás Leiva Díaz, Nicolás Bastías Campos, Francine Montecinos Puente, Carla Quitral Monardes, and Catalina San Martín Rodríguez who have been instrumental in setting up applied examples and online resources, and Kathya Tapia Schythe, Daniel Pailañir, and Marcelo Gómez Ramírez, who provided useful input and feedback in earlier versions of this book. Many students have raised illuminating questions that have improved this book across its earlier iterations as teaching notes and made the process of developing this text a far richer experience. Thank you to my past students. In particular, I am grateful to master's students at the University of Chile and the University of Santiago de Chile who have cast careful and inquisitive eyes over this project in earlier stages.

The themes I discuss in this book have been shaped by my own econometric formation, studying under a number of professors who have been influential in the way I view these problems. In particular, these include Eduardo Fajnzylber, Andrea Repetto, Nicolas Van de Sijpe, Simon Quinn, Sonia Bhalotra, Andrew Zeitlin, Steve Bond, and Michael Keane.

I have gained considerably from my coauthors, with whom frequent collaborations and research discussions have been instrumental in the adoption of the methods discussed here in my work in practice. In particular, I am grateful to Sonia Bhalotra, my constant coauthor and friend, who I have worked with from the early days of my graduate training and who has been influential in my career. I have also gained substantially, both personally and professionally from collaborations with many other coauthors including Atheendar Venkataramani, Andrea Bentancor, Benjamín Matta, Sonia Oreffice, Climent Quintana-Domeque, Hanna Mühlrad, Kathya Tapia Schythe, Daniel Pailañir, Joseph Gomes, Pilar Larroulet, Francisco Pino, Nicolás Paris Torres, Rudi Rocha, Michel Szklo, Nicolás Lillo Bustos, and Viviana Salinas. This is only a partial list, as I owe considerably to all my coauthors and collaborators, including many not listed here but who have worked with me on the themes discussed in the pages of this book.

A number of colleagues and friends have provided feedback related to this book. In particular I thank Alejandro Robinson-Cortes, Simon Quinn, Climent Quintana-Domeque, and Rudi Rocha for deep comments and suggestions after reading draft versions of the book, and thank Sam Engle, Felipe González, Jaime Ruíz-Tagle, Pablo Muñoz, and Stephane Hliami for conversations, feedback, and encouragement.

I do not wish to implicate any of the previously mentioned people in any shortcomings of this book. Any errors in these pages are my own, while the useful portions of this book owe in large part to the people who have supported me throughout my career as an applied econometrician.

I am grateful to the Millennium Institute for Labour Market Imperfections and Public Policy, funded by Chile's Agencia Nacional de Investigación y Desarrollo for supporting my work for a number of years, and in particular providing support during the writing of this book. I also wish to acknowledge FEN University of Chile, which has supported the writing of this book.

This work has been written nearly entirely on free software. Thanks in particular to developers and maintainers of Ubuntu, Python, R, TeX/XeTeX, Quarto, and emacs, as well as many statistical and scientific libraries that exist within these languages.

Finally, the deepest thanks are to my family who have motivated me and supported me constantly. Without them, this would not have come to fruition.

D.C.
2025

1

Identifying Causal Effects

> I saw my life branching out before me like the green fig tree ... From the tip of every branch, like a fat purple fig, a wonderful future beckoned and winked.
>
> —Silvia Plath, *The Bell Jar*

1.1 Introduction

What shapes human well-being? Do more engaged teachers increase children's learning? Do minimum wage hikes reduce employment? Does democracy cause growth? The study of economics is the study of human behavior, and in practice, many of the questions we wish to answer are related to causal effects. This book describes how causal methods are employed in economics, and more broadly within the social sciences, to answer questions such as these.

One thing that distinguishes economics from other fields interested in causal methods, such as physics or medicine, is that a considerable proportion of the phenomena whose causal effect we wish to isolate may not be easily manipulable by researchers. For example, consider variables such as exposure to changing climates or extreme weather events, whether a country adopts a democratic regime, or the total amount of schooling an individual accrues during their life. These variables are of major relevance to economic policy, but there is no way for these to be precisely manipulated by researchers in a laboratory. At the same time, there are many creative studies that *have* experimentally manipulated variables that are of first-order importance for policies, ranging from settings as broad as race and labor market outcomes (Bertrand and Mullainathan 2004) to the national-level application of conditional cash transfers (Schultz 2004). The breadth of phenomena under study, and the need to interact with both observational and experimental settings, points to the importance of having a clearly defined framework of causal analysis.

The importance of questions of causality has been reflected in at least two recent Nobel Memorial Prizes in Economics. In 2019, Abhijit Banerjee, Esther Duflo, and Michael Kremer were awarded this prize for applying experimental methods to questions related to global poverty, and in 2021 the work of Joshua Angrist and Guido Imbens, who were awarded the prize alongside David Card, was explicitly highlighted for its "methodological contributions to the analysis of causal relationships." These are unlikely to be the last Nobel Prizes in this vein. However, beyond these specific themes elevated by the Nobel committee, work on causality is seen in fundamental questions in all fields of economic endeavor where microeconometric methods are used. To consider a number of emblematic examples that employ methods we will discuss throughout this book, Miguel and Kremer (2004) and Baird et al. (2016) consider the causal effect of deworming treatments on child well-being in the short and long term, Dell (2015) studies how a government's decision to fight drug crime can fuel large-scale violence, LaLonde (1986) and Dehejia and Wahba (1999) wish to isolate the impacts of labor training programs on subsequent earnings, Dobbie, Goldin, and Yang (2018) seek to isolate the effect of pretrial detention on conviction and future crime, and Acemoglu, Johnson, and Robinson (2001) and Chernozhukov et al. (2018) tackle the question of whether institutions affect economic output in the long run. These are of course just a select few examples. Indeed, if you open up a recent issue of one of your favorite economics journals, it is exceedingly likely that empirical findings purporting to isolate causal effects of *some variable* on *some other variable* will be reported. And the confluence of improved computational tools, considerable advances in microeconometric methods, and a massive increase in data collection and availability has meant that these methods are growing in importance across analyses in microeconomics as documented by Currie, Kleven, and Zwiers (2020).

What's more, these questions are of importance not only for the way we understand human behavior but also for the way policies are designed and the way the world is run. Organizations such as J-PAL, an academic center focused on poverty alleviation, work to map evidence into policy changes, seeking to both evaluate policy and scale up successful programs. Many governments have their own policy analysis units and interact closely with academic research. Private companies are increasingly incorporating causal tools into their product design and workflow—for example, using A/B testing to compare between potential features in products.

In this chapter we will lay out a general framework for considering causality that is widely adopted in economics, given its flexibility to interact with the range of settings in which causal effects are of interest. This chapter will be entirely focused on outlining this theory and key assumptions and definitions that will be required throughout the rest of the book, while the remaining chapters will refer back to this theory when relevant in discussing how to estimate effects in practical settings.

1.2 A Framework for Causal Analysis

In the early days of studies of causality in observational settings, the pioneers developed a robust and flexible framework for thinking about causal relationships. The workhorse framework for causal analysis in microeconometrics is the so-called Rubin Causal Model

(RCM). At its heart, this model is relatively simple, but as we will see throughout this book, it provides a powerful way to help us think about causality across a very broad range of observational and experimental settings.

The RCM breaks down our understanding of causality into two separate parts. A first part of the model is the *potential outcome* framework, which provides us with a way to think about causal effects. And a second part is an *assignment mechanism*, which describes how treatments are assigned to units, and the nature of the "experiment" or event that generated the data with which we work. We will examine these two parts in turn.

1.2.1 Potential Outcomes

The first part of the RCM is the potential outcome framework. The most primitive elements we require to begin defining causal effects are three: units, treatments, and potential outcomes. Units refer to physical objects, such as individuals or firms, at a specific point in time. A treatment refers to some action or manipulation that can be applied to or withheld from units. And potential outcomes refers to some theoretical measure of interest for each unit under alternative states of treatment.

To provide some notation to describe this, we will define W_i as a random variable for each individual i that takes a value of 1 if unit i receives some particular treatment of interest, and 0 if they do not. You will note here that we are working with a binary measure of treatment, and throughout much of this book we will focus on the binary treatment setting given its practical importance. However, it is worth highlighting that this notation can be expanded to consider multivalued treatments, as we lay out in section 1.3.2. While often $W_i = 1$ is assumed to imply some particular active version of treatment and $W_i = 0$ is assumed to represent some control condition where treatment is not assigned, this setting can also house alternative situations, such as individuals exposed to two alternative treatment regimes.

Depending on the phenomenon under study, we will be interested in some particular outcome, which we will denote as Y_i. The logic of the potential outcomes framework is that each individual i will have two potential outcomes. These outcomes are denoted using random variables $Y_i(1)$: the outcome for individual i should they receive treatment, and $Y_i(0)$: their outcome should they not receive treatment. You will note that this definition simply refers to the two possible states of the world for individual i, and refers to outcomes *that could* eventually be observed if an individual were exposed to a particular treatment regime. We are not yet discussing the outcomes that are *actually* observed, but rather simply defining, at an individual level, a theoretical quantity under the two potential treatment states, regardless of which treatment state is eventually assigned. Throughout this book we will adopt this notation of $Y_i(0)$ and $Y_i(1)$ to refer to potential outcomes, though you may also see this written in varying ways in the literature, such as Y_{i0} and Y_{i1}.

These potential outcomes are very useful, because they allow us to formally define what we mean by a causal effect. A causal effect of treatment for an individual i is simply defined as the following quantity:

$$\tau_i = Y_i(1) - Y_i(0). \tag{1.1}$$

This quantity τ_i is a theoretical object of interest for us. If we were able to observe it, it would tell us for any particular individual what was the effect of having received treatment W_i instead of the control condition. This is our definition of a causal effect, and it would be a remarkably useful quantity to be able to isolate if we were able to observe it for every individual.

While this setting likely feels very broad, you may note that we are already placing some limits on what we can consider as a causal effect. Specifically, we are requiring that the states of the world are able to differ. Making causal statements requires that the treatment is *able* to be manipulated. This is expressed by Holland (1986, 959) with the motto that he also attributes to Rubin of "No causation without manipulation" (indeed, a similar though less pithy statement of this is provided in Rubin [1978, 38]). What this aims to make clear is that if some characteristic cannot be manipulated in the sense that an individual could not—in theory—be observed in two states of the world, then it is not correct to talk about this characteristic being a cause.

While this may seem like it could substantially limit the factors we can consider as treatments, creativity in the design of manipulations, including work in both the lab and field, has meant that often phenomena that at first glance may appear to be outside of the scope of causal analysis are now widely viewed as questions that can be cast in causal terms. To see one illustrative example, consider the "manipulation" of individual characteristics such as gender or race and their impact on labor market outcomes like job offers. Such individual characteristics are not obviously manipulable, at least in the way that is feasible in an economic study on labor market outcomes. However, if focus is slightly changed from manipulating individual characteristics to manipulating responses to questions on job application forms, it becomes apparent that questions of this scope could absolutely be considered in a causal fashion.[1] Such questions have been taken up in a number of influential papers where race, gender, or other factors such as ethnicity are manipulated on résumés holding other factors constant (Bertrand and Mullainathan 2004; Neumark 2018). These studies, known as correspondence studies or audit studies, are examples of cases where the "no causation without manipulation" lemma can be respected in an empirical design, despite the fact that the underlying factor of interest is not easily manipulable.

While (1.1) provides us with our formal definition of a causal effect, this does not imply that we can simply *estimate* a causal effect in this way. Indeed, in looking at (1.1) and thinking about the potential outcome framework, we come across a problem. This problem is that at any point in time, only one of these potential outcomes will actually be observed. We now define as Y_i the observed realization of the outcome for unit i. Ex post, observed Y_i will be:

$$Y_i = \begin{cases} Y_i(1), & \text{if } W_i = 1 \\ Y_i(0), & \text{if } W_i = 0. \end{cases} \tag{1.2}$$

At this point it is worth explicitly making note that both of these outcomes together will never exist for a given i. If an individual is assigned to treatment, we observe $Y_i(1)$, which precludes us from observing the counterfactual state $Y_i(0)$. Conversely, if an individual is not assigned to treatment, we will never observe the counterfactual state in which the same unit has received treatment. The mechanics of translating potential outcomes into observed data can also be seen via the following "switching" equation:

$$Y_i = Y_i(0) + (Y_i(1) - Y_i(0))\, W_i. \tag{1.3}$$

When treatment "switches on," $W_i = 1$, and the realization of $Y_i = Y_i(1)$. But when treatment is "switched off," $W_i = 0$, and the realization of $Y_i = Y_i(0)$. This is what Holland (1986) calls the "fundamental problem of causal inference": For the individuals whom we observe under treatment, we have to form an estimate of what they would have looked like if they had not been treated. This is a point that we will discuss in theory in section 1.4, and then in a more practical way for the rest of this book.

1.2.2 The Assignment Mechanism

Thus, while the potential outcomes portion of the RCM allows us to define a theoretical causal effect, we do not yet have the mechanics worked out about how to isolate this effect from data we actually observe in the real world. For this, we must understand the assignment mechanism. Simply stated, the assignment mechanism describes how treatment is assigned in terms of both potential outcomes, as well as covariates. Unlike the potential outcomes framework, which is based on a theoretical construct, the assignment mechanism is actually a probabilistic model of how treatment is assigned.

That assignment may depend on potential outcomes themselves was a point first noted in Rubin (1975). Following the notation defined previously, and using X_i and ε_i to define observed covariates and unobserved factors, in general we have that the assignment mechanism can be represented as follows:

$$W_i = f\,(X_i, Y_i(1), Y_i(0), \varepsilon_i), \tag{1.4}$$

where $f(\cdot)$ is the function that describes how treatment is assigned (the "assignment mechanism"). The fact that the assignment mechanism *may* depend on observable characteristics does not mean that it *must* do so. Assignment mechanisms can be features of an experimental design: For example, individuals could be randomly assigned to one treatment or another by us as researchers, in which case, by virtue of randomization, there would be no relationship between treatment and observable characteristics or potential outcomes. Alternatively the assignment mechanism may be a more complicated economic or political decision-making process. For example, if individuals are freely allowed to determine whether they sort in to some treatment, we would expect that they should precisely consider their potential outcomes when deciding whether to opt into treatment or not. We also may sometimes have a mixture of the two—for example, when we have a randomized controlled trial (RCT) but where individuals can opt out of receiving treatment (i.e., an RCT with imperfect compliance).

Another way to look at this is as in Rubin (1974), where he describes causal inference as a missing data problem. Our challenge is in imputing what would have happened to the treated unit had they not received treatment, and the assignment mechanism describes the missing data mechanism: Which observations are missing data on what would have happened had they *received* treatment, and which observations are missing data on what would have happened had they *not* received treatment? This view of the assignment mechanism as a missing data mechanism is useful, as it allows us to think about potential selection into or selection out of treatment. As we will see throughout the rest of this book, the appropriateness of alternative estimators will hinge crucially on whether our assumptions related to the assignment mechanism are correct. For example, if we assume that a treatment is randomly assigned, where instead there is some sort of nonrandom selection into treatment, our estimates of the impact of receiving treatment will presumably be biased given that we will assume that apart from treatment, all else will be equal between treated and untreated units. A similar conception is provided by Heckman and Vytlacil (2007), who seek to carefully separate the "the evaluation problem" (the fundamental problem of causal inference) and the "selection problem," which refers to the fact that the assignment mechanism may depend on individual choice to select into or out of treatment.

1.3 Treatment Assignment and the Stable Unit Treatment Value Assumption

Inherent in the idea of an assignment mechanism is the assumption that a unit is effectively assigned to either treatment or control status. It turns out that we need to be quite careful with what we mean about this, and it is important to formalize the details of treatment assignment and think about some potential issues that may crop up regardless of the empirical setting examined.

1.3.1 SUTVA

A key assumption that we will employ throughout this book (unless otherwise indicated), and which is generally applied either explicitly or implicitly in papers, is the stable unit treatment value assumption. This assumption, typically referred to as SUTVA, was first defined in Rubin (1980b) and formalized in Rubin (1986). Formally, the SUTVA can be stated as follows:

Assumption 1. Stable Unit Treatment Value Assumption (SUTVA)

(A) The potential outcomes $Y_i(0), Y_i(1)$ for any unit i are independent of W_j, $\forall j \neq i$, namely:

$$Y_i(W_i, \boldsymbol{W}_{-i}) = Y_i(W_i)$$

for all possible values of $\boldsymbol{W}_{-i}$, where $\boldsymbol{W}_{-i}$ refers to the vector of treatment assignments for all units apart from i.

(B) The potential outcomes are the same no matter what mechanism is used to assign treatment to unit i.

This assumption then nests two subcomponents, each of which places certain limits on the nature of treatment.

The first consideration, labeled (A) above, is that there can be no interference between units: An individual responds to their own treatment status, W_i, but the treatment assignment of other individuals, $\boldsymbol{W}_{-i}$, has no bearing on what happens to individual i, and hence can be omitted from the potential outcome.[2] This rules out situations that may be empirically relevant in certain settings. Most importantly, this no-interference condition in SUTVA requires a number of circumstances to hold. Firstly, it requires that there are no externalities from treatment—that is, no benefits or costs from treatment spillover from treated units to control units, or from one treated unit to another. When treatment is localized to units that are quite geographically or otherwise disperse, this assumption is likely to be reasonable, but when units are exposed to other treated and untreated units in close proximity, this may be questionable in certain settings. For example, consider the case of vaccination campaigns. Part of the goal of vaccination is to induce a response of herd immunity, where the fact that some other individuals are vaccinated makes it less likely that any particular individual will be exposed to a disease, and hence there are gains from direct spillovers, implying SUTVA would be violated.[3] Secondly, the no-interference condition implies that there must not be general equilibrium effects of the policy. General equilibrium effects refer to cases where the impact of the policy itself at the micro level in aggregate is large enough to generate macro-level impacts, which potentially reinforce or crowd out micro-level impacts. One such example is discussed by Heckman, Lochner, and Taber (1998). They note that a large subsidy program for university tuition—while likely raising wages for individuals who go to university—would alter the productive structure of the economy. If many more individuals begin attending higher education, the wage premium for higher education would go down, which is an example of a general equilibrium effect. This is at odds with the partial equilibrium effect of a tuition policy, which is the effect maintaining all else constant.

Beyond this no-interference element of SUTVA, there is a second element, labeled as (B) in assumption 1. This part of the assumption requires that there are no hidden or "unrepresented" (Rubin 1986) versions of treatment. It refers to the fact that there must be a single type of treatment, and no matter how treatment is assigned, the same potential outcome will be observed. If, on the other hand, there are actually different versions of treatment (for example, a high-dose and a low-dose response), this assumption will not be met. Other situations in which we may be concerned that this second element of SUTVA is violated is if there is a single type treatment, but the treatment is delivered by more or less efficient providers such that there is "hidden variation" in treatment. If we are concerned that such violations exist in practice, treatment will likely need to be either redefined into a more general definition or the problem will need to be restated as a multivalued treatment (refer to section 1.3.2).

Failures of SUTVA When SUTVA fails, there are a number of ways in which we may proceed. A first typical response is to change the unit of analysis, so as to internalize the externality. For example, if we are concerned that spillovers or treatment externalities may occur, but that these spillovers only occur locally, we may wish to aggregate our treatment up to a higher level. For example, if we are interested in assessing some educational policy but are concerned that there may be interactions among students in a classroom, we may wish to randomize treatment at the level of the classroom rather than the student; see, for example, Chetty et al. (2011) for an analysis of a classroom-level treatment. Similarly, if we are concerned that spillovers may occur more broadly, we may wish to consider treatments assigned at the level of villages or communities; see, for example, Schultz (2004) for an analysis of Mexico's PROGRESA conditional cash transfer program targeted at the community level. A second option where SUTVA fails is to seek to estimate the externalities directly. For example, we may consider that there are some units that can act as pure controls, others that are directly treated, and others that are potentially exposed to some treatment spillovers. See in particular Miguel and Kremer (2004) for a paper that grapples with such externalities. Further discussions related to SUTVA and policy evaluation are available in Angelucci and Di Maro (2016). Unless otherwise specified, throughout this book we will assume that SUTVA holds, and we provide a complete discussion of loosening this assumption in chapter 8.

1.3.2 More on Treatment

1.3.2.1 Multivalued treatments In certain circumstances, rather than being binary in nature, a treatment may be multivalued or even continuous. For example, rather than considering treated and untreated units, we may wish to consider treatments of both high and low intensity, as well as an untreated control. In cases such as these, the effects of treatment can be thought of as a dose, and the resulting impacts as giving a dose response function, where we wish to determine what will be the impact of receiving a higher dose of treatment compared with a lower dose of treatment.

In cases where we wish to house potentially multiple treatment levels, we can slightly generalize the notation from the potential outcomes laid out in section 1.2.1. To do this, we define a set of potential outcomes $Y_i(t)$ for $t \in \mathcal{T}$. Up to this point, we have considered $\mathcal{T} = \{0, 1\}$ as the standard binary treatment setup. However we may also be interested in cases where treatment can be multivalued: $\mathcal{T} = \{0, 1, \ldots, K\}$, as laid out in Imbens (2000) or even continuous, which is implemented as $\mathcal{T} \in [t_0, t_1]$ in Hirano and Imbens (2004). Note in this case that whereas previously we had two potential outcomes and we only observed one of these, now we will have multiple potential outcomes (and we observe only one), where observed Y_i is simply the potential outcome for each individual in their realized treatment assignment: $Y_i \equiv Y_i(T_i)$.

For the time being, we will note that extending the workings of the RCM is not necessarily notationally challenging as we can see here, but additional complications are likely to arise when we wish to quantify the effect of exposure to varying treatments. The degree of complexity will depend on how the assignment mechanism operates, and throughout the rest of the book, while principally focusing on binary treatments as a workhorse case, we will provide some consideration of multivalued treatments where relevant, including formal definitions of quantities of interest in section 1.4 below.

1.3.2.2 The nomenclature of treatment The language of the RCM lends itself to thinking about a particular "treatment," where assignment refers to the receipt of treatment. Often, this will gel perfectly with the particular setting we are interested in studying. For example, in a randomized control trial, often one group of individuals will be assigned a particular treatment of interest. Such cases include assignment to receive vocational training receipt (Attanasio, Kugler, and Meghir 2011), or even cases where treatment refers to some medical treatment (Miguel and Kremer 2004). In these settings it is easy to see that treatment is an active state, and this will be compared to a passive state in which treatment is not received or where only some sort of placebo treatment is assigned. In such cases where there is clearly a treated and an untreated group, the term "control" is often used to refer to the untreated group. However, at other times it is not necessarily true that one group will receive an active treatment and another will be in a passive control group. For example, we may wish to compare between two states, such as entering one profession rather than another, or opting to continue with studies versus entering the labor market. In such cases, what is important is that we are clear that we are considering two potential outcomes, and our "treatment effect" will refer to the impact of having been assigned to one group rather than another.

1.3.2.3 Undesired effects of treatment assignment: John Henry effects, Hawthorne effects, and experimenter demand While not explicitly built into SUTVA, the importance of effects and one's *own* treatment status is something that we will want to think carefully about when considering the scope of results. Both John Henry effects and Hawthorne effects will lead to a situation where we may assign to the treatment an effect that is not actually due to the substance of the treatment, but rather due to the assignment of treatment and control *status* itself. Hawthorne effects, also known as placebo effects, refer to the case where individuals simply respond to receiving a treatment, regardless of what the treatment may be. The converse of Hawthorne effects are John Henry effects. John Henry effects refer to cases where individuals respond to the fact that they are assigned to the status of control group. Both situations are named for circumstances in which such effects are popularly believed to have occurred, one for research occurring in the early twentieth century at the Hawthorne Western Electric plant in Illinois and the other the legendary railroad steel-driver John Henry, who worked on the US railroads in the late nineteenth century. In the case of Hawthorne Electric, a number of studies were conducted where levels of illumination were changed in the plant, and worker output was observed. The popular narrative (though refer to Levitt and List [2011] for a reexamination) is that when light levels were varied, productivity increased, even when illumination returned to original levels. What's more, productivity was observed to decline when individuals were no longer study participants. This led to the conclusion that workers were actually responding to the fact that they were being studied, rather than to the particular inputs being varied. And in the case of John Henry effects, the narrative (see Saretsky [1972]) is that when steam drills were experimentally introduced to potentially replace human steel drivers in the construction of railroads, the steel driver John Henry worked with such intensity that, while he was more effective than the steam drill, he died of overexhaustion, suggesting that he altered his behavior as a response to being the "control" in the study of the steam drill. In both cases, it is important to note that if such patterns occur, this will confound the true impact of the underlying treatment of interest.

Related concerns exist if data collection occurs in a way that makes experimental subjects believe that they are expected to behave in certain ways, which are different to the way they would behave if they were not being studied. For example, individuals may respond to a treatment in the way they believe researchers would like, a situation known as experimenter demand effects, or may generally present themselves in data in a way they believe is expected, a situation known as social desirability bias. While lab evidence suggests that experimenter demand effects may be limited (Quidt, Haushofer, and Roth 2018) evidence shows that individuals respond to enumerator characteristics (see for example Cilliers, Dube, and Siddiqi [2015]). A range of actions that can be taken to potentially minimize such effects have been proposed as discussed in Dupas and Miguel (2017) and Zizzo (2010), among others.

1.4 Estimands of Interest

1.4.1 Average Causal Effects

You will note in equation 1.1 that the RCM refers to individual-level causal effects, but given that we always have one missing counterfactual outcome to infer, estimation of treatment effects can *only* occur based on grouped data. While it is not possible to observe information on treated and untreated potential outcomes for a single observation, it *is* possible to observe averages over treated and untreated units within groups, and, depending on assumptions related to the assignment mechanism, these quantities may be useful to allow us to estimate the impact of treatment at a group level. However, when moving from individual- to group-level data, there are a number of possible treatment effects that may interest us.

In the general framework laid out so far, we have not assumed that potential outcomes $(Y_i(0), Y_i(1))$ are the same across all individuals, or even that the *difference* between the potential outcomes is constant across individuals. In practice, the impact of exposure to some treatment may be highly heterogeneous across individuals, which opens up a range of potential quantities that may be of interest.

The two most frequently reported quantities of interest are the average treatment effect (or ATE) and the average treatment effect on the treated (ATT, at times also referred to as ATET). These quantities are defined as follows:

$$\tau_{\text{ATE}} = \mathbb{E}[Y_i(1) - Y_i(0)], \tag{1.5}$$

for the ATE, and:

$$\tau_{\text{ATT}} = \mathbb{E}[Y_i(1) - Y_i(0) | W_i = 1] \tag{1.6}$$

for the ATT. The first of these, the ATE, represents the average improvement that would be experienced by all members of the population under study, if they were all treated. The ATT, on the other hand, is the average treatment effect *actually experienced* in the sub-population of those who received treatment. Depending on the setting we are considering, the statistic we will be interested in will likely vary. For example, if we are interested in assessing the impact of a targeted antipoverty program, it seems unlikely that we would be interested in the ATE in the whole population, many of whom are not eligible for the program, and would likely prefer the ATT. On the other hand, if we were aiming to assess the impact of a program that is planned to roll out to the whole population over time, the ATE is precisely what we would like to know. Except in particular circumstances, the ATE and the ATT will generally not be the same. To see why this is the case, consider analyzing the effect of obtaining secondary schooling on subsequent income. The returns to secondary schooling will vary by individual: Those with greater natural ability or connections in the labor market may be better placed to benefit from additional schooling. If it is also the case that those who end up receiving schooling are those with higher returns, then the ATT will be greater than the ATE. Such concerns are central to the "*scaling up*" of successful interventions: If the ATT and the ATE differ, then intervening to obtain complete coverage may not yield the expected results.

It is also important to note the difference between the ATE and the ATT in a practical sense. If we wish to isolate an ATE, we must infer a counterfactual untreated state for each treated unit *and* a counterfactual treated state for each untreated unit. That is, for the entire population, we must infer the counterfactual outcome. However, if we wish to isolate an ATT, we only need to infer the counterfactual (untreated) outcome for each treated unit, as we are simply concerned about average effects on the treated. The fact that the ATE "requires more" than the ATT can be seen by rewriting the ATE from (1.5) in terms of the ATT in (1.6):

$$\tau_{\text{ATE}} = \mathbb{E}[Y_i(1) - Y_i(0) | W_i = 1] \cdot \Pr(W_i = 1) + \mathbb{E}[Y_i(1) - Y_i(0) | W_i = 0] \cdot \Pr(W_i = 0). \tag{1.7}$$

In the above we clearly see that the first quantity in the ATE *is* the ATT, along with additional quantities, namely the probability of treatment receipt, and another treatment effect.

In comparing (1.7) to (1.6), it is thus clear that arriving to an ATE requires information (and most likely) assumptions that are not required to arrive to an ATT.

While the ATE and ATT are the most frequently encountered quantities of interest, and are likely what we wish to estimate in many cases, we may certainly be interested in other alternatives. A counterpart to the ATT is the ATU, or average treatment effect on the untreated, which it turns out is the second component of our ATE defined in (1.7). This is defined exactly like the ATT, however in this case for the *un*treated:

$$\tau_{\text{ATU}} = \mathbb{E}[Y_i(1) - Y_i(0) | W_i = 0], \tag{1.8}$$

implying that we must seek the treated counterfactual ($Y_i(1)$) for all untreated individuals. What's more, treatment effects of interest need not stratify only on an individual's treatment status. We may also be interested in how these effects vary over some other covariate of interest. In this case, we will be interested in a conditional average treatment effect (CATE), as defined below:

$$\tau(x) \equiv \mathbb{E}[Y_i(1) - Y_i(0) | X_i = x], \tag{1.9}$$

where we use $\tau(x)$ to note the dependence of the treatment effect on a particular realization of covariates. Such treatment effects may be of interest if we believe our treatment is likely to be particularly efficacious for certain groups, or if we are concerned about particular distributional implications of policies.

You may note that all the above treatment effects assume a binary treatment, implying that for a particular type of effect, we can speak of one average treatment effect. In the case of multivalued treatments, there are potentially multiple shifts we may be interested in considering. The shifts can be summarized from the mean dose response function, $\mu_t = \mathbb{E}[Y_i(t)]$, also sometimes known as the average structural function (Cattaneo 2018). While we may wish to estimate a dose response function directly, we may also wish to estimate particular treatment effects of interest that describe shifts across doses of treatment. For example, Lechner (2001) defines a number of treatment effects of interest, such as the effect of moving from (arbitrarily chosen) treatment level l to (arbitrarily chosen) treatment level m, for particular groups of the population:

$$\tau^{m,l}_{\text{ATE}} \equiv \mathbb{E}[Y_i(m) - Y_i(l)], \tag{1.10}$$

$$\tau^{m,l}_{\text{ATT}_m} \equiv \mathbb{E}[Y_i(m) - Y_i(l) | W_i = m], \tag{1.11}$$

$$\tau^{m,l}_{\text{ATU}_l} \equiv \mathbb{E}[Y_i(m) - Y_i(l) | W_i = l]. \tag{1.12}$$

Here superscript m, l terms on treatment effects refer to movements at these particular treatment margins, while the definition of these effects as ATE (1.10), ATT_m (1.11), or ATU_l (1.12) refers to the fact that these are isolated to particular groups, as in the case of the binary measures laid out above. In the case of the ATE, we are interested in impacts should we be able to move the entire population from l to m; in the case of the ATT, we are interested in impacts of moving only those particular individuals who received treatment dose m; and in the case of ATU_l, we are interested in what would happen if individuals who received treatment dose l but were not treated by treatment m were now exposed to treatment m. In this case, there are potentially many treatment effects of interest, and depending on our particular interest, certain groups may be of particular relevance, such as specifically focusing on some untreated counterfactual $Y_i(0)$ as the comparison group instead of arbitrary potential outcomes $Y_i(l)$ (Imbens and Wooldridge 2009).

Beyond the quantities introduced here, throughout the rest of this book we will encounter a number of other types of treatment effects, which may be useful in particular situations, or in specific empirical designs. You may note that the above treatment effects all refer to average—that is, mean—treatment effects. Often mean treatment effects will hide substantial variation in effects *beyond* the mean, and this heterogeneity is something we turn to later in this book (chapter 8).

1.4.2 A Note on Jargon: Estimands, Estimators, Estimates, and Parameters

You will note above that when referring to the average treatment effects we have introduced, we have referred to these as "quantities." Formally, these "quantities" are known as estimands. The term "estimand" simply refers to a quantity we wish to estimate. Thus, in the sense that we will wish to estimate an ATE, or ATT, or other type of treatment effect, these will be the estimands we seek. These estimands are of interest to us because they describe the behavior of some population of interest that we are studying.

More generally, we may read the term "parameter," which also refers to some fixed quantity that characterizes some population or model. While, our estimands often seek to simply target parameters, estimands do not need to necessarily always target parameters, as estimands can also seek to nail down functions of parameters, or nonparametric quantities, which cannot be reduced to a single parameter. Generally speaking, we will use the term "estimand" to emphasize some particular parameter or parameters of interest in our analysis, while the term "parameter" may include a larger range of values that characterize our model of the population. In certain settings, we may require several parameters to define a model, even if we are ultimately interested in only a subset of them—the estimands. Parameters that are necessary for estimation but not directly of interest are often called "nuisance parameters." Such nuisance parameters must be accounted for in order for us to arrive at our estimand, but we do not necessarily care about them per se.

To avoid confusion, it is important to differentiate between estimands and the related terms "estimators" and "estimates." An "estimator" refers to the specific way in which we will calculate an estimand from a sample of data, and hence can be seen as a mechanical process or mathematical function required to actually generate our estimand. Thus, while our estimand may be an ATT or an ATE, and we will refer to this as τ_{ATE} or similar, our estimator may be something like ordinary least squares, a comparison of means, or any other number of procedures. To differentiate from our estimand, our estimator will be referred to

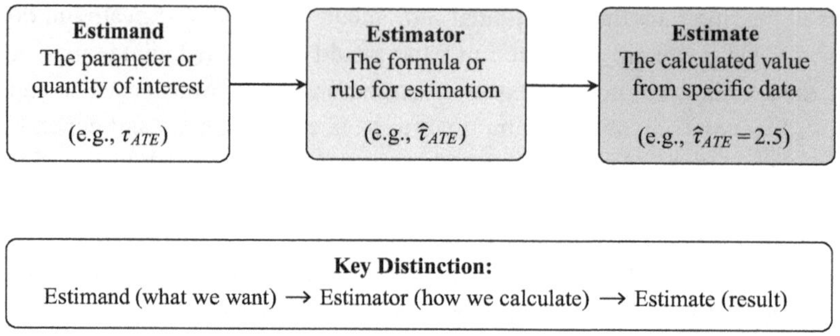

Figure 1.1
Relationships between estimands, estimators, and estimates.

as $\widehat{\tau}_{\text{ATE}}$. Up to this point we have simply been interested in defining our estimands, and not actually estimating them, and as such we have not yet encountered an estimator. However, the rest of this book will be full of estimators. And it is when introducing an estimator that we will need to carefully consider the assumptions that are required for this estimator to actually isolate a causal effect, and hence the suitability of the proposed estimator. Finally, the term "estimate" will refer to the numerical result produced by the estimator, when the estimator is applied to data. This is summarized in figure 1.1, which seeks to make clear that the general way in which we will work will be to first define an estimand of interest, then propose an estimator, and finally, apply this estimator to data, resulting in an estimate.

While an estimand is simply a fixed but unknown quantity, as an estimator is applied to random samples of data, our estimators are random variables, and so come with uncertainty. Thus, beyond simply estimating certain quantities of interest, we will be interested in conducting inference for these quantities of interest. Indeed, we will often read the term "causal inference" to refer to settings where we wish to make statements about the impact of exposure to treatment on some outcome(s) of interest. When we extend into inference we will be concerned about making probabilistic statements about the likelihood that some treatment impacts outcomes, and as such will generally find that we are testing hypotheses about effects, or reporting confidence intervals. Thus, this requires that we do not simply estimate parameters but also that we can say something about the variance of these estimates. Throughout this book, whenever we discuss estimators, we will also discuss the estimation of variance of corresponding estimates, as well as the theoretical underpinnings on which inference is based.

1.5 What We Mean When We Talk About "Identification"

What we wish to do with the RCM and the estimands discussed above is "identify" some causal effect of interest. Here, "identification" is a formal term, and a causal effect is said to be identified if it can be uniquely determined from the distribution of observable data under a given model of the world.[4] When we say that a parameter or a causal effect is identified, we mean to say that in theory, if we observed infinite data, our model of the world would let us speak of "a causal effect" that we could isolate from the data (refer to Lewbel [2019] for a comprehensive discussion of identification in econometrics).

It is important to note that this does not imply that any particular treatment effect cannot have heterogeneity across units, but rather that when we define a parameter of interest (say the ATT), this can be uniquely estimated in our data. Identification relies on some underlying model about how we believe that the data we observe is generated. That is, we must have some idea about the underlying data generating process, or DGP. Often this DGP will include assumptions about functional form and relationships between variables and unobserved factors, and assumptions about what we can and can't measure. These assumptions, when combined with data, are what allow us to actually propose to estimate causal quantities. It is important to note that identification refers to the theoretical ability to estimate a parameter, rather than the practicalities of actually estimating it, so in this sense, it precedes estimation and inference.

In certain settings, parameters of interest will not be identified, and in this case we refer to the parameters being unidentified. For example, consider if we wished to identify the returns to primary schooling in some population where primary school is mandatory and everyone completes primary school. Here we would be in a situation where the causal effect is unidentified, because even if we observed the full distribution of wages in the population and we had a model that explained wages as a function of primary school attendance, there would be many values for the return to primary education that could rationalize the distribution of observed wages, given that we don't observe variation off of which to drive identification.

In practice, we may often read about the identifying variation or the source of identification that allows us to arrive at a causal estimate.[5] Thinking about how to credibly achieve identification is the starting point in our work in empirical economics. This is often referred to as determining an "identification strategy," or proposing an empirical strategy. Indeed, in his 2021 Nobel Prize lecture, Angrist (2022) states that "the term *identification* is shorthand for research design," in reference to his and Krueger's Handbook chapter (Angrist and Krueger 1999), which discusses the identification of causal relationships in labor economics in particular. What this aims to make clear is that to be able to credibly identify a causal effect, we must have a particular strategy in mind that will let us in some way isolate variation in the treatment of interest from other movements in the data, and hence isolate, or identify, the impact of treatment, above and beyond other movements of interest.

Throughout the rest of this book, we will think about the particular research designs or identification strategies that will allow us to isolate causal effects of interest. As we will see, different identification strategies will generally imply the need to make more or less demanding assumptions in our models, and so the suitability of any particular strategy will depend on whether or not we (and ultimately the readers of our research) find such assumptions credible.

Historical Context and Selected Further Reading

The Rubin Causal Model (RCM) is generally ascribed to Rubin (1974), and this naming was first used in Holland (1986, 946). In naming this as Rubin's Model for Causal Inference in the title of his section 3, Holland (1986) states:

> I refer to this as "Rubin's model" even though Rubin would argue that the ideas behind the model have been around since Fisher. I think that Rubin (1974) was the place where these ideas were first applied to the study of causation.

However, the genesis of this model is considerably longer, dating back to ideas introduced by Splawa-Neyman (1923,1990) in his master's thesis and Fisher (1925), both applied to randomized trials. A very nice discussion of the history of the RCM is available in Imbens and Rubin (2015, chapter 2).

There are alternative conceptualizations of causality that interested readers may wish to consult for further discussion and alternative views. This includes the work of graphical models and causality of Pearl and colleagues, discussed, among many other places, in Pearl's (2009) *Causality* book. A discussion of causality and econometrics with a link to structural parameters, as well as a coverage of how this differs to the Rubin Causal Model and other approaches, is available in Heckman and Pinto (2024). Further (recommended) reading specifically on identification in econometrics can be found in Lewbel (2019).

2

Ignorable Treatment Assignment: Experiments and Random Assignment

All is experiment and adventure. We are for ever mixing ourselves with unknown quantities. What is to come? I know not.

—Virgina Woolf, *The Waves*

2.1 Introduction

Experimental assignment of treatment has a long history in research in economics and the social sciences—and a far longer history in the natural sciences, dating back to the Renaissance. R. A. Fisher's book "*The Design of Experiments*" is often suggested to be a precursor of the current wave of experimental papers in the social sciences. Relatively early examples of field experiments in economics have included large-scale social experiments in the United States in the 1960s and beyond, which have shaped how we understand factors such as income tax and child welfare (Ross 1970) and health insurance and health care usage (Manning et al. 1987). More recently, Mexico's experimental evaluation of the PROGRESA cash-transfer scheme (Schultz 2004) has been highly influential in thinking about a government's role in development. Randomized assignment of treatment is now a mainstay in economics research (see for e.g., the discussion in Ravallion 2020).

The growth and success of randomized assignment of treatment in economics comes from both its simplicity as an experimental design and its credibility when conducted cleanly (Banerjee, Chassang, Montero, et al. 2020). If units assigned to treatment and control are randomly selected from a larger group, there will no systematic differences *on average* between individuals in both groups, *except* for their program receipt. Of key importance is that individuals with high potential outcomes for a particular treatment assignment will be no more likely to be assigned to this treatment than individuals with low potential outcomes, allowing us to abstract away from concerns related to selection into treatment that will be present throughout the rest of this book.

Of course this does not imply that randomizing treatment is necessarily easy or cheap. Randomization requires that researchers are able to implement some particular treatment, ensure a valid assignment to the treatment and control statuses, and measure outcomes of individuals in both groups. While laboratory experiments exist in economics, where all of this can be manipulated in highly controlled settings (see, for example, A. E. Roth [1986] for an early discussion) many experiments of interest to economists are conducted "in the field," implying considerable design challenges (Duflo 2006). While implementation is a challenge and is often costly, in some sense, "paying" the cost of randomization "buys" identification. In this chapter we will discuss the details behind random assignment and identification, considerations related to estimation and inference in these settings, and a number of practical considerations related to experimental design.

2.2 Identification with Random Assignment

To begin, we will assume that we have some sample of N observations. At random, N_T of these will be randomly drawn to receive treatment, and the remaining $N_C = N - N_T$ of these will hence be randomly assigned to control status. This is a completely randomized setting in the sense that randomization occurs at the individual, rather than some more highly aggregated, level. We assume that we will observe each individual's assigned treatment status, W_i, outcome Y_i, and that as laid out in chapter 1, each individual has two theoretical potential outcomes $\big(Y_i(0), Y_i(1)\big)$.

The simplest case in the analysis of treatment effects occurs when the following two assumptions hold, combined with assumption 1 (SUTVA):

Assumption 2. Unconditional Unconfoundedness: $\big(Y_i(0), Y_i(1)\big) \perp\!\!\!\perp W_i$.

Assumption 3. Overlap: $0 < \Pr(W_i = 1) < 1$.

The first of these assumptions (assumption 2) implies that treatment assignment is independent of potential outcomes. This precludes any type of systematic selection into treatment: Individuals with high potential outcomes for treatment are just as likely to receive treatment as they are to receive control, and the same goes for individuals with high potential outcomes for control. It is important to note that this assumption *does not* rule out the fact that treatment receipt can have a substantial effect on observed outcomes Y_i. It simply implies that individuals with systematically high or systematically low potential outcomes are not more likely to receive treatment. To see a worked example of this, refer to exercise 5 at the end of this chapter. This definition of independence ($\perp\!\!\!\perp$) was first provided in Dawid (1979) and is equivalent to stating $\Pr\big(W_i | Y_i(0), Y_i(1)\big) = \Pr(W_i)$, making clear that knowing something about the potential outcomes gives us no information whatsoever about treatment assignment.

Assumption 3 above, "overlap," simply implies that there is variation in treatment status. This latter assumption is mechanically required for us to be able to estimate treatment effects. If all individuals are assigned to treatment or all are assigned to control, there will be no variation off of which to estimate treatment effects. Of these two assumptions, assumption 3 is something that can be observed in the data; however, assumption 2 is unobservable. How may we expect that these two assumptions could be fulfilled in practice? We require that treatment assignment is independent of unobserved potential outcomes. It is unlikely that we would ever make an assumption as strong as assumption 2 unless we are sure that treatment is randomly assigned, for example via an RCT.

The value of these assumptions 1–3 together is that now, for the first time, we can move from theoretical quantities (the potential outcomes we defined in chapter 1) to observable quantities. To see this, we will start with the defined estimand τ_{ATE} from (1.5):

$$\tau_{\text{ATE}} = \mathbb{E}[Y_i(1) - Y_i(0)] = \mathbb{E}[Y_i(1)] - \mathbb{E}[Y_i(0)] \tag{2.1}$$

$$= \mathbb{E}[Y_i(1)|W_i = 1] - \mathbb{E}[Y_i(0)|W_i = 0] \tag{2.2}$$

$$= \mathbb{E}[Y_i|W_i = 1] - \mathbb{E}[Y_i|W_i = 0]. \tag{2.3}$$

Here, (2.1) simply applies the linear expectations operator. Arguably the most important step is in moving from (2.1) to (2.2). We can write $\mathbb{E}[Y_i(1)] = \mathbb{E}[Y_i(1)|W_i = 1]$ (and similar for $\mathbb{E}[Y_i(0)]$) because of our unconditional unconfoundedness assumption. Given that there is no selection into treatment, individuals who receive treatment provide a valid snapshot of average potential outcome $Y_i(1)$ in the population of interest, and similarly, individuals who receive control assignment provide a valid picture of average potential outcome $Y_i(0)$. Finally, in moving to (2.3) we note that these theoretical quantities are what we actually observe with Y_i, simply following (1.3). The fact that both of these quantities are indeed observed (given the overlap assumption) means that now we can formally identify a treatment effect from real data.

An alternative way to think about identification in cases with random assignment—and why observed differences between treated and control units will not generically return unbiased estimates of treatment effects, can be seen from an emblematic example presented in Angrist and Pischke (2009, 22). They note that the observed difference in average outcomes (2.3) can be decomposed as follows:

$$\underbrace{\mathbb{E}[Y_i|W_i = 1] - \mathbb{E}[Y_i|W_i = 0]}_{\text{Observed difference in average outcomes}} = \underbrace{\mathbb{E}[Y_i(1)|W_i = 1] - \mathbb{E}[Y_i(0)|W_i = 1]}_{\text{average treatment effect on the treated}} + \underbrace{\mathbb{E}[Y_i(0)|W_i = 1] - \mathbb{E}[Y_i(0)|W_i = 0]}_{\text{selection bias}}. \tag{2.4}$$

The right-hand side of this equality simply results from adding and substracting the middle term (you may note that these two terms are the same!). By grouping terms, we can see that by definition, the first quantity on the right-hand side is the ATT, leaving a second quantity:

$$\mathbb{E}[Y_i(0)|W_i = 1] - \mathbb{E}[Y_i(0)|W_i = 0].$$

This quantity is the bias potentially inherent in the assignment mechanism. What would have happened to the treated had they not been treated ($\mathbb{E}[Y_i(0)|W_i=1]$) may be quite different to what actually happened to the untreated group in practice ($\mathbb{E}[Y_i(0)|W_i=0]$). In the case of randomized assignment, we essentially "randomize away" this treatment bias; given that treated units are a random sample of all units, their untreated potential outcome will be no different on average to that of control units. As a matter of fact, if assumption 2 holds, then this implies that in an infinitely large sample $\mathbb{E}[Y_i(0)|W_i=1]=\mathbb{E}[Y_i(0)|W_i=0]$. On the other hand, if we *are not* in a randomized trial with perfect compliance, this selection bias term will likely remain, which is a point we return to in all chapters following this one.

One thing that you may have noted above is that in (2.1) we referred to an ATE, while in (2.4) we referred to an ATT. This equivalence of the ATT and the ATE comes *only* because there is nothing special about individuals who receive treatment: They are a random selection of the full population. In the special case where there is random assignment to treatment, because treated and control units will, on average, be alike, the ATT will equal the ATE. This should not be seen as implying either (a) that generally speaking the ATT and the ATE will be equal or (b) that treatment effects are homogeneous across all units when assignment to treatment is randomized. In the first case, as we will see throughout the rest of this book, from here on out we will need to be quite careful in considering exactly what type of treatment effect we are capturing. And in the case of the second point, while the ATE and the ATT will be the same given that treated and controls are the same on average, within these treatment effects—that is, across units i, effects may be heterogeneous.

2.3 Estimation with Unconditional Unconfoundedness

Once we make assumptions of unconditional unconfoundedness, we have a number of estimation methods at our disposal. As unconfoundedness solves the business of the assignment mechanism by making it completely observable, all we have left is to recover estimates of these treatment effects by using data. This is now a technical issue, which we turn to here.

2.3.1 Unconditional Unconfoundedness: Comparison of Means

Simply by looking at (2.3), a first option is likely apparent. Given that our treatment effect can be written as two expectations, the ATE can be estimated by a difference-in-means estimator. This is simply:

$$\widehat{\tau}_{\text{ATE}}=\frac{1}{N_T}\sum_{i:W_i=1}Y_i-\frac{1}{N_C}\sum_{i:W_i=0}Y_i, \tag{2.5}$$

which can alternatively be written as follows, if we wish to omit the notational dependence on N_T and N_C:

$$\widehat{\tau}_{\text{ATE}}=\frac{\sum_{i=1}^N W_iY_i}{\sum_{i=1}^N W_i}-\frac{\sum_{i=1}^N(1-W_i)Y_i}{\sum_{i=1}^N(1-W_i)}. \tag{2.6}$$

This second notation, while equivalent to the first, simply allows for W_i to act as an indicator to select treatment and control units in each term, and by definition $N_T = \sum_{i=1}^{N} W_i$ and $N_C = \sum_{i=1}^{N}(1 - W_i)$.

This estimator is extremely simple. All we need to do to calculate our estimate is simply take two averages. Of course the simplicity of the estimator owes to the fact that W_i is randomly assigned, and much of the complexity of studies where assumptions 1–3 hold is precisely in generating this experimental variation. We delay discussion of these issues until section 2.5.2.

2.3.2 Regression Analysis

In practice, a differences-in-means estimator can be estimated directly by simple linear regression. Thus far, the language of treatment effects may seem a bit foreign to the regression framework that is frequently at the center of econometrics courses. This need not be so. In fact, starting from the potential outcomes framework can help to clarify the assumptions underlying regressions used for causal inference.

To see this, we will define the population means of the potential outcomes $Y_i(0)$ and $Y_i(1)$ as $\mu(0)$ and $\mu(1)$, respectively. Given this, we know that the average treatment effect will simply be the difference between these two values—that is, $\tau_{\text{ATE}} = \mu(1) - \mu(0)$. For any specific individual, we can write their potential outcome as this population mean plus a mean zero individual-specific error ($\varepsilon_i(0)$ and $\varepsilon_i(1)$ below):

$$Y_i(0) = \mu(0) + \varepsilon_i(0)$$
$$Y_i(1) = \mu(1) + \varepsilon_i(1).$$

We can substitute these quantities into (1.3), and thus rewrite the observed outcome as

$$Y_i = \mu(0) + \underbrace{[\mu(1) - \mu(0)]}_{\tau_{\text{ATE}}} W_i + \underbrace{\varepsilon_i(0) + [\varepsilon_i(1) - \varepsilon_i(0)]W_i}_{\varepsilon_i}. \tag{2.7}$$

Thus we can see that a regression of Y on W will produce an unbiased estimate of the ATE only if W is uncorrelated with the compound error term, ε_i.[1] Of course, this is exactly what we get from the assumption of unconditional unconfoundedness. If W_i were systematically correlated with realizations of $\varepsilon_i(1)$ or $\varepsilon_i(0)$ that were particularly high or low, this would be a violation of unconditional unconfoundedness as stated in assumption 2.

In practice, when we are interested in estimating causal effects in situations where we believe that unconditional unconfoundedness holds, we will generally proceed in estimating the regression laid out in (2.7). Simply regressing our observed outcome Y on W along with an intercept term allows us to recover the comparison of means estimate (2.5) as the coefficient on W in the regression. The constant term allows us to capture the mean among untreated units ($\mu(0)$), and if we wish to determine the mean among treated units from regression coefficients, we can do so by simply summing the intercept term and the coefficient on treatment assignment.

2.3.3 Regression with Unconditional Unconfoundedness: Benefits and Extensions

While it may seem like overkill to estimate a regression model if we are simply interested in a comparison of means, there are a number of additional benefits from estimating (2.3) in a regression framework rather than mechanically estimating two means. One of these is related to the incorporation of heterogeneity by observable characteristics, and a number of other benefits are related to inference and efficiency. We will focus on incorporating heterogeneity here and discuss inferential considerations in the following section.

One immediate benefit of regression models is that it is easy to incorporate covariates in analysis. Given a maintained assumption of unconditional unconfoundedness, it is never *necessary* to include covariates to arrive at unbiased estimates of treatment effects. However, in many cases, covariates may be of interest as a means of describing heterogeneous results. To see this, consider a covariate X_i. For ease of exposition, define $\bar{X}$ as the sample average of X such that $(X_i - \bar{X})$ will be centered around 0. Now, let's assume that these covariates are relevant in explaining potential outcomes and that potential outcomes are defined according to the following data-generating process:

$$Y_i(0) = \mu(0) + \beta_0(X_i - \bar{X}) + \varepsilon_i(0) \tag{2.8}$$

$$Y_i(1) = \mu(1) + \beta_1(X_i - \bar{X}) + \varepsilon_i(1). \tag{2.9}$$

Notice here that we allow the coefficients, β_0 and β_1, to vary according to treatment status, implying that the effect of X_i on potential outcomes can be more or less valuable depending on an individual's treatment status. Such a case (where in particular, $\beta_1 > \beta_0$) is illustrated in figure 2.1.

In this case, the ATE is still given by $\mu(1) - \mu(0)$, given that this will capture the *average* effect across all realizations of X_i. We can also directly include X as a regressor in any regression models we estimate (the reasons for doing so are discussed in the next section). But we may now want to take explicit care to let the relationship between X and Y depend on treatment status, and to incorporate this into our estimates of the treatment effect. This allows us to flexibly model the situation in which $\beta_0 \neq \beta_1$ in equations (2.8) and (2.9). There are many real-life examples where this might be the case: For example, the effect of social networks on earnings might be stronger among those with secondary education (a treatment of interest) than among those without, or the effects of some training program may be greater for individuals with more labor market experience.

To see how this can be constructively captured in a regression model, we need simply to substitute these expressions of $Y_i(0)$ and $Y_i(1)$ into the switching equation (1.3):

$$\begin{aligned} Y_i &= Y_i(0) + (Y_i(1) - Y_i(0))W_i \\ &= \mu(0) + \beta_0(X_i - \bar{X}) + \underbrace{[\mu(1) - \mu(0)]}_{\tau_{\text{ATE}}} W_i + \underbrace{(\beta_1 - \beta_0)}_{\text{Heterogeneity}} (X_i - \bar{X})W_i \\ &\quad + \underbrace{\varepsilon_i(0) + [\varepsilon_i(1) - \varepsilon_i(0)]W_i}_{\varepsilon_i}. \end{aligned} \tag{2.10}$$

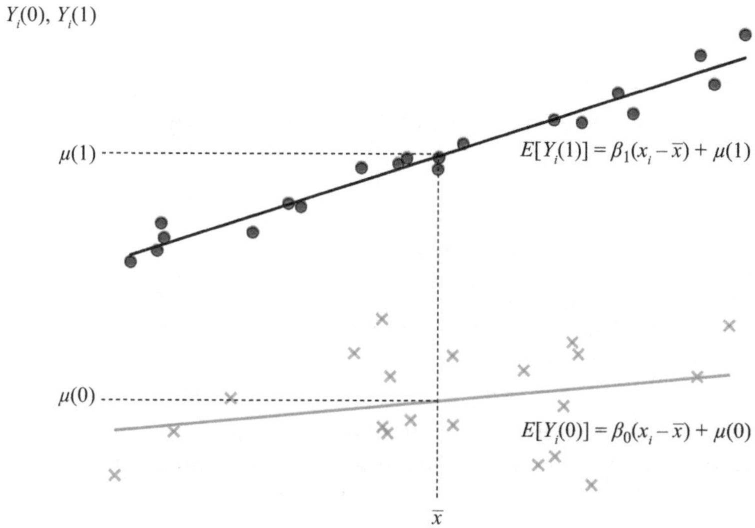

Figure 2.1
Treatment effect heterogeneity based on an observable characteristic X.

This will look even simpler if you substitute some single letter for $(X_i - \bar{X})$, but makes clear that it is straightforward to capture treatment effect heterogeneity in some particular covariate of interest by regressing the outcome variable Y_i on an indicator for treatment receipt, the covariate of interest, as well as an interaction between treatment receipt and the covariate of interest. You may note here that if there is no treatment effect heterogeneity in terms of X, this will be captured in the fact that $\beta_0 = \beta_1$, and so the "Heterogeneity" term in (2.10) can simply be removed. We will return to a much more extensive discussion of heterogeneity in treatment effects in chapters 8 and 9 of this book.

Code Callout 2.1: Regression, Comparison of Means, and Covariates
We will explore the equivalence between regression and a comparison of means in a binary regression setup, as well as the incorporation of covariates to capture heterogeneity in code callout 2.1. There we work with data from a randomized control trial examining the impact of microfinance access on the success of small businesses in Pakistan from Bari et al. (2024).

2.4 A Number of Approaches to Inference

If assignment to treatment is random, we have seen that estimating a treatment effect can be quite straightforward following (2.5) or alternatively regressing observed outcomes Y

on an indicator of treatment receipt. However, beyond arriving at a treatment effect, we will wish to conduct inference on this parameter, either to generate confidence intervals, estimate standard errors, report a p-value, a t-statistic, or so forth. In practice, a number of approaches to inference may be taken in cases where assignment to treatment is random. Here we will consider these approaches and potential benefits and costs of respective alternatives.

2.4.1 Design-Based Versus Sampling-Based Uncertainty

A first distinction worth noting is that the way in which we wish to proceed will likely depend on our view of the uncertainty inherent in our estimators. One way to conceive of uncertainty is in terms of sampling-based variation. This is "the dominant approach to inference in social sciences" (Abadie et al. 2020, 265) and views uncertainty as a result of only observing a random sample of data from a much larger population. Under this view, our uncertainty about the parameter of interest stems from the fact that we observe only one of many possible samples; had we observed a different sample, we would likely have obtained a different estimate.

An alternative perspective is to view uncertainty as stemming from design-based variation. Here, uncertainty arises from the fact that, for each unit, we only observe one potential outcome. Under a different treatment assignment, we would have observed a different potential outcome—and thus likely estimated a different treatment effect. Design-based uncertainty therefore refers specifically to variation arising from the way in which treatment is assigned that is, from "the (experimental) design."

An illustration of the difference between sample-based uncertainty and design-based uncertainty can be viewed in tables 2.1 and 2.2. A similar representation is presented in Abadie et al. (2020). Table 2.1 presents a representation of sample-based uncertainty. Here we consider a population of N individuals, a proportion of which are randomly sampled. Individuals randomly sampled are indicated as $R_i = 1$, while nonsampled individuals (shaded in gray) are denoted $R_i = 0$. For sampled individuals, we observe both their treatment status W_i as well as their outcome Y_i. Based on these observations, we can estimate a treatment effect of interest. However, we could just have likely observed alternative sampling schemes such as those indicated as alternative sample 1, and so forth. Uncertainty in our estimate thus owes to uncertainty related to unobserved observations from the sample. Table 2.2, on the other hand, presents a representation of design-based uncertainty. In this case, for each of the N individuals in the population, one of two potential outcomes is observed but not the other (unobserved outcomes are shaded in gray). Which of the two potential outcomes is observed is determined by the assignment mechanism, represented by treatment status W_i. In this case, uncertainty owes to the fact that alternative realizations of the assignment mechanism, such as those indicated in alternative sample 1, and so on would have resulted in alternative observed outcomes and, as such, alternative estimates of treatment effects.

Table 2.1
A pictoral example of the source of sample-based uncertainty

	True sample			Alternative sample 1			Alternative sample 2			⋯	Alternative sample ∞		
i	Y_i	W_i	R_i	Y_i	W_i	R_i	Y_i	W_i	R_i	⋯	Y_i	W_i	R_i
1	✓	✓	1	×	×	0	✓	✓	1	⋯	×	×	0
2	✓	✓	1	✓	✓	1	×	×	0	⋯	✓	✓	1
3	×	×	0	×	×	0	✓	✓	1	⋯	×	×	0
4	✓	✓	1	×	×	0	×	×	0	⋯	✓	✓	1
5	×	×	0	✓	✓	1	✓	✓	1	⋯	×	×	0
⋮	⋮	⋮	⋮	⋮	⋮	⋮	⋮	⋮	⋮	⋱	⋮	⋮	⋮
N	×	×	0	✓	✓	1	×	×	0	⋯	✓	✓	1

Table 2.2
A pictoral example of the source of design-based uncertainty

	True sample			Alternative sample 1			Alternative sample 2			⋯	Alternative sample ∞		
i	$Y_i(0)$	$Y_i(1)$	W_i	$Y_i(0)$	$Y_i(1)$	W_i	$Y_i(0)$	$Y_i(1)$	W_i	⋯	$Y_i(0)$	$Y_i(1)$	W_i
1	✓	×	0	✓	×	0	×	✓	1	⋯	×	✓	1
2	×	✓	1	✓	×	0	✓	×	0	⋯	✓	×	0
3	✓	×	0	×	✓	1	×	✓	1	⋯	✓	×	0
4	✓	×	0	✓	×	0	✓	×	0	⋯	✓	×	0
5	×	✓	1	×	✓	1	✓	×	0	⋯	×	✓	1
⋮	⋮	⋮	⋮	⋮	⋮	⋮	⋮	⋮	⋮	⋱	⋮	⋮	⋮
N	×	✓	1	×	✓	1	×	✓	1	⋯	×	✓	1

These two conceptions of uncertainty give rise to alternative views related to inference. Sampling-based inference procedures seek to account for sampling processes when considering the variation of the estimator of interest. Design-based inference procedures instead aim to use information about the assignment process to determine the variance of the estimator across assignments. As we lay out below, inference procedures in each case follow quite different logic. Given the focus on the Rubin Causal Model and potential outcomes in chapter 1, the design-based inference setting will likely feel particularly familiar. A very complete handbook chapter focusing on randomized experiments by Athey and Imbens (2017) puts design-based inference at its core. However, given the frequency of use of sampling-based methods in the economic literature, it is important to understand inference in this setting also.

2.4.2 Randomization Inference

Randomization inference, originally laid out in Fisher (1925, 1935), provides quite a clean way of thinking about design-based uncertainty. What's more, it is valid in small samples, providing a p-value without the need for any distributional assumptions or large sample asymptotics. Fisher's method allows for the testing of sharp null hypotheses. A sharp null hypothesis refers to the test where the null imposes a precise treatment effect for every individual. Often, this is that the impact of treatment is zero for every unit, namely $H_0 : Y_i(0) = Y_i(1)\ \forall\ i \in \{1, \ldots, N\}$; however, alternative conceptions can be considered—see, for example, Young (2019) and Imbens and Wooldridge (2009, 21). The alternative hypothesis in this case is that, for at least one observation, $Y_i(0) \neq Y_i(1)$. It is important to note that this is a stronger null than the null that some treatment effect $\tau_{\text{ATE}} = 0$, and p-values resulting from randomization inference should be considered in line with this demanding null hypothesis.

The logic of randomization inference is that under the sharp null hypothesis, all the values of unobserved potential outcomes are known. If, for example, $Y_i(1) = Y_i(0)$, then the observed value can be used to infer the unobserved value *under the null*, and, as a result, any alternative sample from table 2.2 be generated. Given this, we can generate a distribution of test statistics that is true under the null hypothesis by permuting the sample assignment mechanism, and recalculating the test statistic of interest (for example, the difference in means) in the resulting alternative sample. Here, permutation refers to taking the treatment assignment and randomly shuffling it around such that units are assigned a potentially different treatment status, and then recalculating the same test statistic based on the original realization of Y_i but the new assignment of W_i. If the treatment does indeed have a large effect, we would expect that the true treatment effect should be substantially larger than versions that are recalculated based on arbitrary assignments of W_i. However, if treatment does not have a substantial effect, we may expect that the true treatment effect is similar to versions calculated off alternative permutations of treatment.

This can be formalized via the calculation of a p-value. Consider now a treatment effect calculated based on the true sample, denoted $\tau(W^{\text{obs}}, Y^{\text{obs}})$, where each individual's outcome Y_i is associated with their true treatment assignment W_i. Also, consider potentially many treatment effects calculated based on alternative permutations of treatment assignments, denoted $\tau(W^{\text{perm}}, Y^{\text{obs}})$, where now the true outcome Y_i of each individiual is associated with randomly re-permuted realizations of W_i. In this case, a p-value can be calculated as the proportion of times that permuted treatment effects exceed the true treatment effect, or:

$$\Pr\left(\left|\tau(W^{\text{perm}}, Y^{\text{obs}})\right| \geq \left|\tau(W^{\text{obs}}, Y^{\text{obs}})\right|\right). \tag{2.11}$$

This p-value is at times referred to as Fisher's exact p-value. In this particular example, the p-value is calculated based on the underlying treatment effect, though alternative test-statistics can also be used; see, for example, Athey and Imbens (2017, section 4.1). A discussion of the incorporation of covariates in the calculation of these p-values can be found in Imbens and Rubin (2015, §5.9).

An element that simplifies randomization inference is that permutation simply respects the original treatment assignment in the data. Thus, if in some sample of N observations N_T receive treatment and N_C receive control, each permutation should randomly reassign a new N_T of these observations to treatment, and N_C to control. In each permutation, the same N observations exist and no units are repeated—treatment assignment W_i is just shuffled around. Given that this is just simply choosing treatment at random without replacement, this implies that there are $\binom{N}{N_T}$ possible ways that treatment could be applied.[2] Where there are quite a small number of units, the p-value (2.11) can be calculated exactly, which is to say that each possible reassignment be considered. For example, in an experiment with six observations, three of which are assigned to treatment, the number of different combinations is $\binom{6}{3} = \frac{6!}{3!\times(6-3)!} = 20$. In settings such as these, we can consider the value of $\tau(W^{\text{perm}}, Y^{\text{obs}})$ under each possible permutation and consider how extreme $\tau(W^{\text{obs}}, Y^{\text{obs}})$ is compared to these twenty realizations. However, where we have a larger number of observations, we cannot easily calculate an exact p-value,[3] and thus generally we simply calculate a relatively large number of permutations at random. As the number of simulations increases, the result of these random permutations will converge to the distribution defined by the exact calculation, in line with the law of large numbers.

Code Callout 2.2: Randomization Inference

It is likely most illustrative to see an example of randomization inference in practice, as this can be quite easily visualized by tabular permutation. To see this, refer to code callout 2.2. This works with a number of simple examples: first where six units are observed, three of whom are randomly assigned to treatment and the rest to control, and second a true experimental assignment of Banerjee, Duflo, and Sharma (2021) who conducted an RCT examining asset transfers to poor households in India based on a larger number of units.

2.4.3 Regression-Based Inference in Experimental Design

Potentially still the most common way of conducting inference in applied settings where treatment is assigned randomly is via regression. When we estimate a regression of the style laid out in (2.7), which we will rewrite in shortened form as:

$$Y_i = \mu(0) + \tau_{\text{ATE}} W_i + \varepsilon_i,$$

if we view uncertainty as flowing from repeated sampling from a large population, then the appropriate variance formula is the standard OLS formula. Specifically, if we assume homoscedastic errors, this is:

$$\widehat{\mathbb{V}(\widehat{\tau}_{\text{ATE}})} = \frac{\widehat{\sigma}^2}{\sum_{i=1}^{N}(W_i - \bar{W})^2} \qquad \text{where} \qquad \widehat{\sigma}^2 = \frac{1}{N-2}\sum_{i=1}^{N}\widehat{\varepsilon}_i^2, \tag{2.12}$$

where $\widehat{\varepsilon}_i$ refers to the regression residual. We may also note that $\widehat{\varepsilon}_i = (Y_i - \widehat{Y}_i)$, which makes clear that variation in realizations of treatment assignment W_i and realized outcomes Y_i is explicitly taken account for, unlike in design-based approaches where we simply consider alternative possible potential outcomes. What's more, the presence of modeled $\widehat{Y}_i$ makes clear the model-based approach to inference here. In this particular setting where W_i is binary, and homoscedasticity is assumed, the variance formula can be further simplified[4] to be written as:

$$\widehat{\mathbb{V}(\widehat{\tau}_{\text{ATE}})} = \widehat{\sigma}^2\left(\frac{1}{N_C} + \frac{1}{N_T}\right).$$

However, the homoscedasticity assumption here is likely to be limiting. In practice, in this particular setting, homoscedasticity implies that the variance of observed Y_i is identical in both treatment and control groups, and in fact, heterogeneity in treatment effects across individuals implies that it is necessary to use a heteroscedasticity-robust variance estimator.[5] Fortunately, the regression-based formula robust to heteroscedasticity has been known since Huber (1967), Eicker (1967), and White (1980). In practice, what is often reported when regressions are estimated to evaluate random assignment to treatment are heteroscedasticity-robust estimates:

$$\widehat{\mathbb{V}_H(\widehat{\tau}_{\text{ATE}})} = \frac{\sum_{i=1}^{N}\widehat{\varepsilon}_i^2(W_i - \bar{W})^2}{\left(\sum_{i=1}^{N}(W_i - \bar{W})^2\right)^2}.$$

Once again, if W_i is a binary treatment measure, this formula can be further simplified to:

$$\widehat{\mathbb{V}_H(\widehat{\tau}_{\text{ATE}})} = \frac{\widehat{\sigma}_0^2}{N_C} + \frac{\widehat{\sigma}_1^2}{N_T}, \tag{2.13}$$

where $\widehat{\sigma}_0^2$ and $\widehat{\sigma}_1^2$ refer to the estimated variance of Y_i among control and treated units respectively, which is:

$$\widehat{\sigma}_0^2 = \frac{1}{N_C - 1}\sum_{i:W_i=0}[Y_i - \widehat{\mu}(0)]^2 \qquad \text{and} \qquad \widehat{\sigma}_1^2 = \frac{1}{N_T - 1}\sum_{i:W_i=1}[Y_i - \widehat{\mu}(0) - \widehat{\tau}_{\text{ATE}}]^2.$$

You may note in comparing between (2.12) and (2.13) the assumption of constant variance in the former with a single global variance estimate, and not the latter.

One point of note with the use of heteroscedasticity-robust estimate $\widehat{\mathbb{V}_H(\widehat{\tau}_{\text{ATE}})}$ is that in small samples, it is downward biased. In practice, this implies that a number of small-sample refinements are used to seek to reduce bias. A comprehensive discussion of this is provided by Imbens and Kolesár (2016), with key points summarized in the endnotes of this book if you are interested in further details.[6] This is a variant of what is known as the Behrens-Fisher problem, and Imbens and Kolesár (2016) note that even in larger samples, issues can arise if the number of treated or control units are small. They suggest implementing a variance estimator proposed by Bell and McCaffrey (2002), which uses a t-distribution with a degree of freedom calculation that is driven by the number of observations in the smaller group (either treated or control). Further details are provided in the previously mentioned endnote. Of course, in general, rather than reporting an estimate along with its variance, standard errors or 95% confidence intervals are reported, although both standard errors and confidence intervals are directly obtained from the variance estimate.[7]

Baseline controls In random assignment, there is no need to include baseline controls in regression models. As randomization "buys us" identification, the inclusion of controls will be superfluous, even if those controls are relevant in explaining outcome Y_i. However, as we noted above, there is potentially a benefit of including baseline controls in cases of random assignment: It allows for greater efficiency when estimating the variance of our estimate. To see this, we can consider a regression model of the form:

$$Y_i = \mu(0) + \tau_{\text{ATE}} W_i + X_i'\beta + \varepsilon_i,$$

and where X_i is a $K \times 1$ vector of pretreatment variables and β are coefficients on these variables. *If* W_i is randomly assigned, then a multivariate regression-based estimate $\widehat{\tau}_{\text{ATE}}$ estimated from the previous model will be a consistent (though not unbiased, except in certain special cases)[8] estimator of τ_{ATE}, regardless of the true functional form between Y_i and X_i. The benefit of including covariates X_i is that it can lead to potentially important reductions in estimated variance terms and, correspondingly, standard errors and confidence intervals. To see why this is the case, note that the variance formula laid out in (2.12) can be written with and without covariates as:

$$\widehat{\mathbb{V}(\widehat{\tau}_{\text{ATE}}|X_i)} = \frac{1}{N-K-2} \frac{\sum_{i=1}^{N}(Y_i - \widehat{\tau}_{\text{ATE}} W_i - X_i'\widehat{\beta})^2}{\sum_{i=1}^{N}(W_i - \bar{W})^2},$$

$$\widehat{\mathbb{V}(\widehat{\tau}_{\text{ATE}})} = \frac{1}{N-2} \frac{\sum_{i=1}^{N}(Y_i - \widehat{\tau}_{\text{ATE}} W_i)^2}{\sum_{i=1}^{N}(W_i - \bar{W})^2},$$

where, apart from the degree of freedom correction $N-K-2$ on the left-hand side, the only difference between these variance formulae owes to the regression residuals, written as $Y_i - \widehat{\tau}_{\text{ATE}} W_i - X_i\widehat{\beta}$ and $Y_i - \widehat{\tau}_{\text{ATE}} W_i$ in the numerator in each case. Given that the inclusion of additional variables X_i can only serve to increase the explanatory power of Y_i, the numerator of the variance on the left-hand side will be at worst identical, and potentially considerably smaller than the numerator on the right-hand side, and this will hold even in large samples. What's more, in cases such as those laid out in (2.10), the incorporation of interactions between the treatment variable and covariates to capture heterogeneity will serve to further increase efficiency should there be heterogeneous effects. Another way to understand this reduction in variance is to see that when covariates X are included in regression models, the resulting variance of standard errors will depend on the *conditional* variance of Y within groups of X, and this variance can be considerably smaller than the *unconditional* variance of Y when X explains a substantial portion of Y. This suggests that the inclusion of covariates is potentially beneficial, with drawbacks only in cases where samples are small, and small-sample bias concerns outweigh gains of efficiency (Samii and Aronow 2012). In practice, the inclusion of baseline controls is frequently observed in studies where treatment is randomly assigned for precisely this reason.

2.4.4 The Bootstrap

An alternative and flexible manner of conducting inference is via the bootstrap. While the bootstrap is not used frequently in randomized control trials given the existence of other simple and easy-to-use alternatives discussed up to this point, it certaintly could be used and would providc asymptotically valid standard errors with relatively few required assumptions. While likely not the first choice in the particular setting of randomized treatment assignment, we will nevertheless briefly introduce the bootstrap here because it *will* be the first choice for inference in various other settings during this book where other forms of inference are either unavailable or not as simple as the bootstrap.

Like randomization inference, bootstrap inference, first introducted by Efron (1979), is based on randomly shuffling the data around. However, *unlike* randomization inference, the bootstrap takes a sample-based approach where uncertainty flows from the fact that we could have observed a different sample of data, with correspondingly different realizations of outcomes (and treatments). In bootstrapping, the idea is then to consider alternative samples of data that we may have observed from the population. However, as we only have one sample of data, we cannot simply generate more samples from the population. Rather, bootstrapping generates new samples of data, with replacement *from the original sample*, and observes how much an estimand of interest varies in resampled data. While potentially surprising at first glance, working in this way results in confidence intervals, standard errors and p-values that are asymptotically valid, and that rely on quite weak assumptions, discussed briefly below.

There are many excellent introductions to the bootstrap, including reviews by Horowitz (2019, 2001) or book-length descriptions in Efron and Tibshirani (1993) and Davison and Hinkley (1997). To fix ideas now, we will consider a simple case where we wish to generate bootstrap standard errors and confidence intervals for an estimated treatment effect. Throughout the book, we will encounter a range of other examples of bootstrap inference. We will note that our treatment effect can be estimated as $\widehat{\tau}_{\text{ATE}}$ (all details are identical for other estimands such as the ATT), and this is estimated from our original sample of data $\{(Y_1, W_1), \ldots, (Y_N, W_N)\}$. A bootstrap resample consists of randomly selecting observations with replacement from the original sample of data, such that an identically sized resampled dataset is built. Thus, while a resampled dataset consists of the same number of observations N, because resampling occurs *with replacement*, this resampled data likely contains multiple realizations of certain observations and no realizations of other observations. We will refer to this as a bootstrap sample and refer to the data in a boostrap sample with the notation: $\{(Y_1^*, W_1^*), \ldots, (Y_N^*, W_N^*)\}$. Based on this bootstrap resample, we can return to estimate our treatment effect of interest, which we will refer to as $\widehat{\tau}^*_{\text{ATE}}$. This bootstrap resampling procedure is also known as a pairs bootstrap, given that resampling consists of selecting observations at random, and collecting their pair of outcome and treatment observations into a new bootstrap sample.

To estimate standard errors and confidence intervals from this procedure, we conduct the above pairs bootstrap many times. For some iteration $b \in \{1, \ldots, B\}$, where B is a large quantity such as $B = 1{,}000$ or $B = 5{,}000$, we begin with our original sample and then generate a random bootstrap sample. From this bootstrap sample, we can generate our estimate of interest, which is denoted $\widehat{\tau}^*_{\text{ATE},b}$. Because each resample is based on a different resample, these estimates will vary, and this variance will reflect the underlying variance of treatment effects in the population. The range of values and the variance of these resample estimates allows for the generating of confidence intervals and standard errors. We can generate a 95% confidence interval simply by taking the range of values between percentiles 2.5 and 97.5 of the empirical distribution of resampled estimates. Using $\widehat{\tau}^*_{\text{ATE},(b)}$ to denote the ordered values of treatment effects, such that $\widehat{\tau}^*_{\text{ATE},(1)}$ is the lowest estimated treatment effect and $\widehat{\tau}^*_{\text{ATE},(B)}$ is the highest, we can write the confidence interval for an arbitrary type one error rate α as:

$$CI_B^{100*(1-\alpha)\%} = \left[\widehat{\tau}^*_{\text{ATE},(B\times\alpha/2)}, \widehat{\tau}^*_{\text{ATE},(B\times(1-\alpha)/2)}\right].$$

Thus, if $B = 5{,}000$ and $\alpha = 0.05$, this confidence interval will be:

$$CI_B^{95\%} = \left[\widehat{\tau}^*_{\text{ATE},(125)}, \widehat{\tau}^*_{\text{ATE},(4{,}875)}\right].$$

Similarly, variance estimates for treatment effects and standard errors can be directly estimated; see, for example, Efron and Tibshirani (1986) for a discussion of the estimation of standard errors. Variance estimates are simply calculated as the variance of resampled $\widehat{\tau}^*_{\text{ATE},b}$ across all bootstrap resamples, and standard errors are simply calculated as the standard deviation across all bootstrap resamples, namely:

$$\widehat{\mathbb{V}_B(\widehat{\tau}_{\text{ATE}})} = \frac{\sum_{b=1}^{B}\left(\widehat{\tau}^*_{\text{ATE},b} - \bar{\widehat{\tau}}^*_{\text{ATE},b}\right)^2}{B-1},$$

where $\bar{\widehat{\tau}}^*_{\text{ATE},b}$ refers to the mean value of $\widehat{\tau}^*_{\text{ATE}}$ across bootstraps. Based on this variance, standard errors can be simply calculated as $\sqrt{\widehat{\mathbb{V}_B(\widehat{\tau}_{\text{ATE}})}}$.

Formal requirements for the validity of bootstrap variance estimators and confidence intervals generally rely on smoothness of the parameter being estimated. Regression parameters of the type we are estimating here are smooth, and thus bootstrap methods are appropriate, unlike, for example, estimates of maxima or minima, where functions are non-smooth. The validity of bootstrap for regression models has been documented as early as D. A. Freedman (1981); see also Mammen (1992) for further details related to asymptotic requirements.

Code Callout 2.3: Bootstrapping a Standard Error Based on Randomized Treatment

For an example of bootstrap inference in practice, refer to code callout 2.3. There we will estimate a standard error using the data from Chong et al. (2016) which studies the impact of iron supplementation on educational outcomes. We will also see how we can estimate 95% confidence intervals (without normality assumptions).

2.4.5 What Type of Inference Procedures Should Be Used?

The fact that various variance estimators exist logically leads to the question of which should be used. The answer to this question depends in part on the conception of uncertainty in a particular setting. In many cases, it will be logical to consider that at least *some* uncertainty flows from sampling-based factors. In particular, this will be the case where there is a clear sampling frame and units are selected with some known probability from a sample of interest. This is the case with representative surveys, though also, at times, it can occur with randomized treatment assignments (see, e.g., Muralidharan and Niehaus [2017] for a discussion of "experimentation at scale"). In other, potentially more infrequent cases, it will be less obvious to see a sampling-based element to uncertainty. In particular, this may be the case if experiments are conducted with all units in a sample (say all schools in school district) or if one considers state-based assignments (Manski and Pepper 2018). In settings such as these, it is likely more logical to consider randomization-based inference procedures. Abadie et al. (2020) introduce an alternative variance estimator that recognizes both sampling- *and* design-based uncertainty, which they suggest is relevant in settings where no clear sampling frame exists (such as in cases where convenience samples are used).

In practice, the vast majority of experimental papers conduct some sort of regression-based estimation procedure. This suggests that, at least in the applied literature, uncertainty appears to be frequently viewed as a sampling-based issue. Influential work by David A. Freedman (2008) notes that such regression-based estimators, if assuming homoscedastic error terms, do not coincide with common randomization-based estimators, and he cautions against the use of regression-based procedures for experimental settings. While this has been influential in driving a range of theoretical studies, Samii and Aronow (2012) show that, in practice, various randomization estimators are not very different, or indeed in some circumstances are identical, to heteroscedasticity-robust regression variance estimates, potentially limiting these concerns. And more recently, formal methods have been documented by Chang, Middleton, and Aronow (2024) that also limit theoretical concerns in applying regression-based methods with covariates should such concerns be viewed as relevant. Empirically, this would suggest that using as a preferred method regression-adjusted variance estimates with appropriate robust standard error adjustments (such as HC2 or Bell-McCaffrey in cases of small samples) is defensible; see endnote 6 of this chapter.

2.5 Experimental Design and Other Considerations

2.5.1 Alternative Assignment Mechanisms

The methods discussed so far in this chapter have assumed that the assignment mechanism is fully random: That is, individuals are assigned to treatment and control with equal probability and independently of other individuals. However, there are alternative ways for treatment to be assigned. This includes stratified randomization and paired randomization, and clustered randomization.

Clustered randomization In clustered randomized control trials, rather than assigning treatment at the level of the individual, treatment is assigned at a more aggregate level, referred to as a cluster. This is common where there are concerns that there may be spillovers between units, for example, in cases where individuals may communicate within villages or within classrooms. In these cases, rather than assign treatment at an individual level, entire clusters are assigned to treatment or control.

The estimation of the ATE in this case is identical to the case where fully randomized assignment is used, and it can be calculated simply as a difference in means following (2.5) or a regression of the outcome of interest on each individual's treatment status following (2.7). However, the fact that treatment is perfectly correlated within groups implies that special care must be taken when conducting inference. Given that, by design, treatment is now shared by all individuals within a cluster, if common shocks occurring at the level of the cluster are ignored, we will underestimate the variance of our estimated treatment effect.

Fortunately, the solution is generally quite simple, and this is to estimate standard errors clustered at the level at which treatment is assigned (Athey and Imbens 2017). Clustered standard errors have been laid out in Liang and Zeger (1986) and allow for us to build in cross-unit dependence between units within clusters when we conduct inference. Specifically, we can refer to the number of clusters as G, indexed by $g = 1, \ldots, G$, and as before assume there are $i = 1, \ldots, N$ observations in total, with N_g of these assigned to each cluster. Then, applying the variance calculations from Liang and Zeger (1986) to the case of a binary treatment operator, we have that the variance estimator for $\widehat{\tau}_{\text{ATE}}$ is as follows:

$$\widehat{\mathbb{V}_C(\widehat{\tau}_{\text{ATE}})} = \frac{\sum_{g=1}^{G}\sum_{i=1}^{N_g}\sum_{j=1}^{N_g}(W_i - \bar{W})(W_j - \bar{W})\widehat{\varepsilon_i}\widehat{\varepsilon_j}}{\left(\sum_{i=1}^{N}(W_i - \bar{W})^2\right)^2}. \tag{2.14}$$

In particular by taking cross-products between residuals $\widehat{\varepsilon}_i$ and $\widehat{\varepsilon}_j$, *within the same cluster* this accounts for joint shocks shared by individuals in the cluster. It may be useful to note that this can be written as below:

$$\widehat{\mathbb{V}_C(\widehat{\tau}_{\text{ATE}})} = \frac{\left(\sum_{i=1}^{N}\sum_{j=1}^{N}(W_i - \bar{W})^2\widehat{\varepsilon}_i\widehat{\varepsilon}_j\mathbb{1}\{i,j \text{ from the same cluster}\}\right)}{\left(\sum_{i=1}^{N}(W_i - \bar{W})^2\right)^2}.$$

In this formula, $\mathbb{1}$ is an indicator function equal to one if two individuals share a cluster, and 0 otherwise. This makes clear that correlation between units are accounted for whenever individuals are indicated as sharing a cluster. Also note that $(W_i - \bar{W})(W_j - \bar{W})$ from (2.14) is written as $(W_i - \bar{W})^2$ above, given that within a cluster treatment is fixed, and hence $W_i = W_j$.

Stratified randomization Stratified randomization, first proposed in Fisher (1926), consists of first dividing the sample by some relevant covariate or covariates and then, within these homogeneous groups, randomizing the assignment of treatment and control. In practice, stratified randomization is common. For example, Bai (2022) notes that in 5,000 RCTs listed on the AEA RCT registry, over 800 involve stratified randomization. Where stratification is used, estimation of the average treatment effect simply requires estimating each within-stratum treatment effect and then weighting these by the proportion of units that are in this stratum to arrive to the global ATE. That is, if there are S stratum, and each stratum s consists of N_s units, $N_{T,s}$ of which are assigned to treatment and the remaining $N_{C,s}$ assigned to control, the average treatment effect can be calculated as:

$$\widehat{\tau}_{\text{ATE}} = \sum_{s=1}^{S}\frac{N_s}{N}\widehat{\tau}_s \qquad \text{where} \qquad \widehat{\tau}_s = \frac{1}{N_{T,s}}\sum_{i:W_{i,s}=1} Y_{i,s} - \frac{1}{N_{C,s}}\sum_{i:W_{i,s}=0} Y_{i,s} \quad \text{for} \quad i \in s.$$

However, if the proportion of units assigned to treatment and control is equal within each stratum, this calculation can be further simplified and is simply the global difference in means estimator laid out in (2.5).

The benefits of stratified randomization follow from the logic of including baseline covariates in a regression model. Where a variable or variables that are relevant in explaining variation in the outcome of interest are used for stratifying, the variance of the estimated treatment effect will be smaller than that of unstratified randomizations. What's more, stratification on X will be more efficient than controlling for X after unstratified randomization, because stratification ensures overlap within each group (Duflo, Glennerster, and Kremer 2007). In practice, the average treatment effect, *as well* as the variance of the parameter, can be estimated by regression, simply by regressing the outcome Y on an indicator of treatment as well as set of strata-specific fixed effects. Alternative design-based variance estimators are also possible. For example, an explanation of randomization inference applied to clustering can be found in Imbens and Rubin (2015, §9.4).

Paired randomization A particular type of stratified randomization is paired randomization. This is a version of stratified randomization where each stratum consists of two observations, one of which is randomly assigned to treatment and the other of which is randomly assigned to control. Like stratified randomization, paired randomization is commonly used in practice. For example, in a particular sample of development economists, Bruhn and McKenzie (2009) report that 56 percent of these have used paired randomization. Paired randomization can be a particularly efficient way to estimate the variance on treatment effects. Indeed, Bai (2022) shows that among all possible options for stratified randomization where half the units are assigned to treatment and half the units are assigned to control, a specific type of matched-pair design is the most optimal.

In practice, there are a number of ways in which matched pair designs may be applied. If a baseline measure of the outcome variable is available, one way is to simply order observations by the value of this variable at baseline and then pair observations off starting with the lowest two values, then the next two values, and so on. Considering a simulation study based on ten particular published RCTs that were either fully randomized or used stratified randomization, Bai (2022) documents that if this ordered baseline procedure is used, the resulting standard error is on average 10 percent lower than the reported standard error in the original study. An alternative option that has also been shown to result in more efficient estimation of treatment effects where multiple baseline covariates are present is to match by minimizing the Mahalanobis distance between each unit i and all other potential units j. This distance, for a particular unit i, is calculated to each unit j as:

$$\mathrm{d}_M(\boldsymbol{X}_i, \boldsymbol{X}_j) = \sqrt{(\boldsymbol{X}_i - \boldsymbol{X}_j)' \widehat{\Sigma}_N^{-1} (\boldsymbol{X}_i - \boldsymbol{X}_j)}, \tag{2.15}$$

where $\boldsymbol{X}$ refers to a vector of variables, and, as such, $\boldsymbol{X}_i$ refers to unit i's values of these variables and $\boldsymbol{X}_j$ refers to unit j's values of these variables. The matrix $\widehat{\Sigma}_N^{-1}$ is the inverse of the variance-covariance matrix across each of these variables across all units. The Mahalanobis distance d_M is a quadratic distance and is lower where two units have variables that are more similar to one another. A description of an efficient algorithm for Mahalanobis matching is provided by King et al. (2007).

In general, once pairs are formed, estimation is quite simple. Estimation can proceed at the pairs level by either taking the difference between pairs as $Y_1 - Y_0$ and then regressing this quantity on a constant—simply capturing the mean between-pair differences across the entire sample. Alternatively, estimation can proceed at the unit level by regressing Y on an indicator of treatment and additionally including a series of fixed effects for each treatment pair. Recent results from Chaisemartin and Ramirez-Cuellar (2024) provide guidance on inference in analyses based on paired randomization, or stratified randomization where strata are very small, which approach the properties of paired randomization. In general, their results suggest that if pair (or stratum) fixed effects are included, then regression standard errors clustered at the pair level (or stratum) level are appropriate, but that degree of freedom corrections made to account for the many pair fixed effects should not be included.

A key point that they note is that if randomization occurs at the cluster level and if clusters are large (for example, if groups of villages are paired and one village in each pair is treated while the other is not, and analysis proceeds at the individual level), then this guidance is particularly important, as if instead one clusters at the level over which randomization occurs, this will lead to severe overrejection of null hypotheses.[9]

2.5.2 Practical Issues in Experimental Design

Beyond issues related to analysis of experimental data, there are many practical issues related to experimental design that are fundamental to consider if actually *conducting* an experiment. This includes issues such as how to find and work with partners to deliver interventions, how to introduce randomization in the field, how to determine the number of control and treatment units to include in an intervention, what data to collect (and how to collect it), piloting and scaling up interventions, as well as, fundamentally, the ethical considerations that may limit work. In her 2017 Presidential Address to the American Economic Association, Duflo (2017) emphasized the importance of taking seriously these practical issues in experimental settings (and more broadly), drawing the analogy of "The Economist as Plumber." Here, we will briefly discuss work that exists to systematize such considerations, though this will be necessarily limited in scope, and point you to more comprehensive resources that exist specifically to work through these issues fully.

An overview of some of the practical issues in setting up a field experiment is given in List (2011). This focuses in particular on how to get started with a field experiment and notes some of the organizational issues that are key in working with partners such as firms within which to randomize interventions. List (2011) also notes the importance of using economic theory to design experimental interventions, a point emphasized in Card, DellaVigna, and Malmendier (2011).

A very applied discussion of implementation of field experiments that goes deeply into the practical considerations of implementation is available in a book by Glennerster and Takavarasha (2013) and the chapter by Duflo, Glennerster, and Kremer (2007) in the *Handbook of Development Economics*. Glennerster and Takavarasha (2013) provide chapter-length discussions of how to formulate questions in this setting, randomization in practice, the measurement of outcomes, and power analysis as an input to the determination of sample sizes. In this book, we delay a discussion of power analyses and sample size until chapter 7. In this chapter we also discuss the importance of preregistration of hypotheses in settings such as experiments where preregistration can be conceivably implemented. Issues related to the practicalities of randomization are also discussed in Bruhn and McKenzie (2009). A particular point to highlight, covered in both of these references, is how one can examine potential random assignments. Frequently, once a proposed random assignment exists, tests are conducted to examine equality of means of some relevant baseline variables across proposed treatment and control groups (Bruhn and McKenzie, 2009, §I.B). In practical terms, both Bruhn and McKenzie (2009) and Glennerster and Takavarasha (2013) recommend using stratification on baseline variables where randomization occurs *within* strata defined by baseline outcomes such as geographic location and demographic characteristics. Bruhn and McKenzie (2009) show that such considerations are particularly relevant for smaller samples of data (of around 300 observations or fewer) but matter less so where larger samples are used.

Further details on randomization, as well as many other relevant implementation and analysis considerations, are also discussed in Duflo, Glennerster, and Kremer (2007). As well as pure randomization, Duflo, Glennerster, and Kremer (2007) note there are other ways that randomization can be induced within a setting of interest. The authors list (1) the oversubscription method, where participants can be chosen randomly from applicants where more applicants than spots exist, (2) randomized order of phase-in, where all individuals eventually receive treatment, but the timing is staggered, (3) within-group randomization, where certain subgroups in each group receive treatment, or (4) encouragement designs, where rather than randomizing the program itself, researchers provide random groups encouragement of some sort to participate in a program. Such methods may be of key importance in settings where ethical or equity considerations limit the use of pure randomization, which is a point we turn to discuss in section 2.5.4.

In general, many of the practical issues that are discussed in these texts owe to the "field" nature of field experiments. A growing use of experimental methods now occurs within online panels where experiments frequently are based on information provision and/or vignettes or other randomly varied characteristics. Haaland, Roth, and Wohlfart (2023) discuss key details of such experiments and provide a discussion of key advantages and disadvantages of online survey panels or labor markets.

2.5.3 Limits in Experimental Settings

Like any method of analysis, random assignment and experimental analysis will not be suitable for all settings and has relevant drawbacks to be aware of. Below we discuss a number of critiques, and responses to criticisms, of the use of experimental methods in economics, and we discuss concerns about the generalizability of findings that are relevant to keep in mind for *any* type of analytic method.

Critiques of experimental analyses While RCTs allow us to quite credibly make the unconfoundedness assumption, such trials are not easy to implement and will not be able to answer all questions. Indeed, for this reason, microeconometrics is more than experimental methods, and other chapters exist in this book. A number of authors have laid out drawbacks of RCTs—for example, Deaton (2009), who focuses also on drawbacks to other nonexperimental techniques, and Deaton and Cartwright (2018).[10] These raise the arguments that RCTs are expensive and potentially time-intensive to run; many big questions of interest can simply not be experimentally manipulated, experimental samples will be limited and potentially not representative of true samples of interest, statistical challenges such as attrition remain, and RCTs are often atheoretical (though need not be). While these drawbacks exist, there appears to be a broad consensus that *no* method should be seen as a catch all or first-best method for *all* questions of interest while, at the same time, a recognition that when well designed, experiments can be a powerful way to test theories and advance knowledge in various ways (Morduch 2020).

Internal and external validity A common theme in critiques of experimental methods is that while they may be well designed to isolate a causal effect in the population under study, they inform us relatively little of how a particular treatment will work in *another* setting. This is often pitched as a case where experiments can offer good *internal validity* but generally provide little in the way of *external validity*. These terms date to at least Campbell and Stanley (1963), who provide a quite clear definition in the case of experimental treatments as referring to deriving a causal effect in the population under study (internal validity), as well as understanding to which "populations, settings, treatment variables and measurement variables" effects generalize (external validity). More recently, internal validity is also understood to refer to identification in a particular setting (see, for example, the definition of Shadish, Cook, and Campbell [2002]).

Of course, questions of internal validity and external validity are relevant for any particular study and method, and in particular, concerns related to external validity are not limited to RCTs and experimental methods. Whether a result observed in one setting is likely to be observed in another setting is a question of considerable interest, both in experimental and nonexperimental literatures, and we will return to discuss this in chapter 8.

2.5.4 Ethical Considerations

Randomized control trials, like any human subject research, raise a range of ethical considerations, and research involving human subjects must be evaluated and approved by institutional review boards (IRBs) charged with considering research ethics and approving or rejecting the implementation of studies on ethical groups. In general, IRBs should be consulted that have in-depth knowledge of local ethical considerations (Glennerster 2017), such as IRBs based in the country where research is conducted.

There are a range of internationally recognized ethical standards, including the Declaration of Helsinki in 1967 by the World Medical Association and the Belmont Report authored by the National Commission for the Protection of Human Subjects of Biomedical and Behavioral Research in the United States in 1974. These standards lay out a number of key principles to consider in human subjects research such as the need to receive informed consent from research subjects, the adoption of a "Do no harm" principle, and the protection of vulnerable populations. Glennerster and Powers (2014) and Glennerster (2017) note the three central principles of the Belmont report of respect for people, beneficence, and justice as guideposts for human subjects research, which generally compare to principles adopted in a range of settings.

Glennerster and Powers (2014) provide a handbook chapter-length discussion on the overarching ethical considerations of human subjects research, in particular focused on RCTs in economics and generally developing countries. They note some of the specific factors that make ethical considerations particularly relevant in an RCT setting, as well as the practical challenges in ensuring that principles such as those laid out in the Belmont report are met. While such discussions generally focus on RCTs conducted with individuals, Bandiera, Barankay, and Rasul (2011) note that similar considerations are relevant when experimenting with firms. The editorial by Bédécarrats, Guérin, and Roubaud (2020) in a book on RCTs in development suggest, that often such principles do not appear to be followed in research, even despite work receiving support of IRBs and being published in journals. The discussion by Deaton (2020, §11) is also relevant in this line, noting among other things that there are often clear power differentials by researchers and research subjects, and these are generally tilted in the favor of researchers, even in developed country settings. Such discussion suggests that serious consideration should be given to the potential benefits of RCTs, and in particular the principle of equipoise is important, where an RCT should truly be seeking to determine uncertainty in potential treatments (Abramowicz and Szafarz 2020).

While there are a range of excellent texts discussing key issues, such as those of Glennerster and Takavarasha (2013), Glennerster (2017), and Glennerster and Powers (2014), and the particularly balanced view presented in Ravallion (2020, §1.4), which is recommended reading, the work Bédécarrats, Guérin, and Roubaud (2020), Baele (2013), and others suggests that this is still an active discussion and an area requiring work, with ethical considerations being, necessarily, ad hoc to every particular proposed experiment.

Historical Context and Selected Further Reading

Discussions of the history of experimental methods in the social sciences can be found in, among other places, Levitt and List (2009) and List and Rasul (2011), noting that *field experiments* have a rich history and have a played an important part in the generation of knowledge in economics for over a century. More broadly, the statistical foundations of experimental design trace back to the work of Fisher (1925, 1935), whose ideas about randomization and design remain central today and can still be considered as "recommended reading."

Key texts on experimental methods are cited throughout this chapter and include Duflo, Glennerster, and Kremer (2007) and Glennerster and Takavarasha (2013), which provide excellent coverage of applied implementation and design considerations. For formal statistical treatments, see Imbens and Rubin (2015) and Athey and Imbens (2017). A number of foundational chapters can be found in the handbook of Banerjee and Duflo (2017) and in later chapters of this book (in particular chapters 7, 8, and 9) we will expand on the themes discussed in this chapter to provide more focus on considerations of statistical power, external validity, and heterogeneity.

Exercises

1. Baranov et al. (2020) study the impact that treatment of maternal depression by cognitive behavior therapy has on women's long-term mental health, financial empowerment, and parenting decisions. In this question, you will work with the data provided by the authors in their official replication material available as `Baranov_et_al_2020.csv` on the Data page to explore an experimental implementation and estimation procedure.
   (a) Open the data and ensure that you understand key variables. In these data, the variable `depressed_x` measures maternal depression at various lengths after childbirth, with `x` indicating these time periods, `Group` is a variable indexing treatment receipt. The variables `depressed` and `depindex_x` measure maternal depression at the year seven follow-up and levels of depression severity for mothers at various lengths after birth, respectively. These variables will be key in the following subquestions. Explore these variables and generate a summary statistics table and/or descriptive plots.
   (b) Using the provided data, examine the impact of the experimental intervention (with treatment group indicated by `Group`) on depression-related variables (`depressed_6m`, `depindex_6m`, `depressed_1y`, `depindex_1y`, `depressed` and `depindex_7y`). Note that the treatment is assigned at the level of the cluster with `uc` indicating treatment clusters. You may wish to consider regression analysis to estimate treatment effects, accounting for clustered assignment.
   (c) Discuss the output from the regression models. What does the significance of the coefficients tell you about the impact of the treatment? How does this depend on the inference procedures used?
   (d) Generate a number of graphs depicting the trend of depression over time. How do you interpret the trends observed in the graph, especially in relation to the treatment and control groups? You may wish to generate a graph with estimated treatment effects and confidence intervals over time to aid in your response.

(e) How might you conduct permutation inference in this setting? Consider an outcome and seek to implement permutation inference as an alternative procedure. How do standard errors and confidence intervals compare to the closed form versions you estimated in part (c)?

2. In this exercise we will examine the experimental estimates from Miguel and Kremer's (2004) study of the impact of deworming on children's educational outcomes in Kenya. Data is provided as `Miguel_Kremer_2004.csv`. As laid out in Miguel and Kremer (2004, 165), the experimental implementation consists of school-level assignment to treatment with three randomized groups: a first group that receives treatment in 1998, a second group that receives treatment in 1999, and a third group group receiving treatment in 2001. Baseline information was collected in early 1998 (prior to first treatments), and post-treatment outcomes are collected between the first and second treatment, and again after the second treatment. This suggests analyses where, in 1998, group 1 schools can be viewed as treated and group 2 and 3 schools can be viewed as controls, and in 1999, group 1 and 2 schools can be viewed as treated and group 3 schools viewed as controls.

   (a) Seek to replicate table I of Miguel and Kremer (2004), which examines the balance of covariates at baseline between group 1 and group 2 schools and group 3 schools. This will require examining the paper and table notes therein. Note that treatment groups are indicated with the variable `wgrp`, and the data provided is at the level of the school, where the number of pupils (relevant for generating pupil averages) is `npupil`. Interpret the balance tests you conduct.

   (b) In panel A of their table VIII, Miguel and Kremer (2004) report experimental results analyzing the impact of deworming treatment in group 1 (indicated by the variable `wgrp1`) on school attendance (`prs`). Seek to replicate this table. It may be useful to consider that `elg98`, `visit`, and `sex` are relevant for conditioning in all or some of the columns.

   (c) In the above question, comparisons of group 1 to groups 2 and 3 are viewed as experimental analyses, and group 2 to group 3 are viewed as placebo tests. Why might we prefer the experimental comparison of group 1 to groups 2 and 3 together, rather than simply comparing group 1 to group 3. In practice, do you see big differences if you compare estimates and their confidence intervals?

   (d) Replicate the analysis from table VIII, however now for panel B (outcomes after two waves of treatment). What does the difference between the results in column 5 between panel A and panel B tell you about the experimental impacts of deworming?

   (e) In panel B, what would happen if we mistakenly compared group 1 (treatment) to group 2 and 3 as controls? Be formal in discussing the bias we may expect and its magnitude.

(f) A key point in the analysis of Miguel and Kremer (2004) is that SUTVA may not hold given externalities in infectious diseases. Seek to analyze the impact of deworming on attendance in both treated schools, as well as among students who live within 3 km of treated schools. How do the estimates among treated students change when considering such (local) spillovers?

3. The data `MacKinnon_et_al.csv` (from MacKinnon, Nielsen, and Webb 2023) is based on the Tennessee Student Teacher Achievement Ratio (STAR) experiment, in which students were assigned to either a small class (`small_1=1`) a regular-sized class with a teacher's aid (`aide_1=1`), or neither (a control group). Because assignment refers to a class-level treatment, the experimental assignment was clustered by class. Consider as the outcome of interest each child's reading score at the end of grade 1 `treadss1`, and follow MacKinnon, Nielsen, and Webb (2023) by consistently conditioning on a vector of dummy variables that capture whether the student was male, nonwhite, received a free lunch, their quarter of birth and year of birth (`male`, `nonwhite`, `freelunch`, `brys*`, `sbq*`), their test score at the end of kindergarten (`treadssk`), as well as controls for the teacher's experience (`totexp1`) and dummies for whether the teacher is nonwhite, as well as their highest degree (`teach_nonwhite`, `hdg*`).

(a) Generate kernel density plots or distributional plots showing grade 1 test scores by the three possible treatment statuses: small class, regular class with aide, and regular class.

(b) Estimate a model of the following form:

$$read\ one_{ic} = \alpha + \tau_1 small_c + \tau_2 aide_c + X'_{ic}\delta + \varepsilon_{ic},$$

where outcomes are measured by individual i and class c, X is the vector of controls mentioned previously, and *small* and *aide* are treatment indicators. Explain how you interpret τ_1 and τ_2?

(c) Consider the model estimated in part (b) if estimating with heterogeneity robust standard errors and with cluster robust standard errors (clustering by class `clsid`). Does your understanding of the success of the program change depending on the nature of standard errors employed? In this setting, which standard error procedure do you believe is correct?

(d) Calculate the standard errors on $\widehat{\tau}_1$ and $\widehat{\tau}_2$ using a clustered bootstrap. How do these standard errors compare to closed form versions of cluster-robust standard errors?

(e) Calculate the standard errors on $\widehat{\tau}_1$ and $\widehat{\tau}_2$ using a permutation-based procedure. Specifically, in this procedure you should seek to permute treatment at the level of classes so that in each permutation an identical number of randomly selected classes are assigned without replacement to `small_1` and `aide_1`.

4. Abel, Burger, and Piraino (2020) conduct an experiment in which individuals are randomly assigned to submit job applications with and without cover letters, and call-back rates from firms are examined. The data `Abel_et_al_2020.dta` contain information from this experiment ("experiment 1" of their paper), where randomization is stratified by individual gender.
   (a) Examine the variable `ref_letter` (the treatment variable). What proportion of observations are treated, and what proportion are control?
   (b) The authors have stratified treatment by respondent gender (`female_d`). Has the stratification worked? How can you confirm this?
   (c) Examine whether treatment is balanced by other characteristics such as individual's age, education level, and the sector in which they work. Is there balance in each of these characteristics? Would you expect this to be the case? Without stratification, is this guaranteed?
   (d) Imagine that these were actually baseline data, and you wished to conduct a stratified randomization based on both an individual's work sector (`sector`) and their gender (`female_d`). Write a simple program to do this. Inspect treatment rates in each of your strata, and confirm that your stratification has worked.
5. Consider the assumption of unconditional unconfoundedness. Simulate a series of data under the following data-generating process:

$$Y_i(1) = 5 + \varepsilon_i(1) \qquad Y_i(0) = 3 + \varepsilon_i(0),$$

   for $i = \{1, \dots, 1{,}000\}$, where $\varepsilon_i(1) \sim \mathcal{N}(0, 1)$ and $\varepsilon_i(0) \sim \mathcal{N}(0, 1)$. Save the realizations of $Y_i(1)$, $Y_i(0)$, $\varepsilon_i(1)$ and $\varepsilon_i(0)$ as a dataset.
   (a) Now randomly assign "treatment" such that around 500 of your 1,000 observations are treated, and the other 500 or so are control. For example, this could be done using the rule: $W_i = 1\{U_i(0, 1) > 0.5\}$, where U is a random uniform draw. Calculate the correlation between $Y_i(1)$ and W_i in your data. Similarly, calculate the correlation between $Y_i(0)$ and W_i in your data. What does this suggest about unconditional unconfoundedness?
   (b) Generate the actual outcome $Y_i = Y_i(0) + [Y_i(1) - Y_i(0)]W_i$. Now estimate the treatment effect using regression or a comparison of means estimator. Is this effect surprising?
   (c) Generate an alternative assignment rule in which there is positive selection into treatment. One possibility is to use an assignment rule such as $W_i = 1\{(\mathcal{U}(0, 1) + \varepsilon_{i1}) > 0.5\}$. (Why will this imply positive selection into treatment?) Now examine the correlation between $Y_i(1)$ and W_i in your data. What does this suggest about unconditional unconfoundedness?

(d) Follow the steps from part (b) of this question but now based on the new assignment rule from part (c). Now estimate the impact of treatment using a regression or comparison of means estimator. Does this capture the true treatment effect?

(e) Return to the data-generating process above, but now additionally simulate a covariate $X_i \sim \mathcal{N}(0, 1)$. This time, generate potential outcomes as:

$$Y_i(1) = 5 + 2X_i + \varepsilon_i(1) \qquad Y_i(0) = 3 + 1X_i + \varepsilon_i(0)$$

and randomly assign treatment as in part (a). Estimate the treatment effect using a regression both controlling for X_i and not controlling for X_i. Is it necessary to control for X_i to estimate an unbiased treatment effect? What do you notice about the precision of the estimated treatment effect in each case? Why does this occur?

3

As Good as Random?: Constructing a Counterfactual with Observables

> She is a friend of mind. She gather me, man. The pieces I am, she gather them and give them back to me in all the right order.
>
> —Toni Morrison, *Beloved*

3.1 Introduction

The use of randomization discussed in chapter 2 considerably simplifies the process of estimation and inference. However, there is a substantial body of work in econometrics that focuses on the case where randomization *is not* assumed unconditionally, but rather only assumed *conditional* on some set of observed variables, which we can call X. The idea in this case is that although treatment is not randomly assigned overall for some reason—either related to treatment design or related to some clearly understood natural or statistical phenomenon—when we focus on observations that have the same realizations of X, treatment is randomly assigned. For our interests, this implies that treatment is "as good as random" once we appropriately control for observable factors X.

Challenges of extending the ideas of randomization into observational settings are long-standing and cross many fields in the social sciences. Essentially, the logic of an RCT is followed, but rather than being considered to randomize treatment overall, the idea is that some random process directs certain observations into treatment and certain observations into control within *each* possible combination of covariates. Methods that are suitable in this case must thus properly account for this covariate-specific assignment mechanism. Such methods have evolved over a substantial period of time. For example, considering one option that we will encounter in this chapter—matching—Heckman et al. (1998) cite as the potential earliest example in this line as dating from the mid-nineteenth century (Fechner 1860). Beyond matching, in this chapter we aim to explore and understand the range of ways which we can move from assumptions which are specific to covariate groups to estimators which allow us to speak of treatment effects more broadly. We will see that in this case both regression estimators and weighting estimators can offer productive ways forward, and understand the differences and similarities between these various options.

Although the methods developed to work in settings where we believe that treatment assignment is random conditional on observable factors X have developed over a long period, a fundamental series of papers circulated during the '80s, '90s, and 2000s. While the theoretical properties of many of the proposed estimators are elegant and insightful, extending the assumption of unconditional unconfoundedness—stemming from controlled random assignment—to conditional unconfoundedness in settings where assignment is not under the researcher's control is fraught with challenges. In such methods, it is fundamental to have some reason to believe that while it is *not* credible to assume random assignment unconditionally, it nevertheless *is* reasonable to assume conditional random assignment. In section 3.6 we will discuss the credibility of such considerations in our empirical work. Before turning to the specific estimators we may seek to apply—and the specific challenges we must have in mind in these settings—we will begin below by laying out key assumptions and discussing identification, as well as introducing a fundamental tool which will be useful for us here, as well as more generally for other estimators where covariates are encountered.

3.2 Moving to Conditional Unconfoundedness: Assumptions and Tools

3.2.1 Identification with Conditional Unconfoundedness: Required Assumptions

In practice, the translation of the assumptions we have been working with previously to those we will work with if we are considering random assignment *conditional* on some series of covariates is relatively straightforward. Previously, identification has required the three assumptions of SUTVA, unconditional uncounfoundedess, and overlap. We will still require SUTVA for identification as well as a variation of unconfoundedness and overlap. Specifically, we will replace assumptions 2 and 3 with their conditional versions below:

Assumption 2′. Conditional Unconfoundedness $(Y_i(0), Y_i(1)) \perp\!\!\!\perp W_i|X_i$.

Assumption 3′. Overlap $0 < \Pr(W_i = 1|X_i) < 1$.

If you compare assumption 2′ with assumption 2, and similarly, assumption 3′ with 3 you will see they look very similar. Indeed, the only difference is that in both cases we are writing $W_i|X_i$ instead of W_i. In practice, however, they mean quite different things. In this case, we are assuming that unconfoundedness and overlap hold among observations with identical realizations of X_i, but not necessarily more generally among observations with different observable characteristics.

Assumptions 2′ and 3′ are sometimes known together as the condition of "strongly ignorable treatment assignment" (Rosenbaum and Rubin 1983). In an identical spirit to

(2.1)–(2.3), from these assumptions we can now show that we can identify a conditional average treatment effect (CATE), $\tau(x)$:

$$\tau(x) = \mathbb{E}[Y_i(1) - Y_i(0)|X_i = x] \tag{3.1}$$

$$= \mathbb{E}[Y_i(1)|X_i = x] - \mathbb{E}[Y_i(0)|X_i = x] \tag{3.2}$$

$$= \mathbb{E}[Y_i(1)|X_i = x, W_i = 1] - \mathbb{E}[Y_i(0)|X_i = x, W_i = 0] \tag{3.3}$$

$$= \mathbb{E}[Y_i|X_i = x, W_i = 1] - \mathbb{E}[Y_i|X_i = x, W_i = 0]. \tag{3.4}$$

As was the case previously, the big step in moving from (3.2) to (3.3) can be taken because of the conditional unconfoundedness assumption. Given this, for members of a particular group $X_i = x$, the potential outcome under treatment is the same in the treated group as it is for the group as a whole, and likewise for potential outcomes among controls. This is to say:

$$\mathbb{E}[Y_i(0)|X_i = x, W_i = 1] = \mathbb{E}[Y_i(0)|X_i = x, W_i = 0] = \mathbb{E}[Y_i(0)|X_i = x], \tag{3.5}$$

and

$$\mathbb{E}[Y_i(1)|X_i = x, W_i = 1] = \mathbb{E}[Y_i(1)|X_i = x, W_i = 0] = \mathbb{E}[Y_i(1)|X_i = x], \tag{3.6}$$

and hence the (unobserved) counterfactual can be generated from outcomes of individuals not exposed to treatment (Heckman, Ichimura, and Todd 1997).

You will note that previously we used our assumptions to arrive at an ATE, whereas here the conditional version of the assumptions mean that we estimate a CATE: an average treatment effect for each covariate group. The analysis from the previous chapter is an extreme case of strong ignorability, given that if assignment is indeed fully random, we can view it as a case of strong ignorability without covariates, or where the covariate vector X is null (Rosenbaum 1984). In this case, our "CATE" actually corresponds to the overall average treatment effect. However, when our identification strategy does require that we condition on some group of covariates X, we must aggregate effects to arrive to a specific treatment effect of interest. For example, if we wish to estimate an ATT, we must aggregate our CATEs by weighting across the distribution of X among the treated population:

$$\tau_{\text{ATT}} = \mathbb{E}_{X_i|W_i=1}\left[\mathbb{E}\left(Y_i(1)|X_i, W_i = 1\right) - \mathbb{E}\left(Y_i(0)|X_i, W_i = 1\right)\right] \tag{3.7}$$

$$= \mathbb{E}_{X_i|W_i=1}\left[\mathbb{E}\left(Y_i(1)|X_i, W_i = 1\right)\right] - \mathbb{E}_{X_i|W_i=1}\left[\mathbb{E}\left(Y_i(0)|X_i, W_i = 0\right)\right] \tag{3.8}$$

$$= \mathbb{E}\left(Y_i(1)|W_i = 1\right) - \mathbb{E}\left(Y_i(0)|X_i, W_i = 0\right) \cdot \Pr(X_i = x|W_i = 1). \tag{3.9}$$

Here, (3.7) simply defines our ATT as the CATE for each covariate group, weighted by the distribution of covariates among the treated. Moving to (3.8) uses the fact from (3.5) that the assumption of conditional unconfoundedness implies that the counterfactual term $\mathbb{E}[Y_i(0)|X_i = x, W_i = 1]$ can be measured by untreated individuals within this group ($\mathbb{E}[Y_i(0)|X_i = x, W_i = 0]$). Finally, we can simplify the expectations operator which conditions over the distribution of covariates among the treated, with the first term (3.9) following from the law of iterated expectations.[1] A similar procedure can be followed if one wishes to arrive to the ATE instead of the ATT.

There are a number of ways in which one can seek to implement these estimators, and conduct inference on estimated treatment effects. In the sections below we will explore three commonly used strategies: matching, regression-based methods, and weighting-based methods.

3.2.2 The Propensity Score as a Foundational Tool with Conditional Unconfoundedness

A key point in the above assumptions and parameters is that we are conditioning on specific realizations of X_i. In practice, this implies conditioning on all possible realizations of X_i which may be observed. If X_i refers to a single discrete covariate this will thus be relatively few points of support, however if X_i refers to many variables, these will interact to form a very large number of potential combinations. For example, even if we consider the simplest case where all variables are binary, if there are p covariates to consider, the support of X_i will consist of 2^p combinations. The fact that the dimensionality of X_i grows as the number of variables increases is a well-known problem, referred to as the "curse of dimensionality": as the dimension of data grows, data will become sparse at many points, implying serious problems for overlap and feasibility of estimation.

The propensity score It turns out that there is a key tool which can be used to address such issues, and which comes up with great frequency in cases where identification relies upon conditioning on covariates. This is the propensity score. The propensity score is defined by Rosenbaum and Rubin (1983) as the probability of receiving treatment conditional on observable characteristics X. Namely:

$$P(X_i) \equiv \Pr(W_i = 1|X_i), \tag{3.10}$$

which provides a summary univariate measure of the probability of treatment receipt given a vector of covariates X_i.

The importance of the propensity score The importance of the propensity score owes to its balancing property. Namely, if we are concerned about balancing covariates X across treated and control units, it is sufficient to balance on the single-dimension propensity score, rather than on multidimensional X itself. This result comes from a famous series of theorems from Rosenbaum and Rubin (1983). Specifically Rosenbaum and Rubin (1983, Theorem 1) states that based on the prior definition of the propensity score:

$$X_i \perp\!\!\!\perp W_i|P(X_i).$$

This is a key property, because it implies that if we are concerned with treatment assignment being correlated with some particular set of covariates X_i, we do not necessarily need to proceed through each potential combination of levels of the high dimensional X_i, but rather only on the uni-dimensional propensity score $P(X_i)$. Thus, $P(X_i)$ summarizes all the information in X_i that is useful for predicting treatment. More importantly in this setting, if we combine the above theorem with a conditional unconfoundedness assumption, this gives Rosenbaum and Rubin's (1983, Theorem 3):

$$(Y_i(1), Y_i(0)) \perp\!\!\!\perp W_i|X_i \Rightarrow (Y_i(1), Y_i(0)) \perp\!\!\!\perp W_i|P(X_i).$$

These theorems are often presented together. For example, Angrist and Pischke (2009) refer to the Propensity Score Theorem, and Proposition 1 in Dehejia and Wahba (1999) does similar work. Proofs of this theorem abound. If you are interested, see for example the proof of Lemma 2.1 in Imbens (2004). Taken together, these provide a key result which can drive estimation. Namely, instead of writing an ATT as a weighted average of CATEs as we have done in (3.8), we can do everything in terms of the uni-dimensional propensity score:

$$\begin{aligned} \tau_{\text{ATT}} = & \mathbb{E}_{P(X)|W_i=1}\left[\mathbb{E}\left(Y_i(1)|P(X_i), W_i = 1\right)\right] \\ & - \mathbb{E}_{P(X_i)|W_i=1}\left[\mathbb{E}\left(Y_i(0)|P(X_i), W_i = 0\right)\right]. \end{aligned} \tag{3.11}$$

As these results establish that it is sufficient to condition only on the propensity score to ensure independence of the assignment mechanism and the potential outcomes, this opens up a range of estimation techniques. One of these is matching, which we will discuss immediately below, however later in this chapter we will see that a number of alternative techniques exist which also take advantage of the propensity score theorem. At various times throughout the rest of this book we will see that the propensity score is a fundamental building block in a range of other techniques, even if we do not wish to assume conditional unconfoundedness.

3.3 Matching as an Identification Strategy

A conceptually elegant solution for estimating treatment effects when assuming conditional unconfoundedness is to use matching estimators. Matching estimators are based on the logic that if for each combination of covariates X_i units are randomly assigned to treatment and control, we should simply find treated and control units *within* each level of covariates and "match" them to estimate treatment effects. In essence, we are thus matching each treated individual to their untreated counterpart, and in this way inferring their counterfactual outcome to estimate a CATE. These can then be aggregated to estimate an ATT or other quantities of interest. This is essentially an exact implementation of what is summarized in (3.9).

In practice, it is not (necessarily) so straightforward as just matching and estimating. Indeed, there is a considerable literature on matching, which we will discuss below, as well as a number of overview papers from within economics (e.g., Imbens [2015] and Caliendo and Kopeinig [2008] for particularly applied examples) and outside of economics (e.g., Stuart

[2010]; Sekhon [2009]) that lay out key elements to consider when implementing matching. A handbook edited by Zubizarreta et al. (2023) provides a broad overview of the literature along with some recent developments in this space.

3.3.1 A General Overview of Matching Estimators

A matching estimator will seek to estimate a counterfactual for each treated unit (if estimating an ATT) or a counterfactual for each unit (if estimating an ATE). Such an estimator can be written as follows:

$$\widehat{\tau}_{\text{ATT}}^{\text{Match}} = \frac{1}{N_T} \sum_{i:W_i=1} \left(Y_i - \frac{1}{M} \sum_{j \in \mathcal{J}_M(i)} Y_j \right) \tag{3.12}$$

for an ATT, or, in the case of the ATE, as:

$$\widehat{\tau}_{\text{ATE}}^{\text{Match}} = \frac{1}{N_T} \sum_{i:W_i=1} \left(Y_i - \frac{1}{M} \sum_{j \in \mathcal{J}_M(i)} Y_j \right) + \frac{1}{N_C} \sum_{i:W_i=0} \left(\frac{1}{M} \sum_{j \in \mathcal{J}_M(i)} Y_j - Y_i \right). \tag{3.13}$$

Here, following a notation similar to Abadie and Imbens (2016), the function $\mathcal{J}_M(i)$ refers to the set of matches for each unit i, and M refers to the number of matches. A nice thing about these matching estimands is that they make very clear the links to potential outcomes from the Rubin Causal Model. Specifically, following, for example, Imbens (2004), imputed potential outcomes can be written as:

$$\widehat{Y}_i(0) = \begin{cases} Y_i, & \text{if } W_i = 0 \\ \frac{1}{M} \sum_{j \in \mathcal{J}_{M(i)}} Y_j, & \text{if } W_i = 1 \end{cases} \tag{3.14}$$

and

$$\widehat{Y}_i(1) = \begin{cases} \frac{1}{M} \sum_{j \in \mathcal{J}_{M(i)}} Y_j, & \text{if } W_i = 0 \\ Y_i, & \text{if } W_i = 1 \end{cases} \tag{3.15}$$

and based on this, the matching estimator in (3.13) can simply be rewritten as:

$$\widehat{\tau}_{\text{ATE}}^{\text{Match}} = \frac{1}{N} \sum_{i=1}^{N} \left(\widehat{Y}_i(1) - \widehat{Y}_i(0) \right). \tag{3.16}$$

This matching function $\mathcal{J}_M(i)$ does the work of defining for us the counterfactual for each unit i. The implementation of a matching estimator thus hinges crucially on the way that this matching function operates. In defining the matching function, there are a number of key choices—specifically, we must define a measure of closeness on which to match, and we then must define some specific matching method to be used. The first of these conditions refers to how we measure the "distance" between two observations in determining which units are considered as matched. And the second condition refers to how we decide to use this distance to match, for example, whether we should match with or without replacement, match each observation to a single or potentially multiple units, and so forth. Following any proposed matching procedure, potentially we must consider issues related to overlap and sample trimming. We consider these factors below discussing particular matching methods laid out in the literature.

3.3.2 Exact Matching

Exact matching is the most straightforward implementation of the ideas laid out in (3.7)–(3.9). Here we simply match by seeking observations that have the exact same realizations of all covariates X. This implies a matching function of the following type:

$$\mathcal{J}_{M(i)} = \{j : W_j = 1 - W_i, \|X_i - X_j\| = 0\}. \tag{3.17}$$

Here this matching function resolves to 1 for units of j only if two specific conditions are met: firstly $W_j = 1 - W_i$, which is to say units which have a different treatment status to i, and if $\|X_i - X_j\| = 0$. This latter condition could be written in other ways, but here $\|\cdot\|$ is a norm,[2] and the implication of this is that this value will only be zero when each covariate X is exactly the same between i and j.

In exact matching, we are considering a measure of closeness that essentially searches *only* for units that are exactly identical on covariates. We consider as "matched" units that are identical and discard as matches all units with even a single difference in a single covariate. This can be viewed as equivalent to matching based on the distance between two observations, where the distance is 0 if all covariates are identical and infinite if any covariates are not identical (Stuart 2010). Once we have generated this distance, the only detail left is how to match, and in this case again the procedure is relatively straightforward, as we simply use as matches all observations that meet the criteria in (3.17). Matching is conducted "with replacement" as if any two treated units have the same set of covariates, they will be matched to the same set of control units. Examples of such matching procedures can be found in Angrist (1998).

While exact matching is conceptually very clear and suggests a logical way forward, in practice, it can be difficult to implement (see, e.g., Heckman, Ichimura, and Todd [1997]) and comes with some inefficiencies. In particular, finding matches can be difficult if the number of covariates is large. For example, if a match is being conducted based on two binary variables, there will only be four cells on which to match, and this will be very tractable. However, as the number of variables and levels increases, the number of cells increases very rapidly, precisely in line with the curse of dimensionality discussed previously. For example, Zhao (2004) discusses an example based on twelve covariates that results in six million distinct cells on which to match, a quantity far in excess of the total number of observations under study. In practice, this means that most cells are empty, and most individuals remain unmatched. Additionally, exact matching requires that variables are categorical rather than continuous.[3]

3.3.3 Other Forms of Covariate Matching

One possible solution to challenges inherent in the exact matching estimator, and the presence of continuous variables in particular, is to still match on covariates but to use some alternative measure of distance on which to match. One such commonly used metric in this case is the Mahalanobis Distance, suggested for use in matching by Rubin (1980a). The Mahalanobis distance, defined as $\mathrm{d}_M(X_i, X_j)$ in (2.15), provides a summary of the distance between two observations i and j in the multidimensional space of X. The specific matching function that is considered in Mahalonobis matching can be written as:

$$\mathcal{J}_{M(i)} = \left\{ j : W_j = 1 - W_i, \left[\sum_{k: W_k = 1 - W_i} \mathbb{1}\left(\mathrm{d}_M(X_i, X_k) \leq \mathrm{d}_M(X_i, X_j) \right) \right] \leq M \right\}. \tag{3.18}$$

This style of matching function is defined in Abadie and Imbens (2016) and for each unit i will indicate the j units that are the M closest matches based on the Mahalanobis distance. Thus, if M is set equal to 1, $\mathcal{J}_{M(i)}$ will indicate the closest unit to i in terms of its Mahalanobis distance. Similarly, if $M=2$, $\mathcal{J}_{M(i)}$ will indicate the two closest units, and so forth. The summation over k implies that j will be chosen such that the required number of units (indexed by k) will be chosen to have a value for the Mahalanobis distance below j. In essence, j is the largest value of the Mahalanobis distance accepted as a match, up to the point that M units are indicated as matched.

This function thus specifies both the distance metric on which to match (Mahalanobis) as well as certain elements related to the precise *way* in which the match is made. If a larger value for M is used, this will imply matching each unit with a larger number of comparison units, reducing variance at the cost of potentially increasing bias, while a smaller value for M matches each unit with fewer "counterfactual" units, increasing noise but working with closer matches. In sections 3.3.7 and 3.3.8 we discuss at more length considerations related to the bias and variance of such estimators.

3.3.4 Matching with the Propensity Score

There are a number of drawbacks with matching on covariates that can be remedied by working with more aggregated matching methods. This is both related to issues with continuous variables and the curse of dimensionality, as well as issues related to overlap in terms of X between treated and untreated units (Heckman, Ichimura, and Todd 1997). Perhaps the most common of these—and the most common matching strategy more generally—leverages the propensity score discussed above to conduct propensity score matching.

The logic of matching with the propensity score is virtually identical to that laid out in (3.18); however, here matching proceeds based on the distance between the propensity scores of units. A particular implementation, following (3.18), as laid out in Abadie and

Imbens (2016) is to use the following matching function:

$$\mathcal{J}_{M(i)} = \left\{ j : W_j = 1 - W_i, \left[\sum_{k: W_k = 1 - W_i} \mathbb{1} \left(|P(X_i) - P(X_k)| \leq |P(X_i) - P(X_j)| \right) \right] \leq M \right\}. \tag{3.19}$$

In their original work, Rosenbaum and Rubin (1983) note that if the propensity score is known, matching on the propensity score is one of a number of techniques that can be used to estimate treatment effects. Matching on the propensity score has been widely adopted, in part because as well as resolving practical issues related to matching when there are potentially many covariates without observed overlap in each cell, it has also been shown to be more efficient than covariate matching in a number of empirically relevant cases (Angrist and Hahn 2004). In settings where the propensity score must be estimated based on covariates X—as is generally the case—these methods also have desirable properties. Generally estimation proceeds via a logit specification that was suggested even in the original work of Rosenbaum and Rubin (1983, 1984) and that can be viewed as the de facto choice, which ensures that the propensity score is bounded between 0 and 1.[4] Applied details related to matching on the propensity score, and the implementation of matching procedures more generally, are discussed below in section 3.3.6.

With the matching function defined in (3.19), estimation of both ATT or ATE parameters can proceed. For example, based on the above methods, the ATE and ATT can be estimated as defined in (3.12) and (3.13). Relatively recent work from Abadie and Imbens (2016) has provided theoretical results related to estimation and inference when the propensity score is estimated rather than known (the most common case in practice), and we will delay our discussion of aspects related to biases and inference in these methods until later subsections.

Code Callout 3.1: Propensity Score Matching and Job Training Programs
Dehejia and Wahba (2002) revisit an analysis of job-training programs described in LaLonde (1986) and document how matching estimators compare to experimentally identified estimates. Refer to code callout 3.1 to see the implementation of such estimators in practice as well as their performance in a particular setting against a benchmark experimental evaluation.

3.3.5 The Technology of Matching

The above procedures consider particular *metrics* on which to match. In the case of propensity score, units will be matched based on the absolute distance between their propensity scores, while in the case of Mahalanobis matching, units will be matched based on a quadratic distance. However, even conditional on a particular matching metric, there are a range of possible matching technologies that can be employed. These issues have been discussed and explored both based on real data as well as Monte Carlo experiments[5] by, among others, Dehejia and Wahba (2002), Smith and Todd (2005), Frölich (2004), and Diaz and Handa (2006).

A range of possible matching procedures have been proposed, and properties of matching estimators depend on these procedures. These procedures can be based simply on relative proximity, where each unit is simply matched to its closest, or k-closest counterfactal units. This is referred to as nearest-neighbor and k-nearest-neighbor matching, respectively. Nearest-neighbor matching consists of setting $M = 1$ in (3.18) or (3.19) for Mahalanobis and propensity score matching, respectively, and k-nearest-neighbor matching consists of setting $M = k$. These procedures do not account for the absolute proximity of units in generating the match; simply matching each unit with its nearest neighbor(s). Alternatively, procedures can be based simply on the absolute proximity, where each unit is matched to units within some specific fixed range. This is referred to by Smith and Todd (2005) and Dehejia and Wahba (2002) as "radius matching," where the match is generated by averaging across all units within a given "radius." Matching can also proceed considering both relative and absolute distance. Caliper matching, defined in Cochran and Rubin (1973), is similar to nearest-neighbor matching in that it matches each unit with the nearest counterfactual but also considers absolute proximity by *not* considering a unit as matched if there are no counterfactuals within a specific distance (the caliper). Such a method gains from being able to include more units in the generation of the counterfactual when there are many observations close to the support of the indicator observation, without sacrificing match quality when fewer observations are available. Similarly, kernel matching, described among other places in Heckman, Ichimura, and Todd (1998, 1997), seeks to gain from matching with more units where there is substantial overlap between a unit and its counterfactuals by generating a weighted average, placing *more* weight on units that are closer to a given unit and less weight on units that are further away. It does so by weighting with a kernel function. These functions integrate to 1 and, depending on the functional form of the kernel used, can place differing weights on units with weights decreasing as the distance between each unit and potential matches increases.

A range of such matching procedures is presented graphically in figure 3.1. This data is simulated in the interests of documenting alternative matching procedures, where here we consider matching by a propensity score (horizontal axis) to estimate an ATT. Indeed, in this particular (made up) example, estimating an ATE would likely not be reasonable, given the substantial lack of overlap across the propensity score of untreated individuals, though note that there *is* good overlap among treated units and controls. We return to the practical considerations behind matching, and discussions related to a lack of overlap, in the following subsection. Each panel documents an alternative procedure such as nearest-neighbor matching based on pairs in panel (a) and a similar procedure based on k units in panel (b).

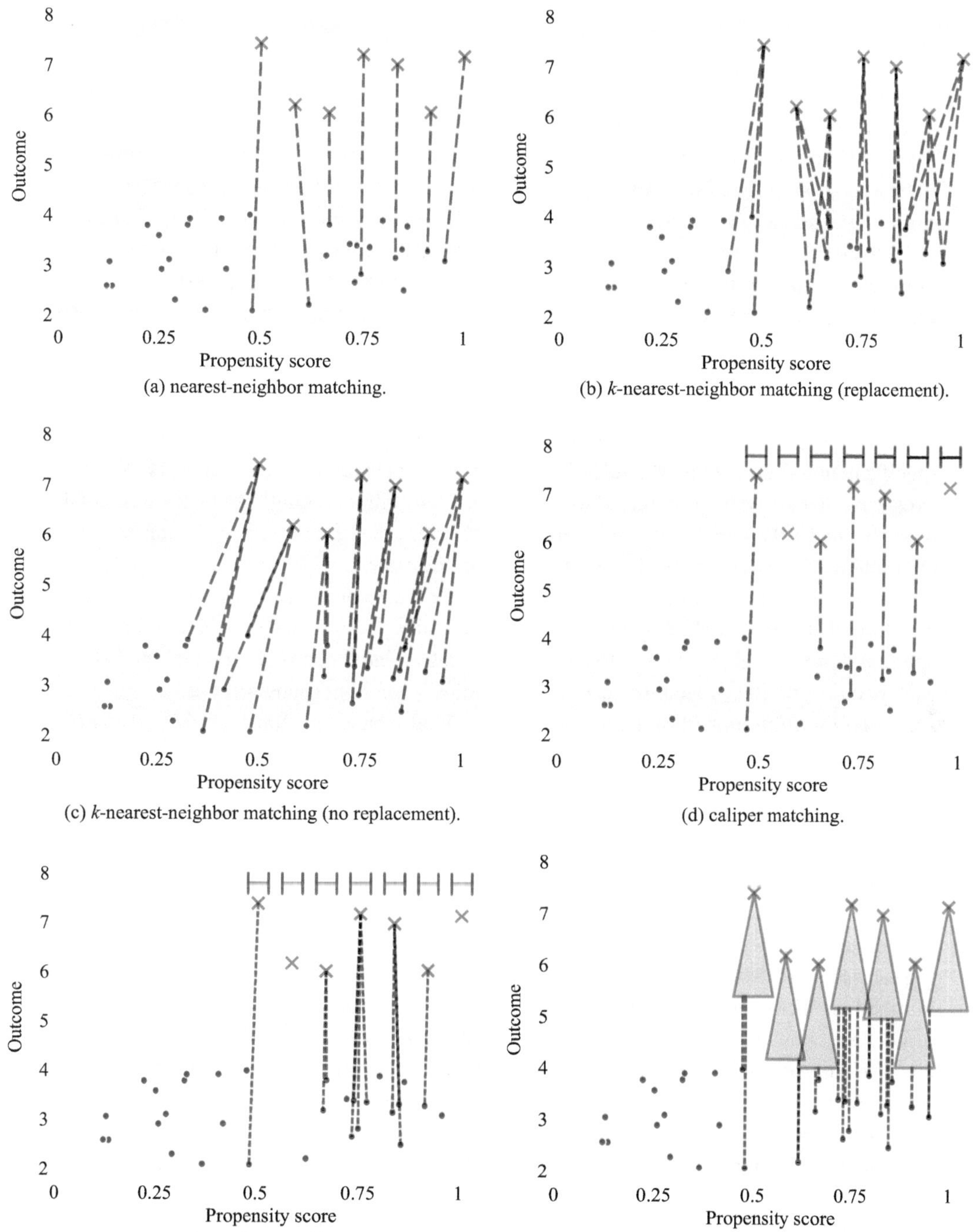

(a) nearest-neighbor matching.

(b) k-nearest-neighbor matching (replacement).

(c) k-nearest-neighbor matching (no replacement).

(d) caliper matching.

(e) radius matching.

(f) kernel matching (triangular kernel).

Figure 3.1
Alternative matching methods.

A key consideration in such procedures is whether matching occurs with or without replacement. In panel (b), matching is conducted with replacement such that units can be "recycled" and used multiple times as counterfactuals. However, in panel (c), a similar k-nearest-neighbor procedure is used, where in this case once a unit is used as a counterfactual it is *not* used again. If matching occurs without replacement, it is important to note the results are sensitive to the order in which matching occurs. If, as in panel (c), matching occurs from highest to lowest propensity scores matches will be better at high propensity scores, and deteriorate as propensity scores fall. Alternatively, matching without replacement may occur in random order, or from lowest to highest. A clear discussion of the implications of such decisions is provided in Dehejia and Wahba (2002), and in exercise 1 of this chapter, you can see the implications of such choices with their data. Such a result occurs because these procedures are "greedy" algorithms, where "greedy" refers to the fact that when a specific match uses a counterfactual observation, it is not available for other units. Alternatives exist that are optimal, referred to as "optimal" or "full matching" (B. B. Hansen 2004; Rosenbaum 1991), which generate matches with replacement in a way that minimizes the total difference across all matched units and their covariates.

Panels (d), (e), and (f) further refine the matching process by considering some maximum matching distance. Panel (d) bases matches on a caliper, and hence considers unmatched any unit that is not close enough to a counterfactual, as indicated by horizontal bars above each point. A similar procedure occurs with "radius" matching (panel e), but here matches are based on *all* units within a specific caliper. Finally, panel (f) considers kernel matching. In this case, counterfactuals are generated based on triangular weighting functions that integrate to 1, and that give most weight to units closest to the specific treated unit. In practice, a range of alternative kernels can be considered such as a normal kernel, which weights based on a Gaussian distribution, or an Epanechnikov kernel, which is symmetric and hump shaped, declining to zero at some particular start and end point.

The consideration of the type of matching procedure entails a trade-off between bias and variance. As a larger number of units are included in counterfactuals, the variance of matching estimators is reduced given that counterfactuals can be estimated with greater precision, but the bias increases, given that units are used that are further from matched pairs. Similarly, if matching occurs *with* replacement, bias is smaller given that units are matched with closer counterfactuals (Abadie and Imbens 2006), but variance increases because potentially fewer units are used in the construction of counterfactuals. We turn to the bias and variance properties of matching estimators in section 3.3.7 and 3.3.8.

More generally though, practical advice on working with matching in small samples suggests no clear advice on an ideal procedure across settings, and so the question of what method to used should be tailored to the nature of the setting under study. Such lessons can be drawn from Monte Carlo simulations, such as those conducted by Frölich (2004) and Zhao (2004). These papers typically consider the performance of estimators in terms of mean-squared bias, which seeks to trade off bias and variance. In general, performance in small samples depends on a number of factors, such as the overlap between treated and control units, the sample size and number of variables considered, the quantity of control units available, and their explanatory power. While lessons can be drawn for specific cases, overall these point to "no clear winner" (Zhao 2004, 100). This is echoed in the fact that surveys such as those of Imbens (2015) note that there is no evidence to suggest that one particular estimator should always be used. Huber, Lechner, and Wunsch (2013), in conducting Monte Carlo studies seeking to mimic real data, similarly report that no specific estimator is superior for all designs and outcomes, though they note that caliper matching appears to work best on average in the cases they consider. This lack of a universally preferred option makes clear the importance of considering the properties of the data to be used, including sample size, overlap, the variables used to generate the propensity, and potentially even beliefs about data-generating processes, in determining the preferred matching technology. Nevertheless, a number of more general practical recommendations do exist, and we discuss these now.

3.3.6 Practical Considerations

When implementing matching-based methods, there are a number of important practical considerations. This includes factors such as what to do if certain observations do not have a close match, evaluating the quality of potential matches, and, in the case of propensity score matching, considerations of exactly how to estimate the propensity score.

Common support and trimming A first fundamental issue in matching is that of overlap, or common support. We have previously made an assumption that we have called overlap (assumption 3′). This overlap assumption refers to population-level behavior. It states that in theory, every unit has some chance of being assigned to treatment and to control. In practice, in any sample of data, we will likely observe units that have covariate combinations not observed in any other units. This is a problem if no close comparison unit can be found for a particular unit. In cases where propensity score or other univariate aggregation methods are used, a lack of exact overlap is overcome by reducing multivariate covariates to a single metric. However, it is fundamental that in such cases, units are matched with counterfactuals that are close in terms of propensity score.

Indeed, Manski (1990), Heckman et al. (1998), Angrist (1998), and Rubin (1977) note that treatment effects are not defined over areas in which there is no common support between treated units and controls, with a lack of overlap potentially resulting in considerable bias in estimates. In the case of propensity score, by definition $P(X_i)$ tends to be higher on average among treated units than among control units given that treated units are more likely to receive treatment given their covariates. However, what is key for estimation is that there exist at least some untreated observations with high propensity scores to match with extreme treated observations, and similarly there exist some treated observations with a low propensity score to match with control observations. In the case of estimates of the ATT, common support is only required across treated units. The illustrative version of matching indicated in figure 3.1 is a case where common support appears reasonable among treated units (justifying the estimation of an ATT) but not among control units (suggesting an ATE will be considerably more questionable). In real examples, often extreme values of propensity scores share no overlap with counterfactual groups. For example, visual inspection of propensity scores in the commonly considered case of evaluating a labor market training program (Dehejia and Wahba 2002; LaLonde 1986) presented in figure 3.2 suggests a small number of low-propensity scores among control units with no close match among treated and a small number of high scores among treated with no close match among controls.

Commonly, considerations of overlap, such as that presented in figure 3.2, are presented, and Lechner (2008) suggests that visual inspection in this way is often sufficient to see lack of overlap without formal tests. A number of procedures have been described to ensure that common support is obtained prior to estimation. Heckman, Ichimura, and Todd (1998) and Smith and Todd (2005), for example, use a trimming procedure that discards observations where the estimated density of propensity scores is zero or very low. Dehejia and Wahba (1999) suggest discarding treated observations for which estimated propensity scores are larger than the highest value among the control group in order to estimate an ATT (and additionally discard control units with propensity scores smaller than the lowest

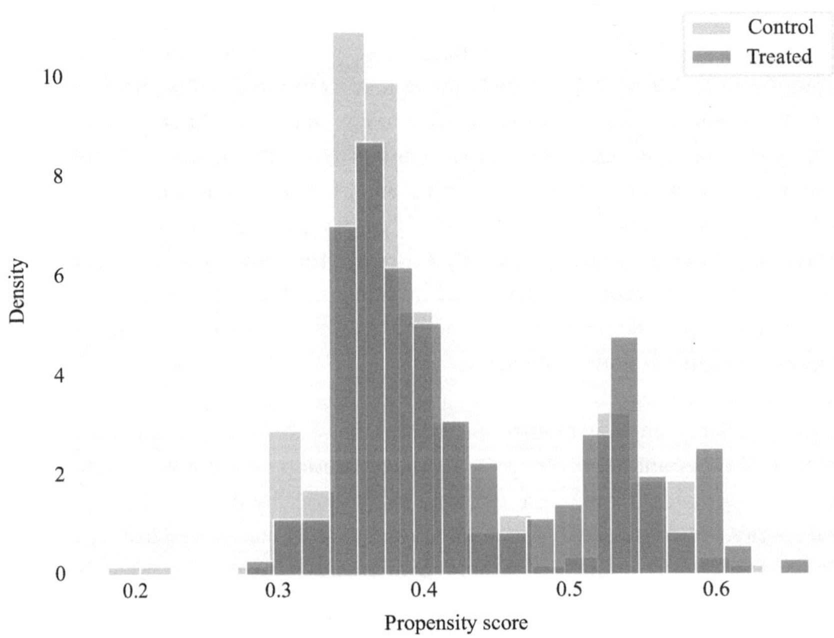

Figure 3.2
Overlap and propensity score: Dehejia and Wahba (2002) data.

value in the treatment group in the case of an ATE [Caliendo and Kopeinig 2008]). In such minima/maxima criteria, Lechner (2002) suggests additionally examining sensitivity to alternative choices, such as dropping from the tenth lowest and tenth highest in this way. Crump et al. (2009) suggest an optimal procedure based on precision of estimated propensity scores, though they note that an approximation to their optimal rule is to drop units with propensity scores outside of the range 0.1–0.9. Such procedures imply that any estimated treatment effects will not be viewed as either ATTs or ATEs, but rather need be interpreted as informative of effects among selected subpopulations (Crump et al. 2009). Lechner (2008) suggests a bounding procedure to return from such quantities to ATT or ATE estimates.

Covariate match A second key consideration in cases where matching is not conducted exactly is in considering whether matching actually achieves the desired covariate balance. Given the propensity score theorem, conditioning on the propensity score should imply that there is no remaining correlation between treatment W_i and covariates X_i. This can be observed by considering balance in covariates X_i across matched treated and control samples. Given that the propensity score theorem makes no statement of the functional form of X_i, Smith and Todd (2005) suggest that finding that covariates are *not* balanced between treatment and control units may be evidence of misspecification of the estimation of propensity score. This suggests the need of some way to suggest testing for balance in matched samples. A number of proposals exist (Caliendo and Kopeinig 2008). One is to consider the standard bias by estimating the standardized difference of mean values of each variable X across matched treatment and control groups. This standardized bias (SB) proposed by Rosenbaum and Rubin (1985) is:

$$SB = 100 \cdot \frac{\bar{X}_{1M} - \bar{X}_{0M}}{\sqrt{\frac{1}{2}\left(\mathbb{V}_{1M}(X) + \mathbb{V}_{0M}(X)\right)}},$$

where $\bar{X}_{1M}$ and $\mathbb{V}_{1M}$ refer to means and variance of X in the matched treated group, and $\bar{X}_{0M}$ and $\mathbb{V}_{0M}$ is the same for the control group. One drawback of this method is that it suggests no criteria by which one can reject hypotheses of balance, which has led to usage of t-tests of balance across group in matched samples, or t-tests within strata of the propensity score (Dehejia and Wahba 1999, 2002). Dehejia and Wahba (2002) propose a procedure (discussed below) in which balance is used to inform the estimation of the propensity score.

Code Callout 3.2: Covariate Balance

In code callout 3.2 we work with data from Almond, Chay, and Lee (2005), who examine the impact of smoking during pregnancy on birthweight. We examine the estimation of the propensity score and overlap across treated and untreated groups, and how covariate balance varies in original and propensity score matched samples.

Estimating the propensity score Generally, propensity scores are unknown and so must be estimated from the data. The problem of estimating a propensity score is essentially the problem of nonparametric estimation of a regression function (Imbens and Rubin 2015) as we seek to flexibly estimate $\widehat{P(X_i)}$ for combinations of X_i. While a number of proposals exist related to estimating the propensity score, there is no explicit rule for this. We do, however, have a general criteria for evaluating estimated propensity scores: Conditioning on the propensity score should result in balance of observable characteristics across treatment and control groups. In other words, we can seek to determine if, at least approximately:

$$W_i \perp\!\!\!\perp X_i | \widehat{P(X_i)}, \tag{3.20}$$

where here the notation $\widehat{P(X_i)}$ refers to the estimated propensity score.

Often, the propensity score is estimated using a logit model. Thus, each individual's treatment status is regressed on a vector of characteristics X_i using a logit model, and predictions are taken from this model. The use of a logit model has the desirable property that all predictions will be bound between 0 and 1. Nevertheless, there is nothing particularly special about the logit compared to other nonlinear estimation procedures such as the probit, and estimates should be assessed to be robust to such decisions (Imbens 2015). By design, the logit places more mass on scores in the tails of the propensity score distribution and is often suggested as the procedure for estimating propensity scores (see, for example, Caliendo and Kopeinig [2008]).

The balancing property described in (3.20) is frequently used as a criteria for assessing the proposed propensity score estimates and conducting further refinement if necessary. Given that the propensity score is not given any causal or structural interpretation, and rather is seen as approximating the conditional expectation, there is no issue if specification searches are used in the definition of this approximation (Imbens 2015). Definitions of procedures that build a propensity score estimation based on covariate balance exist—for example, see the appendix of Dehejia and Wahba (2002). Their proposal is to estimate propensity score using baseline covariates as well as interactions between covariates and higher-order (e.g., quadratic) terms. They suggest that any propensity score can then be evaluated by considering strata (ranges of values) of the propensity score in which the average propensity score does not differ between treated and control units, and then within each of these strata, assess whether covariates are balanced using a simple t-test. If covariates are observed to be balanced in all strata, the propensity score is accepted; otherwise further higher-order terms and interactions are added. A similar procedure is discussed by Imbens and Rubin (2015) and Imbens (2015), where additionally a stepwise procedure is defined with specific criteria used to judge whether a marginal variable or interaction should be included in model based on testing whether the variable has a null impact on treatment.

Other procedures have also been proposed such as the use of shrinkage estimators like the Lasso (Belloni, Chernozhukov, and Hansen 2014b), which will automatically select groups of variables for inclusion in the propensity score model from among a larger pool of potential variables. We will return to discuss the Lasso and related methods in chapter 9 of this book. Similarly, other criteria exist for matching that seek to explicitly achieve balance across covariates. This includes a procedure discussed in Díaz, Rau, and Rivera (2015), where both matched units and their weights are selected to maximize balance, and "genetic matching" proposed by Diamond and Sekhon (2013) where covariates are allowed to take on different weights. In general, sensitivity testing to techniques such as these should be considered, and if results are observed to be highly sensitive to reasonable methods of estimating propensity scores or conducting matching, this will suggest that estimates should not be viewed as credible (Imbens 2015).

Multiple treatment levels So far throughout this chapter, we have assumed that there is a single binary treatment that we are concerned with modeling. *However*, such analyses can be extended to multiple treatment levels (Lechner 2001) or to cases where treatments are viewed as dose responses (Imbens 2000). In these cases, any propensity score estimation will need to account for multiple treatment levels, which can either be modeled with a multinomial or nested logit if there is no clear ordering in doses or levels, or as a smoother function such as a linear regression if these doses are ordered (Imbens 2000). Estimation of effects can thus proceed by considering matched samples across dose levels at arrive to estimates such as those laid out in (1.11). Given the relative infrequency of this setting in applied work, we will not delve into these issues here, but we direct you to Imbens (2000) and Lechner (2001) if you would like to see more.

3.3.7 Bias in Matching

Understanding bias in matching I—estimation The value of multivariate matching procedures, such as Mahalanobis matching and propensity score matching, is that they allow for matching even where the full set of covariates on which to match is large, precluding the possibility of using exact matching. However, such matching methods are not, in general, unbiased, even if assumptions related to conditional unconfoundedness hold. If we consider an ATT, following the notation of Abadie and Imbens (2006), the bias in matching estimators can be written as follows:

$$B_M = \frac{1}{N_T} \sum_{i=1}^{N} W_i \frac{1}{M} \sum_{m=1}^{M} \left(\mu_0(X_i) - \mu_0(X_{jm(i)})\right), \tag{3.21}$$

where $\mu_0(X_i) \equiv \mathbb{E}[Y(0)|X = X_i]$. Similar expressions for bias can be written if one wishes to calcuate an ATE; see, for example, Abadie and Imbens (2006, 243) Thus, any bias comes from the fact that for any particular treated unit with characteristics X_i, the expectation of Y_0 at their particular values of X_i may not be the same as expectation of $Y(0)$ at the particular values of $X_{\mathcal{J}_M(i)}$ of matched units j. Of course, if exact matching is used, then, by definition, $X_i = X_{J_M(i)}$, and hence $\mu_0(X_i) - \mu_0(X_{\mathcal{J}_M(i)}) = 0$, and any bias disappears. However, if treated units are matched to counterfactual units with different realizations of X_i, as generally occurs in multivariate matching, bias will not necessarily disappear, even as the sample grows without limit.

Abadie and Imbens (2006) analyze this formally in a case where matching is conducted using k nearest neighbors with replacement. They show that if more than a single continuous covariate exists, then the order of the bias in (3.21) is increasing in the number of (continuous) covariates, and standard large sample theory for variance estimation cannot be used, as the bias will not disappear, even with as few as two continuous covariates, and will overwhelm the variance term with three or more continuous covariates. However, such biases *can* be ignored either in cases where all variables X_i are discrete (as, in the limit, this will converge to exact matching), where only a single continuous covariate exists, or, in the case of an ATT, if the number of controls is considerably larger than the number of treated units. However, bias corrections also exist (as laid out below) that address this issue directly.

Understanding bias in matching II—unobservables In cases where *unobservable* selection occurs, any procedures posited on conditional uncounfoundedness will not be sufficient to eliminate bias. Heckman et al. (1998) examine the bias in matching estimators where, as well as potential differences owing to mismatch in covariates, note that bias depends on mismatch in terms of any variables *not* being conditioned upon. They propose that such a bias can be directly estimated in a particular empirical setting if some randomized experiment is conducted, and the control is compared to a matched "control" group drawn from the general population. This relates to an important line of work starting with LaLonde (1986) where observational estimators are compared to experimental estimates. Based on a particular empirical example and using propensity score-based methods, they suggest that bias owing to selection is *less important* than bias owing to differences in support of covariates; pointing to benefits of propensity score matching, they nevertheless document bias owing to selection on unobservables that is relevant compared to the size of experimental estimates. We return to discuss selection, and whether assumptions of conditional unconfounding are reasonable, at more length in section 3.6.

Bias correction procedures Procedures exist that can be used to correct biases owing to mismatches in observed covariates as laid out in Abadie and Imbens (2006). The key element in such procedures is that biases present in matching estimators occur because the expectation of $Y_i(0)$ for each treated unit may not actually be the same as $Y_i(0)$ for matched untreated counterfactuals given that the two groups have different baseline covariates X_i (i.e., bias occurs as in (3.21)).

Abadie and Imbens (2011) show that the solution to this is to simply incorporate the estimation of this bias into the matching estimator. Previously, we have seen that a matching estimator can be expressed as the difference between observed outcomes and matched counterfactuals, as (3.16). A bias correction term can be directly incorporated in such a setting as laid out below:

$$\tilde{Y}_i(0) = \begin{cases} Y_i, & \text{if } W_i = 0 \\ \frac{1}{M} \sum_{j \in \mathcal{J}_{M(i)}} \left(Y_j + \widehat{\mu}_0(X_i) - \widehat{\mu}_0(X_j) \right), & \text{if } W_i = 1 \end{cases} \tag{3.22}$$

and

$$\tilde{Y}_i(1) = \begin{cases} \frac{1}{M} \sum_{j \in \mathcal{J}_{M(i)}} \left(Y_j + \widehat{\mu}_1(X_i) - \widehat{\mu}_1(X_j) \right), & \text{if } W_i = 0 \\ Y_i, & \text{if } W_i = 1. \end{cases} \tag{3.23}$$

Here, $\widehat{\mu}_0(X_i)$ and $\widehat{\mu}_1(X_i)$ are regression-based imputations of mean outcomes where treatment is equal to 0 and 1, respectively. Later in this chapter (section 3.5), we will return to consider regression-based imputation estimators. Note here that for cases where $X_j = X_i$, $\widehat{\mu}_0(X_i) = \widehat{\mu}_0(X_j)$, and hence the second and third term in (3.22) will cancel out (and similar for cases μ_1 in (3.23)). However, in cases where X_i is not equal to X_j, the above procedure allows for the direct correction of the bias, leading to the bias-corrected matching estimator defined as:

$$\widehat{\tau}_{\text{ATE}}^{\text{BCM}} = \frac{1}{N} \sum_{i=1}^{N} \left(\tilde{Y}_{i(1)} - \tilde{Y}_{i(0)} \right). \tag{3.24}$$

The results from Abadie and Imbens (2011) prove that this estimator is consistent if $\widehat{\mu}_0(X_i)$ is a consistent estimator of $\mu_0(X_i)$. Recent work from Lin, Ding, and Han (2023) suggests additionally that if the number of matches considered is allowed to grow with the sample size, this estimator also has very attractive efficiency properties.

3.3.8 Inference

In the previous chapter, we saw that there were a number of alternative manners one could follow to conduct inference where treatment is randomly assigned, with correct inference procedures depending on the nature of treatment assignment, as well as views on whether the source of uncertainty is sampling or design based. Inference in the case of matching estimators has additional complexity, both because we must take into account the fact that matches can potentially be recycled (in cases where matching with replacement is used) and because we must consider that the the propensity score is estimated, rather than known (in cases where propensity score is used as a distance metric).

If the propensity score *were* known or if some other known distance such as the Mahalanobis metric is used for matching, Abadie and Imbens (2006) provide a valid sample based variance estimator for cases where matching occurs with replacement. This is a complicated problem because units can potentially be used as matches multiple times, and Abadie and Imbens (2006) note that the distribution of the number of times units are reused is an important component in variance estimates. Abadie and Imbens (2006) show that, nevertheless, there is a closed-form solution for this variance. This variance depends on two terms. A first term, referred to as $\mathbb{V}^{\tau(X)}$ is simply the variance of the conditional average treatment effect $\mathbb{E}[(\tau(x)-\tau)^2]$. Additionally, the variance depends on a second term that is based on unexplained variation in the outcome at each particular point of the data. This is referred to as $\mathbb{V}^E$, where $V^E = N \cdot \mathbb{V}(\widehat{\tau}_{\text{ATE}}|X, W)$, with:

$$\mathbb{V}\left(\widehat{\tau}_{\text{ATE}}|X, W\right) = \frac{1}{N^2}\sum_{i=1}^{N}\left(1+\frac{K_M(i)}{M}\right)^2 \sigma^2(X_i, W_i),$$

where $K_M(i) = \sum_{l=1}^{N} \mathbb{1}\{i \in J_M(l)\}$ is the sum of times that unit i is used as a match and $\sigma^2(X_i, W_i)$ is the variance of outcome Y_i at X_i, W_i. The key point here is to note that the variance must account in an explicit way for the fact that matches are potentially reused, such that increasing the number of matches considered will increase the variance of estimates. Abadie and Imbens (2006) show how each element of these variance terms can be estimated, resulting in a consistent estimator for the variance of ATT and ATE estimates, and Abadie and Imbens (2011) note its suitability for inference for bias-corrected estimates such as (3.24). Computational implementations of these estimators are made available by the authors of the papers; however, they are now implemented as default in various computational languages.

In practice, however, generally the propensity score is unknown and must be estimated. In cases such as these, Abadie and Imbens (2016) have derived a closed-form variance formula for use with both the ATT and the ATE that accounts for the estimation of the propensity score. While these formulae are derived for cases where it is assumed that propensity score matching occurs with replacement, they are also suitable for other matching procedures Abadie and Imbens (2016, 793). Interestingly, adjustments to the variance to account for the fact that the propensity score is estimated will, if anything, result in reductions to the variance for ATE estimates, implying that even if the propensity score were known, estimating the propensity score is more efficient. While such a result holds for the ATE, Abadie and Imbens (2016) show that for the ATT, adjustments may result in either larger or smaller variance estimates.

Often in cases where estimators are based on various stages of estimation, the bootstrap provides a tractable way forward. However, for matching estimators, the standard bootstrap does *not* generally provide a consistent estimate of the variance. This is shown in Abadie and Imbens (2008), with the crux of the issue being that in bootstrapping, units are resampled multiple times, and each time they are resampled they will be matched with the same counterfactual. Nevertheless, a number of recent papers have proposed further refinements to bootstrap procedures (Otsu and Rai 2017; Bodory et al. 2020) that account for this and that have been shown to have particularly good properties in small samples (Bodory et al. 2020). This suggests that, with some care, such bootstrap methods can also provide a good way forward for matching estimators.

3.4 Weighting as an Identification Strategy

An alternative way to estimate treatment effects by means of the propensity score is to see that the problem can be cast as an issue of weighting. In a setting of conditional unconfoundedness, if we were to return to our *simple* difference in means estimator from the previous chapter (2.6):

$$\widehat{\tau}_{\text{ATE}} = \frac{\sum_{i=1}^{N} W_i Y_i}{\sum_{i=1}^{N} W_i} - \frac{\sum_{i=1}^{N}(1-W_i)Y_i}{\sum_{i=1}^{N} 1-W_i},$$

we know that the estimator would not return an average treatment effect. This is precisely because we are *not* accounting for the fact that treatment assignment is only as good as random when conditioning on covariates, implying that the balance of covariates in the treatment and control group are different. However, we can seek to reweight this estimator to correct for the fact that certain units are underrepresented in treatment or control. This leads to a reweighting estimator written as follows, where IPW is used to denote "inverse propensity score weight":

$$\tau_{\text{ATE}}^{\text{IPW}} = \frac{1}{N}\sum_{i=1}^{N}\left(\frac{Y_i W_i}{P(X_i)} - \frac{Y_i(1-W_i)}{1-P(X_i)}\right). \tag{3.25}$$

You will note the clear analogue between (3.25) and the (unweighted) difference in means estimator written above. Indeed, you could note that if treatment assignment is completely random, implying that (in theory) $P(X_i)$ is a constant, you can quite easily work from (3.25) back to the simple comparison of means estimator. Some related discussion is available in Hirano, Imbens, and Ridder (2003, section 3). While we are still essentially estimating a difference of means estimator in (3.25), here means are scaled (or weighted) by the inverse of the probability that they receive their particular treatment status. Roughly, the idea behind this is that for individuals with propensity score $P(X_i)$, we wish to compare them with their counterfactual among nontreated units. If there are few individuals with propensity score $P(X_i)$ among treated units, and many individual with this propensity score among control units, then treated units should be effectively weighted upward to match the size of the control units. This upward weighting occurs because if there are few individuals treated, a low value for the propensity score will be contained in the denominator on the left-hand side of (3.25). A similar logic holds for untreated units. Untreated units with *high* values of the propensity score will be scarce, and hence will receive more weight given their greater importance as counterfactuals for treated units. Indeed, Hahn (1998) highlights the property of estimators of this style as imputation estimators, given that weighting can be used to impute missing counterfactuals.

The fact that weighting by the inverse of the propensity score can be used to make a sample representative of the population of interest is underpinned by results first shown by Horvitz and Thompson (1952). Horvitz and Thompson (1952) proved such a result for cases where data is generated by sampling where different units have a different probability of selection. This is referred to as inverse probability weighting. The link between the results of Horvitz and Thompson and inverse propensity score weighting is such that at times (3.25) is referred to as a Horvitz-Thompson estimator (see, e.g., Imbens and Rubin [2015, 274]). This result owes to the fact that the two terms in (3.25) can be shown to be equal means of potential outcomes. This is to say:

$$\mathbb{E}\left[\frac{Y_iW_i}{P(X_i)}\right]=\mathbb{E}[Y_i(1)] \qquad \text{and} \qquad \mathbb{E}\left[\frac{Y_i(1-W_i)}{(1-P(X_i))}\right]=\mathbb{E}[Y_i(0)]. \tag{3.26}$$

To see why this is the case, note for the first equality above we can resolve as follows.

$$\begin{aligned}\mathbb{E}\left[\frac{Y_iW_i}{P(X_i)}\right]&=\mathbb{E}\left[\mathbb{E}_X\left(\frac{Y_iW_i}{P(X_i)}\middle|X_i\right)\right]=\mathbb{E}\left[\mathbb{E}_X\left(\frac{Y_i(1)W_i}{P(X_i)}\middle|X_i\right)\right]=\mathbb{E}\left[\frac{\mathbb{E}_X[Y_i(1)|X_i]\mathbb{E}_X[W_i|X_i]}{P(X_i)}\right]\\&=\mathbb{E}\left[\frac{\mathbb{E}_X[Y_i(1)|X_i]P(X_i)}{P(X_i)}\right]=\mathbb{E}[\mathbb{E}_X[Y_i(1)|X]]=\mathbb{E}[Y_i(1)].\end{aligned} \tag{3.27}$$

The first step of this applies the law of iterated expectations, before the second step uses the key result of conditional unconfoundedness, which means that *conditional on* X_i $\mathbb{E}[Y_i|W_i=1]=\mathbb{E}[Y_i(1)]$. The following steps then resolve the law of iterated expectations and substitute terms. An analogous series of steps can be conducted to arrive to the second expectation $\mathbb{E}[Y_i(0)]$.

While there is a little bit of algebra above, this should not distract from the fact that this result suggests that we can use the propensity score to arrive at an imputed counterfactual outcome by weighting upward those units that—according to their propensity score—are underrepresented within treatment or control groups. And once we have counterfactual outcomes, we can very simply arrive at our ATE by simply subtracting $\mathbb{E}[Y_i(0)]$ from $\mathbb{E}[Y_i(1)]$.

In practice, if the propensity were known, then the weighting estimator described in (3.25) would be very simple to implement. Generally, however, the propensity score is not known and must be estimated. Somewhat surprisingly, even if the propensity were known, estimates of the ATE based on the true propensity score would not be efficient (Hahn 1998), but estimates of the ATE based on the *estimated* propensity score can be efficient (Hirano, Imbens, and Ridder 2003). In particular, Hirano, Imbens, and Ridder (2003) suggest a slightly modified estimator based on inverse propensity score weighting. This is written as follows:

$$\widehat{\tau}_{\text{ATE}}^{\text{IPW}}=\left(\frac{\sum_{i=1}^N\frac{W_iY_i}{\widehat{P}(X_i)}}{\sum_{i=1}^N\frac{W_i}{\widehat{P}(X_i)}}\right)-\left(\frac{\sum_{i=1}^N\frac{(1-W_i)Y_i}{1-\widehat{P}(X_i)}}{\sum_{i=1}^N\frac{1-W_i}{1-\widehat{P}(X_i)}}\right). \tag{3.28}$$

Here, firstly, $P(X_i)$ is substituted for its estimated version allowing us to estimate $\widehat{\tau}_{\text{ATE}}^{\text{IPW}}$, and additionally a normalization is used to ensure that weights among treated and control units sum to one. Further discussion of this point is provided in the review paper of Imbens (2004). This normalization can be seen in the denominator in each term of (3.28). Hirano, Imbens, and Ridder (2003) show that in theory this estimator is consistent and efficient if the propensity score is estimated in a rich nonparametric manner, and Busso, DiNardo, and McCrary (2014) show that in practical implementations, the estimator performs well when the propensity score is estimated with a logit.

What's more, we can use a similar setup to arrive to an ATT estimate based on reweighting (Hirano, Imbens, and Ridder 2003). Because we are interested now only in the treated units, we must match the distribution of X_i among untreated units to that in the treated group, and we can write our ATT as follows:

$$\tau_{\text{ATT}}^{\text{IPW}} = \frac{1}{\Pr(W_i = 1)} \frac{1}{N} \sum_{i=1}^{N} \left(Y_i W_i - \frac{Y_i(1 - W_i)}{1 - P(X_i)} P(X_i) \right) \tag{3.29}$$

If the propensity score were known, we could thus estimate this as (see Imbens [2004]):

$$\hat{\tau}_{\text{ATT}}^{\text{IPW}} = \left(\frac{\sum_{i=1}^{N} W_i Y_i \frac{P(X_i)}{\hat{P}(X_i)}}{\sum_{i=1}^{N} W_i \frac{P(X_i)}{\hat{P}(X_i)}} \right) - \left(\frac{\sum_{i=1}^{N} (1 - W_i) Y_i \frac{P(X_i)}{1-\hat{P}(X_i)}}{\sum_{i=1}^{N} (1 - W_i) \frac{P(X_i)}{1-\hat{P}(X_i)}} \right). \tag{3.30}$$

Here the inclusion of the true propensity score ensures that the estimator recovers the ATT, while the use of the estimated propensity score owes to the efficiency point, and follows (3.28). When the propensity score is instead estimated, the known propensity score is simply replaced by its estimate, resulting in the simplified formula:

$$\hat{\tau}_{\text{ATT}}^{\text{IPW}} = \left(\frac{\sum_{i=1}^{N} W_i Y_i}{\sum_{i=1}^{N} W_i} \right) - \left(\frac{\sum_{i=1}^{N} (1 - W_i) Y_i \frac{\hat{P}(X_i)}{1-\hat{P}(X_i)}}{\sum_{i=1}^{N} (1 - W_i) \frac{\hat{P}(X_i)}{1-\hat{P}(X_i)}} \right). \tag{3.31}$$

Variance estimation for inverse propensity score weighting of the ATT or ATE is relatively straightforward and is implemented as standard in most computational languages. These variance estimators are typically based on generalized method of moments (GMM) but can also be implemented using bootstrap techniques. Formulae and discussions are presented in, among other places, Bodory et al. (2020), who also note that in small samples, standard bootstrap procedures appear to be more efficient than GMM-based counterparts in empirically relevant simulations.

3.5 Regression as an Identification Strategy

3.5.1 Understanding Regression as an Estimation Strategy

Under conditional unconfoundedness, our interest is in isolating the effect of treatment on some outcome *after* conditioning on a set of covariates X_i. Perhaps the most common way in which we are accustomed to conditioning in econometrics is via the use of regression. This thus suggests a logical third type of estimator, which is to simply run a regression. While this is indeed a valid option, the nature of the covariates and the way that the regression is specified will be important in considering the properties of this estimator as well as precisely *what* the estimator returns to us.

To see this, let's return to the potential outcomes framework with covariates that we defined in (2.8) and (2.9). For simplicity, we can begin by considering a single covariate X_i, though the nature of conditioning variables will be important, and so while presented initially as a single covariate case, below we discuss general principals. As noted in (2.10), this leads to a regression written as:

$$\begin{aligned} Y_i &= \mu_0 + (\mu_1 - \mu_0)W_i + \beta_0(X_i - \bar{X}) + (\beta_1 - \beta_0)(X_i - \bar{X})W_i + [\varepsilon_{0i} + (\varepsilon_{1i} - \varepsilon_{0i})W_i] \\ &\equiv \mu_0 + \tau^{\text{reg}} W_i + \beta_0(X_i - \bar{X}) + (\beta_1 - \beta_0)(X_i - \bar{X})W_i + \varepsilon_i. \end{aligned} \tag{3.32}$$

We likely remember from prior work with regressions that we can attach a causal interpretation to τ^{reg} when estimated by OLS under the assumption of exogeneity. This assumption implies that ε_i is independent of X_i and W_i. The key identifying assumption we have maintained here has been unconfoundedness, which states that $Y_i(0)$ and $Y_i(1)$ are independent of W_i conditional on X_i. Given that we have previously defined $Y_i(0)$ and $Y_i(1)$ as simply a function of X_i and $\varepsilon_i(0)$ and $\varepsilon_i(1)$, respectively (you may wish to refer back to (2.8)–(2.9)), unconfoundedness will imply exogeneity—and a causal interpretation for τ^{reg}—provided that we are adequately controlling for X_i. However, this implies that we must be correctly capturing the functional form that describes the relationship between X_i and $Y_i(0)$ and $Y_i(1)$. If we fail to capture some relevant covariate, or nonlinearity in included variables, this will induce a correlation between ε_i and X_i and W_i, resulting in bias when estimating τ^{reg}. As a matter of fact, given the propensity score theorem, rather than regression Y_i on all X_i, in cases of multidimensional X_i it would be sufficient to control for the propensity score (Heckman et al. 1998), though this is not in general efficient (Hahn 1998).

While an unconfoundedness assumption plus a correct functional form to model the dependence of Y_i on covariates provides identification and we can view τ^{reg} as a causal parameter, it is important to consider *what* treatment effect this captures. It turns out that this can be viewed as a reweighted matching estimate. Indeed, Angrist (1998) states that the "differences between regression and matching strategies for the estimation of treatment effects are partly cosmetic." To see why this is the case, consider a version of (3.32) with a single binary covariate X_i. We denote:

$$\mathbb{E}[Y_i(1) - Y_i(0)|X_i = 1, W_i = 1] = \tau_{x_1} \qquad \text{and} \qquad \mathbb{E}[Y_i(1) - Y_i(0)|X_i = 0, W_i = 1] = \tau_{x_0}.$$

These quantities are thus the covariate-specific treatment effects for each level of the covariate. Angrist (1998) demonstrates that the coefficient τ^{reg} from the regression:

$$Y_i = \mu_0 + \tau^{\text{reg}} W_i + \beta X_i + \varepsilon_i$$

generates a weighted combination of these two covariate-specific effects. Particularly, regression weights the effects in the following way:

$$\tau^{\text{reg}} = \frac{\tau_{x_0}\mathbb{V}(W_i = 1|X_i = 0)\Pr(X_i = 0) + \tau_{x_1}\mathbb{V}(W_i = 1|X_i = 1)\Pr(X_i = 1)}{\mathbb{V}(W_i = 1|X_i = 0)\Pr(X_i = 0) + \mathbb{V}(W_i = 1|X_i = 1)\Pr(X_i = 1)}.$$

Thus, while regression aggregates covariate-specific treatment effects, it does so in a way that provides greater weight to observations that have more variation in the treatment variable in that particular cell. Incidentally this behavior of regression helps explain why OLS estimators are the most efficient class of linear estimators—precisely because they place more weight on cells in which more treatment variation is observed and more can be learned, and less weight on cells where there is relatively little variation and less can be learned. Nevertheless, this weighting is different to the way that treatment effects are aggregated in matching estimators, where weights are simply based on the relative frequency of X_i among the group of interest. Angrist (1998) shows that this result holds for any combination of variables X_i provided that a dummy variable is included for every possible combination of X_i in the regression. This is known as saturating the model in X_i, and provided that this is done, OLS estimands will always aggregate the treatment effect for each covariate group, weighting by the variance of treatment within this group. If, on the other hand, variables X_i are continuous or models are not fully saturated in X_i, regression estimates extrapolate to arrive to the final treatment effect.

It is useful to see that the regression estimator can also be couched in terms more clearly corresponding to the potential outcomes framework. Following the notation of Imbens (2004), note that the regression estimator can be written as follows:

$$\begin{aligned}\widehat{\tau}^{\text{reg}}_{\text{ATE}} &= \frac{1}{N}\sum_{i-1}^{N}\left[\widehat{\mu}_1(X_i) - \widehat{\mu}_0(X_i)\right] \\ &= \frac{1}{N}\sum_{i=1}^{N} W_i\left[Y_i - \widehat{\mu}_0(X_i)\right] + (1 - W_i)\left[\widehat{\mu}_1(X_i) - Y_i\right].\end{aligned} \tag{3.33}$$

Here $\widehat{\mu}_1(X_i)$ is a regression-based estimator of $\mathbb{E}[Y|W = 1, X = X_i]$ and $\widehat{\mu}_0(X_i)$ is a similar regression-based estimator of $\mathbb{E}[Y|W = 0, X = X_i]$. When we write (3.33) we can see that regression effectively acts as an imputation estimator, or a model based estimator, given the importance of modeling how Y_i depends on covariates X_i. This is in contrast to matching estimators that are design-based, given their central consideration of identifying an untreated counterpart for each treated unit (and vice versa). For each treated unit Y_i, we subtract the regression-imputed counterfactual $\widehat{\mu}_0(X_i)$ to arrive at a treatment effect, and similarly, for each control outcome, we consider their regression-imputed treated counterfactual $\widehat{\mu}_1(X_i)$, implying their treatment effect would be $\widehat{\mu}_1(X_i) - Y_i$. The fact that the left-hand term of (3.33) is written in terms of Y_i and not $\widehat{\mu}_1(X_i)$ simply owes to the fact that we assume that the average prediction from regression equals the average true value in a sample.[6]

In practice, we can see that this estimator is thus tracing out the mean difference across two regression lines over all points of support in the sample. For a visual representation of the univariate case, this simply allows us to capture the mean difference across the two regression lines plotted in figure 2.1. The fact that estimation flows from the regression-based imputation allows us another way to understand the point mentioned previously. If linear regression is used to estimate $\widehat{\mu}_0(X_i), \widehat{\mu}_1(X_i)$ estimates will be variance weighted due to the mechanics of the regression, and these regression fits will give more weight to certain observations with higher treatment variation. Observing the estimator in this way makes it simple to see how an ATT can be encapsulated in this framework. In this case, we simply consider the regression-based counterfactual estimate for the treated units only:

$$\widehat{\tau}^{\text{reg}}_{\text{ATT}} = \frac{1}{N_T} \sum_{i=1}^{N} W_i \left[Y_i - \widehat{\mu}_0(X_i) \right].$$

Apart from subsetting to treated units, all other details follow those in (3.33).

These estimators (3.33)–(3.34) raise a more subtle point about the stability of the regression estimator and potential model misspecification. If we consider the quantity $\widehat{\mu}_0(X_i)$ in (3.34), we are using this to estimate the counterfactual outcome $\mathbb{E}[Y_i(1)|W_i=0]$. This quantity thus seeks to inform us of counterfactual outcomes for *treated* units with some particular value of X_i, but parameters used to estimate $\mathbb{E}[Y_i(1)|W_i=0]$ are based on the distribution of X_i among *control* units. In practice this implies that bias can be introduced in regression estimators if the distribution of covariates is very different between treated and control groups unless functional form assumptions are exactly correct (see, e.g., Imbens [2004, 12–13]). The importance of correctly capturing relationships between the outcome covariates has also led to the use of richer models to estimate $\widehat{\mu}_0(X_i)$ and $\widehat{\mu}_1(X_i)$. This includes a range of nonparametric techniques such as efficient series estimators described in Hahn (1998) and local linear kernel regression described in a series of papers by Heckman, Ichimura, and Todd (1997, 1998) and Heckman et al. (1998).

Code Callout 3.3: Matching, Weighting, and Regression
We examine the differences between matching, weighting and regression with data from Millimet and Tchernis (2009), which explores the environmental impact of countries' entry into trade organization memberships. We report estimates of ATEs and ATTs in each case, seeing how estimation for each procedure varies, both in terms of form and in terms of results in this particular case.

3.5.2 Combining the Above Techniques: Double-Robustness

The previous methods have taken alternative approaches to conditioning on the presence of covariates X_i while maintaining a conditional unconfoundedness assumption.

Regression-based strategies seek to correct for the influence of X_i on outcomes Y_i directly, by modeling the outcome itself, and isolate treatment effects by comparing regression-adjusted outcomes across treated and untreated groups. Propensity score–based methods seek to model the influence of X_i on the likelihood of receiving treatment by estimating propensity scores and, in this way, isolate the effect of treatment by comparing uncorrected outcomes and, correct for differences in the likelihood of having been treated. Often, the prior approach is referred to as the outcome regression (OR) approach, while the latter is referred to as the inverse propensity score (IPW) approach. What is key from the above methods is that provided that regression models are correctly specified (in the prior case) or that propensity score models are correctly specified (in the latter case), these procedures can provide unbiased estimates of treatment effects as discussed above.

However, this dual approach begs the question of whether we may gain anything from seeking to combine these methods. It turns out that we can, and this is the idea of double-robust or doubly robust (DR) methods, introduced by Robins, Rotnitzky, and Zhao (1994) and named in Robins, Rotnitzky, and Laan (2000). Formally, DR methods are methods that rely on the estimation of two "nuisance" functions, and that remain consistent even if one of those two specifications is incorrect (Rothe and Firpo 2019). In this particular case, if we are concerned that we do not know the precise functional form of either the propensity score or the outcome regression (two nuisance functions), a doubly robust estimator is an estimator that will be based on models for both of these functions and will remain consistent even if one of these is modeled incorrectly. This is the idea of the augmented inverse-probability weighting (AIPW) estimator of Robins, Rotnitzky, and Zhao (1994):

$$\widehat{\tau}_{\text{ATE}}^{\text{AIPW}} = \frac{1}{N}\sum_{i=1}^{N}[\widehat{\mu}_1(X_i) - \widehat{\mu}_0(X_i)] + \left[\frac{W_i(Y_i - \widehat{\mu}_1(X_i))}{\widehat{P}(X_i)} - \frac{(1-W_i)(Y_i - \widehat{\mu}_0(X_i))}{1-\widehat{P}(X_i)}\right]. \tag{3.34}$$

While this estimator is slightly more elaborate in its notation than both the regression estimator presented in (3.33) and the inverse propensity score weight estimator in (3.25), it is clearly related to each of these. Indeed, the representation in (3.34) is of a regression-based estimator (the first term), as well as an adjustment factor that corrects for any residual-mismeasurement of the regression adjustment based on an IPW estimator. In this way, we can see the double-robustness property in (3.34). If the regression model is correctly specified, both $\mathbb{E}[Y_i - \widehat{\mu}_1(X_i)] = 0$ and $\mathbb{E}[Y_i - \widehat{\mu}_0(X_i)] = 0$, and the estimator will be unbiased even if the propensity score is mismeasured. On the other hand, if the regression model is incorrectly specified but the propensity score is correctly specified, the second term will correct for any residual mismeasurement in the regression term to the degree that this measurement is relevant for any selection into treatment.

The AIPW estimator can be similarly expressed as an IPW estimator with a regression-based adjustment to correct for mismeasurement of the propensity score. Similarly, an ATT estimator can be defined (see, e.g., Mercatanti and Li [2014, equation 5]). In general, there have been various extensions of these doubly robust methods to develop more efficient estimators. What's more, a range of other procedures exist that seek to leverage multiple estimation methods, such as regression-adjusted matching estimators discussed in Heckman, Ichimura, and Todd (1997) and Heckman et al. (1998). The double-robustness property of the AIPW estimator has been particularly influential however, and we will come across doubly robust estimators in a range of settings later in the book, beyond this specific setting of conditional unconfoundedness.

3.6 The Credibility of Identifying Variation from Conditional Unconfoundedness

A drawback with the methods laid out in this chapter is the central importance of the *conditional* unconfoundedness assumption. While the methods discussed are without doubt elegant econometric constructions, the plausibility of identifying assumptions is far less elegant in most circumstances we encounter in applied microeconometrics. Conditional unconfoundedness is also referred to as ignorable treatment assignment, the "conditional independence assumption" Lechner (2001), or "selection on observables." The "selection on observables" moniker makes clear that identification *requires* that any selection into treatment can only be related to observed variables X_i, and not unobserved factors. This is closely related to the exogeneity assumptions you have likely come across in prior econometrics courses, with precise statements of equivalence available in Imbens (2004, 7). This suggests that if you were not in a situation where you would believe that exogeneity holds, you should also not believe in conditional unconfoundedness.

There *are* ways that these assumptions can be loosened. For example, Heckman, Lochner, and Taber (1998) shows that if we wish to identify an ATE, really all that is needed is mean independence of the type:

$$\mathbb{E}[Y_i(1)|X, W] = \mathbb{E}[Y_i(1)|X] \qquad \text{and} \qquad \mathbb{E}[Y_i(0)|X, W] = \mathbb{E}[Y_i(0)|X]$$

rather than the full distributional version implicit in conditional unconfoundedness, and further, if we are only interested in the ATT, then assumptions $2'$ and $3'$ can be replaced with versions that hold for control units only.

Assumption 2*. Conditional unconfoundedness for controls $Y_i(0) \perp\!\!\!\perp W_i|X_i$.

Assumption 3*. Weak overlap $\Pr(W_i = 1|X_i) < 1$.

This is logical given that for the ATT we only need to form a single counterfactual based on control units. Nevertheless, all of these assumptions still imply a strong type of selection on observables at least for certain groups.

Whether these assumptions are reasonable—as in the case of any assumptions—is entirely context dependent. In general, these methods should certainly not be seen as a catch-all solution when you do not believe in random assignment. But rather, these methods should be used when there is a justifiable reason to believe that while assignment is not random, it is random conditional on some X. For example, Rubin (1977) discusses an example where assignment to treatment is randomized conditional on some baseline test scores. In this case, if we failed to control for baseline test scores, we would fail to identify a causal effect, but once we condition on baseline test scores, all that is left is random variation.

The key point in methods such as this is that we will want to have a theoretical reason to believe that once we have conditioned on X, any remaining variation in treatment is truly random. Here we can observe some type of tension between assumptions $2'$ and $3'$. From assumptions $2'$ we want observables X to be the only factors that systematically explain treatment assignment. But from assumption $3'$ we *do not* want these factors to perfectly predict treatment. Random assignment thus still plays a key role here: On top of observable factors X, some random process must occur that directs observably identical units into both treatment and control, and based on this random assignment, we can use the methods in this chapter to estimate treatment effects.

A useful thought here comes from Smith and Todd (2005):

> More generally, our findings make it clear that propensity score matching does not represent a "magic bullet" that solves the selection problem in every context. The implicit search for such an estimator in the literature cannot succeed. Instead, the optimal non-experimental evaluation strategy in a given context depends critically on the available data and on the institutions governing selection into the program. (Smith and Todd 2005, 307)

While they are discussing propensity score matching in particular, their point is valid for all of the methods discussed in this chapter, and indeed in this book. Such a message can be found echoed in a range of studies focusing on selection on observables (see, for example, Sekhon [2009]; Dehejia [2005]). While propensity score and other methods based on conditional unconfoundedness assumptions may be useful in certain settings, they should not be viewed as an alternative to thinking carefully about the assignment mechanism, and are likely not relevant if we are concerned that substantial selection into treatment occurs for reasons that are difficult to capture in data. Throughout the rest of this book, we will extend into a range of methods that *do* allow for such (self-)selection.

A closing point on this discussion, however, is that even if we suspect that we may not often have models where our identification will be driven by assumptions of unconditional uncounfoundedness, it turns out that understanding the mechanics of the techniques discussed in this chapter is nevertheless very important. This is because in many other empirical designs, we may wish to account for the presence of covariates, and the tools we have discussed here are extremely useful there also. We will see this in practice in a range of settings throughout this book, including when we encounter instrumental variables, difference-in-differences methods, and quantile treatment effects (among other themes). There we will see that even if our identifying assumptions are quite different from those laid out in this chapter, the tools described here—and in particular the propensity score—can be quite helpful for our work there.

Historical Context and Selected Further Reading

As laid out throughout this chapter, many important results related to conditional unconfoundedness were proven in influential papers published in the 1980s and 1990s. Interestingly, a number of these papers shared a special issue in the *Review of Economic Studies*, with volume 64, issue 4 focused on "Evaluation of Training and Other Social Programmes."

From particularly applied viewpoints, the papers of Caliendo and Kopeinig (2008) and Imbens (2015) both provide excellent practical guidance and are go-to references in this regard. A nice illustration of the complexities of conditional unconfoundedness in practice can be viewed by reading the foundational text of LaLonde (1986), revisitation from Dehejia and Wahba (1999, 2002), and then discussion of the credibility of identifying assumptions in Smith and Todd (2005) and Dehejia (2005).

While fundamental for the estimation of the propensity score, the use of nonlinear models such as the logit and probit are discussed only in passing in this chapter. Formal details of such models are provided in most modern foundational econometrics texts, or a much earlier book-length coverage of these methods is available in Maddala (1983).

Exercises

1. In Dehejia and Wahba (2002), a number of types of matching procedures are considered when matching on the propensity score. In their figures 3–6 they document how the comparison across propensity scores varies under four different procedures: (1) matching without replacement in random order, (2) matching without replacement from lowest to highest propensity score; (3) matching without replacement from highest to lowest propensity score; and (4) matching with replacement using the closest match.

    (a) Use the data `Dehejia_Wahba_1999.csv` and guidance from code callout 3.1 to replicate these four matching procedures. Note that you should only focus on treated units (`treat=1`) and control units (`data_id="CPS1"`) to do this.

(b) Based on the matches, replicate figures 3–6 from Dehejia and Wahba (2002), which plot the propensity score of treated units and their matched controls against the propensity score of the treated unit of interest. Explain the observed behavior and which method you think may be preferable here.

(c) How may we expect these results to differ if instead of using a single matched control we use multiple matched controls. Show how the plots to part (b) change if we use three controls instead of one control for each treated unit, and discuss the implications of this for the different strategies considered.

2. We will return to the data of Almond, Chay, and Lee (2005) used in code callout 3.2 to explore doubly robust estimation techniques. We will use the data `Almond_et_al_2005` and consider the impact of smoking during pregnancy (`mbsmoke`) on an infant's birth weight in grams (`bweight`). Based on the covariates `mmarried, mage, medu, fage, fbaby, monthslb` (mother's marital status, age, educational level, father's age, and an indicator for first birth and the months since last birth, respectively), seek to implement the following:

   (a) Estimate the impact of smoking on birth weight using the outcome regression (regression-based model) in (3.33).

   (b) Estimate a propensity score model that seeks to examine how these covariates predict whether a mother smokes during pregnancy. Estimate treatment effects using inverse propensity score weighting following (3.28).

   (c) Examine the overlap in part (b). Does this look reasonable, and are estimates robust to trimming any extreme observations?

   (d) Finally, seek to combine parts (a) and (b) using double-robust methods. In particular, implement the AIPW estimator described in (3.34). Do this by hand to ensure that you understand each of the component steps. If there is an automated library for the estimation of AIPW in the language you use, compare this with your "manual" estimate.

3. Imbens, Rubin, and Sacerdote (2001) study the impact of a financial windfall (a lottery win), on subsequent labor supply. The data `Imbens_et_al_2001.dta` consists of the sample of 237 winners in their paper, who can be divided into treated individuals who are "big winners," with prizes of more than $100,000 per year (`prize>100`), and smaller winners. Imbens, Rubin, and Sacerdote (2001) note that while a lottery win is based on randomness, misbalance in characteristics is observed given that certain individuals are likely to buy more tickets.

   (a) Open these data and define the "treatment" variable to distinguish between big prize winners and small prize winners. Examine the earnings reported by treated and untreated individuals in the years prior to winning. Do these suggest random assignment?

(b) Calculate the propensity score for each individual using logistic regression. The propensity score estimates the probability of winning a large prize based on observed characteristics.

(c) Match each big prize winner with a small prize winner or nonwinner who has the most similar propensity score (matching with replacement). Repeat this procedure where instead of matching based on the nearest propensity score, matching is conducted using units that are closest in terms of the Mahalanobis distance.

(d) Examine the balance in characteristics in each of the two cases above. How do these methods compare in their ability to balance observable characteristics used to match?

(e) Estimate the average treatment effect on the treated (ATT) to assess the impact of winning on subsequent earnings based on each of these methods with the matched samples. How do the results vary?

4. In equations (3.7)–(3.9) we show how a series of CATEs can be aggregated to arrive at an ATT.

   (a) Show similar calculations where instead of the ATT, we wish to calculate the ATT.

   (b) Show that we actually require a slightly weaker form of conditional unconfoundedness and overlap if we wish to estimate an ATT compared to an ATE.

   (c) Generally, why would we require weaker assumptions to estimate an ATT compared to an ATE?

5. Here we will examine some simulated data in which conditional unconfoundedness holds. Specifically, simulate 1,000 observations with three covariates X_{i1}, X_{i2}, X_{i3} each being distributed as uncorrelated standard normal $\mathcal{N}(0,1)$ variables. Now, simulate a probability $P_i = \frac{1}{(1+\exp(-1+1X_1+0.8X_2-0.3X_3))}$ and a treatment variable $W_i = \mathbb{1}\{U_i < P_i\}$, where U_i is a variable drawn from the random uniform distribution. This should result in around 30% of units receiving treatment. Finally, generate $Y_i(1)$ and $Y_i(0)$ as follows:

$$Y_i(0) = 0.5X_1 + 0.2X_2 - 0.1X_3 + \varepsilon_i(1) \qquad Y_i(1) = 2 + 2X_1 + 1.5X_2 - 0.1X_3 + \varepsilon_i(1),$$

   where $\varepsilon_i(0)$ and $\varepsilon_i(1)$ are standard normal. Generate Y_i as each observations observed value (based on W_i).

   (a) Use propensity score weighting to estimate the treatment effect τ. How does this perform with your simulated data?

   (b) Seek to estimate the treatment effect by regression Y_i on $W_i, X_{i1}, X_{i2}, X_{i3}$?. Why does this perform poorly?

(c) Estimate the treatment effect τ using a regression adjustment as in (3.33). Why does this perform better than your estimate in part (b)?

(d) Examine the overlap of the propensity score. Trim the propensity score at 0.02 and 0.98 and reestimate the treatment effect with inverse propensity score weighting. Does this recover the treatment effect we simulated above? Why or why not?

(e) Repeat the procedure in part (a), but now omitting X_2 from our estimate of the propensity score. Are these results surprising?

4

Difference-in-Differences, Synthetic Controls, and Their Derivatives

There are years that ask questions and years that answer.
—Zora Neale Hurston, *Their Eyes Were Watching God*

4.1 Introduction

Often we may be unwilling to assume that unconfoundedness holds, even if we condition on covariates and use any of the techniques discussed up to this point in this book. In this case, we say there is selection on unobservables, where these unobservables may be any of the factors defined in the assignment mechanism (1.4). These unobservable factors are frequently actually known (or partially known) to individuals themselves, but the key concern is that we, as researchers, cannot observe the full range of relevant factors in our data. This opens up an entirely new set of techniques that must be used to potentially estimate consistent effects of treatment. In the coming chapters we turn to these.

One particular case that we frequently encounter in which we may no longer believe in selection on unobservables is that of "natural experiments," or naturally occurring events that strike certain units of a sample but not others. To take one simple example, imagine that we wish to estimate the impact of a natural disaster, such as an earthquake, on school completion rates. Earthquakes are, to some degree, geographically localized, and it seems reasonable to think that they are not endogenously determined by affected individuals. However, this does not imply that it is appropriate to treat them as if they are randomly assigned and simply compare the outcomes of affected individuals with those of unaffected individuals. One important factor is that an event such as an earthquake hits an area that is potentially quite different at baseline to areas that are not hit by an earthquake, and as such, any difference following the earthquake may owe to the event itself, or also to baseline differences in affected areas.

Another particular example are policy decisions where some reform of interest may be put in place in certain areas but not others, or may be rolled out differentially over time. It may be that individuals living in different states are exposed to different policy environments for reasons that they do not determine but that nevertheless do owe to relevant unobservable characteristics. For example, if some policymaker is resource constrained and has to offer a particular policy to only some states, they may logically decide to implement the policy in the area they perceive has the most to gain from the policy, or, in other words, assign a policy in terms of expected potential outcomes $\mathbb{E}[Y_i(1)]$. Similarly, they may seek to implement policies in areas they view as particularly open to interacting with the policy or amenable to reform (see, e.g., Besley and Case [2000]), which are potentially quite hard-to-measure factors but are likely relevant for the policy's final effect.

In both the cases discussed previously, while we clearly would not believe that we are able to observe the relevant unobservable factors we are concerned about, we *may* nevertheless believe that such factors do not vary over time. For example, we may believe that certain areas are more prone to natural disasters such as earthquakes, but this does not vary from one time period to the next. Similarly, we may believe that certain states or regions in a country are particularly likely to gain from certain policies, or have institutions that make them particularly amenable to policy reform, but that these factors are sufficiently slow to evolve that they are fixed under some period under study. If this is the case, rather than seeking to observe and control for unobservables, we can seek data on pretreatment periods that will allow us to determine the impact that such unobservables have on outcomes *entirely before* a policy is put in place. If the impact of these unobservables is indeed time-invariant, we will see that such a data setup will provide us an elegant alternative way to reach causal inferences.

In particular, if we are concerned about *time-invariant* confounders, the challenge in finding an appropriate counterfactual simply requires that we account for any differences between treated and untreated areas at baseline. In cases like this, designs such as "difference-in-differences" or related methods provide an attractive way forward. We turn to this setting in this chapter, discussing the required assumptions, when such designs are appropriate, when such designs will *not* isolate a causal parameter, and a range of potentially more flexible models that may provide a way forward where standard difference-in-differences designs are likely to fail. Throughout this chapter, we will assume that we are in a setting where certain units are exposed to treatment in certain time periods, and that repeated observations are available for units over time. We will discuss this formally below, but the key thing to note is that this all *requires* either the availability of panel data on exposed and unexposed units, or repeated cross-sections of data following units over time. Provided that such data are available, a range of methods may be appropriate, depending on the true nature of unobservables. In the course of this chapter, we will first encounter difference-in-differences designs and related methods, before moving on to "synthetic" methods such as synthetic control.

This has been an area of tremendous recent growth. This is the case when considering empirical papers—with a nearly linear increase in the frequency of reference to "Difference-in-differences" documented by Currie, Kleven, and Zwiers (2020) between the 1990s and the 2020s—but *also* when considering theoretical advances in modeling. In particular, a number of theoretical advances documented in the late 2010s and published from 2019 onward have pointed to substantial nuance required in designs based on time-varying treatment exposure and has led to a revisitation of methods that were previously used in these settings. Many of these theoretical advances have been discussed in recent survey papers, such as Roth et al. (2023), Chaisemartin and D'Haultfœuille (2022), and Arkhangelsky and Imbens (2023), who each take a slightly different tack but note key challenges and modeling solutions. The authors of these surveys have been at (slightly different areas of) the frontier of these recent advances, so they provide an excellent alternative range of takes on the methods laid out here.

4.2 The Canonical Difference-in-Differences Design

The basic underpinnings of the difference-in-differences design (also known as diff-in-diff, DiD, DD, or double-difference) is the case where we have observations for a pair of units across time, one of which is exposed to some policy or "treatment" of interest, and another of which is not. For example, for the case discussed above in which a natural disaster occurs, imagine if we observed average high-school completion rates in two areas across two periods, and in one of the areas an earthquake occurred between the two periods, while in the other it did not. Even in the case that the standard assumption of unconfoundedness is not met (assumption $2'$ from the previous chapter), difference-in-differences allows us to recover an unbiased causal estimate if certain, weaker, assumptions are met.

Namely, difference-in-differences no longer requires that unconfoundedness holds, but it does require that it holds in first differences, or that selection only owes to a fixed difference at baseline. Consider the schematic example laid out in figure 4.1. While we will lay out the notation formally below, the key elements are that there is some treatment that occurs at the moment indicated "Intervention," where units shaded more lightly are exposed to treatment and units shaded more darkly are unexposed. In the top panel (4.1a), we can see that these two groups of units are identical at baseline in terms of their outcomes as we would expect to occur if treatment were assigned randomly. In cases such as this, treatment effects can be inferred simply by comparing the difference between outcomes at the end line between the two groups. However, this setting is unlikely *unless* treatment is assigned randomly (or if we get lucky).

The setting in panel (b), on the other hand, shows a case in which treatment is not necessarily assigned randomly and as such, even at baseline, treated units are quite different to control units in terms of their outcomes. If we were to ignore this difference and assume unconfoundedness, this difference would be quite disastrous for any treatment effect we estimate. However, if the *difference* between treated (light) and control (dark) units would have remained constant over time in the absence of treatment, we can infer that without treatment, the treated unit would simply have followed the dashed line. Clearly the setting in (a) is a special case of the setting in (b), but (b) allows for any arbitary shift not permitted in (a). This case in figure 4.1(b) is, in a nutshell, the idea behind difference-in-differences designs.

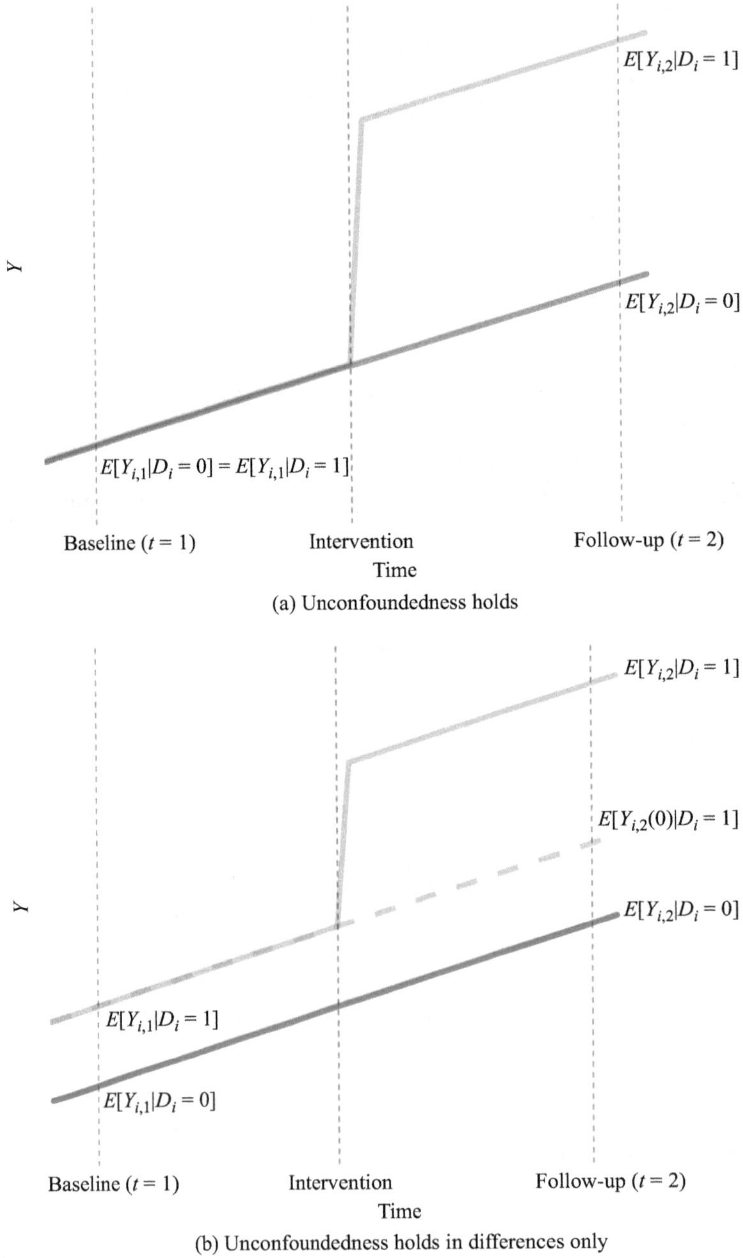

Figure 4.1
Repeated observations over time: Levels and difference.

4.2.1 Notation, Assumptions, and Estimands of Interest

To lay out key details of the difference-in-differences design, we will introduce notation that is suitably flexible to capture all key elements in a simple 2×2 setting, and also extends to other more complicated settings we will encounter below. For this baseline 2×2 design we will observe data in two time periods, denoted, as in figure 4.1, as $t = 1, 2$. A sample of N individuals or units will be observed in each time period and are denoted as $i \in \{1, \ldots, N\}$. Observed outcomes will be denoted as $Y_{i,t}$, capturing the logic that each unit i will be observed in each period t (we will discuss unbalanced samples in section 4.5.4).

Some, but not all, members of this group will receive treatment, and those units that receive treatment will be indicated with W_i, where $W_i = 1$ indicates treatment receipt and $W_i = 0$ indicates no treatment receipt. Treatment receipt will "switch on" between period $t = 1$ and $t = 2$ such that no units will be exposed to the treatment in period $t = 1$, while treated units will be exposed to treatment in period $t = 2$. In this notation W_i is a time-invariant measure that indicates whether a unit is eventually treated. At times we will also wish to work with a measure indicating that treatment is "switched on" at a particular time period. In cases where we wish to actually refer to this time-variant treatment measure, we will use the notation $W_{i,t}$. This measure will then take the value of 1 only for treated units during the post-treatment period. In this particular 2×2 setting, $W_{i,t} = W_i \times \mathbb{1}\{t = 2\}$.[1]

Potential outcomes The potential outcomes notation previously laid out will also provide a framework for difference-in-differences designs. We will denote as $Y_{i,t}(W_{i,1}, W_{i,2})$ the potential outcome for unit i in period t, such that $Y_{i,2}(0, 1)$ and $Y_{i,2}(0, 0)$ refer to potential outcomes for individual i in the respective states of the world in which they do and do not receive treatment in period 2. Here we are now allowing potential outcomes to depend upon the entire history of treatment for the individual, although it is important to note that in this particular case where $W_{i,1}$ is never equal to 1, we can rule out certain potential outcomes.

DD estimands Ideally, we would like to estimate an ATT of the following type:

$$\tau_2^{DID} = E\left[Y_{i,2}(0, 1) - Y_{i,2}(0, 0) \middle| W_i = 1\right]. \tag{4.1}$$

You will note that here we are already making two particular restrictions on this estimand. Firstly, we are proposing to estimate an ATT rather than an ATE, which is common in difference-in-differences designs, and which we will discuss at more length when we lay out key identifying assumptions below. Secondly, we are proposing to estimate this in the second time period, as noted by the sub-index on τ_2^{DID}. Indeed, in this case that the quantity τ_1^{DID} cannot be estimated given that there are no treated units in $t = 1$, which makes clear the importance of defining the temporal nature of the estimand.

As we have discussed in section 1.2.1, the problem we face to arrive to a causal estimand is that we only observe one of the two potential outcomes. In particular in (4.1), $\mathbb{E}[Y_{i,2}(0, 1) | W_i = 1]$ is observed while $\mathbb{E}[Y_{i,2}(0, 0) | W_i = 1]$ is not. Thus, while we would like to observe the counterfactual outcome for treated individuals in the post-treatment period, this is, by definition, never observed. For this reason, identification of a treatment effect will require a number of assumptions.

Assumptions Firstly, we will require that SUTVA holds. This can be stated analogously to assumption 1 such that $Y_{i,t}(W_{i,1}, W_{i,2}, \boldsymbol{W}_{-i,1}, \boldsymbol{W}_{-i,2}) = Y_{i,t}(W_{i,1}, W_{i,2})$, where $-i$ refers to all units except i, which rules out spillover or general equilibrium effects. The second required assumption is the most salient, and arguably the most discussed, assumption in identification in these settings. This is the so-called parallel trends assumption:

Assumption 4. Parallel Trends Assumption

$$\mathbb{E}[Y_{i,2}(0,0) - Y_{i,1}(0,0) | W_i = 1] = \mathbb{E}[Y_{i,2}(0,0) - Y_{i,1}(0,0) | W_i = 0]. \tag{4.2}$$

In words, this states that in the absence of treatment, the evolution of outcomes in the treated areas would have been the same as that observed in untreated areas. You may note that this assumption is thus a counterfactual assumption, but it is an assumption *only* about what would have happened to the *treated units*. In assumption 4, the second term $\mathbb{E}[Y_{i,2}(0,0) - Y_{i,1}(0,0) | W_i = 0]$ can be estimated from data. What is not observable is the first term because we can never observe $\mathbb{E}[Y_{i,2}(0,0)]$ for units with $W_i = 1$. Thus, we are assuming that the changes observed over time between period 1 and 2 in the control group are informative of changes that would have occurred in the treated group in the absence of treatment.

This immediately implies that this assumption can *only* return us an ATT. This is because we are assuming something about the counterfactual of treated units but *not* something about counterfactuals for untreated units. It is worth thinking through this, and thinking what types of assumptions we would require if we actually wished to estimate an ATE rather than an ATT.[2] As in the case with earlier unconfoundedness assumptions, we can *never* test the parallel trends assumption because we never observe the untreated potential outcome for treated units. For this reason it is important to never state that the parallel trend assumption can be empirically validated.

It may also be illustrative to note that the parallel trend assumption also can be given by an additive structure for a potential outcomes model, and at times is indeed stated in this way (see, e.g., Borusyak, Jaravel, and Spiess [2024, Assumption 1]). For example, consider a model of the following form:

$$\mathbb{E}[Y_{i,t}(0,0) | i, t] = \alpha_i + \beta_t. \tag{4.3}$$

This simply states that in the absence of treatment, the outcome consists of a time-invariant unit effect (α_i) and a time-fixed effect (β_t) that is common across all units. The key requirement here is that the systematic temporal component β_t is common across units. While it is perfectly permissible that each unit has its own specific level effect (or fixed effect) α_i, and indeed, treatment could be correlated with these level effects, the time-specific components are shared across units. What would generally violate parallel trends is if there were some interactive effect between α_i and β_t, such as unit-specific time trends.

A final identifying assumption is that there can be no policy anticipation as discussed by, among others, Abbring and Van Den Berg (2003). Specifically:

Assumption 5. No Anticipation Assumption $Y_{i,1}(0,1) = Y_{i,1}(0,0)$ for all $W_i = 1$.

This assumption requires no anticipation in the sense that units cannot behave differently precisely *because* a policy will be implemented in the future. Here we require that what we are observing in the pretreatment period $Y_{i,1}(0,1)$ for units that eventually receive treatment is a true representation of what would have happened had they not received treatment in the second period. While this may sound slightly convoluted, we are simply ruling out units responding to future treatment, for example, by employing strategic behavior in which treated units delay or expedite actions given knowledge that a policy will be put into place.

Identification To see that we can identify the ATT from DD assumptions, we can return to our estimand of interest (4.1). The challenge in identification is that $\mathbb{E}[Y_{i,2}(0,0)|W_i = 1]$ is unknown. Below, we will see that step by step, we can use the stated assumptions to isolate an estimate of τ_2^{DID} based on observable quantities. In each step of the below, it is useful if you note which quantities can be estimated from data and which cannot, as it helps make clear where assumptions come in:

$$\begin{aligned}
\tau_2^{\text{DID}} &= \mathbb{E}\left[Y_{i,2}(0,1) - Y_{i,2}(0,0) \middle| W_i = 1\right] && (4.4)\\
&= \mathbb{E}\left[Y_{i,2}(0,1) \middle| W_i = 1\right] - \mathbb{E}\left[Y_{i,2}(0,0) \middle| W_i = 1\right] && (4.5)\\
&= \mathbb{E}\left[Y_{i,2}(0,1) \middle| W_i = 1\right] - \left(\mathbb{E}[Y_{i,1}(0,0)|W_i = 1] + \mathbb{E}[Y_{i,2}(0,0) - Y_{i,1}(0,0)|W_i = 0]\right) && (4.6)\\
&= \mathbb{E}\left[Y_{i,2}(0,1) \middle| W_i = 1\right] - \left(\mathbb{E}[Y_{i,1}(0,1)|W_i = 1] + \mathbb{E}[Y_{i,2}(0,0) - Y_{i,1}(0,0)|W_i = 0]\right) && (4.7)\\
&= \mathbb{E}\left[Y_{i,2} - Y_{i,1} \middle| W_i = 1\right] - \mathbb{E}[Y_{i,2} - Y_{i,1}|W_i = 0]. && (4.8)
\end{aligned}$$

The key steps here are noting that in moving from (4.5) to (4.6), we can use the parallel trends assumption, which implies that $E\left[Y_{i,2}(0,0) \middle| W_i = 1\right] = \mathbb{E}[Y_{i,1}(0,0)|W_i = 1] + \mathbb{E}[Y_{i,2}(0,0) - Y_{i,1}(0,0)|W_i = 0]$. To move to (4.7) we require no anticipation, and from there, simple rearrangement results in an estimable quantity laid out in (4.8). This derivation also makes clear the importance of the no-anticipation assumption. We can estimate $\mathbb{E}[Y_{i,1}(0,1)|W_i = 1]$, which is the pretreated outcome for treated units in the counterfactual state in which they are treated. However, we wish to use this to measure $\mathbb{E}[Y_{i,1}(0,0)|W_i = 1]$, which is the pretreatment outcome in the counterfactual state in which they did not receive treatment. Thus, if for some reason treated units behave differently in the pretreatment period as a result of their future treatment assignment, this will be confounded in the treatment effect given that we assume that $\mathbb{E}[Y_{i,1}(0,1)|W_i = 1]$ is entirely unrelated to any impacts of treatment (yet).

While it requires a couple of lines of algebra to get from $\mathbb{E}[Y_{i,2}(0,0)|W_i = 1]$ to an estimable quantity, the deeper point is that with the parallel trend (and no-anticipation) assumptions, we can build up this single unobserved quantity from three observable quantities. This is also clearly observable if one returns to the graphical conception of the 2×2 difference-in-differences setup laid out in figure 4.1(b). While we would *like* to observe the quantity indicated by the dashed line of this figure, what we actually observe are the solid dark lines at baseline and post-treatment and the baseline lighter-coloured period. With parallel trends and the no-anticipation assumption, we can infer what the dashed line is by calculating the global temporal difference from the evolution of the dark lines over time and summing it to the baseline for treated units.

4.2.2 Estimation and the Two-Way Fixed Effect Model

The above stylized setting defines the difference-in-differences design. In this design, there is a pre-period, a post-period, a treatment that affects certain units and not others, and a parallel trends assumption. There are many ways to *estimate* parameters from a difference-in-differences design, and it is important to separate out the estimation of parameters from the DD design itself. In the simplified 2×2 setting, there are two commonly used estimation procedures (each estimating the same parameter), and we lay these out below. Later in this chapter, we will see that when the treatment setting is more complex, there are a dizzying range of estimators that one may wish to consider, each of which interact with this DD design and assumptions to arrive to a reasonable treatment effect estimate.

The simplest way to estimate the quantity τ_2^{DID} is to simply take (4.8) to data. Using N_T to indicate observations for which $W_i = 1$, and N_C to indicate observations for which $W_i = 0$, this estimator can be written as follows:

$$\hat{\tau}_2^{\text{DID}} = \frac{1}{N_T} \sum_{i:W_i=1} \left(Y_{i,2} - Y_{i,1}\right) - \frac{1}{N_C} \sum_{i:W_i=0} \left(Y_{i,2} - Y_{i,1}\right). \tag{4.9}$$

You may note the similarity of this estimator to the standard difference in means estimator assuming unconfoundedness laid out in (2.5). The difference here is that we now take the double difference by first subtracting $Y_{i,1}$ from $Y_{i,2}$ in each group, before estimating the DID estimand as the relative change among treated compared to any change among controls.

While this estimator is the most straightforward way of estimating (4.8), and is unbiased under assumptions 1, 4, and 5, in practice DD is more frequently estimated by regression. The most common form to estimate in difference-in-differences designs is via the two-way fixed effects regression. This consists of estimating the following model by ordinary least squares:

$$Y_{i,t} = \alpha + \beta_t + \gamma_i + \tau W_{i,t} + \varepsilon_{i,t}, \tag{4.10}$$

where β_t are time fixed effects, γ_i are unit fixed effects, and $W_{i,t}$ is the binary indicator for treatment defined previously. This is known as the two-way fixed effect estimator (at times denoted TWFE, or two-way FE) because it includes two dimensions of fixed effects, which are the two dimensions over which the difference-in-difference design operates. The $\varepsilon_{i,t}$ term capture stochastic unobserved factors.

In the 2×2 setting, this two-way FE estimator is equivalent to (4.9). To see this, note that if we are including full fixed effects for all levels of i and t, we must always omit a single fixed effect to avoid perfect multi-colinearity or omit the regression constant. If we include a constant and have a single treated and single control unit, it is sufficient to include a single unit fixed effect. Similarly, if we have a single pre and single post period, it is sufficient to include a single time fixed effect. Thus, in the 2×2 setting, and arbitrarily selecting the inclusion of a fixed effect for treated units, and for post-treatment periods for units and time FEs respectively, we can rewrite (4.10) as:

$$Y_{i,t} = \alpha + \beta \mathbb{1}\{t=2\} + \gamma W_i + \tau^{2\times 2} W_{i,t} + \varepsilon_{i,t}, \tag{4.11}$$

If the vector of parameters $(\alpha, \beta, \gamma, \tau^{2\times 2})$ are estimated by OLS, we can show $\tau^{2\times 2} \equiv \tau_2^{\text{DID}}$.

There are a number of ways to see this, but one particularly illustrative way is to examine the parameters that would be recovered in particular groups and time periods from this model, and see that this maps precisely into the difference-in-differences framework described in (4.8). This is laid out in table 4.1 below, where binary indicators for relevant dummy variables are substituted into the regression model for each group. For example, the second row of panel A is simply calculated as $\mathbb{E}[Y_{i,t}|W_i = 1, t = 1] = \alpha + \beta 0 + \gamma 1 + \tau^{2\times 2}(1 \cdot 0) = \alpha + \gamma$. From panel A, it is quite clear why a single difference using temporal variation within the treated group *will not* isolate a causal effect of treatment. In this case, $\mathbb{E}[Y_{i,2} - Y_{i,1}|W_i = 1]$ will be confounded by the time-fixed effect β. However, under a parallel trends assumption, this time-fixed effect can be estimated with $\mathbb{E}[Y_{i,2} - Y_{i,1}|W_i = 0]$, and unlike the single-difference estimator, difference-in-differences will isolate *just* the treatment effect $\tau^{2\times 2}$.

Table 4.1
A regression interpretation of a difference-in-differences estimator

Estimand	Estimate		
Panel A: $W_i = 1$			
$\mathbb{E}[Y_{i,t}\|W_i = 1, t = 2]$	$\alpha + \beta + \gamma + \tau^{2\times 2}$		
$\mathbb{E}[Y_{i,t}\|W_i = 1, t = 1]$	$\alpha + \gamma$		
Single Difference	$(\alpha + \beta + \gamma + \tau^{2\times 2}) - (\alpha + \gamma)$	$=$	$\beta + \tau^{2\times 2}$
Panel B: $W_i = 0$			
$\mathbb{E}[Y_{i,t}\|W_i = 0, t = 2]$	$\alpha + \beta$		
$\mathbb{E}[Y_{i,t}\|W_i = 0, t = 1]$	α		
Single Difference	$(\alpha + \beta) - \alpha$	$=$	β
Difference-in-differences	$(\beta + \tau^{2\times 2}) - \beta$	$=$	$\tau^{2\times 2}$

One reason why this regression-based estimator for a difference-in-differences design is convenient is that it generalizes *in some ways*. It also allows for the direct estimation of standard errors, confidence intervals, and testing of hypotheses directly in a regression framework. However, both of these points are more nuanced than they might first appear. We will discuss these points in the sections below.

If we look back at the equation (4.10), we have already alluded to one way in which our standard 2×2 estimator generalizes. Provided that we have a single transition from pre- to post-treatment, we can have as many groups i and as many time periods t as we wish, and these can all be housed in a two-way FE model with a full set of time- and unit-fixed effects. Indeed, *provided that we only have a single transition into treatment*, there is no major additional nuance required in moving from estimating with two groups and time periods to multiple groups and time periods.[3] In practice, all that is required is now to include a full set of fixed effects for all time periods and units, as laid out in (4.10). As before, our identifying assumptions will still be parallel trends *on aggregate* between groups, as well as no anticipation among the treated.

In empirical practice, difference-in-differences designs are frequently based on settings where treatment is assigned at the level of some aggregate areas like states or municipalities within a country. If our treatment of interest occurs at a single date, and we have potentially multiple pretreatment and post-treatment periods, and some proportion of states or municipalities that receive treatment and the remainder that do not, this is precisely a case where two-way FE will perform admirably in isolating the ATT. At times, if we have multiple observations within a more highly aggregated group-level treatment of this type, we may see our two-way fixed effect specification explicitly written to note these three levels of observations:

$$Y_{i,g,t} = \alpha + \beta_t + \gamma_g + \tau^{2\times 2} W_{g,t} + \varepsilon_{i,g,t}, \tag{4.12}$$

where it is now apparent that treatment $W_{i,g}$ is assigned at the level of the group g, and hence we can write this as W_g, and refer to the time-varying group-level treatment indicator $W_{g,t}$. What's more, in certain cases our unit of interest may actually be simply some more highly aggregated (e.g., state- or municipal-level) average of outcomes across all units within a group, in which case we may prefer to entirely omit the i subscript in (4.12), noting a group by time design. If we wish to conduct analysis based on repeated cross-sections of data aggregated to some group-specific mean where treatment is assigned at the level of the group, this is also not an issue (Heckman, Lalonde, and Smith 1999) provided that we treat our assumptions as referring to these group averages (a point noted long ago in a different setting by Deaton [1985]).

However this requires considerably more nuance in two particular dimensions. Firstly, in cases where there is not a single transition from pre- to post-treatment, the regression-based estimation procedure can be highly problematic. We turn to examine this in section 4.3. And secondly, for inference, the number of treated units and time periods is highly relevant, and as we will see below, moving from two units to more units considerably simplifies things. We discuss this shortly.

The inclusion of covariates An additional benefit of the regression-based framework for estimation of a difference-in-differences design is that it lends itself to the incorporation of covariates. In empirical practice, this often consists of the inclusion of time-varying covariates $X_{i,t}$ in the regression model (4.11), with the justification that parallel trends is believed to hold *conditional on* these time-varying factors but may not hold in the absence of these controls. Provided that covariates do effectively vary both across units and across time, they will not be perfectly colinear with time- or unit-fixed effects, and hence there is no mechanical reason why they cannot be included in this way. However, the theoretical literature raises a number of important caveats in this regard.

A first point is related to the inclusion of time-varying controls. The prototypical justification of the inclusion of controls is that parallel trends must then only hold after conditioning out the effect of time-varying factors (see, for example, Heckman et al. [1998, § 3.3]). Caetano and Callaway (2023) discuss the identifying assumptions under which TWFE models with a single pre-and post-treatment period can isolate an ATT in the presence of time varying controls and note that this requires three specific assumptions. Firstly, trends in untreated potential outcomes *must not* also depend on time-invariant covariates. Secondly these trends must only depend on changes in time-varying covariates, *not* on the levels of time-varying covariates. Thirdly the dependence of trends on changes in covariates must indeed be linear. They also note that even if these assumptions are met, estimates from a two-way fixed effect regression conditioning on time-varying covariates will aggregate treatment effects in a way that gives *more* weight to observations with covariate values that are less common in the estimation sample. They refer to this as a "weight-reversal" property, which has been shown by Słoczyński (2022) to be a general property in OLS estimates.

This leads to a number of proposals relating to the inclusion of time-varying controls in DD models. A first consists of estimating the coefficients on covariates in a first step among untreated units only and then implementing a regression adjusted estimator, which is a point also discussed in Powell (2021). A second consists of the use "double-robust strategies," which estimate separately the impact of covariates on the likelihood of receiving treatment in a propensity score step, as well as on the outcome itself. These strategies are able to isolate consistent effects provided *either* the relationship between covariates and outcomes is correctly modeled *or* the relationship between covariates and outcomes are correctly modeled. We turn to discuss double-robust procedures at more length below, though we note that the Caetano and Callaway (2023) procedure is specifically focused on adjusting for time-varying controls.

The discussion above also raises the question of what one should do if outcome trends are actually believed to be related to time-invariant covariates. Specifically, what should be done if we believe that parallel trends does not hold generically in the full population, but *does* hold within subpopulations consisting of observations with particular characteristics? If these characteristics are indeed time-invariant measures X_i, clearly we cannot control for them in models like (4.11) because they will be perfectly colinear with (and absorbed by) fixed effects α_i. But at the same time, if parallel trends only holds within these groups, we must account for these covariates in some way. Fortunately, there a number of established and accepted ways to do this.

A common way is that documented by Abadie (2005), who shows that even under only a *conditional* parallel trends assumption, which can be written (assuming the same two-period design as above) as:

Assumption 4′. Conditional Parallel Trends Assumption

$$\mathbb{E}[Y_{i,2}(0,0) - Y_{i,1}(0,0)|X_i, W_i = 1] = \mathbb{E}[Y_{i,2}(0,0) - Y_{i,1}(0,0)|X_i, W_i = 0], \tag{4.13}$$

an aggregate ATT can be recovered. Interestingly, this is done using propensity-score reweighting methods, much as discussed in chapter 3. The key result from Abadie (2005) is that under a conditional parallel trends assumption as well as a standard overlap assumption like assumption 3*, we have that:

$$\mathbb{E}[Y_{i,2}(0,1) - Y_{i,2}(0,0)|W_i = 1] = E\left[\frac{1}{\Pr(W_i = 1)} \cdot \frac{W_i - \Pr(W_i = 1|X_i)}{1 - \Pr(W_i = 1|X_i)}(Y_{i,2} - Y_{i,1})\right]. \tag{4.14}$$

This result shows that we can estimate an ATT using a propensity score reweighting estimator! As we have seen previously, this reweighting seeks to assign more weight to changes in outcomes over time for untreated units that have values of covariates that are relatively uncommon among the untreated, thus resulting in a matched distribution of covariates among treated and control units.[4] Abadie (2005) proposes an implementation of this estimator, simply requiring taking (4.14) to data, with a flexible estimate of the propensity score.

However, propensity score–based methods are not the only way that one can proceed. Rather than seeking to condition on X_i via the treatment variable W_i, we can condition the outcome itself Y_i on X_i. This is known as the outcome regression (OR) approach, and is described in Heckman, Ichimura, and Todd (1997). The idea of this OR approach is that we should simply form the DD estimate for each treated unit by comparing it to control units with the same covariates. We can see the idea of this estimator by noting that we can write our ATT as follows:

$$\begin{aligned}\mathbb{E}[Y_{i,2}(0,1) - Y_{i,2}(0,0)|W_i = 1] &= \mathbb{E}[Y_{i,2} - Y_{i,1}|W_i = 1] \\ &\quad - \mathbb{E}_X\big\{\mathbb{E}[Y_{i,2} - Y_{i,1}|W_i = 0, X_i]\big|W_i = 1\big\},\end{aligned} \tag{4.15}$$

which is simply a generalization of (4.8), though now noting that we need to take care to ensure that our untreated units are weighted to match the distribution of X_i among treated units. In writing (4.15), the outer expectations on the final quantity is taking expectations over the distribution of X_i among treated units, while the inner quantity is simply the difference among treated units with this specific value of X_i.

In practice, this can be implemented along the lines of the notation for (4.9), as:

$$\widehat{\tau}_2^{\text{DID,OR}} = \frac{1}{N_T} \sum_{i:W_i=1} \left(Y_{i,2} - Y_{i,1}\right) - \frac{1}{N_C} \sum_{i:W_i=0} \left(\widehat{Y}_{i,2}(X_i) - \widehat{Y}_{i,1}(X_i)\right), \tag{4.16}$$

where we are consistently working with treated units both in the left-, and right-hand differences, *but* $\widehat{Y}_{i,t}(X_i)$ is a regression based estimate using data from untreated units. In effect, the idea of (4.16) is that we can estimate regression models with untreated observations in each period, and then use the resulting parameters from these regression models to ask what a treated unit with a specific value of X_i would have looked like had it been untreated, in effect balancing the covariates of the control sample to the treated samples.

More recently, Sant'Anna and Zhao (2020) propose a doubly robust method, which incorporates both the propensity score method and the outcome regression method. While the proposals above will do a good job if the propensity score model is correctly specified in the first case, or if the outcome regression is correctly specified in the second case, the value of double-robust methods is that they will capture causal effects if *either* the propensity score *or* the outcome regression are correctly specified. This "double-robustness" property, which we discussed in section 3.5.2, allows for one of the two models to be incorrect in a way that would cause breakdowns of the above methods. For the sake of completion, we can see the idea of doubly robust DD methods by writing our ATT as:

$$\mathbb{E}[Y_{i,2}(1) - Y_{i,2}(0) | W_i = 1] = \mathbb{E}\left[\omega_i(Y_{i,2} - Y_{i,1} - \mathbb{E}_X[Y_{i,2} - Y_{i,1} | W_i = 0, X_i])\right], \tag{4.17}$$

where ω_i is a weight based on the propensity score, which follows the logic of propensity score reweighting as laid out in (4.14).[5] The key point to see here is that this procedure shares elements with both propensity score weighting via the inclusion of weights, and regression adjustment, via the inclusion of modeled outcomes. Estimation and inference procedures for these double-robust methods are defined in Sant'Anna and Zhao (2020), with software available for implementation.

4.2.3 Inference in Difference-in-Differences Designs

4.2.3.1 Cluster-robust inference Up to this point, we have principally focused on the estimation of parameters in a difference-in-differences design. However, there is a long literature pointing to important inferential considerations that must be taken into account for the estimation of appropriate standard errors and the construction of appropriate confidence intervals. Given the regression-based framework that is commonly employed for the estimation of parameters in DD designs, the estimation of regression-based standard errors will be trivial. However, it is highly unlikely that the sampling assumptions underlying standard regression-based standard errors are reasonable. In particular, it is highly likely that outcomes are correlated over time *within* groups i, introducing auto-correlation in unobservable errors. This is a point first made by Bertrand, Duflo, and Mullainathan (2004), who noted that the reporting of uncorrected standard errors from regression, which was a frequent practice up to this time, likely results in downward-biased standard errors. This resulted in the widespread adoption of corrections for within-group dependence of standard errors since the paper's appearance.

The most common solution to account for within-group correlations of outcomes across time is to simply cluster standard errors by treatment groups. This solution is one of those espoused by Bertrand, Duflo, and Mullainathan (2004) and works well provided that the number of groups and number of time periods is sufficiently large. In practice, this cluster-robust variance-covariance estimator (CRVE) simply allows arbitrary correlations among unobserved components of all units within a single group—including both cross-sectional dependence in a particular time period among multiple individuals in a treatment cluster and temporal dependence among errors over time within a particular group. This CRVE takes the form:

$$\widehat{\mathbb{V}}_{\mathrm{CR}} = (\boldsymbol{X}'\boldsymbol{X})^{-1}\left(\sum_{g=1}^{G}\boldsymbol{X}_g\hat{\epsilon}_g\boldsymbol{X}'_g\right)(\boldsymbol{X}'\boldsymbol{X})^{-1}, \tag{4.18}$$

where following (4.12), we are using $g \in \{1, \ldots, G\}$ to indicate clusters. Here, $\boldsymbol{X}$ includes time-fixed effects, group-fixed effects, as well as a treatment indicator and $\hat{\epsilon}_g$ is a vector of regression residuals. This is the well-known cluster-robust formula used for estimating standard errors (Liang and Zeger 1986; M. Arellano 1987).[6] For reference, this variance term is typically larger than the "standard" variance term of OLS, and the degree to which the cluster robust variance inflates the (overly precise) standard variance is known as the "Moulton factor," after the paper that laid this out (Moulton 1986). While full discussion can be found in Moulton (1986, equation 1), the Moulton factor shows that the variance of the clustered standard errors will be larger than that in unclustered errors provided that there is a positive intra-group correlation, and unclustered standard errors will tend to understate the true variance more in cases where (a) the number of clusters is smaller, (b) the within-cluster variation in covariates is larger, and (c) within-cluster correlation between variables is larger. Thus, in cases like clustered treatments, where treatment is constant within clusters and high degrees of auto-correlation of outcomes exist over time, the use of clustered standard errors is likely to be important.

However, as has been extensively documented (see, for example, Donald and Lang [2007] and Cameron and Miller [2015]), standard CRVEs are only asymptotically valid, where the asymptotic behavior depends on the number of clusters $G \to \infty$. When standard clustering is used based on "too few" clusters, the CRVE is generally downward biased, resulting in overrejection of null hypotheses. This bias occurs because $E(\hat{\epsilon}_g\hat{\epsilon}_g') \neq \epsilon_g\epsilon_g'$ in (4.18), with the latter term being the true intra-cluster variation. For this reason, small-sample corrections are generally used. For example, common computational implementations tend to make a small-sample correction by pre-multiplying (4.18) by $\frac{G}{G-1}$ or $\frac{G}{G-1}\frac{N-1}{N-K}$, with the $\frac{G}{G-1}$ correction effectively inflating standard errors to correct for downward biases where few clusters exist. Alternative corrections for bias in clustered standard errors have been proposed by Bell and McCaffrey (2002) and Imbens and Kolesár (2016), which behave better in certain cases (see Imbens and Kolesár [2016]), but these are viewed as bias-reduction rather than bias-correction methods.

4.2.3.2 Cluster-robust inference and the number of clusters The aforementioned discussion suggests a clear solution if "enough" clusters are observed in data. But with few clusters, even the bias-correction methods above can result in poor coverage of standard errors. In particular, for CRVE to perform well in DD designs, a sufficient number of treatment and nontreatment groups must exist.

In practice, knowing how many clusters are "too few" depends on a number of factors. While there are rules of thumb such as the (somewhat facetious) rule of 42 laid out in Angrist and Pischke (2009), which suggests that standard clustering provides a good approximation if $G \geq 42$ clusters, or the suggestion of fifty clusters as a rough benchmark for state-year panels in the survey of Cameron and Miller (2015), in practice these recommendations depend on a number of factors. This includes the relative size of clusters (Mackinnon and Webb 2017b), the variation of the size of clusters (Djogbenou, MacKinnon, and Nielsen 2019), and the relative number of treated and control clusters (Mackinnon and Webb 2017a, 2018). For this reason, MacKinnon, Nielsen, and Webb (2022) report that depending on conditions such as these, cluster-robust inference can be relatively reliable in certain cases with values of G as small as 20, but in other cases not until G is at least 200.

This leads to the question of what we should do if we have an application in which we would like to cluster our standard errors but don't have a "large enough" number of clusters. It is important to note that the answer most certainly *is not* "just cluster anyway." If we use traditional clustered standard errors with a small number of clusters, we will very likely *underestimate* our standard errors given that the variance estimate is downward biased (Cameron, Gelbach, and Miller 2008; Kézdi 2004), justifying the degree-of-freedom correction discussed above. Fortunately, alternative solutions do exist. The most common solution is to use bootstrap-based solutions, which have been documented by Cameron, Gelbach, and Miller (2008) and in subsequent work to perform well, even in cases with a very small number of clusters such as $G=5$.

While we have discussed bootstrap-based methods for inference previously in section 2.4.4, there are two particular reasons why a "standard" pairs bootstrap is not the solution for inference in this particular case. Firstly, we wish to allow for arbitrary correlations within clusters, and so we need resamples that work at the cluster level. Secondly, given that our variable of interest is a binary treatment measure with potentially few clusters, certain bootstrap resamples may result in data where either all units are treated or all are untreated, implying that estimation cannot proceed. In the particular case of difference-in-differences with few treatment clusters, Cameron, Gelbach, and Miller (2008) have shown that the wild cluster bootstrap has particularly good properties. The wild cluster bootstrap is a generalization of the wild bootstrap, which was first laid out in Wu (1986)[7] and which is a residual-based resample procedure. The idea of a residual-based bootstrap is that rather than resampling original data $\{(Y_1,X_1),\dots(Y_N,X_N)\}$ to result in resampled pairs $\{(Y_1^*,X_1^*),\dots(Y_N^*,X_N^*)\}$, dependent variables are held fixed and *residuals* $\widehat{\varepsilon}_i$ are resampled, providing for each observation i a resampled outcome $\widehat{Y}_i^* = X_i\widehat{\beta}+\widehat{\varepsilon}_i^*$. This results in resampled data that respects the original treatment assignment but brings in sampling variation from across the original data—that is, $\{(\widehat{Y}_1^*,X_1),\dots(\widehat{Y}_N^*,X_N)\}$.

The wild bootstrap in particular seeks to consider resampled versions of residuals that either take the value of $\widehat{\varepsilon}_i$ or $-\widehat{\varepsilon}_i$ with a probability of 0.5. The wild bootstrap brings in a clustered element by assigning the values of $+1$ or -1 that are used to multiply each residual at the level of the cluster. These values, known as Rademacher weights, ensure that across many resamples, different distributions of $\widehat{Y}_i^*$ will be generated, however, where a specific value ($+1$ or -1) is chosen for a given cluster, the realizations of $\widehat{Y}_i^*$ for that cluster will be the same as in any other replicate where the same value ($+1$ or -1) is chosen. It is potentially clearest to see the entire way this algorithm is written. Below, this is adapted for the notation here (a general presentation is available in Cameron, Gelbach, and Miller [2008, Appendix B]), assuming that we wish to test the null that $\tau^{2\times 2}=0$:

1. Estimate (4.12) to obtain $\widehat{\tau}^{2\times 2}$ along with its cluster-robust standard error $se(\widehat{\tau}^{2\times 2})$ and residuals $\widehat{\varepsilon}_{i,g,t}$. Calculate the t-statistic of interest as $t=(\widehat{\tau}^{2\times 2}-0)/se(\widehat{\tau}^{2\times 2})$.
2. Impose the null hypothesis $\tau=0$ and reestimate (4.12) to obtain "restricted" estimates $\tilde{\alpha}_g$ and $\tilde{\beta}_t$, as well as restricted residuals $\tilde{\varepsilon}_{i,g,t}$.
3. Conduct the following step a large number B times, indexing with b:
   (a) Assign a value of $a_g=1$ or $a_g=-1$ for each cluster g, with probability 0.5 for each.
   (b) Generate a new set of bootstrap errors $\varepsilon_{i,g,t}^{*,b}$, where $\varepsilon_{i,g,t}^{*,b}=a\tilde{\varepsilon}_{i,g,t}$.
   (c) Form the value $\widehat{Y}_{i,g,t}^{*b}=\tilde{\alpha}_g+\tilde{\beta}_t+\varepsilon_{i,g,t}^{*,b}$ from resampled errors and the estimates we generated above with the null imposed.
   (d) Estimate $\widehat{\tau}^{2\times 2,*b}$ and its cluster robust standard error $se(\widehat{\tau}^{2\times 2,*b})$ using resampled data, and calculate $t^{*b}=(\widehat{\tau}^{2\times 2,*b}-0)/se(\widehat{\tau}^{2\times 2,*b})$.
4. Reject the null that $\tau^{2\times 2}=0$ at the level of α if $|t|>|t^*_{[1-(\alpha/2)]}|$, where $t^*_{[q]}$ refers to the qth quantile of the distribution of resampled t values.

While this looks slightly complicated, the idea itself is that if we "impose the null hypothesis" that $\tau^{2\times2}=0$ in each bootstrap resample, we should see that in general the estimated parameters $\widehat{\tau}^{2\times2*b}$ cluster around this null, giving us some idea of the standard sampling variation we may expect if the null were true. In the final step above we then ask whether our true parameter is extreme compared to the distribution observed under the null, and if it is, we conclude that it is unlikely that the estimated quantity is consistent with the null hypothesis.

Code Callout 4.1: Wild Cluster Bootstrap Implementation
We examine the performance of the wild cluster bootstrap with data from Porter and Serra (2020), comparing *p*-values and confidence intervals from this procedure with those from a standard clustered bootstrap. In order to gain insight to wild cluster bootstrapping, we set this up "by hand" and compare this to avaiable libraries.

This method has been shown to perform well under a range of situations, even with as few as five clusters (Djogbenou, MacKinnon, and Nielsen 2019; Cameron, Gelbach, and Miller 2008; Cameron and Miller 2015). What's more, it can be implemented in a very computationally efficient way, implying that it is generally trivial to conduct tests with a large number of bootstrap replicates, such as $B=9,999$ or $B=99,999$ (Roodman et al. 2019). One small point to note is that the use of Rademacher weights implies that the total number of possible different datasets that can be drawn is in effect capped at 2^G, which can be a relevant limit when G is small. In practice, what is required for the generation of residuals is that weights are centered on 0 and have a variance of 1 and so where G is small alternative weighting schemes may be useful. Other options exists, such as the six-point weighting scheme discussed in Webb (2023).

4.2.3.3 Cluster robust inference with very few groups A situation that at times arises is that there are an *even smaller* number of clusters present in one particular group, often the treatment group. A situation such as this is discussed by Conley and Taber (2011), who note that at times, the number of treated clusters is small and fixed, in limits consisting of cases where a single treated unit exists, with a potentially larger number of control groups. Because asymptotic considerations in clustering are based on both the number of treated and the number of control units increasing, it turns out that such a case requires its own consideration. Specifically, Conley and Taber (2011) consider the case where the number of treated clusters is very small and fixed, and T is considered fixed, and so asymptotics simply consider increasing the number of nontreated clusters. Interestingly, in this case they show that even though DD methods are unbiased, they *will not* be consistent, because even as sample sizes become very large, noise will remain due to the differencing between treated units over time.

In this case, Conley and Taber (2011) propose an inference procedure for DD with few treated units. This procedure is based on randomly reassigning treatment and control units and reestimating test-statistics to infer information about the distribution of the noise owing to the small number of treated units. This is closely related to randomization inference, and MacKinnon and Webb (2020) show that the procedure performs very similarly to effectively conducting randomization inference to reestimate the treatment effect (or t-statistic based on this parameter) of interest many times. MacKinnon and Webb (2020) document in a number of settings that these procedures work well, even in cases with one treated cluster, so long as the treatment cluster is similar in size to untreated clusters, though they caution against such procedures if treatment clusters are very different in size to control clusters. A quite different take on these settings, which is potentially more suited to the very few treated cluster setting, are the synthetic control and related methods, which will be discussed in section 4.6 below.

4.3 Generalizations of the 2 × 2 Design

Until relatively recently, the two-way fixed effects model was thought to be an adequate way to estimate parameters in a difference-in-differences design extending to multiple time periods and treated states without major issues. For example, Angrist and Pischke (2009, 234) state that "it's also easy to add additional states or periods to the regression setup," and Bertrand, Duflo, and Mullainathan's (2004) seminal paper on inference in difference-in-differences models discuss the multi-period multi-state model as a "common generalization of the most basic DD setup." While these statements are indeed true in certain cases like those discussed above, a burst of work published from around 2020 and onward has shown that considerably more nuance is required in many common empirical settings. Specifically, in a multiple-group, multiple-period setting, this will only be true if *either* there is a single date of treatment adoption *or* treatment effects are homogeneous across time (or both).

The two-way fixed effect models we have encountered so far, for example (4.10), have assumed a single policy adoption. In this setting, treatment "switched on" only between the first and second period, implying that we could write our time-varying treatment measure $W_{it} = W_i \times Post_t$, where $Post_t$ varies only over time, referring to periods after which treatment has been switched on. Of course, in general, there is nothing that limits the binary measure $W_{i,t}$ or $W_{g,t}$ in (4.10) and (4.12) to behave in this way. Indeed, if these time-varying treatments vary by group and time, we can write our two-way fixed effect models as:

$$Y_{i,t} = \gamma_i + \lambda_t + \tau^{\text{twfe}} W_{i,t} + \varepsilon_{i,t}, \tag{4.19}$$

where treatment varies by unit i and time t, or alternatively, as:

$$Y_{i,g,t} = \gamma_g + \lambda_t + \tau^{\text{twfe}} W_{g,t} + \varepsilon_{i,g,t}, \tag{4.20}$$

if we wish to explicitly note that treatment is assigned to units i by aggregate group g. You may note that the manner in which we have written these models is precisely the same as the two-way fixed effect model we discussed in the 2×2 setting (4.10). We have explicitly noted τ^{twfe} to refer to this more general design with time-variant treatment adoption, though we note that the 2×2 design is just the most simple version of this model. Such models are frequently encountered in empirical economics "in the wild." According to Chaisemartin and D'Haultfœuille (2020), around 20% of empirical papers published in the *AER* between 2010 and 2012 are based on this type of model. The body of recent work re-examining difference-in-differences designs, often with accompanying new methods and computational implementations, show that in the case of heterogeneous treatment effects, these standard "single coefficient" models may produce estimates of $\hat{\tau}^{\text{twfe}}$ that are quite different to what we would like to capture. We turn to this point now.

4.3.1 Time-Varying Treatment

In looking at (4.19), we may think that estimates $\hat{\tau}^{\text{twfe}}$ will capture mean differences between outcomes in treated and untreated areas, holding constant all unit-invariant and time-invariant factors. This will be true where treatment adoption occurs at a single moment in time. This implies that if the nature of the setting being studied is indeed a two-by-two setting with treated and untreated units in pre- and post-treatment period, this model will be perfectly adequate. Similarly, if we have a single adoption date where multiple units move into treatment and multiple units remain untreated, no estimation issues exist. Schematically, these two settings are described in tables 4.2 and 4.3. The former is often referred to simply as a two-by-two difference-in-differences design, and the latter is known as a "block adoption design" (see, e.g., Athey and Imbens [2019]).

But in practice, in many cases treatment will effectively "roll out" over time. This is what Athey and Imbens (2022), among others, refer to as the "staggered adoption design." This case, presented schematically in table 4.4, sees different units exposed to treatment, with treatment adoption occurring across a number of *different* time periods. You may note that in both the block-adoption design and staggered adoption design, we assume that once put in place, treatment is fixed thereafter, which is also at times referred to as an "absorbing" treatment (Sun and Abraham 2021). In section 4.5.3, we will briefly discuss "intertemporal

Table 4.2
A two-by-two difference-in-differences design

	Time Period	
	t_1	t_2
State A		
State B		

Dark gray cells indicate treatment, gray cells indicate control.

Table 4.3
A block adoption design

	Time Period			
	t_1	t_2	t_3	t_4
State A				
State B				
State C				
State D				
State E				
State F				
State G				
State H				

Dark gray cells indicate treatment, gray cells indicate control.

Table 4.4
A staggered adoption design

	Time Period					
	t_1	t_2	t_3	t_4	t_5	t_6
State A						
State B						
State C						
State D						
State E						
State F						
State G						
State H						
State I						

Dark gray cells indicate treatment, gray cells indicate control.

designs" where treatment is not assumed to be an absorbing state. In practice, in these cases where adoption is staggered, the mechanics of ordinary least squares mean that (4.19) *will not* simply capture mean differences between treated and untreated units holding constant unit-specific factors and time-specific factors. Rather, as we will see below, OLS will do something quite different and undesired.

4.3.2 Diagnosing Estimation Issues

Issues with this estimator have been clearly documented in a number of papers, perhaps most influentially by Goodman-Bacon (2021) and Chaisemartin and D'Haultfœuille

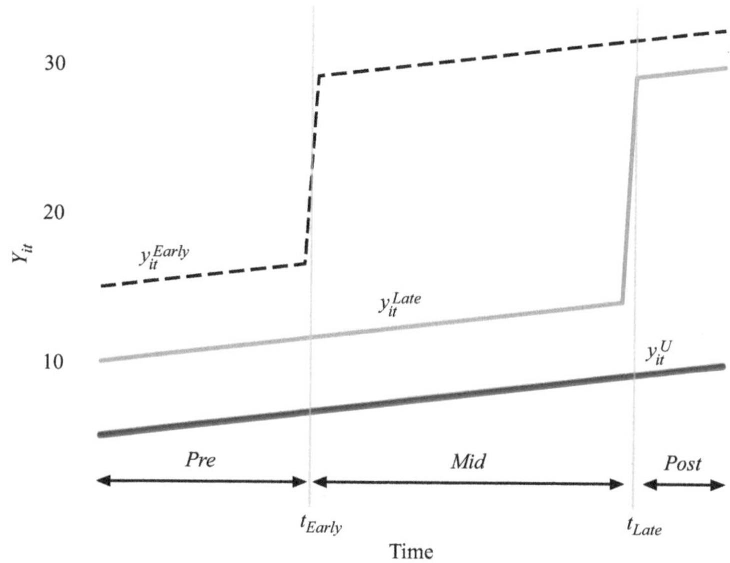

Figure 4.2
Goodman-Bacon's (2021) graphical setup with three treatment groups.

(2020). In a broad sense, the identifying variation in estimating $\widehat{\tau}^{\text{twfe}}$ in (4.19) comes from the moment when units change treatment status, from untreated to treated. A key stumbling block in these models occurs if there are multiple time periods, given how OLS views the variation in the treatment of interest. Specifically, where a unit has already *changed* treatment status and is treated across multiple periods, this (already treated unit) will incorrectly be seen as a control unit in these periods given the lack of variation in $W_{i,t}$.

This has been laid out graphically in a clear way in Goodman-Bacon (2021), which allows us to visualize the problems in using (4.19) in a DD design with time-varying treatment exposure. Consider a very simple staggered adoption design documented in figure 4.2. Here there are three groups. One, indicated with a dashed line is an early treated state. A second, indicated with a solid light line is a later-treated state, which receives treatment after the early treatment state. And finally, there is an untreated state indicated with the thick solid dark line. Thus, we are clearly in a staggered adoption design with two particular treatment transitions, indicated as t_{Early} and t_{Late} on the horizontal axis.

As Goodman-Bacon (2021) shows, the estimated parameter from (4.19) will consist of all possible combinations of "2 × 2" comparisons. These 2 × 2 comparisons are indicated in figure 4.3 (a)–(d) using dark colors in each subpanel to highlight the relevant 2 × 2 comparison. In particular, here there are two concerns. Firstly, and most importantly, there is

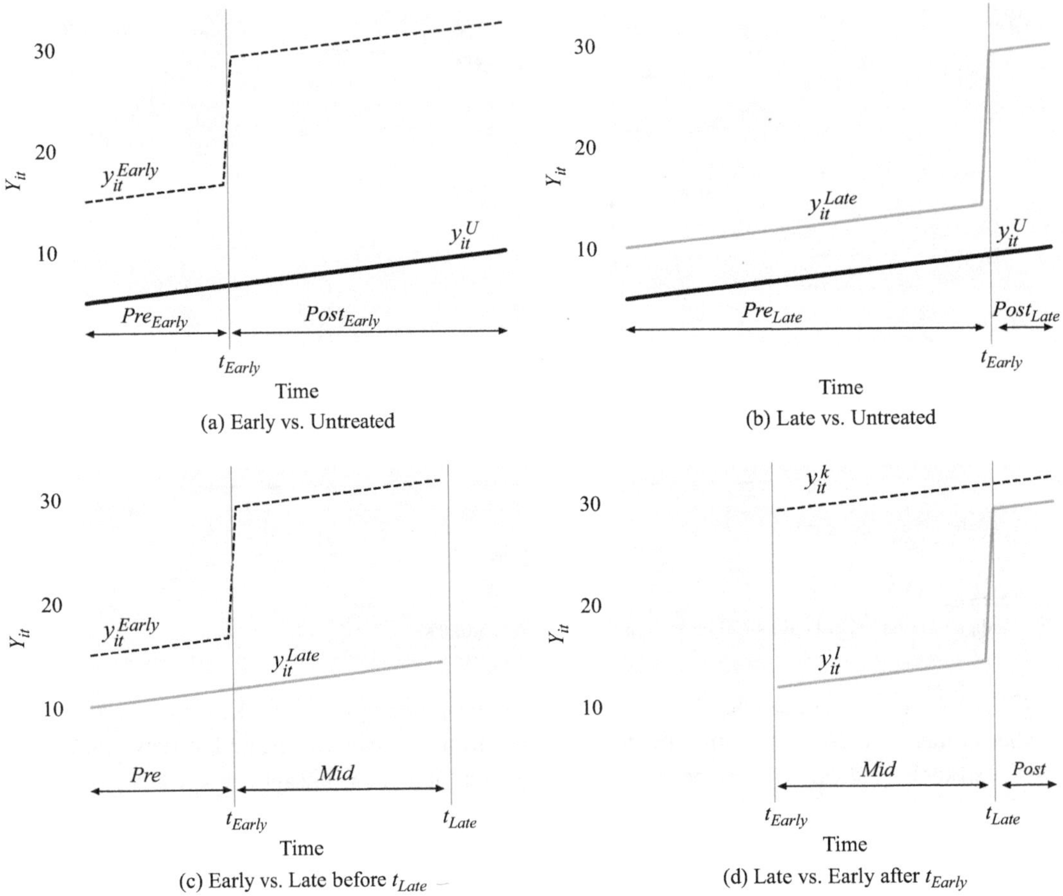

Figure 4.3
Decomposing the two-way fixed effect estimator.

one comparison that is quite strange, and that is the comparison indicated in panel (d). Here the "control" group refers to the early treatment group, which does not change status in its own post-treatment period, and the "treatment" group refers to the late treatment group, which does change treatment status in this period. Indeed, this comparison is now known as the "forbidden comparison" (see, e.g., Chaisemartin and D'Haultfœuille [2022]; Roth et al. [2023]),[8] and solutions discussed in section 4.3.3 propose estimators precisely to avoid its inclusion. And the second issue is that these four "2 × 2" comparisons will not be given equal weight when arriving to a single coefficient estimate $\widehat{\tau}^{\text{twfe}}$.

This latter issue is that each possible "2 × 2" comparison will receive a different weight, with this weight not being linked to some logical property of a treatment effect estimator we wish to uncover, but rather the mechanical properties of the OLS estimator. This is laid out formally in Goodman-Bacon (2021, proposition 1), and we will apply this to the notation adopted in this chapter here. To see what $\widehat{\tau}^{\text{twfe}}$ does, consider a balanced panel of observations for groups indicated $g = 1, \ldots, G$, which are ordered based on the time they receive treatment, such that $g \in (1, T)$, as well as potentially an untreated group denoted U. Note that here g refers to treatment adoption groups, rather than individual units. The OLS estimate of equation 4.19 is a weighted average of all possible 2×2 DD estimators written as follows:

$$\widehat{\tau}^{\text{twfe}} = \sum_{g \neq U} \omega_{gU} \cdot \widehat{\tau}_{gU}^{2\times 2} + \sum_{g \neq U} \sum_{l > g} \left[\omega_{gl}^{g} \cdot \widehat{\tau}_{gl}^{2\times 2,g} + \omega_{gl}^{l} \cdot \widehat{\tau}_{gl}^{2\times 2,l} \right], \tag{4.21}$$

where here l refers to all units that adopt treatment later than unit g. Thus, the OLS estimate of the two-way fixed effect estimate actually consists of a weighted mean of three groups of estimates (each of the three types of $\widehat{\tau}^{2\times 2}$ terms from (4.21), and the weights are indicated by ω). These estimates are precisely those laid out in panel (b)–(e) of figure 4.3. Specifically:

$$\widehat{\tau}_{gU}^{2\times 2} \equiv \left(\bar{Y}_g^{\text{Post}(g)} - \bar{Y}_g^{\text{Pre}(g)} \right) - \left(\bar{Y}_U^{\text{Post}(g)} - \bar{Y}_U^{\text{Pre}(g)} \right) \tag{4.22}$$

$$\widehat{\tau}_{gl}^{2\times 2,g} \equiv \left(\bar{Y}_g^{\text{Mid}(g,l)} - \bar{Y}_g^{\text{Pre}(g)} \right) - \left(\bar{Y}_l^{\text{Mid}(g,l)} - \bar{Y}_l^{\text{Pre}(g)} \right) \tag{4.23}$$

$$\widehat{\tau}_{gl}^{2\times 2,l} \equiv \left(\bar{Y}_l^{\text{Post}(l)} - \bar{Y}_l^{\text{Mid}(g,l)} \right) - \left(\bar{Y}_g^{\text{Post}(l)} - \bar{Y}_g^{\text{Mid}(g,l)} \right), \tag{4.24}$$

where $\bar{Y}$ refers to mean estimates over time in pre-treatment, post-treatment, or between-treatment ("Mid") periods. In particular $\widehat{\tau}_{gU}^{2\times 2}$ refers to comparisons between untreated units, and each treated unit (panels a and b of figure 4.3), $\widehat{\tau}_{gl}^{2\times 2,g}$ refers to comparisons between later treated groups and earlier treated groups around the period of adoption of early adopters (panel c), and $\widehat{\tau}_{gl}^{2\times 2,l}$ refers to comparisons between early treated groups and later treated groups around the period of adoption of late adopters (panel d). In understanding the global estimate, it is key to understand the weights that result from OLS and are given to each of the groups of estimates listed in equations 4.22, 4.23, and 4.24. These sum to one and are:

$$\omega_{gU} = \frac{\left(\frac{N_g + N_U}{N}\right)^2 \widehat{\mathbb{V}}_{gU}^{W}}{\widehat{\mathbb{V}}^{W}} \tag{4.25}$$

$$\omega_{gl}^{g} = \frac{\left[\frac{N_g + N_l}{N}(1 - \bar{W}_l)\right]^2 \widehat{\mathbb{V}}_{gl}^{W,g}}{\widehat{\mathbb{V}}^{W}} \tag{4.26}$$

$$\omega_{gl}^{l} = \frac{\left[\frac{N_g + N_l}{N}\bar{W}_g\right]^2 \widehat{\mathbb{V}}_{gl}^{W,l}}{\widehat{\mathbb{V}}^{W}}, \tag{4.27}$$

where quantities N_g and N_l and N_U refer to sample sizes of groups, N to the total sample, and $\bar{W}$ refers to the share of time that the sample is treated. Finally, the terms $\widehat{\mathbb{V}}_{gU}^{W}$, $\widehat{\mathbb{V}}_{gl}^{W,g}$, and

$\widehat{\mathbb{V}}^{W,l}_{gl}$ refer to how much treatment varies in each subsample and $\widehat{\mathbb{V}}^{W}$ to how much treatment varies overall. This weighting implies that even if *potential outcomes* are identical in two particular settings, if treatment timing varies, $\widehat{\tau}^{\text{twfe}}$ would generally return a different treatment effect estimate. In particular, (4.25)–(4.27) implies that the weight assigned to a given comparison will be higher when (a) it is between two groups of similar sizes and (b) when the variation of treatment within a comparison is higher, which will occur when treatment is adopted closer to the middle of the considered time period.

While this weighting of the two-way fixed effect estimator is itself interesting, what is perhaps more key is that where there is heterogeneity in the effects over time, the OLS estimate may be a considerably biased estimate of a weighted average of underlying ATTs. While the full derivations are provided in Goodman-Bacon (2021, section II) and explored in code callout 4.2 below, the logic comes from the comparison between "already treated units" and newly treated units, which is the "forbidden comparison." If the impact of treatment is changing over time and already treated units are used as "control" units in future periods, this change in treatment effect will be mistakenly included as part of the control group. This is problematic, as, if treatment effects grow over time, it will result in effects that are too small, and may even result in an estimated effect that is of the wrong sign altogether.

To see the reasoning behind this, imagine a case where the impact of treatment was growing over time and, in particular, what this would imply about the comparison between late and early treatment groups presented in panel (d) of figure 4.3. In this case, even if there is a clear jump in the outcome following treatment in the late treated group, we may estimate a *negative* impact of treatment, given that the outcomes for the "control" group may be growing at a faster rate over time. But this change in the "control" group is not actually something that we wish to consider, because it is not actually a control group, but rather a "previously treated" group, and the growth in the outcome in this group occurs precisely because of earlier treatment receipt. We work through this case at more length in code callout 4.2, where we see a number of numerical examples that let us see cases where positive but heterogeneous treatment effects result in negative values of $\widehat{\tau}^{2\times 2,l}_{g,l}$.

The key result from Goodman-Bacon (2021) is that if treatment adoption is staggered, and if treatment effects are heterogeneous over time in the sense that they are not simply one-off jumps at the moment when treatment is adopted, then the two-way fixed effect estimator is unlikely to be a good estimator. This result has actually been shown in a number of ways by a number of papers that evolved in parallel. This includes the breakdown in Chaisemartin and D'Haultfœuille (2020), who demonstrate the result based on the difference-in-differences design itself and parallel trends assumptions, noting that the two-way FE regression might result in certain treatment effects being given negative weights.[9] Similarly, a somewhat related decomposition is provided in Athey and Imbens (2022, Lemma 5) (who additionally go on to discuss a number of very important points on inference); however, their baseline assumptions and final result are somewhat different. It was also noted, in particular in line with the negative weighting point, in an early working paper of Borusyak and Jaravel (2018), which was later published as Borusyak, Jaravel, and Spiess (2024). Regardless of where one looks, what is clear is that in cases of staggered adoption, unless very stringent homogeneity assumptions are met, it is better to seek an alternative estimator to pin down treatment effects in difference-in-differences designs. We consider a range of such "heterogeneity-robust" estimators now.

Code Callout 4.2: Two-Way Fixed Effects and Parameter Decompositions
In this code callout we will work with a simulated staggered adoption design considering cases both with and without time-varying treatment effects, exploring the resulting two-way fixed effect decomposition "by hand" following Goodman-Bacon (2021). We also show the equivalence of this result to the group by time-specific treatment effect derivations of Chaisemartin and D'Haultfœuille (2020).

4.3.3 Solutions and Some New Estimators

This has been an area of active development in recent years, and fortunately, there are now various solutions to these issues. A number of the most commonly used solutions are discussed below, along with key assumptions. It is important to note that in each case, these methods explicitly allow for heterogeneous treatment effects over time, which would be problematic in the two-way fixed effect estimator discussed above. They also all maintain parallel trends assumptions of some type.

4.3.3.1 Explicitly building control groups Various of these methods seek to avoid the "forbidden comparison" discussed above by explicitly defining control groups for each treatment adoption of interest. One such estimator, proposed in Chaisemartin and D'Haultfœuille (2020), is the DID_M estimator. This estimator considers the moment when units adopt treatment and compares temporal differences among units that adopt treatments with similar temporal differences among units that have not yet adopted. Formally, they consider groups g observed in time periods $t = 1, \ldots, T$, where treatment adoption may occur in any periods $t = 2, \ldots, T$. Treatment cannot be adopted in $t = 1$ because some baseline period is required for each unit. They then define two quantities:

$$\tau^{\text{DID}_{+,t}} = \sum_{g: W_{g,t}=1, W_{g,t-1}=0} \frac{N_{g,t}}{N_{1,0,t}} \left(Y_{g,t} - Y_{g,t-1}\right) - \sum_{g: W_{g,t}=W_{g,t-1}=0} \frac{N_{g,t}}{N_{0,0,t}} \left(Y_{g,t} - Y_{g,t-1}\right),$$

which compares the evolution of average outcomes in units changing treatment status between $t-1$ and t with those who remain unchanged. Similarly, if relevant,

$$\tau^{\text{DID}_{-,t}} = \sum_{g: W_{g,t}=W_{g,t-1}=1} \frac{N_{g,t}}{N_{1,1,t}} \left(Y_{g,t} - Y_{g,t-1}\right) - \sum_{g: W_{g,t}=0, W_{g,t-1}=1} \frac{N_{g,t}}{N_{0,1,t}} \left(Y_{g,t} - Y_{g,t-1}\right).$$

Note that in the cases we are considering here where treatment is staggered and absorbing, units do not switch from treated to untreated, and hence there will be no cases where $W_{g,t}=0$ and $W_{g,t-1}=1$, and so $\text{DID}_{-,t}$ is set to 0.

Then, they propose their DID_M estimator as the weighted average of these quantities over all time periods:

$$\tau_{\text{ATT}}^{\text{DID}_M}=\sum_{t=2}^{T}\left(\frac{N_{1,0,t}}{N_G}\text{DID}_{+,t}+\frac{N_{0,1,t}}{N_G}\text{DID}_{-,t}\right). \tag{4.28}$$

They show that with a balanced panel of groups with at least some untreated units, and with assumptions related to parallel counterfactual trends between $t-1$ and t and no treatment anticipation, this provides an unbiased estimate of the average treatment effect across all switchers—that is, all units that change treatment between $t-1$ and t. This thus "resolves" the impact of treatment effect heterogeneity over time by considering instantaneous effects when treatment is adopted. However, this estimator also avoids the problem of forbidden comparisons by explicitly constructing a control group from units that have not (yet) adopted treatment, and as such, this estimator can be extended to consider dynamic effects beyond periods surrounding $t-1$ and t. Below, in section 4.4, we discuss the extension of this to dynamic settings. A similar estimator is proposed in Imai and Kim (2021).

An alternative solution in which estimators are built up from finer "building blocks" in staggered adoption designs is that laid out in Callaway and Sant'Anna (2021). However, the solution of Callaway and Sant'Anna (2021) starts from a different building block allowing for a potentially different (heterogeneity robust) estimator. To see the solution of Callaway and Sant'Anna (2021), we introduce the idea of a cohort. A cohort is simply a group of units that adopt treatment at the same moment of time t. Specifically, we can define an adoption date for each unit, G_i, which gives the period when treatment is first adopted by that unit. Formally, this is defined as:

$$G_i=\min\{t:W_{i,t}=1\}. \tag{4.29}$$

If a unit does not receive treatment, $G_i=\infty$, based on the idea that this is not exposed at all during all periods t considered. In a staggered adoption design there are thus multiple cohorts with different adoption dates, and here we will index these cohorts as g, which follows the notation of Callaway and Sant'Anna (2021).

Callaway and Sant'Anna (2021) thus start their analysis considering cohort- and time-specific treatment effects, defining $\text{ATT}(g,t)$ as the average treatment effect for a specific cohort at different time periods t. While Callaway and Sant'Anna (2021) discuss a more complex estimator when controls are required, if a parallel-trend and no-anticipation assumption hold, they note that

$$\text{ATT}^{\text{nev}}(g,t)=\mathbb{E}[Y_t-Y_{g-1}|G_i=g]-\mathbb{E}[Y_t-Y_{g-1}|G_i=\infty]. \tag{4.30}$$

In Callaway and Sant'Anna's terminology this quantity $\text{ATT}(g,t)$ is the "Group Average Treatment Effect" as it will (potentially) be different for each treatment group g and time period t. This ATT in (4.30) is referred to as $\text{ATT}^{\text{nev}}(g,t)$ as it is generated by comparing treated units to units that are never treated. However, alternatively, Callaway and Sant'Anna also note that such quantities could be based off all *not yet* treated units, which includes both never treated as well as units that adopt treatment at some point in the future. In this case, the group-specific effect of interest would be:

$$\text{ATT}^{\text{ny}}(g,t) = \mathbb{E}\left[Y_t - Y_{g-1}\middle|G_i = g\right] - \mathbb{E}\left[Y_t - Y_{g-1}\middle|W_{i,t} = 0\right],$$

where $W_{i,t} = 0$ implies individuals for whom treatment will not yet have switched on by t.

Among other things, starting with group- and time-specific treatment effects allows for the consideration of various types of heterogeneity, including heterogeneity by time of adoption, and by time since adoption. Indeed, if one were to average over all $\text{ATT}^{\text{ny}}(g,g)$ parameters (i.e., setting t precisely at the moment that each group adopts), this would correspond to the DID_M estimator proposed by Chaisemartin and D'Haultfœuille (2020). More generally, however, one can seek to focus on particular aggregate treatment effects of the form:

$$\tau^{\text{CS}} = \sum_{g \in \mathcal{G}} \sum_{t=2}^{T} w(g,t) \cdot \text{ATT}(g,t), \tag{4.31}$$

where $w(g,t)$ are weights assigned so that (4.31) aggregates certain $\text{ATT}(g,t)$ group effects into an estimand of interest. For example, among various other aggregate estimands of interest laid out by Callaway and Sant'Anna,

$$\tau_W^{\text{CS}} = \frac{1}{\kappa} \sum_{g \in \mathcal{G}} \sum_{t=2}^{T} \mathbb{1}\{t \geq g\} \text{ATT}(g,t) \Pr(G = g), \tag{4.32}$$

where $\kappa = \sum_{g \in \mathcal{G}} \sum_{t=2}^{T} \mathbb{1}\{t \geq g\} \Pr(G = g)$, so that τ_W^{CS} captures an aggregate treatment effect over all post-adoption periods for all treatment groups, with groups weighted by their size.

In their paper, Callaway and Sant'Anna discuss a range of other estimands, including some we will discuss below when considering treatment effect dynamics. They also note that alternative estimands can be written that loosen no-anticipation assumptions, if instead of using Y_{g-1} as the baseline period for ATT quantities, $Y_{g-\delta-1}$ for values of $\delta \geq 0$ is used. Additionally, they discuss how one can incorporate dependence on observable covariates by applying inverse propensity score weighting, regression adjusted, or double robust versions of each ATT. They also prove the asymptotic normality of their estimators and lay out an efficient bootstrap procedure to calculate confidence intervals for both ATT quantities as well as summary quantities like τ^{CS}.

4.3.3.2 Imputation-based estimators An alternative, potentially more efficient, manner of dealing with the forbidden comparison problem has been proposed by Borusyak, Jaravel, and Spiess (2024). These methods take advantage of the fact that the parallel trend assumption can be written as laid out in (4.3), or more generally as:

$$\mathbb{E}[Y_{i,t}(\mathbf{0}|i,t) = \alpha_i + \beta_t],$$

where $\mathbf{0}$ refers to the full path of treatment indicators $(W_{i,1}, W_{i,2}, \ldots, W_{i,T})$ being equal to 0. This suggests that untreated counterfactuals for each unit i and t can be estimated by a regression of outcomes $Y_{i,t}$ on unit-fixed effects and time-fixed effects using *only* observations in which treatment has not (or not yet) been switched on. This is written as:

$$\widehat{Y}_{i,t}(\mathbf{0}) = \widehat{\gamma}_i + \widehat{\mu}_t. \tag{4.33}$$

Note that the fact that these parameters must be estimated with untreated observations only implies that units can neither be treated in all periods (in which case their γ_i would be unidentified) nor can all units eventually be treated (as this would imply some late μ_t parameters would be unidentified).

However, provided that (4.33) is identified, then, under a parallel trend and no-anticipation assumption, for a given treated unit i in period t, their treatment effect is simply their observed outcome minus their imputed (untreated) counterfactual:

$$\widehat{\tau}_{i,t} = Y_{i,t} - \widehat{Y}_{i,t}(\mathbf{0}). \tag{4.34}$$

You will note that this takes us back very much to the Rubin Causal Model laid out in chapter 1. What's more, given that both $\widehat{\gamma}_i$ and $\widehat{\mu}_t$ are estimated off of untreated units only, there is no contamination from previous treatment adoption, as would be observed in a single step regression. Essentially, the forbidden comparison problem is avoided by imputing only the comparisons we want into $\widehat{Y}_{i,t}$. Finally, based on some prespecified weighting function, a grouped treatment effect can be estimated as:

$$\widehat{\tau}^{\text{DID,imputation}} = \sum_{i,t:W_{i,t}=1} \omega_{i,t}\widehat{\tau}_{i,t}, \tag{4.35}$$

where $\omega_{i,t}$ simply defines how unit- and time-specific treatment effects should be aggregated. For example, if an ATT is desired, $\omega_{i,t} = \frac{1}{N_T}$.

The idea of estimators based on imputation have been proposed in a number of other settings. A similar idea has been proposed by Gardner (2022) as "two-stage difference-in-differences" as well as by Liu, Wang, and Xu (2024) in their counterfactual estimators. In chapter 9 we will see a machine learning approach of Athey et al. (2021), where a related counterfactual logic underlies estimation. Borusyak, Jaravel, and Spiess (2024) show that *all* unbiased estimates, including those discussed previously in this section, can be written as imputation estimators, and they note that their procedure is efficient under the (strong) assumption of homoscedasticity, or known error structures. This greater efficiency comes from the fact that unlike other estimators up to this point, all pretreatment units are used in generating imputed outcomes $\widehat{Y}_{i,t}(\mathbf{0})$. However, this comes at a cost in terms of assumptions, as Borusyak, Jaravel, and Spiess (2024) require a parallel trend assumption across all periods, while other estimators require parallel trends only across periods that are used when generating particular comparisons of interest.

A somewhat related procedure comes from Wooldridge (2021). One key result from Wooldridge is that that the estimator $\widehat{\tau}^{\text{twfe}}$ commonly recovered from a two-way fixed effect regression such as (4.19) is actually equivalent to the "Mundlak" regression, first described in Mundlak (1978). This consists of estimating:

$$Y_{g,t} = \alpha + \widehat{\tau}^{\text{Mundlak}} W_{g,t} + \gamma \bar{W}_g + \lambda \bar{W}_t + \varepsilon_{g,t}, \tag{4.36}$$

where rather than including unit- and time-specific fixed effects, a single covariate is included that averages treatment across each group ($\bar{W}_g$), and a single covariate is included that averages treatment across each period ($\bar{W}_t$). Wooldridge (2021) shows that in the two-way FE setting, $\widehat{\tau}^{\text{Mundlak}} \equiv \widehat{\tau}^{\text{twfe}}$, which leads to the proposition that if we are concerned about staggered adoption designs with treatment heterogeneity, we could simply fully estimate the treatment effect heterogeneity in a model like (4.36), which could be done by including a single treatment indicator for each post-treatment period for each treatment adoption group. This will estimate a group-specific treatment effect for each period since treatment, and in the spirit of the interpretation of standard dummy variables, each of these treatment effects are understood as the comparison to the omitted baseline category, which in this case would be all units in which treatment has not yet been adopted. Wooldridge (2023) also shows that such a procedure is useful for nonlinear models, including (among others) the probit and logit.

4.3.3.3 Stacked designs An additional estimator, initially driven by applied papers such as Cengiz et al. (2019), is the stacked difference-in-differences design, which in their setting is based on 138 separate minimum wage law adoptions. The idea of a stacked design is for a staggered adoption design to be broken down into a series of "clean" comparisons where each treatment adoption date is lined up with all available untreated units in the period surrounding treatment adoption. These separate clean comparisons are then stacked, and a two-way fixed effect model is run where group-specific time- and state-fixed effects are included. This essentially seeks to recenter the staggered adoption design so that it looks like a block adoption design.

This can be viewed schematically as in table 4.5, where here we imagine a case with three separate treatment adoptions, occurring at t_3, t_4, and t_5. The original data structure is displayed in table 4.5(a), and in table 4.5(b) we see how this can be lined up in three separate sub-groups, resulting in a larger "stack" of comparisons. In order to compare across events, pre- and post-treatment periods must be trimmed, resulting in each comparison being based on identical relative times but different calendar times.

Table 4.5
A stacked design: Original data and stacked data

(a) Original Data

	Time Period					
	t_1	t_2	t_3	t_4	t_5	t_6
State A						
State B						
State C						
State D						
State E						
State F						
State G						

Dark gray cells indicate treatment, gray cells indicate control.

(b) Resulting stacked data

	Relative Time Period			
	−2	−1	0	1
	Event 1			
State A	t_1	t_2	t_3	t_4
State B	t_1	t_2	t_3	t_4
State D	t_1	t_2	t_3	t_4
State E	t_1	t_2	t_3	t_4
State F	t_1	t_2	t_3	t_4
State G	t_1	t_2	t_3	t_4
	Event 2			
State C	t_2	t_3	t_4	t_5
State F	t_2	t_3	t_4	t_5
State G	t_2	t_3	t_4	t_5
	Event 3			
State D	t_3	t_4	t_5	t_6
State E	t_3	t_4	t_5	t_6
State F	t_3	t_4	t_5	t_6
State G	t_3	t_4	t_5	t_6

In order to estimate a treatment effect in a stacked design, a model of the type

$$Y_{c,p,g,t} = \alpha + \tau^{\text{stacked}} W_{c,p} + \lambda_{c,g} + \mu_{c,p} + \varepsilon_{c,p,g,t} \tag{4.37}$$

is estimated, where this notation follows Gardner (2022, Appendix A) in using c as indexing stacked datasets, and p as indexing periods within a stacked dataset. Thus, rather than including a single set of year- and group-fixed effects, a separate set of year-fixed effects is included for each dataset in the stack as $\mu_{c,p}$, and a separate set of state-fixed effects is included for each dataset as $\lambda_{c,g}$. While this design allows for the avoidance of undesired comparisons, Gardner (2022) notes that this strategy will potentially lead to undesired weighting of ATTs, as it will weight each ATT in the data by the number of treated units and the variance of treatment in each particular dataset.

4.4 Dynamics and Panel Event-Study Designs

The above methods have made clear that treatment effects may be time dependent. This can be seen in temporally-defined DD estimates such as that defined in (4.9), as well as heterogeneity-robust methods, such as Callaway and Sant'Anna (2021), which explicitly aggregate effects over time. While building blocks such as ATT(g, t) point to a range of possible time-specific treatment effects of interest, one particularly important dimension of treatment effect heterogeneity in difference-in-difference style settings refers to dynamic effects with regards to treatment adoption. When we refer to dynamic effects, we will thus refer explicitly to effects cast in terms of time to treatment, allowing us to consider whether estimated effects grow, shrink, or remain stable over time.

Richer analyses of treatment effects in difference-in-differences style designs can explicitly consider such dynamics provided that multiple time periods of data are available. Perhaps the most common way to test for and visualize dynamic effects is via panel event-study designs. Such analyses seek to both visually display the temporal emergence of treatment effects and study the evolution of outcomes between treated and untreated areas in the pre-reform period when treatment was not *yet* assigned. Consider two particular descriptive examples. In figure 4.4 we consider two particular groups of treated and control units. In the left-hand panel, we observe a case where outcomes appear to be evolving approximately on parallel paths between a treated and control group up until the moment some treatment is assigned, and then jump in treated units, remaining essentially on trend for nontreated units. In the right-hand panel, we observe a case where outcomes were diverging even in the pre-treatment period. Panel event studies, documented below each set of raw trends, capture the dynamics of changes over time compared to an (arbitrary) pretreatment period. These figures thus allow us to descriptively assess two things at once. Firstly, we can graphically observe whether outcomes were approximately trending in a parallel manner in the pretreatment period by examining pretreatment point estimates and confidence intervals. And secondly, we can observe whether there are any clear dynamics in post-treatment periods by considering whether post-treatment "effects" grow, shrink, or remain stable over time.

These designs have grown considerably in frequency in empirical work. Schmidheiny and Siegloch (2023) find that event studies were mentioned in around 5% of papers published in The *American Economic Review*, The *Quarterly Journal of Economics*, and The *Journal of Political Economy* in recent years. Currie, Kleven, and Zwiers (2020) note a sharp increase in their frequency from around 2010 onward. Below we lay out these models before discussing how such methods relate to the assumptions in difference-in-differences designs, as well how they interact with issues related to staggered adoption and heterogeneous treatment effects discussed above.

4.4.1 The Panel Event Study Model

There is a burgeoning literature discussing panel event study methods, and multiple notations have been employed to lay out event study models, though all generally imply the same model. Alternative ways of writing the same thing can be found in Borusyak and Jaravel (2018); Freyaldenhoven, Hansen, and Shapiro (2019); Borusyak, Jaravel, and Spiess (2024); Schmidheiny and Siegloch (2023); and D. L. Miller (2023), among other places. One way to lay out event study models is to work with the adoption date for each unit, which we have

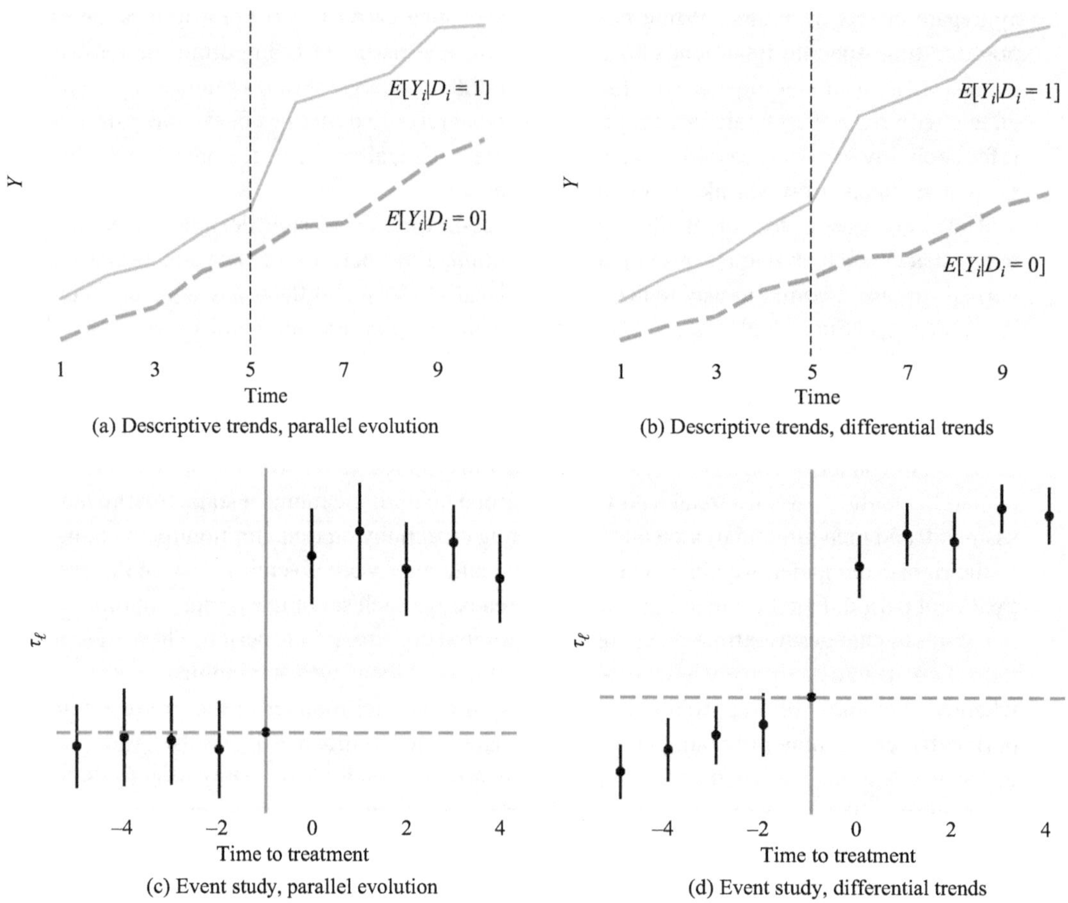

Figure 4.4
Outcome trends and event studies under simulated dynamics.

referred to as G_i in (4.29) above. The event study then includes a series of indicators for relative time to treatment, along with unit-specific and time-specific fixed effects:

$$Y_{i,t} = \alpha_i + \beta_t + \sum_{\substack{\ell=-L \\ \ell \neq -1}}^{K} \tau_\ell^{\text{event}} \mathbb{1}\{t - G_i = \ell\} + \varepsilon_{i,t}. \tag{4.38}$$

In the above, the indicator function $\mathbb{1}\{\cdot\}$ resolves to define a series of "leads" in which treatment has not yet been adopted and in which the relative time to adoption $t - G_i$ can vary from $-L$, which is assumed to be the largest lead observed in data, up to periods -2 (two periods prior to treatment). Similarly, a series of post-treatment "lags" exist for relative time periods $t - G_i = 0, \ldots, K$, with 0 referring to the period of adoption, and K assumed to be the most distant lag observed in data. Because units that are never treated have values of $G_i = \infty$, the condition $\mathbb{1}\{t - G_i = \ell\}$ will never be met, and the indicator function will always resolve to 0. Note that this specification can be viewed as a fully interacted version of (4.19). Here, rather than a single post-treatment indicator, which takes 1 if $W_{i,t} = 1$ (or in other words, if $t - G_i \geq 0$), a full series of pre- and post-treatment indicators is included. As in the two-way fixed effect model discussed previously, a full set of unit-specific and time-specific fixed effects are included to capture all time-invariant and unit-invariant factors.

The idea of the event study is to observe how outcomes $Y_{i,t}$ change over time since treatment compared with baseline differences between treated and untreated units. For this reason, some baseline reference period must be omitted in the time to treatment indicators, which is indicated as $\ell = -1$ in (4.38). While a reference period of 1 unit prior to treatment is often used in practice and is generally the default in such models, alternative periods may be desired for a number of reasons. Firstly, the use of multiple pre-periods as a reference may result in more tightly estimated standard errors (G. Miller 2008). Such a procedure of defining multiple periods as the baseline reference can be achieved by either omitting multiple time to treatment dummies from (4.38) or by estimating constrained regressions where coefficients across multiple periods are constrained to average to zero. Because a full set of treatment lags and leads are included, at least one category must be omitted to avoid multicolinearity, or alternatively, some other exclusion restriction can be imposed to anchor the interpretation of all coefficients. An option that may be useful in certain cases would be to estimate a constrained regression in which all leads must average out to zero, allowing for each lead to be separately estimated while, at the same time, providing a base reference exclusion restriction. Secondly, using leads before period -1 may allow for the loosening of the no-anticipation assumption, as laid out later in this section.

For a clear illustration of what the coefficients τ_ℓ^{event} in an event study capture, we can consider a case with a single treatment adoption date (i.e., a block adoption design). In this case, given that there will be a single treatment adoption date G_i, and that at this date units will either adopt treatment if $W_i = 1$, or remain untreated if $W_i = 0$, the binary nature of dummy variables implies that regression coefficients can be interpreted as follows:

$$
\begin{aligned}
\widehat{\tau}_{-L}^{\text{event}} &= \left(\mathbb{E}[Y_{i,G-L}|W_i=1] - \mathbb{E}[Y_{i,G-L}|W_i=0]\right) - \left(\mathbb{E}[Y_{i,G-1}|W_i=1] - \mathbb{E}[Y_{i,G-1}|W_i=0]\right) \\
&\ldots \\
\widehat{\tau}_{-2}^{\text{event}} &= \left(\mathbb{E}[Y_{i,G-2}|W_i=1] - \mathbb{E}[Y_{i,G-2}|W_i=0]\right) - \left(\mathbb{E}[Y_{i,G-1}|W_i=1] - \mathbb{E}[Y_{i,G-1}|W_i=0]\right) \\
\widehat{\tau}_{0}^{\text{event}} &= \left(\mathbb{E}[Y_{i,G}|W_i=1] - \mathbb{E}[Y_{i,G}|W_i=0]\right) \qquad - \left(\mathbb{E}[Y_{i,G-1}|W_i=1] - \mathbb{E}[Y_{i,G-1}|W_i=0]\right) \\
\widehat{\tau}_{1}^{\text{event}} &= \left(\mathbb{E}[Y_{i,G+1}|W_i=1] - \mathbb{E}[Y_{i,G+1}|W_i=0]\right) - \left(\mathbb{E}[Y_{i,G-1}|W_i=1] - \mathbb{E}[Y_{i,G-1}|W_i=0]\right) \\
&\ldots \\
\widehat{\tau}_{K}^{\text{event}} &= \left(\mathbb{E}[Y_{i,G+K}|W_i=1] - \mathbb{E}[Y_{i,G+K}|W_i=0]\right) - \left(\mathbb{E}[Y_{i,G-1}|W_i=1] - \mathbb{E}[Y_{i,G-1}|W_i=0]\right),
\end{aligned}
$$

which is simply the lag- and lead-specific double-difference compared to the baseline omitted time category.

In practice, various elements of event studies may vary. Often, rather than considering all possible lags and leads, beyond certain points lags and leads are "binned" (Schmidheiny and Siegloch 2023) or "capped" (D. L. Miller 2023). This implies that only a certain number of lags or leads are included, and periods more extreme than these lags and leads are indicated in a single dummy taking 1 for all periods prior (in the case of leads) or posterior (in the case of lags) to this point. One way to rewrite (4.38) to bin end points is as follows:

$$\begin{aligned} Y_{i,t} = \alpha_i + \beta_t &+ \tau_{-L}^{\text{event}} \mathbb{1}\{t - G_i \leq -L\} \\ &+ \sum_{\substack{\ell=-L+1 \\ \ell \neq -1}}^{K-1} \tau_\ell^{\text{event}} \mathbb{1}\{t - G_i = \ell\} + \tau_K^{\text{event}} \mathbb{1}\{t - G_i \geq K\} + \varepsilon_{i,t}, \end{aligned} \tag{4.39}$$

where τ_{-L}^{event} captures the binned lead and τ_K^{event} captures the binned lag. In a review of twelve particular empirical implementations of event studies, Sun and Abraham (2021, table 1) note that six of them do such binning. It is important to note that if treatment adoption is staggered, binning event studies implies an assumption of stability of treatment effects following these periods; which is potentially reasonable if effects converge to some particular value over time (Schmidheiny and Siegloch 2023). It is also important to note that while binning may be a reasonable empirical choice, simply omitting dummies for lags and leads beyond a certain point is unlikely to be a reasonable choice and should be avoided. Such a choice will result in the inclusion of these periods as part of the baseline comparison, and in effect assumes that dynamic treatment effects drop to zero beyond the included lags.

A stylized example of the generation of event study lags and leads with binned end points is described in table 4.6. This particular example considers four units forming a balanced panel of years from 2000 to 2009. Treatment is adopted at varying times among units 1, 2 and 4, while unit 3 is untreated. Here both four leads and four lags are included, such that $L = K = 4$. Lead and lag 4 (exclusively) are binned. If binning had not occurred, additional lags and leads would exist (such as lag 5 for unit 1 in 2009).

Units in which the event never occurs (such as unit 3 in table 4.6) act as pure controls. These units have 0s in all lead and lag terms and act as the counterfactual on which the estimation of impacts is based. Differences between these pure control states and states that adopt the event of interest are anchored at 0 in the omitted base period—that is, the first lead in equation 4.38. Hence, leads and lags capture the difference between treated and control states, compared to the prevailing difference in the omitted base period. Unbiased estimation of post-event treatment effects thus relies fundamentally on the parallel trends assumption (as well as the no-anticipation assumption). In the absence of treatment, it is assumed that treated and control states would have maintained similar differences as in the baseline period. For this reason, these models have been demonstrated to be under-identified, or identified

Table 4.6
A stylized example of a panel event study

Unit (i)	Year (t)	Event (G_i)	$W_{i,t}$	Time to Event	Lead 4	Lead 3	Lead 2	Lead 1	Lag 0	Lag 1	Lag 2	Lag 3	Lag 4
Unit 1	2000	2004	0	−4	1	0	0	0	0	0	0	0	0
Unit 1	2001	2004	0	−3	0	1	0	0	0	0	0	0	0
Unit 1	2002	2004	0	−2	0	0	1	0	0	0	0	0	0
Unit 1	2003	2004	0	−1	0	0	0	1	0	0	0	0	0
Unit 1	2004	2004	1	0	0	0	0	0	1	0	0	0	0
Unit 1	2005	2004	1	1	0	0	0	0	0	1	0	0	0
Unit 1	2006	2004	1	2	0	0	0	0	0	0	1	0	0
Unit 1	2007	2004	1	3	0	0	0	0	0	0	0	1	0
Unit 1	2008	2004	1	4	0	0	0	0	0	0	0	0	1
Unit 1	2009	2004	1	5	0	0	0	0	0	0	0	0	1
Unit 2	2000	2005	0	−5	1	0	0	0	0	0	0	0	0
Unit 2	2001	2005	0	−4	1	0	0	0	0	0	0	0	0
Unit 2	2002	2005	0	−3	0	1	0	0	0	0	0	0	0
Unit 2	2003	2005	0	−2	0	0	1	0	0	0	0	0	0
Unit 2	2004	2005	0	−1	0	0	0	1	0	0	0	0	0
Unit 2	2005	2005	1	0	0	0	0	0	1	0	0	0	0
Unit 2	2006	2005	1	1	0	0	0	0	0	1	0	0	0
Unit 2	2007	2005	1	2	0	0	0	0	0	0	1	0	0
Unit 2	2008	2005	1	3	0	0	0	0	0	0	0	1	0
Unit 2	2009	2005	1	4	0	0	0	0	0	0	0	0	1
Unit 3	2000	∞	0	.	0	0	0	0	0	0	0	0	0
Unit 3	2001	∞	0	.	0	0	0	0	0	0	0	0	0
Unit 3	2002	∞	0	.	0	0	0	0	0	0	0	0	0
Unit 3	2003	∞	0	.	0	0	0	0	0	0	0	0	0
Unit 3	2004	∞	0	.	0	0	0	0	0	0	0	0	0
Unit 3	2005	∞	0	.	0	0	0	0	0	0	0	0	0
Unit 3	2006	∞	0	.	0	0	0	0	0	0	0	0	0
Unit 3	2007	∞	0	.	0	0	0	0	0	0	0	0	0
Unit 3	2008	∞	0	.	0	0	0	0	0	0	0	0	0
Unit 3	2009	∞	0	.	0	0	0	0	0	0	0	0	0
Unit 4	2000	2007	0	−7	1	0	0	0	0	0	0	0	0
Unit 4	2001	2007	0	−6	1	0	0	0	0	0	0	0	0
Unit 4	2002	2007	0	−5	1	0	0	0	0	0	0	0	0
Unit 4	2003	2007	0	−4	1	0	0	0	0	0	0	0	0
Unit 4	2004	2007	0	−3	0	1	0	0	0	0	0	0	0
Unit 4	2005	2007	0	−2	0	0	1	0	0	0	0	0	0
Unit 4	2006	2007	0	−1	0	0	0	1	0	0	0	0	0
Unit 4	2007	2007	1	0	0	0	0	0	1	0	0	0	0
Unit 4	2008	2007	1	1	0	0	0	0	0	1	0	0	0
Unit 4	2009	2007	1	2	0	0	0	0	0	0	1	0	0

This examples is based on the example provided in Clarke and Tapia Schythe (2022).

only up to a linear trend, when all units adopt treatment at some point in time (Schmidheiny and Siegloch 2019; Borusyak and Jaravel 2018). Schmidheiny and Siegloch (2019) show that, in this case, it is necessary to bin leads and lags beyond certain maximum lead (L) and lag (K) periods.

A graphical example of how event studies are frequently presented is provided in figure 4.4(c). Here, each point estimate $\widehat{\tau}_{\ell}^{\text{event}}$ from (4.38) is presented along with 95% confidence intervals generally estimated to allow for arbitrary correlations within clusters over time (either with cluster robust variance covariance estimators or wild cluster bootstrap procedures). These graphs allow us to focus on how outcomes evolve in the pretreatment period, as well as the dynamics in any treatment effects in the post-treatment period.

A key focus in event studies is on pretreatment leads, as these allow us to inspect whether units that are eventually treated and those that remain untreated are approximately following parallel trends in the pretreatment period. Because we are omitting a baseline period at -1 in this figure, this acts as a standardization to capture any level differences, such as that between treated and control units at time period 5 in figure 4.4(a). And because all dummies are now cast in terms of comparisons with this baseline reference period, we can simply observe whether there are systematic changes in the difference in levels between treated and controls in the pretreatment period by examining each of the coefficients and confidence intervals on leads -2 to -5. In cases like that presented in panel (c), the fact that all point estimates are tightly clustered around 0 suggests that treated and control units were trending in an approximately parallel way, while in cases like that presented in panel (d), the clear divergence of trends is visible on the plot, suggesting that treated units were actually increasing their outcomes by more than control units even in advance of treatment.

However, these patterns must be treated with caution for two reasons. A first reason is that even though we can speak of parallel pre-trends, this does *not* allow us to test the identifying assumption of parallel trends laid out in assumption 4. This is because the parallel trends assumption refers to counterfactual outcomes between treated and control units in the post-treatment period, in which case $Y_{i,t}(\mathbf{0})$ is entirely unobservable for treated units. Thus, we may see evidence consistent with parallel pre-trends in the pretreatment period when neither group was treated, but this does not necessarily imply that such trends would have remained in the post-reform period (Kahn-Lang and Lang 2019). Nevertheless, the existence of parallel pre-trends may be considered as supportive auxiliary information, and at the very least if trends in treated and untreated areas were not parallel even pre-event, it would seem unlikely that they would be parallel post-event.

A second point of caution related to tests of dynamics, and specifically tests of pre-trends in the event study and related design, is noted by J. Roth (2022). He documents, based on 12 empirical studies published in highly visible economics journals, that often given imprecision in estimates of pretreatment coefficients, which manifests as wide confidence intervals, tests of parallel pre-trends may not actually be very powerful. Specifically, he conducts a simulation exercise and seeks to determine what the most extreme linear trend would be that would still "pass" pre-trend tests, in the sense that in 80% of simulations, all pre-event confidence intervals would include 0. What he finds is that under this condition, in seven of the 12 studies considered, the actual bias in estimated treatment effects under such "passing" pre-trends would be larger than the estimate itself, and in the other five cases, the bias is still meaningful.

One particular case in which these parallel pre-trends will not hold is the case of the so-called "Ashenfelter dip." This Ashenfelter dip, named for the labor economist Orley Ashenfelter, and particularly the results in Ashenfelter (1978), recognizes that often participants in labor market training programs have a reduction in earnings immediately *before* participation in the program. The logic of this is that if individuals self-select into training programs, many of those who select in will be those who have lost their job and, hence, participate in the training program as part of a job search. This pattern of outcomes has been shown in a wide array of labor market training programs (see, for example, Heckman and Smith [1999]). Such a setting would clearly be in violation of the no-anticipation assumption, though fortunately it is something that can be visually inspected in an event study provided sufficient pretreatments are available.

4.4.2 Heterogeneous Treatment Effects and Event Study Models

4.4.2.1 Interaction weighted event studies As is the case in standard two-way fixed effect models, if there is both staggered adoption *and* unrestricted heterogeneity in treatment effects, event study models can also suffer from undesired aggregation in regression parameters. In particular, Sun and Abraham (2021) show that concerns will exist in staggered adoption designs if there is heterogeneity in effects across treatment groups in particular lag and lead terms. Specifically, they are concerned with heterogeneity in treatment effects across "cohorts," where cohorts refer to units that share a common treatment adoption date G_i. Interestingly, they show that if treatment effects are heterogeneous across time *but* all cohorts in a staggered adoption design have the same time path of effects, this would not be an issue for the parameters estimated in event studies. This is important, as such temporal dynamic effects themselves were an issue in two-way fixed effect models. Rather, in the case of event studies, issues will be encountered if there are both time-varying effects *and* these effects vary by cohorts that adopt at different periods.

The work of Sun and Abraham (2021) has been influential firstly because it has documented exactly what this bias is and how it comes about, and additionally because it proposes an alternative method of generating estimates in the spirit of event studies, which are robust to heterogeneous treatment effects. In order to document what the parameters of a standard event study along the lines of (4.38) incorporate, Sun and Abraham (2021) define as a basic building block the notion of a "Cohort Average Treatment Effect on the Treated," which for each cohort (adoption group) is defined as:

$$\text{CATT}_{g,\ell} = \mathbb{E}[Y_{i,g+\ell} - Y(0)_{i,g+\ell} | G_i = g].$$

Here g refers to the adoption period—in other words, the values that can be taken by G_i defined above. The CATT is also defined in terms of ℓ, where ℓ refers to periods since treatment. For example, for a group such as unit 1 in table 4.6, which adopted treatment in year 2001 and for whom we wanted to calculate the impact of treatment in year 2005, this would be defined as $\text{CATT}_{2001,4} = \mathbb{E}[Y_{i,2005} - Y(\mathbf{0})_{i,2005} | G_i = 2001]$. Here the term Y_i refers to the observed outcome for this cohort at this time period, and $Y(\mathbf{0})$ refers to the counterfactual under a situation in which the unit *would never have been treated*. This CATT, if estimable, is a relevant parameter, as it can be used to consider many questions, such as for a given adoption cohort, how treatment effects respond to policies over time, and similarly, CATTs could be weighted across adoption cohorts to generate some sort of aggregate time path of treatment effect, which is what we desire to capture in the baseline standard event study design described previously.

One of the key results from Sun and Abraham (2021) is that *even* under a parallel trends assumption and a no-anticipation assumption, if there is heterogeneity in treatment effects across cohorts, then the coefficients on the lags and leads in event studies such as (4.38) will *not* recover a weighted estimate of CATTs for this lag or lead length. Instead, they will be partially contaminated by treatment effects from other lags and leads. Specifically, they note that for a specific lag ℓ in (4.38), we have that:

$$\tau_\ell^{\text{event}} = \sum_g \omega_{g,\ell} \text{CATT}_{g,\ell} + \sum_{\ell' \neq \ell, \ell' \geq 0} \sum_g \omega_{g,\ell'} \text{CATT}_{g,\ell'}, \tag{4.40}$$

where ω are weights that sum to 1 in the case of the first term $\omega_{g,\ell}$, and that sum to zero in the case of the second term $\omega_{g,\ell'}$. This formula is actually a simplification of the formula presented as Sun and Abraham (2021, equation 16), given that here we are assuming that each treatment lag and lead are a single period (a fully dynamic specification). Nevertheless, a key point to highlight here is that without restricting treatment effect heterogeneity, τ_ℓ^{event} will *not* just consist of a weighted average of each adoption specific CATT (the first term) but *also* will include a second series of terms that are drawn from each *other* post-treatment lag $\ell' \neq \ell$.

Similarly to weighting cases discussed previously, when estimating parameters by regression, these weights will be set to minimize variance. Specifically, Sun and Abraham (2021) note that these weights simply come from regressing a binary indicator of each specific treatment lag or lead on the same two-way fixed effect model. The fact that the first set of weights $\omega_{g,\ell}$ sums to one makes sense as we are weighting up lag-specific treatment effects. The fact that the second set of weights $\omega_{g,\ell'}$ sums to zero is also desired, as these are effects from other lags which will "contaminate" τ_ℓ^{event}. However, even though these weights sum to zero, this term is not guaranteed to average out to zero *unless* treatment effects from other leads ℓ' are homogeneous.

A key implication of this is that not only will it be complicated to understand exactly what the empirical content is of a specific post-treatment lag or lead in standard event studies but *also* that standard pretreatment tests of stability of coefficients from event studies may not actually allow us to examine whether treated and untreated units were following identical trends prior to treatment. This is because both pre- and post-treatment indicators suffer from the contamination problem noted in (4.40), unless one is willing to assume away heterogeneity of treatment effects across treatment cohorts.

Fortunately, the authors suggest an alternative specification that does not suffer from this issue, and additionally that recovers a meaningful set of CATTs for each post-treatment indicator. This is their "Interaction-weighted (IW) estimator." This IW estimator consists of the following three steps, laid out at more length in Sun and Abraham (2021, §4.1):

1. Estimate each $\text{CATT}_{e,l}$ for each adoption period in a two-way FE framework, additionally controlling for relative time indicators for each cohort.
2. Estimate weights for each lag and lead term that assign more importance to units that make up a larger proportion of each lag and lead
3. Use the weights from 2 and the estimated CATTs from 1 to generate the IW estimator.

Sun and Abraham (2021) show that the IW estimator is a consistent estimator for the weighted average of each CATT term, and additionally that it is asymptotically normal, implying that standard (analytical) variance-covariance estimators to conduct inference, without needing bootstrap or other procedures.

> **Code Callout 4.3(a): Event Study and Interaction-Weighted Estimators**
> To see details of this interaction-weighted estimator at more length, refer to code callout 4.3. Here we consider a real empirical example based on data from Stevenson and Wolfers (2006) documenting both the estimation and plotting of a standard event study as well as the estimation of an interaction-weighted version.

4.4.2.2 Alternative time-varying treatment effects Along with Sun and Abraham's (2021) IW estimator, the estimators discussed earlier in this Chapter of Chaisemartin and D'Haultfœuille (2020); Callaway and Sant'Anna (2021); and Borusyak, Jaravel, and Spiess (2024) similarly offer solutions to the issues identified by Sun and Abraham (2021). In particular, the heterogeneity-robust estimators can be applied to focus on effects aggregated at particular lags and leads. Consider, for example, the case of the DID_M estimator defined in (4.28). This is based on the quantity $\text{DID}_{+,t}$, which compares changes from the period of adoption t and the period prior to adoption $t-1$. However, an analogous estimator could be defined where rather than aggregating over differences between t and $t-1$, lags can be produced by comparing differences between $t+1$ and $t-1$, between $t+2$ and $t-1$, and so forth. Similarly, placebo treatment leads can be produced by comparing differences between $t-2$ and $t-1$, between $t-3$ and $t-1$, and so forth (Chaisemartin and D'Haultfœuille

2020, 2024). This results in output that is similar in structure and substance to a panel event study, while at the same time being robust to issues with heterogeneous treatment effects with a staggered adoption design.

Similarly, note that precisely the same argument can be made with the aggregate estimators from Callaway and Sant'Anna (2021). In this case, event study coefficients correspond to averaging over all quantities $\text{ATT}(g, g+\ell)$ for lags and leads in ℓ. Using the notation from Callaway and Sant'Anna (2021), a lag- or lead-specific term can be defined as follows:

$$\tau_{\ell}^{\text{CS,event}} = \sum_{g \in \mathcal{G}} \mathbb{1}\{g+\ell \leq T\}\text{ATT}(g, g+\ell)\Pr(G=g|G+\ell \leq T). \tag{4.41}$$

Here, all details are defined as laid out in (4.31); however, you will note that we are considering ATT terms defined at period $g+\ell$. In (4.41) we simply aggregate these terms $\text{ATT}(g, g+\ell)$ over all adoption periods, weighted by their relative frequency. The indicator term $\mathbb{1}\{g+\ell \leq T\}$ simply implies that we will only consider ATTs that actually exist, and (for example) could not consider a term for $\ell = 3$ if a unit only adopts treatment two periods before the end of our observed data. For this reason, it is important to be clear about the composition of groups when estimating lags and leads, as changes in composition over time may result in changes in effects that reflect these changes, rather than temporal dynamics themselves. With this definition of (4.41), we can generate an equivalent event study specification where we estimate $\tau_{\ell}^{\text{CS,event}}$ for a full set of lags and leads of interest, noting that for consistency with the idea of event studies, we should ensure that ATT terms for lags and leads are cast with respect to period $g-1$, as in (4.30).

Finally, note that the methods of Borusyak, Jaravel, and Spiess (2024) also allow for effects to be cast in terms of an event study; however, in this case, the idea of event leads (i.e., pre-treatment estimates) requires some tweaking. The definition of event lags for Borusyak, Jaravel, and Spiess (2024) is straightforward, simply averaging imputation-based quantities from (4.34) at specific lags:

$$\widehat{\tau}_{\ell}^{\text{DID,imputation}} = \mathbb{E}[\widehat{\tau}_{i,t}|g-t=\ell],$$

where, as standard, g is used to indicate treatment adoption dates. However, in this case, note that such a quantity cannot be generated for (pretreatment) leads, given that $\widehat{\tau}_{i,t}$ is *only* estimated for units that are treated, and hence does not exist prior to treatment adoption. For this reason, Borusyak, Jaravel, and Spiess (2024) propose an alternative pre-trend test that consists of estimating a regression sub-setting to units that are not (or not yet) treated, and including a set of K indicators capturing periods until treatment along with unit- and time-fixed effects. Namely, this consists of estimating:

$$Y_{i,t} = \alpha_i + \beta_t + \sum_{\ell=-K}^{-1} \tau_{\ell}^{\text{pretrend,imputation}} \mathbb{1}\{g-t=\ell\} + \varepsilon_{i,t} \tag{4.42}$$

for all $(i,t): W_{i,t}=0$. By jointly testing the significance of the $\tau_{\ell}^{\text{pretrend,imputation}}$ terms, or presenting them along with $\widehat{\tau}_{\ell}^{\text{DID,imputation}}$ in an event study–style plot, one can consider the existence of any pre-trends. It is important to note, however, that the logic of this pre-treatment test and the nature of the post-treatment estimates is different, as pre-trend tests are based on comparisons in changes over time compared with a reference group of never-treated units and time periods more than K units before treatment. Borusyak, Jaravel, and Spiess (2024) do not suggest an optimal criteria for choosing K, but instead suggest that a large enough quantity be chosen to judge for the existence of pre-trends while also leaving enough comparison units to maintain power in joint tests of coefficients in (4.42).

Code Callout 4.3(b): Alternative Time-Varying Treatment Effect Estimators
To see these methods in practice, we return to the example discussed in code callout 4.3(a) above, implementing event study analogues for Chaisemartin and D'Haultfœuille (2017), Callaway and Sant'Anna (2021), and Borusyak, Jaravel, and Spiess (2024) using software provided by the authors of each routine.

4.5 Other Extensions to Difference-in-Differences Methods

4.5.1 Difference-in-Difference-in-Differences

Difference-in-differences estimates frequently provide a good test for the impact of some reform. However, what can we do if we think that simply capturing a baseline difference in treatment and nontreatment areas is not enough? One option is to extend the difference in-differences approach to a difference-in-differences-in-differences (also known as triple differences, or DDD) approach! This follows the logic of difference-in-differences; however, estimates the differences-in-differences model for two groups: one that is affected by the reform and one that isn't. If the group that is not affected by the reform has any change over time, this is then subtracted from the main difference-in-differences estimate to give a triple difference estimate.

This estimator is formalized in Olden and Møen (2022), who credit its introduction to Gruber (1994). Applying their setup to the notation used here, consider a reform that arrives at the level of groups g, with groups indicated as $T_g=1$ when treated, and 0 otherwise. Within treated and nontreated groups, assume there are two types of individuals, one of whom will receive treatment in the treated group. This beneficiary group is indicated as $B_b=1$ if individuals are in the beneficiary group (whether or not individuals live in a group in which $T_g=1$). Finally, assume there is a pre- and post-treatment period, with $Post_t=1$ (for all groups, untreated or not) in the period when treatment arrives. Olden and Møen

(2022) note that the DDD equivalent to (4.11) above is:

$$Y_{b,g,t} = \beta_0 + \beta_1 T_g + \beta_2 B_b + \beta_3 Post_t + \beta_4 (T_g \cdot B_b) + \beta_5 (T_g \cdot Post_t) + \beta_6 (B_b \cdot Post_t) + \tau^{\text{DDD}} (T_g \cdot B_b \cdot Post_t) + \varepsilon_{b,g,t}, \tag{4.43}$$

where the triple difference estimator is captured by τ^{DDD}. They show this in a parameter-by-parameter interpretation of equation 4.43, similar to the approach taken in table 4.1. This is a relatively straight forward calculation, but it is somewhat notationally cumbersome and so is left as an activity for you to work through, or it can be consulted in Olden and Møen (2022, 5).

Specifically, they show that the triple difference estimator captures:

$$\widehat{\tau}^{\text{DDD}} = \left[(\bar{Y}_{b,g,t}^{T=1,B=1,\text{Post}=1} - \bar{Y}_{b,g,t}^{T=1,B=1,\text{Post}=0}) - (\bar{Y}_{b,g,t}^{T=0,B=1,\text{Post}=1} - \bar{Y}_{b,g,t}^{T=0,B=1,\text{Post}=0}) \right] \tag{4.44}$$

$$- \left[(\bar{Y}_{b,g,t}^{T=1,B=0,\text{Post}=1} - \bar{Y}_{b,g,t}^{T=1,B=0,\text{Post}=0}) - (\bar{Y}_{b,g,t}^{T=0,B=0,\text{Post}=1} - \bar{Y}_{b,g,t}^{T=0,B=0,\text{Post}=0}) \right], \tag{4.45}$$

which, as the name suggests, is made up of the difference between difference-in-differences estimates. The first difference-in-differences estimate is captured in the first line, and is the pre- versus post-DD estimate between treated and nontreated groups for individuals with $B = 1$, while the second DD estimate is for the same difference, but for individuals with $B = 0$. It is useful to understand that the triple difference must capture all the single-interaction, double-interaction, and the triple-interaction term as laid out in (4.43), but at times it may be easier to estimate the triple differences design by *first* taking group and time differences for outcomes between groups $B = 1$ and $B = 0$, and then simply estimating the double differences model. This effectively begins by taking one difference by transforming the outcome variable and then generates the second and third difference with the regression model as below:

$$(Y_{g,t}^{B=1} - Y_{g,t}^{B=0}) = \alpha_0 + \alpha_1 T_g + \alpha_2 Post_t + \tau^{\text{DDD}} (T_g \cdot Post_t) + \eta_{g,t}. \tag{4.46}$$

The parameter τ^{DDD} in (4.46) is identical to the parameter in (4.43), and if we like we could find the equivalence between parameters such as α_0 and the β parameters in (4.43). The key thing to see here is that in both models we are taking the three differences we require, and so both are equivalent ways to estimate the triple difference parameter.

Note that if we were to impose the standard parallel trend assumption from our previous double-difference model, it would be sufficient to identify the causal impact of policy T using the first double difference estimate for the beneficiary group $B = 1$. However, if parallel trends does not hold between treated and untreated states for group $B = 1$, a causal estimate can still be recovered by using the triple difference estimator provided that these same nonparallel trends are also present in group $B = 0$. In this sense, the triple difference estimator can be considered as using group $B = 0$ to estimate the violation of standard parallel trends in group $B = 1$, allowing us to subtract this bias from the double-difference estimate from $B = 1$, thus isolating the causal effect. If parallel trends assumptions *are* indeed present between treated and untreated states for groups $B = 0$ and $B = 1$, this is entirely fine as well, as in this case, the first double-difference term in the triple difference (equation 4.44) will capture the treatment effect, while the second difference (equation 4.45) will be zero, given that the untreated group $B = 0$ does not receive treatment in either state. Given that the triple difference estimator nests the DD estimator when parallel trends are met in both groups but also captures a causal effect of treatment if parallel trends is violated in a similar way in both groups, this leads Olden and Møen (2022) to suggest that "there is little to lose, and some to gain, by using the triple difference relative to difference-in-differences." However, note that there are conceivably cases where a DD estimator could lead to a causal estimate, while the DDD estimator does not, if parallel trends are met in group $B = 1$ but are violated in group $B = 0$, so, as always, judicious consideration of identifying assumptions should be employed.

4.5.2 Continuous Treatment Variables

So far we have focused on cases where we have a binary treatment versus control distinction: Those individuals who receive treatment can be indicated with $W_{it} = 1$, while control individuals consistently have $W_{it} = 0$. However, in practice, treatments at times take on a "dose response," where rather than switching from 0 to 1 for treated units, they may switch from 0 to some continuous value, where higher values imply higher exposure. To consider such cases, we define here D_{it} as the continuous dose response measure, that is:

$$D_{it} = \begin{cases} 0 & \text{if unit is untreated in period } t \\ d_{it} & \text{if unit is treated in period } t, \end{cases}$$

where d is the continuous value of the Dose received.

Recent work of Callaway, Goodman-Bacon, and Sant'Anna (2021) suggests that it is not simply a case of estimating the regression

$$Y_{it} = \alpha + \theta_t + \eta_i + \tau D_{it} + \varepsilon_{it}$$

to understand the impact of a marginal change in the dose D_{it} on the outcome Y_{it}, or an average treatment effect of receiving a particular dose d. Perhaps the key message from the paper of Callaway, Goodman-Bacon, and Sant'Anna (2021) is that to understand causal effects in this setting, one needs to make substantially more demanding assumptions than in the binary treatment case. For example, they show that if we wish to estimate some parameter such as $\text{ATE}(d) = \mathbb{E}[Y_t(d) - Y_t(0)]$, where $Y_t(d)$ and $Y_t(0)$ simply refer to potential outcomes under dose d and no dose, we require what they refer to as the "strong parallel trends assumption."

This assumption states that *for all possible values of* d,

$$\mathbb{E}[Y_t(d) - Y_{t-1}(0)] = \mathbb{E}[Y_t(d) - Y_{t-1}(0)|D=d].$$

This is likely a much stronger assumption than standard parallel trends in the binary case. What it states is that for all observed doses d, the average change across time for all units had they been assigned treatment (the first term) is the same as the average change in outcomes across time for all units that effectively experienced that dose (the term on the right-hand side). Specifically, this assumption entirely limits selection into treatment effects, in the sense that units that effectively received dose d are assumed to be representative of the impact of d of all other units, including those that received no dose, those that received some lower dose, and those that received some higher dose. Under this assumption, Callaway, Goodman-Bacon, and Sant'Anna (2021) show that the ATE is identified, and interestingly, that one can also identify other estimands of interest, such as the impact of a marginal change in treatment from some value d_{j-1} to d_j, referred to as an Average Causal Response (ACR).

Chaisemartin et al. (2024) also propose estimators in this line for cases where the treatment dose is continuous at each time period (changing over time) but remains fixed for some units over time. They do so with a version of a parallel trends assumption that fixes period 1 treatment doses (referred to as D_1) and states that changes given their specific treatment dose in period 2 (D_2) would have been the same for other units had they also been treated with this dose in period 2. In essence, this parallel trends assumption is that the change over time is unrelated to the second period treatment dose conditional on the first period treatment dose. They show that under this assumption, it is possible to estimate an "Average of Slopes" parameter defined as:

$$E\left[\frac{Y_{i,2}(D_2) - Y_{i,1}(D_1)}{D_2 - D_1}\middle|S_i = 1\right],$$

where $Y_{i,t}(D)$ refer to potential outcomes given a dose D, and S_i is a binary variable which takes the value of 1 for individuals who change treatment doses between period 1 and 2. This quantity thus captures how much outcomes change over time as treatment doses increase, which is informative for individuals who change treatment, and only for the specific treatment doses observed in period 1 and 2. Chaisemartin et al. (2024) show how this quantity can be estimated by comparing changes over time between switchers and stayers, and lay out estimation and inference procedures. They extend the estimator in a number of dimensions, including to more than two periods (discussing parallel pre-trend tests), and to a version weighted to reflect true treatment doses in the population. This estimator requires that stayers are observed, which are individuals whose treatment dose does not change over time, though they relax this requirement to only require "pseudo-stayers" (individuals with similar treatment doses across time) in Chaisemartin, D'Haultfœuille, and Vazquez-Bare (2024).

4.5.3 Intertemporal Treatment Effects and "Non-Absorbing" Treatments

The staggered adoption design, which has been the focus to this point, implies that once treatment switches on, it is assumed to remain on. The majority of the literature focuses on this case where a unit's treatment status can be considered as "absorbing." However, Chaisemartin and D'Haultfœuille (2024) discuss how we may proceed in cases where treatment adoption is not absorbing but can switch on and off. They also allow for treatment exposure in previous periods to have effects on contemporaneous outcomes implying inter-temporal treatment effects, which implies the need to carefully consider dynamics even if parallel trends are assumed to hold.

To allow for unbiased estimation in such a setting, we can return to potential outcomes written in terms of an individual's full treatment history $Y_{g,t}(W_{i1}, \ldots, W_{i,t})$. Now, given that treatment is no longer non-absorbing, potential outcomes permit cases where an individual is treated in one period: say $W_{i,2} = 1$, but then move out of treatment in a later period, say $W_{i,4} = 0$. Chaisemartin and D'Haultfœuille (2024) propose building up an estimator that they denote $\text{DID}_{g,\ell}$ which aggregates treatment effects across units who had adopted treatment at period ℓ, comparing their outcomes with the period immediately before they *first* adopted treatment, and double differencing with similar changes across units that had unchanged treatment statuses over this entire period, and the same initial treatment as treated units. This effect can thus be viewed as an effect versus the "status quo" counterfactual that a specific unit would never have changed their treatment status. Chaisemartin and D'Haultfœuille (2024) lay out formal assumptions and discuss estimation and inference for treatment effects in this setting. They note a number of strategies of interest, including estimating trajectory-specific treatment effects (the effect of having been exposed to a specific treatment path), presenting grouped estimates that are standardized by the total number of treatment increments, and estimating a weighted total effect, considering the total periods exposed to a treatment increment. While this design is more complicated given the larger range of underlying treatment effects, the authors provide computational tools to implement each of these quantities of interest.

4.5.4 Difference-in-Differences with Unbalanced Panels

A conceptually clear difference-in-differences design is based on panel data, in which individuals are followed over time, and we observe both pre- and post-treatment outcomes for treated and untreated individuals. However, in cases where repeated cross-sections of data are available, identical conceptualizations can be set up based on group-level aggregates, and unbiased results can be estimated. It is important to note that such models *do* of course require assumptions about random samples, namely that both in the pre- and post-treatment periods a random sample of data is available (see, for example, the statement in Abadie [2005, Assumption 3.3]). Interestingly, Sant'Anna and Zhao (2020) note that if panel data is available, estimators for the ATT will be more efficient than in cases with repeated cross-sections, and also note that if repeated cross-sections are available, it is most efficient to have identical sample sizes in both the pre- and post-treatment periods.

However, one point that is not addressed in this discussion is what happens if there is imbalance in panels over time, perhaps because of attrition, or because the composition of panels regularly changes with refresher samples. If such an unbalanced panel is used for analysis, and if difference-in-differences models are based on mean differences between all observed treated units and all observed control units in pre- and post-treatment periods, imbalance can result in contamination bias of estimates unless such imbalance occurs at random. One solution to such a method is to simply implement difference-in-differences methods with the subset of units that are observed in all time periods, as this will avoid contamination altogether. Such an approach may imply substantial loss of data, particularly in cases of rotation panels where refreshment samples are added over time, in which case alternative methods such as the "chained difference-in-differences" estimator of Bellégo, Benatia, and Dortet-Bernadet (2024) also provide approaches to estimate unbiased ATTs without balance in panels.

4.5.5 Loosening the Parallel Trends Assumption

So far we have laid out the importance of the parallel trends assumption but not discussed what one should do if it seems unlikely that the parallel trends assumption is met. One way to proceed is laid out by Rambachan and Roth's (2023). This method takes as a baseline case the panel event study (though the framework also applies to methods such as Callaway and Sant'Anna [2021] and Sun and Abraham [2021]), and propose a way for researchers to loosen the parallel trends assumption. In short, their suggestion is that rather than assuming that parallel trends hold exactly, leading to point-estimated treatment effects, we could allow for there to be different violations of (unobservable) post-treatment counterfactual trends between treated and control units, where these differences are informed by observed pretreatment trends between these groups. They suggest that instead of dogmatically assuming that parallel trends are exactly equal to zero, we can allow parallel trends to be violated over some specific range. The cost of this increased flexibility, and realism, in the parallel trends assumption is that instead of resulting in exactly estimated treatment effects, it results in partially identified (or bounds) estimates.

While a technically demanding paper, the logic of Rambachan and Roth (2023) is very intuitive: Given the importance of parallel trends to unbiasedness in DD estimates, and given that we can never formally prove parallel trends, it makes sense to consider how the estimates would look under a range of assumptions that are similar in style to parallel trends but leave slightly more room for movement around this very specific assumption. What's more, while this procedure can be conducted for a specific treatment effect or post-event coefficient, it can similarly be run on all post-event coefficients in event study–style models and analogous dynamic models. The paper provides a clear section on practical guidance for empirical applications and can be used for both standard panel event studies, as well as heterogeneity robust methods such as Callaway and Sant'Anna (2021).

4.6 Synthetic Control and Related Methods

4.6.1 "Classic" Synthetic Control

4.6.1.1 Definition An alternative take on the problem, which moves entirely away from the need for parallel trend assumptions in aggregate data, is the synthetic control method. The synthetic control method was borne out of an interest in "comparative case studies" in which a single unit is exposed to treatment with multiple possible unexposed units to act as controls. Early work in this line was conducted by Abadie and Gardeazabal (2003) and was formalized in the canonical reference of Abadie, Diamond, and Hainmueller (2010). However, more recently, considerable advances in synthetic control methods have occurred, with extensions to cases with multiple treated units.

These synthetic control methods aim to construct a "synthetic" (i.e., algorithmically produced) control unit for comparison with the true treatment unit. The synthetic control group is—similar to matching—formed using just a subset of all potential controls, which are also known as donor units. These donor units are combined in a manner to track as closely as possible the trend in the true treatment group in the *pre*-reform periods. The logic behind the method is to form a comparison group as similar as possible to the control group considering only the pretreatment data and observe what happens once the treatment has taken place. If the synthetic control is a good match with the treatment group, all else constant, they should follow identical paths in the post-reform period. However, given that only the treatment group is affected by treatment receipt, we infer that any post-treatment divergence in trends is due to the receipt of treatment itself.

Graphically, figure 4.5 provides an example of the synthetic control process. This is drawn from the example of Abadie, Diamond, and Hainmueller (2010) and considers the passage of a tobacco control policy "Proposition 99," which levied an excise tax on cigarette sales in California from 1989 onward. The data from Abadie, Diamond, and Hainmueller (2010), which we discuss at more length in code callout 4.4, consists of records of state cigarette sales from 1970–2000 in California, as well as thirty-eight other untreated states. We wish to infer the impact of California's excise tax on sales in California, which is to say, we wish to calculate an ATT. However, in panel (a), we observe that outcomes in the treatment area (California) clearly diverge from those in the rest of the US well before treatment occurs, and this divergence occurs in a way that presumably violates the parallel trend assumption. However, in figure (b), we see that a "synthetic control" can be formed based on a constantly weighted subgroup of the untreated states that tracks the true outcomes in the treated area very well in the pre-reform period. By comparing California with its synthetic control in the post-reform period, we can infer a treatment effect as a simple difference of means.

The standard notation for synthetic control methods was presented in Abadie, Diamond, and Hainmueller (2010) (see also the review paper of Abadie [2021], which does this) and has often been adopted as a starting point in more recent extensions discussed in section 4.6.1.5 below. The traditional synthetic control analysis is based on a balanced panel of units

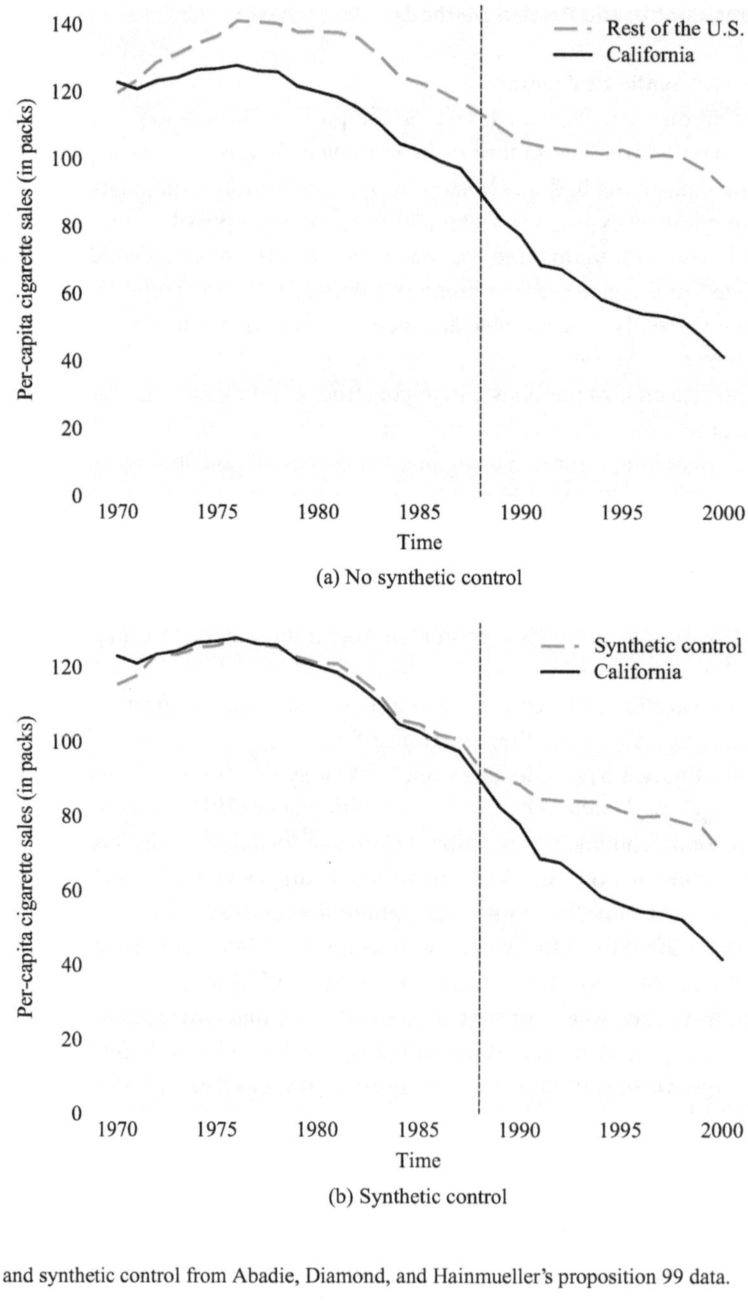

Figure 4.5
Raw trends and synthetic control from Abadie, Diamond, and Hainmueller's proposition 99 data.

observed over time. This considers $j = 1, 2, \ldots, J + 1$ units, with the treated unit (arbitrarily) labeled as $j = 1$, and the remaining J units, $j = 2, \ldots, J + 1$ being control units, also referred to as potential "donor units," or the "donor pool" as these will be potentially used to generate the synthetic control. The panel consists of T time periods, and $t = 1, \ldots, T_0$ is the pretreatment period, with the remaining $T - T_0$ time periods being the post-treatment period.

We will denote outcomes of interest as $Y_{j,t}$. Based on a standard potential outcomes notation in which $Y_{j,t}(1)$ refers to potential outcomes in cases where j is treated at t and $Y_{j,t}(0)$ is the untreated potential outcome, the interest in synthetic control is in estimating:

$$\tau^{\text{sc}}_{\text{ATT},t} = Y_{1,t}(1) - Y_{1,t}(0). \tag{4.47}$$

Here, there are two things to note. The first is that τ^{sc} is an ATT because we are explicitly interested in evaluating this effect for the treated state $j = 1$. The second is that because we have multiple time periods of interest, τ^{sc} depends on time period t. The synthetic control methodology seeks to estimate this quantity in particular for periods in which treatment is switched on, which is $t > T_0$.

Here we of course once again face the fundamental problem of causal inference given that for cases where $j = 1$ and $t > T_0$ we will only observe $Y_{j,t} = Y_{j,t}(1)$. Thus, the challenge is in determining how the treated unit would have evolved in the absence of treatment: $Y_{j,t}(0)$ for $t > T_0$. Because we are interested in modeling $Y_{j,t}(0)$, and because $Y_{j,t}(0)$ is observed for both the treated units and all potential donors in the *pre*treatment period, the proposal of the synthetic control method is to find a specific group of units from the donor pool that do a good job of matching $Y_{1,t} = Y_{1,t}(0)$ in the pre-reform period. This same group of donors will then be used to estimate $Y_{1,t}(0)$ in the post-treatment period.

A synthetic control is represented by a series of weights that are assigned to each potential donor unit. These weights sum to 1 and may potentially be 0, but they cannot be negative. The weights are chosen to form a single aggregate synthetic control from all underlying donor units that matches as closely as possible the pre-reform levels in the outcome variable (and potentially other controls) in the treated area. Formally, we will follow Abadie, Diamond, and Hainmueller (2010) in defining weights as $\boldsymbol{W} = (w_2, \ldots, w_{J+1})$, where $w_j \geq 0$ and $w_2 + \ldots + w_{J+1} = 1$. We can note that these weights are time-invariant, implying that our synthetic control will be a single aggregate unit consisting of the same underlying proportions of certain donor units. In order to find these weights, we will consider that for each unit j a set of K predictors is available, which we can denote $X_{1j}, \ldots, X_{Kj}$. We will then denote as $\boldsymbol{X}_1$ the $1 \times K$ vector containing all predictor variables for the treated unit, and $\boldsymbol{X}_0$ the $J \times K$ matrix containing all predictor variables for each of the donor variables. Commonly, these predictor variables simply consist of all pretreatment realizations of the outcome, but this need not be the case, and additional predetermined covariates could in principle be used as predictors for generating a synthetic control. However, to fix ideas, the common case in which a synthetic control is generated using all pre-intervention information on Y is represented as below:

$$\begin{pmatrix} Y_{1,1} & Y_{1,2} & \cdots & Y_{1,T_0} & Y_{1,T_0+1} & \cdots & Y_{1,T} \\ Y_{2,1} & Y_{2,2} & \cdots & Y_{2,T_0} & Y_{2,T_0+1} & \cdots & Y_{2,T} \\ \vdots & \vdots & \ddots & \vdots & \vdots & \ddots & \vdots \\ Y_{N,1} & Y_{N,2} & \cdots & Y_{N,T_0} & Y_{N,T_0+1} & \cdots & Y_{N,T} \end{pmatrix}$$

$$\equiv \left(\begin{array}{cccc|ccc} X_{1,1} & X_{1,2} & \cdots & X_{1,T_0} & Y_{1,T_0+1} & \dots & Y_{1,T} \\ \hline X_{2,1} & X_{2,2} & \cdots & X_{2,T_0} & Y_{2,T_0+1} & \dots & Y_{2,T} \\ \vdots & \vdots & \ddots & \vdots & \vdots & \vdots & \vdots \\ X_{N,1} & X_{N,2} & \dots & X_{N,T_0} & Y_{N,T_0+1} & \dots & Y_{N,T} \end{array}\right)$$

$$\equiv \left(\begin{array}{c|c} \mathbf{X}_1 & \mathbf{Y}_1 \\ \hline \mathbf{X}_0 & \mathbf{Y}_0 \end{array}\right). \tag{4.48}$$

Such a representation is provided in Ben-Michael, Feller, and Rothstein (2021), where each row represents the evolution of outcomes for a particular unit j over time. The top row represents the treated unit, while the remaining rows represent donor units. Time periods are thus represented as columns, and while we are including here post-outcome periods as $\boldsymbol{Y}_0$ and $\boldsymbol{Y}_1$, the entire generation of the synthetic control is based off of $\boldsymbol{X}_0$ and $\boldsymbol{X}_1$.

The proposal in synthetic control is to choose weights that minimize the "distance" between the synthetic control and the treated unit across all covariates in a mean-squared distance sense. This mean squared distance can be variously written as follows:

$$\begin{aligned} \|\boldsymbol{X}_1 - \boldsymbol{X}_0'\boldsymbol{W}\|_V &= \sqrt{(\boldsymbol{X}_1 - \boldsymbol{X}_0'\boldsymbol{W})'\boldsymbol{V}(\boldsymbol{X}_1 - \boldsymbol{X}_0'\boldsymbol{W})} \qquad (4.49) \\ &= \left[\sum_{k=1}^{K} v_k \left(X_{k1} - w_2X_{k2} - \cdots - w_{J+1}X_{KJ+1}\right)^2\right]^{1/2}, \end{aligned}$$

for a positive definite diagonal matrix $\boldsymbol{V}$. Here we can see that for a given set of weights $\boldsymbol{W}$ and matrix $\boldsymbol{V}$ (discussed below), this quantity will return to us the scalar value summarizing the distance between $\boldsymbol{X}_1$ and $\boldsymbol{X}_0$. This is precisely the root mean square prediction error (RMSPE), which is a loss function that takes higher values when weighted aggregates of $\boldsymbol{X}_0$ are further from realizations of $\boldsymbol{X}_1$. The weights that minimize this quantity are denoted as $\boldsymbol{W}^* \equiv (w_2^*, \cdots, w_{J+1}^*)$ and are used to generate the synthetic control as $\boldsymbol{X}_0'W^*$ in the pretreatment period, and $\boldsymbol{Y}_0'W^*$ in the post-treatment period. By definition of the optimization problem, $\boldsymbol{X}_0'W^* \approx \boldsymbol{X}_1'$ resulting in a close fit such as that observed in figure 4.5(b) in the pretreatment period, while $\boldsymbol{Y}_0'W^*$ will reflect mean outcomes for this same synthetic control in the post-treatment period. If we believe that the synthetic control that historically predicts outcomes for treated units when treatment had not yet occurred *also* would predict outcomes for treated units in the absence of treatment in the post-treatment period, we can compare our treated unit with this synthetic control to infer treatment effects.

Thus, once we have calculated our synthetic control weights, this suggests a simple way to calculate a treatment effect. We can infer potential outcomes for treated units as:

$$\widehat{Y}_{1,t}(0) = \sum_{j=2}^{J+1} w_j^* Y_{j,t},$$

and estimate the quantity laid out in (4.47) as follows:

$$\widehat{\tau}^{SC}_{ATT,t} = Y_{1,t} - \sum_{j=2}^{J+1} w_j^* Y_{j,t}. \tag{4.50}$$

This quantity will simply trace out for each t the difference between the outcome for the treated unit (the solid line in figure 4.5) and the outcome for the synthetic control (the dashed line in figure 4.5).

Before turning to discuss the assumptions that underlie synthetic control estimates in section 4.6.1.2, it is important to note that while the key element of interest in synthetic control is to find weights $\boldsymbol{W}^*$, these weights will depend upon the matrix $\boldsymbol{V}$ that is used in the optimization problem (4.49). In practice, this matrix $\boldsymbol{V}$ simply acts to indicate the importance of any differences between each of the k predictors that are used to form the synthetic control. If an identity matrix 1_k is used, this will ensure that each unit of difference between a particular element X_{k1} and the value of the weighted comparison $\boldsymbol{X}_k\boldsymbol{W}$ will contribute identically to the loss function (4.49). While a choice such as the identity matrix may make sense if only pretreatment $Y_{j,t}$ variables are used for generating the synthetic control as in (4.48), it is unlikely to make sense if additionally some series of covariates are included that might have quite a different scale to the outcome of interest. In cases such as this, rather than the identity matrix, a matrix may be used that replaces all elements on the main diagonal with the variance of each predictor variable in the data. However, empirically, the most common procedure (Ferman, Pinto, and Possebom 2020) sets $\boldsymbol{V}$ as the solution to a nested optimization problem originally laid out in Abadie and Gardeazabal (2003, Appendix A) where:

$$\widehat{\boldsymbol{W}}(V) = \arg\min_{\boldsymbol{W}} (\boldsymbol{X}_1 - \boldsymbol{X}_0'\boldsymbol{W})'(\boldsymbol{X}_1 - \boldsymbol{X}_0'\boldsymbol{W})$$

and

$$\widehat{\boldsymbol{V}} = \arg\min_{V \in \mathcal{V}} (\boldsymbol{X}_1 - \boldsymbol{X}_0'\widehat{\boldsymbol{W}}(V))'(\boldsymbol{X}_1 - \boldsymbol{X}_0'\widehat{\boldsymbol{W}}(V)).$$

Here $\mathcal{V}$ is the set of all positive definite diagonal matrices where the diagonal term sums to one, which implies that $\mathcal{V}$ is optimized within $\boldsymbol{W}$, and hence $\widehat{\boldsymbol{V}}$ is that which minimizes the RMSPE in the pretreatment period. Alternative options have been proposed, including choosing using training and validation periods (see, e.g.,

Abadie, Diamond, and Hainmueller [2015]), but Abadie (2021) notes that in practice, researchers should show that estimated treatment effects do not vary substantially by $\boldsymbol{V}$.

4.6.1.2 Assumptions and properties of synthetic control estimators Abadie, Diamond, and Hainmueller (2010) lay out the underlying assumptions in synthetic control mechanisms, along with the properties of the estimator under these assumptions. Firstly, they note that synthetic control relies on a no-anticipation assumption for all periods $t = 1, \ldots, T_0$. Secondly, and as standard, synthetic control methods require that SUTVA holds. A third assumption relates to the nature of the donor pool. In particular, there must be weights that allow for $\boldsymbol{X}_0\boldsymbol{W}^*$ to approximate $\boldsymbol{X}_1$. This is stated as the convex hull assumption, or the assumption that the set of predictor variables among treated units $(X_{11}, X_{21}, \ldots, X_{K1})$ is contained within the convex set of all donor units $\{(X_{12}, X_{22}, \ldots, X_{K2}), \ldots, (X_{1J+1}, X_{2J+1}, \ldots, X_{KJ+1})\}$. In practice, this implies that no particular predictor variable for treated units is extreme compared to all donor variables. In general, $\boldsymbol{X}_0\boldsymbol{W}^* \neq \boldsymbol{X}_1$ exactly implying that the convex hull assumption will not hold exactly, but provided $\boldsymbol{X}_0\boldsymbol{W}^* \approx \boldsymbol{X}_1$ the convex hull assumption is likely a reasonable approximation. This can be examined formally by examining the RMSPE defined in (4.49) and the difference between the synthetic control and treated unit in a variable-by-variable fashion.

The properties of synthetic control are discussed by Abadie, Diamond, and Hainmueller (2010) assuming a particular (flexible) data generating process. Thus, commonly discussed properties of synthetic control methods are not generally applicable to all possible situations, but rather should be viewed as representative of particular assumptions related to data generating processes. In particular, they note that if one starts with a flexible model for untreated potential outcomes as follows:

$$Y_{j,t}(0) = \delta_t + \boldsymbol{\theta}_t\boldsymbol{Z}_j + \boldsymbol{\lambda}_t\boldsymbol{\mu}_j + \varepsilon_{j,t}, \tag{4.51}$$

results can be derived on the degree of bias that may exist in a synthetic control estimator. This model is known as a linear factor model, and the key thing to note is that it is a very flexible model, allowing for unobserved factors that vary by unit, unobserved factors that vary by time, and unobserved factors that vary by unit *and* by time. In this particular setting, Abadie, Diamond, and Hainmueller (2010) assume that $\boldsymbol{Z}_j$ is a vector of common observed covariates, and $\boldsymbol{\theta}_t$ a corresponding vector of parameters that allow the effect of covariates to vary over time. Similarly, $\boldsymbol{\lambda}_j$ and $\boldsymbol{\mu}_t$ are unobserved common factors and covariates. As common, $\varepsilon_{j,t}$ is a stochastic mean zero error term.

The key thing that Abadie, Diamond, and Hainmueller (2010) demonstrate is that if $\boldsymbol{X}_1$ contains $\boldsymbol{Z}_1$, *even without observing unobserved factors*, then the bias on $\widehat{\tau}_{j,t}$ can be bounded, and this bias will be close to zero if the number of pre-intervention periods used to generate the synthetic control T_0 is large compared to unobserved shocks $\varepsilon_{j,t}$. This result is important because it suggests that if a long enough pre-intervention period is available off of which to estimate a synthetic control, bias will be minimal provided that unobserved shocks are not too large. The formal details of this result are discussed in Abadie, Diamond, and Hainmueller (2010, see, e.g., formula 3), and are also summarized in Abadie (2021). However the logic behind this result is that if the synthetic control estimator manages to do a good job in modeling $\widehat{Y}_{1,t}(0)$ in periods $t = 1, \ldots, T_0$ despite the presence of time-varying unobservables, it will also do a good job in modeling $\widehat{Y}_{1,t}(0)$ in post-treatment periods, unless it has managed to compensate to model $\widehat{Y}_{1,t}(0)$ principally with noise $\varepsilon_{j,t}$. The likelihood that this is the case will fall as the degree of unobserved noise falls, and as the length of the pretreatment period increases.

This result justifies the use of synthetic control provided that one has a sufficient number of pretreatment periods, provided that one believes that a flexible factor model like (4.51) is a reasonable model of unobserved potential outcomes and provided that the synthetic control manages to appropriately fit pretreatment data. In the discussion of practical considerations below, we return to discuss the number of pretreatment periods that may be sufficient in synthetic control methods. If the linear factor model is not an appropriate model for potential outcomes, these results cannot be assumed.[10] However, it is clear that if pretreatment fit is not good, synthetic controls are likely not a good option (Abadie, Diamond, and Hainmueller 2010; Ferman and Pinto 2021).

4.6.1.3 Inference Typically, inference in synthetic control models is based on permutation-based methods. To have an idea of whether the difference between a treated unit and its synthetic control is larger than that which may be observed by chance, similar comparisons can be conducted between each untreated unit and its *own* synthetic control, and these can be compared with the original effect. This procedure is laid out in Abadie, Diamond, and Hainmueller (2010) and follows the logic of permutation tests we have discussed previously in section 2.4.2. In the case of synthetic controls, such permutation-based inference simply consists of reassigning treatment to each control state starting from the true time of treatment, calculating a synthetic control for this (placebo) treatment, and comparing the true path of synthetic control effects $\widehat{\tau}^{sc}_{ATT,t}$, with all placebo estimates $\widehat{\tau}^{sc}_{j,t}$ for $j = 2, \ldots, J$. The idea with such permutations is that if the effects of the real treatment assignment are simply driven by random noise, they will likely not be dissimilar to effects seen in placebo estimates. However, if true treatment effects are unusually large compared to placebo distributions, this will lend credence to the idea that such effects are real, and do not simply owe to noise. In general, placebo effects of this type are presented graphically, as they lead to figures that are immediately able to summarize whether real effects are larger than effects observed by change, see, for example, figures 4–6 of Abadie, Diamond, and Hainmueller (2010).

One potential issue with permutation-based inference for synthetic control methods is that while a good synthetic control may exist for a given treated unit, there is no guarantee that a good synthetic control will exist for each untreated unit. Thus, certain permutations may result in extreme placebo "treatment effects" simply because the synthetic control does not do a good job of matching the placebo unit even in the pretreatment period. To guard against this, Abadie, Diamond, and Hainmueller (2010) propose a refinement in which rather than basing inference on the treatment effects themselves, inference is based on a consideration of whether the treatment effect is particularly large for some particular time period (namely the post-treatment period), compared with the difference between predicted and observed outcomes for the same unit in the pretreatment period. This procedure, which is based precisely on observed deviations between treated and synthetic control units defined in (4.49) (the RMSPE), consists of calculating for each unit:

$$r_j = \frac{\sum_{t=T_0+1}^{T}(Y_{j,t} - \widehat{Y}(0)_{j,t})^2/(T-T_0)}{\sum_{t=1}^{T_0}(Y_{j,t} - \widehat{Y}(0)_{j,t})^2/T_0} \equiv \frac{\text{RMSPE}_j^{T_0+1,T}}{\text{RMSPE}_j^{1,T_0}}. \tag{4.52}$$

This quantity r_j summarizes the deviation between the treated outcome and the synthetic control in the post-treatment period, compared to the deviation in the pretreatment period. A unit with a large treatment effect but a small pretreatment difference would thus return a very large value for r_j, and this quantity also gains from the fact that if a synthetic control is generally poor, we would expect that both the pre-period and post-period RMSPE would be large. What's more, we can generate a p-value for tests of null effects by considering how large this quantity r_j is for the true treated unit r_1 compared to placebo treatments:

$$p = \frac{\sum_{j=1}^{J+1} \mathbb{1}(r_j \geq r_1)}{J+1}. \tag{4.53}$$

In general, inference following synthetic control presents graphical output based on permuted treatment effects, or permutation inference following (4.52)–(4.53). Sergio and Vitor (2018) note how this can be used to generate confidence intervals for synthetic control estimands. There are, however, recent alternative proposals based on permutations of time variation in treatment adoption (Chernozhukov, Wüthrich, and Zhu 2021) or directly considering uncertainty owing to synthetic control weights and unobserved errors (Cattaneo, Feng, and Titiunik 2021).

4.6.1.4 Practical considerations One question when applying synthetic control methods is precisely which variables should be used when seeking to match across matrices $\boldsymbol{X}_1$ and $\boldsymbol{X}_0$. One paper that touches on this is Ferman, Pinto, and Possebom (2020). There, the authors suggest that there is no broad consensus on this question on this in theoretical or applied work. They document quite varied practice in published papers using synthetic control methods, with papers typically using some type of pretreatment outcomes, though not necessarily all pretreatment periods, and at times additional covariates. What's more, they suggest that this question is not innocuous, finding in both Monte Carlo simulations and real empirical examples that different choices in how synthetic controls are generated can lead to cases where a given intervention or treatment is found to be significant, or insignificant. Fortunately, this paper makes quite concrete recommendations related to the practice of synthetic control estimation. They suggest that synthetic control should use all pretreatment periods when generating a match. This has the benefits that it minimizes the difference between synthetic controls and the treatment unit in the pretreatment period, and additionally avoids other arbitrary decisions related to the number of pretreatment periods to include. They suggest that the only exception to this is if for some reason there is a strong prior that specific covariates are *required* for the generation of a reasonable synthetic control. Even so, they suggest that should other specifications be considered, this baseline of using full pretreatment periods as predictors should always be documented.

The review paper by Abadie (2021) provides a rich discussion of relevant considerations in terms of data requirements in synthetic controls and should be viewed as required reading for individuals wishing for a very complete discussion of practical recommendations. A number of these recommendations are directly related to assumptions, namely the convex hull assumption, which implies that analysis cannot proceed if outcomes are extreme compared to control units, and no anticipation and no spillovers between units can occur, though note that if anticipation is assumed over only a certain period, analysis can proceed by generating the synthetic control only up to this period. Additional practical considerations relate to the properties or mechanical implications of estimation, namely, synthetic control is of limited use if a synthetic control is not available that closely matches pre-trends or predictor variables, and if unobserved components are particularly relevant, as this will affect bias and limit the feasibility of estimating even quite large effects.

Another particularly relevant point in synthetic control modeling relates to the number of pretreatment periods for which data is available. The result discussed in 4.6.1.2 relates bias (inversely) to the availability of long pretreatment periods. For this reason, long pretreatment time frames should be sought, and longer pretreatment time frames should be preferred to shorter ones if data is available. One exception to this, discussed in Abadie (2021), is cases where there are structural breaks in pretreatment outcomes that complicate the modeling of a synthetic control, and that occur many periods before treatment adoption, as the inclusion of these will likely not improve the bias in synthetic control methods. In general, a precise rule for the number of required pretreatment periods does not exist, as bias results depend upon the assumed DGP. Indeed, evidence from simulation points to quite variable results, with Abadie and Vives-i-Bastida (2026) documenting overfitting bias even with twenty pretreatment periods when the number of donors is large. If the pretreatment fit is poor, even having extremely large pretreatment periods can result in very poor results (Ferman, Pinto, and Possebom 2020). For this reason, Abadie (2021) discusses the use of backdating or a training and validation period (Abadie, Diamond, and Hainmueller 2010), which consists of fitting a synthetic control up to only some lagged ("backdated") pretreatment year, and using the remaining pretreatment periods in which the synthetic control was not fit as a test of any potential bias, given that no effect should emerge before any treatment occurs.

4.6.1.5 Extensions to synthetic control methods The literature on synthetic control methods is active, and a range of new methods have been developed that maintain the underlying spirit of synthetic control, while proposing a number of extensions, formalizations or generalizations of the original methods. Many of these advances were published in a special issue of *The Journal of the American Statistical Association* in 2021, around ten years after the publication of the original formalization of synthetic controls at the journal in 2010. This special issue is introduced by Abadie and Cattaneo (2021), who provide a rundown of all contributions. Among other recent extensions—from alternative takes on inference methods to high-dimensional implementations—an important focus has been on cases where a well-matched pretreatment synthetic control cannot be constructed. This has led to a number of suggestions such as de-meaning variables prior to applying synthetic controls (Ferman and Pinto 2021), permitting level shifts and extrapolations outside of the original support of the data (Doudchenko and Imbens 2016), and implementing de-biasing methods that seek to estimate pretreatment differences between treated units and synthetic controls, and adjust for these with bias-correction methods (Ben-Michael, Feller, and Rothstein 2021; Abadie and L'Hour 2021). These estimators also generalize for cases with multiple treated units, rather than the single treated unit view taken in the original comparative case study work of synthetic controls.

4.6.1.6 Understanding differences between synthetic control, difference-in-differences, and unconfoundedness-based approaches While both synthetic control and difference-in-differences designs are based on a setting in which treatment varies over time in a panel, the conceptualization of the estimators that we have seen here is quite different. Difference-in-differences are often based on a setting in which we have relatively few time periods T, a larger number of observations N, a large number of which can be treated, and relatively few post-treatment periods. Synthetic control, on the other hand, is often based on relatively fewer units N, often a single treated unit, and a larger number of time periods T. Athey et al. (2021) lay this out graphically as in figure 4.6, where we consider potential outcomes $Y(0)$. Here, check marks indicate observations and time periods not exposed to treatment, and in which case potential outcomes $Y(0)_{i,t}$ will be observed. Question marks, on the other hand, indicate units and time periods exposed to treatment, and as such, $Y(0)_{i,t}$ will be unknown. Differences-in-differences will generally be appropriate in cases where we work with "thin" matrices: We will have many units who are treated and untreated, estimators will inherit good properties in terms of precision and inference, and will be clearly based on parallel trend assumptions across units. Synthetic control, on the other hand, will be appropriate where we have "fat" matrices, as we will have many periods off of which to determine an appropriate counterfactual.

It turns out that synthetic control can also be understood through the lens of regression, as discussed in Abadie, Diamond, and Hainmueller (2015), Ferman and Pinto (2021), and Athey et al. (2021). Abadie, Diamond, and Hainmueller (2015) note that if we wanted to

$$
Y(0)_{N\times T} = \begin{matrix} i_1 \\ i_2 \\ \vdots \\ i_3 \\ i_4 \\ i_N \end{matrix}
\overset{\begin{matrix} t_1 & t_2 & t_T \end{matrix}}{\begin{pmatrix} \checkmark & \checkmark & \checkmark \\ \checkmark & \checkmark & \checkmark \\ \vdots & \vdots & \vdots \\ \checkmark & \checkmark & ? \\ \checkmark & \checkmark & ? \\ \checkmark & \checkmark & ? \end{pmatrix}}
\qquad
\begin{matrix} i_1 \\ i_2 \\ i_N \end{matrix}
\overset{\begin{matrix} t_1 & t_2 & \dots & t_{T-1} & t_T \end{matrix}}{\begin{pmatrix} \checkmark & \checkmark & \dots & \checkmark & \checkmark \\ \checkmark & \checkmark & \dots & \checkmark & \checkmark \\ \checkmark & \checkmark & \dots & ? & ? \end{pmatrix}}
$$

Figure 4.6
"Thin" matrices, "fat matrices," difference-in differences, and synthetic control.

generate a counterfactual outcome based on regression, we could take control units and regress outcomes in post-treatment periods on outcomes in pretreatment periods. Using the estimated coefficients from this regression, we could predict a counterfactual for treated units by using these coefficients and pretreatment outcomes to predict the post-treatment counterfactual. Abadie, Diamond, and Hainmueller (2015) note that this is also a weighting calculation like in synthetic control where weights sum to one, but weights can be negative. Ferman and Pinto (2021), on the other hand, points out that a synthetic control estimator can also be estimated by regressing outcomes of treated units in the pretreatment period on outcomes on untreated units in the same period, and using the estimated coefficients on each of the untreated units as weights to form the synthetic control. These two approaches are what Athey et al. (2021) refer to as horizontal and vertical regression. The prior idea comes from the idea of unconfoundedness. If we believe in unconfoundedness, treatment and control units will be identical on average, and so changes over time in untreated units would provide a guide to how changes would have occurred in treated units in the absence of treatment, and this can be estimated from horizontal regression. Synthetic control, however, takes the view of vertical regression, which is that if treated and control units had historically looked similar before treatment, they would have also looked similar in the post-treatment period had treatment not been applied. Shen et al. (2023) summarize these alternative approaches as unconfoundedness considering that "history is a guide to the future," while synthetic control is based on the premise that "similar units behave similarly."

4.6.2 Synthetic Difference-in-Differences

Up until recently, where the treatment state had outcomes that were universally higher or universally lower than the donor states, synthetic control methods could not be used. However, work from Doudchenko and Imbens (2016) extended synthetic control methods and loosened the estimation requirements. Principally, this allows for a constant difference in levels between the treatment area and the synthetic controls. Doudchenko and Imbens (2016) document their updated methods using the same case as Abadie, Diamond, and Hainmueller (2010) and also a number of other applied examples.

A particularly flexible estimator, going beyond Doudchenko and Imbens (2016), is the synthetic DID procedure, hereafter SDID, as developed in Arkhangelsky et al. (2021). As input, SDID requires a balanced panel of N units or groups, observed over T time periods. An outcome, denoted Y_{it}, is observed for each unit i in period t. Some, but not all, of these observations are treated with a specific variable of interest, denoted W_{it}. This treatment variable $W_{it} = 1$ if observation i is treated by time t, otherwise, $W_{it} = 0$ indicates that unit i is untreated at time t. Here, we assume that there is a single adoption period for treated units, i.e. a "block treatment assignment." In an appendix, the authors note how this can be extended to a "staggered adoption design", where treated units adopt treatment at varying points. This is laid out in Clarke et al. (2024) upon which the below presentation is based. For estimation to proceed, we require at least two pretreatment periods off of which to determine control units.

The goal of SDID is in consistently estimating the causal effect of receipt of policy or treatment W_{it}, (an average treatment effect on the treated, ATT) even if we do not believe in the parallel trends assumption between all treatment and control units on average. Estimation of the ATT proceeds as follows:

$$\left(\widehat{\tau}^{\text{sdid}}, \widehat{\mu}, \widehat{\alpha}, \widehat{\beta}\right) = \underset{\tau,\mu,\alpha,\beta}{\arg\min} \left\{ \sum_{i=1}^{N} \sum_{t=1}^{T} (Y_{it} - \mu - \alpha_i - \beta_t - W_{it}\tau)^2 \widehat{\omega}_i^{\text{sdid}} \widehat{\lambda}_t^{\text{sdid}} \right\}, \tag{4.54}$$

where the estimand $\widehat{\tau}$ is the ATT, generated from a two-way fixed effect regression, with optimally chosen weights $\widehat{\omega}_i^{\text{sdid}}$ and $\widehat{\lambda}_t^{\text{sdid}}$ discussed below. Note that here, this procedure flexibly allows for shared temporal aggregate factors given the estimation of time-fixed effects β_t and time invariant unit-specific factors given the estimation of unit-fixed effects α_i. The presence of unit-fixed effects implies that SDID will simply seek to match treated and control units on pretreatment trends, *not* both pretreatment trends and levels, allowing for a constant difference between treatment and control units.

In this setting, it is illustrative to consider how the SDID procedure compares to the traditional synthetic control method discussed previously, as well as the baseline difference-in-differences procedure. The standard difference-in-differences procedure consists of precisely the same two-way fixed effect estimation procedure, simply assigning equal weights to all time periods and groups:

$$\left(\widehat{\tau}^{\text{did}}, \widehat{\mu}, \widehat{\alpha}, \widehat{\beta}\right) = \underset{\tau,\mu,\alpha,\beta}{\arg\min} \left\{ \sum_{i=1}^{N} \sum_{t=1}^{T} (Y_{it} - \mu - \alpha_i - \beta_t - W_{it}\tau)^2 \right\}. \tag{4.55}$$

The synthetic control, on the other hand, maintains optimally chosen units weights ω (as laid out below); however, it does not seek to optimally consider time periods via time weights, and omits unit fixed effects implying that the synthetic control and treated units should maintain approximately equivalent pretreatment levels, as well as trends.

$$\left(\widehat{\tau}^{\text{sc}}, \widehat{\mu}, \widehat{\beta}\right) = \underset{\tau,\mu,\beta}{\arg\min} \left\{ \sum_{i=1}^{N} \sum_{t=1}^{T} (Y_{it} - \mu - \beta_t - W_{it}\tau)^2 \widehat{\omega}_i^{sc} \right\} \tag{4.56}$$

From equations 4.55–4.56, it is clear that the SDID procedure offers greater flexibility than both the difference-in-differences and SC procedures: in the case of difference-in-differences by permitting a violation of parallel trends in aggregate data, and in the case of SC by both additionally seeking to optimally weight time periods when considering counterfactual outcomes and allowing for level differences between treatment and control groups.

The selection of unit weights, ω, as inputs to equation 4.54 (and 4.56) seeks to ensure that a comparison is made between control and treatment units that were approximately following parallel trends prior to the adoption of treatments. The selection of time weights, λ, in the case of SDID seeks to draw more weight from pretreatment periods that are more similar to post-treatment periods, in the sense of finding a constant difference between each control unit's post-treatment average, and pretreatment weighted averages across all selected controls. Specifically, as laid out in Arkhangelsky et al. (2021), unit-specific weights are found by resolving:

$$\left(\widehat{\omega}_0, \widehat{\omega}^{\text{sdid}}\right) = \underset{\omega_0 \in \mathbb{R}, \omega \in \Omega}{\arg\min} \sum_{t=1}^{T_{\text{pre}}} \left(\omega_0 + \sum_{i=1}^{N_C} \omega_i Y_{it} - \frac{1}{N_T} \sum_{i=N_C+1}^{N} Y_{it} \right)^2 + \zeta^2 T_{\text{pre}} ||\omega||_2^2, \tag{4.57}$$

where

$$\Omega = \left\{ \omega \in \mathbb{R}_+^N, \text{ with } \sum_{i=1}^{N_C} \omega_i = 1 \text{ and } \omega_i = \frac{1}{N_T} \text{ for all } i = N_C + 1, \ldots, N \right\},$$

and ζ is a regularization parameter laid out in Arkhangelsky et al. (2021, 4091–4092). This leads to a vector of N_C weights plus an intercept ω_0. The weights ω_i for all $i \in \{1, \ldots, N_C\}$ imply that absolute difference between control and treatment trends units should be minimized over all pretreatment periods, while ω_0 initially allows for a constant difference between treatment and controls over time. Together, these imply that units will follow parallel pre-trends, though provided $\omega_0 \neq 0$, not identical pre-trends.

In the case of time weights, a similar procedure is followed, finding weights that minimize the following objective function:

$$\left(\widehat{\lambda}_0, \widehat{\lambda}^{\text{sdid}}\right) = \underset{\lambda_0 \in \mathbb{R}, \lambda \in \Lambda}{\arg\min} \sum_{i=1}^{N_C} \left(\lambda_0 + \sum_{i=1}^{T_{\text{pre}}} \lambda_t Y_{it} - \frac{1}{T_{\text{post}}} \sum_{t=T_{\text{pre}}+1}^{T} Y_{it} \right)^2 + \zeta^2 N_C ||\lambda||^2, \tag{4.58}$$

where

$$\Lambda = \left\{ \lambda \in \mathbb{R}_{+}^{T}, \text{ with } \sum_{t=1}^{T_{\text{pre}}} \lambda_t = 1 \text{ and } \lambda_t = \frac{1}{T_{\text{post}}} \text{ for all } t = T_{\text{pre}} + 1, \ldots, T \right\},$$

and the final component in 4.58 is a very small regularization term to ensure uniqueness of time weights.

This estimation procedure is summarized in Arkhangelsky et al. (2021, algorithm 1). The authors also prove that the estimator is asymptotically normal and centered on zero, suggesting that confidence intervals on τ can be constructed as $\widehat{\tau}^{\text{sdid}} \pm z_{\alpha/2}\sqrt{\mathbb{V}_{\tau}}$, where $z_{\alpha/2}$ refers to the inverse normal density function at percentile $\alpha/2$ should one wish to compute 1-α confidence intervals. These confidence intervals thus simply require an estimate of the variance of τ, $\widehat{\mathbb{V}}_{\tau}$, and they propose three specific procedures to estimate this variance: via bootstrap, jackknife, or placebo. While we won't delve into this too deeply here (it is available in algorithms 2–4 of Arkhangelsky et al. [2021]), note that these are all computationally based resampling or placebo-based estimation procedures, and so, in practice, simply consist of reestimating $\widehat{\tau}^{\text{sdid}}$ over many resamples of data, or over permutations of the treatment variable, and observing the variance of these many reestimates.

Code Callout 4.4: Synthetic Control, Difference-in-Differences, and Synthetic Difference-in-Differences

We examine details of the implementation of synthetic controls, as well as differences between synthetic control, difference-in-differences, and synthetic DID procedures in code callout 4.4. Here we use data from Abadie, Diamond, and Hainmueller (2010), which is based on the passage of a reform that raised tax rates on cigarettes in California, and seeks to determine the impact of this increased tax rate on cigarette sales. As well as implementing SC, DID, and SDID procedures, we explore the nature of weights that result from each of these and discuss considerations related to inference.

Historical Context and Selected Further Reading

The origins of difference-in-differences are often traced back to Snow's 1855 study of cholera in London (see, for example, Hamad, Collin, and Rehkopf [2020]). Snow proposed that cholera was waterborne—a radical idea at the time—and to test this, he studied two neighboring water companies: the Southwark & Vauxhall Company and the Lambeth Company, which drew water from different points of the Thames. A natural experiment occurred when Lambeth moved its water intake upstream to a cleaner source, while Southwark & Vauxhall continued to draw water from a more contaminated part of the river. The origins of synthetic methods are far more recent, with key elements of synthetic control being laid out in Abadie and Gardeazabal (2003) and formalized in Abadie, Diamond, and Hainmueller (2010).

While the focus on this chapter has been on the use of repeated realizations of data within units over time with a particular focus on difference-in-differences or synthetic methods, there is much work in econometrics in causality in panel data models that is not covered. Coverage of such methods is available in Arellano (2003), among other places.

Exercises

1. In this exercise we will work with the paper of Deryugina (2017) that examines the impact of hurricanes in the US on government aid receipt in affected US counties. We will use the database `Deryugina2017.csv`, which contains a measure of exposure to hurricanes in each US county between 1979 and 2002, along with mean salaries and government transfers observed in a given county and time period.

   (a) Estimate the following two-way FE model:

   $$y_{st} = \phi_s + \lambda_t + \tau post_t + X'_{st}\Gamma + \varepsilon_{st},$$

   where s and t refer to counties and years, respectively, and ϕ_s and λ_t are county- and time-fixed effects. The measure $post_t$ takes 1 following the first occurrence of a hurricane in county s. A series of control variables X_{st} is described by Deryugina (2017) in her paper. Estimate the specification for the two outcome variables (1) the natural logarithm of per capita government transfers (`logTransfers`) and (2) the natural logarithm of mean salaries (`logSalary`). Follow Deryugina (2017) with regard to the use of controls, which are contained in the provided data file.

   (b) Document that the standard errors and 95% confidence intervals on the parameter τ vary when using (1) the "standard" OLS variance-covariance estimate, (2) a heteroscedasticity-robust variance-covariance estimate, (3) a variance-covariance estimator clustering by county and (4) a wild cluster bootstrap estimate clustering by county. Which of these estimates do you believe is preferable in this case?

   (c) Repeat the exercise from part (a), however now evaluating impacts in the short, medium, and long term. To do this, generate a series of binary exposure groups indicating short term as the three years after a hurricane, medium term indicating years four to six following a hurricane, and long term as years seven to nine following a hurricane. Include these in a single model, where all other details follow those in part (a).

(d) Similar to the models estimated in the paper, estimate a full panel event study where each counties treatment status is interacted with treatment lags and leads. Consider ten years pre- and post-hurricane as lags and leads, where the tenth period in each case accumulates all periods greater than or equal to ten periods to the event. After estimation, present estimated coefficients and 95% confidence intervals graphically, approximately following the structure of figure 4.4.

(e) Estimate and graph each "2 × 2" individual difference-in-differences estimate along with their weight according to the derivations provided by Goodman-Bacon (2021). (*Hint:* computational packages may be useful here). Present these estimates and weights graphically as a scatterplot. Interpret the various types of comparisons defined by Goodman-Bacon and their implications in this case.

(f) Implement the alternative DID_M estimator proposed by Chaisemartin and D'Haultfœuille (2020). Consider both dynamic effects as well as placebo effects surrounding the arrival of hurricanes in each county. Compare and contrast this with the event-study estimates you presented previously.

2. Consider the paper by Muralidharan and Prakash (2013), which examines the impact of a program launched in 2006 that provides bicycles to girls in the state of Bihar in India if they continue on to secondary education. The data `Muralidharan_Prakash_2013.csv` contains individual survey data from a household survey in 2007 and 2008 covering individuals living in the state of Bihar where the program was implemented (`bihar=1`) and the contiguous state of Jharkhand. These data contain information on individual's gender (`female=1` are exposed to the program), and age, where fourteen- and fifteen-year-olds are exposed (`treat1=1`) and sixteen- and seventeen-year-olds are not.

(a) Estimate an equation like (4.43) with these data where the outcome variable is `enrollment_secschool`. Confirm that with this model you can replicate the results in table 2 of Muralidharan and Prakash (2013).

(b) Estimate a simple difference-in-differences that compares girls and boys in Bihar who are of treated and untreated ages. How does this compare to the triple-differences estimate in part (a), and what does this suggest about the triple-differences estimator.? Why do Muralidharan and Prakash (2013) prefer the triple-differences estimator? (*Note:* If you would like, you may wish to refer to the data `Muralidharan_Prakash_2013_extra.csv`, which contains enrollment data for Bihar and Jharkhand in the pre-policy period to answer this question). These are the data used by the authors to generate their table 1.

   (c) Replicate the difference-in-differences estimates from part (b), but now using identical groups in the state of Jharkhand. Show that you can combine the estimates from parts (b) and (c) to replicate the estimates in part (a).

3. In this exercise we will work with the paper by Abadie, Diamond, and Hainmueller (2015), which uses synthetic control methods to seek to estimate the economic impact of the 1990 German Reunification. We will use the database `Abadie_et_al_2015.csv`, which contains country-level data from West Germany and other sixteen OCDE countries such as real GDP per capita, inflation rate, industry share of value added, investment rate, schooling, and a measure of trade openness.

   (a) In a line plot, graph the evolution of the real GDP per capita (`gdp`) for West Germany and the mean of the other countries. What difference can you see in the trend of both series?

   (b) Calculate the synthetic West Germany. Do this using the full set of pretreatment outcomes from 1960 to 1990. Which countries make up the synthetic control in this case?

   (c) With the synthetic West Germany computed in the previous question, repeat the first plot but instead the mean of all other countries, use synthetic West Germany. Discuss key differences between the plots.

   (d) Plot the gap between West Germany and Synthetic West Germany's real GDP per capita. What is the effect of the 1990 reunification?

   (e) Seek to follow the discussion from Abadie, Diamond, and Hainmueller (2015) and precisely replicate the results in figure 2. Note that this will be similar but not identical to the results in (b) and (c).

   (f) Consider only the sample from 1960 to 1990, and repeat the previous exercises for a placebo reunification in 1975. What effect do you find, and does this lead support to your previous estimates?

4. In this question, we will consider data from Bhalotra et al. (2023), which studies the passage of parliamentary gender quotas that reserve seats for female leaders on the proportion of women in parliament, and on rates of maternal mortality. The data `Bhalotra_et_al_2023.csv` consists of an unbalanced panel covering the maximum sample of countries with measurements of maternal mortality rates over the period of 1990–2015.

   (a) Implement a two-way fixed effect model controlling for country and year-fixed effects examining the outcomes `womparl` (women in parliament) and `lnMMR` (the natural logarithm of maternal mortality, or $\ln(MMR)$). In doing so, ensure that you cluster standard errors by country. Why might this model be a problem in this setting?

(b) Now, implement the range of dynamic heterogeneity robust estimators that present lags and leads to treatment adoption with $\ln(MMR)$. Specifically, implement the estimators of Callaway and Sant'Anna (2021), Chaisemartin and D'Haultfœuille (2020), and Borusyak, Jaravel, and Spiess (2024) to present both pretreatment leads or placebo tests and post-treatment lags. You will likely wish to use packages available in languages such as R, Stata, or Python for this. Explain carefully how these quantities differ. Depending on the estimator considered, you may need to consider what to do with a single country that is always treated.

(c) Refer to the papers which define each of the estimators you have applied in part (b). Clearly define the precise nature of the required form of the parallel trends assumption which corresponds to each estimator, as well as the required no-anticipation assumption. Discuss whether you find any set of assumptions most credible for this setting, and whether based on these assumption, you would have a preferred estimation strategy.

(d) Return to each of the papers discussed above and discuss the inference procedures laid out by the authors. Are there any issues with inference that should be considered if reporting time-to-treatment specific estimates?

(e) Now focus on the balanced panel of countries for which observations are available for each of the twenty-six years studied. Implement a synthetic difference-in-differences estimator with these balanced panel data. How do these results differ to the estimators implemented in part (b)?

5. In this question we will simulate some data with treated and untreated units observed over time where parallel trends does not hold among all units, and explore a number of methods to estimate treatment effects. To begin, simulate a dataset with 50 units i observed over 20 time periods t. For each i, generate a unit fixed effect μ_i drawn from a standard normal $\mathcal{N}(0, 1)$ (this should just be a constant for each unit). Randomly split these 50 units into five groups of ten. The first three groups are treated units, and set their treatment adoption as occurring at $t = 14, 15, 16$, respectively. The last two groups are control units, and we will refer to these units as $control_i$ and $problem_i$. Generate a variable $post_{it}$ which takes 1 following treatment assignment for the treated units and 0 otherwise, and simulate outcomes as:

$$Y_{it} = \mu_i + 10 \times post_{it} + 0.2 \times t + 0.5 \times problem_i \times t + \varepsilon_{it}, \qquad \text{where } \varepsilon_{it} \sim \mathcal{N}(0, 1).$$

(a) Implement the two-way FE model to seek to estimate the effect of treatment receipt by regressing Y_{it} on $post$ and unit- and time-fixed effects. Are we close to recovering our true estimate? What issue do we encounter here? Be careful in explaining which of the assumptions underlying difference-in-differences are violated and whether we should be concerned about the staggered adoption setting here.

(b) Estimate an event study that corresponds to the model in part (a) but now including full treatment lags and leads. Are we close to recovering our true estimate? Confirm that if we remove from our estimation sample those units for which $problem_i = 1$ that we do indeed recover the true ATT.

(c) Using the full sample and the event study from part (b), explore the methods of Rambachan and Roth (2023). Specifically, follow the authors' proposal where rather than assuming parallel trends, we assume that trends do not deviate much from observed pre-trends. Does the procedure manage to bound this parameter? Consider how the bounds behave as you allow for divergence from this parallel pre-trend.

(d) Instead of the methods of Rambachan and Roth (2023), consider the use of synthetic methods. Seek to estimate the treatment effect using both synthetic controls and synthetic DID. Examine the units selected in the synthetic control, and comment on the resulting estimates. Examine how the estimator and its performance changes if rather than using 20 time periods, 30 time periods are used, and treatment adoption occurs in periods 24, 25 and 26. Explain these results.

5

Estimation with Local Manipulations I: Instrumental Variables and LATE

First you learn the instrument, then you learn the music, then you forget all that shit and just play.
—Attributed to Charlie Parker (source uncertain)

5.1 Introduction

The use of methods based on panel data or repeated cross-sections discussed previously provides one potential route to the identification of treatment effects even when we do not believe that exposure to treatment occurs randomly. However, the data requirements in these cases are not trivial, and the identifying assumptions need not be met in many circumstances. Fortunately, even in cases where treatment receipt may owe to unobservable factors *and* when we don't necessarily have multiple periods of data to work with, a range of alternative paths to identification exist. One of these is via the use of instrumental variables (IVs). In this chapter we will see that such IVs, if they exist, can allow for the identification of some type of treatment effect *even without requiring multiple periods of data*. However, as we will see in the pages ahead, one cost of such methods is that if we allow treatment effects to be heterogeneous as in (1.1), the nature of the treatment effect identified is potentially quite different to those that we have discussed up to this point.[1]

The logic behind instrumental variables is that, even when treatment assignment depends on unobserved factors, we can still identify a causal effect if there exists an external variable—an instrument—that induces random variation in treatment but does not directly affect the outcome except through treatment. If this external factor acts to "shift" treatment in some way, we can grab on to this random shift to help us back out a treatment effect. This external factor is referred to as an instrumental variable, generally denoted as Z_i, a notation also adopted here.

The prototypical example of this is random treatment assignment with imperfect compliance. Consider, for example, a case where individuals are assigned to treatment and control in a randomized experiment. But then imagine that among those assigned to treatment, only those who perceive a large return to treatment—that is, those for whom their perceived

$Y_i(1) > Y_i(0)$—actually comply with their treatment status. Unless individuals are in some way obliged to comply with their treatment status, it would be illogical for them to accept a treatment assignment unless they perceive benefits from treatment (Heckman 1997). In this case, because individuals elect to comply with treatment given their perceived potential outcomes, potential outcomes will be correlated with treatment, and hence even conditional unconfoundedness will be an unreasonable assumption. *However*, the fact that treatment was originally assigned randomly provides a source of variation off of which to isolate some type of well-defined treatment effect. Essentially, the random assignment of the original treatment will imply that similar individuals are separated into groups that are eligible for treatment and groups that are not, and using the mechanics of IV estimation laid out here provides a route forward. What is more, these IV methods can be applied in any setting where treatment assignment owes to unobservable factors provided that some external factor is available that shifts treatment in observable ways.

The crux of IV models is that if we wish to estimate the impact of some treatment on an outcome of interest, and even if the assignment mechanism is *not* as good as random, we can proceed if we can locate an instrumental variable. An IV, is a variable that is related to our treatment of interest but is not itself related to unobservable factors that are relevant to treatment receipt. If such a variable is available, there are a number of ways to estimate causal effects of treatment on the outcome of interest, where the "clean" variation imposed by the IV is essentially leveraged to estimate treatment effects. While we will encounter a range of methods for IV estimating in this chapter, including commonly encountered strategies such as two-stage least squares (2SLS) and the IV estimator, in the case that a binary instrument is available, perhaps the simplest way to understand IV estimation is via the Wald estimator. The Wald estimator, which is equivalent to other IV estimation methods when IVs are binary (see section 5.2.4), is written as follows:

$$\tau^{\text{Wald}} = \frac{\mathbb{E}[Y_i|Z_i=1] - \mathbb{E}[Y_i|Z_i=0]}{\mathbb{E}[D_i|Z_i=1] - \mathbb{E}[D_i|Z_i=0]}. \tag{5.1}$$

The Wald estimator provides a way to measure causal effects by leveraging the IV Z_i. At its core, the approach is elegantly simple: We calculate the causal effect of treatment D_i on the outcome Y_i by taking the ratio of two quantities—how much the instrument affects the outcome divided by how much the instrument affects treatment participation. Provided that the instrument is indeed generating "clean" variation in treatment, this ratio effectively isolates the causal pathway we care about, filtering out confounding factors that would otherwise bias our estimates.

You may note a slight variation in notation here, as we are referring to treatment as D_i rather than W_i. Previously, we have referred to an individual's treatment status as W_i. In this chapter, D_i still refers to an individual's treatment status, though we have adopted this notation to emphasize the fact that treatment now depends on an individual's choice of whether or not to adopt treatment. This also aligns with the broad literature on instrumental variables where, overwhelmingly, instruments are denoted as Z_i, and generally (endogenous) treatment variables as D_i.

We will formalize all of this below and discuss precisely *what* IV methods estimate as well as the precise nature of the identifying assumptions required. While IV methods have emerged from a long literature in econometrics and structural equation modeling, more recent advances, and in particular hugely influential work of Imbens and Angrist (1994), has cast the assumptions of the IV model within the framework of the Rubin Causal Model. This work has highlighted the importance of the nature of the resulting treatment effect if the effect of treatment is heterogeneous across individuals, as we will generally wish to permit.[2] For this reason, throughout this chapter we will not assume that treatment effects are homogeneous, implying that, as always, our model begins with the notion that treatment effects vary across individuals i as laid out in (1.1).

Perhaps the key challenge across all instrumental variable methods will be in identifying, and measuring, a variable that meets the assumptions required. In this chapter, we will begin by working with the example discussed previously where random *assignment* to treatment acts as an instrument Z_i, for nonrandom *receipt* of treatment D_i. This has the desirable property that the IV is clearly independent of relevant unobservables due to its random assignment. However, more generally a large number of IVs have been proposed, and all of the mechanics discussed throughout this chapter work regardless of the IV—provided of course that the IV meets the assumptions we will see shortly. After introducing key design features of IV based on this particular example, we will turn to a range of practical considerations in which other instruments will be discussed.

5.2 Instrumental Variables and the Local Average Treatment Effect

5.2.1 A Broader Causal Framework

A beautiful exposition of the Rubin Causal Framework incorporating instrumental variables is laid out in Angrist, Imbens, and Rubin (1996a). In this case, we add an instrumental variable, defined as Z_i, to the Rubin Causal Model we defined previously. In this section, we will assume that the instrument $Z_i \in \{0, 1\}$ is discrete, though in section 5.4 we show how this extends to other settings. To fix ideas here, we will consider the setting where Z_i is an individual's random assignment to treatment. However, we assume that an individual's *actual* treatment receipt is not random. Once individuals receive their random assignment to treatment, they may seek to comply with their treatment status or not comply with treatment.

Following the notation in section 1.2, we will consider an individual's treatment adoption, which here is denoted D_i. This will also be binary, though similarly can be generalized as we will see below. We are interested in the causal effect of this treatment D_i on some outcome Y_i, which is precisely the estimand defined in (1.1). In order to house the instrument in our Rubin causal model, we now note that there are potential outcomes for treatment receipt D_i.

We write $D_i(Z_i)$ as the treatment status of the individual given their instrumental assignment Z_i.[3] This is a potential outcome, simply defining what an individual would do in terms of their treatment in a setting in which they are randomly assigned to a treatment condition ($D_i(1)$), or randomly assigned to a control condition ($D_i(0)$). These values need not vary: For example a person who has no interest in receiving treatment may be assigned to treatment but elect not to receive treatment in which case their $D_i(1)=0$, where similarly, had this person been assigned to control, they would have happily agreed not to receive treatment—that is, $D_i(0)=0$. In practice, only one of these potential outcomes will be observed based on the realized value of the IV:

$$D_i = \begin{cases} D_i(1), & \text{if } Z_i = 1 \\ D_i(0), & \text{if } Z_i = 0. \end{cases} \tag{5.2}$$

Alternatively, this can be written in terms of the switching equation

$$D_i = D_i(0) \cdot (1 - Z_i) + D_i(1) \cdot (Z_i), \tag{5.3}$$

which we have seen previously in the case of potential outcomes defined in (1.3).

Similarly, potential outcomes will *also* exist for the outcome of interest Y_i. However, now given that treatment assignment is *itself* written in terms of potential outcomes, we write $Y_i(Z_i, D_i)$ as the potential outcome for individual i when their value for the instrument is Z_i and their treatment status is D_i. So there are now *four* potential outcomes for each individual, associated with all possible combinations of Z_i and D_i. We can write these potential outcomes as laid out in table 5.1, where the explanation states in words what this means in terms of a setting of treatment with imperfect compliance. In practice, we will observe only one of these potential outcomes as Y_i, which implies that we cannot yet estimate anything without further assumptions.

Table 5.1
Potential outcomes with a randomized treatment and imperfect compliance

Potential Outcome	Z_i	D_i	Explanation
$Y_i(0,0)$	0	0	Outcome in the state of the world where i is not assigned to treatment, and does not receive treatment.
$Y_i(0,1)$	0	1	Outcome in the state of the world where i is not assigned to treatment, but somehow accesses treatment.
$Y_i(1,0)$	1	0	Outcome in the state of the world where i is assigned to treatment, but does not elect to receive treatment.
$Y_i(1,1)$	1	1	Outcome in the state of the world where i is assigned to treatment, and elects to receive treatment.

5.2.2 Instrumental Variable Assumptions and the Rubin Causal Model

To see what we can estimate in this setting, we will lay out the key IV assumptions. Most of these assumptions clearly cross over with the "textbook" assumptions we likely have come across in presentations of IV models under homogeneous treatment effects; however, here they will be couched in terms of the Rubin Causal Model exposition.

As we have generally required throughout this book, SUTVA will be imposed. SUTVA, as we have stated it previously, has required that the potential outcomes for any unit i are not affected by the treatment status of any other unit $j \neq i$. Because in this setting we have defined potential outcomes for both treatment receipt $D_i(Z_i)$, and outcomes $Y_i(D_i, Z_i)$, the version of SUTVA required here states that an individual's treatment receipt decision cannot depend on the treatment assignment status of anyone but themselves and, similarly, that their outcome Y_i cannot depend on treatment assignment (or receipt) of other units.

Likely the most salient, and most questioned, assumption in IV settings is that of independence, or the required unconfoundedness assumption. This assumption states that for an instrument to be valid, it must be independent of potential outcomes. Again, because there are potential outcomes both for treatment receipt and for outcomes themselves, we can write this assumption in extensive form as follows:

Assumption 6. Independence

$$\left[Y_i(1,1), Y_i(1,0), Y_i(0,1), Y_i(0,0), D_i(1), D_i(0)\right] \perp\!\!\!\perp Z_i. \qquad (5.4)$$

This is analogous to the independence assumption we made in chapter 2 as assumption 2; however, here we no longer require independence of treatment receipt D_i, but rather, the independence of some IV (such as treatment *assignment*), Z_i.

While we are placing no restrictions on how potential outcomes for treatment D_i and potential outcomes Y_i are related among themselves, we *are* imposing a strong assumption about the nature of the IV. The IV is assumed to be independent of *all* potential outcomes, implying that individuals who are exposed to the instrument cannot be selected in any way in terms of their theoretical likelihood to take up treatment, or their theoretical potential outcomes. For example, if treatment is offered to those individuals who are more likely to take up treatment, (i.e., there is a positive correlation between Z_i and $D_i(1)$), this will violate assumption 6, implying that any estimates flowing from the methods discussed in this chapter will be biased and inconsistent. In some cases, such assumptions will be met by definition. If the instrument Z_i is indeed a randomly assigned treatment status, then assumption 6 will be fulfilled. What's more, in cases such as these, the IV assumptions can be explicitly defined in terms of random assignment, as for example, is laid out in Angrist, Imbens, and Rubin (1996a, assumption 2). However, in other cases, arguments related to the independence assumption require substantive knowledge and can generate substantial discussion. We will discuss this in section 5.5, where we consider a number of frequently encountered IVs beyond random treatment assignment.

Note that even if independence holds, this does *not* guarantee that the causal channel through which the instrument affects outcomes is limited to the treatment under study. For this reason, we add an exclusion restriction assumption, which is written as follows:

Assumption 7. Exclusion restriction

$$Y_i(0, d) = Y_i(1, d) \tag{5.5}$$

for $d = 0, 1$.

This states that for a given treatment receipt status, what matters is treatment *receipt*, rather than the instrument itself. In other words, this implies that the instrument has no effect on outcomes *except* for via treatment receipt. The notion (and nomenclature) of the "exclusion restriction" generally comes from regression modeling, where the fact that the instrument has no effect on Y_i apart from its effect via D_i means that Z_i can be "excluded" from the equation of interest. This assumption is in effect an *attribution* restriction (Imbens and Rubin 2015, 527) in that it allows us to attribute eventual treatment effects we estimate to D_i, rather than other variables that may respond to the instrument Z_i.

Whether an exclusion restriction holds is actually a separate argument from whether an instrument fulfills the independence assumption, and even if unconfoundedness holds, the exclusion restriction need not. Indeed, even in cases of random assignment where independence holds by definition, the exclusion restriction does not necessarily hold. Clear examples of this would occur if some treatment assignment—even though randomly assigned—affects both treatment uptake as well as other relevant outcomes that go on to affect Y_i. This essentially boils down to a question of whether the nature of the instrument is to simply push individuals into treatment without additionally containing any other substance. Useful discussion of the difference between these two assumptions can be found in Angrist, Imbens, and Rubin (1996a, section 4.1), and we will return to discuss this slightly more in Section 5.5.

At times, these two assumptions (6 and 7) can be combined into one, and the notation is no more cumbersome (see, for example, Imbens and Angrist [1994], and the exposition of Imbens and Wooldridge [2009] among others).[4] However, because the assumptions have quite separate empirical content, it useful to consider them separately, and we do so in this way throughout this Chapter. You may note that because of the exclusion restriction, instead of writing potential outcomes as $Y_i(Z_i, D_i)$, we can exclude Z_i and simply write $Y_i(D_i)$. Thus, if we ever see notation along the lines of $Y_i(1)$ and $Y_i(0)$ in an IV setting, we can safely conclude that (1) this refers to potential outcomes in terms of treatment D_i rather than the instrument Z_i, and (2) the exclusion restriction assumption has already been made, allowing for the exclusion of Z_i from potential outcomes.

A standard requirement of instrumental variables is that of relevance. The IV must actually act to shift at least some individuals' treatment status. This can be written as follows:

Assumption 8. Relevance

$$\mathbb{E}\left[D_i(1) - D_i(0)\right] \neq 0. \tag{5.6}$$

This may also be referred to as a first-stage assumption, or as an assumption that there is a nonzero average causal effect of Z_i on D_i (Angrist, Imbens, and Rubin 1996a). At first glance this may look strange because we just recently made an assumption that the IV *cannot* be correlated with potential outcomes $D_i(0)$ and $D_i(1)$. However, on closer thought, it is clear that these assumptions are entirely consistent. If an instrument acts to randomly assign treatment and most people comply with their treatment, then for most people, $D_i(1) = 1$ and $D_i(0) = 0$. If there is imperfect compliance, some people who are assigned to treatment will not actually take up treatment, and thus for these people $D_i(1) = 0$. What the relevance condition implies is simply that on average, the instrument must do something to shift individuals toward or away from treatment. What it rules out are cases where individuals may be assigned to treatment, but this random assignment does nothing to convince *any individuals at all* to take up treatment, in which case the instrument will be irrelevant in explaining variation in D_i. On the other hand, what the independence assumption says is something quite different. Namely, among those who are (randomly) selected to receive the instrument, their potential outcomes $D_i(1)$ and $D_i(0)$ should be no different to those potential outcomes of individuals who do not receive the instrument.

Notice that this is a statement about the expected value for the population as a whole. It of course does not guarantee that any specific individual is "moved" by the instrument to change their treatment status. It does not even guarantee that all individuals are "moved" in the same direction: Some may be induced by the instrument to take up treatment, whereas they otherwise would not have done so, while others may be induced by the instrument not to take up treatment, whereas they otherwise would have done so.

Classic work on instrumental variables assumption gets around this issue by assuming that treatment effects are homogeneous, and in these cases, as we will see in the next sub-section, the preceding assumptions are sufficient to nail down a parameter of interest. Of course, we generally do not want to assume treatment effect homogeneity, and for this reason the work starting with Imbens and Angrist (1994) has been influential in suggesting a way forward even in the presence of treatment effect heterogeneity. The cost of this way forward is the requirement of one further assumption, known as monotonicity. In particular, we require that *all individuals in the population* are uniformly more (or less) likely to be treated when they have $Z_i = 1$.

Assumption 9. Monotonicity $D_i(1) \geq D_i(0), \forall i$.

Notice that if the instrument takes the form of a discouragement from taking up the treatment, we can always define a new variable $Z_i' = (1 - Z_i)$, which will satisfy monotonicity as defined above, or restate monotonicity as $D_i(1) \leq D_i(0), \forall i$. What is important here is that the instrument acts on all individuals in a (weakly) similar direction. The monotonicity assumption rules out settings where, for example, being assigned to treatment makes certain individuals more likely to actually receive treatment but somehow *discourages* others from taking up treatment. With these assumptions in hand we can now define estimands of interest, but we will turn to think a lot more more about the implications of monotonicity when we consider the empirical content of the estimands discussed below.

Putting these assumptions together, we would hope that an IV generates something like the situation schematically represented in figure 5.1. In this figure, individuals colored more lightly are those who receive treatment—that is, those for whom $D_i = 1$—while individuals shaded more darkly are those who do not receive treatment ($D_i = 0$). Individuals have different (unobservable) combinations of $D_i(0)$ and $D_i(1)$, but individuals with particular combinations of $D_i(0)$ and $D_i(1)$ are just as likely to be observed in groups exposed to the instrument as those not exposed to the instrument. This is seen given balanced frequencies of the number of individuals in each of the three permitted types of potential outcome groups in cases where $Z_i = 0$ and $Z_i = 1$. In this figure, relevance is observed in that there are *some* individuals for whom $D_i(1) = 1$ and $D_i(0) = 0$ implying that the rate of individuals treated when $Z_i = 1$ is higher than the treatment rate when $Z_i = 0$. And monotonicity is observed given that there are no individuals for whom $D_i(1) = 0$ and $D_i(0) = 1$. The key element of the IV is that it "switches on" treatment for some group, and for this reason, we can learn something about the effect of treatment from our IV. Exactly *what* we can learn is the point we turn to now.

5.2.3 The Local Average Treatment Effect and Other New Estimands

5.2.3.1 The intent to treat effect Before we jump into instrumental variables estimates themselves, it is worth noting that there are other estimands of interest that we may wish to consider. Specifically, note that in the case of randomized treatment with imperfect compliance, we may *actually* be interested in estimating (or willing to accept the estimation of) the effect of treatment *assignment* rather than treatment receipt. This may make sense in cases where we are directly interested in understanding what the effect of treatment assignment (or any other instrument, Z_i) was on our outcome of interest. For example, in cases where the assignment process itself is costly, we may wish to consider whether the assignment of individuals to treatment has been successful in changing outcomes of interest, regardless of whether or not individuals actually adopt treatment.

This estimand is known as the intent to treat effect, or the ITT. We can define our ITT as:

$$\tau_{\text{ITT}} = \mathbb{E}\left[Y_i\big(1, D_i(1)\big) - Y_i\big(0, D_i(0)\big)\right]. \tag{5.7}$$

Note that this estimand in effect bundles two things. The first is the impact of assignment to treatment or control on actual exposure to treatment of control. The second, is the impact of exposure to treatment on outcomes Y_i. If we observe that some ITT is small, this may owe to the fact that the treatment effect itself is small, for example, $\mathbb{E}[Y_i(1, 1) - Y_i(0, 0)]$ is close to zero, implying that even though the instrument shifts individuals into treatment, this

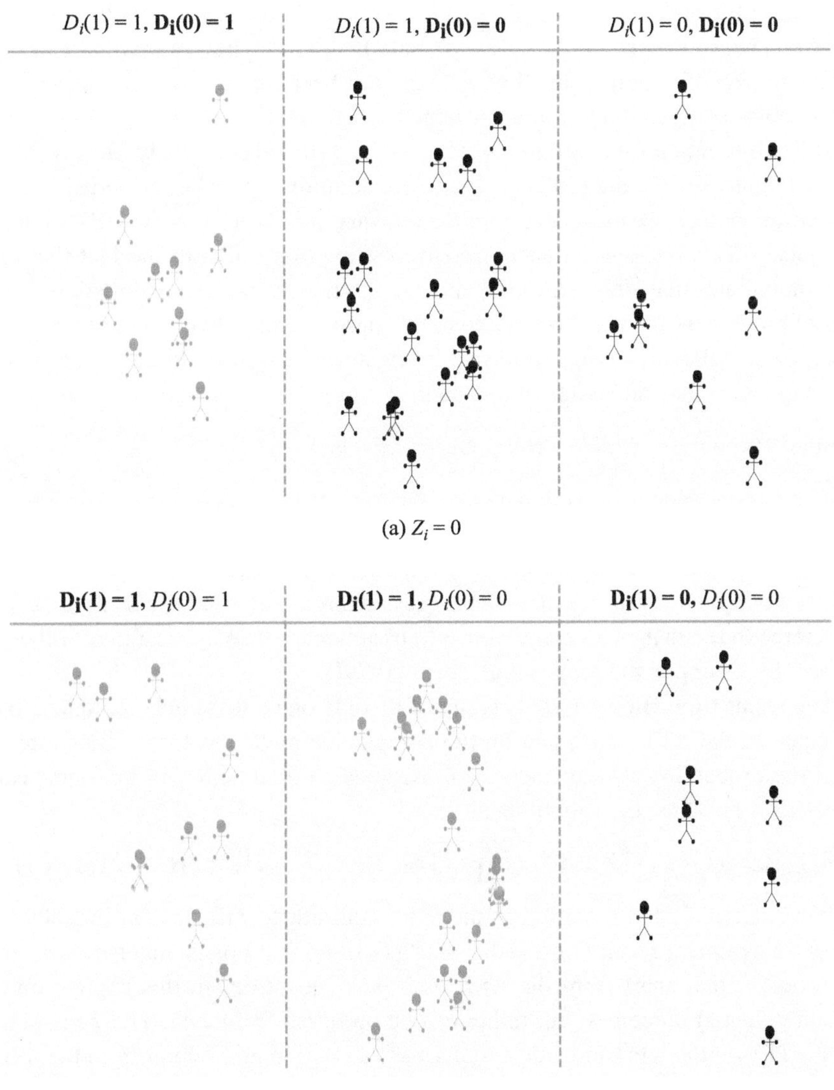

Figure 5.1
A schema of IV independence and relevance.
Note: Individuals colored gray receive treatment ($D_i = 1$). Individuals colored black do not ($D_i = 0$).

treatment has little effect, *or* to the fact that the treatment does relatively little to encourage adoption, and hence $\mathbb{E}[D_i(1)] - \mathbb{E}[D_i(0)]$ is small. In this latter case, a small ITT may persist even if the impact of treatment itself were large, just because rates of treatment take-up do not differ substantially among groups for which $Z_i = 1$ and $Z_i = 0$.

The ITT is a different estimand to those we have discussed previously. However, a useful result documented by Bloom (1984) is that if we additionally add a one-sided noncompliance assumption, then we can actually relate this quantity directly to the ATT we have laid out previously. This one-sided noncompliance assumption refers to the fact that in some settings, individuals may only not follow their assignment status in one direction. Typically, in cases of random assignment to treatment, this permits individuals to elect not to receive treatment even if they are assigned to receive treatment but does not allow individuals to access treatment if they are assigned to a control group.

Assumption 10. One-sided Non-compliance $D_i(0) = 0 \ \forall i$.

Whether or not one-sided noncompliance exists is entirely context-specific, though in many real cases one-sided noncompliance is observed. In many experimental implementations a researcher or organization may be able to set up their experiment to ensure that individuals who are not assigned to treatment cannot access treatment, but, at the same time, are not able to coerce individuals who are assigned to treatment to take up treatment if they prefer not to (see, for example, the proposal of Zelen [1979]).

The key result from Bloom (1984) is that if there is one-sided noncompliance, then the ITT is equal to the ATT multiplied by the compliance rate. The compliance rate simply refers to the probability that an individual assigned to treatment will take up treatment, $\Pr(D_i = 1 | Z_i = 1)$. Thus, the Bloom result is:

$$\mathbb{E}(Y_i | Z_i = 1) - \mathbb{E}(Y_i | Z_i = 0) = \left(\mathbb{E}\big[Y_i(1) - Y_i(0) \big| D_i = 1\big]\right) \times \Pr(D_i = 1 | Z_i = 1).$$

Here we have simplified the notation on the right-hand side to write the dependence of $Y_i(1)$ and $Y_i(0)$ on treatment receipt only—that is, $Y_i(D_i)$—so that this is understood as an ATT. It is noteworthy that apart from the ATT, both other quantities in this expression do not depend on potential outcomes, but rather can be observed from data. These quantities are simply the ITT on the left-hand side (we discuss estimation and inference in the following subsection) and the probability of treatment receipt conditional on having been assigned to treatment on the right-hand side. This result is quite logical given that, with one-sided noncompliance, the only treated individuals are those who are assigned to treatment, and the ITT will thus consist of a weighted average of the effect of treatment assignment for those individuals who comply with their treatment status (the ATT), diluted with the null effect of treatment assignment on individuals who are assigned to treatment but do not actually take up treatment. A numerical example that helps to illustrate this point is provided in Bloom (1984), and formal proofs abound (see, e.g., Angrist and Pischke [2009, Theorem 4.4.2]), though perhaps the key point is really that the ITT is an interesting parameter in its own right.

While a useful result, this *only* holds because of the one-sided noncompliance assumption. Because we are able to rule out that people assigned to control can access treatment, we can actually link parameters related to treatment *assignment* (Z_i) such as the ITT to parameters related to treatment *receipt* (D_i), such as the ATT. More generally though, if we are not in a setting of one-sided noncompliance, this opens the question about what we can say about parameter estimates, and how this all links to the long literature on instrumental variables which we began this chapter talking about.

5.2.3.2 The local average treatment effect The key theorem of Imbens and Angrist (1994) defines the local average treatment effect. Much of the work coming before Imbens and Angrist that sought to link instrumental variables methods to underlying treatment effect parameters of interest had noted that to do so *without imposing treatment effect homogeneity assumptions* requires either structural models or parametric assumptions (Heckman 1990; Manski 1994; Heckman and Honoré 1990), bounds estimates (Manski 1994), or limits to the nature of compliance such as those discussed previously (Angrist and Imbens 1991; Efron and Feldman 1991).

However, the success of the paper of Imbens and Angrist (1994), and its broad usage thereafter, owes to its identification of the fact that under the five assumptions discussed above (SUTVA and assumptions 6–9), but even without one-sided noncompliance, instrumental variables estimates will have a clear link to a specific type of average treatment effect, namely a *local average treatment effect*, or LATE. This LATE, is an average treatment effect for a specific subpopulation. For example, this can be laid out as in Angrist, Imbens, and Rubin (1996a):

$$\frac{\mathbb{E}\left[Y_i\left(1,D_i(1)\right)-Y_i\left(0,D_i(0)\right)\right]}{\mathbb{E}\left[D_i(1)-D_i(0)\right]}=\mathbb{E}\left[\left(Y_i(1)-Y_i(0)\right)\middle|D_i(1)-D_i(0)=1\right]. \tag{5.8}$$

This is important because you will note that the term on the left-hand side actually just defines the Wald estimator that we have previously laid out in (5.1). That is:

$$\frac{\mathbb{E}\left[Y_i\left(1,D_i(1)\right)-Y_i\left(0,D_i(0)\right)\right]}{\mathbb{E}\left[D_i(1)-D_i(0)\right]}=\frac{\mathbb{E}\left[Y_i|Z_i=1\right]-E\left[Y_i|Z_i=0\right]}{\mathbb{E}\left[D_i|Z_i=1\right]-\mathbb{E}\left[D_i|Z_i=0\right]}\equiv\tau^{\text{Wald}},$$

which implies that the Wald estimator has the interpretation of a well-defined treatment effect in (5.8). This treatment effect $\mathbb{E}\left[\left(Y_i(1)-Y_i(0)\right)\middle|D_i(1)-D_i(0)=1\right]$ is the effect of treatment for individuals who are induced by the instrument to move into treatment. This is made clear by the fact that $D_i(1)-D_i(0)=1$ *only* for individuals who will receive treatment when assigned the instrument, $D_i(1)=1$, and who will not receive treatment when not assigned the instrument, $D_i(0)=0$.

This also implies that while our treatment effect is informative for some individuals, we can say nothing at all about what the treatment effect is for individuals who would always have been exposed to treatment regardless of their instrumental assignment or individuals who would never have been exposed to treatment regardless of their IV assignment. This is summed up in quite a pithy way, making clear the links to IV, by Imbens and Angrist (1994, 467) who state: "LATE is an average treatment effect for individuals whose treatment status is influenced by changing an exogenous regressor that satisfies an exclusion restriction." For this reason, rather than referring to an ATE or an ATT, the treatment effect is referred to as "Local" to a specific group of individuals. We return to discuss the nature of this group, and what we can (and cannot) say about them at more length in section 5.3.

Based on the maintained assumptions, seeing how the Wald estimator is linked to the LATE is relatively straightforward, though it does require some careful thinking about potential outcomes. Below we can see in a number of steps how such a link is made.

$$\tau^{\text{Wald}} = \frac{\mathbb{E}[Y_i(0)+(Y_i(1)-Y_i(0))D_i|Z_i=1]-\mathbb{E}[Y_i(0)+(Y_i(1)-Y_i(0))D_i|Z_i=0]}{\mathbb{E}[D_i(0)+(D_i(1)-D_i(0))Z_i|Z_i=1]-\mathbb{E}[D_i(0)+(D_i(1)-D_i(0))Z_i|Z_i=0]} \tag{5.9}$$

$$= \frac{\mathbb{E}[Y_i(0)+(Y_i(1)-Y_i(0))D_i(1)]-\mathbb{E}[Y_i(0)+(Y_i(1)-Y_i(0))D_i(0)]}{\mathbb{E}[D_i(1)]-\mathbb{E}[D_i(0)]} \tag{5.10}$$

$$= \frac{\mathbb{E}[(Y_i(1)-Y_i(0))(D_i(1)-D_i(0))]}{\mathbb{E}[D_i(1)-D_i(0)]} \tag{5.11}$$

$$= \frac{\mathbb{E}[(Y_i(1)-Y_i(0)|D_i(1)>D_i(0))\cdot \Pr(D_i(1)>D_i(0))]}{\Pr[D_i(1)>D_i(0)]} \tag{5.12}$$

$$= \mathbb{E}[(Y_i(1)-Y_i(0)|D_i(1)>D_i(0))]. \tag{5.13}$$

Such a result can be documented in a range of ways; see, for example, Angrist and Pischke (2009, 114) or Imbens and Angrist (1994, 467–470). While it may take a little bit of thinking to confirm that the notation in each step makes sense, each step flows from our definition of the Rubin Causal Model, one of the assumptions 6–9, or simple algebraic rearrangement. In (5.9) we simply rewrite our Wald estimator in terms of the switching equations that define potential outcomes as flowing from realizations of D_i and Z_i. We can remove the condition on Z_i in each case of (5.10) given the independence assumption. We then rearrange terms in (5.11), which requires no assumptions. Noting that $D_i(1)-D_i(0)$ in (5.11) can only take values of 1 or 0 (given that monotonicity rules out the case where $D_i(1)-D_i(0)=-1$), and noting that $D_i(1)-D_i(0)=0$ in cases where $D_i(1)=D_i(0)$ we can rewrite the numerator and denominator in (5.11) as shown in (5.12). Finally, provided that the denominator is nonzero and (5.12) is estimable (the relevance assumption), we resolve to arrive to the LATE in (5.13). Given the exclusion restriction, we can attach a causal interpretation to the LATE as flowing from treatment receipt D_i rather than some other factor related to assignment Z_i.

5.2.4 Estimation and Inference

5.2.4.1 Estimation of an ITT Estimating the ITT is straightforward, in the spirit of the estimation of an ATT or ATE with unconditional unconfoundedness laid out in section 2.3. As the instrument Z_i is exogenously assigned, and the ITT simply seeks to isolate the effect of treatment *assignment* on the outcome of interest, the ITT can be estimated using a simple comparison of means. Namely:

$$\widehat{\tau}_{\text{ITT}} = \frac{\sum_{i=1}^{N} Z_i Y_i}{\sum_{i=1}^{N} Z_i} - \frac{\sum_{i=1}^{N}(1-Z_i)Y_i}{\sum_{i=1}^{N}(1-Z_i)}. \tag{5.14}$$

Alternatively, and in practice what is generally done, is a simple regression of Y_i on Z_i. This will identically return $\widehat{\tau}_{\text{ITT}}$ as the coefficient on Z_i, along with standard errors permitting valid inference, as laid out in section 2.4.3.

5.2.4.2 Estimation of a LATE We have motivated our definition of the LATE as an IV parameter by beginning with the Wald estimator, and as such it will likely not be surprising that one way to estimate the LATE will be by using the Wald estimator! With a sample of data of N observations, we can write this in a similar notation to (5.14) as follows:

$$\widehat{\tau}_{\text{LATE}}^{\text{Wald}} = \frac{\frac{\sum_{i=1}^{N} Z_i Y_i}{\sum_{i=1}^{N} Z_i} - \frac{\sum_{i=1}^{N}(1-Z_i)Y_i}{\sum_{i=1}^{N}(1-Z_i)}}{\frac{\sum_{i=1}^{N} Z_i D_i}{\sum_{i=1}^{N} Z_i} - \frac{\sum_{i=1}^{N}(1-Z_i)D_i}{\sum_{i=1}^{N}(1-Z_i)}}. \tag{5.15}$$

If you are observant, you will note that the numerator of (5.15) is precisely the same as (5.14), which we have said can also be generated by a regression of Y_i on Z_i. Examining the denominator, we see that this is written identically, but now in terms of the impact of the instrument Z_i on treatment receipt D_i.

This leads to a key point, which is that the LATE can also be estimated as the ratio of two regression coefficients. The LATE is simply the ITT divided by the impact treatment assignment has on treatment adoption. Given that (in the binary treatment case), this quantity will be bounded between 0 and 1, and the LATE will thus be a scaled-up version of the ITT, where the scaling depends inversely upon the strength the instrument has in shifting individuals into treatment.

This also allows us to see that the Wald estimator is equivalent to the more standard IV estimator you have likely come across before. Note that the standard IV estimator is defined as follows (see, for example, Clarke and Windmeijer [2012] or a standard econometrics textbook):

$$\widehat{\tau}_{\text{LATE}}^{\text{IV}} = \frac{\mathbb{C}\text{ov}(Y_i, Z_i)}{\mathbb{C}\text{ov}(D_i, Z_i)}. \tag{5.16}$$

The numerator of the Wald estimator is simply the coefficient on Z_i from a bivariate regression of Y_i on Z_i, and we may remember that such a regression parameter can be written as $\mathbb{C}\text{ov}(Z_i, Y_i)/\mathbb{V}(Z_i)$. Similarly, we can write the denominator as the regression coefficient from the regression of D_i on Z_i. This allows us to quite simply see the correspondence between the Wald estimator and the IV estimator as follows:

$$\widehat{\tau}_{\text{LATE}}^{\text{Wald}} = \frac{\mathbb{C}\text{ov}(Y_i, Z_i)/\mathbb{V}(Z_i)}{\mathbb{C}\text{ov}(D_i, Z_i)/\mathbb{V}(Z_i)} = \frac{\mathbb{C}\text{ov}(Y_i, Z_i)}{\mathbb{C}\text{ov}(D_i, Z_i)} = \widehat{\tau}_{\text{LATE}}^{\text{IV}}. \tag{5.17}$$

The result from (5.17) thus states the equivalence of the Wald estimator, the IV estimator, as well as an "indirect least squares" implementation of the IV estimator. You may note that the equivalence of the Wald estimator and the indirect least squares estimator in the binary case is, essentially, the analogue to the case laid out in chapter 2, where we noted that one could equivalently estimate a treatment effect with unconfoundedness using a difference in means, or a bivariate OLS regression.

Note also in the case where we have a single instrument Z_i and single treatment variable D_i, the IV estimator is identical to the 2SLS estimator. That is, a two-stage least squares estimator:

$$\widehat{\tau}_{\text{LATE}}^{\text{2SLS}} = \frac{\mathbb{C}\text{ov}(Y_i, \widehat{D}_i)}{\mathbb{C}\text{ov}(D_i, \widehat{D}_i)} \tag{5.18}$$

will identically return the LATE. Note here that we are using $\widehat{D}_i$ to denote the predicted value for D_i following a first-stage projection of the treatment on the instrument. This is precisely what gives the two-stage least squares its name. The estimator can be generated in two steps: a first stage in which the following model is estimated by OLS:

$$D_i = \pi_0 + \pi_1 Z_i + \eta_i \tag{5.19}$$

and a second stage in which the predicted values from this regression, which are calculated as:

$$\widehat{D}_i = \widehat{\pi}_0 + \widehat{\pi}_1 Z_i \tag{5.20}$$

are substituted in place of D_i:

$$Y_i = \mu_0 + \tau_{\text{LATE}}^{\text{2SLS}} \widehat{D}_i + \varepsilon_i. \tag{5.21}$$

Estimating this second-stage regression results in the 2SLS estimand $\widehat{\tau}_{\text{LATE}}^{\text{2SLS}}$, which is equivalent to $\widehat{\tau}_{\text{LATE}}^{\text{IV}}$ and $\widehat{\tau}_{\text{LATE}}^{\text{Wald}}$ in this setting with a single binary IV.

In practice, 2SLS is generally the preferred estimation method because it is the most flexible of the three previous estimation procedures. By definition, the Wald estimator can only be written for a binary IV. Thus, while in these cases it is identical to IV and 2SLS, if an instrument is *not* binary, the Wald estimator can no longer be employed, leaving either IV or 2SLS. We will return to discuss the case of continuous instruments in section 5.4.2. What's more, this equivalence between IV and 2SLS is only the case with a single instrumental variable. In a setting with more than one instrumental variable, 2SLS can easily incorporate a second instrument in the first-stage 5.19, something that is not true in the case of the IV estimator, which is defined for a single instrument. We will return to discuss the case of multiple instruments in section 5.4.4.

Code Callout 5.1: Treatment Assignment with Imperfect Compliance
We will explore a real experiment and dataset to see that each of these ways of estimating IV is identical when instruments are binary, and also to explore the relationship between the intent to treat effect, the first stage, and the LATE. To do so, we will use data from Finkelstein et al. (2012), which comes from the Oregon Health Insurance Experiment, where insurance access was randomly assigned but where noncompliance resulted in nonrandom treatment adoption.

Properties of IV estimators In previous chapters we have generally worked with estimators that are unbiased, or worked with bias correction methods if bias remains. IV estimators, while consistent, are biased, implying that most formal results related to the properties of IV rely on the asymptotic behavior of the estimator. Indeed, as N goes to infinity, the IV estimate is known to converge to the true parameter of interest following a normal distribution with known variance. Namely, Imbens and Angrist (1994, theorem 3) show that:

$$\sqrt{N}(\widehat{\tau}^{\text{IV}}_{\text{LATE}} - \tau^{\text{IV}}_{\text{LATE}}) \xrightarrow{\text{d}} \mathcal{N}\left(0, \frac{\mathbb{E}[\varepsilon^2(Z - \mathbb{E}[Z])^2]}{[E(Z - \mathbb{E}[Z])E(D - \mathbb{E}[D])]^2}\right), \tag{5.22}$$

where $\varepsilon_i = Y_i - \mu_0 - \tau^{\text{IV}}_{\text{LATE}} D_i$. This implies that in the limit as the sample size goes to infinity, the distribution of $\widehat{\tau}^{\text{IV}}_{\text{LATE}}$ is centered on the true parameter $\tau^{\text{IV}}_{\text{LATE}}$ and is normal with a known variance. It is important, nevertheless, to understand the nature of the bias, given that in practice all samples are finite, and we would like to understand when we may worry about this bias and when it may be less of a concern.

Early work alerting to the importance of this bias pointed out that in empirically relevant cases, the bias was large, with standard errors suggestive of overly precise effects, and this situation is aggravated when the effect of Z_i on D_i in the first stage regression is weaker (Nelson and Startz 1990b). In cases of many instruments, the bias has been shown to be substantial, even in cases with hundreds of thousands of observations (Bound, Jaeger, and Baker 1995), suggesting that seeking large datasets is not always an immediate solution to the problem.

Conceptually, the bias in IV comes from the fact that the first stage must be estimated, and it will be estimated with some error due to sampling variation. Because the idea of the instrumental variables is that variation from the instrument will provide "clean" variation, $\widehat{D}_i$ from (5.20) should be purged of endogenous factors. However, in practice, when a sample is not infinitely large, the first-stage estimates will not capture the true parameters, but rather will be estimated with some noise. This is a problem because any variation *not* coming from the IV will contain variation from the endogenous component of D_i, resulting in bias in IV estimates. We will discuss this bias further when discussing tests of instrumental relevance in section 5.5.1, but even this brief conceptual discussion is useful to understand the nature of the bias.

Firstly, because the bias in IV will owe to noise in the first stage driven by the original endogenous variable, the bias in IV will be in the direction of the OLS estimate (Sawa 1969; Nelson and Startz 1990a; Buse 1992). Indeed, as IVs become less and less correlated with an endogenous variable the expectation of the IV estimator approaches that of OLS (Bound, Jaeger, and Baker 1995). Secondly, the bias in IV depends upon the strength of the instrument in the first stage. This makes sense intuitively because if an instrument is more relevant, the noise in the first stage will be relatively less important than the explained portion from the IV. Indeed, the bias can be shown to depend inversely upon the population analogue of the F statistic of the test that parameters in the first stage are equal to 0. This has led to formal tests of finite sample bias developed by Staiger and Stock (1997) being based on this first-stage F-statistic. We discuss these tests in section 5.5.1. Finally, the bias depends positively upon the number of instruments used. As the number of instruments grows (all else constant), the bias increases (Bound, Jaeger, and Baker 1995). This also intuitively makes sense given the conceptual discussion above. This is because as more instruments are used, a larger number of first-stage parameters will be estimated, implying more space for noise from the endogenous component of D_i to creep into $\widehat{D}_i$. In particular, these last two facts suggest that concerns are greatest when multiple weak instruments are used, which has resulted in a rich literature on weak instruments and multiple instruments reviewed in Andrews, Stock, and Sun (2019), which we discuss in section 5.5.1.

5.2.4.3 Inference Estimating the variance of the LATE is relatively straightforward, and in the case of the Wald estimator the variance was provided even in Wald's 1940 original paper. In (5.22), one version of the asymptotic variance of $\widehat{\tau}^{\text{IV}}_{\text{LATE}}$ is already shown, which is:

$$\mathbb{V}(\widehat{\tau}^{\text{IV}}_{\text{LATE}}) = \frac{\frac{1}{N}\mathbb{E}[\varepsilon^2(Z - \mathbb{E}[Z])^2]}{[E(Z - \mathbb{E}[Z])E(D - \mathbb{E}[D])]^2}. \tag{5.23}$$

The only important thing to note about this variance is that ε_i refers to the quantity based on the IV estimand itself, which will have its own uncertainty, which is to say that $\varepsilon_i = [Y_i - E(Y_i) - \tau^{\text{IV}}_{\text{LATE}}(D_i - E(D_i)]$, where you can note that this depends upon $\tau^{\text{IV}}_{\text{LATE}}$. If it is assumed that this $\mathbb{E}[\varepsilon_i^2|Z_i]$ in (5.23) is a constant term σ^2 (homoscedasticity) then this can be removed from the expectation in the numerator and (5.23) can be rewritten as:

$$\frac{\frac{\sigma^2}{N}\mathbb{E}[(Z - \mathbb{E}[Z])^2]}{[E(Z - \mathbb{E}[Z])E(D - \mathbb{E}[D])]^2} = \frac{\frac{\sigma^2}{N}\mathbb{V}(Z)}{\mathbb{C}\text{ov}(Z, D)},$$

which is the well-known IV variance estimator. However, one need not assume homoscedasticity, and as such it is easy to arrive at heteroscedasticity-robust and cluster robust versions of 5.23 by placing this restriction on ε_i, and each of these variance estimators are widely available in computational implementations.

In cases where multiple IVs and/or multiple endogenous variables are included in a 2SLS model, or if covariates are included in an IV model, IV and 2SLS estimators are often rewritten in a vector form that we will encounter in section 5.5, and this leads to the standard representation of the variance of IV or 2SLS that is available in most econometrics textbooks.

5.2.4.4 A note on jargon: Reduced form, first stage, and IV estimation We have already referred to some terms above, and it is worth highlighting a number of elements of jargon that frequently come up in IV estimation. We often may be interested in some relationship of interest:

$$Y_i = \mu_0 + \tau D_i + \varepsilon_i.$$

If this describes the data generating process, or underlying economic model of interest, we may see it referred to as the structural equation, reflecting the fact that τ is the true causal parameter we wish to capture. However in implementing IV estimation, we also come across the first stage (5.19), which is the regression of the endogenous variable of interest on the IV, and the second stage (5.21), which is the regression of the outcome on the predicted value from the first stage. You may also read that the first stage consists of a linear projection of the instrument on the endogenous variable. This projection simply refers to the fact that we are predicting $\widehat{X}$ from the underlying variation of Z using least squares.[5]

One piece of notation that has not been introduced above is the "reduced-form" regression. The reduced form refers to the regression of the outcome of interest Y_i on the instrument itself. Above we have noted that in the case where the instrument is treatment *assignment* and the endogenous variable is treatment receipt, the reduced form regression itself returns a parameter of theoretical and empirical relevance, namely the ITT. More generally however, for other instrumental variables, it is often of interest to consider the reduced form regression. Based on assumptions of independence and the exclusion restriction, this allows us to simply understand the causal impact of the IV, which may be a parameter of interest.

5.3 Understanding the Composition of the LATE

5.3.1 LATE and the Compliant Subpopulation

The LATE theorem tells us that the Wald/IV estimator provides a consistent estimate of treatment effects for some subpopulation—the subpopulation for whom $D_i(1) \neq D_i(0)$. Who are these people? The answer depends on the instrument that we are using and its ability to affect the eventual treatment status of individuals in the sample. Relative to a given instrument, we can categorize individuals in four groups. These are listed in Table 5.2.

Notice here that the assumption of monotonicity rules out the existence of "defiers." This language of defiance was introduced in Balke and Pearl (1993, see, e.g., §7.3). While the

Table 5.2
Compliance types with IV

Group	Definition	Words
Compliers:	$D_i(1)=1, D_i(0)=0$	Participate when assigned to participate, don't participate when not assigned to participate
Never-takers:	$D_i(1)=0, D_i(0)=0$	Never participate, whether assigned to or not
Always-takers:	$D_i(1)=1, D_i(0)=1$	Always participate, whether assigned to or not
Defiers:	$D_i(1)=0, D_i(0)=1$	Participate when assigned not to participate, don't participate when assigned to participate

monotonicity assumption implies that defiers must not exist, compliers, always-takers, and never-takers certainly can. Indeed, given our first-stage assumption, compliers *must* exist, or else the instrument will have no power. And it is precisely this group of compliers we are most interested in here. This is because our LATE is *only* informative of the effect on this group. The LATE does not tell us anything about the effect on always-takers or never-takers, precisely because the IV does not generate any variation in treatment for these groups, and hence we cannot learn anything about the treatment effects for these groups by comparing across individuals randomly assigned to receive the instrument and those assigned not to receive the instrument.

For this reason we may want to be able to say something about who exactly these compliers are. Under the assumption of monotonicity with a binary instrument, the size of the compliant subpopulation is given by the first stage of our IV estimation. We can see this quite simply by noting that the proportion of compliers can be written as $\Pr\big(D_i(1) > D_i(0)\big)$, which in turn can be written (noting that D_i is binary) as:

$$\begin{aligned}\Pr\big(D_i(1) > D_i(0)\big) &= \mathbb{E}[D_i(1) - D_i(0)]\\ &= \mathbb{E}[D_i(1)] - \mathbb{E}[D_i(0)]\\ &= \mathbb{E}[D_i|Z_i=1] - \mathbb{E}[D_i|Z_i=0]. \end{aligned} \tag{5.24}$$

The last line here is the most important jump, and it makes use of the independence assumption. The idea here is that because Z_i is randomly assigned, we can use the expectation of D_i among those individuals who were assigned treatment to provide a general estimate of $D_i(1)$, and similarly, we can use the expectation of D_i among individuals assigned to control to estimate $\mathbb{E}[D_i(1)]$. This final line is simply a difference in means, or the quantity π_1 defined in the first-stage regression (5.19).

Another way to see that we can estimate the rate of compliance without ever "observing" compliance is to note that, because of monotonicity, there are only three types of individuals (compliers, always-takers, and never-takers), and the proportion of these individuals must sum to 1. If we consider the first term in (5.24), this will only differ from 1 due to the presence of never-takers. And if we consider the second term in (5.24), this will only differ from 0 due to the presence of always-takers. What's more, because we have ruled out defiance, we can directly estimate the rate of never-takers as individuals for whom $Z_i = 1$ but $D_i = 0$. The proportion of such individuals can be written as ϕ_n. We can directly estimate the rate of always-takers as individual's for whom $Z_i = 0$ but $D_i = 1$, and this proportion will be written ϕ_a. Precisely *because* Z_i is assumed independent, it does not matter that we can only estimate the rate of never-takers among individuals with $Z_i = 1$, and always-takers among individuals with $Z_i = 0$: These proportions will be representative for individuals in both groups. Finally, because there are only three types of individuals, and because we can estimate the probability that individuals are always-takers and never-takers from data, we can infer the probability that an individual is a complier as: $\phi_c = 1 - \phi_a - \phi_n$.

As a first approach to considering whether the LATE is an informative parameter, we can ask whether a considerable portion of the sample are compliers. If a high proportion of treated individuals are compliers, we may be relatively happy that even though the LATE is a "local" estimand, it is local to a relatively large group of individuals. This is a point made by, among others, Oreopoulos (2006), who states that the fact that the particular IV used is a mandatory law with which most of the population complies allows us to learn quite a lot about the ATE rather than a LATE.

A separate, but no less important, point about compliers is that they are instrument-specific. Different instruments will have different populations of compliers, and so different LATEs. This insight has important lessons for tests used elsewhere for the validity of instruments such as the Sargan-Hansen J test that are based on assumptions of homogeneous effects. If treatment effects are heterogeneous, and we estimate very different effects using two different instruments, we may not be able to tell whether this is due to heterogeneity in treatment effects or due to the invalidity of one of the instruments.

5.3.2 What Can We Say About the Compliers?

5.3.2.1 Examining compliance rates by groups While the above suggests that it is simple to know what proportion of observations are compliers, we probably would like to be able to say more about this group to better interpret the LATE. Of course, we cannot simply "look at" the compliers and summarize their observations, given that one's status as a complier is unobservable. However, as a first approach at the problem, we can quite simply ask whether compliance rates are higher among certain groups than others. This allows us to ask questions such as: "Are the compliers more likely to have a secondary education than the general population?" or any such question relating to observed characteristics. It turns out that we can do this relatively easily, using the first-stage estimates for different groups. To see this, note that (as, for example, discussed in Angrist and Pischke [2009, 171]), for a binary variable X_{1i}:

$$\frac{\Pr\left(X_{1i}=1 \middle| D_i(1)>D_i(0)\right)}{\Pr\left(X_{1i}=1\right)} = \frac{\Pr\left(D_i(1)>D_i(0) \middle| X_{1i}=1\right)}{\Pr\left(D_i(1)>D_i(0)\right)}$$
$$= \frac{\mathbb{E}[D_i|Z_i=1, X_{1i}=1] - \mathbb{E}[D_i|Z_i=0, X_{1i}=1]}{\mathbb{E}[D_i|Z_i=1] - \mathbb{E}[D_i|Z_i=0]}.$$

This final line is likely not too surprising, as it simply states that if the relative strength of a first stage is higher among a particular group than in the entire population, then this group has a greater proportion of compliers than the general population. Because we assume the instrument is randomly assigned, there is no issue in estimating the first stage by group, and the logic of (5.24) will similarly hold.

5.3.2.2 Mean characteristics of compliers: Abadie's kappa It is useful to know that we can say something about compliance rates of different groups, but can we say anything more precise about what compliers "look like"? For example, with the first-stage result above, we could say if compliance is more likely for individuals with secondary education, or individuals with primary education (and so forth). But could we say what the mean educational level of compliers are? It turns out that we can, but to do so requries some mechanics that we have not come across so far. In particular, we can describe mean characteristics of compliers—and indeed, other descriptive properties—using what is now known as Abadie's Kappa. Abadie's Kappa was described in Abadie (2003) and crops up in a number of settings which we will encounter here and in the rest of the book, including that of describing compliers.

Abadie (2003) laid out a theorem that defines the following quantities:

$$\kappa_i(0) = (1-D_i)\frac{(1-Z_i) - \Pr(Z_i=0|X_i)}{\Pr(Z_i=0|X_i)\Pr(Z_i=1|X_i)} \tag{5.25}$$

$$\kappa_i(1) = D_i\frac{Z_i - \Pr(Z_i=1|X_i)}{\Pr(Z_i=0|X_i)\Pr(Z_i=1|X_i)} \tag{5.26}$$

$$\kappa_i = \kappa(0)\Pr(Z_i=0|X_i) + \kappa(1)\Pr(Z_i=1|X_i)$$
$$= 1 - \frac{D_i(1-Z_i)}{\Pr(Z_i=0|X_i)} - \frac{(1-D_i)Z_i}{\Pr(Z_i=1|X_i)}, \tag{5.27}$$

and then states (in a slightly abridged form here) that the following result holds. For any finite measurable function of interest $g(Y, D, X)$, where Y, D, and X refer to outcomes, treatment, and predetermined covariates X, then:

$$\mathbb{E}[g(Y,D,X)|D_i(1)>D_i(0)] = \frac{1}{\Pr\left(D_i(1)>D_i(0)\right)}\mathbb{E}[\kappa g(Y,D,X)]. \tag{5.28}$$

While there is a fair bit of algebra, the take-home message is very nice. This message is that the quantity κ essentially "finds" compliers. That means that if we have some arbitrary quantity that we would like to observe and this quantity is a function of any observable quantities Y_i, D_i, or X_i, we can estimate this quantity by using Abadie's Kappa! This allows us to do many things, including estimating the mean of variables for compliers. For example, imagine that we would like to estimate the mean of some specific observable variable X_1 among compliers. Setting $g(Y,D,X)=X_1$, we can sub this into (5.28) to estimate the complier average as follows:

$$\mathbb{E}[X_1|D_i(1)>D_i(0)]=\frac{1}{\Pr\left(D_i(1)>D_i(0)\right)}\mathbb{E}[\kappa X_1].$$

It turns out that we can similarly use $\kappa_i(0)$ and $\kappa_i(1)$ to find never-takers and always-takers too, and this is useful for a range of things, including describing mean characteristics of these groups and also implementing richer estimators, as discussed by Tymon Słoczyński and Wooldridge (2025).

Code Callout 5.2: Characterising Compliers
We will examine the data and setting of Clingingsmith, Khwaja, and Kremer (2009), who study the Hajj pilgrimage to Mecca. In their paper, they instrument making the pilgrimage with a random lottery with imperfect compliance and study how making this pilgrimage shapes beliefs and views. In code callout 5.2, we consider the composition of compliers in terms of a range of covariates, in particular documenting complier means using Abadie's Kappa.

5.3.2.3 Characterizing the outcomes of compliers Finally, it is worth noting that given the maintained assumptions, and in particular the assumption of instrumental independence, we can actually describe the entire distribution of both $Y_i(1)$ and $Y_i(0)$ for compliers! This may seem surprising given that whether an individual is a complier or not is an unobservable characteristic, but it turns out that the result can be "backed out" given instrumental independence, and given other things which can be observed in data.

The crux of the argument is laid out in Imbens and Rubin (1997b). They note that, as discussed above, the probability that an individual is a complier is: $\phi_c=1-\phi_a-\phi_n$, where each of ϕ_a and ϕ_n can be estimated from data. By a similar argument, the entire distribution of outcomes Y can be estimated for both always-takers and never-takers. Imbens and Rubin (1997b) define as $f_{zd}(Y)$ the distribution of Y for specific values of Z and D, such that, for example, $f_{00}(Y)$ refers to the distribution of outcomes Y among individuals with $Z_i=0$ and $D_i=0$. They note that the distribution of outcomes among never-takers, which they call $g_n(y)$, can be inferred from individuals for which $Z_i=1$ and $D_i=0$, which is to say $g_n(Y)=f_{10}(Y)$. Similarly, the distribution of outcomes for always-takers $g_a(Y)$ can be inferred from individuals with $Z_i=0$ and $D_i=1$, or $g_a(Y)=f_{01}(Y)$.

However, the distribution of outcomes for compliers is not directly observable, but rather needs to be inferred. Note that among individuals with $Z_i = 0$ and $D_i = 0$, these may either be compliers or never-takers. Thus, the distribution of outcomes Y among such individuals, $f_{00}(Y)$ is a mixture of the distribution of outcomes among compliers and never-takers. Specifically:

$$f_{00}(Y) = \frac{\phi_c}{\phi_c + \phi_n} g_{c0}(Y) + \frac{\phi_n}{\phi_c + \phi_n} g_n(Y). \tag{5.29}$$

Here, all elements of (5.29) can be observed from data, or have been defined previously, except for $g_{c0}(Y)$, the distribution of outcomes Y among compliers where their instrumental assignment $Z_i = 0$. Similarly, the distribution of outcomes Y among individuals assigned to treatment and who also receive treatment, $f_{11}(Y)$, is a mixture of compliers and always-takers, and analogously to (5.29), $f_{11}(Y)$ can be written as:

$$f_{11}(Y) = \frac{\phi_c}{\phi_c + \phi_a} g_{c1}(Y) + \frac{\phi_a}{\phi_c + \phi_a} g_a(Y). \tag{5.30}$$

All elements of (5.29) and (5.30) are now known, with the exception of the distribution of outcomes among the compliers in cases where compliers are assigned to treatment ($g_{c0}(Y)$) and control ($g_{c1}(Y)$), respectively. Thus, by rearranging (5.29) and (5.30), we can characterize the complier distributions as follows:

$$g_{c0}(Y) = \frac{\phi_n + \phi_c}{\phi_c} f_{00}(Y) - \frac{\phi_n}{\phi_c} f_{10}(Y) \tag{5.31}$$

$$g_{c1}(Y) = \frac{\phi_a + \phi_c}{\phi_c} f_{11}(Y) - \frac{\phi_a}{\phi_c} f_{01}(Y). \tag{5.32}$$

In each case, all elements can be estimated either directly or indirectly from data.

While these quantities are written in terms of the distribution functions $f_{zd(Y)}$, Abadie (2002) shows that arbitrary functions of Y can be estimated directly as follows:

$$\mathbb{E}[h(Y_i(1))|D_i(1) > D_i(0)] = \frac{\mathbb{E}[h(Y_i)D_i|Z_i = 1] - \mathbb{E}[h(Y_i)D_i|Z_i = 0]}{\mathbb{E}[D_i|Z_i = 1] - \mathbb{E}[D_i|Z_i = 0]} \tag{5.33}$$

$$\mathbb{E}[h(Y_i(0))|D_i(1) > D_i(0)] = \frac{\mathbb{E}[h(Y_i)(1 - D_i)|Z_i = 1] - \mathbb{E}[h(Y_i)(1 - D_i)|Z_i = 0]}{\mathbb{E}[(1 - D_i)|Z_i = 1] - \mathbb{E}[(1 - D_i)|Z_i = 0]} \tag{5.34}$$

This suggests a simple way to estimate mean outcomes for compliers among treatment and control assignment if $h(\cdot) = \cdot$ on the right-hand side of 5.33 and 5.34, or across the entire distribution if $h(\cdot)$ is set to return empirical percentiles. We will consider an example of such a calculation in the end-of-chapter exercises.

5.3.3 LATE with One-Sided Noncompliance

It is worth noting that while generally the LATE is not informative of any of the treatment effects we have previously encountered, there are some specific cases where the LATE *will*

Table 5.3
The LATE is equal to the ATT with one-sided noncompliance

	Assigned to Treatment ($Z_i = 1$)	Assigned to Control ($Z_i = 0$)
Always-takers	$D_i(1) = 1, D_i(0) = 1$ $D_i = 1$	$D_i(1) = 1, D_i(0) = 1$ $D_i = 0$
Compliers	$D_i(1) = 1, D_i(0) = 0$ $D_i = 1$	$D_i(1) = 1, D_i(0) = 0$ $D_i = 0$
Never-takers	$D_i(1) = 0, D_i(0) = 0$ $D_i = 0$	$D_i(1) = 0, D_i(0) = 0$ $D_i = 0$

be equal to some other more clearly defined treatment effect. Specifically, in cases of one-sided noncompliance, the LATE will be equal to the ATT or the ATU (average treated effect on the untreated). If one-sided noncompliance occurs such that individuals assigned to treatment can elect to be untreated, but individuals assigned to control cannot elect to be treated, then the LATE will actually provide the ATT. And similarly, if one-sided noncompliance occurs in the other direction (individuals not exposed to the instrument can be treated, but individuals exposed to the instrument cannot remain untreated), then the LATE will actually provide the ATU. This result is related to the Bloom (1984) results discussed previously, and was noted in Imbens and Angrist (1994) and earlier work such as Heckman (1990).

Essentially, the reason for this is *not* because it limits the compliers in any way, but rather because it limits the types of individuals who can receive treatment. In particular, consider the case of one-sided noncompliance where individuals not assigned to treatment cannot receive treatment. This implies that $D_i(1) = 0$ is not possible, ruling out the existence of always-takers. If we consider the compliance types laid out in table 5.3, the fact that we are ruling out always-takers implies that there is now only one type of individual for whom $D_i = 1$: the compliers. Because the instrument is randomly assigned, the LATE is the same for individuals assigned $Z_i = 1$ or $Z_i = 0$, and thus we can write:

$$\begin{aligned}\mathbb{E}[Y_i(1) - Y_i(0)|D_i(1) > D_i(0)] &= \mathbb{E}[Y_i(1) - Y_i(0)|D_i(1) > D_i(0), Z_i = 1] \\ &= \mathbb{E}[Y_i(1) - Y_i(0)|D_i = 1], \qquad (5.35)\end{aligned}$$

which starts with the LATE, and arrives to the ATT. If one-sided noncompliance were to occur in the other direction, this would rule out never-takers. In this case, we could conduct an analogous process to see that the LATE would inform us of the ATU.

Examples of the case where the LATE provides an ATT exist in many real settings, given that one-sided noncompliance is often observed where treatment can be assigned but not enforced. However, in these settings, it generally *is* enforceable that individuals not assigned to treatment cannot access treatment. One frequently cited example of such a case is Sommer and Zeger (1991), where individuals are randomly assigned to receive vitamin A supplementation, but not all assigned individuals actually received treatment. Another case where an ATT is reported based on imperfect uptake of an experimentally assigned treatment is in Chetty, Hendren, and Katz (2016), who study a housing voucher offered to individuals in which they can move neighborhoods. Similarly, examples exist in which LATE estimates are actually interpreted as ATUs (Oreopoulos [2006]; Angrist, Lavy, and Schlosser [2010], for example). In the case of Oreopoulos (2006) a compulsory schooling law passed in the UK in the 1940s obliged all individuals to study until at least fifteen years of age, and the interest of the study was to understand the effect of studying at least fifteen years on labor market outcomes. Because the reform was compulsory, there was no scope for never-takers (all individuals must study until at least fifteen if they are exposed to the reform), but there is scope for always-takers, as certain individuals would have studied until at least fifteen years of age even without the reform. Thus, Oreopoulos (2006) notes that the LATE returned will provide an ATU (and argues that this will be quite representative of the ATE, given that most of the population were indeed compliers).

5.3.4 Discussions of the (Dis-)Utility of the LATE

Few estimands in applied econometrics generate as much discussion as the LATE. The Local Average Treatment Effect is what is delivered from a binary instrumental variable with heterogeneity provided that monotonicity holds. However, in most cases, this is likely not the quantity that we are specifically interested in estimating for deep theoretical or policy reasons. While the precise nature of the compliers will depend on each IV, conceptually simple quantities such as the ATE or ATT offer potentially quite different estimands, and policy-relevant quantities are likely based on entirely different criteria, such as the impact of the policy on the entire population or the impact on some particular group that is of relevance to target for treatment, or for scaling up treatment.

There is a robust discussion of the utility of the LATE, focusing on (among other things) the relative importance of the (good) internal validity of the estimates under the maintained assumptions, versus the parameter's more questionable use in an external population, or whether the (valid) parameter returned actually identifies a quantity of interest to us as researchers. This discussion has been apparent since early work on LATE. For example, in a comment on Angrist, Imbens, and Rubin's work on LATE in *The Journal of the American Statistical Association*, Heckman (1996a) states:

> LATE is a controversial parameter because it is defined for an unobservable subpopulation. Its use as an evaluation parameter thus is of questionable value.

While subsequent work described above shows that plenty can be learned about this population, it is still true that unlike previously encountered estimands like the ATT, ATE and ATU, we cannot know, even ex post which specific individuals are compliers.

In their rejoinder, Angrist, Imbens, and Rubin (1996b) respond that the focus on the LATE is not due to its particular appeal, but rather because it is what the instrumental variables estimator identifies.

> our focus on the complier average causal effect is not incidental, nor do we view compliers as the only interesting group. Rather, we focus on the average causal effect for compliers because this is the only directly estimable causal effect of the treatment.

This focus on feasibility and the importance of understanding what an estimator *actually* returns has been emphasized in many other settings, including those discussed at more length below.

But perhaps the main focus of critiques of the LATE has been that it requires that we accept a parameter which we may not be looking for (see, for example, the widely cited critiques of Deaton [2009]; Heckman and Urzúa [2010]). The standard practice in econometrics, and indeed, the way that this book has generally been structured, has been to propose an estimand such as an ATT or ATE, and then seek an estimator to return this estimand. However, in the case of the LATE, it is the estimand that is defined after the estimator (and you may note that this Chapter has also proceeded in this manner!).

However, this is not to say that the LATE cannot be a parameter of interest in and of itself. Whether it is depends entirely on the nature of compliers. In cases where an instrument may be drawn from exogenous variation in policy implementation, the LATE is likely to be an especially interesting parameter (Heckman 1997). If instruments are drawn from availability of different policies, the LATE is defined in terms of the response to some policy change for individuals induced to participate in a policy. And these individuals are likely to be precisely the people we would like to learn about. In cases such as this, the LATE is defined as the impact of treatment for some particular group that a policy Z invokes to move into treatment. For example, in a setting studied by Kline and Walters (2016), the question of interest is the effect of an early childhood policy in the US (Head Start) on cognitive outcomes. They note that the LATE estimated from random assignment to the program will capture the effect of treatment on children who are drawn by the random offer to join Head Start centers, moving away from other childcare centers or from no preschool into a preschool program. Because we have relatively little interest in identifying impacts for children who would not change into the program if offered a spot, this parameter is intuitive and appealing.

Later in this book we will return to other quantities estimated based on similar types of models when returning to discuss heterogeneity in more detail (chapter 8). There we will see that we can say far more about such policy-relevant treatment effects (PRTEs) as well as learn about other treatment effects of interest. Nevertheless, regardless of your own opinion of the use of LATE, it is important to understand exactly what is being estimated in these models, given their frequency of appearance in economics papers and the success of the LATE framework as a lens through which we can understand instrumental variables methods.

5.4 Covariates, Multiple IVs, and Continuous IVs

5.4.1 Treatments with Multiple Levels

So far, we have been considering the case where D_i, the endogenous (treatment) variable of interest, is a binary variable. In this case, when we estimate a LATE, although the parameter is "local" to some specific group, it is clear that this parameter refers to the impact of a shift from 0 to 1 in the binary variable D_i. However, how does the interpretation of the LATE change when we consider a multilevel treatment variable (or multilevel endogenous variable more generally)? For example, what if the treatment variable of interest is years of schooling, or total fertility in a family? The response to this question turns out to require thinking not just about *who* the instrument causes to shift behavior, but also about *at what margin* of the endogenous variable the instrument induces shifts.

For example, consider a case where we wish to examine the impact of fertility on child educational outcomes. Here a frequently used instrument is the twin birth instrument. In particular, let's consider a twin birth at birth order 3. This could cause families to move from having had three children without the twin to four children with the twin, but similarly, could also cause higher margin shifts in fertility, for example a family that would have had four births now has five births. In the case of a multileveled treatment variable, as the instrument can cause shifts at multiple margins of the treatment variable, we can no longer talk of a single class of complier.

In cases such as these, Angrist and Imbens (1995) show that the interpretation of the IV estimand can now be conducted in terms of the "Average Causal Response" function, or in terms of the entire shift of the distribution of the endogenous variable of interest caused by receipt of the instrument. To see precisely what this implies, we have to slightly expand our notation. To do so, we will consider a multilevel treatment variable, that is, a D_i which can take multiple values (results for the fully continuous case can be found in Angrist, Graddy, and Imbens [2000]). We will continue assuming that we have a binary IV Z_i. Now, because D_i can take multiple levels, which we will refer to as $j \in 1, \ldots, J$, we have *multiple* potential outcomes, which we will refer to as $Y_i(j)$. For example, $Y_i(1)$ refers to the potential outcome if individual i has $D_i = 1$, and similarly $Y_i(2), Y_i(3), \ldots, Y_i(J)$ refer to potential outcomes at treatment levels $D_i = 2, 3, \ldots, J$. You may note that here, unlike in section 5.2.1, we are omitting the dependence of potential outcomes on Z_i for ease of notation, as we will be maintaining an exclusion restriction implying that the action of Z_i can only be channeled through D_i. Note also that we will follow our previous notation in defining potential outcomes for the endogenous variable of $D_i(1)$ and $D_i(0)$ as the level of the endogenous variable in cases where an individual is exposed to the instrument or not exposed to the instrument, respectively. For each i we will observe only one level of $Y_i(j)$ and either $D_i(0)$ or $D_i(1)$.

Nevertheless, under an independence assumption that states that $D_i(0)$, $D_i(1)$ and all $Y(j)$ are independent of Z_i, and a monotonicity assumption that states that $D_i(1) - D_i(0) \geq 0$ for each individual, Angrist and Imbens (1995) show that the IV estimand with a continuous treatment has a logical parallel to the case with a binary treatment. In particular, they lay out the so-called average causal response (ACR) theorem as follows:

$$\frac{\mathbb{E}[Y_i|Z_i=1]-\mathbb{E}[Y_i|Z_i=0]}{\mathbb{E}[D_i|Z_i=1]-\mathbb{E}[D_i|Z_i=0]}=\sum_{j=1}^{J}\omega_j\mathbb{E}[Y_i(j)-Y_i(j-1)|D_i(1)\geq j>D_i(0)]\equiv\tau_{\text{LATE}}^{\text{Continuous } D}$$

$$\text{where}\quad \omega_j=\frac{\Pr[D_i(1)\geq j>D_i(0)]}{\sum_{j=1}^{J}\Pr[D_i(1)\geq j>D_i(0)]}. \tag{5.36}$$

This notes that we can break down the Wald Estimator (i.e., the IV estimator) into two components for each particular treatment intensity j. A first component is the quantity $\mathbb{E}[Y_i(j)-Y_i(j-1)|D_i(1)\geq j>D_i(0)]$, which is the ACR of moving from level $j-1$ of the treatment to level j. In particular, and in line with the LATE we have observed previously, this ACR will be considered *only* for individuals who are *compliers* for this level of treatment, in the sense that if exposed to the IV, their treatment dose $D_i=D_i(1)\geq j$, while if not exposed to the IV, their treatment dose $D_i=D_i(0)<j$. This is where the average causal response component of the theorem comes from: The IV simply aggregates over the entire average causal response function for all levels of j based on compliers at each level. However, the second component notes that weights will not be evenly assigned, but rather based on the relative importance of compliers at each level of the treatment variable. This is captured by the weighting scheme ω_j. If an IV is more likely to shift compliance at a particular treatment level j, movements of the endogenous variable at this level will be particularly relevant in the estimated parameter $\tau_{\text{LATE}}^{\text{Continuous } D}$ from (5.36).

This result thus suggests that our estimates will be local in two senses. Firstly, estimates will be local to compliers, and secondly, they will be local to the particular points of the distribution over which an IV induces variation. Fortunately, even though $D_i(1)$ and $D_i(0)$ are never observed together, given the assumption of independence, we can estimate $\Pr[D_i(1)\geq j>D_i(0)]$ from data in the same sense that we could estimate compliance previously. Specifically, we can estimate reduced-form models where an indicator equal to 1 if $D_i\geq j$ is regressed on the instrument, and this indicates the likelihood that the instrument induces variation at each point j of the distribution of D_i. These weights can perhaps be illustrated most simply with an example. Consider the case mentioned briefly above, where we wish to estimate the impact of the number of children in a family (a multivalued treatment) on children's educational outcomes. In figure 5.2, we show plots that present the estimated weights assigned to each point of the ACR function corresponding to shifts in fertility induced by a twin birth. These show how twin birth at birth order 3 (a proposed IV, as discussed at more length in section 5.5) shift total completed fertility in a family in a developing country sample (top panel) and in the United States (bottom panel). While in both cases a twin at birth order 3 causes the biggest shift in fertility when considering families exceeding four children, it also has higher-order impacts, up to as much as 9+ births in a developing country sample, while only shifting fertility at lower levels in the United States. Note that here, even using the same instrument, the LATE will be interpreted quite differently depending on the context examined.

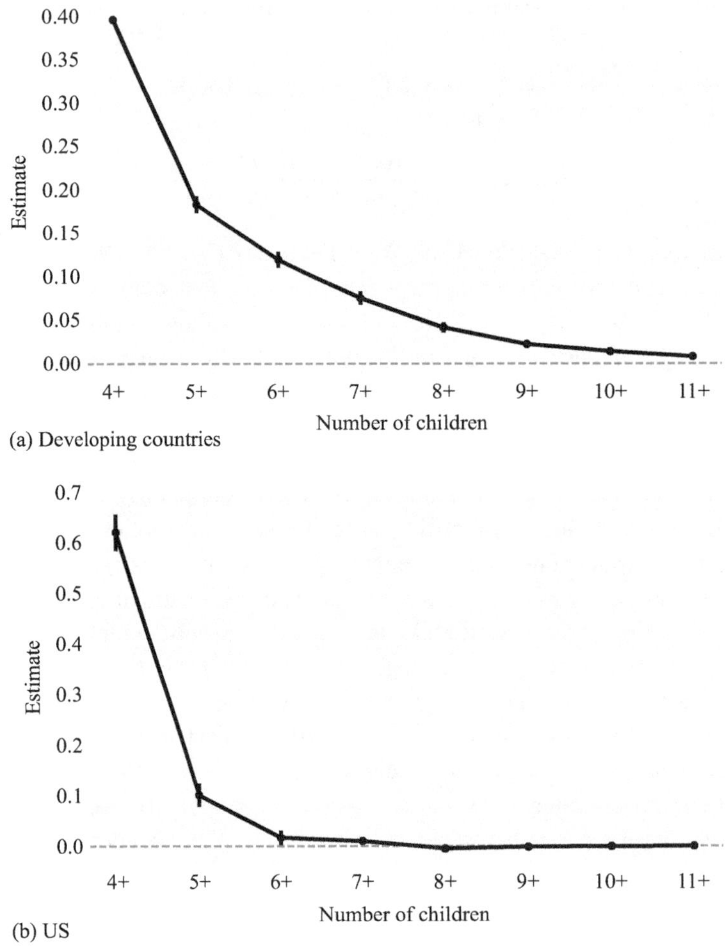

Figure 5.2
Average causal response functions for twin birth.

Code Callout 5.3: Average Causal Response Functions
In code callout 5.3, we consider the estimation of these average causal response functions using data from Bhalotra and Clarke (2020). We estimate curves as presented in figure 5.2 and note how these correspond to weights on LATEs with a continuous treatment as described by ω_j in (5.36).

5.4.2 Instruments with Multiple Levels

A logical counterpoint to the question of how things change when the endogenous variable of interest is multileveled instead of binary, is the question of how things change when the instrument itself is multileveled instead of binary. The LATE theorem laid out above has at its heart a Wald estimator, which is by definition based on a binary IV. Fortunately, the results for multileveled rather than binary IVs are a simple extension to the LATE theorem, and indeed were laid out in the original paper where LATE was defined by Imbens and Angrist (1994).

In that paper, they note that under the same four conditions as laid out above, an IV estimator based on a multileveled IV taking values $\{z_0, z_1, \ldots, z_K\}$ will estimate:

$$\tau_{\text{LATE}}^{\text{Continuous } Z} = \sum_{k=1}^{K} \lambda_k \tau_{z_k, z_{k-1}} \tag{5.37}$$

where $\tau_{z_k, z_{k-1}}$ is a local average treatment effect for compliers when moving from level z_{k-1} to z_k, that is:

$$\mathbb{E}[Y_i(1) - Y_i(0) | D(z_k) = 1, D(z_{k-1}) = 0],$$

and λ_k are a series of weights which are non-negative and sum to 1. Note that here, the monotonicity assumption needs to be stricter, as there are multiple levels of the instrument. Specifically, monotonicity in this case requires that for each value of the instrument, arbitrarily z and w, either $D_i(z) \geq D_i(w)$ or $D_i(z) \leq D_i(w)$ for each individual i.

Thus, with a multivalued IV, we observe that the IV estimate is just a weighted average of LATE estimates when moving across the support of the IV. The weights, denoted λ_k in (5.37) are defined as:

$$\lambda_k = \frac{[\Pr(z_k) - \Pr(z_{k-1})] \cdot \sum_{l=k}^{K} \pi_l \cdot (Z_l - \mathbb{E}[Z]))}{\sum_{m=1}^{K} (\Pr(z_m) - \Pr(z_{m-1})) \cdot \sum_{l=m}^{K} \pi_l \cdot (Z_l - \mathbb{E}[Z])}, \tag{5.38}$$

where $\pi_k = \Pr(Z = Z_k)$. Thus, a specific LATE is given relatively more weight in two circumstances, as can be observed in the numerator of the above fraction. Firstly, and logically, a LATE will be given more weight if a larger proportion of individuals are shifted into compliance precisely at this point, in which case $\Pr(z_k) - \Pr(z_{k-1})$ will be relatively larger. And secondly, and more obscurely, LATEs will receive more or less weight depending on the underlying mechanical variation of Z, as summarized by the second term in the numerator. Among other things, we can see that this weight increases as the realization of Z_l is more common in data, and gives greater weight to realizations of Z_l that are close to the center of the distribution of Z.

5.4.3 What Changes If We Add Controls?

In general, when discussing the LATE, the Wald estimate is considered as a starting point, but, in practice, the assumptions leading to consistency in IV estimates may only hold conditional on covariates. For example, the frequently used twin instrument is thought to require (at least) controls for maternal age, given that the likelihood of a twin birth increases as women become older (Rosenzweig and Wolpin 1980). In practice, this implies that we are replacing the independence assumption (6) with a conditional independence version:

Assumption 6′. Conditional Independence

$$(Y_i(1,1), Y_i(1,0), Y_i(0,1), Y_i(0,0), D_i(1), D_i(0)) \perp\!\!\!\perp Z_i | X_i, \tag{5.39}$$

along with a conditional version of the exclusion restriction, first stage, and monotonocity (see Abadie [2003, assumption 2.1] for a statement of these assumptions). Specifically, we are now simply assuming that *within covariate groups* indicated by X_i, instrumental assignment is independent of potential outcomes, and similarly, the exclusion restriction, first stage, and monotonicity assumption hold. Abadie (2003) notes that this implies that the instrument Z is "as good as randomly assigned" (quotation marks in original) once conditioning on X.

Fortunately, the arguments of LATE also go through when independence assumptions *only* holds conditional on covariates, though nuance and care is required. Specifically, Angrist and Imbens (1995) note that when including a series of covariates X_i in a 2SLS specification, the resulting estimate is simply a weighted average of each group-specific LATE. Specifically, we can start with the basic building block of a group-specific LATE:

$$\tau^{\text{LATE}}(X_i) \equiv \mathbb{E}[Y_i(1) - Y_i(0) | X_i, D_i(1) > D_i(0)]. \tag{5.40}$$

Here X_i refers to a specific combination of levels across all covariates, and we can thus view $\tau^{\text{LATE}}(X_i)$ as describing a single treatment effect for each possible covariate combination. Note that this can be summarized in a design matrix, which is a matrix that generates dummy variables for each level of X_i, thus effectively breaking out X_i into "fully saturated" dummies for each variable.

The result from Angrist and Imbens (1995, theorem 3) is that the estimated parameter from a 2SLS specification, where the fully saturated set of variables is included in the first and second stage, can be written as follows:

$$\tau^{\text{2SLS}}_{\text{LATE}(x)} = \sum_{x \in \mathcal{X}} \tau^{\text{LATE}}(x) \cdot \omega(x), \tag{5.41}$$

where $\mathcal{X}$ refers to all levels of X_i. Thus, 2SLS returns a weighted average of covariate-specific LATEs, where weighting depends upon the function $\omega(x)$. These weights are positive and sum to one, and there are multiple ways to write these weights; see, for example, Angrist and Imbens (1995, theorem 3) and Angrist and Pischke (2009, theorem 4.5.1). However, one way to write the weights is as follows:

$$\omega(x) = \frac{\Pr(X_i = x)\mathbb{V}\left(\widehat{D}_i | X_i = x\right)}{\sum_{x' \in \mathcal{X}} \Pr(X_i = x')\mathbb{V}\left(\widehat{D}_i | X_i = x'\right)}, \tag{5.42}$$

where $\widehat{D}_i$ refers to the first-stage predicted value. We have seen in a number of settings that regression models result in weights that assign more importance to observations with greater underlying variance of the independent variable of interest (e.g., see sections 3.5 and 4.3.2), and (5.42) is no different. In this case, given that key variation is that which is traced from the instrument to the endogenous variable, we see that units with more variation in the first-stage prediction are given more weight in the single-parameter estimate $\tau^{2SLS}_{LATE(x)}$.

This result has been popularized as the "saturate and weight" theorem by Angrist and Pischke (2009), because of the importance of fully saturating the model with a full set of dummies to capture all levels of X_i. In practice, however, in many empirical applications, rather than fully saturating with covariates, covariates may be entered linearly in a model, or using some particular functional forms but without fully saturating the model. Indeed, Blandhol et al. (2022) conducted a systematic review of papers published between 2000 and 2018 in highly visible economic journals that used IV methods. They find that of ninety-nine papers meeting their search criteria and using 2SLS with covariates, only one of these papers consistently estimates a fully saturated model in all specifications. The nature of fully saturated models is demanding, as it implies, firstly, that not only are any categorical variables fully discretized but also, that all possible interactions between such dummies must be included in models. Secondly, the fully saturated model consists of a separate first stage for each level of X, thus, in effect, allowing the instrument to have a heterogeneous effect on the treatment variable of interest for each level of X_i.

What is more, Blandhol et al. (2022) shows that if a functional form is used for X that does *not* actually adequately capture the relationship between covariates and the instrument, this may result in serious problems for the resulting estimand. This can be worrying, and, as the authors show, empirically relevant in real cases. The key requirement that Blandhol et al. (2022) show for a 2SLS specification to actually capture a weighted average of the LATE is that the functional form for X must correctly capture $\mathbb{E}[Z|X=x]$. If, for example, some overly simple linear model is used in which the regression prediction for Z at particular values of X is different to the true value for Z, this will result in undesired results. This result is most clearly documented for IV with a binary treatment and binary instrument, where Blandhol et al. (2022) show that if controls are not adequately captured, the resulting estimate can be conceptualized as a weighted average of both always-takers and compliers, and the weights assigned to always-takers are strictly *negative*. This may be a major concern, especially if always-taker effects are large, as these will be effectively subtracted away from the estimated treatment effect. While Blandhol et al. (2022) fully work this through in cases without binary instruments and treatments, the key takeaway is that for a regression-based implementation of IV estimation, covariates must be entered in a rich enough way for the model to accurately capture the true functional form.

Code Callout 5.4: Fully Saturating a Model with Controls
We will examine the implications of fully saturating a model in IV using data from Duflo, Kiessel, and Lucas (2024) who examine the impact of a number of school-level interventions in Ghana on student achievement, instrumenting intervention uptake with random assignment. We will use controls from Duflo, Kiessel, and Lucas (2024) and see how this "fully saturated" specification works, seeing that it manually approximates the 2SLS estimate as laid out in (5.41).

5.4.4 Multiple IVs

In cases where multiple IVs are available, we have noted previously that 2SLS estimators do not have any mechanical challenges in estimating IV models. What's more, even early work on the LATE theorem suggested that *provided monotonicity holds*, then incorporating multiple instruments into a LATE setup with 2SLS was a perfectly valid strategy. Indeed, in cases with multiple binary instruments, we already have all of the ingredients to understand parameter estimates based on the results we have seen in a setting with an IV with multiple levels in section 5.4.2. There, we noted that when an IV shifts individuals across multiple margins, a two-stage least squares estimator will simply capture a series of weighted LATEs following (5.37).

Note however, that we can "recycle" this result, using the fact that multiple IVs can be re-considered as a series of points of support $\{z_0, z_1, \ldots, z_k\}$. For example, consider a case where we have two IVs, which we can call Z_{1i} and Z_{2i}. If we rewrite $z_i = (Z_{1i}, Z_{i2})$, if these IVs are mutually exclusive, we can see that the points of support to consider are: $z_0 = (0,0)$, $z_1 = (1,0)$ and $z_2 = (0,1)$. Similarly, if the variables are *not* mutually exclusion, we can consider $z_0 = (0,0)$, $z_1 = (1,0)$, $z_2 = (0,1)$, and $z_3 = (1,1)$. Writing the setup in this way makes clear that we can view the multiple IV setting as analogous to the multilevel IV setting, and the result in (5.37) suggests that 2SLS will simply return to us a weighted average of LATE. This result is defined in Imbens and Angrist (1994), and the result is extended to multiple continuous IVs by Angrist and Imbens (1995) in their theorem 2.

While the weighting of each LATE is defined in (5.38) it is particularly informative to see the weighting in a case with two mutually exclusive IVs, as laid out with Z_{i1} and Z_{i2} previously. If we do that, we can start with τ^{2SLS} and substitute in the first-stage equation based on these two instruments, and resolve as follows:

$$\tau^{2SLS} = \frac{\mathbb{C}\text{ov}(Y_i, \widehat{D}_i)}{\mathbb{C}\text{ov}(D_i, \widehat{D}_i)} \tag{5.43}$$

$$= \frac{\mathbb{C}\text{ov}(Y_i, \pi_0 + \pi_1 Z_{i1} + \pi_2 Z_{i2})}{\mathbb{C}\text{ov}(D_i, \widehat{D}_i)} \tag{5.44}$$

$$= \frac{\pi_1 \mathbb{C}\text{ov}(Y_i, Z_{i1})}{\mathbb{C}\text{ov}(D_i, \widehat{D}_i)} + \frac{\pi_2 \mathbb{C}\text{ov}(Y_i, Z_{i2})}{\mathbb{C}\text{ov}(D_i, \widehat{D}_i)} \tag{5.45}$$

$$= \frac{\pi_1 \mathbb{C}\text{ov}(D_i, Z_{i1})}{\mathbb{C}\text{ov}(D_i, \widehat{D}_i)} \frac{\mathbb{C}\text{ov}(Y_i, Z_{i1})}{\mathbb{C}\text{ov}(D_i, Z_{i1})} + \frac{\pi_2 \mathbb{C}\text{ov}(D_i, Z_{i2})}{\mathbb{C}\text{ov}(D_i, \widehat{D}_i)} \frac{\mathbb{C}\text{ov}(Y_i, Z_{i2})}{\mathbb{C}\text{ov}(D_i, Z_{i2})}. \tag{5.46}$$

Initially, (5.44) comes from simply substituting in the first stage, while (5.45) comes from rearranging the covariance in the numerator. Finally, (5.46) is obtained by multiplying and dividing each fraction in (5.45) by a constant term and rearranging.

It may not be apparent yet, but this give us a nice result. In particular, note that $\mathbb{C}\text{ov}(Y_i, Z_{i1})/\mathbb{C}\text{ov}(D_i, Z_{i1})$ in the first term is simply the IV (LATE) estimate based on just Z_{i1}, which we will call $\tau_{\text{LATE}}^{Z_1}$, and similarly, $\mathbb{C}\text{ov}(Y_i, Z_{i2})/\mathbb{C}\text{ov}(D_i, Z_{i2})$ in the second term is the IV estimate based on just Z_{i2}, here $\tau_{\text{LATE}}^{Z_2}$. Thus, we can rewrite (5.46) as:

$$\tau^{2\text{SLS}} = \frac{\pi_1 \mathbb{C}\text{ov}(D_i, Z_{i1})}{\mathbb{C}\text{ov}(D_i, \widehat{D}_i)} \tau_{\text{LATE}}^{Z_1} + \frac{\pi_2 \mathbb{C}\text{ov}(D_i, Z_{i2})}{\mathbb{C}\text{ov}(D_i, \widehat{D}_i)} \tau_{\text{LATE}}^{Z_2} \tag{5.47}$$

$$= \lambda_1 \tau_{\text{LATE}}^{Z_1} + \lambda_2 \tau_{\text{LATE}}^{Z_2}, \tag{5.48}$$

where λ_1 and λ_2 are simply weighting terms. This shows that 2SLS based on two instruments is just a weighted average of each individual LATE. What's more, we may note that the numerator of each weighting term sums to produce the denominator given that $\mathbb{C}\text{ov}(D_i, \widehat{D}_i) = \pi_1 \mathbb{C}\text{ov}(D_i, Z_{i1}) + \pi_2 \mathbb{C}\text{ov}(D_i, Z_{i2})$. Thus, we can see that these weights sum to one, with relatively larger weights assigned to a particular instrument-specific LATE when either (a) this instrument shifts more individuals into compliance (π_k is larger), or (b) where the variance of the instrument is larger, explaining relatively more of the variation in D_i. It turns out that this is exactly the same result that we had arrived to previously in (5.38) when discussing the weighting function in multivalued IVs, however here perhaps providing an even more intuitive way to see the weights.

While this is useful, it is important to remember that this result relies on a monotonicity assumption that states that there is a strict ordering for each combination of IVs. While this may be well-suited to the continuous or multileveled discrete IV case where higher values correspond to higher "doses" of an instrument, it is less clear-cut in the multiple IV case. This is a fact emphasized by Mogstad, Torgovitsky, and Walters (2021), who point out that the required assumptions of monotonicity may be quite restrictive here, and actually imply a form of homogeneity that is highly undesired. If we consider the case of two binary IVs Z_{i1} and Z_{i2}, with the ordering of $z_0 = (0,0)$, $z_1 = (1,0)$, $z_2 = (0,1)$, and $z_3 = (1,1)$, monotonicity implies that $D_i(z_0) \leq D_i(z_1) \leq D_i(z_2) \leq D_i(z_3)$ for all i. In particular, the ordering $D_i(z_1) \leq D_i(z_2)$ suggests a homogeneity in which a particular instrument universally is more convincing than some other. Mogstad, Torgovitsky, and Walters (2021) discuss a particular example in which college attendance is instrumented with proximity to a college, as well as tuition subsidies. Monotonicity in this case means that *all* individuals must either be more influenced by tuition than by proximity (or vice versa), which they note is an assumption related to homogeneous choice behavior. They suggest that one could adopt a weaker version of monotonicity to consider *only* shifts of one IV holding other IVs constant, which effectively rules out assumptions about ordering of $D_i(z_1)$ and $D_i(z_2)$ above. They call this assumption partial monotonicity and note that if instruments are positively correlated, 2SLS will still return a positively weighted average of causal effects on compliers, but need not do so if instruments are negatively correlated.

5.5 Testing IV Assumptions

We have previously laid out five central assumptions related to IV, namely SUTVA plus assumptions 6–9. Independently of *what* parameter an IV estimator returns to us, if we are to believe that estimates based on instrumental variables return to us any causal parameter, it is fundamental that we consider these assumptions and what we can say about each.

Some of these assumptions can be formally tested, others can be falsified, but not proven definitively, and others cannot be formally tested at all, instead requiring substantive knowledge on our part as researchers. In general, carefully considering the nature of assumptions in any particular setting will be as, if not more, important than considering the estimate itself. While there has been substantial developments since, Angrist, Imbens, and Rubin (1996a) discuss the nature of assumptions, note the implications of these assumptions breaking down, and provide an assessment for a specific empirical example. We discuss the testing of these assumptions below.

5.5.1 First Stage

A logical place to start is with the "first stage" of a 2SLS estimator, or the assumption of relevance. Because the relevance assumption is entirely related to observable quantities, it can be formally tested, and there are rich guidelines on empirical practice, which we discuss here. In essence, in the case of a single binary instrument, we simply require that:

$$\Pr(D_i = 1|Z_i = 1) \neq \Pr(D_i = 1|Z_i = 0),$$

which is testable. This can be easily tested directly in the first-stage regression (5.19) itself, which has the added benefit that it can seamlessly work for both binary and continuous instrumental variables.

A test of relevance in this single IV case is just a test that $\pi_1 \neq 0$ from the first-stage regression. However, it turns out that more nuance is required in this statement, and that this first stage test also has implications for our confidence in the IV results themselves. The reason for this owes to the bias in IV models. As we alluded to in section 5.2.4.2, IV estimators are consistent, but in finite samples they may be substantially biased. All else constant, this bias is worse when the first stage is weak, and when more IVs are present. Thus, generally, rather than *just* being concerned about relevance, we need to ensure that instruments are sufficiently strong so that estimates are not likely to suffer from substantial bias. For this reason, tests of the first stage will focus both on whether relevance holds (i.e., whether our IV estimator is even identified) as well as whether we can rule out problems related to weak instruments.

Generically, it is important to consider tests in settings where we may have (potentially) multiple variables of interest and multiple IVs, and as such, both tests of relevance (or "under-identification" tests) and tests of instrument strength (or "weak instrument" tests) are based on two-stage estimators such as 2SLS. Thus, commonly, the model is written as:

$$Y_i = \boldsymbol{D}_i'\boldsymbol{\tau} + \boldsymbol{X}_i'\boldsymbol{\beta} + \varepsilon_i \tag{5.49}$$

$$\boldsymbol{D}_i' = \boldsymbol{Z}_i'\boldsymbol{\pi} + \boldsymbol{X}_i'\boldsymbol{\gamma} + \boldsymbol{V}_i', \tag{5.50}$$

where (5.49) is a structural equation of interest relating a scalar outcome Y_i to a $p \times 1$ vector of endogenous treatment variables $\boldsymbol{D}_i$, and an $r \times 1$ vector of controls $\boldsymbol{X}_i$. A $k \times 1$ vector of instruments is available, written $\boldsymbol{Z}_i$, and these are used in a series of first-stage equations (5.50). There are thus p first-stage equations, each containing the k instrumental variables $\boldsymbol{Z}_i$ along with the same controls as the structural equation and a stochastic error. While this includes the setting a of single treatment variable and single IV as a simple limiting case (in which case (5.50) will be a single first stage with a single instrument and corresponding coefficient π_1), it allows more complex cases too.

5.5.1.1 Tests of under-identification Identification in this case requires, firstly, that there are at least as many instruments as there are endogenous variables—that is, $k \geq p$. If this identification condition is not met (i.e., $k < p$), we refer to under-identification, rather than just identification ($k = p$) or over-identification ($k > p$). However, additionally we require that each IV must explain some relevant independent variation in endogenous variables, and each endogenous variable must draw some independent variation from the IVs. This amounts to a rank test on the $k \times p$ matrix of first-stage coefficients $\boldsymbol{\pi}$. If the rank of this matrix is less than k, this implies that the instruments do not generate independent variation in all of the endogenous variables of interest. In the case that there is a single IV and single endogenous variable, this simply collapses to a test that $\pi_1 \neq 0$.

Thus, tests of under-identification are tests of whether the matrix $\widehat{\boldsymbol{\pi}}$ is of rank k (known as "full rank"). Tests of the rank of a matrix were developed by T. W. Anderson (1951) and are presented in terms of under-identification in an IV setting by Cragg and Donald (1993). Both the tests of T. W. Anderson (1951) and Cragg and Donald (1993) are based on the assumption of independent and identically distributed errors, while heteroscedasticity- and cluster-robust versions were developed by Kleibergen and Paap (2006). These tests are reported as standard in most econometric implementations of instrumental variable regression and are based on the null that the matrix is not full rank. Thus, if the null is not rejected, this suggests that instruments do not pass the relevance condition we require. While these tests are all appropriate for cases with multiple endogenous variables, in special cases where a single endogenous variable is considered, they are equivalent to estimating the first stage by OLS, and conducting joint tests of significance of the instruments with a standard OLS variance estimator (in the case of Cragg and Donald [1993]), or heteroscedasticity- or cluster-robust variance estimator (Kleibergen and Paap 2006).

5.5.1.2 Weak instrument tests and weak-IV robust inference Even if under-identification tests can be rejected, this does not necessarily mean that instruments will deliver trustworthy parameter estimates. Additionally, weak instrument tests need to be passed, and weak-IV robust inference to be considered. There is a substantial literature on the considerations of weak IVs and their implications, and here just a number of key points will be laid out. For a recent much more comprehensive summary, the review papers of Andrews, Stock, and Sun (2019) and Keane and Neal (2023) are a valuable source.

As discussed previously, if instruments are weak, this can result in substantial bias (Staiger and Stock 1997), even with very large samples when multiple instruments are used (Bound, Jaeger, and Baker 1995). While, in general, we have been considering cases with a single IV and many IVs may not feel like a major concern, there are cases, such as the fully saturated model discussed in section 5.4.3 in which the instrument is interacted with each and every control combination, and hence where multiple instruments will be used in practice. Staiger and Stock (1997) show that weak instruments can result in both bias in estimated parameters $\widehat{\boldsymbol{\tau}}$ from (5.49) in the direction of OLS estimates, as well as confidence intervals for $\boldsymbol{\tau}$ that are too narrow, suggesting overrejection of null hypotheses.

A standard solution is to test whether instruments are weak. If instruments are observed to be "too" weak, then we can conclude that any resulting parameter estimated from these IVs will be 'too biased', and confidence intervals too narrow, for these IVs to be reasonable candidates. Staiger and Stock (1997) derive tests for such a circumstance, leading to the well-known rule of thumb that in the case of a single endogenous variable, instruments should be deemed weak if the first-stage F-test of joint significance of the instruments produces an F-statistic less than 10. This rule of thumb is based on the idea that instruments should only be considered if the relative bias of IV estimates is some small proportion (say 10 percent) of the bias of OLS estimates. Stock and Yogo (2005) provide a full set of tabulations showing that this $F = 10$ rule of thumb is very much just an approximation.[6] Stock and Yogo (2005) document two tests and provide critical values for the first-stage F-statistic for each. A first type of test considers the maximal relative bias that IV can have compared to OLS. A second test considers the maximum rate of overrejection of null hypotheses. In these latter tests, they show that with a single endogenous variable and a single IV, if we wish to ensure that a hypothesis test related to τ at the 5 percent level actually rejects "only" 10% of null hypotheses incorrectly, we would require a first-stage F-statistics of 16.38, with these values growing considerably as the number of IVs grows. These tests are widely reported with statistical software, but they rely on homoscedastic error terms. In cases where errors are not assumed homoscedastic, Montiel Olea and Pflueger (2013) provide a robust testing option if a single endogenous variable is considered, and this is recommended as a go-to test.

While testing for weak instruments provides one way forward and should be viewed as a required test when IV is used in practice, Andrews, Stock, and Sun (2019, §4.3) note that if IVs are discarded when minimum F-statistics are not observed, this introduces bias in published estimates. A long-standing solution to this issue is to instead conduct weak-IV robust inference on parameters and implement tests that provide valid (i.e., wider) confidence intervals and rejection rates even in the presence of weak IVs. Anderson and Rubin (1949) provide one such procedure that is efficient in just-identified cases. To see this, we will consider the just-identified version of (5.49)–(5.50) where $k=p=1$ and, for simplicity, assume other controls are not required:

$$Y_i = \tau D_i + \varepsilon_i \tag{5.51}$$

$$D_i = \pi Z_i + V_i. \tag{5.52}$$

Our interest in IV methods is the parameter τ. The idea of Anderson and Rubin's test procedure is that rather than conducting tests about τ in (5.51) by using 2SLS and a t-test that is subject to bias and problems with standard errors if instruments are weak, we can seek alternatives tests that are robust to weak instruments. Specifically, they note that the reduced form regression of Y_i on Z_i can be written as follows, which simply comes from substituting (5.52) into (5.51):

$$\begin{aligned} Y_i &= \tau\pi Z_i + (\tau V_i + \varepsilon_i) \\ &= \xi Z_i + \upsilon_i. \end{aligned}$$

The final equality simply rewrites $\tau\pi \equiv \xi$ and $(\tau V_i + \varepsilon_i) \equiv \upsilon_i$. Noting that instrumental relevance implies that $\pi_1 \neq 0$ and independence rules out correlations between the instrument and the compound error term υ_i, this implies that a direct test for the hypotheses $H_0 : \tau = 0$ is the test $H_0 : \xi = 0$. Thus, the Anderson-Rubin test consists of estimating the reduced form regression and conducting a joint F-test of the coefficients on all instruments. As such, the parameter $\widehat{\tau}$ is viewed as significant if Z_i is significant in the reduced form regression. This can also be viewed in terms of the exclusion restriction: If the exclusion restriction holds and if Z_i is found to be significant in the first stage, this *must* be because of the relationship between D_i and Y_i. Because this test does not rely on the correlation between Z_i and D_i, it is robust to weak IVs.

This test can generalized to cases where τ is hypothesized to be some other nonzero value, τ_0 by simply implementing the regression of $Y - D_i\tau_0$ on Z_i (see, e.g., Chernozhukov and Hansen [2008]). Tests for overidentified settings have been proposed in a number of places, such as by Kleibergen (2002) and Moreira (2003), with relevant discussion in Andrews, Stock, and Sun (2019). What's more, these tests also suggest how one can arrive at valid confidence intervals on a parameter even in cases of weak IV. This can be done by test inversion, which consists of building a confidence interval from all values of τ_0 that cannot be rejected in null hypotheses. The robustness of these tests to weak instruments makes them ideal candidates for inference in this setting (Keane and Neal 2023; Andrews, Stock, and Sun 2019) rather than using t-tests following 2SLS with instruments found to have strong first stages, which are more commonly implemented. Lee et al. (2022) have documented that in the case where t-tests are used following weak instrument F-tests, alternative procedures can be employed that adjust confidence intervals for second-stage t-statistics based on the strength of first-stage F statistics, which they refer to as a tF procedure. These confidence intervals are shown to be substantially wider, pointing to the importance of either proceeding with weak instrument robust confidence intervals or adjustments of this style.

5.5.2 Independence

5.5.2.1 Arguments for and against independence The assumption of validity requires that potential outcomes are independent of the instrument. Unlike the first stage where we can observe whether the assumption is met given that all relevant quantities are observable, we cannot observe counterfactual potential outcomes for each unit and, as such, cannot directly observe whether validity holds.

Given the central importance of validity in identification, discussions of instruments require clear arguments of why an instrument may be related to a treatment variable of interest but, at the same time, *not* related to potential outcomes themselves. In the case of randomized assignment, or other randomization-based designs like IVs based on random assignment to judges (Frandsen, Lefgren, and Leslie 2023; Chyn, Frandsen, and Leslie, Forthcoming), such validity is credibly related to random assignment. However, in other settings, substantial discussion about validity occurs both within papers proposing IVs as well as papers discussing potential concerns or falsification tests.

A challenge with the proposition of an IV is that validity cannot be proven, but it can be disproven (a formal test of this will be discussed later in this chapter). At times, this can be seen within developments over time within literatures. For example, proposals to use season of birth to instrument school attainment (Angrist and Krueger 1991) were later questioned owing to selection into birth month based on parental characteristics (Buckles and Hungerman 2013). Similarly, proposals to use sex mix of the first children (Angrist and Evans 1998) or the birth of twins (Rosenzweig and Wolpin 1980) to instrument fertility are sensitive to nonrandom assignment of child gender (Dahl and Moretti 2008) and selective survival of twins during gestation Bhalotra and Clarke (2020). In general, such arguments are ad hoc to specific instruments, and as such, it is useful to consider what types of patterns may be problematic for any particular IV and whether specific falsification tests can be conducted. A nice example of a paper that considers both the identification requirements and falsification tests is Goldsmith-Pinkham, Sorkin, and Swift (2020), who discuss Bartik, or shift-share instruments, and the conditions under which they work and can be partially tested.

5.5.2.2 A formal test of instrumental validity While typically, IV validity is argued in terms of substantive knowledge, as discussed above, formal tests of IV validity *have* recently been developed. In particular, Kitagawa (2015) shows that in cases where a single binary instrumental variable Z_i is available, IV validity can be tested formally, where IV validity refers to the three assumptions of independence, the exclusion restriction, and monotonicity. Kitagawa (2015) defines a formal test that, if rejected, implies the rejection of IV validity.

For a full definition of the test, see Kitagawa (2015), but in essence the test is based on the distributional results laid out in Imbens and Rubin (1997b) discussed in section 5.3.2.3. If we refer to (5.31) and (5.32), we may remember that under the assumption of IV validity, the distribution of outcomes for the compliers can be written in terms of the difference between two observable distributions. In the case of treated outcomes, this is the difference between the distribution of outcomes for units with $Z_i = 1$ and $D_i = 1$ and the distribution of outcomes for units with $Z_i = 0$ and $D_i = 1$. Kitagawa (2015) notes that for all points B that are contained in Y_i, these results can be written as follows:

$$\Pr(Y_i \in B, D_i = 1|Z_i = 1) - \Pr(Y_i \in B, D_i = 1|Z_i = 0) = \Pr(Y_i(1) \in B|D_i(1) \geq D_i(0)) \tag{5.53}$$

$$\Pr(Y_i \in B, D_i = 0|Z_i = 0) - \Pr(Y_i \in B, D_i = 0|Z_i = 1) = \Pr(Y_i(0) \in B|D_i(1) \geq D_i(0)). \tag{5.54}$$

The key point here is that the quantities on the left-hand side of each equality in (5.53) and (5.53) are observable, and the quantities on the right-hand side of each equality are densities and, hence, must be greater than or equal to 0. This implies that the following inequality holds for all points B in the distribution of Y_i, which is a point also noted in Balke and Pearl (1997):

$$\Pr(Y_i \in B, D_i = 1|Z_i = 1) \geq \Pr(Y_i \in B, D_i = 1|Z_i = 0) \tag{5.55}$$

$$\Pr(Y_i \in B, D_i = 0|Z_i = 0) \geq \Pr(Y_i \in B, D_i = 0|Z_i = 1). \tag{5.56}$$

Kitagawa (2015) provides a formal test that examines whether the conditions in (5.55)–(5.56) hold. While in practice the test is based formally on the equality of distributions that can be tested using a Kolmogorov-Smirnov test statistic descriptively, the test considers whether the conditional distribution on the left-hand side of each equation in (5.55)–(5.56) envelopes the conditional distribution on the right-hand side. Thus, graphically, one would not reject IV validity if distributions looked like those presented in panels (a) and (b) of figure 5.3, while one would reject IV validity if the distributions crossed, as laid out in panels (c) and (d). We can see that in the bottom case, subtracting one distribution from

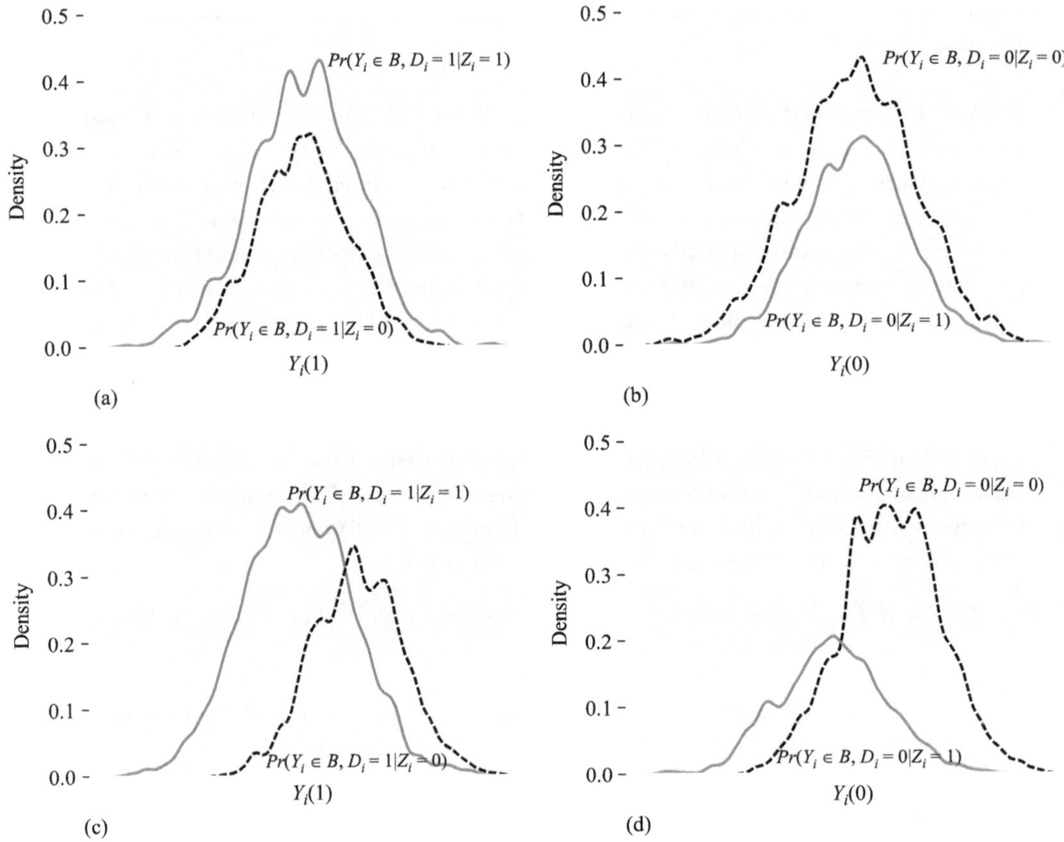

Figure 5.3
Testing for instrumental validity (Kitagawa 2015). (a) treated outcomes (validity not rejected). (b) control outcomes (validity not rejected). (c) treated outcomes (validity rejected) (d) control outcomes (validity rejected).
Note: Plotted distributions in each subplot are conditional on $Z_i = 1$ and $Z_i = 0$, for $D_i = 1$ (left-hand side) or $D_i = 0$ (right-hand side). Thus, summing the area under both curves on each plot integrates to 1 ($f_{Y(1)}(y)$ at left, and ($f_{Y(0)}(y)$) at right).

the other will result in a probability that becomes negative at certain points of the potential outcome distribution, which is inconsistent with the idea of probabilities.

The test laid out in Kitagawa (2015) provides a formal way to examine IV validity, though the logic has been laid out previously, for example by Imbens and Rubin (1997b) who discuss that negativity of complier distributions they estimate in practice may owe to violations of the exclusion restriction (or independence or monotonicity). Similar results have been laid out in terms of partial identification in Balke and Pearl (1997), leading to related tests such as that proposed by Huber and Mellace (2015).

5.5.3 The Exclusion Restriction

Considerations of the exclusion restriction are quite separate to considerations of instrumental independence, even though both are required for instrumental validity. Indeed, even in settings where instruments are randomly assigned (and hence clearly independent of potential outcomes), the exclusion restriction can be violated if the instrument itself in some way shapes outcomes. Regardless of the setting, considerations of the exclusion restriction require careful thought about whether such channels exist.

This distinction is particularly clear in cases where random assignment occurs. For example, Angrist, Imbens, and Rubin (1996a) discuss the case of draft numbers drawn by lottery that impact the likelihood that an individual is drafted. In a study that seeks to identify the effect of military service on later-life economic outcomes, such draft numbers based on random lotteries are clearly independent from unobserved potential outcomes. However, Angrist, Imbens, and Rubin point out that individuals who draw numbers that make them more likely to be drafted may stay in formal education to avoid being drafted, which will have its own effect on economic outcomes.

Considerations of the exclusion restriction require thinking carefully about outcomes, the treatment variable of instruments, and the IV itself. One such illustration is the work of Sarsons (2015) based on the proposal of using rainfall as an IV for income shocks in a study of how conflict depends on income shocks. While rainfall is potentially unrelated to potential outcomes, Sarsons (2015) documents that rainfall is observed to correlate as highly with conflict in areas downstream from dams (in which rainfall has small affects on income) as those upstream from dams (in which rainfall more strongly affects income). Such a pattern is problematic if rainfall can only affect conflict through income, as such patterns suggest that something else must be driving this relationship. A more general point here is that to believe an exclusion restriction, the IV must *not* be linked with other relevant outcomes. In the case of weather IVs like those discussed by Sarsons (2015), later work has made clear that there are substantial concerns about the exclusion restriction in particular, with a literature survey finding 194 outcomes linked to weather-based IVs (Mellon 2024), which is inconsistent with an exclusion restriction holding in any one case.

5.5.4 Monotonicity

Finally, monotonicity rules out the presence of defiers. If monotonicity does not hold, rather than identifying a LATE, IV estimation captures a weighted average of treatment effects on compliers and defiers, with the weight on defiers being *negative*. Specifically, Angrist, Imbens, and Rubin (1996a) show that with defiers that Wald estimate captures:

$$(1+\lambda)\mathbb{E}[Y_i(1)-Y_i(0)|D_i(1)-D_i(0)=1]+\lambda\mathbb{E}[Y_i(1)-Y_i(0)|D_i(1)-D_i(0)=-1]$$

with $\lambda = \Pr(\mathit{Defier})/[\Pr(\mathit{Complier}) - \Pr(\mathit{Defier})]$. Thus, violations of monotonicity are concerning, specifically if substantial defiance is suspected, or if compliance rates are low.

Note, however, that if the causal effect $Y_i(1) - Y_i(0)$ is identical for compliers and defiers, the presence of compliers will not complicate estimates.

Tests of monotonicity exist for cases where treatments are multivalued, as in this case, the cdf of outcomes Y_i for individuals with $Z_i = 1$ should be weakly greater than the cdf for individuals with $Z_i = 0$ at all points of support of the treatment (Angrist and Imbens 1995). In cases with binary treatments, while no tests of monotonicity alone exist, the test of Kitagawa (2015) discussed previously, as well as tests described by Huber and Mellace (2015) and Mourifié and Wan (2017) are tests of monotoncity, independence, and exclusion together. Discussion of cases where defiance is unlikely to hold is available in Chaisemartin (2017), who additionally proposes alternative assumptions and estimation strategies for cases where concerns exist about the presence of defiers.

Historical Context and Selected Further Reading

Instrumental variables have a long history in economics, indeed far predating the emergence of the Rubin Causal Model laid out in chapter 1. The earliest developments of IV were propelled by challenges in estimating elasticities despite simultaneous movements in demand and supply curves. The genesis of such strategies as a solution to problems of identification has been traced to a particular technical work *The Tariff on Animal and Vegetable Oils* (Wright 1928). Interesting discussions of the history, authorship, and key precursors to this work are discussed in (among various other places) Stock and Trebbi (2003) and Angrist and Krueger (2001). The early emergence of these methods as possible routes to identification in observational settings has meant a considerable adoption in the economic literature even in advance of many of the other methods discussed in this text up to this point (Currie, Kleven, and Zwiers 2020, refer to the online appendix).

More recently, the fundamental papers identifying LATE are very nicely written, and Angrist, Imbens, and Rubin (1996a) is absolutely recommended reading in this regard. This paper was published in the *Journal of the American Statistical Association* along with a series of comments that provide a very interesting view on the takes regarding the paper at the time.

This chapter has focused on heterogeneous treatment effects, though many classic econometrics texts provide a rigorous discussion of IV estimation and inference where effects are assumed to be constant (see, among others, Bruce Hansen [2022]). Such texts also lay out the benefit of alternative estimation methods such as limited information maximum likelihood, which is not discussed here but is particularly useful in settings with weak instruments or small samples.

Exercises

1. In this question, you will work with the data from Thornton (2008). In this paper the author studies an experiment in which individuals were randomly assigned monetary incentives to learn their HIV status after being tested, as well as their behavior following learning their HIV status. The data `Thornton_2008.csv` contains a measure of whether an individual was randomly assigned an incentive (`any`), their decision of whether or not to learn their HIV status (`got`), and their decision of whether or not to purchase condoms `anycond`.
   (a) Estimate the most simple first stage in which an individual's decision to get their results is regressed on their incentive assignment. What does this suggest about the first stage?
   (b) Now estimate the reduced form and the IV model where the outcome is an individual's decision of whether or not to purchase condoms. Show that the IV model can also be constructed using indirect least squares.
   (c) What does the first-stage regression suggest about compliance rates in this setting? What do the compliers look like in terms of their characteristics? Answer this question using the ideas of Abadie's Kappa and variables such as age, education, and distance from the results center (`age`,`educ2004` and `distvct`).
   (d) Thornton (2008) shows important heterogeneity by whether or not individuals learn that they are HIV positive. Implement a 2SLS model with two endogenous variables *GotResults* and *GotResults* × *HIVpositive*, which allow for differential responses by an individual's HIV status, with similar interactions for the instruments. Discuss the IV assumptions here, providing the results of any tests to provide partial support for these.
2. In this question we will consider the data from Lochner and Moretti (2015), who implement an IV strategy studying the impact of educational attainment (`educ`) on the likelihood of being in prison (`prison`). In their paper educational attainment is instrumented by a series of compulsory schooling laws (`ca9`, `ca10` and `ca11`) for compulsory attendance at different levels. These data are available as `Lochner_Moretti_2015.csv`.
   (a) Estimate a model like that presented in column 2 of the top panel of the authors' table 1, where education is instrumented with compulsory schooling, but here using only the variable `ca11`. Ensure that you additionally include state, year, age and birth place fixed effects (`state`, `year`, `rage` and `birthpl`).
   (b) Educational attainment is not a binary variable. How should we interpret the LATE in this setting?

(c) Estimate the average causal response curve that underlies this instrument, and plot the result.

(d) Now repeat the analysis above, but using reforms to compulsory schooling at age ten as an IV (`ca10`). Comment on the differences between results in part (c) and (d).

(e) Seek to implement the test related to monotonicity discussed by Angrist and Imbens (1995) using the reform to compulsory schooling up to the age of eleven. Comment on the results.

3. In this question we will work with an IV that is not binary. Specifically, we will work with data from Riaño and Valencia Caicedo (2024), who study the impact of historical exposure to conflict in Laos on long-term development, as measured by night light intensity (`Lights`). The data `Riaño_ValenciaCaicedo_2024.csv` contains the information used in the IV analysis of their paper. They propose a number of continuous IVs to instrument the intensity of bombing (`log_bombs`) during the US "Secret War" of the 1960s–1970s.

   (a) Estimate the main specifications in panel A of table 6 in which the distance to unmapped parts of the Ho Chi Min Trail and distance to the closest historical air base (`dist_nearest_hochi`,`dist_nearest_base`) are used to instrument bombing intensity. Note that this specification requires a series of location controls (`inside_x`, `inside_y`, `dist_dmz`, `dist_vnm_border`, `dist_popcenter`), geographic controls (`avgalt`, `avgtemp`, `avgprec`), and year-fixed effects (`year`).

   (b) Discretize the endogenous variable (exposed to bombing above the median level) and re-estimate the model using this "high-intensity" dummy as the endogenous variable of interest, with only the `dist_nearest_hochi` IV. Explain how the interpretation differs between the coefficients from part (a) and here.

   (c) Now generate a categorical IV where rather than using `dist_nearest_hochi`, the distance rounded to the nearest one hundred units is used. Reestimate the IV model. In order to understand this model, estimate the weights from (5.38). Which units are given the most weight in the resulting IV estimate?

   (d) Comment on the strength of the first stage using tests such as Montiel Olea and Pflueger (2013). Can we conclude that there is likely to be substantial bias?

   (e) Compare the confidence intervals of your IV estimate with confidence sets from weak-instrument-robust procedures such as Anderson and Rubin (1949). Are these results surprising given your results from (d)?

4. In this question we will work with a quite frequently examined setting in which educational attendance is instrumented by proximity to a college. In particular, we will work with the data documented in Card (1995) which consists of 3,010 observations,

consisting of an individuals log(wage), their total years of education, and whether they live close to a two-year of four-year college (`lwage`, `educ`, `nearc2`, and `nearc4`, respectively). These data, which also include a number of covariates, are provided as `Card_2005.csv`.

(a) Estimate a simple IV model by 2SLS without covariates in which log(wage) is regressed on education and education is instrumented by the binary variables `nearc2` and `nearc4`.

(b) Show that the point estimate from this regression can be replicated by regressing log(wage) on $\widehat{\text{educ}}_i$, where $\widehat{\text{educ}}_i = \widehat{\pi}_0 + \widehat{\pi}_1 \text{nearc2}_i + \widehat{\pi}_2 \text{nearc4}_i$. Discuss why the point estimate in models estimated in parts (a) and (b) are equal but the standard errors are not. If you would like an advanced challenge, seek to replicate the standard errors presented in part (a) manually.

(c) Estimate an IV regression with each instrument separately. Show that you can exactly replicate the 2SLS estimate from part (b) by weighting each estimate as described in (5.47).

(d) Document the compliance rates of these two instruments and discuss what this may imply about the compliers in each case laid out in (c).

(e) How can you replicate the result in part (c) when controls are also included? Seek to do so including a full set of controls. *Hint:* If you wish to calculate quantities such as $\mathbb{C}\text{ov}(D_i, Z_{i1})$ conditional on controls, you can do so by first regressing each variable on the controls and then taking the regression residual of each variable $\tilde{D}_i$ and $\tilde{Z}_{i1}$, and calculate $\mathbb{C}\text{ov}(\tilde{D}_i, \tilde{Z}_{i1})$.

(f) Discuss the assumptions of IV and whether you believe they are met in this case. You may wish to support your answer with readings and (in certain cases) formal tests.

5. In this question we will consider some simulated data that allows us to explore compliers, treatment effects, and the IV estimate, as well as estimating the distribution of $Y_i(1)$ and $Y_i(0)$ for compliers using results from Imbens and Rubin (1997b). To do so, we will simulate 1,000 observations for which:

$$Y_i(0) = 5 + 0.5\theta_i + \varepsilon_i \qquad \text{and} \qquad Y_i(1) = 6 + 2\theta_i + \varepsilon_i,$$

where $\theta_i \sim \mathcal{N}(0, 1)$, and $\varepsilon_i \sim \mathcal{N}(0, 1)$. Imagine that θ_i were unobserved, but that treatment takeup correlated with θ_i in the sense that individuals with $\theta_i > 0.5$ were compliers, while individuals with $\theta_i \leq 0.5$ were randomly split into always-takers and never-takers with 50 percent probability. Finally imagine that treatment assignment Z_i is randomly assigned $Z_i \sim \text{Bernoulli}(0.5)$.

(a) Simulate these data, and assign an individual's observed treatment status D_i as 1 if individuals are always-takers, Z_i if individuals are compliers, and 0 if individuals are never-takers. Also define observed outcomes as $Y_i = Y_i(0) + D_i(Y_i(1) - Y_i(0))$. Estimate the treatment effect by regressing Y_i on D_i. Does this recover the ATE? Why or why not?

(b) Why is Z_i a valid IV in this setting? Estimate the LATE using IV, the Wald Estimator, or 2SLS, and show that this is very close to the true treatment effect $\tau_i = Y_i(1) - Y_i(0)$ among compliers.

(c) Show that we can estimate complier means of $Y_i(1)$ and $Y_i(0)$ applying the formulae in (5.33) and (5.34) using only information that is observed as Y_i, D_i, Z_i. Show that in this case where we have simulated $Y_i(1)$, and so can also observe the quantities $E[Y_i(1)|D_i(1) > D_i(0)]$ (and similarly with $Y_i(0)$), our estimated values line up with these quantities.

(d) Finally, use the results from (5.31) and (5.32) to show that we can indeed approximate the entire distribution of $Y_i(1)$ and $Y_i(0)$ among compliers and that these agree with the actual distributions simulated in data. Note that here the estimated distributions may be slightly negative at certain points, but what is key is showing that this closely approximates the actual complier distributions from simulated data.

6

Estimation with Local Manipulations II: Regression Discontinuity Designs

> A line so delicate a sparrow might have
> picked it up in its beak.
>
> Not an artist's line, or a line of writing.
>
> A line between birth and non-being.
> —Moniza Alvi, *The Line*

6.1 Introduction

In the previous chapter, we encountered one way of identifying local treatment effects. We have seen that even without assuming unconfoundedness globally, provided that some form of random variation generated shifts in treatment probabilities, we could estimate a parameter local to some particular group. The idea of local identification to resolve issues with global identification is also seen in regression discontinuity and related designs, which we will turn to now. In this case, the local nature of the estimator will be even more apparent. Regression discontinuity designs (RDDs) are based on treatment assignment rules, which can be viewed as essentially random at some particular jump point.

For example, if we were interested in examining the effect of different types of politicians on the outcomes in their constituencies, we would be very hard-pressed to make the claim that politicians are randomly assigned to localities, given that they are explicitly chosen (elected) by constituents! However, we may be willing to assume that there is nothing particularly special about a politician gaining one vote more or one vote fewer. But if this additional vote comes exactly at the 50% vote margin in many democratic systems, the politician will be elected and the constituency will be exposed to this politician rather than their competitor.

Such local unconfoundedness-type assumptions are at the heart of the regression discontinuity approach. It turns out that such arbitrary discontinuities are found with some frequency in the real world, as often formal decision rules are needed where various individuals seek access to limited spots. For example, discontinuities are encountered in educational admissions based on test scores, diagnostic decisions to define medical care, access to means tested public programs, and a whole host of other circumstances. The idea of regression discontinuity is attributed to Thistlethwaite and Campbell (1960), though applications in economics began in earnest in the late 1990s and early 2000s. In a relatively early review paper on RDDs, Lee and Lemieux (2010) compile around sixty examples of studies based on these designs covering themes across applied microeconometrics, namely education, labor markets, political economy, health, crime, and the environment. The use of this method has exploded since then, and by 2019 was being referred to in over 10% of NBER working papers (Currie, Kleven, and Zwiers 2020).

Alongside the burgeoning empirical literature in which RDDs are employed, there have been notable theoretical advances over the last decade or so. While the idea behind RDD is quite simple—essentially some smooth score or forcing variable generates a discontinuous jump in some variable of interest at a certain threshold, and we can use this discontinuity to infer treatment effects—the tools required to do this formally are theoretically very interesting. Unlike other settings where we ostensibly wish to learn as much as we can from as much data as possible, in RDD we wish to focus only on certain points and ignore data that is too far from this point to justify its inclusion. The fact that we are zooming in on certain areas, and are particularly interested in extreme points around a discontinuity, means that a range of new tools is required, perhaps most centrally weighted nonparametric regression.

The success of the regression discontinuity as an empirical design owes to a number of factors. One key point in its favor is the ability to make compelling identification arguments that are visually salient. Generally, the discontinuities that are used for identification can be clearly expressed in terms of verifiable treatment rules, and often results can appreciated visually with jumps observed in treatment assignments and outcomes of interest precisely around these discontinuities. Another point in favor of the RDD is that often the discontinuity is of interest in its own right. Treatment assignment rules often reflect (malleable) policy decisions, and thus, even if we are focused on the treatment that these rules manipulate, RDDs allow us to consider underlying policy effects themselves.

In this chapter we will define RDDs as well as consider estimation, inference, graphical presentations, and partial identification tests. We will see variations in the way that RDDs are implemented and understood as local estimands when treatment is perfectly assigned at the cutoff compared to when jumps are discontinuous but do not imply perfect compliance. We will discuss a number of extensions to standard RDDs, including the regression kink design where rather than treatment likelihood jumping at some cutoff, the slope of treatment intensity changes.

6.2 Identification and Regression Discontinuity Designs

6.2.1 The Regression Discontinuity Design and the Evaluation Problem

Let's begin by laying out a standard notation for RDDs. As typical, we will have potential outcomes $Y_i(1)$, $Y_i(0)$ corresponding to outcomes for unit i under treatment and control exposure. However, what is new in RDDs is a score, or running variable that acts to assign units to treatment. This running variable, which we will denote as Z_i, assigns units to treatment based on some specific cutoff, which we will refer to as κ. At times, Z_i is referred to as X_i (see, e.g., Calonico, Cattaneo, and Titiunik [2014a]), but here we will use notation Z_i to denote the running variable. In the simplest case, adherence with the assignment rule is perfect, such that any units with $Z_i \geq \kappa$ are assigned to treatment; otherwise units remain as untreated.

This case in which the cutoff κ perfectly defines treatment assignment—known as the "sharp design," given that treatment jumps sharply from 0 to 1—implies a treatment assignment rule, or assignment mechanism, of the following type:

$$W_i = \mathbb{1}(Z_i \geq \kappa). \tag{6.1}$$

Based on this rule, we can rewrite the switching equation (1.3) as:

$$Y_i = Y_i(0) + \big(Y_i(1) - Y_i(0)\big)W_i = \begin{cases} Y_i(0) & \text{if } Z_i < \kappa, \\ Y_i(1) & \text{if } Z_i \geq \kappa. \end{cases} \tag{6.2}$$

This makes clear that the observed outcome relates to potential outcomes through the running variable and the threshold κ. While the above notation is based on a sharp treatment discontinuity occurring at κ, regression discontinuity need not require such sharp treatment discontinuity. Alternatively, RDDs can be based on cases where treatment exposure jumps sharply around κ, but without perfect adherence to the rule at each side, in which case we will refer to "fuzzy designs." In the following two subsections we will see that we can define estimands of interest in both these cases under broadly similar assumptions, though how we understand the two estimands differ.

Early work by Hahn, Todd, and Klaauw (2001) laid out the assumptions that allow us to identify treatment effects in an RDD. Key to this were arguments about limits of conditional means as the running variable approaches the cutoff value κ. For example, consider the quantities $\mathbb{E}[Y_i(1)|Z_i = z]$ and $\mathbb{E}[Y_i(0)|Z_i = z]$. These are simply conditional means of potential outcomes at specific points of the running variable Z_i. In RDDs, we will be particularly interested in the point where the discontinuity occurs. Specifically, we will be interested in conditional means at points infinitesimally close to the cutoff, namely:

$$\lim_{z \uparrow \kappa} \mathbb{E}[Y_i(0)|Z_i = z] \qquad \text{and} \qquad \lim_{z \downarrow \kappa} \mathbb{E}[Y_i(0)|Z_i = z], \tag{6.3}$$

where the left-hand quantity in (6.3) refers to quantity $\mathbb{E}[Y_i(0)|Z_i = z]$ as z approaches κ from below, while the right-hand quantity refer to the the expectation as z approaches κ from above.

Hahn, Todd, and Klaauw (2001) show the identification of treatment effects relies on assumptions related to conditional means of a number of quantities at these limits. They first note a mechanical assumption:

Assumption 11. Regression Discontinuity
The quantities $\lim_{z\uparrow\kappa}\mathbb{E}[W_i|Z_i=z]$ and $\lim_{z\downarrow\kappa}\mathbb{E}[W_i|Z_i=z]$ exist, and $\lim_{z\uparrow\kappa}\mathbb{E}[W_i|Z_i=z]\neq\lim_{z\downarrow\kappa}\mathbb{E}[W_i|Z_i=z]$,

which states that a regression discontinuity *is* observed, with treatment W_i effectively jumping at the cut-point κ. Of course, in the case of a sharp design discussed above, if some assignment rule is explicitly defined, such as an electoral victory at 50%+1 votes, $\lim_{z\uparrow\kappa}\mathbb{E}[W_i|Z_i=z]=0$ and $\lim_{z\downarrow\kappa}\mathbb{E}[W_i|Z_i=z]=1$, clearly fulfilling the condition above. This assumption also acts to ensure identification in cases where treatment is not sharp, as we will see in section 6.2.3, where we introduce the fuzzy design formally.

However, the key point for identification is a second assumption that relates to the continuity of potential outcomes at the cut-point. Specifically,

Assumption 12. Continuity of Potential Outcomes
The quantities $\mathbb{E}[Y_i(0)|Z_i=z]$ and $\mathbb{E}[Y_i(1)|Z_i=z]$ are continuous in z at the cut-off point κ.

This assumption (restated as in D. S. Lee [2008]) is interesting, as it emphasises that the approach to identification here will really just depend upon the continuity of potential outcomes at the cutoff. In essence, Hahn, Todd, and Klaauw (2001) note that if we consider a very small value $e>0$, this continuity assumption implies that $\mathbb{E}[Y_i(0)|Z_i=\kappa-e]\approx\mathbb{E}[Y_i(0)|Z_i=\kappa+e]$, meaning that we can infer that differential effects in observed Y_i owe to treatment receipt, rather than differences in potential outcomes. This shifts the burden of identification onto the fact that apart from treatment, *other factors* should be trending smoothly around the cutoff, and the only sharp change occurring at the cutoff is the shift in treatment assignment itself.

This presence of this new assumption—which is quite different to our identifying assumption in previous chapters—relates in some way to the fact that assumptions we had previously been making for identification no longer make much sense here. Specifically, while we will maintain SUTVA, we will no longer ever maintain an overlap assumption, which was key in experimental and observational-based methods such as matching discussed in chapters 2–3. You will likely have already noted that when assignment of treatment status varies according to strict rules along a single observable dimension, z, then we have a special problem for experimental or matching-based methods. Here we will, *by definition*, violate assumptions of common support, as the discontinuity we are using for identification rules out overlap. Thus, rather than base identification off overlap and conditional unconfoundedness assumptions, we will rely on some sort of limited extrapolation, assuming continuity of underlying unobservables around the cutoff point of interest. In section 6.5.1 we will discuss an alternative local randomization-based view of these identifying assumptions noted by D. S. Lee (2008, among others), which provides a different conceptualization of identification in RDDs, viewing the design as a very local experiment.

As we will formalize in the subsections immediately following this one, if we are willing to make continuity assumptions like those laid out in assumption 12, then we can isolate a treatment effect by approximating the expectation of observed outcomes Y_i (and W_i) on either side of the cutoff. However, the key evaluation problem in RDD is that it is based on arguments about limits. Here, identifying assumptions say nothing about the running variable being irrelevant in explaining potential outcomes. Indeed, because the running variable will generally reflect some underlying phenomenon of interest that is relevant over a broader range in both explaining treatment access and outcomes, we will generally expect there to be a considerable relationship between the running variable and outcomes across the distribution of the running variable. For example, consider later-life earnings as an outcome, school test scores as a running variable, and university entry as a treatment. Even if there is some test score threshold that defines university entry in an RDD, the running variable itself (school test scores) will have its own effect on outcomes more generally, because school test scores likely captures a range of factors such as knowledge, family resources, test-taking ability, and so forth, which themselves will affect labor market outcomes. The identifying assumptions laid out above (and assumption 12 in particular) do not state that the running variable is unrelated to potential outcomes, but rather simply that it affects potential outcomes in a continuous way around the cut-point. Given this, if we focus our attention on an infinitely small window around the cut-point, potential outcomes will be equal on each side even though they are not over a broader range.

The challenge will thus be in taking this theoretical design to practice when confronted by real data. Consider, for example, the illustrative case in figure 6.1. Here outcomes Y_i are plotted against a running variable, and a visual discontinuity is observed at the point $\kappa = 0$. While we clearly see a jump in these data, we also see a clear relationship between Z_i and Y_i away from the discontinuity, which is what we will generally expect. Indeed, even eyeballing these (simulated) data it seems that we could infer the effect of treatment with some degree of accuracy. But in practice, it is not clear exactly how we should do this. Because we do not rule out relationships between potential outcomes and the running variable, we should clearly focus on points very close to the discontinuity to infer treatment effects. However, if we focus on points *infinitely* close to the cutoff, eventually we will focus on a range so short that no data remains. Thus, we will want to focus on some bandwidth small enough that the role of the running variable is limited, but not so small that we remain with too few observations to estimate our treatment effect precisely. As we will see below, in practice estimation will seek to resolve a bias-variance trade-off.

In effect, we will seek to focus our attention on the areas "local" to the cutoff, where the only justification of considering more than an infinitesimally small local area is that we need sufficient data to estimate any parameters precisely. The implication of this is that we will only ever estimate a treatment effect that is informative for observations with Z_i approximately equal to κ. When treatment effects are heterogeneous, this will thus not correspond to an ATE or an ATT, but rather the ATT(κ). Of course, there is nothing that will imply that this treatment effect will tell us anything about treatment effects at other points of the running variable. This will depend entirely upon how partially unobservable potential

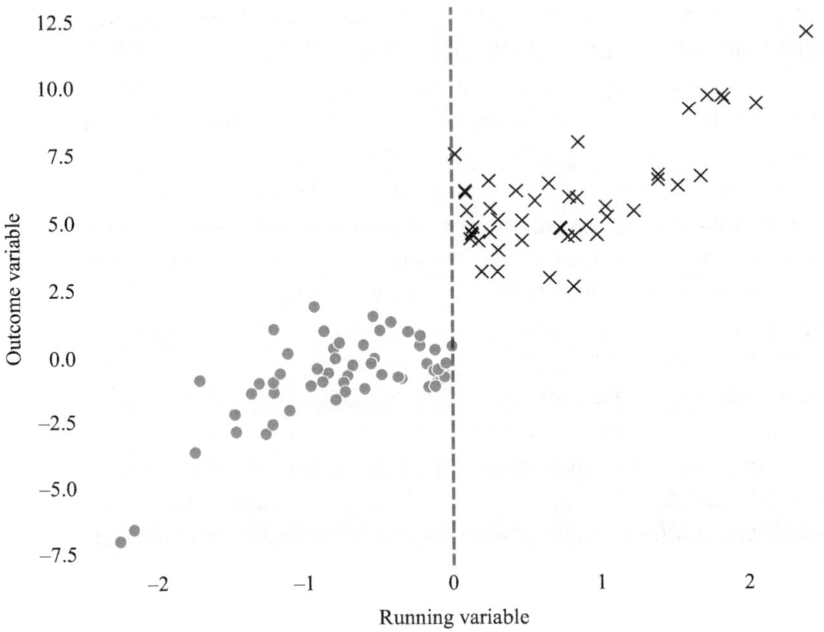

Figure 6.1
Observed outcomes, the running variable, and a discontinuity.

outcomes track across the distribution of the running variable. Consider, for example, the illustrative example documented in figure 6.2, where potential outcomes $Y_i(0), Y_i(1)$ are defined in lighter and darker colors, respectively, while simulated observed data are plotted as points. Here, the quantity $\tau(\kappa)$ corresponding to the jump in potential outcomes at the discontinuity turns out to be relatively informative for treatment effects at points lower in the distribution of the running variable, but quite uninformative for τ at points higher in the distribution, given the shape of potential outcome curves. Of course, in practice, we will never observe such curves, and so we generally have to satisfy ourselves in accepting a specific local treatment effect (we discuss external validity in chapter 8).

6.2.2 Sharp RDDs

We now turn to consider the formal definition of parameters of interest. To begin, we will consider the case of the Sharp regression discontinuity as described in (6.1). In this case, treatment assignment is perfectly manipulated at the cutoff, proving a quite direct route to identification based on the maintained assumptions. A clear example of this could be an election between two candidates (say an incumbent versus a challenger for some political office). If our treatment is that a constituency is assigned to a new politician, we know that this will only occur if in this constituency the new candidate receives at least 50%+1 vote,

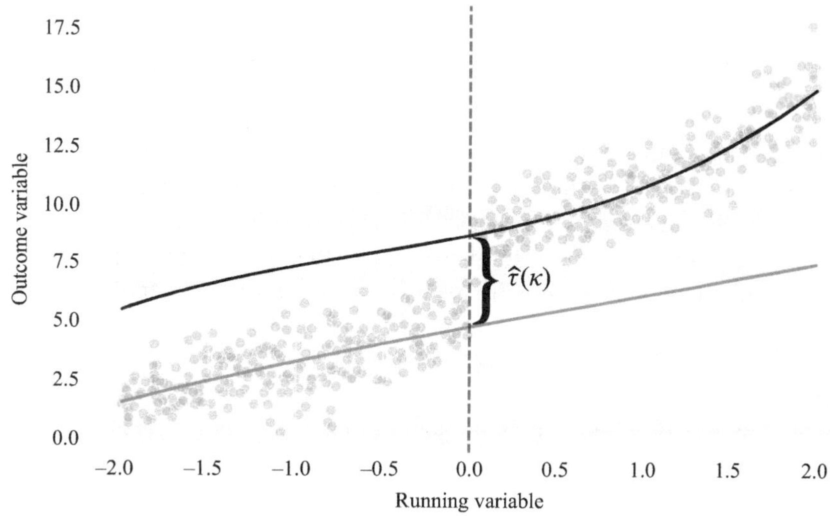

Figure 6.2
Regression discontinuity and heterogeneity over the distribution of z.

while if the new candidate receives 50%−1 vote, the constituency will be assigned to the control group. The important thing here is that there is absolutely no discretion: If a majority of votes is received, a candidate is chosen; otherwise said candidate is not chosen.

Given the assignment mechanism described in (6.1), the impact of being assigned to treatment can be isolated easily given that the variable of interest jumps from 0 to 1 precisely when moving across point κ. Specifically, we can write our sharp RDD estimand as (6.4) (or (6.5)), which, given the continuous nature of the underlying potential outcomes, can be written in terms of observable quantities in (6.6).

$$\tau^{\text{SRD}}_{\text{ATT}(\kappa)} = \mathbb{E}[Y_i(1) - Y_i(0)|Z_i = \kappa] \tag{6.4}$$

$$= \mathbb{E}[Y_i(1)|Z_i = \kappa] - \mathbb{E}[Y_i(0)|Z_i = \kappa] \tag{6.5}$$

$$= \lim_{z \downarrow \kappa} \mathbb{E}[Y_i|Z_i = z] - \lim_{z \uparrow \kappa} \mathbb{E}[Y_i|Z_i = z]. \tag{6.6}$$

While a proof is available in Hahn, Todd, and Klaauw (2001), we can also see the logic of this by combining assumption 12 with our switching equation (6.2) as follows:

$$\mathbb{E}[Y_i(0)|Z_i = \kappa] = \lim_{z \downarrow \kappa} \mathbb{E}[Y_i(0)|Z_i = z] = \lim_{z \uparrow \kappa} \mathbb{E}[Y_i(0)|Z_i = z] = \lim_{z \uparrow \kappa} \mathbb{E}[Y_i|Z_i = z].$$

Here, the first equality simply comes from the definition of limits. The second equality owes to the continuous nature of the expectations of potential outcomes around the discontinuity as implied by assumption 12. Finally the latter equality comes from the switching equation, which implies that when approaching κ from below, treatment will not yet be switched on, and so the limit from below will allow us to estimate $\mathbb{E}[Y_i(0)|Z_i=\kappa]$. A similar argument can be made simply taking limits from above, in which case the quantity $\tau^{\text{SRD}}_{\text{ATT}(\kappa)}$ is identified at the point κ.

You will note that formally, this quantity is indicated as an ATT rather than an ATE, and this is because, based on the definition in (6.1), when $Z_i=\kappa$, treatment is switched on, and we are thus considering effects for the treated. However, for untreated units very close to the point κ, this effect is likely also informative, and so this ATT is akin to an ATE for areas very close to the cutoff. This point will also be clear when we return to discuss the local randomization approach to RDD in section 6.5.1.

6.2.3 Fuzzy RDDs

In the "sharp" regression discontinuity design examined so far, the probability of receiving treatment jumps deterministically from zero to one at the cutoff. Such is the case, for example, with simple majority elections discussed previously, where crossing the threshold of the vote majority automatically results in a candidate being elected. Perhaps even more common than pure regression discontinuities are situations in which the probability of treatment jumps at the cutoff, but treatment assignment is not deterministic. In these cases, not everyone above the cutoff is treated and not everyone below the cutoff is untreated. Nevertheless, there is *some* local manipulation that occurs at this point that can be leveraged for the identification of a treatment effect. Essentially, now rather than the likelihood of treatment jumping by one at the cutoff, we observe the relevance of assumption 11:

$$\begin{aligned} &\lim_{z\downarrow\kappa}\mathbb{E}(W_i|Z_i=z) > \lim_{z\uparrow\kappa}\mathbb{E}(W_i|Z_i=z) \\ \Leftrightarrow &\lim_{z\downarrow\kappa}\Pr(W_i=1|Z_i=z) > \lim_{z\uparrow\kappa}\Pr(W_i=1|Z_i=z), \end{aligned} \tag{6.7}$$

with a jump in treatment receipt occurring, but this not necessarily being from 0 to 1.

Graphically, the difference in these designs can be observed in figure 6.3. Here we consider a simulated example of data, where are each point of the distribution of the running variable the quantity $\Pr(W_i=1)$ is plotted. In the case of sharp designs displayed in panel (a), there is no discretion in the application of the assignment rule. To the left of the threshold, no individual receives treatment, and to the right of the threshold, everybody receives treatment. However, in the case of the Fuzzy design, treatment is discretionary. While in Fuzzy designs, the threshold *does* have an impact and does shift behavior, this shift is not absolute, with certain individuals either opting into treatment below the cutoff set here at $Z_i=0$ or opting out of treatment above the cutoff, in which case the observed change does not jump sharply from 0 to 1, but rather in a "fuzzy" way from some value greater than or equal to 0, to some value less than or equal to one. This fuzzy design can be viewed as a case of treatment assignment with imperfect compliance (see, e.g., Calonico, Cattaneo, and Titiunik [2014a]; Dong [2015; 2018]; Arai et al. [2022]).

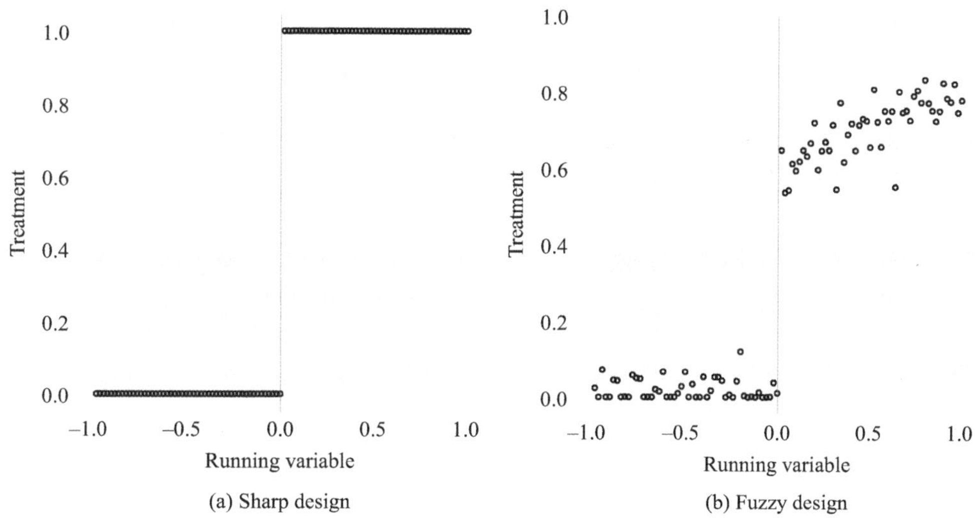

Figure 6.3
Fuzzy versus sharp RDD designs.

For example, Ozier (2018) uses a cutoff (eligibility) rule in primary exam scores to estimate the impact of secondary education in Kenya (we work with these data in an end of chapter question). While individuals who achieve greater than this cutoff score are eligible to attend secondary, there is of course not obligatory, as individuals can opt to not continue with their studies. Similarly, if individuals achieve a score below the cutoff, while they are not eligible for public secondary schools, they can still access secondary school via paying for private schools or elect to retake the exam the following year, resulting in two-sided noncompliance.

This language of treatment assignment with imperfect compliance harks back to the ideas we explored in the previous chapter with instrumental variables, and it turns out that the fuzzy regression discontinuity design can be viewed precisely in this way! To see this, consider that we can view the fuzzy RDD as owing to the same treatment assignment rule from (6.1) but now also define a treatment take up measure D_i with potential outcomes $D_i(1)$, corresponding to an individual's treatment take up when assigned $W_i = 1$, and $D_i(0)$ corresponding to their treatment take up when assigned $W_i = 0$. In line with (6.2), this results in a switching equation for treatment receipt around the cutoff written as follows:

$$D_i = D_i(0) + (D_i(1) - D_i(0))\, W_i = \begin{cases} D_i(0) & \text{if } Z_i < \kappa, \\ D_i(1) & \text{if } Z_i \geq \kappa. \end{cases} \tag{6.8}$$

We can take this to the logical conclusion following our previous discussion of IV with imperfect compliance in noting that now potential outcomes can depend on treatment assignment, and treatment receipt $Y_i(W_i, D_i(W_i))$. Because we have now introduced potential outcomes for treatment, we will lay out an analogous assumption to the continuity assumption 12, however now for treatment receipt itself:

Assumption 13. Continuity of Potential Outcomes for Treatment Receipt
The quantities $\mathbb{E}[D_i(0)|Z_i=z]$ and $\mathbb{E}[D_i(1)|Z_i=z]$ are continuous in z at the cutoff point κ.

The introduction of potential variation in both assignment and receipt suggests a number of estimators in the setting of Fuzzy RDD. A first simple estimator considers what the impact of treatment *assignment* is on outcomes Y_i. This is, of course, an intent to treat (ITT) estimate as discussed in section 5.2.4. This can be written as follows:

$$\tau^{\text{FRD}}_{\text{ITT}(\kappa)} = \mathbb{E}\big[Y_i\big(1, D_i(1)\big) - Y_i\big(0, D_i(0)\big)|Z_i=\kappa\big] \tag{6.9}$$

$$= \lim_{z\downarrow\kappa} \mathbb{E}[Y_i|Z_i=z] - \lim_{z\uparrow\kappa} \mathbb{E}[Y_i|Z_i=z], \tag{6.10}$$

where arguments laid out above when discussing the Sharp RDD also hold here. The logic of this estimand is that if we wish to simply assess the impact of treatment *assignment*, we can ignore the question of imperfect take-up altogether and simply revert to an estimand like (6.6), which is identified off of the continuity assumptions (12) and (13).

However, if we wish to consider the effect of treatment receipt itself, we must account for the fact that the discontinuity only produces a fuzzy increase in treatment receipt, rather than a deterministic jump from 0 to 1. This is done precisely by using the logic of the LATE defined previously. In particular, note that we can define a parameter of interest $\tau^{\text{FRD}}_{\text{LATE}(\kappa)}$ as below.

$$\tau^{\text{FRD}}_{\text{LATE}(\kappa)} = \mathbb{E}[Y_i(1) - Y_i(0)|Z_i=\kappa, D_i(1) - D_i(0) = 1] \tag{6.11}$$

$$= \frac{\lim_{z\downarrow\kappa} \mathbb{E}[Y_i|Z_i=z] - \lim_{z\uparrow\kappa} \mathbb{E}[Y_i|Z_i=z]}{\lim_{z\downarrow\kappa} \mathbb{E}[D_i|Z_i=z] - \lim_{z\uparrow\kappa} \mathbb{E}[D_i|Z_i=z]}. \tag{6.12}$$

The quantity in (6.12), is of course, the Wald estimator we have worked with extensively in IV models previously. That this quantity actually captures $\tau^{\text{FRD}}_{\text{LATE}(\kappa)}$ requires both continuity assumptions 12 and 13 as well as the RDD relevance assumption 11. *However*, we also require an exclusion restriction as defined in assumption 7, and, because we are now defining this in the LATE framework, we also require a monotonicity assumption. There are a number of ways this monotonicity assumption can be defined. For example, it can be defined as "local monotonicity," in which we assume that $D_i(1) \geq D_i(0)$ in some local window around the cutoff as in Hahn, Todd, and Klaauw (2001) and Arai et al. (2022), thus ruling out that defiers exist locally, or alternative can be based on smoothness assumptions of potential outcomes for each complier type, as well as a lack of selection of complier types to either side of the cutoff, as in Dong (2015) and Dong and Lewbel (2015).

The key point is that under these assumptions, and as in section 5.3.1, this allows us to estimate a treatment effect, but this treatment effect holds *only* for the subpopulation of compliers. In this case, compliers are the units who would get the treatment if their score were at κ or above but would not get the treatment if their score were lower than κ. For example, in the Ozier (2018) example mentioned previously, they are those students who would go on to secondary school if they achieve a score above the cutoff in the Kenyan Certificate of Primary Education, but would leave school if they do not achieve a score over the minimum cutoff.

6.3 Visualization, Estimation, and Inference with RD

6.3.1 Graphical Representations

Arguably, one of the reasons why RD is such a successful identification strategy is that it often leads to visually striking representations of the causal effect under study. A shift owing to some arbitrary crossing rule in the running variable generates exogenous variation in the exposure to some particular phenomenon, and this shift can be graphed quite simply in two dimensions. When examining how some outcome of interest moves along the support of the running variable, we can observe both a general pattern describing the relationship between the running variable and the outcome of interest, and importantly, visually inspect for any discontinuities at the assignment threshold. Similarly, in the case of a fuzzy RDD, we can inspect graphical functions of the probability of treatment receipt, plotted against the running variable.

Thus, generally, in any study involving an RDD, we should see a plot documenting the underlying variation between the running variable and outcome of interest (as well as potentially other patterns described in section 6.4). Generally, rather than plotting the full dataset, some smoothed function is plotted of averages of outcomes at various points of the running variable. For example, consider the simulated data presented in figure 6.4(a). Here a simple discontinuity exists at 0, and the running variable plotted on the horizontal access ranges from more negative to more positive values. In panel (a) raw data is plotted, where the discontinuity is clearly visible, though the nature of the jump is somewhat disguised by the underlying variation at each point. Remaining panels (b)–(d) present alternative plots, commonly referred to as "RD plots," where instead of presenting raw data, binned averages are presented in varying numbers of points. In these graphs, each point refers to the average outcomes in small ranges of mutually exclusive points of support of the running variable, also referred to as binned scatterplots (Cattaneo et al. 2024). Here, the size of points refers to the number of individuals contained in each group, and these are presented without any fit line.

While these bins could be chosen arbitrarily (for example using ten bins on either side of the discontinuity as in panel b of figure 6.4), there are principled ways to select both bins, as well as any regression fit line. The work of Calonico, Cattaneo, and Titiunik (2015) proposes a data-driven rule for bin selection, as well potentially allowing for the suggestion of an

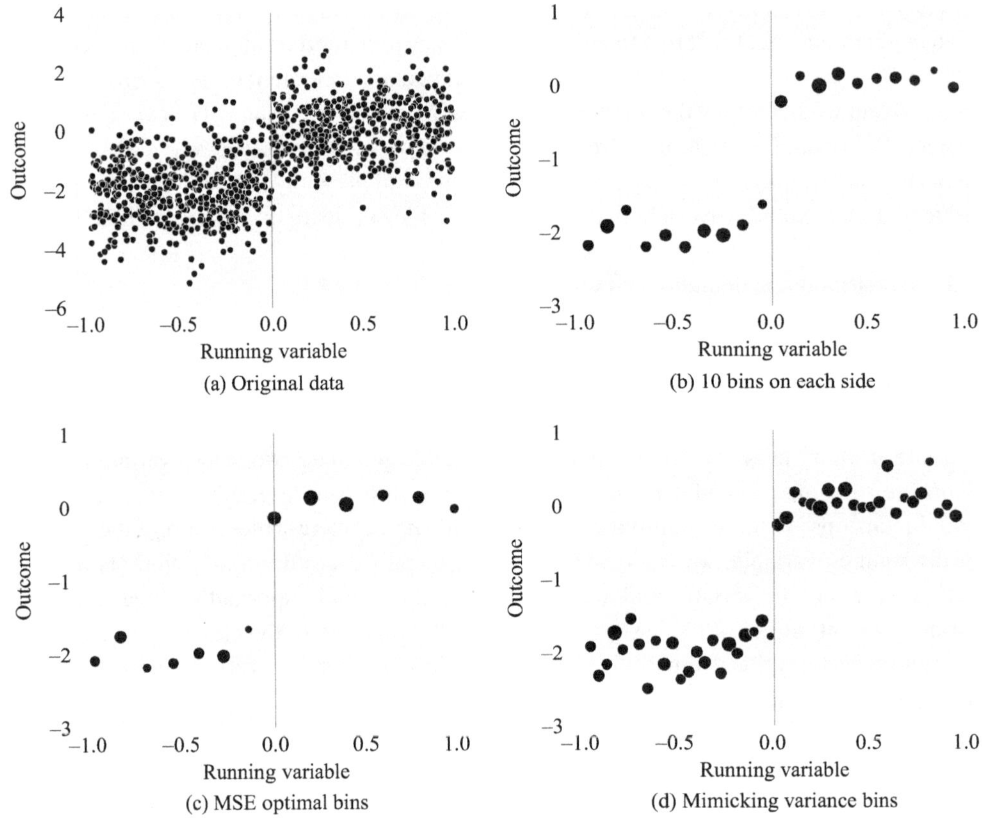

Figure 6.4
Graphical representation in an RD design.

optimally defined polynomial fit to describe the relationship between the running variable and outcomes on either side of the cutoff.

Calonico, Cattaneo, and Titiunik (2015) suggest a number of procedures by which bins can be constructed: These can either be evenly spaced, or quantile-spaced. Evenly spaced refers to bins that are spaced at an equal absolute difference in the running variable, while quantile-spaced refers to bins defined to be evenly distributed across percentiles of the observed data (taking into account that data may be more sparse at different values of the running variable). What's more, they suggest a number of ways of determining the optimal numbers of bins: the first an integrated mean-squared error (IMSE) minimizing procedure and the latter a variance-mimicking procedure. Given that the mean-squared error is a function of the variance and bias squared, the first of these procedures seeks to choose bins in a way which trades off bias and variance. Bias exists given that local bins simply take means of outcomes across the entire bin-width rather than capturing the true functional form in this bin. This bias can be reduced when smaller bins are used as local means will be based on smaller ranges of the running variable, but will generally be noisier estimates, as they are based on fewer data points. An alternative approach is to seek to generate a binned scatterplot whose variance is similar to the variance of underlying data, hence providing a clearer representation of the uncertainty in original data. This is what Calonico, Cattaneo, and Titiunik's "mimicking variance" (MV) procedure does, and, in general, this results in substantially more bins (see figure 6.4d compared to panel c). While full formal details are laid out in Calonico, Cattaneo, and Titiunik (2015), a key takeaway is that the MV procedure should likely be preferred if the idea of the plot is to describe underlying data, while IMSE optimal graphs may be produced if one wishes to consider underlying regression functions, for example, if seeking to consider whether discontinuities are more broadly observed in data.

Even based on the above guidance, there is considerable discretion related to which of these methods should be used, whether regression fit lines should be included on plots, whether a vertical line should be used to indicate the discontinuity (κ), axis scaling, and so forth. While the goal of graphical presentations in RDDs is simply to visually present information in a way that allows readers to grasp central elements of the design, there is no definitive rule for such choices. However Korting et al. (2023) provide a creative way to offer concrete guidance on these choices. By consulting expert and non-expert readers, and experimentally varying the way that RD plots are displayed, they consider the way that such choices influence the likelihood that readers make "type I" errors (seeing a discontinuity where there is in fact none) and "type II' errors (not seeing a discontinuity where there is one). They find that in their particular sample, using the smaller MV bin selector defined above outperforms the larger IMSE bin selector in terms of reducing type I error, as does presenting graphs without fit lines. This leads to a concrete recommendation to use smaller (i.e., MV) bins, and omit fit lines, while suggesting that reasonable discretion in other choices does not appear to sway readers one way or the other.

6.3.2 Estimating Regression Discontinuity Effects

6.3.2.1 Global vs. local methods In principle, if we consider the assumptions made to this point, we *could* seek to estimate the treatment effect τ^{SRD} (or τ^{FRD}) by fully modeling the relationship between the running variable and the outcome. In essence, if we are able to correctly capture this relationship on both sides of discontinuity, all we need to do is allow for a separate level effect at the discontinuity to capture the impact of treatment "switching on" at this point. Such a procedure for estimating the RDD is known as a global parametric or global polynomial approach (see, e.g., Lee and Lemieux 2010; Van Der Klaauw 2008) because it seeks to use all data (global) and parameterize the relationship between the outcome and the running variable. While this method is discussed, particularly in early literature on regression discontinuity designs, it is not a recommended estimation procedure and should generally not be adopted, as we will discuss below.

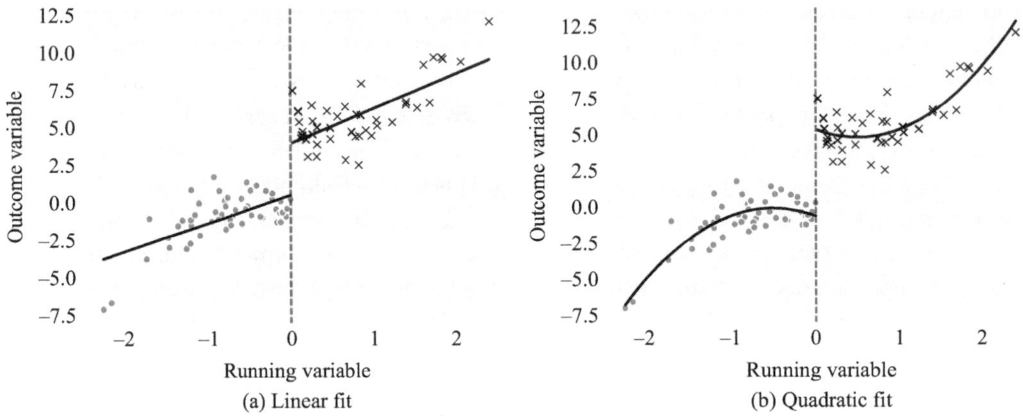

Figure 6.5
Modeling relationships between outcomes and the running variable in regression discontinuity estimates.

The idea of the global parametric approach is to estimate some sort of flexible model such as:

$$Y_i = m(Z_i) + \tau^{\text{SRD,global}} \mathbb{1}(Z_i \geq \kappa) + \varepsilon_i, \tag{6.13}$$

where $m(Z_i)$ is a function that captures the relationship between the running variable and the outcome Y_i. It is clear that we *must* capture the relationship between Y_i and Z_i because Z_i will typically have an important effect on Y_i, even in the absence of its sharp effect on treatment at the point κ. For example, if Z_i is a standardized test score allowing admission to some competitive degree program at point κ and Y_i is future labor market outcomes, we would expect that even without the admission to the degree program, individuals with very different test scores would likely have quite different labor market outcomes in the future. Indeed, even locally, assumption 12 allows the running variable to affect potential outcomes. Thus, global methods require us to correctly capture the global relationship between Y_i and Z_i by correctly specifying the functional form for $m(Z_i)$ such that we can separate any discontinuity at κ from general effects of Z_i on Y_i.

Van Der Klaauw (2008) notes that this is, in essence, a "control function"[1] approach as we are controlling for the (endogenous) relationship between Z_i and Y_i. The reason why this approach is no longer used in practice in the empirical literature is that we generally do not know how to model $m(Z_i)$, and reasonable decisions about this function can lead to quite different estimates of $\tau^{\text{SRD,global}}$. In practice, suggestions for the modeling of $m(X_i)$ typically consist of fitting separate polynomials on either side of the cutoff κ. For example, if we consider the simulated data displayed in figure 6.1, we may seek to approximate the function $m(Z_i)$ using a split linear or split quadratic function, as displayed in figure 6.5.

This approach in which separate polynomials are fit on each side of the discontinuity is straightforward to implement (see, e.g., Lee and Lemieux 2010 for further discussion) and simply consists of parameterizing $m(Z_i)$ with said split polynomials. This can be written as in (6.14) below and then defined using some particular polynomial, such as a first-order (linear) polynomial,[2] which is written in (6.15):

$$Y_i = \mu_0 + f^-(Z_i)(1 - W_i) + f^+(Z_i)W_i + \tau^{\text{SRD,global}} W_i + \varepsilon_i \quad (6.14)$$

$$= \mu_0 + \beta_1^-(1 - W_i)(Z_i - \kappa) + \beta_1^+ W_i(Z_i - \kappa) + \tau^{\text{SRD,global}} W_i + \varepsilon_i. \quad (6.15)$$

Here, β_1^- captures the linear fit on the left-hand side of the cutoff, and β_1^+ captures the linear fit on the right-hand side of the cutoff. We have re-centered our running variable as $(Z_i - \kappa)$ such that any points below 0 are on the left of the cutoff, while any points above 0 are to the right of the cutoff. We can thus see from (6.14) that as we approach the cut-point from the left $(Z_i - \kappa)$ approaches 0, and we are left with $Y_i = \mu_0 + \varepsilon_i$. Similarly, as we approach the cutoff from the right, we are left with $Y_i = \mu_0 + \tau^{\text{SRD,global}} W_i + \varepsilon_i$, and $\tau^{\text{SRD,global}}$ thus simply captures the jump in intercepts of our polynomials on either side of the cutoff.

While this is easy to estimate in practice, the challenge is that we do not actually know what the correct model for $m(Z_i)$ is and whether it even *can* be approximated by a global polynomial. For example, if we consider the linear and quadratic polynomials displayed in figure 6.5, we can see that even though both seem to do a reasonable job of approximating the relationship between the running variable and the outcome Y_i on either side of the cut-off, their implications for the discontinuity estimate are quite different.[3] In the linear case, the left-hand intercept μ_0 is approximately 0, while the right-hand intercept is around 4, suggesting $\widehat{\tau}^{\text{SRD,global}}$ of around 4, while in the quadratic case, the left and right intercepts are approximately -0.5 and 5, suggesting a $\widehat{\tau}^{\text{SRD,global}}$ of around 5.5.

Early literature notes that while methods can be chosen to select polynomials that seek to minimize some sort of objective criteria related to the model's explanatory power, such criteria will be global. The drawback of these methods is that even if polynomial are chosen that provide some global best fit, this doesn't actually say anything about how well $m(Z_i)$ approximates the functional form at the cut-point κ, which is what we require to estimate the parameters τ^{SRD} and τ^{FRD}. What's more, Gelman and Imbens (2019) document quite clearly that the use of global estimation samples and high-order polynomials leads to an overreliance on data far away from the discontinuity point, and substantial sensitivity of the intercepts at the discontinuity, which is precisely the point of relevance for estimating the parameter of interest.

For this reason, current literature warns against such practice, (see, e.g., Imbens and Wager [2019]; Cattaneo and Titiunik [2022]; Cattaneo, Nicolas Idrobo, and Titiunik [2024]; Cattaneo, Nicolás Idrobo, and Titiunik [2020]). The far more common approach, and that which lines up with the theory related to *local* continuity assumptions, is to focus on data local to the cutoff, minimizing the importance of any mistakes we make in modeling the relationship between the running variable and the outcome of interest. Such "local" approaches require a new set of tools, which we turn to discuss now.

6.3.2.2 Nonparametric local linear and polynomial methods The idea behind local polynomial methods is that—in line with identifying assumptions—we will focus our attention on areas "local" to the cutoff. We will then control for Z_i within this local area only, discarding observations that are too far from the cutoff to merit consideration. We call the interval around the cutoff that is used for estimation the bandwidth. The limiting argument above in assumption 12 hints at a key feature of the argument that underlies the RD approach: The bandwidth should be as small as the sample allows. Indeed, the only reason we will include points beyond an infinitely small bandwidth is because as the bandwidth shrinks, the number of points we have to work with shrinks, and the variance of any resulting estimator grows. As we will see below, principled choices related to the bandwidth with which we work seek to optimally trade off bias and variance.

The idea behind local regression discontinuity methods is that even though we will still impose certain polynomial fits, we will be quite hands off in modeling assumptions, and allow the data to inform us about how local to the discontinuity we should work. We will do this by using nonparametric estimation procedures. These procedures will be nonparametric in the sense that we make no assumptions about the functional form that describes relationships between running variables and outcomes, rather allowing data to suggest the optimal observations close to the bandwidth used for estimating means on either side of the cutoff, which can be estimated in a data-driven form discussed below. These nonparametric methods have been initially described in an earlier statistical literature (Fan and Gijbels 1992; Fan 1992) with their adaption for use in regression discontinuity estimation by Hahn, Todd, and Klaauw (2001). Porter (2003) shows that the optimal results from the statistical literature also hold with RD estimation. Before turning to the implementation of nonparametric local regression discontinuity estimators in particular, we will briefly introduce the idea of nonparametric local linear estimation, and the importance of kernels and estimation bandwidths.

6.3.2.3 Nonparametric estimation Imagine that we wish to describe the distribution of some variable Z_i. We may be happy to do so using histograms if, for example, the variable takes a number of discrete values, but alternatively, we might seek to estimate the distribution of this variable using observations "close" to each distributional point, while discarding information from observations that are further away. The idea of a kernel density estimator is simply to provide a nonparametric method to estimate the probability density function of a random variable. This is "nonparametric" in the sense that we impose no assumptions on the distribution of our variable Z_i, simply allowing the data to "speak for itself." Formally, a kernel density estimator can be described as follows:

$$\widehat{f}(z) = \frac{1}{Nh} \sum_{i=1}^{N} K\left(\frac{z - Z_i}{h}\right), \tag{6.16}$$

where Z_i are observed data, $K(\cdot)$ is a kernel function, and h is a bandwidth parameter. The idea of the kernel function $K(\cdot)$ is that we select a kernel to define weights for each

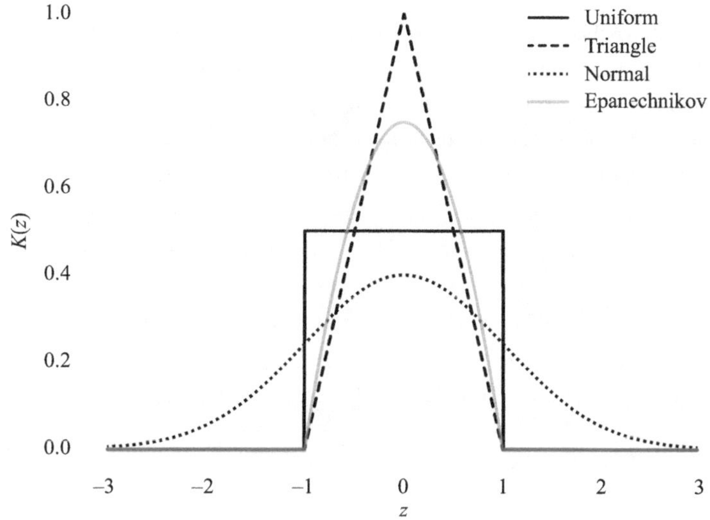

Figure 6.6
Common kernel densities.

observation Z_i. This kernel function is typically a symmetric and nonnegative function that integrates to one. A range of common kernel density functions is plotted in figure 6.6. Around some particular point, these kernels give more or less weight to observations, often falling to zero weights beyond a specific point.

In (6.16), the quantity h is the bandwidth, which acts to control a specific kernel. If a large value for a bandwidth is chosen, the scaled distance $(z - Z_i)/h$ becomes smaller in magnitude, meaning that even observations relatively far from the target point z will receive substantial weight from the kernel function. In contrast, a smaller bandwidth increases the scaled distance, causing the kernel to assign less weight—or none at all—to observations farther from z.

In regression discontinuity estimators, rather than estimating densities themselves, we are actually interested in estimating mean outcomes on either side of a discontinuity as per (6.6). One possibility for estimating means is to use the Nadaraya-Watson estimator (for Nadaraya 1964; Watson 1964), which is a nonparametric regression method similarly based on Kernel weighting. Specifically, this can be used to estimate the expectation of a random variable Y_i at points of another variable Z_i and is defined as:

$$\widehat{m}(z) = \frac{\sum_{i=1}^{N} K\left(\frac{z-Z_i}{h}\right) Y_i}{\sum_{i=1}^{N} K\left(\frac{z-Z_i}{h}\right)}.$$

This quantity $\widehat{m}(z)$ allows us to provide a nonparametric approximation for the mean of Y in some zone "close" to z where the kernel function K defines weights, and the bandwidth h determines the nature of what is "close" to the point z.

However, in regression discontinuity estimation, we are particularly interested in the boundary points where the discontinuity is met on both sides of the cutoff. Fan (1992) shows that in cases such as these, using local linear regression is optimal in minimizing the mean squared error near the end points. Local linear regression allows us to nonparametrically estimate a regression model locally. For a given point z, the local linear regression estimate $\widehat{m}(z)$ is obtained by minimizing the weighted sum of squared residuals:

$$\min_{\alpha,\beta} \sum_{i=1}^{N} [Y_i - \alpha - \beta(Z_i - z)]^2 K\left(\frac{Z_i - z}{h}\right).$$

Here, as above, the idea of this is two-fold. With the kernel we can place weights on observations based on their distance to some specific point z, and with the bandwidth h we can vary the degree of what is considered "close" to the point of interest z.

Code Callout 6.1: Nonparametric Estimation Procedures
In code callout 6.1, we consider simulated data and explore the implications of different kernel choices and bandwidths for estimating densities such as (6.16). We then consider Nadaraya-Watson estimation as well as local linear regression, illustrating the point that local linear regression performs better at boundaries than Nadaraya-Watson.

6.3.2.4 Local linear regression discontinuity estimation To see how these nonparametric methods come into regression discontinuity estimation, we can note that the estimand in (6.6) requires the estimation of two limit points. The first is the intercept when approaching the cutoff from the left, and the second is the intercept when approaching the cutoff from the right. Based on the local linear procedure defined previously, and assuming some specific kernel $K(\cdot)$ and bandwidth h, we can proceed to estimate on each side of the cutoff. The treatment effect of interest then consists of comparing conditional expectations at the limits on either side of the cut-point.

Specifically, using local linear regression on the left-hand side of the cutoff, we can estimate

$$\widehat{\boldsymbol{\beta}}_{-} = \arg\min_{\boldsymbol{\beta}} \sum_{i=1}^{N} \mathbb{1}\{Z_i < \kappa\} [y_i - \beta_0 - \beta_1(Z_i - \kappa)]^2 K\left(\frac{Z_i - \kappa}{h}\right), \tag{6.17}$$

where $\widehat{\boldsymbol{\beta}}_{-}$ refers to the vector of parameter estimates $\widehat{\beta}_{+,0}, \widehat{\beta}_{+,1}$. Similarly, on the right-hand side of the cutoff we can estimate:

$$\widehat{\boldsymbol{\beta}}_{+} = \arg\min_{\boldsymbol{\beta}} \sum_{i=1}^{N} \mathbb{1}\{Z_i \geq \kappa\} [y_i - \beta_0 - \beta_1(Z_i - \kappa)]^2 K\left(\frac{Z_i - \kappa}{h}\right). \tag{6.18}$$

with $\widehat{\boldsymbol{\beta}}_+$ defined analogously to $\widehat{\boldsymbol{\beta}}_-$. Based on these estimates, the regression discontinuity estimator $\widehat{\tau}$ is the difference of the intercept at the cutoff point:

$$\widehat{\tau}^{\text{SRD,LL}} = \widehat{\beta}_{+,0} - \widehat{\beta}_{-,0}. \tag{6.19}$$

What is nice about this estimator is that it is clear that we are interested in the intercepts on either side of the cutoff—that is, the regression estimates at the points where the discontinuity occurs. Under the assumption of local unconfoundedness, $\widehat{\tau}^{\text{SRD,LL}}$ from (6.19) is a consistent estimate for τ from 6.6.

In this procedure, and in (6.19) in particular, it is clear that what we care about is the jump in the intercept when moving across the discontinuity. However, we *also* allow for a local effect of the running variable Z_i on the outcome of interest via the incorporation of the linear relationship $\beta_1(Z_i - \kappa)$. Because these are estimated separately above and below the cutoff, we are not imposing that such relationships be identical. However, more generally, we may wish to allow for more flexible relationships even locally, and in these cases rather than imposing a linear relationship on each side of the cutoff, we may allow for a higher order polynomial to be specified. This can be done quite simply for a polynomial of order p by adding higher-order terms:

$$\begin{aligned}\widehat{\boldsymbol{\beta}}_- = \arg\min_{\boldsymbol{\beta}} \sum_{i=1}^{N} \mathbb{1}\{Z_i < \kappa\} \Big[y_i - \beta_0 - \beta_1(Z_i - \kappa) - \beta_2(Z_i - \kappa)^2 \\ - \cdots - \beta_p(Z_i - \kappa)^p \Big]^2 K\left(\frac{Z_i - \kappa}{h}\right)\end{aligned}$$

in the case of (6.17), and similarly for (6.18). We delay the discussion of these considerations, as well as discussions about the choice of the Kernel to section 6.3.2.6 below. What is key, and what we will turn to immediately following this subsection, is the choice of bandwidth h.

While illustrative to see that the estimation of (6.6) simply consists of estimating two separate local linear regressions as in (6.17) and (6.18), in practice we can simply estimate this in a single model, provided that the same bandwidth is employed in each of (6.17) and (6.18). This allows for direct estimation of the regression discontinuity parameter $\widehat{\tau}^{\text{SRD,LL}}$ as:

$$\begin{aligned}\left(\widehat{\tau}^{\text{SRD,LL}}, \widehat{\boldsymbol{\beta}}\right) = \arg\min_{\tau,\boldsymbol{\beta}} \sum_{i=1}^{N} \big[Y_{it} - \beta_{-,0} - W_i\tau - (Z_i - \kappa)\beta_{-,1} \\ - (Z_i - \kappa)W_i\beta_1 \big]^2 K\left(\frac{Z_i - \kappa}{h}\right),\end{aligned} \tag{6.20}$$

where the incorporation of the interaction with W_i allows us to separately estimate the intercept and slope in the below cutoff sample as $\beta_{-,0}$ and $\beta_{-,1}$, as well as any *changes* in intercept and slope when crossing the cutoff. For this reason, we may see the local linear estimator written in either of these ways (see, for example, Abadie and Cattaneo [2018] who present the joint specification, or Cattaneo and Titiunik [2022] who present separate estimators).

6.3.2.5 Selection of bandwidth Bandwidth selection in regression discontinuity estimators has been the focus of substantial research progress over the past decade. Choosing a bandwidth h generally implies that estimation is conducted using *only* those observations for which $Z_i \in [\kappa - h, \kappa + h]$.[4] The primary reason for using a larger-than-infinitesimal bandwidth is, of course, sample size. This is a perfect example of the bias-variance trade-offs we often come across in econometrics. While we would like to use only those observations which are *just* above or just below the cutoff, if we restrict to too small a sample, estimates will be too imprecise to permit any constructive inference. We will thus prefer to marginally increase the bandwidth provided that the gains from allowing slightly more bias into estimation is offset by a reduction in the variance of the resulting estimators.

Fortunately, there is a considerable amount of work on how to optimally balance this trade-off. Early work by Imbens and Kalyanaraman (2012), sometimes called first-generation bandwidth estimators, provides specific guidelines for bandwidth choice. Imbens and Kalyanaraman (2012) proposed to estimate the bandwidth in a mean-squared error (MSE) optimal way. The idea of this is that a reasonable criteria for judging models is to find one that results in estimates that are close to the true parameter. In a mean-squared error criteria, we can define:

$$MSE(h) = \mathbb{E}[(\hat{\tau}^{\text{SRD}} - \tau^{\text{SRD}})^2],$$

where this is viewed as a loss function for a particular bandwidth choice h where the loss is greater to the degree that the estimated parameter $\hat{\tau}^{\text{SRD}}$ diverges from the true parameter of interest τ^{SRD}. The mean squared error is often used as a criteria for judging modeling choices precisely because the MSE can be written as the variance of an estimator plus the square of its bias, and hence trades off variance and bias. Imbens and Kalyanaraman (2012) propose an optimal bandwidth h^{opt}, which satisfies:

$$h^{\text{opt}} = \arg\min_h MSE(h). \tag{6.21}$$

Imbens and Kalyanaraman (2012) (and the restatement in Calonico, Cattaneo, and Titiunik [2014a]) show that in the case of the local polynomial regression discontinuity estimator, this can be approximately written as:

$$MSE(h) \approx h_N^{2(p+1)} \mathcal{B}_p^2 + \frac{1}{Nh_N} \mathcal{V}_p, \tag{6.22}$$

where p refers to the polynomial order of the local RD estimate, $\mathcal{B}$ refers to the bias in the RD estimate, and $\mathcal{V}$ refers to the variance of the parameter $\hat{\tau}^{\text{SRD}}(h_N)$. An exact statement can be found in Imbens and Kalyanaraman (2012, equation 5) or Calonico, Cattaneo, and

Titiunik (2014a, Lemma 1), but the key takeaway from this is that to consider the optimal bandwidth in an RDD according to the Imbens and Kalyanaraman (2012) criteria, we seek to trade off the bias and variance terms we will discuss at more length below. By minimizing (6.22) in terms of h, this suggests the following optimal bandwidth parameter:

$$h^{\text{opt}}(N,p) = \left(\frac{\mathcal{V}_p}{2(p+1)\mathcal{B}_p^2}\right)^{\frac{1}{(2p+3)}} \times N^{\frac{-1}{(2p+3)}}. \tag{6.23}$$

A number of results are immediately clear from this, and they are logical if we think of the trade-offs we will be facing in estimating an RDD. Firstly, as the number of observations N grows, the bandwidth will fall. This is because (6.23) is scaled by $N^{-1/5}$ (in the case where $p=1$, implying a linear fit on both sides of the discontinuity). Secondly, the bandwidth will increase as the variance of data grows. This is because in cases with high variance, if a small bandwidth is chosen, it is unlikely that we will be able to say much about any treatment effect because standard errors of resulting estimates will simply be too large, and so we will prefer more data, even at the cost of slightly more bias. And thirdly, the bandwidth will fall as the bias increases. As we will discuss at more length below, bias in RD estimation comes from seeking to approximate unknown relationships between the running variable and outcome of interest with polynomial functions. To the degree that smaller bandwidths are used, any approximation errors will fall, vanishing entirely as the range for the running variable shrinks to 0. Thus, to the degree that the bias in our regression approximations on each side of the cutoff becomes more relevant, we will prefer to shrink the bandwidth to minimize the space for bias to creep in. However, one concern noted by Imbens and Kalyanaraman (2012) is that if this bias term is small or imprecisely estimated, the denominator may be close to 0, which will result in very large optimal bandwidths in small samples. This motivates the inclusion of a positive regularization term R in the denominator, which avoids very small denominators and the resulting very large bandwidths $h^{\text{opt}}(N,p)$, resulting in the generally used optimal bandwidth calculation:

$$\widehat{h}_{\text{IK}} = \left(\frac{\widehat{\mathbb{V}}_{\text{IK}}}{2(p+1)\widehat{B}_{\text{IK}}^2 + \widehat{R}_{\text{IK}}}\right)^{\frac{1}{(2p+3)}} \times N^{\frac{-1}{(2p+3)}}, \tag{6.24}$$

where, as above, N is the sample size, p is the degree of the polynomial included on each side of the discontinuity, $\widehat{\mathbb{V}}$ is an estimate of the variance of the RD parameter $\widehat{\tau}$, $\widehat{B}$ is an estimate of the bias of this parameter, and $\widehat{R}$ is a regularization term to avoid small denominators when the sample size is not large.

This thus suggests an empirically justified bandwidth estimator provided that estimates are available for $\widehat{\mathbb{V}}_{\text{IK}}$, $\widehat{B}_{\text{IK}}^2$, and $\widehat{R}_{\text{IK}}$. While Imbens and Kalyanaraman (2012) propose estimates for these quantities, the estimates themselves rely on an initial bandwidth, at times referred to as a "pilot bandwidth," which is itself not optimally chosen. The idea of this is that we can estimate these quantities within some arbitrarily chosen "plug-in" bandwidth,

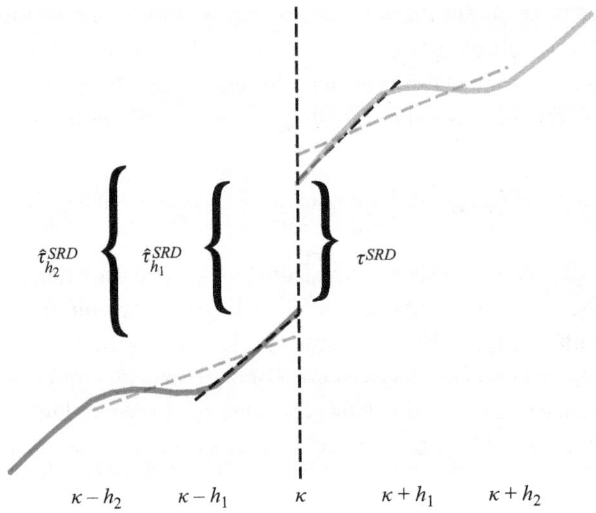

Figure 6.7
Local linear regression and bandwidth choice.

then, based on these estimates, calculate the optimal quantity (6.24). However, more recent work from Calonico, Cattaneo, and Titiunik (2014a) has provided enhancements to the plug-in bandwidth of Imbens and Kalyanaraman (2012), suggesting that these variance, bias, and regularization terms can themselves be estimated optimally, leading to an updated optimal bandwidth $\hat{h}_{\text{CCT}}$ which follows (6.24), simply replacing $\widehat{\mathbb{V}}_{\text{IK}}$, $\widehat{B^2_{\text{IK}}}$, and $\widehat{R}_{\text{IK}}$ with optimal quantities $\widehat{\mathbb{V}}_{\text{CCT}}$, $\widehat{B^2_{\text{CCT}}}$, and $\widehat{R}_{\text{CCT}}$. While the precise formulae for these estimates are provided in the appendix of Calonico, Cattaneo, and Titiunik (2014a) and we will not define them in full here, it is worth discussing the principles behind these terms, in particular the bias and variance terms, because as well as allowing us to understand the nature of the optimal bandwidth used ubiquitously in empirical practice, they will also be relevant for inference discussed in section 6.3.3.1.

As noted briefly above, the bias in regression discontinuity estimates comes from approximations in local regression functions, which do not correctly capture the true functional form of the underlying relationship between the running variable and outcomes of interest. Consider figure 6.7 for a specific example. Here we can consider what would happen if we sought to fit a linear relationship on either side of the cutoff when the true relationship between the running variable and the outcome is nonlinear. In this particular case, using a wider bandwidth of $\kappa \pm h_2$ results in quite poor fits while using a narrower bandwidth of $\kappa \pm h_1$ results in an improved fit given that close to the cut-point, nonlinearities become less extreme. While this illustration is based on a specific functional form and, of course, nothing guarantees that local linear fits will actually capture the correct end points when moving

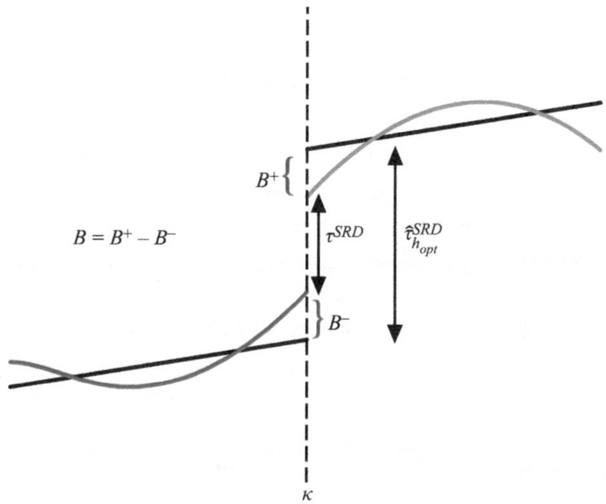

Figure 6.8
Bias in local linear regression discontinuity.

between any two arbitrary bandwidths, it is guaranteed that for a given polynomial degree, the fit of a relationship will never get worse, and will generally improve, as the bandwidth falls, and in the limit, as the bandwidth becomes miuscule, this local fit will capture the true intercepts.

Of course, in general, bias will occur, in particular if there is excess curvature in the true regression function that is *not* captured by our local model. An illustrative example of this is documented in figure 6.8. As we can observe in figure 6.8, the bias term will depend upon the excess curvature of the true dark and light polynomial functions, and can be approximated by the leading polynomial term *not* included in the black local polynomial fit. For example, if we observe relatively little excess curvature such that the values B^+ and B^- are small, then bias will be minimal. Similarly, if the curvature is such that both fit lines will intercept the discontinuity at above or below the true intercepts, these will counteract each other, and the bias term will be smaller given that the total bias B depends upon the bias at each point $B = B^+ - B^-$. Given this, the proposal in Imbens and Kalyanaraman (2012) and Calonico, Cattaneo, and Titiunik (2014a) is to approximate this bias as a function of $\widehat{\mu}_+^{(p+1)} - \widehat{\mu}_-^{(p+1)}$, where $\widehat{\mu}_+^{(p+1)}$ and $\widehat{\mu}_-^{(p+1)}$ refer to estimates of the curvature of the leading polynomial term not captured in the original local regression model. Because the optimal bandwidth for estimation is not yet known (this will depend upon the bias we are seeking to estimate), we will estimate the bias in a larger ("pilot") bandwidth than the one used for the main local polynomial fit, allowing us to obtain stable estimates of the higher-order curvature terms.

The estimation of the variance term also requires focusing on observations close to the threshold. In particular, we are interested in some variance $\mathbb{V}(n,p) = \mathbb{V}(N,p)_+ + \mathbb{V}(N,p)_-$. Here $\mathbb{V}(N,p)_+$ and $\mathbb{V}(N,p)_-$ depends upon the variance of data at either side of the discontinuity: $\sigma_+^2 = \lim_{z\downarrow\kappa} \mathbb{V}[Y_i(1)|Z_i = z]$ and $\sigma_-^2 = \lim_{z\uparrow\kappa} \mathbb{V}[Y_i(0)|Z_i = z]$, respectively, as well as the density of the running variable, and kernel used. The key unknown quantities are the variance terms σ_+^2 and σ_-^2, and Calonico, Cattaneo, and Titiunik (2014a) note that these can be estimated from the underlying variation of observed observations Y_i around the predicted values $\widehat{\mu}_+$ and $\widehat{\mu}_-$. Specifically, defining $\varepsilon_{i,+} = (Y_i - \widehat{\mu}_+^{(p)}(Z_i))$ (and similarly for below cutoff observations), variances can be estimated as $\sigma_+^2 = \mathbb{E}[\varepsilon_{i,+}^2|Z_i]$. Calonico, Cattaneo, and Titiunik (2014a) discuss a number of ways in practice to define these variance terms, either via a "plug-in" route where $\widehat{\mu}_+^{(p)}(Z_i)$ and $\widehat{\mu}_-^{(p)}(Z_i)$ are estimated using some pilot bandwidth, or using a matched pair approach drawing on matching procedures laid out in Abadie and Imbens (2006).

Precise formulae for all optimal bias, variance, and regularization terms are laid out in the appendix of Calonico, Cattaneo, and Titiunik (2014a) or online supplementary material to this paper (Calonico, Cattaneo, and Titiunik 2014b). These formulae are somewhat cumbersome given that they are developed for any choice of local polynomial p both for fuzzy and sharp designs, and are not reproduced in full here. The good theoretical properties of these procedures, the fact that they have been documented to work well in practice (Hyytinen et al. 2018), and given that a robust set of computational tools that implement the methods has been provided by the authors and actively developed over time, has meant that these methods are by far the most common bandwidth selection procedures in practice today. There are, however, also alternative proposals for bandwidth selection from earlier literature, in particular a cross-validation approach first laid out in Ludwig and Miller (2000) and developed in Imbens and Kalyanaraman (2012) and Calonico, Cattaneo, and Titiunik (2014a). Generally however, this procedure is not optimal (Imbens and Kalyanaraman 2012, 944–945) and so is no longer frequently used.

6.3.2.6 Selection of polynomial ordering and kernels The estimator defined in (6.19) requires three particular choices. A first choice is the bandwidth, and, as we discuss above, there is solid theoretical grounding and clear empirical guidance for this choice. The other two choices are related to the kernel $K(\cdot)$ and polynomial ordering p used in local polynomial regressions. In general, the choice of the kernel or the polynomial estimate should be much less important, and if the choice of kernels or polynomial degrees from among a series of reasonable options *does* significantly effect estimated results, this suggests that considerable caution should be employed when interpreting estimated parameters. Generally, the baseline choice is to employ a triangular kernel and a first-order polynomial, and these seem to be a reasonable starting place for most estimation procedures.

Selecting a kernel The logic of using a triangular kernel is that this kernel gives greater weight to observations that are closest to the cutoff, and that are of the most interest for estimation in RDDs. However, similar-shaped kernels, such as the Epanechnikov kernel documented in figure 6.6, also impose weights of this type. Nevertheless, it turns out that the triangular kernel is optimal in terms of minimizing the MSE of point estimates (Fan and Gijbels 1992), which leads to a preference for employing this kernel in practice. There are also arguments in favor of employing a uniform kernel. For one, such a kernel is practically very simple to implement, as it implies estimating an unweighted regression within the optimal bandwidth. What's more, this kernel is also optimal in terms of the asymptotic variance of the point estimator at the boundary (Cattaneo, Nicolas Idrobo, and Titiunik 2024). The fact that a uniform kernel is optimal in terms of asymptotic variance while a triangular kernel is optimal in terms of MSE makes sense in that a triangular kernel will lose some efficiency from giving less weight to observations further from the cut-off. Thus, in practice, either a triangular or uniform kernel seem perfectly justifiable, and robustness should be checked to both choices.

Selecting a polynomial degree The default behavior in selecting a polynomial order is to set $p=1$, and indeed this is implemented in widely used regression discontinuity software, which implements the methods laid out in Calonico, Cattaneo, and Titiunik (2014a). In a review of RDD studies published in a number of journals between 1999 and 2017, Pei et al. (2021) document that of the seventy-six papers employing local polynomial estimation, forty-five implement linear models as their main specification. Arguments against setting $p=0$ and in favor of $p=1$ were laid out in early work on regression discontinuity estimation by Hahn, Todd, and Klaauw (2001) and justified given the smaller bias of these methods.

In general, the correct choice for polynomial ordering in local linear models, of course, depends on the true nature of the unknown underlying data generating process, which describes the relationship between the running variable and the outcome around the cutoff, and becomes irrelevant asymptotically as the bandwidth shrinks to zero. However, when the bandwidth is not infinitely small, the choice of polynomial itself—even in local polynomial approaches—encounters a trade-off between bias and variance. This point is laid out by Pei et al. (2021), who suggest that one can seek to determine the polynomial degree in a data-driven way, following the MSE optimal logic employed in bandwidth selection. They find that there is no universally preferred polynomial ordering, with optimal polynomial choices depending on sample sizes within optimal bandwidths, and the excess curvature of local polynomial estimates, in much the same way as occurs with optimal bandwidth selection. In exploring a number of simulated data generating processes, they find that at times locally optimal polynomials can reach well beyond $p=1$, even up to a maximum degree of $p=4$. In practice, because all results are based on asymptotic approximations, sensitivity should be tested to alternative polynomial choices, though the results (and accompanying software) of Pei et al. (2021) suggest one theoretically justified option for a baseline choice.

6.3.3 Inference in Regression Discontinuity Designs

6.3.3.1 Bias in RDDs and bias-corrected methods The above procedures to estimate the parameters $\widehat{\tau}^{\text{SRD}}$ or $\widehat{\tau}^{\text{FRD}}$ are optimal in terms of the point estimates and are consistent estimators of τ^{SRD} and τ^{FRD}, respectively. The consistency comes from the fact that as the sample grows, the bandwidth will shrink, and any bias term will disappear as the importance of the local approximation to the unknown regression function on each side of the cutoff becomes less and less relevant. For this reason, the parameter $\widehat{\tau}^{\text{SRD}}$ is the best estimate in a mean squared error sense, while additionally enjoying the benefits of consistency, and, as such, is the estimator generally reported in empirical applications.

However, the presence of the bias term in this estimator poses challenges for inference. This issue is addressed in the path-breaking work of Calonico, Cattaneo, and Titiunik (2014a), who note that while the MSE-optimal bandwidth discussed above is suitable for minimizing mean squared error of the point estimate, it is not optimal for inference—specifically for estimating standard errors and constructing confidence intervals—because it tends to be *too large*. They highlight that consistency of the RD estimator $\widehat{\tau}^{\text{SRD}}$ requires the bandwidth to shrink as the sample size N increases, but not too quickly: In particular, we require $h_N \to 0$ and $Nh_N \to \infty$. However, for valid inference, a more stringent condition is needed: $Nh_N^5 \to 0$ and $Nh_N \to \infty$. Under these conditions, Calonico, Cattaneo, and Titiunik (2014a) show that:

$$\widehat{\tau}^{\text{SRD}}(h_N) \xrightarrow{\text{d}} \mathcal{N}\left(\tau^{\text{SRD}}, \mathbb{V}^{\text{SRD}}(h_N)\right). \tag{6.25}$$

This result suggests that *if such converge criterion are met*, then based upon the selection of an appropriate variance estimator for $\mathbb{V}^{\text{SRD}}(h_N)$, asymptotically valid confidence intervals for the parameter τ^{SRD} could be constructed as standard:

$$CI_{\text{SRD}}^{95\%} = \left(\widehat{\tau}^{\text{SRD}}(h_N) - z_{0.975} \times \sqrt{\widehat{\mathbb{V}^{\text{SRD}}(h_N)}}, \widehat{\tau}^{\text{SRD}}(h_N) + z_{0.975} \times \sqrt{\widehat{\mathbb{V}^{\text{SRD}}(h_N)}}\right). \tag{6.26}$$

A problem that may be apparent if we return to inspect the MSE optimal bandwidths laid out as in (6.24) above is that they generally *do not* meet the criteria $Nh_N^5 \to 0$. Rather, because these can be written as some constant $c \times N^{-\frac{1}{5}}$, MSE-optimal bandwidths will be "too large," instead fulfilling $Nh_N^5 \to c$, where c is some positive constant.What this means in practice is that the bias term does not disappear from the asymptotic distribution of the regression discontinuity parameter, and instead of the convenient representation in (6.25), the resulting limit distribution is written as:

$$\widehat{\tau}^{\text{SRD}}(h_N) \xrightarrow{\text{d}} \mathcal{N}\left(\tau^{\text{SRD}} + h_N^2 B_N(h_N), \mathbb{V}^{\text{SRD}}(h_N)\right). \tag{6.27}$$

This is problematic, because the existence of the bias term B_N in (6.27) means that any confidence intervals constructed as in (6.26) will not be centered on the true parameter τ^{SRD}, but rather will be shifted by the existence of any bias, generally resulting in inflated rejection rates of null hypotheses (see, e.g., Calonico, Cattaneo, and Titiunik [2014a], §6).

This leads to a number of possible solutions. A first is to simply use a smaller-than-optimal bandwidth such that the condition $Nh_N^5 \to 0$ is actually met. This process is known as "undersmoothing," though in practice this is not the route typically taken because this requires arbitrary choices of smaller than optimal bandwidths. A second—and the recommended and widely applied solution—is to employ bias correction methods that simply estimate this bias and remove it when constructing confidence intervals. Namely, this consists of calculating the "bias corrected" quantity:

$$\widehat{\tau}^{\text{SRD,bc}} = \widehat{\tau}^{\text{SRD}} - h_N^2 \widehat{B}(b_N, h_N)^{\text{SRD}},$$

which simply corrects for an estimate of the bias. A convenient point for calculating such bias-correction methods is that we already have an estimate $\widehat{B}(b_N, h_N)^{\text{SRD}}$, which was derived when discussing optimal bandwidth calculations, and this is precisely what is used here. Based on this, Calonico, Cattaneo, and Titiunik (2014a) show that if $Nh_N^7 \to 0$ and $h_N/b_N \to 0$, then:

$$\widehat{\tau}^{\text{SRD,bc}}(h_N) \xrightarrow{d} \mathcal{N}\left(\tau^{\text{SRD}}, \mathbb{V}^{\text{SRD}}(h_N)\right), \tag{6.28}$$

suggesting that the following bias-corrected confidence intervals are valid for inference in RDDs:

$$CI_{95\%}^{\text{SRD,bc}} = \left(\widehat{\tau}_{\text{bc}}^{\text{SRD}}(h_N) - z_{0.975} \times \sqrt{\widehat{\mathbb{V}^{\text{SRD}}(h_N)}}, \widehat{\tau}_{\text{bc}}^{\text{SRD}}(h_N) + z_{0.975} \times \sqrt{\widehat{\mathbb{V}^{\text{SRD}}(h_N)}}\right). \tag{6.29}$$

There is, however, one final issue with this, which leads to the most empirically relevant way to conduct inference in RDDs. While the bias-corrected CIs in (6.29) are an elegant solution to the problem of bias in local polynomial methods, these are asymptotically valid, but in practice, in small samples, the fact that bias is estimated rather than known needs also to be accounted for. Thus, to ensure that confidence intervals adequately capture the fact that the estimation of bias itself introduces uncertainty, Calonico, Cattaneo, and Titiunik (2014a) propose a version of (6.29) that is robust to the estimation of the bias. These are the so-called robust bias-corrected inference methods. In practice, all that changes in this case is that the variance used to construct confidence intervals in (6.29) is replaced with a variance term that accounts for the variability of the bias-corrected estimate. This consists of replacing (6.28) with:

$$\widehat{\tau}^{\text{SRD,bc}}(h_N) \xrightarrow{d} \mathcal{N}\left(\tau^{\text{SRD}}, \mathbb{V}^{\text{SRD,bc}}(h_N)\right), \tag{6.30}$$

where

$$\mathbb{V}^{\text{SRD,bc}}(h_N) = \mathbb{V}^{\text{SRD}}(h_N) + C^{\text{SRD,bc}}(h_N, b_N),$$

where C is a correction factor to account for this uncertainty in the bias estimate. This, finally, leads to the robust bias-corrected confidence intervals we will generally wish to use:

$$CI_{95\%}^{\text{SRD,bc}} = \left(\hat{\tau}^{\text{SRD,bc}}(h_N) - z_{0.975} \times \sqrt{\widehat{\mathbb{V}^{SRD,bc}(h_N)}}, \hat{\tau}^{\text{SRD,bc}}(h_N) + z_{0.975} \times \sqrt{\widehat{\mathbb{V}^{\text{SRD,bc}}(h_N)}} \right). \tag{6.31}$$

Before—briefly—discussing the estimates of these variance terms, it is worth highlighting a number of points here. Firstly, as laid out above when discussing estimation, the bandwidth optimal estimate $\hat{\tau}^{\text{SRD}}$ is both consistent and MSE minimizing, and hence when considering *estimation*, we are interested in this quantity rather than the bias corrected quantity. Thus, bias correction should generally not be reported in point estimates, and standard computational implementations of these packages, which we will explore in code callouts, do not report bias-corrected point estimates by default. However, robust bias-correction *is* preferred for confidence intervals, and as such, one should report the non-bias corrected parameter estimate along with the robust bias-corrected confidence intervals. The crux of the argument for this is that the parameter itself is consistently identified, while the (finite sample) point estimates do not suffer from the presence of any bias, resulting in good properties for hypothesis tests.

To complete the discussion of inference with bias correction, we thus just need an estimate for the variance term $\widehat{\mathbb{V}^{\text{SRD,bc}}(h_N)}$. This term depends upon the typical variance owing to variation in data around the cutoff ($\widehat{\mathbb{V}^{\text{SRD}}(h_N)}$) as well as a second variance that owes to the estimation of the bias. We have previously noted that the prior term can be estimated (and is estimated) when determining the optimal bandwidth as laid out in section 6.3.2.5. This can proceed using either the plug-in or matched-pairs procedure laid out in Calonico, Cattaneo, and Titiunik (2014a). The second term is also defined in Calonico, Cattaneo, and Titiunik (2014a). They note that the resulting variance terms are "straightforward to derive but notationally cumbersome," and if you are interested in consulting the full details, they are laid out in Calonico, Cattaneo, and Titiunik (2014a, §5). Following the standard variance formula described for optimal bandwidths, both a plug-in and matched-paired approach is proposed, and can be easily implemented in accompanying software discussed in code callout 6.2.

Code Callout 6.2: Implementing Regression Discontinuity Estimators

Using data from Benjamin Hansen (2015) on DUI charges and recidivism, we will consider the implementation of RDDs, comparing implementations "by hand" with widely used computational routines that implement optimal bandwidth selection procedures and robust bias correction. We will see that estimating RDD "by hand" replicates point estimates (but not CIs) when similar bandwidths are used.

6.3.3.2 Alternative inference procedures for RDD

While these bias-corrected methods are a leading choice for RDDs, alternative valid proposals exist. A first approach, which is somewhat different in nature to bias correction procedures but both conceptually elegant and potentially more efficient in terms of the resulting confidence intervals, is defined by Armstrong and Kolesár (2020). They propose that rather than recentering the confidence intervals with the bias estimate as discussed above, we can work with the original estimate and simply adjust the standard error by a critical value which reflects the estimator's bias. This procedure effectively inflates standard errors, resulting in so-called "honest" confidence intervals, or honest inference on parameters.

This idea of "honest" inference is related to "minimax" procedures, and is drawn from a quite long-standing literature from statistics and nonparametric estimation (see, e.g., Stein [1956]; Lai and Robbins [1985]; Li [1989]; Donoho [1994], for influential early works in this domain) which seek to ensure that inference performs well over a range of potential circumstances. In particular, in the case of regression discontinuity designs with optimal bandwidths, confidence intervals are sought that will contain the true parameter with some level of significance (such as 95%) even if the worst-case scenario for bias occurs. While the complete notation will not be laid out here in full, Armstrong and Kolesár's work provides quite straightforward recommendations for applications with RDD. Namely, if local linear models are estimated and the previously defined optimal MSE-optimal bandwidth is used for estimation, inference can proceed with a 95% confidence level by replacing the standard normal critical value of $z_{0.975} = 1.96$ with an inflated critical value of 2.18. What's more, these procedures can be easily adapted to alternative polynomial degrees and confidence levels, simply resulting in alternative calculable critical values. A key takeaway from the work is that despite the use of inflated critical values, confidence intervals resulting from honest inference are generally shorter than robust bias-corrected counterparts. We will explore this in an end-of-chapter question.

A second approach to variance estimation, which seeks to produce confidence intervals that are more efficient than those resulting from the robust-bias corrected procedure, is laid out by Calonico, Cattaneo, and Farrell (2020). These seek to improve on bias-corrected methods by defining a new "coverage error" (CE) optimal bandwidth. The idea of this CE optimal bandwidth is that it should lead to confidence intervals for some confidence level $(1-\alpha)$ that contain the true parameter as close as possible to $100 \times (1-\alpha)\%$ of the time (for example, as close to 95% of the time in the case of a 95% confidence interval). Calonico, Cattaneo, and Farrell (2020) show how this CE optimal bandwidth can be calculated and propose a procedure in which after using an MSE optimal bandwidth for point estimation, a new CE optimal bandwidth can be used for inference.

6.3.4 What Changes in Fuzzy Designs?

We have generally focused on the sharp RDD when laying out estimation and inference procedures above, but fortunately this does not come at much of a cost if we instead wish to consider fuzzy designs! It turns out that the beauty of many of the mechanics introduced above is that they hold for FRD designs as well. The Fuzzy RDD estimand laid out in (6.7) is simply the ratio of two sharp RDDs: a numerator that is an RDD of the reduced form (the impact of Z_i on Y_i), and a denominator that is an RDD of the first stage (the impact of Z_i on treatment adoption D_i). This suggests that estimation can quite simply proceed by taking the ratio of each of the corresponding sharp estimates, namely:

$$\widehat{\tau}^{\mathrm{FRD}}_{\mathrm{LATE}(\kappa)} = \frac{\widehat{\tau}^{\mathrm{SRD}}_{Y}}{\widehat{\tau}^{\mathrm{SRD}}_{D}}, \tag{6.32}$$

where sub-indices for Y and D in the sharp RD parameters indicate estimation where Y and D act as outcomes.

Calonico, Cattaneo, and Titiunik (2014a) lay out the theory for local polynomial estimation of the quantity $\widehat{\tau}^{\mathrm{FRD}}_{\mathrm{LATE}(\kappa)}$ and fully develop robust bias correction procedures for inference in cases with Fuzzy RDD. While the technical details are all laid out in Calonico, Cattaneo, and Titiunik (2014a) and supplementary appendices, one key point to note is that optimal bandwidth selection in this case refers to the one bandwidth that minimizes the mean square error when considering the estimated quantity $\widehat{\tau}^{\mathrm{FRD}}_{\mathrm{LATE}(\kappa)}$, and not an optimal (different) bandwidth for each of the quantities in the numerator and the denominator. Similarly, when considering inference, robust bias correction is conducted directly with the estimate of interest $\widehat{\tau}^{\mathrm{FRD}}_{\mathrm{LATE}(\kappa)}$. As in the case of sharp designs, software is available to implement these procedures, and we will explore a number of elements of Fuzzy RDD estimation with real data in code callout 6.3.

Code Callout 6.3: Fuzzy RDD, First Stages, and Reduced Forms
We will explore the implementation of a fuzzy RDD using data from Angrist and Lavy (1999), who look at the impact of class size on educational outcomes, using a discontinuity in class sizes when the number of students in a school passes a maximum class size threshold. We will see that fuzzy RDD parameters can be estimated by scaling the reduced form by the first stage, and we will explore the automated implementation of robust (fuzzy) methods with bias correction.

6.4 Diagnostic Tests in RDDs

The elegance of the RDD and the fact that effects can be graphically seen and understood is a key benefit of these methods. What's more, this design lends itself well to a series of similarly visually understandable diagnostic, falsification, or robustness tests.

As noted in section 6.2, the key identifying assumption for the estimands defined up to this point is that the expectation of potential outcomes is smooth around the cutoff (assumption 12). This is, of course, not something that can be tested given the unobserved nature of potential outcomes. However, we can seek to examine whether observed data suggests that these assumptions should be doubted. In effect, if we observe sharp differences in (predetermined) characteristics of individuals on either side of the cutoff, or evidence of manipulation of the running variable itself, this may make us doubt that continuity assumptions may be met.

In essence, these tests, and in particular the first two tests discussed below, seek to consider whether there is evidence that there may be some unexpected imbalance around the cutoff. The logic is that if we observe that individuals on either side of the cutoff are very different—either in terms of their observable characteristics or their frequency—we may be concerned that there is some sort of manipulation of the running variable. If such manipulation exists, *and* if individuals nonrandomly manipulate the running variable based on their potential outcomes then this will lead to discontinuities in the potential outcomes and failures of the identifying assumption. However, formally, the tests we discuss below are neither sufficient nor necessary for proving the validity of an RDD. They are not sufficient in the sense that we may fail to detect manipulation, but nevertheless (unobservable) potential outcomes may jump at the cutoff point. And failing the below tests does not *necessarily* imply that potential outcomes jump discontinuously at the cutoff, if for example heaping occurs, but this heaping is entirely unrelated to potential outcomes. Some specific examples of such cases are mentioned in McCrary (2008, 701). Nonetheless, the below tests all provide a reasonable consideration of whether we may be concerned about manipulation of the running variable or other elements of the empirical design, and are widely viewed as key diagnostic tests to support an RDD.

6.4.1 Balance Tests and Placebo Tests

A first relatively simple test is to consider whether there is balance in predetermined covariates on either side of the regression discontinuity. The logic of this test is that if we fail to observe balance in certain predetermined variables just above and just below the discontinuity, this is evidence to suggest that certain *types* of individuals are managing to access treatment at greater rates than others. And unless these types of individuals have precisely the same potential outcomes as all other individuals, this will result in a failure of assumption 12. This test is in some sense analogous to the balance tests often implemented prior to analyzing data from a randomized controlled trial.

As an example, we may consider the influential class size RD proposed by Angrist and Lavy (1999), which we explore in code callout 6.3. In this setting, class size caps set at forty students per class imply that students in grades with forty students are split into two classes of twenty, while students in grades with thirty-nine students are in a much larger class. Based on the logic of an RDD, we could identify the effect of class size on academic outcomes by taking advantage of the discontinuity in class size determined by the running variable of students in a grade. However, an example in which balance tests are used to document fatal flaws in this design is described by Urquiola and Verhoogen (2009), who seek to implement this design in Chile. They show that in this context, parental education and income drop discontinuously at the cutoff, which suggests that better-educated and higher-income parents are more responsive to this rule, sorting their children into smaller classes. It seems very likely that the potential outcomes of these children are different to those of other children, which will result in violations of assumption 12.

In practice, the implementation of these tests is relatively straightforward. As we are interested in balance precisely at the cutoff of interest, we should seek to test balance in a small window around the discontinuity. And in the same way as laid out in section 6.3.2, we can seek to estimate these balance tests using optimal local polynomial methods, as well as present graphical plots that summarize the variables around the cutoff of interest. In formal tests, this is simply a reestimation of the procedure we use for the main RD analysis, where instead of considering the true outcome, we consider a range of predetermined variables, resulting in a series of point estimates and (robust) confidence intervals. Because this test will be based on optimal RD methods, and because different variables will have different variances and bias estimates, the optimal bandwidth for each balance test will vary, and standard practice is to report a balance test for each variable based on its own optimal bandwidth. It is worth noting that while we would expect variables to be balanced if manipulation does not occur, and thus consider whether the confidence intervals of each balance test contain 0, if a large number of covariates are available, we should not expect all confidence intervals to contain 0 *even if* manipulation does not occur. The reason for this is that under the null hypothesis, valid confidence intervals will contain the parameter of interest in $(1\text{-}\alpha)\times 100\%$ of the time. Thus, if we conduct a large number of tests and see approximately $\alpha \times 100\%$ of variables that suggest misbalance, this is in line with expected type I error rates and should not necessarily be viewed as failure of balance tests. We return to discuss these points at considerably more length in chapter 7.

6.4.2 Running Variable Density and Direct Tests of Manipulation

A related test, first proposed by McCrary (2008) is to consider the distribution of the running variable itself. The logic of this test is that if we observe systematic discrepancies in the density on the left- and right-hand side of the discontinuity, then it is likely that individuals were able to precisely manipulate their value of the running variable Z to choose on which side of the cutoff they were located. In general, if we observe such evidence of sorting across the cutoff, we will have significant concerns about the continuity of the underlying potential outcomes, unless such sorting occurs in a way that is completely orthogonal to potential outcomes.

Initial versions of this test were formalized by McCrary (2008), and, indeed, tests of this type are generally known as McCrary tests. As in the case of many elements of regression discontinuity methods, key elements can be displayed descriptively. Consider figure 6.9 based on data from M.-J. Lee (2008), which plots victory margins in US house elections

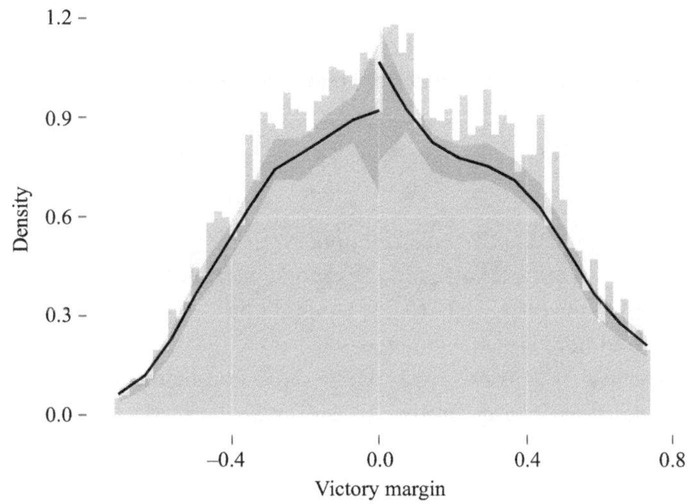

Figure 6.9
McCrary test of heaping of running variable (house election victory margin).

between 1948 and 1998. Here we can see a histogram displaying the density of the victory margin for Democratic representatives, and this histogram is overlaid with an estimate of the density (solid line) and confidence intervals on each side of the cutoff. The key idea of the test is that we should not see a jump in the density of the running variable directly at the cutoff, as otherwise we may be concerned with nonrandom manipulation of the running variable, which will cast doubts on assumptions about the continuity of the potential outcomes at this point. We can test this formally by considering whether there is a break in the density estimate just at the right and just at the left of the cutoff point.

Formal implementations of the test were first laid out in McCrary (2008), and this implementation consists of, first, generating a binned histogram of the running variable on each side of the cutoff, and secondly estimating local linear (kernel-based) regressions on each side of the cutoff, before testing whether there is a discontinuity in the intercept of these two functions at the cutoff. This procedure was widely adopted but required choices related to how the binned histogram was defined on each side of the cutoff in the first step (i.e., the bin sizes) as well as the bandwidth over which the test should be conducted.

Recent extensions by Cattaneo, Jansson, and Ma (2020) suggest an alternative way forward that proceeds without binning, based simply on local polynomial nonparametric estimation of densities. This version of the test also takes advantage of optimal bandwidth selection methods, and it is laid out here. Generally, these methods seek to test the following hypothesis, where $f(z)$ refers to the density of the running variable:

$$H_0: \lim_{z \uparrow \kappa} f(z) = \lim_{z \downarrow \kappa} f(z) \qquad \text{versus} \qquad H_1: \lim_{z \uparrow \kappa} f(z) \neq \lim_{z \downarrow \kappa} f(z).$$

Rejection of the null implies that there is excess mass on one side of the discontinuity, suggestive of manipulation or sorting into treatment. In the version of the test proposed by Cattaneo, Jansson, and Ma (2020), under the null, the quantity

$$T_p(h) = \frac{\frac{N_+}{N}\widehat{f}_+(\kappa) - \frac{N_-}{N}\widehat{f}_-(\kappa)}{\sqrt{\frac{N_+}{N}\frac{1}{Nh_+}\widehat{\mathbb{V}}_+(\kappa) - \frac{N_-}{N}\frac{1}{Nh_-}\widehat{\mathbb{V}}_-(\kappa)}} \tag{6.33}$$

is shown to follow a standard normal distribution, suggesting that this quantity can be calculated and compared with critical values of the normal distribution to test the null of equality of distributions. While the quantity in (6.33) looks slightly elaborate, in essence the numerator simply refers to differences in estimated densities at the cutoff approaching from above and below ($\widehat{f}_+(\kappa)$ and $\widehat{f}_-(\kappa)$), respectively, while the denominator depends on the variances of each of these densities. The quantities N_+ and N_- refer to the number of observations above and below the cutoff with $N = N_+ + N_-$, and similarly the bandwidth above and below the cutoff for testing is referred to as h_+ and h_-, with $h = h_+ + h_-$.

Cattaneo, Jansson, and Ma (2020) propose methods to estimate the distributions $\widehat{f}_+(z)$ and $\widehat{f}_-(z)$ and variances $\widehat{\mathbb{V}}_+(z)$ and $\widehat{\mathbb{V}}_-(z)$. These are based on local polynomial regression (where p refers to the polynomial degree that is used to model the density of z), which work particularly well at boundary points, as is of interest here. In practice, this test requires determining this bandwidth, and Cattaneo, Jansson, and Ma (2020) show that these procedures can be employed with an optimal bandwidth and bias-corrected methods. This consists of estimating an optimal bandwidth in the spirit of the results discussed in the previous section with some polynomial p (suggested to be $p = 2$) and estimating densities with a higher-order polynomial $p + 1$ for bias correction. Finally, the test statistic $T_{p+1}(\widehat{h}_p^{\text{opt}})$ is calculated, which is asymptotically valid. Software exists to implement these methods (as explored in code callout 6.4), and Cattaneo, Jansson, and Ma (2018) show that these methods have particularly good size and power properties when employing bias-correction methods.

Other tests exist to test for potential manipulation of the running variable, perhaps most notably Frandsen (2017) who proposes a test for cases where the running variable is discrete, and Cattaneo, Titiunik, and Vazquez-Bare (2017), who consider a version of the test for RD based on a local randomization framework. In sections 6.5.3 and 6.5.1, we discuss these settings more generally and note that if such settings are of relevance, these tests should replace that of Cattaneo, Jansson, and Ma (2020) laid out above; however, the logic of the test is identical to that laid out above.

6.4.3 Other Tests in Regression Discontinuity Designs

Another empirical test often considered in the battery of RD tests is to consider placebo cutoff points and test whether there is any evidence of jumps in outcomes at points of the running variable where no discontinuity in treatment actually occurs. The idea of such tests is that if placebo RD estimates are implemented at points where treatment access does not actually vary, this allows us to test whether continuity assumptions are met in other points of support of the data. If we observe evidence of jumps in outcomes at other false treatment points, we will likely be concerned that continuity assumptions may also not be met at the true discontinuity. While there is, as yet, no accepted procedure for assigning placebo treatment points in the running variable, for tests of this nature we would ideally like to consider points that may suffer from similar concerns as the main cutoff. For example, if considering educational test scores where a cutoff occurs at some value rounded to 10, we may wish to consider as placebo cutoffs all multiples of 10 in a nearby window, as these may similarly be subject to concerns about rounding of scores. Often such a placebo test will consist of estimating multiple parameters, using precisely the same design as that used around the true cutoff, and presenting resulting estimators in a tabular or graphical form that can be easily compared to the main estimate.

A final canonical RD test encountered, particularly in cases where there may be concern of minor violations of assignment or manipulations very close to the discontinuity, is the so-called donut RD model (Barreca et al. 2011). The donut model consists of reestimating the parameter corresponding to an RDD, however removing the observations that are in the most immediate proximity of the cutoff. This is particularly relevant if there are concerns that there may be nonrandom heaping or sorting very close to the cutoff. For example, Barreca et al.'s (2011) initial use of this model was in response to a setting where interventions were provided to very low-birth-weight infants, based on a 1,500-gram birthweight threshold. They noted that there was substantial heaping in weights at multiples of 100, which would be particularly concerning if such heaping owes to factors related to potential outcomes, such as being more likely in infants born in hospitals with lower technical capacities to precisely record weights. The donut RD thus proceeds by discarding those observations closest to the cutoff and examining the sensitivity of parameter estimates to their exclusion. Noack and Rothe (2023) formalize the details of this test, noting that if donut holes are sufficiently small, both robust bias correction methods and honest confidence intervals (Armstrong and Kolesár 2020) maintain appropriate coverage. In current empirical practice, sensitivity testing is often provided in which estimate stability is considered over a range of small "donut holes."

Code Callout 6.4: Manipulation and Balance Tests in RDD

In this code callout, we will work with data from Holden (2016), who studies the assignment of funding to purchase textbooks, which is assigned if average test schools are below a specific cutoff. We will examine a range of tests, including McCrary tests, balance tests, and donut RDs.

6.5 Extensions to the Standard Regression Discontinuity Design

6.5.1 A Local Randomization Approach

Often, statements related to the regression discontinuity design focus on some sort of local randomization or local unconfoundedness approach. For example, D. S. Lee (2008) notes that because of uncertainty in voting patterns, we may view outcomes in certain types of election as "essentially randomized among elections decided by a narrow margin." And generally, it is appealing to view treatment assignment in regression discontinuity as owing to randomness *local to the cutoff*, even though we would not view movements of the running variable as randomly assigned across a wider window. For example, we may perfectly well recognize that individuals with a higher test score are quite different to those with a lower test score, but at the same time recognize that very close to some arbitrary score κ the fact that someone scores one point more or one point fewer may be effectively random, given that a whole sum of events that strike more or less randomly can feed into test scores, such as factors like good luck on a particular draw of questions, the weather on the day of a test, distractions that may occur, and so forth. Under this logic, we may believe that for individuals quite close to some specific cutoff, if a test were taken many times, they may sometimes place just over the cutoff and sometimes place just under the cutoff, and these differences are as good as random in a very small window.

Such thought experiments suggest an alternative manner of viewing RDDs, with somewhat different implications for the underlying identifying assumptions, estimation methods, and inference procedures. Instead of employing the continuity approach, one can view the entire RDD through the lens of a "local" randomization, and key texts that define the way to conceptualize RDD through local randomization are M.-J. Lee (2008), Cattaneo, Frandsen, and Titiunik (2015), Cattaneo, Titiunik, and Vazquez-Bare (2017), and Sekhon and Titiunik (2017). We lay out here the key elements of this design and how to proceed with estimation and inference, and we discuss a number of settings where this manner of thinking about regression discontinuity may be useful.

Identifying assumptions Formally, this randomization approach can be justified as viewing that within some area local to the cutoff, the score an individual is assigned for the running variable is randomly assigned (Cattaneo, Frandsen, and Titiunik 2015). This is different to viewing treatment itself as being randomly assigned (Sekhon and Titiunik 2017), though via conceptualizing randomly assigned running variable values local to the cutoff, this allows for the "random" treatment assignment to flow directly from this randomly assigned value. The value of assuming random assignment of realizations of the running variable within some local area is that—by nature of randomization—the running variable will thus be unrelated to potential outcomes.

Cattaneo, Frandsen, and Titiunik (2015) lay out the key identifying assumption-underlying local randomization as follows. To start, we can consider potential outcomes for each value of the running variable, defined as $Y_i(z)$. Thus, while an individual will have only a specific realization Z_i of the running variable, they will have a vector of potential outcomes for all possible realizations. In practice, their observed outcome will be $Y_i = Y_i(Z_i)$. Of course, as standard in an RDD if we assume a sharp design, treatment will depend deterministically upon an individual's realization Z_i and the cutoff point κ following $W_i = \mathbb{1}\{Z_i \geq \kappa\}$. Here we will lay out notation for a sharp design, though a fuzzy design can be considered with slightly more notation, as laid out in Cattaneo, Frandsen, and Titiunik (2015, §6.1). Finally, we define $F_{Z_i|Z_i \in W_0}(z)$ as the cdf of the score provided that $Z_i \in W_0$. The idea of this cdf is that at each point in W_0 we could observe a distribution of values for the running variable, and this distribution of the running variable is described by $F(\cdot)$. Based on this notation, Cattaneo, Frandsen, and Titiunik (2015) lay out the following two-part identifying assumption:

Assumption 14. Local Randomization
There exists some neighborhood $W_0 = [\underline{z}, \overline{z}]$ with $\underline{z} < \kappa < \overline{z}$ in which the following holds for all observations i with scores $z_i \in W_0$:

(a) Identical distribution of running variables: $F_{Z_i|Z_i \in W_0}(z) = F(z)$.

(b) Potential outcomes depend on treatment, not on the value of the running variable: $Y_i(z) = Y_i(w)$.

Part (a) of this assumption states that the distribution of the running variable for all units within W_0 is identical, and it is what allows us to talk of "local randomization." While ex-post a specific realization of Z_i will be observed for each individual, ex-ante any value could have been observed as described by $F(z)$. Part (b) of the assumption is essentially an exclusion restriction. This simply states that what matters for potential outcomes is the treatment received and not the value of the running variable itself.

If a local randomization assumption is maintained, this implies that the value of the running variable can thus be ignored, and we can view analysis as—locally—equivalent to an experiment. In particular, this implies that we can identify a treatment effect of interest based on data observed in the range W_0:

$$\begin{aligned}\tau^{\text{SRD,LR}} &\equiv \mathbb{E}[Y_i(1) - Y_i(0)|Z_i \in W_0] \\ &= \mathbb{E}[Y_i|W_i = 1, Z_i \in W_0] - \mathbb{E}[Y_i|W_i = 0, Z_i \in W_0]. \end{aligned} \tag{6.34}$$

One key difference between this estimand and the estimand based on the continuity approach is that in (6.34) we do not explicitly refer to limit arguments. What's more, if W_0 is known, we can simply take (6.34) to data, estimating a differences in means. Perhaps the key implication is that unlike the case in the continuity approach where outcomes may depend upon the running variable in a complex way, here *by assumption* the running variable can only affect Y_i via the treatment, and so we can ignore the running variable entirely. It is important to note that this is a stronger assumption than we have made in the continuity-based approach, as it is equivalent to assuming that $Y_i(0)$ and $Y_i(1)$ are constant.

Estimation and inference The analogy to randomized experiments drives estimation and inference procedures. Estimation can be based on differences of means within the area local to the cutoff in which random assignment is assumed to hold. For inference, a range of procedures can be considered depending on the specific view of the nature of the local randomization, and related uncertainty. Cattaneo, Frandsen, and Titiunik (2015) originally laid out an inference procedure that takes a design-based approach in which the sample of individuals close to the cutoff was viewed as fixed, with uncertainty flowing from the fact that only one potential outcome is observed. This led them to proposing a randomization-based approach with randomization inference based on sharp null hypotheses, as discussed in section 2.4.2. While this procedure will work well particularly with small samples, it is important to note its use of the sharp null hypothesis of a precise zero effect for each individual, which is more demanding than typical tests. However, alternative sampling-based inference views can also be taken, in which case a null hypothesis about average effects can be taken, and inference can proceed as standard in an experimental setting (see Cattaneo et al. [2024, §2] for further details).

Selecting an estimation window A key final consideration in this approach is in what window we may truly believe that a local randomization assumption is reasonable. The leading approach for selecting the window W_0 is laid out in Cattaneo, Frandsen, and Titiunik (2015), who suggest that this can be based explicitly on the identifying assumptions. Because we are assuming *local* but not global randomization, the idea of this method is to consider a range of predetermined covariates (or placebo outcomes that are assumed unaffected by treatment) and seek to select the largest window in which these covariates are found to be balanced on each side of the cutoff. This is very much related to the logic of balance tests in an experimental design. If we observe that covariates are balanced in two arms of an experimental intervention, we may be willing to believe that the randomisation was successful. Similarly in a local randomization approach, if we observe balance between treated and controls in some local area we may be willing to accept that scores are as good as random in that range. However, once we expand the window and consider a range that is "too large," the effect of the running variable will begin to be seen in covariates, and we will reject this window.

In effect then, the procedure of window selection consists of considering a range of covariates and a small window. If covariates are all observed to be balanced within that small window, then this small window will be accepted as a potential window W_0. Then a larger window will be considered, and if balance is still observed, then the larger window will become the potential window W_0. This procedure will continue up until the point when any covariate is observed to be unbalanced, at which point the candidate window will be accepted as W_0. A formal definition of this algorithm is provided in Cattaneo, Titiunik, and Vazquez-Bare (2016).

6.5.2 Multidimensional RDDs

The cannonical RDD is based on a single known cutoff implying that implementation requires knowledge of a single score or running variable and focus on a critical discontinuity point we have called κ. At times, however, treatment assignment rules may be more complicated, resulting in multidimensional designs. In particular, we may come across cases with a single running variable but multiple cutoffs around which treatment assignment varies, or cases where treatment assignment varies based on multiple running variables with criteria on more than one running variable at a time. The first of these is a "multiple cutoff" setting, while the latter is a "multiple running variable" or "multiple-score" setting.

Multiple running variables A statement of the problem of regression discontinuity with multiple running variables is provided in Papay, Willett, and Murnane (2011), with further formalization discussed in Imbens and Zajonc (2011) and Wong, Steiner, and Cook (2013). This considers cases where treatments depend upon two running variables, including cases where grade progression or enrollment in remedial education may depend upon threshold scores in multiple tests (see, e.g., Jacob and Lefgren [2004]), where publicly offered programs or subsidies may depend upon a needs-based score and some other eligibility criteria (for example Londoño-Vélez, Rodríguez, and Sánchez 2020), or on geographic boundaries conceptualized by cutoffs defined in latitudinal and longitudinal space (e.g., Dell [2010]).

A challenge in this setting is that because there are multiple criteria that define cutoff points, there are potentially multiple estimands of interest. Consider, for example, the case where an individual passes a grade if they achieve over 50% on two tests (say a reading test and a mathematics test). If we wish to consider the effect of passing a grade based on an RDD in this setting, we could think of multiple counterfactual exercises. Consider, for example, the cases in table 6.1. Clearly in each case, if the key distinction is falling below 50%, treated units "just" pass, and control units "just" fail. However, the nature of the experiment is quite different in each case. For example, the first case considers a treated unit that barely passes both math and reading, compared to a control case that barely passes reading and fails math. The second case will similarly result in a treatment discontinuity owing to the math test, but both units achieve quite a high score on reading. We could, of course, consider an entire continuum of cases where the key discontinuity is observed in one of the running variables, while the other running variable is allowed to vary.

This results in a definition of treatment effects across a continuum of points. Imbens and Zajonc (2011) define a boundary $\mathcal{B}$ as areas that surround the treatment discontinuity. They then note that we can consider a boundary regression discontinuity estimand for each point $\boldsymbol{b} \in \mathcal{B}$ as:

$$\tau^{\text{BSRD}}(\boldsymbol{b}) = \mathbb{E}[Y_i(1) - Y_i(0)|\boldsymbol{Z}_i = \boldsymbol{b}], \tag{6.35}$$

Table 6.1
Multiple experiments with multiple running variables

	Treated unit		Control unit	
	Math score (Z_{1i})	Reading score (Z_{2i})	Math score (Z_{1i})	Reading score (Z_{2i})
Marginal math "low"	50	50	49	50
Marginal math "high"	50	75	49	75
Marginal reading "low"	50	50	50	49
Marginal reading "high"	75	50	75	49
Marginal both	50	50	49	49

which, based on continuity assumptions, can be treated in a standard way with limit arguments to give:

$$\tau^{\text{BSRD}}(\boldsymbol{b}) = \lim_{z \downarrow \boldsymbol{b}: z \in \mathcal{B}_1} \mathbb{E}[Y_i|\boldsymbol{Z}_i = z] - \lim_{z \uparrow \boldsymbol{b}: z \in \mathcal{B}_0} \mathbb{E}[Y_i|\boldsymbol{Z}_i = z],$$

where $\mathcal{B}_1$ and $\mathcal{B}_0$ refer to treated and control units respectively within the boundary. A similar approach is defined in Keele and Titiunik (2015), who explicitly note how this applies to a case of geographic discontinuities based on latitudes and longitudes. In these settings, the explicit dependence on the environment at the boundary where units are located implies that we can produce a range of treatment effects. For example, considering the cases in table 6.1, we may write $\tau^{\text{BSRD}}(50, 50)$, $\tau^{\text{BSRD}}(50, 75)$, and $\tau^{\text{BSRD}}(75, 50)$ as three separate local ATTs. The above notation assumes a sharp RDD but can be similarly defined in the case of a fuzzy RDD, as laid out in Imbens and Zajonc (2011).

While such point-specific estimands fully describe treatment effects that exist in cases with multiple running variables—and extend to arbitrary numbers of running variables—in practice, estimands will generally be considered at a reduced number of points. The implementation of such estimands can interact with optimal bandwidth choices, and frequently-used software is available to do this (Cattaneo, Titiunik, and Vazquez-Bare 2020). Alternatively, average effects can be produced in a more aggregate way. Imbens and Zajonc (2011) suggest an integrated procedure that weights across treatment effects (6.35) to produce a single aggregate effect. In effect, this produces a single mean effect τ^{BSRD} by integrating $\tau^{\text{BSRD}}(\boldsymbol{b})$ across all support points $\boldsymbol{b}$. Wong, Steiner, and Cook (2013) suggest alternative aggregates, defining "frontier effects" as mean effects by considering a discontinuity in a single boundary at a time, and averaging across all points on this boundary. Alternative quite simple-to-implement procedures consist of converting multidimensional boundaries into unidimensional distances, such as generating the distance to the *nearest* boundary and then conducting a standard regression discontinuity analysis. This is referred to as the recentering approach in Wong, Steiner, and Cook (2013) and is frequently employed in practice, though Wong, Steiner, and Cook (2013) note that the weighting of specific estimands (6.35) is unlikely to be optimal in this recentering approach.

Multiple cutoffs An alternative case where multiple dimensions comes into regression discontinuities is where rather than confronting multiple *running variables*, a single running variable is present, but multiple cut-points κ exist. In cases such as this, rather than resulting in boundary-specific treatment effects, the result is cutoff specific treatment effects.

This case is studied in Cattaneo et al. (2016). We can follow Cattaneo et al. (2016) and introduce a notation for a cutoff that is itself a random variable having J distinct cut-off points. Thus, what was previously simply κ now can take multiple levels, written as $\mathcal{C} = \{c_1, c_2, \ldots, c_J\}$. These levels are stored in a random variable denoted C_i, which records the cutoff a given individual is exposed to. The precise nature of the treatment effect depends upon the nature of the multiple cutoffs. In particular, two specific situations may be encountered. A first is a case of "noncumulative cutoffs" in which different individuals may be exposed to different treatment thresholds for a single given treatment. For example, cases where individuals have different treatment thresholds based on specific characteristics result in noncumulative cutoffs. Alternatively, regression discontinuities may be based on "cumulative cutoffs" where an individual's score for the running variable defines some level of treatment. In these cases, individuals will receive treatment 1 if $Z_i < c_1$, treatment 2 if $c_1 \leq Z_i < c_2$, and so on for the remaining treatment levels. The difference in these designs is that in the noncumulative case, individuals below a specific cutoff will always be unexposed while those above the cutoff will be exposed to treatment, where as in the cumulative case, individuals below a threshold will be exposed to one level of treatment, while those above will be exposed to another level of treatment.

If we begin by considering the noncumulative case, we can define multiple cutoff specific treatment effects. Namely,

$$\tau^{\text{SRD,MC}}(c) = \lim_{z \downarrow c} \mathbb{E}[Y_i | Z_i = z, C_i = c] - \lim_{z \uparrow c} \mathbb{E}[Y_i | Z_i = z, C_i = c], \tag{6.36}$$

where it is clear that this results in a single estimand for each of the J cut-points observed in data. These can be estimated precisely as laid out previously in this chapter using local nonparametric methods. Commonly, these treatment effects are pooled, and this can be done using the "normalizing-and-pooling" strategy (Cattaneo et al. 2016). Specifically, if a normalized running variable is defined as $\tilde{Z}_i = Z_i - C_i$, this will now be centered around 0, and measure the distance of each observation to their own cutoff. An RDD based on this normalized variable can be written as follows:

$$\tau^{\text{SRD,P}} = \lim_{z \downarrow 0} \mathbb{E}[Y_i | \tilde{Z}_i = 0] - \lim_{z \uparrow 0} \mathbb{E}[Y_i | \tilde{Z}_i = 0]. \tag{6.37}$$

Perhaps unsurprisingly, Cattaneo et al. (2016) show that this re-centered estimand simply generates a weighted average of the underlying quantities $\tau^{\text{SRD,MC}}(c)$. Specifically,

$$\tau^{\text{SRD,P}} = \sum_{j=1}^{J} \tau(c_j)\omega(c_j),$$

where $\omega(c_j) = \Pr(C_i = c_j | \tilde{Z}_i = 0)$ (Cattaneo, Titiunik, and Vazquez-Bare 2020).

In the the cumulative case, one can again provide a clear definition of cutoff-specific treatment effects, however now must define this based on specific levels of treatment. To see this, let's define as $w_1, w_2, \ldots, w_J$ specific levels of treatment. Then,

$$\tau_j^{\text{SRD,MCC}} = \mathbb{E}[Y_i(w_j) - Y_i(w_{j-1}) | Z_i = c_j] \tag{6.38}$$

$$= \lim_{z \downarrow c} \mathbb{E}[Y_i | Z_i = z, C_i = c] - \lim_{z \uparrow c} \mathbb{E}[Y_i | Z_i = z, C_i = c], \tag{6.39}$$

We may note that while the definition of the estimator in (6.38) makes explicit that the interpretation of our treatment effects in this case are based on changes in treatment from w_{j-1} to w_j, the estimator itself in (6.39) is identical to that laid out in (6.36). One benefit of such cutoff-specific estimands is that we can learn about effects beyond a single local cutoff, suggesting that broader treatment effects may be achievable (Bertanha 2020; Cattaneo et al. 2021). We will return to consider this point in chapter 8 when we explore external validity.

6.5.3 Discrete Running Variables

In some cases, the running variable in regression discontinuity is discrete. This may be encountered, for example, in settings where some passing grade is key for progression in an educational setting, and grades have discrete intervals (for example $49, 50, 51, \ldots$). Similarly, examples where assignment depends upon an individual's date of birth clearly have a discrete running variable. While this is still perfectly compatible with an assignment rule such as (6.1), it implies certain complications for identifying assumptions. One clear issue is that in this discrete setting is that the coarseness of the running variable will mean that continuity-based approaches break down, as limits cannot be taken. This is discussed by Lee and Card (2008) who note that identification in this setting can be achieved if assumptions are made about the functional form of the running variable. They suggest a strategy that incorporates uncertainty about the functional form into inference that provides further flexibility in this setting.

Alternatively, the randomization approach is valid in this setting (Cattaneo, Frandsen, and Titiunik 2015) and may be particularly well suited to the case when there are relatively few points of support for the running variable, when modified continuity methods are most challenged. In practice, Cattaneo and Titiunik (2022) suggest that if the number of points of support for the running variable are large, continuity-based approaches may be acceptable, though the number of effective observations should be viewed as the number of points of support of the running variable, and not the number of total observations which make up these mass points. Other procedures have also been defined that permit estimation and inference including Dong (2015) who proposes viewing discretization as a type of rounding error, and Imbens and Wager (2019) who suggest estimation routines that bound quadratic terms on relationships between the running variable and outcomes that they document for both continuous and discrete running variables.

6.5.4 Regression Discontinuity with Covariates

In previous chapters we have seen that covariate-adjustment can be required for identification in cases where conditional unconfoundedness assumptions are made, or can improve the efficiency of estimation when unconditional unconfoundedness is assumed—that is, in cases where treatment is randomly assigned. In the case of regression discontinuity, given that the nature of identifying assumptions are different to those we have made previously, it is important to consider the role that covariates play, and whether they have a productive role in RDDs.

Calonico et al. (2019) discuss the relevance of covariates in achieving efficiency in estimation. As discussed in section 2.4.3, the inclusion of baseline controls in regression models where treatment is randomly assigned increases efficiency of estimates without affecting identification. Calonico et al. (2019) show that under the continuity-based assumptions for RDDs, a similar result holds, and Cattaneo, Keele, and Titiunik (2023) note that this is also the case if a local randomization approach to identification is taken. A key result from Calonico et al. (2019) is that under continuity assumptions about potential outcomes and provided a number of standard regularity conditions, provided that the RD has no effect on covariates, the inclusion of covariates can substantially increase power. Specifically, their recommendation is for covariates to be adjusted identically above and below the threshold, which provides a consistent estimator provided that covariates are indeed not themselves affected by the discontinuity.

A separate point is whether covariate adjustment can be used if there are problems with the assignment of the running variable itself. This is a point related to estimation rather than inference, and this has been addressed by Frölich and Huber (2019). Frölich and Huber (2019) show that even in cases where covariates exist that are both unbalanced around the threshold and have effects on the outcome variable, identification of unconditional treatment effects can be recovered. Frölich and Huber (2019) propose an estimator that recovers this treatment effect by incorporating covariates into local linear regressions and show that this method works well provided that all relevant covariates are indeed included. The technical demands of this estimator are not trivial, given that separate bandwidths must be considered for estimating nonparametric relationships between outcomes and the running variable, and for estimating nonparametric relationships between outcomes and covariates.

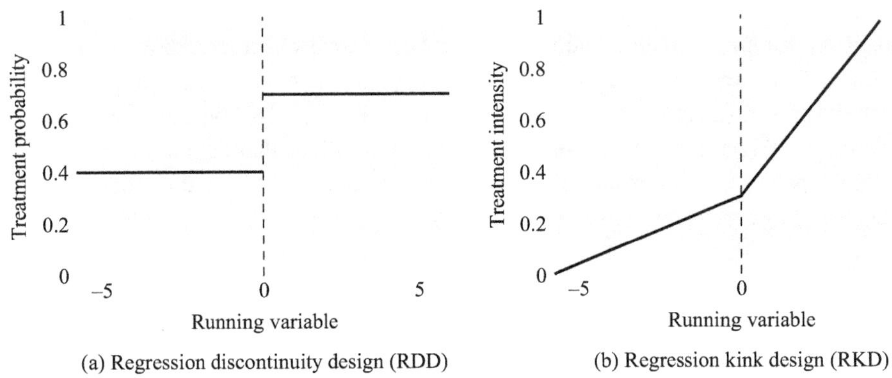

Figure 6.10
Comparison of regression discontinuity and regression kink designs.

Further discussion of covariates in RDD can be found in the chapter of Cattaneo, Keele, and Titiunik (2023), which focuses on the number of reasons one may wish to include covariates in RDDs and when this will and will not be effective.

6.6 Regression Kink Designs

The RD design draws identification from a sudden discontinuous jump in treatment assignment at a specific cut-point. Another set of methodologies exist when rather than an appreciable jump in treatment, we encounter an appreciable change in the slope of treatment assignment. In essence, these designs are based on the fact that there is some treatment measure that has a regular assignment pattern, but then this assignment has a "kink" at some specific cutoff point, as we can see in figure 6.10. While in panel (a), we see a schematic typical of regression discontinuity where the likelihood of treatment jumps around the cutoff indicated at 0, in the panel (b) there is no jump at the cutoff, but rather the rate with which some treatment of interest shifts sharply.

Perhaps unsurprisingly given the kink in the treatment assignment schedule, designs of the type described in figure 6.10 are referred to as "regression kink designs" (RKDs). Examples of kinks from the economic literature include changes in rates of unemployment benefits by time out of work (Landais 2015), changes in drug reimbursement rates as spending increases (Simonsen, Skipper, and Skipper 2016), changes in marginal tax rates by income levels, and various other applications (see table 1 from Ganong and Jäger [2014] for a list of early studies in which kinks were employed). While the underlying treatment assignment mechanism is clearly different in these two cases, it turns out that we can adapt many of the mechanics of RDD to the RKD setting. Indeed, while in regression discontinuity we are seeking to determine whether there is a corresponding sharp change in the outcome of interest at the discontinuity, in RKD we seek to determine whether there is a sharp change in the first differential.

Initial formalizations of the RKD are provided in Card et al. (2015) along with details on the estimation methods and assumptions underlying the regression kink design. In practice, the regression kink design consists of estimating the change in the slope of the outcome variable of interest at the discontinuity and scaling this quantity by the change in the slope of the treatment intensity at this point. Noting from (6.20) that we already have parameters for the slope on either side of the cutoff as $\beta_{-,1}$ and $\beta_{+,1}$, we can capture changes in the slope of outcomes as $\widehat{\beta}_{+,1} - \widehat{\beta}_{-,1}$. In certain settings, we will know precisely how the treatment intensity changes at the cutoff, if, for example, kinks owe to explicit rules such as changes in marginal tax rates. However, at other times, we may need to estimate the change in treatment intensity, which we can do by simply estimating (6.20) where Y_i is replaced by the treatment of interest. If we refer to the parameters of this model as $\gamma_{+,1}, \gamma_{-,1}$, and so forth, we can write our regression kink estimator as follows:

$$\hat{\tau}_{\text{RKD}} = \frac{\widehat{\beta}_{+,1} - \widehat{\beta}_{-,1}}{\widehat{\gamma}_{+,1} - \widehat{\gamma}_{-,1}}. \tag{6.40}$$

In cases when the change in slope of treatment is known (and hence the denominator is known), this is simply replaced by the known scalar value $\gamma_{+,1} - \gamma_{-,1}$, and the design is referred to as sharp regression kink designs. Whereas in cases where the changes in the slope of treatment intensity are not known and hence must be estimated, as in (6.40), this is referred to as fuzzy RKDs.

You will note that the procedures in (6.20) and (6.40) are analogous to the RDD; however, instead of focusing on intercepts, we focus on slopes. Given this, it also turns out that many of the considerations, such as optimal bandwidth calculations, polynomial order, bias correction, and so forth, are very similar to those in regression discontinuity designs. Indeed, one of the impressive elements of Calonico, Cattaneo, and Titiunik (2014a) is that they fully develop these results for both regression discontinuities and regression kinks, meaning that the estimation points discussed previously also hold here. Perhaps the main difference in the kink design is that rather than local linear models, local quadratic models are typically preferred for estimation (Calonico, Cattaneo, and Titiunik 2014a).

The parallels between RDDs and RKDs also imply that the identification relies on similar continuity assumptions as those laid out in the RDD, namely that potential outcomes are assumed to evolve smoothly around the kink point (formally, they are required to be at least four times differentiable), along with other regularity conditions. This also implies that many of the diagnostic tests described for RDDs that were discussed in section 6.4 remain relevant in the case of RKDs.

Historical Context and Selected Further Reading

There are a series of historical texts that first lay out the elements of the regression discontinuity design, including the text of Thistlethwaite and Campbell (1960) mentioned in the introduction and work of Trochim (1984). While this chapter seeks to cover much of the current state of the art in this setting, recent book-length overviews of RDD are also available from Cattaneo, Nicolás Idrobo, and Titiunik (2020) and Cattaneo, Nicolas Idrobo, and Titiunik (2024), providing an even broader coverage.

Much of the basis of the most recent optimal-bandwidth RD strategies draws heavily on semiparametric and nonparametric econometrics. If you are interested in reading more deeply on these foundations, classic resources include Fan and Gijbels (1996) for nonparametric regression and Härdle (1990) for a general introduction to smoothing techniques. These texts provide the mathematical underpinnings for kernel methods, local polynomial regression, and bandwidth selection strategies central to RD estimation.

More generally beyond the regression discontinuity and regression kink design, there is work that seeks to take advantage of any bunching that would be problematic for such designs. A recommended jumping-off point for such work is Kleven (2016).

Exercises

1. This exercise is based on Meyersson (2014), who studies the effect of Islamic political representation in Turkish municipal elections on women's educational achievements. These data are provided as Meyersson_2014.csv. In this study, the units are municipalities and the running variable is the margin of victory of the (larger) Islamic group in the 1994 Turkish elections. The cutoff point of the running variable is zero, with the treated on the right and the controls on the left.
   (a) To graphically analyze the above, obtain the following two scatterplots: (1) the percentage of women who completed school in the year 2000 against the Islamic margin of victory in 1994 Superimpose the sample mean obtained on each side of the discontinuity. (2) the percentage of women who completed school in the year 2000 vs. Islamic margin of victory in 1994 within 50 pp from the discontinuity. Superimpose a polynomial fit line for each side of the discontinuity.
   (b) In this case, what does the McCrary (2008) test consist of? Perform this test and generate the standard McCrary plot. What is the result of this test?
   (c) Estimate the regression discontinuity where the impact of a close victory by an Islamic candidate on the proportion of women in secondary education in 2000 is estimated. To do this, follow the methods of Cattaneo et al. (the `rdrobust`

command) using a uniform kernel and the optimal bandwidth. Demonstrate that this estimator can be exactly replicated (but not the standard errors) by estimating a model of the form:

$$y_i = \beta_0 + \beta_1 \text{Votes}_i + \beta_2 (\text{Votes} \times \text{Victory})_i + \tau \text{Victory}_i + u_i, \tag{6.41}$$

in the optimal bandwidth, and also by estimating

$$y_i = \beta_0 + \beta_1 \text{Votes}_i + u_i \tag{6.42}$$

on both sides of the cutoff point (within the optimal bandwidth) and subtracting the intercept on the left side from the intercept on the right side. Explain why the estimates are identical but the standard errors are not.

(d) There are a number of covariates in this dataset. Explain whether these may be useful in implementing an estimation procedure based on a local randomization approach. Implement a local randomization procedure using these data.

2. In this question we will use data from Ozier (2018), contained in `Ozier_2018.csv`. Ozier studies the impact of secondary education (`finishsecondary`) on later life outcomes, namely early pregnancy (`pregnant_by_18`) and the likelihood to be employed in informal work (`self_employed`). To do so, he uses the discontinuous likelihood of entering secondary education based on a cutoff score in the Kenyan Certificate of Primary Education.

   (a) Generate plots of the first stage and the reduced form where the outcome considered is high school completion (for the first stage) and whether the individual is working informally (for the reduced form). Consider a number of ways to present these graphs, and comment on whether these choices appear to be important.

   (b) Implement a McCrary test using administrative data of individual's first test scores around the cutoff of 250 points (`kcpe_self_recent`). Do these results support the idea of an RDD?

   (c) Implement a similar test with self-reported scores based on any tests an individual has taken (`kcpe_confirmed_first`). What does this result suggest about challenges with RDDs?

   (d) Considering the results from part (c), should we be concerned about nonrandom heaping at the threshold? In your answer, consider how information on other covariates in the data may be useful in assessing this?

   (e) What do the compliance rates in this setting tell you about the generalizability of this result? What does the author note about compliance rates in his paper?

   (f) Implement a Fuzzy RDD in which the test score cutoff from the first test recentered on 0, as described in the paper (`rkcpe`), is used to instrument high school completion, focusing on the two outcomes mentioned above.

3. Data from Clarke, Lillo Bustos, and Tapia-Schythe (2026) provided as `Clarke_et_al_2026.csv` consists of a large sample of births with their birth weights in grams (`bweight`), an indicator of death during the first year of life (`infmort`) and a number of key covariates. This study is based on discontinuous medical treatment receipt for babies born at less than 1,500 grams, originally studied in Bharadwaj, Løken, and Neilson (2013).
   (a) Using these data, generate histograms showing the frequency of birth weights across the entire distribution, as well as when zooming in on quantities within around 500 grams of the cutoff. Do you see evidence suggestive of any heaping in birth weights? Is this specific to the 1,500 gram cutoff, or evidence of rounding more generally?
   (b) Considering a number of characteristics such as mother's and father's age and education (`mage`, `fage`, `meduc`, `feduc`), and examine whether these characteristics also vary with any heaping you documented in part (a).
   (c) Estimate a local linear model in which survival is considered as an outcome, and generate plots showing how this outcome varies in bins around the cutoff.
   (d) Why may a donut model be useful in this setting? Estimate a donut version of the RDD you implemented above. What sort of trade-offs do we face in setting the size of the donut hole?
4. Landais (2015) uses a regression kink design to study labor market responses to changes in rates of benefits in unemployment insurance. The large microdata available to conduct these analyses is available at http://doi.org/10.3886/E114581V1.
   (a) Read section IIA of Landais (2015) and explain in your own words what the kink exists of in this setting as well as why we may expect a change in labor supply decisions at the kink point.
   (b) Use these data, and in particular the data from Louisiana, to generate a plot showing a kink in the duration of unemployment around the kink point you discuss in (a). This should look something like figure 6a from Landais (2015).
   (c) Seek to replicate the estimate displayed as α in row one of some panel of table 2 of the paper. Replicate this "by hand" using a linear specification and bandwidth of $2,500 for the highest quarter of earnings.
   (d) Estimate your model using optimal local linear methods using a routine such as rdrobust. How do the bandwidths vary here compared to part (c)? Document how your estimates vary if you consider alternative kernel choices and polynomials for local regressions.
5. In this question we will simulate a discontinuous and nonlinear relationship and examine whether local linear regression is able to capture the discontinuity. We will then compare the performance of alternative estimation and inference procedures.

Specifically, simulate data from the following DGP:

$$Y_i = 0.6X_i^3 + 5W_i + \varepsilon.$$

Here Y_i is the outcome variable, X_i is the running variable, and W_i is the treatment variable. Both X and ε are standard normal variables. Treatment will only be received by individuals for whom $X \geq 0$, so W is defined as equal to 1 if $X \geq 0$ and 0 if $X < 0$.

(a) Simulate 100 data points that follow the above specification and plot the resulting data points.

(b) Manually estimate an RDD with a split linear trend to capture the relationship between the running variable using the observations in the range $x \in (-2, 2), x \in (-1.9, 1.9), \ldots, x \in (-0.1, 0.1)$ resulting in twenty different estimates. Comment on these estimates, and what we may conclude from this.

(c) Now, repeat the simulation in part (a) one hundred times, and estimate the twenty different estimates from part (b) in each simulation. Examine the mean treatment effect estimated across all simulations for each of these twenty estimates, and comment on these results.

(d) Using a single simulation, estimate the parameter using local linear bandwidth and Calonico, Cattaneo, and Titiunik's (2014) optimal bandwidth selection procedures. What bandwidth is used for estimation?

(e) Repeat the simulation conducted in part (d), however now varying the number of observations $N \in \{1000, 10000, 100000, 1000000\}$ observations. Comment on the bandwidth selected in each simulation and the estimated RDD parameter.

(f) Consider the data you simulated in part (e) with 1,000 observations. Now generate two covariates that are related to X_i, namely generate $X_{i2} = 0.2X_i + \varepsilon_{2i}$ and $X_{i3} = 0.2X_i + \varepsilon_{3i}$, where each of ε_{2i} and ε_{3i} are (separate) standard normal variables. Implement local randomization-based RD methods using the logic of Cattaneo, Titiunik, and Vazquez-Bare (2016) and the covariates X_{i2} and X_{i3} for the selection of the local estimation window. How does this method compare to that above in terms of bandwidth and estimation? And how do results change if the relationship between X and X_{i2} and X_{i3} is stronger?

(g) Finally, considering the data you used above in part (e) and (f), explore how your estimates vary if using Honest RD methods of Armstrong and Kolesár (2020), using their rule of thumb for selecting input smoothness parameters. Simulate this one hundred times and explore the 95% confidence intervals each time. Comment on your results.

7

Testing, Testing: Hypothesis Testing in (Quasi-)Experimental Designs

Do I contradict myself?
Very well then, I contradict myself.
(I am large, I contain multitudes.)
—Walt Whitman, *Song of Myself*

7.1 Introduction

The nature of frequentist statistical tests implies that we will at times make mistakes. Indeed, this is built directly into the framework that we have also used in inference up to this point. When we refer to a parameter being significant *at 95%*, we acknowledge that there is a 5% probability of rejecting the null hypothesis when it is actually true. Similarly, because our parameters are estimated with uncertainty, and we seek a high degree of certainty in order to reject a null hypothesis, we may often fail to reject a null hypothesis even though it is false. These types of errors are fundamental to hypothesis testing and influence the trade-offs we must consider when designing studies and interpreting results.

In general, these errors are not a problem as long as our inference respects the nature of these tests, and our findings are taken in light of this chance. However, in this chapter, we will consider a number of situations in which this *may* be a problem. The first: how to consider hypothesis tests when we have multiple dependent variables, is a technical issue for which, fortunately, there are many solutions. The second, abuse of the notion of frequentist testing owing to incentives to report a significant result, is a far deeper problem related to research in social sciences, to which a lot of attention is only quite recently being placed.

Because hypothesis testing—or some procedure to account for the uncertainty of our estimates—is fundamental in nearly all types of quantitative analyses we will conduct, we will delve more deeply into these considerations here. In this chapter, we will begin by recapping the ideas behind the basic hypothesis test, the types of errors and uncertainty that exists, and factors that affect the power we have to detect effects. Then we will discuss how these tests can be extended to take into account the use of multiple dependent variables, which is an empirically relevant concern in many settings. We will then close discussing some particular ways that are increasingly being used to avoid concerns about the selective reporting problem alludeded to above, namely, the use of a pre-analysis plan or to preregister analyses before data are in hand, thus removing so called "researcher degrees of freedom" (Simmons, Nelson, and Simonsohn 2011) from analysis.

7.2 Frequentist Hypothesis Testing and Error Rates

In order to think about hypothesis testing and the way that we would like to be able to classify treatment effects, we will start by briefly returning to the typical error rates from simple hypothesis tests. Let's consider a hypothesis test of the type:

$$H_0 : \tau = k \qquad \text{versus} \qquad H_1 : \tau \neq k.$$

In the above, our parameter of interest is τ, and k is just some value that we (the hypothesis tester) fix based on our hypothesis of interest.

Because τ is a population parameter, we can never know with certainty whether the null hypothesis H_0 holds. The best we can do is ask how likely it is that the observed data would arise if the null hypothesis were true. In simple terms, an estimate of τ that is far from k—all else equal—provides stronger evidence against the null and in favor of rejecting it.

Classical hypothesis testing then consists of deciding to reject or not reject the null hypothesis given the information available to us. Although we will never know if we have correctly or incorrectly rejected a null, there are four possible states of the world before a hypothesis test is conducted, as laid out in table 7.1. If the null is true, we can either correctly not reject the null, which will occur with probability $(1-\alpha)$, or incorrectly reject the null, which occurs with probability α. And if the null is not true, we either correctly reject the null, or incorrectly fail to reject the null. These two errors are commonly referred to as type I and type II errors, which we will discuss in turn below. In an ideal world, we would like to perfectly classify hypotheses, never committing either types of the errors above. However, given that in applied econometrics we never know the true parameter τ (outside of simulations), and that hypothesis tests are based on stochastic (noisy) realizations of data, we can never simultaneously eliminate both types errors.

Table 7.1
Decisions in hypothesis testing

		True State of the World	
		H_0 True	H_1 True
Result of test	Do not reject H_0	Correct (1-α)	Type II error (β)
	Reject H_0 in favor of H_1	Type I error (α)	Correct (1-β)

7.2.1 The Size of a Test

The size of a test refers to the probability of committing a type I error. A type I error occurs when the null hypothesis is rejected, even though it is true. In the above example, this is tantamount to concluding that $\tau \neq k$ despite the fact that τ actually *is* equal to k. Such a situation could occur, for example, if by chance a sample of the population is chosen who have higher than average values for a treatment effect of interest, even if the treatment effect is on average equal to 0 in the entire population. This situation could also occur if by chance units with unexpectedly high or unexpectedly low realizations of the outcome end up being assigned to treated or control groups.

The rate of type I error (or the size of the test) is typically denoted by α. We then refer to $1-\alpha$ as the confidence level. Typically we focus on values of α such as 0.05, implying that if we repeated a hypothesis test many times when the hypothesis was indeed true (with different samples of data, of course) in expectation, 5 out of every 100 times we would incorrectly reject the null. Lehmann and Romano (2005, 57) report that standard values for α were originally chosen given that it allowed for fewer statistical tables to be produced when critical values were generally tabulated. Currently, given the ease of generating critical values with a computer, this is no longer necessary, but the practice has stuck. There is, of course, absolutely nothing magic about this 0.05 threshold, and many arguments exist suggesting that smaller thresholds could be used, specifically in the case of big data (Leamer 1978; Deaton 1997; Benjamin et al. 2018), or questioning the logic of focusing on an arbitrary significance level in isolation of context or magnitudes (Ziliak and McCloskey 2008). Nevertheless, often the starting point of hypothesis testing is to impose an arbitrary rejection criteria, and this criteria is set considering the case in which the null hypothesis is true.

A simple graphical example of such a case is presented in the top panel of figure 7.1. Here we imagine that we wish to test a hypothesis that $\tau = k$, where we assume that our estimator $\widehat{\tau}$ follows a normal distribution with a standard deviation of σ. Starting from the assumption that the H_0 is true (and, hence, the true parameter lines up precisely with the hypothesized value k), we will consider as evidence against the null any value of $\widehat{\tau}$ that is outside of the range $k \pm 1.96\sigma$. This is the area colored in light gray. We do this knowing full well that if the null hypothesis does indeed hold precisely, in certain samples from the true population (in 5% of them to be exact!) we will be unlucky enough to reject the null *even though* $\tau = k$. Of course, if we are concerned that we will commit too many type I errors, then we can simply decrease the size of our test to, say, $\alpha = 0.01$, effectively demanding stronger evidence from our sample before we are willing to reject the null.

7.2.2 The Power of a Test

This leads us to ask why we might accept any type I error at all if we can decide to set this threshold at any arbitrary size that we like. Why might we not seek tests with a size very close to 0? The answer to this question owes to the fact that the size of the test relates to cases where the null is true, but does not consider the converse case where the null is

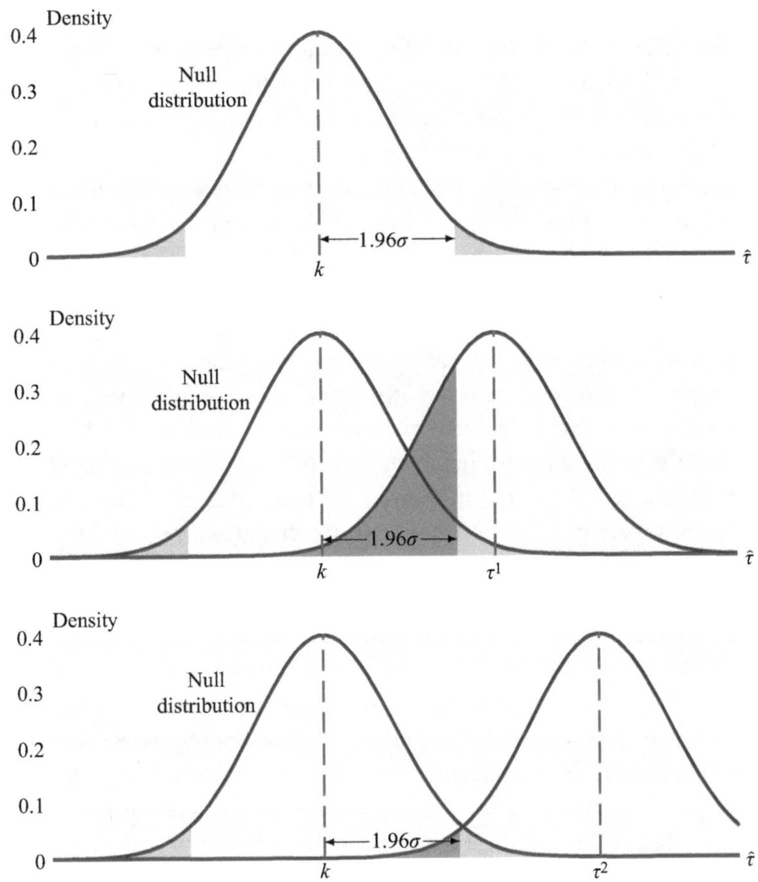

Figure 7.1
Type I and type II errors.

false. We could of course require infinitely strong evidence to reject a null hypothesis. This would mean that we would never incorrectly reject a true null hypothesis. However, this would also mean that we would also never (correctly) reject any *false* null hypothesis. We would thus eliminate all type I error if null hypotheses are true, but this would come at the (considerable) cost of always failing to reject the null when the null is false.

7.2.2.1 Power in detecting impacts versus a scalar null hypothesis This type of error is referred to as a type II error. We define the power of a statistical test as the probability that the test will correctly lead to the rejection of a false null hypothesis. We can then think of the power of a test as the ability that a test has to detect an effect if the effect actually exists. For example, in the above example imagine if the true population parameter were k plus some very tiny value ε. It seems unlikely that we would be able to reject a null that $\tau = k + \varepsilon$, even though it is not true. As we will see below, considerations of the power of a test are particularly common when deciding on the sample size of an experiment or RCT with the ability to detect a minimum effect size.

The statistical power of a test is denoted by $1 - \beta$, where β refers to the type II error. Often, tests with power of greater than 0.8 (or $\beta \leq 0.2$) are considered to be sufficiently powerful (see, for example, proposals in Cohen [1988]). An illustration of the concept of statistical power is provided in the bottom panels of figure 7.1. Now, let's imagine that our estimator still is normally distributed with a standard deviation of σ, and we wish to test the null that $\tau = k$. However, suppose that instead of being true, the null does not hold. In the middle panel, we see a case where $\tau^1 > k$ (where τ^1 is some true treatment effect), and hence the distribution of true effects we are likely to see is shifted to the right. Here, nevertheless, there is a substantial proportion of true effects we may see in a given sample of data that fall within the area of the null distribution that would lead us to *not* reject the null. Indeed, all of the area shared in darker gray would lead us to commit a type II error. This area shaded in blue is the quantity β. All else constant, as the true effect size increases, this area decreases, and we see that in the final panel, if the true effect τ were even higher (now τ^2), our power to (correctly) reject the null increases substantially, and it seems quite likely that we would not make a type II error.

In looking at figure 7.1, we can distinguish a number of features of the power of a test. Firstly, the power of a test will increase as the distance between the null and the true parameter increase. This is to say that we would have greater power when considering the effect τ in the lower-most panel, to that in the middle panel (all else equal). Secondly, we will have greater power when the standard error of the estimate is smaller. As the standard error gives the dispersion of the two distributions, as these dispersions shrink, we will be more able to pick up differences between parameters. As the standard error depends (positively) on the standard deviation of the estimate and (negatively) on the sample size, the most common way to increase power is by increasing the sample size. Finally, we can see that by *increasing* the size of the test (i.e., changing the significance level from $p = 0.05$ to $p = 0.10$), we *increase* the power of the test. We can see this in figure 7.1, as by increasing the light gray area (that is, increasing the likelihood of making a type I error), we shrink the size of the dark gray area (we reduce the likelihood of a type II error). Here we see an interesting and important fact: We cannot simultaneously both increase the power and reduce the size of the test simply by changing the significance level. Indeed, the opposite is true, as there exists a trade-off between type I and type II errors in this case.

Power functions Since the work of Neyman and Pearson (1933)—foundational in the Neyman-Pearson approach to inference[1]—the argument exists that for a given test size, we should always prefer the testing procedure that provides us with the greatest power to detect true effects. An explicit consideration of the power of tests, capturing the features noted in figure 7.1 above, can be summed up in what we know as a power function or power curve. Although figure 7.1 only considers the power we would have to reject the null against two specific values (τ^1 and τ^2 in the middle and bottom panels), we can consider a similar power calculation for a whole range of values. This in effect traces out for us the area not shaded dark gray when the true effect varies, summarizing the power of the test at each alternative value, conditional on the sample size, standard deviation, and value for α.

As above, suppose we wish to test the null hypothesis that some parameter of interest τ is equal to a scalar value k. We can write the t-statistic corresponding to this test as:

$$T_N = \frac{\widehat{\tau} - k}{\widehat{\sigma}/\sqrt{N}}, \tag{7.1}$$

where $\widehat{\tau}$ and $\widehat{\sigma}/\sqrt{N}$ refer to the parameter estimate and standard error, respectively. However, assume now that the true effect τ is actually equal to k'. Generally, the estimator minus the true effect divided by its standard error has a standard t distribution, which for simplicity can be approximated by a normal distribution, and so we can approximately write:

$$\frac{\widehat{\tau} - k'}{\widehat{\sigma}/\sqrt{N}} \sim \mathcal{N}(0, 1). \tag{7.2}$$

By starting from (7.2) and rearranging, we can derive the distribution of the t-statistic in (7.1) given that τ is *actually* equal to k':

$$\frac{\widehat{\tau}}{\widehat{\sigma}/\sqrt{N}} \sim \mathcal{N}\left(\frac{k'}{\widehat{\sigma}/\sqrt{N}}, 1\right)$$

$$\frac{\widehat{\tau} - k}{\widehat{\sigma}/\sqrt{N}} \sim \mathcal{N}\left(\frac{k' - k}{\widehat{\sigma}/\sqrt{N}}, 1\right)$$

$$T_N \sim \mathcal{N}\left(\frac{k' - k}{\widehat{\sigma}/\sqrt{N}}, 1\right). \tag{7.3}$$

With the quantity (7.3) in hand, we can ask ourselves how likely we are to reject the null that $\tau = k$, when in fact $\tau = k'$. This simply corresponds to the likelihood that T_N will be greater than some critical value, which below we arbitrarily set as 1.96, corresponding to $\alpha = 0.05$. We are interested in calculating the power, $1 - \beta$, which below we refer to as B, to detect a given real effect k':

$$B(k') = \Pr\left(|T_N| > 1.96 | \tau = k'\right) = \Pr\left(T_N > 1.96 | \tau = k'\right) + \Pr\left(-T_N < -1.96 | \tau = k'\right). \tag{7.4}$$

This quantity $B(k')$ is referred to as a power function, given that we can map out the power to detect a range of real effects by varying the quantity k' considered. Noting that T_N is normally distributed, and that for a normally distributed variable X with mean μ

and standard deviation σ, this can be converted to a standard normal distribution by simply taking $Z = (X - \mu)/\sigma$, using the properties of the standard normal distribution, we can calculate the probabilities in (7.4) as:

$$\Pr\left(T_N > 1.96 \middle| \tau = k'\right) + \Pr\left(-T_N < -1.96 \middle| \tau = k'\right) = \Phi(-1.96 + T_N) + \Phi(-1.96 - T_N). \tag{7.5}$$

Finally, simply rearranging and substituting T_N back in the expression provides us a standard representation of the power function for a test of the null that $\tau = k$, when instead $\tau = k'$:

$$B(k') = \Phi\left(\frac{k' - k}{\widehat{\sigma}/\sqrt{N}} - 1.96\right) + \Phi\left(-\frac{k' - k}{\widehat{\sigma}/\sqrt{N}} - 1.96\right). \tag{7.6}$$

Noting that above we have (arbitrarily) set α at 0.05 resulting in the critical value of 1.96, we could also write this for any α as follows:

$$B(k') = \Phi\left(\frac{k' - k}{\widehat{\sigma}/\sqrt{N}} - \Phi^{-1}(1 - \alpha/2)\right) + \Phi\left(-\frac{k' - k}{\widehat{\sigma}/\sqrt{N}} - \Phi^{-1}(1 - \alpha/2)\right). \tag{7.7}$$

Similarly, if we would prefer not to make the normal approximation in (7.2) instead using the t-distribution, we can replace the normal cdf with that of the t-distribution with $N - 1$ degrees of freedom.

The idea of this formula is summarized in the power functions presented in figure 7.2. Here we consider the test of the null that $\tau = 4$, when in reality the true value of τ is plotted on the x-axis. In the top panel we observe the power function under varying sample sizes (and values for k'), observing that all else constant, power increases as we consider the detection of effects that are further from the null hypothesis, and power increases to detect a given effect as the sample size increases. Both of these patterns are apparent in the power curve formula (7.7). And in the bottom panel we observe the power functions where the size of the test, α, changes (and once again, for a range of values for k'). Here, we observe the trade-off between size and power.

7.2.2.2 Power in detecting differences between groups A particular case where power is often discussed is in the design of RCTs, where, ex ante, one must decide on a required sample size, with larger sample sizes implying larger costs in terms of the implementation of any treatments, enumeration, and so forth, but bringing with them improved power. Generally, the sample size is chosen to ensure a power to detect some minimum desired effect size between a treatment and a control group, which has a quite standard calculation (see, for example, Cohen [1988]; Murphy, Myors, and Wollach [2014]) that we lay out here.

For a given effect τ we can note that[2]:

$$\frac{\bar{Y}_1 - \bar{Y}_0 - \tau}{\sqrt{\sigma_0^2/N_0 + \sigma_1^2/N_1}} \sim \mathcal{N}(0, 1). \tag{7.8}$$

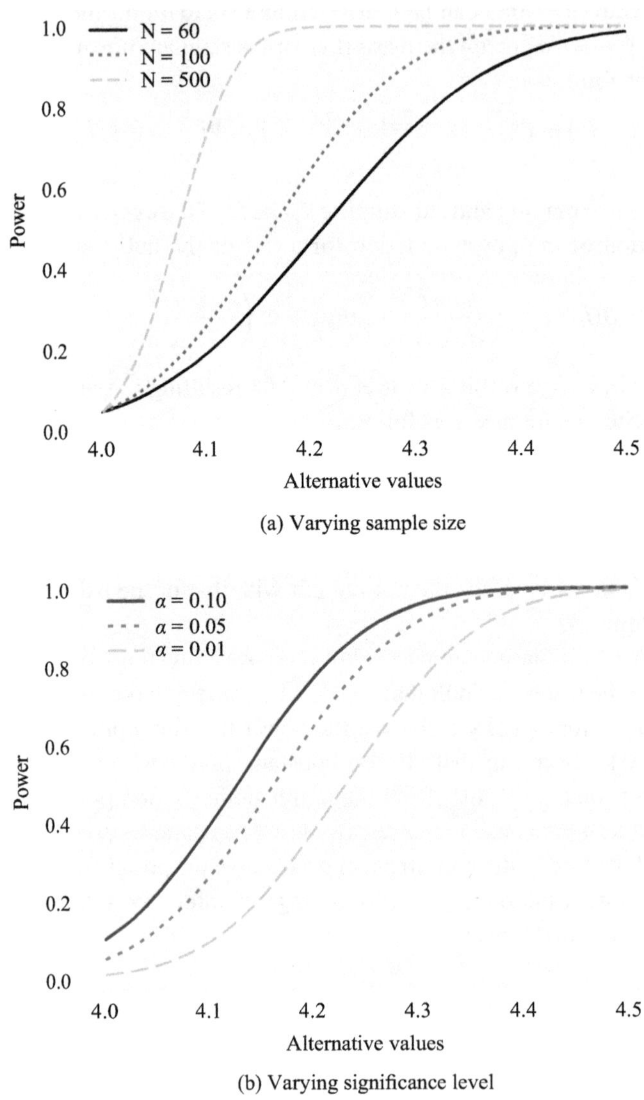

Figure 7.2
Power curves.

If we consider the power to detect this effect against the null that $\bar{Y}_1 - \bar{Y}_0 = 0$, we can consider the t-statistic observed corresponding to the null hypothesis, which is:

$$T_N = \frac{\bar{Y}_1 - \bar{Y}_0}{\sqrt{\sigma_1/N_1 + \sigma_0/N_0}}. \tag{7.9}$$

As above, by rearranging (7.8) and (7.9), we infer that

$$T_N \sim \mathcal{N}\left(\frac{\tau}{\sqrt{\sigma_1^2/N_1 + \sigma_0^2/N_0}}, 1\right).$$

Following the logic of the derivations from the previous subsection, the power to detect the true effect τ against the null can thus be written as:

$$\begin{aligned} B(\tau) &= \Pr(|T_N| > \Phi^{-1}(1-\alpha/2)) \\ &= \Phi\left(\frac{\tau}{\sqrt{\sigma_1^2/N_1 + \sigma_0^2/N_0}} - \Phi^{-1}(1-\alpha/2)\right) \\ &\quad + \Phi\left(-\frac{\tau}{\sqrt{\sigma_1^2/N_1 + \sigma_0^2/N_0}} - \Phi^{-1}(1-\alpha/2)\right) \\ &\approx \Phi\left(\frac{\tau}{\sqrt{\sigma_1^2/N_1 + \sigma_0^2/N_0}} - \Phi^{-1}(1-\alpha/2)\right), \end{aligned} \tag{7.10}$$

where the final step comes from the fact that this latter term will be small, indeed at most $\alpha/2$, and smaller than that for larger values of τ, and so will be ignored in the calculations below.

To consider the minimum sample size to detect an effect of τ with power $1-\beta$, we will begin by simplifying to assume that the variance in each group is identical, and hence $\sigma_0^2 = \sigma_1^2 = \sigma^2$. We will also assume that the proportion of units assigned to treatment and control will be identical, such that the number of units per treatment arm is $N_a = N_0 = N_1$. In this case, we we can rewrite (7.10) as:

$$(1-\beta) = \Phi\left(\frac{\tau}{\sqrt{2\frac{\sigma^2}{N_a}}} - \Phi^{-1}(1-\alpha/2)\right). \tag{7.11}$$

We can then rearrange this expression in terms of the number of units per treatment arm as:

$$N_a = 2\frac{\left(\Phi^{-1}(1-\beta) + \Phi^{-1}(1-\alpha/2)\right)^2}{\tau^2/\sigma^2}, \tag{7.12}$$

providing a simple formula for determining the total number of observations required to detect some minimum effect size τ with a given level of power $(1-\beta)$ provided that we have some credible estimate of the variance of outcomes σ.

It is also simple enough to lay out this formula in terms of separate variance terms σ_0^2, σ_1^2, and/or allow different sample sizes among treatment and control units. List, Sadoff, and Wagner (2011) lay out this formula for cases with different variances among treated and control units, showing that the group with greater variance should be assigned a greater proportion of the sample. Athey and Imbens (2017, 102–104) document that a general form of (7.12) can be written in which the sample is allowed to vary in each group as:

$$N = \frac{\left(\Phi^{-1}(1-\beta) + \Phi^{-1}(1-\alpha/2)\right)^2}{(\tau^2/\sigma^2)\cdot\gamma(1-\gamma)}, \tag{7.13}$$

where γ refers to the proportion assigned to treatment. This makes clear that for a common variance σ, the greatest power will be achieved when assigning half of the sample to treatment and control, given that $\gamma(1-\gamma)$ is maximized for 0.5. However, this does not imply necessarily that half of a sample *should* be assigned to treatment given that the cost of treatment and control units likely varies. Indeed, if the costs of treatment and control units varies, the optimal proportion of units to be assigned to treatment can be shown (Hsu 1994) to be inversely related to the ratio of the cost of treatment to the cost of control:

$$\frac{N_1}{N_0} = \sqrt{\frac{C_0}{C_1}}.$$

There are a range of additional considerations when calculating power, even in experimental settings. The standard formula laid out in (7.12)–(7.13) assume an individual level randomization. If randomization is instead clustered, Teerenstra et al. (2012) show that instead of writing power functions as in (7.11), the power curve is written as:

$$(1-\beta) = \Phi\left(\frac{\tau}{\sqrt{\sigma^2\left[\frac{1+(N_{c0}-1)\rho}{N_{c0}c_0} + \frac{1+(N_{c1}-1)\rho}{N_{c1}c_1}\right]}} - \Phi^{-1}(1-\alpha/2)\right), \tag{7.14}$$

where the difference owes to the variance of the clustered estimate which is a function of the number of units in treated and control clusters (N_{c1} and N_{c0}), the number of treated and control clusters c_1 and c_0, and the intra-cluster correlation between outcomes ρ. A number of relevant points related to this and other considerations of power in experimental settings are provided in List (2011).

> **Code Callout 7.1: Power Curves**
> We will explore the calculation of minimum effect sizes based on preregistered effect size calculations from Alan and Kubilay (2025). There we can explore power curves both with clustered and nonclustered randomization, and consider minimum sample sizes to achieve 80% power.

7.2.2.3 Power analysis in other settings Given the design-choices inherent in RCTs, and in particular the definition of the number of observations, much of the focus on power comes in cases where experimental analyses are conducted. Nevertheless, results related to power are also known in other settings. This includes closed-form solutions for power curves or minimum detectable effects given a specific power for panel data estimators and difference-in-differences settings (Burlig, Preonas, and Woerman 2020), regression discontinuity designs (Cattaneo, Titiunik, and Vazquez-Bare 2019), and instrumental variable estimators (Burgess 2014). Power analysis can also proceed in other types of tests like tests related to multiple coefficients via an F-test, with closed form power solutions (see, e.g., Cohen [1988, chap. 9]). Power functions for these range of cases, as well as those discussed above, are provided in table 7.2. What is key to note in this table is that in essence, the nature of these power functions are very similar, though in seeking to determine power, we will wish to consider different elements of the variance of parameter estimates.

More generally, while closed-form solutions such as those discussed here are well suited to a range of common designs, not all designs will necessarily line up with such ideal settings, and we may not wish to make distributional assumptions such as those laid out previously. In cases such as these, simulated power analysis can be conducted to calculate minimum detectable effect sizes. The idea of simulated power calculations are that we can simulate data that we believe describes the variation inherent in our setting, and introduce treatment effects of a certain size into these data. We then use these simulated data to estimate the treatment effect and test the null hypothesis of interest. If we repeat these simulations many times, we can determine the proportion of times that we reject this null given our specific simulated treatment effect, in effect determining the power we have to reject the null, and detect the true (simulated) effect.

Such simulation-based power analysis can either work entirely with simulated data or with real data that reflects the setting under study, but in which treatment effects are added. A discussion of such a setting where real-world data is used for power analysis is provided by Black et al. (2022) in a specific observational setting in which closed-form power analyses may be complicated. They note that in an observational setting in which pretreatment periods are observed in which no treatment has yet been applied, artificial treatment effects

Table 7.2
Representations of common power functions

Model	Power function $(1-\beta)$	Definitions
Comparison of means	$\Phi\left(\frac{\tau}{\sqrt{\sigma_1^2/N_1+\sigma_0^2/N_0}}-\Phi^{-1}(1-\alpha/2)\right)$	σ_1^2 and σ_0^2 are variance for treated and control, respectively.
Comparison of means (clustered)	$\Phi\left(\frac{\tau}{\sqrt{\sigma^2\left[\frac{1+(N_{c_0}-1)\rho}{N_{c_0}c_0}+\frac{1+(N_{c_1}-1)\rho}{N_{c_1}c_1}\right]}}-\Phi^{-1}(1-\alpha/2)\right)$	N_{c_0} and N_{c_1} are number of units in treated and control clusters, c are clusters, and ρ is intra-cluster correlation.
Difference-in-differences	$\Phi\left(\frac{\tau}{\sqrt{\left(\frac{1}{P(1-P)J}\right)\left[\left(\frac{m+r}{mr}\right)\sigma_\omega^2+\left(\frac{m-1}{m}\right)\Psi^B+\left(\frac{r-1}{r}\right)\Psi^A-2\Psi^X\right]}}\right)$	Panel with J groups, m pre-treatment and r post-treatment periods, proportion P of groups are treated. Ψ^B, Ψ^A, and Ψ^X are mean pretreatment, posttreatment and cross-period error covariance terms, and σ_ω^2 is variance. See Burlig, Preonas, and Woerman (2020).
Instrumental variables	$\Phi\left(\frac{\tau}{\sqrt{\frac{\sigma^2}{N}\cdot\frac{\mathbb{V}(Z)}{\mathbb{C}\mathrm{ov}(Z,D)}}}-\Phi^{-1}(1-\alpha/2)\right)$	$\mathbb{V}(Z)$ refers to variance of IV, and $\mathbb{C}\mathrm{ov}(Z,D)$ covariance between IV and endogenous variable.
Regression discontinuity	$\Phi\left(\frac{\tau}{\sqrt{\mathbb{V}^{bc}}}-\Phi^{-1}(1-\alpha/2)\right)$	$\mathbb{V}_{bc}$ refers to bias-corrected variance. Refer to Cattaneo, Titiunik, and Vazquez-Bare (2019).

can be introduced in many simulations, allowing for such simulation-based power analyses, while maintaining the realism of data. We will consider a simplified example of simulation-based power analysis in end-of-chapter exercise 1.

7.3 Multiple Hypothesis Testing

7.3.1 Multiple Hypothesis Testing and Error Rates

In the previous sections we have thought about hypothesis tests where we are interested in conducting a single test based on a single parameter (for example a t-test), and these ideas also hold for tests of whether there are relationships between a single outcome and multiple independent variables (via the use of an F-test). Setting the rejection rate of a simple hypothesis test of this type at α leads to an unequivocal rule with regards to acceptance or rejection of the null, and a similarly clear understanding of the rate of type II errors. If the test statistic exceeds the critical value at α, reject H_0, otherwise do not reject.

However, we may not always have a single hypothesis to test. For example, what happens if we have a single experiment (leading to one treatment of interest) that we hypothesize may have an effect on *multiple* outcome variables? This is what we refer to as "multiple hypothesis testing,"[3] and it brings about a series of new challenges. To see why, consider the case of a single independent variable and two outcome variables, where we assume that the null hypothesis holds in each case. If we run our analysis once using the first outcome variable and test our hypothesis of interest, we will have a type I error rate of α. However, if we then also conduct our analysis a second time using the second outcome variable, the chance of making *at least one* type I error in these tests now exceeds α (provided cases in which errors will be committed with each variable are not perfectly correlated), as both tests contribute their own risk of falsely rejecting a null. This may have very important consequences for the way that we think about the effect of a policy. If we consider that evidence of an effect of the policy on any variable in a broad class is suggestive that the policy is worthwhile, the accumulation of type I errors will make us more likely to find that a policy is worthwhile as the number of variables examined increases.

More generally, assuming for simplicity that each hypothesis test is independent (this is something we will relax below), the likelihood of falsely rejecting *at least* one null incorrectly in a series of m tests when all the null hypotheses are true is equal to $1-(1-\alpha)^m$. Thus, if ten hypotheses relating to ten outcome variables are tested, the likelihood of at least one true null hypothesis being rejected is $1-(1-0.05)^{10}=0.401$. This is clearly problematic and something that we need to think about. However, before continuing to examine a series of proposed solutions, we will discuss a series of alternative error rates that are relevant when working with multiple hypotheses.

When considering multiple rather than single hypothesis tests, it is not clear that there is only one way to think about the type I error rates associated with hypothesis tests. For example, should we demand that our hypothesis tests with multiple variables set error rates based on falsely rejecting *any one* of the hypotheses in a group, or the *total percent* of all hypotheses in a family, or some other rejection rate? This gives rise to different error rates. Among these, the familywise error rate (FWER), the generalized FWER (k-FWER), and the false discovery rate (FDR). The familywise error rate (FWER) gives the probability of rejecting at least one null hypothesis in a family when the null hypothesis is actually true. The generalized familywise error rate (k-FWER) is similar to the familywise error rate, however, now instead of the probability of falsely rejecting at least *one* null hypothesis, it now refers to the probability of rejecting at least k null hypotheses, where k is a positive integer. Finally, the false discovery rate (FDR) refers to the proportion of all expected "discoveries" (rejected null hypotheses) in which the null is actually true, and hence the proportion of nulls that are wrongly rejected.

These different error rates capture different conceptualizations of size, with the FWER being more demanding than the FDR. In the familywise error rate, we demand that were we to test *all* our multiple hypotheses many times using separate draws from the DGP, only in α% of the cases would we falsely reject any of the true hypotheses. On the other hand, with the FDR, we know that with a significantly large number of findings, $\alpha\%$ will actually be false. To consider one setting where the difference becomes obvious, imagine a case where we wish to test many outcomes, say 1,000, and let's imagine that half of the nulls were true. To achieve a FWER of 5%, we would require that in 95% of tests we do not falsely reject any one of the 500 true null hypotheses. However, if we wish to achieve an FDR of 5%, we would require that on average, 95% of the individuals tests we report as significant actually are significant. If we were somehow able to correctly reject the 500 false null hypotheses, this would imply that we could also additionally reject around 26 of the true null hypotheses, such that 95% of the tests we actually reject are true discoveries that should indeed be rejected.

There exist a range of methods to control the FWER or the FDR. The type of method used will depend largely on the context. There is trade-off between size and power in this choice, as while the FWER offers a more demanding notion of error rates, it does so at the cost of power of detecting true effects. Thus, if decisions to reject the null are particularly instrumental, for example in determining whether a costly intervention be scaled up, we may wish to employ the more demanding size criteria of the FWER. However, if we are interested in testing many potential outcomes in an exploratory way: Perhaps to consider potential further confirmatory analyses, we may be willing to accept the cost of some fixed proportion of false discoveries given the gains in terms of power of also detecting true effects. More generally, although the FWER is more demanding and hence gives rise to stronger evidence where a null is rejected, it should be recognized that there will be circumstances in which the FWER is simply too demanding to work in practice, specifically when the number of hypotheses in a family is so large that it will be very difficult to avoid falsely rejecting any hypothesis. We should also note that the distinction between these error rates declines as the number of true effects becomes smaller. Indeed, in the limit where not a single null hypothesis is false, the definitions of the FDR and the FWER will converge.

A very nice discussion of these error rates and their distinction in an applied context is provided by M. Anderson (2008) in his canonical paper on multiple hypothesis testing.[4] Viviano, Wuthrich, and Niehaus (2025) document the increasing relevance of such corrections in economic journals, pointing to FWER as the most common method in a recent sample of papers. In the sections below we discuss different correction methods to control for these two rates.

7.3.2 Multiple Hypothesis Testing Correction Methods

7.3.2.1 Controlling the FWER There are a number of proposed ways to adjust significance levels or testing procedures to account for multiple hypothesis testing by controlling the FWER. Some of these date from as far back as the first half of the twentieth century and are still widely used today. As we will see below, alternative procedures introduced over time have improved on the earliest methods, maintaining the desired size of tests while increasing their power.

In what follows, let's consider a series of S hypothesis tests, which we label $H_1, \ldots, H_S$. Thus, the family of tests consists of S null hypotheses, and we will assume that S_0 of these are true null hypotheses. In the traditional sense, each of the S hypotheses is associated with their own p-value labeled $p_1, \ldots, p_S$.

The earliest type of multiple hypothesis adjustment is the Bonferroni (1935) correction. The Bonferroni correction simply consists of adjusting the rejection level from each of the tests in an identical way. Rather than rejecting each test if $p_s < \alpha$, the rejection rule is set to reject the null if $p_s < \frac{\alpha}{S}$. It can be shown that under this procedure, the familywise error rate is *at most* equal to α (though likely much lower). To see why, consider the following:

$$FWER = \Pr\left[\bigcup_{s=1}^{S_0}\left(p_s \leq \frac{\alpha}{S}\right)\right] \leq \sum_{s=1}^{S_0}\left[\Pr\left(p_s \leq \frac{\alpha}{S}\right)\right] \leq S_0\frac{\alpha}{S} \leq S\frac{\alpha}{S} = \alpha. \tag{7.15}$$

In the above, even if all the tested hypotheses are true (i.e., $S = S_0$), we will never falsely reject a hypothesis in greater than α% of the families of tests.[5] However, this is a particularly demanding correction. Imagine, for example, if we are testing $S = 5$ hypotheses and would like to determine for each whether their exists evidence against the null at a level of $\alpha = 0.05$. In order to do so, we must adjust our significance level and *only* reject the null at 5% for those hypothesis for which $p_s < 0.01$. It is simple to see that as we add more and more hypothesis to the set of tests, the global significance level required to reject each null quickly rises.

However, one benefit of the Bonferroni (1935) correction is that it is extremely easy to implement. It requires no complicated calculations, and can be done "by eye" even where a paper's authors may not have reported it themselves. Further, this procedure does not require any assumptions about the dependence between the p-values or about the number of true null hypotheses in the family. Of course, this flexibility comes at a cost ... We see below how we can increase the efficiency of multiple hypothesis testing by taking these into consideration.

Single-step and stepwise methods The Bonferroni (1935) correction is unnecessarily underpowered for two reasons. The first reason is that it seeks to conduct all hypothesis tests in a single step, which it turns out is overly stringent. For this reason, stepwise methods can be applied that can still limit the FWER to at most α while potentially gaining power to reject true nulls. The idea of stepwise methods was introduced by Holm (1979). The idea of Holm's procedure is that rather than seeking to make a one-shot decision based on the worst-case scenario that all null hypotheses are true, we can work sequentially refining our test in each step.

To see how this works, we will follow the notation above but now also introduce the notation $p_{(j)}$, and $H_{(j)}$, which refers to our S null hypothesis ordered in terms of the strength of evidence against them. Thus we can order our p-values $p_{(1)} < p_{(2)} \cdots < p_{(S)}$, corresponding to hypothesis $H_{(1)}, H_{(2)}, \ldots H_{(S)}$. The Holm stepdown procedure starts by considering the hypothesis test with the smallest p-value, and determining whether this would be significant at the Bonferroni significance level: $p_{(1)} < \frac{\alpha}{S}$. If this is not significant, the null hypothesis will not be rejected, as will all other null hypotheses. However if it is significant, we can move on to the second hypothesis. Given that we've already determined that at least one null hypothesis is true, we can refine the penultimate step of (7.15) and use a less demanding rejection rule. Namely, now we test if $p_{(2)} < \frac{\alpha}{(S-1)}$. Once again, if we cannot reject the null, all remaining nulls are not rejected and the procedure ends, while if we can reject the null, we pass to the next step, using an even less demanding rejection rule. This testing procedure can then be summarized as rejecting null hypotheses up to the point that the following inequality no longer holds:

$$p_{(j)} \leq \frac{\alpha}{(S-j+1)} \qquad \forall j = 1, \ldots, S. \tag{7.16}$$

While this method begins with a similar idea to the Bonferroni correction (and for the first test has the same criteria as Bonferroni), it progressively becomes less conservative (and correspondingly more powerful). If reaching the final step, the procedure is identical to a single hypothesis test of size α, given that the denominator of (7.16) is equal to $S - S + 1 = 1$. Holm's test achieves a FWER of at most α, and is more powerful than the single-step Bonferroni correction. Indeed, it is a "universally more powerful" testing procedure, meaning it will reject all the false nulls rejected by Bonferroni, and perhaps more. What's more, it maintains the simplicity of Bonferroni in that it can be conducted by eye with nothing more than the p-values corresponding to each test. We can thus view the Holm procedure as a preferred simple method for FWER correction.

Resampling-based testing procedures The second reason that the Bonferroni (1935) (and indeed the Holm [1979]) correction are overly conservative owes to the fact that they assume the near worst-case scenario that all hypothesis tests will be independent. This assumes that errors will build up in an additive way as the number of tests increases. However, in practice, it is likely that outcomes of interest may be quite highly correlated, and as such, when we falsely reject the null for one test, we are also more likely to falsely reject the null for other tests. If we can account for this dependence between tests, noting that at times errors may be shared across tests, it would offer a more powerful alternative.

We can think of an extreme illustration of this by considering a multiple hypothesis correction procedure with ten *identical* variables. Here, if we were to accept the logic of the Bonferroni (1935) test, we should employ a critical value of $\frac{\alpha}{10}$ to control the FWER, even though this test is precisely equivalent to the single test with just one of the ten repeated variables. Indeed, because the ten tests are identical, when we make an error in one of the tests, we will make an error in another, and when we are correct in one, we will be correct in all others. In practice, we would likely be far more satisfied with a procedure that could recognize this dependence among tests and gain power while maintaining the required size.

It turns out that we can do this, but to do so requires knowing about the dependence among our hypothesis tests. While this seems like it may be difficult to determine a priori, early work summarized and further developed in the book by Westfall and Young (1993) shows that resampling procedures offer a way forward. In effect, these resampling methods seek to use permutations or bootstrap-based methods to generate many iterations of data that respect the underlying correlations between variables, and hence test statistics. From these resampling-based methods, we can learn about the dependence among hypothesis tests and offer (potentially substantial) refinements to multiple testing procedures that assume independence.

Romano-Wolf stepdown testing While early developments of these methods, and original multiple hypothesis correction algorithms, were described in Westfall and Young (1993), the current state-of-the art resampling-based multiple hypothesis correction procedure is the Romano-Wolf algorithm. The Romano-Wolf step-down testing procedure, described in Romano and Wolf (2005a, 2005b), is increasingly used in the economic literature—for example, see Gertler et al. (2014) and Dobbie and Fryer (2015) as early adopters. The wide spread use of this method owes to the fact that it offers the benefits of methods that account for dependence among hypothesis tests, while also dispensing with certain assumptions and inefficiencies in earlier iterations of resample-based multiple hypothesis corrections.

To see how the Romano-Wolf method works, consider the same S hypotheses laid out above, ordered again from most to least significant as $H_{(1)}, H_{(2)}, \ldots, H_{(S)}$. Imagine that each of these tests are based on a parameter estimate, which we will denote $\widehat{\tau}_s$, and a standard error, which we will denote $\widehat{\sigma}_s$. Based on these quantities, we can generate a t-statistic of a test of the null hypothesis of no effect as:

$$t_s = \frac{\widehat{\tau}_s}{\widehat{\sigma}_s}.$$

To see where resampling comes in, imagine now that we take a large number B of bootstrap resamples. In each resample $b \in 1, \ldots, B$ we can calculate each of the s parameter estimates and standard errors as $\widehat{\tau}_s^{*b}$ and $\widehat{\sigma}_s^{*b}$ respectively, and calculate the recentered "null statistic":

$$t_s^{*b} = \frac{\widehat{\tau}_s^{*b} - \widehat{\tau}_s}{\widehat{\sigma}_s^{*b}}. \tag{7.17}$$

This quantity, t_s^{*b}, is referred to as a null statistic given that it is centered on the null hypothesis of a zero effect across resamples[6] as the numerator consists of the resample estimate minus the original estimate. If we were to consider the entire distribution of these t-statistics for a given outcome t_s^{*b}, we would observe the natural variation of the t-statistic in our data when the null effect has been imposed (i.e., when the t-statistic is centered on the null). While this null distribution is useful in understanding our data for a single outcome and resulting test, where it is truly useful in the setting of multiple hypothesis testing is that it *also* allows to understand how test-statistics move together. For example, we can understand the relationship between test-statistics for the first two hypotheses by considering how the distributions of t_1^{*b} and t_2^{*b} move together, and so on, with other statistics. Given this, we can dispense with the assumption of independence across statistics and use our data to learn about this dependence.

The Romano Wolf testing procedure is then based on using the information from all of these resampled distributions to correct for the fact that multiple hypotheses are tested at once. Specifically, to do this we consider the construction of null distributions that are based on the maximum t values across multiple tests. We define

$$\max_{t,j}^{*b} = \max\left\{\left|t_{(j)}^{*b}\right|, \ldots, \left|t_{(S)}^{*b}\right|\right\},$$

which captures the maximum t-statistic in each resample b across tests j to S. For example, if we had three tests, $\max_{t,1}^{*b}$ would generate a vector of B test-statistics that is the maximum across $\left(|t_{(1)}^{*b}|, |t_{(2)}^{*b}|, |t_{(3)}^{*b}|\right)$, while $\max_{t,2}^{*b}$ would generate a vector of maxima across $\left(|t_{(2)}^{*b}|, |t_{(3)}^{*b}|\right)$.

The Romano-Wolf multiple hypothesis correction then consists of comparing each true test-statistic t_s with the distribution of null test-statistics in a step-down manner, at each step asking whether the true test-statistic is extreme compared to the null. Specifically, starting with $H_{(1)}$, compare t_s with the distribution of $\max_{t,1}^{*b}$. If $|t_s|$ is greater than percentile $(1-\alpha)$ of $\max_{t,1}^{*b}$, reject $H_{(1)}$, and continue on to $H_{(2)}$. If $H_{(1)}$ is not rejected, stop and accept all alternative hypotheses. We continue in this way, comparing each $H_{(s)}$ with $\max_{s,1}^{*b}$ up to the point that any null is not rejected.

The nice thing about this procedure is that we can clearly see that the step-down procedure allows for us to become progressively less demanding in our tests. For example, in the first test, $\max_{t,1}^{*b}$ consists of the maximum across S t-statistics, while in the final test $\max_{S,1}^{*b}$ consists of simply the t-statistic for the last (single) test. At each stage we *only* consider the t^{*b}-values coming from the hypotheses that have not yet been tested. However, we also gain from the fact that if outcomes are highly correlated, these $\max_{t,j}^{*b}$ will tend to be less demanding. And indeed, if we return to the stylized example of testing ten *identical* hypotheses, the test at each step will be exactly identical, as $\max_{t,1}^{*b} = \cdots = \max_{t,10}^{*b} = |t_{(1)}^{*b}|$. We will explore the Romano-Wolf multiple hypothesis correction, and more generally the differences between the FWER-based procedures described here in code callout 7.2 and end-of-chapter exercises.

Code Callout 7.2: Bonferroni, Holm, and Romano-Wolf Procedures

We will work with data from Charness and Gneezy (2009), who measure the effects of incentives to exercise on seven distinct biometric measures to understand each of these multiple hypothesis correction procedures.

FWER-adjusted *p*-values In general, the procedures we have laid out above lead us to a decision related to our tests: Should we reject or not reject each null hypothesis? However, these procedures can also be used to report multiple-hypothesis testing adjusted *p*-values. The idea of such multiplicity-adjusted *p*-values is that they provides us—for each H_i—the smallest significance level for which we still reject the hypothesis (given the multiple-correction procedure of interest). Formally, this is defined as (see, e.g., Westfall and Young [1993, § 1.3]):

$$p_i^{\text{adj}} = \inf\{\alpha \mid H_i \text{ is rejected at } FWER = \alpha\},$$

where inf refers to the infimum. With Bonferroni, this is simply $p_i^{\text{adj}} = \frac{p_i}{S}$, and with Holm this is simply $p_{(j)}^{\text{adj}} = \frac{p_j}{(S-j+1)}$. The logic of this idea for Romano Wolf is formally defined in Romano and Wolf (2016), and effectively consists of determining the proportion of $\max_{t,j}^{*b}$ greater than the true *t*-statistic $t_{(j)}$.

7.3.2.2 Controlling the FDR Procedures to control for the false discovery rate came to the fore much later than those to control the familywise error rate. Generally, these methods are viewed as flowing from a desire to test very many hypotheses, as is common in the bio-statistics literature where a very large number of variables are considered (think for example of trying to detect gene sequences in DNA that predict some realization). Indeed, the definition of the FDR was first laid out by Benjamini and Hochberg (1995) as a less conservative but more powerful alternative to FWER-based correction methods.

The earliest suggestion of controlling for the expected proportion of falsely rejected hypotheses (the FDR) comes from the work of Benjamini and Hochberg (1995) in which this concept was defined. They suggest the following procedure, where as above we refer to S hypothesis tests: $H_{(1)}, H_{(2)}, \ldots, H_{(S)}$, ordered from most to least significant, with $p_{(1)} \leq p_{(2)} \leq \cdots \leq p_{(S)}$. Suppose that we define some significance level for rejection (such as 0.05) which we will denote q. Then, let k be the largest value of j for which:

$$p_{(j)} \leq \frac{j}{S} q. \tag{7.18}$$

This leads to the rejection rule to reject all $H_{(j)}$ such that $j = 1, 2, \ldots, k$, and do not reject any of the remaining hypotheses. It is important to note that this is actually a *step-up* rather than step-down procedure, as we start with the least significant hypothesis and step up until we meet the condition in equation (7.18). Perhaps the key insight to note here is that this draws on the logic of what we might think the distribution of *p*-values would look like if the null were indeed true. In this case, we would expect that *p*-values would be uniformly distributed, and hence the criteria in (7.18) would do a good job in adjusting for multiplicity. However, if we instead see much more weight low in the distribution of *p*-values, this would suggest there are indeed true effects, and the criteria will allow us to reject these true effects (along with some small proportion α of hypotheses that should not be rejected).

This correction is actually slightly restrictive, as it assumes that p-values are independent or in families with positively dependent test-statistics (Benjamini and Yekutieli 2001, §1.3). While such a property is likely reasonable in many cases where multiple outcomes are positively related (such as, for example, if outcomes consist of measures of health and labor market productivity), later refinements have been proposed that avoid such dependency assumptions. Specifically, Benjamini and Yekutieli (2001) note that if instead of (7.18) the following criteria is used:

$$p_{(j)} \leq \frac{j}{S} \frac{q}{\sum_{i=1}^{S} \frac{1}{i}} \tag{7.19}$$

following the same step-up criteria, this will control the FDR under arbitrary dependence structures including negative dependence among tests. Additional refinements have been proposed in Benjamini, Krieger, and Yekutieli (2006) who note that somewhat analogously to the improvements when moving from Bonferroni to Holm, similar improvements in power can be made if rather than assuming that all null hypotheses are true, refinements are made to account for rejected null hypotheses. They provide a "sharpened" two-stage procedure that offers potential improvements in power over the criteria in (7.18).

This criteria is in general significantly more lenient than FWER-based methods. Figure 7.3 provides a particular illustration of this point, plotting critical values for tests in a setting with $S = 25$ tests. FWER-based critical values are plotted in darker shades, and FDR-based

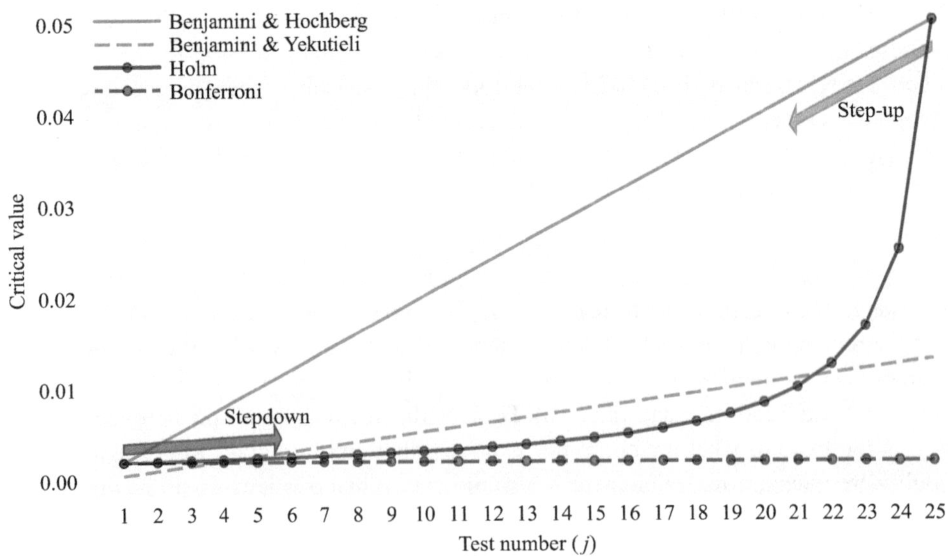

Figure 7.3
Critical values for common multiple hypothesis correction methods.

critical values are plotted in lighter shades. In general, we can see that FDR-based methods permit rejections of p-values that are greater than their FWER-based counterparts. What's more, the stepdown procedure (Holm) starts at the lowest p-value and only rejects null hypotheses up to the point when the first null is found to be not rejected. Step-up procedures on the other hand start at the highest p-value and reject all remaining p-values as soon as the first null is found to be rejected.

Finally, note that as in the case with the FWER, p-values can also be reported where rather than a binary reject vs. do not reject decision, the FDR-adjusted p-value reports the smallest significance level at which the criteria above are met for each test. The tradition in FDR-based tests is to use q (or Q) to denote the error rate to emphasize that this is a quite distinct concept to the α used in FWER and traditional hypothesis tests (this is also adopted in (7.18) and (7.19)). As such, these p-values are often referred to as q-values (see, for example, the discussion in Storey [2002]), or sharpened q-values.

7.3.3 Reducing the Dimensionality of the Problem by Using Indexes

A final common method to avoid the pitfalls of multiple hypothesis testing is to avoid conducting multiple tests altogether by reducing all outcomes to a single summary measure. The logic here is that if we view our multiple outcomes as a representing the sum effects of the policy, we can seek to aggregate these into a single summary index and simply test whether a treatment of interest moves this index in its entirety.

The challenge in this setting is precisely how to generate such an index. Indeed, there are a number of procedures that have been proposed and that are commonly adopted in this line. The most simple procedure is to simply generate a summary index based off of standardized variables. This procedure consists of generating Z-scores for each variable considered, and, if necessary, rescaling variables by multiplying by -1 so that all variables imply similar movements. For example, if considering whether a treatment affects standardized test scores and school dropout decisions, school dropout would be multiplied by -1 so that all positive outcomes are viewed as good. This equally weights all variables, regardless of their contents or how they correlate with one another. Alternatively, M. Anderson (2008) (following O'Brien [1984]) proposes a similar method where rather than weighting variables equally, variables are weighted by the inverse of their variance-covariance matrix. In this way, variables that are similar are given relatively less weight individually, while variables that bring more independent information are given relatively more weight in the aggregate.[7] A conceptually distinct approach, discussed by Filmer and Pritchett (2001), is to use principal component analysis (PCA) to construct this index. This method leverages the data reduction property of PCA, where the first principal component captures the maximum variance in underlying variables. By using PC1 to generate the index, the resulting measure provides a weighted linear combination of the original variables that best explains differences in the family of measures.[8]

Decisions about indexes should be made with careful consideration of the nature of the underlying elements of interest. Is it that we view these as various signals of a deeper underlying phenomena? If so, we will likely prefer principal components. Or is it that we view each element of the index as a separate measure within a family that a policy may impact, and we want to avoid overweighting measures that are highly correlated? In these cases we would clearly prefer the option espoused by M. Anderson (2008). However, if we believe certain elements may be subject to substantial measurement error and for this reason may appear to move in quite different ways to other measures, we will likely prefer to avoid the M. Anderson (2008) index that will weight up such "independent" variation. The decision on which index to use is not innocuous as we will see in code callout 7.3 below. For this reason, the justification of a specific index should be made clearly in line with the nature of the underlying phenomena or problem under study. Recent work has proposed more clearly linking weighting in indexes to a deeper economic argument, for example, an index in Bhatt et al. (2023) where elements are weighted by their social costs.

Code Callout 7.3: Principal Components, Summary Indexes, and Anderson's Index

We will consider the relevance of considerations of the type of index one uses in a situation in which we *know* whether hypotheses should be rejected or not. Based on simulated data generating processes, we will see that the result of such tests can be very sensitive to the index used.

7.4 Precommitting Analyses: Preregistration, Pre-Analysis Plans, and Registered Reports

7.4.1 "p-hacking" and Publication Bias

When working on an empirical research paper, a researcher generally faces many relatively banal choices, but some specific choice must be made in order to arrive to models. To give one simple example, variables can be treated in levels or logs, and at times both options may be reasonable (or not, depending on the context [Chen and Roth 2023]). Many other empirical choices need be made, such as whether and how to treat outliers, precisely how to measure outcomes, which functional forms relationships should take, and so forth. While we should always seek to use rigorous economic or statistical arguments to justify choices, there is some degree of reacher choice required at many points of analyses owing to the "unpleasant realities of real-world data" (P. E. Kennedy 2002). While one can seek to apply a general set of rules to drive these decisions (as indeed, is discussed in P. E. Kennedy [2002], among other places), it is impossible to lay out a proscriptive set of recommendations that cover all choices in empirical work.

Nevertheless, provided that such decisions are made and justified ex ante, the existence of choice in modeling decisions is not an issue per se. However, if output to statistical models is examined *in order* to justify the choice made—that is, if estimation is put before model specification—this is highly problematic as standard testing rates will no longer make sense. If researchers are selectively more likely to report positive results, or if there are strong incentives in place which mean that statistically significant findings are viewed by researchers as being "more valuable," the nature of our traditional hypothesis tests breaks down entirely. Olken (2015) poses the example of a "nefarious researcher, who is interested only in showing that [an] experiment has an effect, choos[ing] to report only the results on the five variables that pass the statistically significant threshold" (from among one hundred potential variables). Clearly this is a problematic abuse of the notion of hypothesis testing. A particularly elegant (graphical) representation of a similar problem is described in figure 7.4 overleaf.

Unfortunately, there is considerable evidence from the literature that such "data snooping" or "p-hacking" does indeed occur. These terms refer to behaviors in which multiple specifications are tested, and only those with statistically significant results are reported by researchers. For example, Brodeur, Cook, and Heyes (2020) collect and plot test statistics on over 20,000 hypothesis tests in nearly 1,000 papers in empirical economics and find evidence of important heaping of reported Z-statistics at points in the probability distribution corresponding to standard significance levels, particularly $Z = 1.96$. There is a substantial body of work pointing to there being an excess of p-values precisely at levels corresponding to commonly invoked definitions of statistical significance (see, among others, Brodeur et al. [2023]; Gerber and Malhotra [2008]). If these patterns do indeed owe to p-hacking, this is particularly concerning given that even if any multiple hypothesis correction procedures are followed, these will not account for hypotheses that were examined and discarded by researchers.

More generally, though, there are other behaviors that may result in the published body of work not being representative of the questions being asked by researchers, and skewing toward results that are "statistically significant." Along with data snooping by researchers, there may also be a selection bias in the types of papers journal editors and referees accept for publication, or researchers may believe this to be the case, resulting in selection in the types of findings that are written up by authors and submitted to academic journals. The first of these is referred to as publication bias, (see, e.g., Abadie [2020]), while that latter is commonly known as "the file-drawer problem" (Rosenthal 1979), referring to authors filing away studies with statistically insignificant results rather than circulating them for publication. Concern with publication bias is somewhat distinct to concerns related to p-hacking given that even if studies were to report results without any snooping, selective publication implies that the published body of work is not representative of effects we may expect in the "real world." There is a growing awareness of these concerns in economics

Figure 7.4
A funny comic but a serious problem (Munroe 2010).

and the social sciences more generally, and a number of mechanisms in place seeking to address them.

7.4.2 Preregistration and Pre-Analysis Plans

One solution, particularly in the case of experimental work, is the use of pre-registration of experiments or pre-analysis plans. Preregistration refers to the process of laying out key details of an experiment in a verifiable way before the experiment is conducted. This is now a standard step in experimental work, and often studies will be preregistered in online systems like the AEA's RCT registry. The details required for preregistration are relatively few. For example, the AEA RCT registry has required fields for details such as the country, intervention dates, objective sample size, outcomes and experimental design, but this leaves considerable space for ex post researcher choice. Indeed, although preregistration is now mandatory in many setting for experimental manipulations, the lack of specificity implies that preregistration alone is not enough to eliminate heaping in test statistics in the published literature (Brodeur et al. 2024).

For this reason, preregistration should be accompanied by pre-analysis plans that more completely lay out the details of empirical designs, the measurement of key variables, the nature of any multiple hypothesis adjustments, and come with a verifiable time-stamp. There has been growing interest in the the use of pre-analysis plans, and these have become mainstream over the last decade, with key overviews focused on these issues provided by Miguel et al. (2014) and Christensen and Miguel (2016).

While the key point with these pre-analysis plans is that main statistical tests and measurement issues should be made explicit entirely before data collection and analysis begins, there is still a question related to precisely what to include in a pre-analysis plan and how extensive these should be. A number of quite concrete suggestions exist such as the proposal in Christensen, Freese, and Miguel (2019) that lists ten key elements, or McKenzie (2012)'s pre-analysis plan checklist. Both of these are broadly in agreement with the elements to be included, and these are laid out in table 7.3, which highlights commonalities and key elements. A pre-analysis plan that covers these elements can thus be viewed as comprehensive.

One relevant counterpoint here is that a pre-analysis plan is unlikely to provide a "full recipe" of a paper. While it may be reasonable to lay out key tests and outcomes, it is likely infeasible to lay out the full set of mechanism tests or heterogeneity analyses when such tests depend, in part, on how or whether prespecified treatments are observed to affect outcomes. Arguments in favor of simplicity are laid out by Olken (2015) and Banerjee, Duflo, et al. (2020), with the latter noting that we may wish to avoid a simple formulaic adherence to a script in an eventual paper by providing a "populated pre-analysis plan" providing the results for prespecified tests, as well as a research paper focusing on key lessons, including non-prespecified exploratory tests, provided that such tests are appropriately indicated. As we will see in considerable more length in chapter 9, there is also substantial space for the

Table 7.3
Key elements for a pre-analysis plan

Element	Christensen, Freese, and Miguel (2019)	McKenzie (2012)
Data details		
Indicate sample	Yes, point 2	Yes, point 1
Data sources	Yes, point 2	Yes, point 2
Measurement	Definitions, indicate primary vs. secondary (point 3)	Provide full variable construction details (point 4)
Other		What will be done if attrition (point 7)? What will be done if limited variation for some outcome? (point 8)
Modeling and estimation choices		
Study Design	Full details of randomization or design (point 1)	Indicate how randomization conducted and balance tests to run (point 1)
Estimation method	Specify precise estimation method (point 8)	Specify equation to be estimated (point 5)
Sequence of outcomes	Indicate outcomes throughout causal chain (point 3)	Indicate tests throughout causal chain (point 3)
Subgroup analysis	List subgroups for analysis (point 6)	Subgroups should be listed for outcomes across causal chain (point 3)
Inference details		
Hypothesis tests	Specify direction of effect (point 7). How are standard errors constructed (point 8)?	How will standard errors be constructed (point 5)?
Multiple hypothesis correction	Indicate how (point 5) and domains of outcomes (point 4)	Indicate how, and domains of outcomes (point 6)
Theory		
Theoretical models	If testing a structural model, include details (point 9)	Indicate any theoretical model in advance (point 9)
Practical details		
Make the pre-analysis credible	Time-stamp using a registry (point 10)	Archive in some registry (point 10)

incorporation of algorithmic processes in research that seek to "learn" about heterogeneity or model selection in rich ways that can be prespecified even where there is uncertainty about precisely which elements should be included in such analyses.

7.4.3 Registered Reports

While the elements discussed above, and in particular a pre-analysis plan, can correct for concerns of researcher manipulation if correctly utilized, they do not entirely address concerns of publication bias. One way to avoid publication bias is for the process of publication—both on the writing and on the reviewing side—to proceed *without* considering results. This is the idea of registered reports, or pre-results review, which is being increasingly adopted by journals.

In registered report, journals allow authors to submit their proposed study, indicating the question, details akin to those in a pre-analysis plan, and any preliminary data required, but not any results themselves. Papers are then evaluated based on whether the question is perceived to be important and the methods sound, and based on this criteria, studies can be conditionally accepted for publication. Following conditional acceptance, the study is implemented as described, actual results are written up, and, provided all agreed processes are followed, the paper is accepted. Details of such processes are available in Arpinon and Espinosa (2023).

The value of such procedures is that they entirely avoid the question of whether the results are surprising, or statistically significant, instead focusing on whether the question moves forward the scientific literature. There is a growing adoption of routes for submitting registered reports. Among other journals, the *Journal of Development Economics*, JPE: Microeconomics, and *Nature* currently have such routes. While each journal has its own specific processes and conditional acceptance pathways, the key element in each of these (as well as similar processes in other journals) is that they are theoretically designed to avoid any incentives for researchers to manipulate statistical tests and avoid concerns that papers may be selected based on the results of such tests.

7.4.4 Observational Analyses

The above procedures in general work well for studies where it is credible to prespecify tests. While this is the case where researchers themselves implement interventions, it is often not feasible or credible to prespecify tests in observational studies. Many such questions will be backward looking, seeking to understand the impact of policies implemented in the past, and so there is no credible way to prove that pre-analysis plans were written prior to data being examined. Nevertheless, in certain cases, even observational studies can be prespecified, and in cases such as these the points in the previous sections hold entirely (see further discussion in Burlig [2018]).

However, at other times, when prespecification cannot be credibly conducted, this places more importance on carefully indicating key choices, documenting robustness to arbitrary choices where possible, and, most importantly, making available carefully documented and fully public replication materials. The publication of replication materials is now mandatory at most economic journals, with many journals implementing formal replication checks of papers before final publication. There is some evidence that suggests that the implementation of data sharing policies results in lower reported significance levels in published findings (Askarov et al. 2022). The role of replication in these cases is key, as it provides some idea of the strength of findings across alternative reasonable empirical models, and organizations such as the Institute for Replicability along with research teams are leading a movement to build the replication of research into the landscape in economics (see, for example, Brodeur, Mikola, and Cook [2024] for one such impressive implementation).

Historical Context and Selected Further Reading

The history of hypothesis testing, and the emergence of the Neyman-Pearson approach integrating considerations of power as a leading approach, is very interesting. While most statistical tests generally have a full rundown of these methods (e.g., Lehmann and Romano 2005), if you are interested in the history itself, E. L. Lehmann (1993) is recommended reading.

For a particular focus on the themes of multiple hypothesis corrections, I recommend chapter 1 of Westfall and Young's (1993) book. The canonical (more recent) applied reference in this area is M. Anderson (2008), where these methods are examined with a particular application to early-life preschool programs. However this paper is illustrative for readers in any field.

There are many excellent papers discussing the practice of "doing" econometrics. Classic examples include Leamer's (1983) "Let's Take the Con out of Econometrics" and P. E. Kennedy's (2002) "Sinning in the Basement," and there are multiple more recent handbook chapters or reviews that can act as further reading on specific themes discussed in this paper such as (multiple) hypothesis testing (Romano, Shaikh, and Wolf 2010), power calculations Athey and Imbens (2017), and reproducibility in economics (Banerjee, Chassang, and Snowberg 2017; Vilhuber 2020).

Exercises

1. In this question we will explore power curves based on simulation. Consider a setting that can be described as follows:

$$Y_i = \tau + \epsilon_i \text{ if } W_i = 1 \qquad Y_i = \epsilon_i \text{ if } W_i = 0.$$

Consider $N = 200$ observations, where 100 observations are randomly assigned $W_i = 1$ and the other 100 observations are randomly assigned $W_i = 0$. Assume that $\epsilon_i \sim \mathcal{N}(0, 1)$.

   (a) Simulate a single realization of these data, setting $\tau = 0.25$, and testing the null $H_0 : \tau = 0$ by regression Y_i on W_i. Can you reject this null hypothesis in this case? Does this tell us anything about the power in this setting to detect true effects against this null?

   (b) Now, repeat the process described in part (a) 1,000 times. In each simulation, record whether the null hypothesis is rejected. Calculate the total proportion of null hypotheses rejected across all of the 1,000 simulations. Does this tell us anything about the power in this setting to detect true effects against this null?

(c) Return to part (b), but now rather than considering only $\tau = 0.25$, consider a range of values of $\tau = 0.01, \ldots, 0.5$. For each of these values, calculate the power in 1,000 simulations and plot this power against the values τ.

(d) How does this simulated power curve compare to power calculations following (7.7)?

(e) Based on the quantities described here, what would be the minimum observations to achieve 80% power in theory?

2. In this question we will explore a randomized intervention from Gallego, Philippi, and Repetto (2024), which provided access to free dental care. The data `Gallego_et_al_2024.csv` contains a number of considered outcome variables, as well as a measure of whether the individual received access to free dental care.

   (a) Consider the thirteen outcome measures used in Gallego, Philippi, and Repetto's (2024) tables 5 and 6, which measure dental health and psychological, economic, and social well-being (i.e., all variables in the data with the exception of treatment). Estimate the treatment effect of each outcome using a simple bivariate regression of the outcome on treatment with robust standard errors.

   (b) Calculate Bonferroni and Holm p-values on the test that each effect is 0 by hand. How do these compare to uncorrected p-values estimated in part (a)?

   (c) Explain why these methods may be unnecessarily demanding in this setting, focusing in particular on the nature of the outcomes considered.

   (d) Calculate Romano-Wolf p-values. You may wish to do this by hand, or with some available libraries. How do these compare to the p-values you calculated above?

   (e) Take the p-values from your estimates in part (a) and apply rules such as those in (7.18) and (7.19) to determine which null hypotheses would be rejected. How do the decisions compare to those if you use p-values from previous parts?

3. In this question we will use data from Bursztyn, Fujiwara, and Pallais (2017), who study whether single women among a group of MBA students avoid engaging in publicly observable ambitious behaviors given concerns that it may affect partnership opportunities. Data in `Bursztyn_et_al_2017.csv` include a treatment variable (`public`), as well as six outcome variables (`salary`, `travelmonth`, `hours_desired`, `tendtolead`, `moreambitious`, `competitive`, and `goodwriter`). The variable `index` contains the summary index as described by Bursztyn, Fujiwara, and Pallais (2017).

   (a) Show that you can replicate the results from table 4, panel A by regressing each of the outcomes above on treatment receipt for single, female respondents (`single==0` and `female==0`).

(b) Generate an Anderson index using the six outcomes above. Plot this to show how they compare to the summary index. What variables are given more weight in this Anderson index?

(c) How do results from this regression look if instead of using the summary index as an outcome, the Anderson index is used?

(d) Generate the first principal component based on the six variables, and consider the regression with this index as an outcome. Should we be surprised by the results in parts (b) and (c) given the stability of results in part (a)?

(e) How do results compare to outcomes for each of the indexes among nonsingle women? How does this line up with the conclusions of Bursztyn, Fujiwara, and Pallais (2017).

4. Many journals now have online repositories of replication materials. This includes the AEA Journals where replication materials are housed on Open ICPSR and listed with the papers online, *The Review of Economics and Statistics*, which has an Harvard Dataverse, and *The Economic Journal*, which has a Zenodo Community.

   (a) Search on repositories such as these (or others) to find a paper that is of interest to you, and aim to follow along with the replication materials.

   (b) Are there any decisions that strike you as potentially arbitrary and subject to reasonable alternative choices? How do the results of this paper change if you consider alternative choices?

8

Beyond Average Treatment Effects and Beyond the Population Under Study ...

> You have brains in your head. You have feet in your shoes. You can steer yourself in any direction you choose!
>
> —Dr. Seuss, *Oh The Places You'll Go!*

8.1 Introduction

The methods discussed so far in this book, and the literature that draws on these methods, focus very carefully on how to infer causality. Explicit questions on what drives observed outcomes—receipt of treatment or selection into treatment—are deeply embedded in this framework. We have encountered this focus throughout this entire book, starting from the Rubin Causal Model first introduced in chapter 1.

In general, while we have been able to clearly define causal parameters of interest in a wide range of settings, we have focused on (a) specific quantities, (b) specific settings, and (c) quite tightly defined notions of treatment assignment. In this chapter, we will begin to explore how and why we might wish to generalize what we know about parameters or contexts, or loosen the assumptions we have made about the nature of treatment assignment.

A first point of focus will be on the treatment effects themselves, which we have defined. Throughout the entirety of this book so far, our treatment effects have been *average* effects. We have wished to quantify mean effects in a specific group (for example, treated units or all units), though of course, much goes on beyond the mean. Indeed, even in the face of equal *average* treatment effects, we may view as very different the impacts of a treatment or policy that generates this effect by lifting up outcomes for individuals at the top of the distribution of some outcome of interest, versus if the policy had lifted up outcomes of those at the very bottom. These distributional questions can be of central importance in thinking about social welfare, and the political economy impacts of a policy (see, for example, the discussion in Heckman, Smith, and Clements [1997]). We will discuss heterogeneity in returns and, in particular, consider how to think about heterogeneity in effects across the distribution of the outcome under study: a particularly relevant type of distributional effect. We will return to consider heterogeneity in treatment effects across *other* dimensions in chapter 9.

A second point we will explore relates to the nature of treatment assignment and how tightly defined this treatment assignment is viewed to be. Specifically, we will focus on SUTVA and ask what happens if we *are not* willing to impose SUTVA. SUTVA has been a fundamental assumption up to this point because it has allowed for us to rule out any interaction between treatment status among users and, in this way, write potential outcomes as simply a function of an individual's own treatment assignment. However, we will see that if we no longer wish to assume such a rigid structure with respect to treatment spillovers, this requires a substantial loosening of our modeling and leads to a number of other estimands and estimation procedures.

We will also turn to questions of *external validity*; namely whether, and if so how, we may seek to extrapolate what we learn from a specific context to a broader setting. The methods we have discussed to this point, of course, do not lay claim to being able to respond to a question without a context. When we estimate a treatment effect using these methods, it holds *only* in the context of the reform or treatment being examined (that is, it is *internally valid*). When we know about schooling in Mexico, or microcredit in Pakistan, or worms in Kenya, do we know anything about these problems in other places in the world? In a strict econometric sense, no. Nevertheless, often this is precisely what we would like to know. Does some treatment that has been shown to work in a specific setting offer us any messages about what may occur in other settings?

Finally, we will close thinking more broadly about further loosening the assignment mechanism we have discussed at length in the previous chapters. Many of the methods throughout the book have leveraged their identification based on some limits to the assignment mechanism: For example, assignment may be random, or subject to some sharp local shock. However, in many circumstances of interest, how an individual interacts with treatment depends entirely upon themselves. We will close discussing a framework where treatment assignment is based upon self-selection, or sorting into treatment, and discuss some resulting treatment effects of interest.

Each of these extensions seeks to loosen certain restrictions we have implicitly or explicitly maintained in our models in previous chapters. Of course, this is not to suggest that all questions of interest will be addressed by such methods, or even should be viewed through the framework discussed here. The key message of this chapter is to note that each of the assumptions we have made up to this point are important, though often with careful thinking we can move beyond these in ways that are empirically meaningful.

8.2 Heterogeneity and Quantile Treatment Effects

The question of *heterogeneity* of treatment effects is swept away when we estimate the parameters we have laid out up to this point. While we may certainly be happy if we manage to credibly estimate an *average* treatment effect, this may still hide substantial information of interest. For example, consider a program targeted to schooling outcomes. If a large average treatment effect is driven only by those with very high test scores, we may consider that the program is actually not doing a good job in addressing problems in the true population of interest, such as children at risk of not progressing or of not learning key skills. Indeed, we may be particularly interested in the impacts among a certain group of the population, such as those in the bottom half or bottom quartile of schooling outcomes, if we are aiming to avoid particularly poor results. In any case, and in general, there are certainly considerations of equality that remain obscured when an average treatment effect is reported.

8.2.1 Quantile Treatment Effects

To consider such heterogeneity, we can define a quantile treatment effect, or QTE. The QTE, first laid out in Doksum (1974) and Erich L. Lehmann (1974), seeks to describe how effects of treatment vary across distributions of the outcome variable Y. To formalize the idea of QTEs and provide a precise definition, we will introduce some key notation. We will use $F_{Y(1)}$ to denote the cumulative distribution function (cdf) of potential outcomes $Y_i(1)$, and $F_{Y(0)}$ to denote the cdf of potential outcomes $Y_i(0)$. Of course, this cdf simply tells us the probability that a potential outcome is below some specific value—that is, $F_{Y(1)}(y) = \Pr[Y_i(1) < y]$, and similar for $F_{Y(0)}$. We can also very simply define the inverse of this function—that is, a function that tells us the minimum value of y that accumulates some specific proportion q of the population beneath it. We will use $F^{-1}_{Y(W)}(q)$ to define this function, which is also known as the quantile function.[1] This can be formally defined as $F^{-1}_{Y(1)}(q) = \inf\{y : F_{Y(1)}(y) \geq q\}$, which while slightly cumbersome in notation, simply turns around the cdf such that we can find values of y that correspond to specific quantiles. Based on these quantities, our QTEs are denoted as follows:

$$\tau_{\mathrm{QTE}(q)} = F^{-1}_{Y(1)}(q) - F^{-1}_{Y(0)}(q). \tag{8.1}$$

We can see an idea of this quite clearly in figure 8.1. Here we consider two theoretical potential outcome distributions for $Y_i(0)$ and $Y_i(1)$. If we wish to calculate a QTE at some particular quantile, say quantile 20, we can invert the quantity $F_{Y(1)}(0.2)$, finding that $F^{-1}_{Y(1)}(0.2) \approx 6.2$, and conduct a similar process for $F_{Y(0)}(0.2)$, resulting in $F^{-1}_{Y(0)}(0.2) \approx 4.1$. Thus, our quantile treatment effect, indicated by the lower black arrow, will be $\tau_{\mathrm{QTE}(0.2)} \approx 2.1$. We can conduct similar exercises at any quantile of interest, for example, a similar effect $\tau_{\mathrm{QTE}(0.8)}$ is plotted.

Analogously, we can define a quantile treatment effect on the treated (QTT, or QTET). This simply applies the similar logic to our definition of an ATT previously, defining an estimand like (8.1), but for treated units only:

$$\tau_{\mathrm{QTT}(q)} = F^{-1}_{Y(1)|D=1}(q) - F^{-1}_{Y(0)|D=1}(q). \tag{8.2}$$

You will note that we have defined our treatment effect in terms of the differences of two distributions, and this choice is not casual. What this quantity thus tells us is how outcomes at some particular point of the distribution vary across assignment to a treatment versus

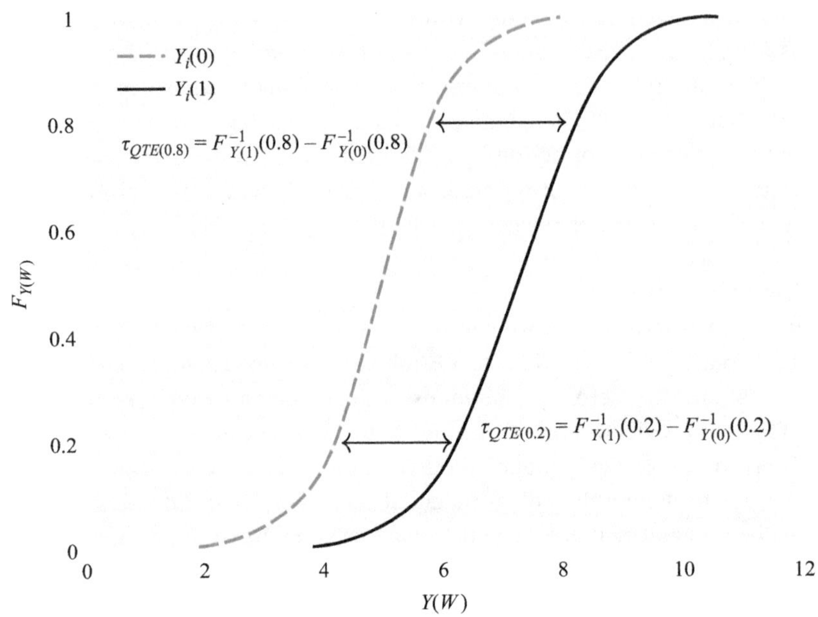

Figure 8.1
Quantile treatment effects: An example.

control condition. What this quantity does *not* tell us is the effect of treatment for some individual located at a specific quantile of the distribution of treatment or control. Indeed, we could define an arguably more useful quantity that is the individual-level quantile treatment effect as: $F^{-1}_{Y_i(1)-Y_i(0)}(q)$. However, even under random assignment, such a quantity will not be identified. The reason why we can not generally observe such a quantity is that it would require that we know the entire distribution of $Y_i(1) - Y_i(0)$, which requires knowing both the counterfactual distribution for an outcome $Y(W)$ *as well as* the position that an individual i would take in that counterfactual distribution, which is something we can never observe. One way we could resolve this is by making assumptions about an individual's position in the counterfactual distribution, in particular an assumption such as rank invariance, or rank preservation. Such an assumption states that an individual's rank in the distribution of outcomes under their actual treatment status is informative of what their rank would also be had they received the alternative treatment assignment. While such an assumption may be met in certain settings such as if individuals have some latent factor that will place them as equally good performers regardless of treatment assignment, it is a strong assumption, and generally not taken. Further details relating to such considerations can be found in Heckman, Smith, and Clements (1997), who provide more discussion of this assumption, as well as discussing how it can be loosened to lead to bounds estimates.

8.2.2 Estimation and Inference for Quantile Treatment Effects

How we should estimate quantile treatment effects, as well as how we should conduct inference on such effects, depends entirely on the nature of treatment assignment. Fortunately, efficient procedures have been well documented for a range of settings, including in cases where treatment is assigned randomly and in cases where conditional unconfoudedness is believed to hold, as well as in cases where treatment is *not* assumed to be randomly assigned such as instrumental variables models, difference-in-differences, and regression discontinuity designs.

8.2.2.1 Unconfoundedness and conditional unconfoundedness

Random treatment assignment If treatment is assigned randomly and we can maintain assumptions 1 (SUTVA), 2 (unconfoundedness), and 3 (overlap), then it is very simple to estimate QTEs (and equivalently, given randomization, QTTs). Provided that quantiles in the data exist (i.e., that distributions are not flat; see Firpo [2007, Assumption 2] for discussion) we can easily estimate these quantities. Noting that unconfoundedness implies that:

$$F_{Y(1)}(y)=F_{Y|W=1}(y) \quad \text{and} \quad F_{Y(0)}(y)=F_{Y|W=0}(y),$$

we can use the observed distributions $F_{Y|W=1}(y)$ and $F_{Y|W=0}(y)$, to estimate the quantities in (8.1) and (8.2), and estimate QTEs or QTTs, which, in the case of random assignment, will collapse to the same quantity.

Quantile regression It is illustrative to note, however, that analogous to the case of the ATE, which can be estimated directly as a difference in means estimator, or equivalently via regression, a similar result holds with the QTE. In the case of the QTE (and QTT), we can proceed to also estimate (8.1) by quantile regression.

In quantile regression, introduced by Koenker and Bassett (1978), parameters are estimated to describe the relationship between dependent variables and *quantiles* of the distribution of that independent variable. The estimation procedure in quantile regression is via an absolute error loss function (rather than a squared error loss function, as in OLS). As a result, quantile regression is less sensitive to outliers than OLS. If we consider a simple bivariate regression of some outcome Y_i on treatment W_i, the quantile regression estimator $\widehat{\tau}(q)$ for percentile q minimizes the following loss function:

$$Q_N(\tau(q))=\sum_{i:Y_i\geq W_i\tau(q)} q\left|Y_i-W_i\tau(q)\right|+\sum_{i:Y_i<W_i\tau(q)}(1-q)\left|Y_i-W_i\tau(q)\right|. \tag{8.3}$$

Note that here we are comparing the dependent variable Y_i to the fitted value $W_i\tau(q)$, and partitioning the sum into observations above and below that fitted value. Also note that we are "tilting" the optimization in favor of the lower or upper percentiles depending on the value of q. If q is a high quantile (e.g., 0.9), more weight is placed on the positive residuals (the first term), and the estimator $\tau(q)$ will reflect the upper part of the outcome distribution, and vice versa for low values of q. In the special case of the median ($q=0.5$), this regression simply collapses to the least absolute deviation estimator. This is often written more compactly using the check function, which is defined (for some quantity u) as:

$$\rho_q(u)=\begin{cases} qu & \text{if } u \geq 0, \\ (q-1)u & \text{if } u < 0. \end{cases}$$

With this function, we can rewrite (8.3) as:

$$Q_N\left(\tau(q)\right)=\sum_{i=1}^{N}\rho_q(Y_i - W_i\tau(q)). \tag{8.4}$$

By simple inspection or rearrangement, we can see that (8.3) and (8.4) are identical.

In cases where unconfoundedness holds, the estimates from quantile regression identify the QTE quantity in (8.1) (and equivalently the QTT quantity in (8.2), given random assignment to treatment). Thus, estimation can proceed simply via the direct estimation of quantiles in each group, or quantile regression. What's more, in cases with randomization, standard variance estimators can be used for quantile regression, including heteroscedasticity-robust versions (Koenker 2005, 73), and bootstrap procedures exist for richer types of randomization procedures such as paired randomization (Jiang et al. 2024).

Conditional unconfoundedness If, rather than assuming unconditional uncounfoundedness, we believe that *conditional* unconfoundedness holds, we can adjust the previous estimation procedures to capture this dependence on covariates X. If we maintain the assumption of SUTVA, but now assume conditional unconfoundedness and overlap (Assumption $2'$ and $3'$), a first alternative is to incorporate relevant covariates X directly into a quantile regression model. Indeed, if we augment (8.4) to include controls, the estimates:

$$\widehat{\tau}(q)=\arg\min_{\tau(q)}\sum_{i=1}^{N}\rho_q\left(Y_i - X_i'\beta - W_i\tau(q)\right) \tag{8.5}$$

will provide us unbiased estimates of *conditional* quantile treatment effects.

However, these conditional QTEs are slightly different to what we laid out in (8.1) and (8.2), as they will be covariate-specific. And the nature of "covariate-specific" in QTEs is actually quite distinct to "covariate-specific" in other regression settings, because here this implies that we are considering the *conditional* quantiles themselves. For instance, when we refer to the conditional 10th quantile, we are estimating the 10th quantile within each covariate-defined subgroup. Suppose we are evaluating the impact of an educational policy, and one covariate of interest is class size. If individuals in small classes tend to perform well, and those in large classes tend to perform poorly, then conditional QTEs at the 10th quantile capture treatment effects for low-performing individuals within each group—that is, individuals at the 10th percentile in small classes (relatively high-performing) and those at the 10th percentile in large classes (relatively low-performing). In this way, conditional QTEs reflect aggregates across the 10th quantiles within each covariate group, rather than the unconditional 10th percentile of the overall outcome distribution.[2]

For this reason, we will likely prefer to consider estimators of unconditional QTEs, which have been developed by Firpo (2007). Firpo shows how we can estimate the quantities in (8.1) and (8.2) under a conditional unconfoundedness assumption. It turns out that we can apply propensity score reweighting methods to directly calculate quantile effects of interest that zoom in precisely on the individuals at specific percentiles of the entire sample, rather than the covariate-specific counterpart discussed above. Firpo (2007) shows that as in reweighting methods we explored previously in section 3.4, in quantile methods we can reweight to balance the distribution of covariates between treated and control units, and hence calculate an unconditonal QTE. Conveniently, Firpo's (2007) QTE estimator is simply a propensity-score reweighted quantile regression function:

$$\widehat{\tau}(q)_{\text{QTE}} = \arg\min_{\tau(q)} \sum_{i=1}^{N} \omega_i \rho_q \left(Y_i - X_i'\beta - W_i \tau(q)\right), \tag{8.6}$$

where:

$$\omega_i = \frac{W_i}{P(X_i)} + \frac{1-W_i}{1-P(X_i)}.$$

We will note that the estimator in (8.6) is very similar to that in (8.5), save for the presence of weights. We may also note that this procedure conducts inverse propensity score weighting exactly as we did with standard implementations of average treatment effects with conditional unconfoundedness in (3.25). Firpo (2007) also shows that along the lines of (3.30), we can similarly define QTTs by simply replacing the weights used for the QTE in (8.6) with:

$$\omega_i = \frac{W_i}{\Pr(W_i = 1)} + \frac{1-W_i}{1-P(X_i)} \cdot \frac{1}{\Pr(W_i = 1)},$$

implying a similar mapping between inverse propensity score weighting in regression models to inverse propensity score weighting in quantile regression models. In this way, we can easily refashion quantile regression to provide us with unconditional quantile treatment effects. Along with these estimands, Firpo (2007) lays out variance estimates for these quantiles.

Code Callout 8.1: Quantile Effects with an Exogenous Treatment
We will explore Quantile Treatment Effects following an example laid out in Firpo (2007). Namely, we will use the data from LaLonde (1986), to see how to estimate and visualize quantile effects, and understand how they are implemented both in cases where unconditional and conditional unconfoundedness are assumed.

8.2.2.2 Instrumental variables Methods for estimating QTEs are also well-characterized in models based on instrumental variables. As we have seen at length in chapter 5, unless we wish to impose quite strict homogeneity assumptions on treatment effects in models based on IVs, parameters from these models will be local average treatment effects (LATEs), informative for individuals whose behavior would be shifted by the instrument in question. The analogue of the LATE for quantile methods is the local quantile treatment effect (LQTE), which allows us to consider how a LATE varies across the distribution of the outcome variable Y_i.

For a binary instrument, we can define our LQTE as:

$$\tau_{\text{LQTE}(q)} = F^{-1}_{Y(1)}\big(q|D_i(1) - D_i(0) = 1\big) - F^{-1}_{Y(0)}\big(q|D_i(1) - D_i(0) = 1\big). \tag{8.7}$$

This follows the definition of the LATE as the difference in potential outcomes for the compliant subpopulation—that is, those for whom $D_i(1) - D_i(0) = 1$, but here instead of considering mean differences, we wish to consider differences in quantiles between treated and untreated compliers.

It turns out that if we maintain our standard IV assumptions of 6–9 presented in Chapter 5, we actually already know a way to get to arbitrary functions of the LATE! This is laid out in Abadie (2002) and defined in (5.33) and (5.34). If we apply the quantities laid out in Abadie (2002) to functions for quantiles, we can write complier-specific quantiles of $Y_i(0)$ and $Y_i(1)$ as follows:

$$F_{Y(1)}\big(y|D_i(1) > D_i(0)\big) = \frac{\mathbb{E}\big[\mathbb{1}(Y_i \leq y)D_i|Z_i = 1\big] - \mathbb{E}\big[\mathbb{1}(Y_i \leq y)D_i|Z_i = 0\big]}{\mathbb{E}\big[D_i|Z_i = 1\big] - \mathbb{E}\big[D_i|Z_i = 0\big]} \tag{8.8}$$

$$F_{Y(0)}\big(y|D_i(1) > D_i(0)\big) = \frac{\mathbb{E}\big[\mathbb{1}(Y_i \leq y)(1 - D_i)|Z_i = 1\big] - \mathbb{E}\big[\mathbb{1}(Y_i \leq y)(1 - D_i)|Z_i = 0\big]}{\mathbb{E}\big[(1 - D_i)|Z_i = 1\big] - \mathbb{E}\big[(1 - D_i)|Z_i = 0\big]}. \tag{8.9}$$

This suggests a direct way to estimate LQTEs in (8.7), as (8.8) and (8.9) can be taken to data, and these can be simply inverted to estimated the LQTEs laid out above.

Now, what about the case with covariates? As in the case of conditional unconfoundedness and the QTE, it turns out that if we assume that instrumental variable assumptions are met conditional on some set of covariates X, separate methods allow us to estimate conditional LQTEs and unconditional LQTEs. A "first-generation" result comes from Abadie, Angrist, and Imbens (2002). They note that if we wish to estimate conditional LQTEs based on an instrument that meets assumptions $6'$ (conditional exogeneity) as well conditional versions of relevance, overlap, and monotonicity conditions, then we can do this with weighted quantile regression, provided that we impose a linearity assumption for potential outcomes among the compliers. Specifically, they show that if we can write complier outcomes distributions as:

$$F^{-1}_{Y(0)}\big(q|X = x, D_i(1) - D_i(0) = 1\big) = X'\beta(q)$$
$$F^{-1}_{Y(1)}\big(q|X = x, D_i(1) - D_i(0) = 1\big) = X'\beta(q) + \tau(q)D_i,$$

then we can proceed to estimate conditional LQTEs with weighted quantile regression. This weighted quantile regression estimator is written as follows:

$$\widehat{\tau}(q)_{\text{LQTE,conditional}} = \arg\min_{\tau(q)} \sum_{i=1}^{N} \omega_i \rho_q \left(Y_i - X_i'\beta - D_i\tau(q)\right), \tag{8.10}$$

where:

$$\omega_i = 1 - \frac{D_i(1-Z_i)}{\Pr(Z_i=0|X_i)} - \frac{(1-D_i)Z_i}{\Pr(Z_i=1|X_i)}.$$

While the quantile regression function (8.10) is written identically to (8.6), what changes in this case is the weighting function. And the weights in this case ω_i are precisely defined as Abadie's Kappa from Abadie (2003), which we discussed at length in section 5.3.2.3. Thus, while this result requires the imposition of a linear restriction on the quantile functions for compliers (which can be quite rich, including interactions with D_i), the value is that it allows us to use all the machinations we have already encountered either in standard LATE models (i.e., Abadie's Kappa) along with a basic quantile regression estimator.

Finally, and analogously to the case of conditional unconfoundedness laid out above, we may very likely be interested in an unconditional LQTE that lets us speak of quantile treatment effects across *unconditional* quantiles of Y_i. This is defined by Frölich and Melly (2013). They show that we can use an alternative weighting scheme and a simple quantile regression *without conditioning* on covariates in the quantile regression. Namely, Frölich and Melly (2013) show that estimating:

$$\widehat{\tau}(q)_{\text{LQTE,unconditional}} = \arg\min_{\tau(q)} \sum_{i=1}^{N} \omega_i \rho_q \left(Y_i - \alpha - D_i\tau(q)\right), \tag{8.11}$$

where

$$\omega_i = \frac{Z_i - \Pr(Z_i=1|X_i)}{\Pr(Z_i=1|X_i)[1-\Pr(Z_i=1|X_i)]} \cdot (2D_i - 1)$$

identifies unconditional LQTEs, and does so without the linearity assumption required in Abadie, Angrist, and Imbens (2002). Frölich and Melly (2013) highlight that the weights in (8.11) are distinct to those in (8.10) in that they serve two purposes: a first purpose that is shared with (8.10)—to find compliers—and a second purpose that allows for the generation of unconditional quantile effects: balancing the covariates between treated and untreated compliers.

Estimation and inference of these models is discussed at length in the original papers, as well as more recent review papers such as Melly and Wüthrich (2017), which is a useful jumping-off point for more advanced considerations related to (local) quantile treatment effects. This review paper also discussed a range of more recent extensions as well comparisons to other approaches to quantile regression (without a direct focus on quantile treatment effects), such as the widely implemented estimator of Chernozhukov and Hansen (2006), which is based on a slightly different approach and method.

8.2.2.3 Difference-in-differences There are a number of ways in which quantile effects have been considered in differences-in-differences designs. Among other procedures, leading alternatives include the changes-in-changes methods developed by Athey and Imbens (2006), which can be applied with repeated cross-sections of data and as few as two time-periods, and QTEs for difference-in-differences developed by Callaway and Li (2019), which require panel data and at least three periods of observations, with quite close links to the assumptions for difference-in-differences designs we laid out in chapter 4.

Changes-in-changes The changes-in-changes (CIC) methods proposed by Athey and Imbens (2006) seek to map the logic of quantile treatment effects into a difference-in-differences style-setting. To wit, Athey and Imbens (2006) begin with a two-by-two design such as that laid out in section 4.2. We will follow this notation of defining the treated group as $W_i = 1$ and the control group as $W_i = 0$, and we assume data on two time-periods, $t = 1$ and $t = 2$, with treatment switched on in the treated group between period $t = 1$ and $t = 2$. We will write outcomes as $Y_{g,t}$ and potential outcomes as $Y_{g,t}(0)$ and $Y_{g,t}(1)$, respectively. Let us denote $F_{g,t}$ by the distribution functions of the outcome for group g (0 for control and 1 for treatment) at time t. The changes-in-changes estimand is defined as:

$$\tau(q)^{\text{CIC}}_{\text{ATT}} = F^{-1}_{Y_{1,2}(1)}(q) - F^{-1}_{Y_{1,2}(0)}(q), \tag{8.12}$$

which asks how treated units respond to treatment in the post-treatment period at specific percentiles of the outcome distribution.

Athey and Imbens (2006) show that under assumptions that are somewhat akin to those we observed in a difference-in-differences setting, we can identify these QTTs. Namely, even if treated and untreated units are observed to have different distributions in the pre-treatment period, we can estimate treatment effects if a number of stability assumptions hold about how these distributions would move in the absence of treatment and the nature of unobservables. Specifically, if a rank-invariance assumption holds within each treatment group, implying that treatment and control units maintain their ranks in their specific group over time, if unobservables do not change within groups over time, and if the distribution of potential outcomes is stable in the absence of treatment, we can write (8.12) in terms of all observable distributions:

$$\tau_q^{\text{CIC}} = F^{-1}_{Y_{1,2}}(q) - F^{-1}_{Y_{0,2}}(F_{Y_{0,1}}(F^{-1}_{Y_{1,1}}(q))). \tag{8.13}$$

The idea of this is that we can infer the unobserved potential outcome $F^{-1}_{Y_{1,2}(0)}(q)$ at quantile q by first finding the same quantile in this group at $t = 2$ and mapping this value into the corresponding quantile among the untreated group. Finally, this $t = 1$ quantile among the control group is mapped into its $t = 2$ value, which provides the counterfactual outcome for treated units. While there are various shifts here, this can perhaps be viewed most clearly in a graphical sense, as documented in figure 8.2. In this figure, if one starts at the darker dashed line and follows corresponding arrows to the darker solid line, then lighter solid line,

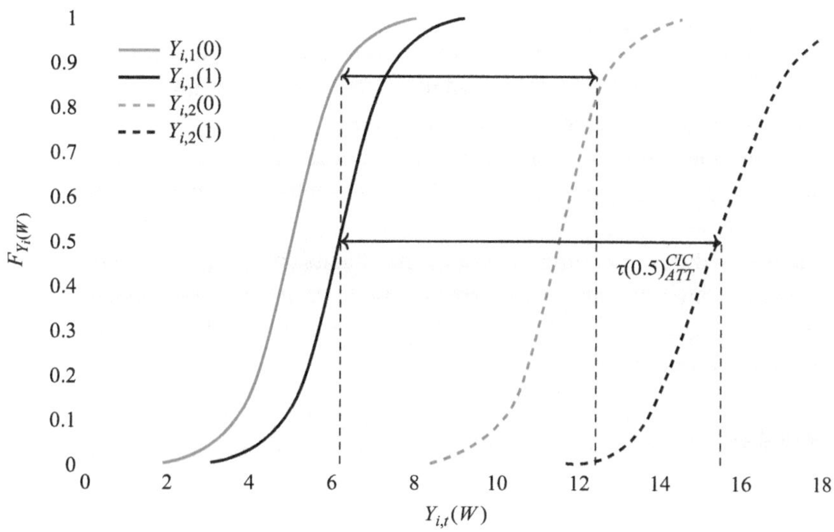

Figure 8.2
An illustrative example: Changes-in-changes.

then lighter dashed line, we can see that we are working from inner to outer functions in the right-hand term of (8.13), finally arriving to the counterfactual value of interest.

Other potential approaches There are other potential approaches that can be taken for quantile methods in a difference-in-differences framework. One more recent proposal from Callaway and Li (2019) is suitable for settings where panel data is available and offers some advantage in terms of weaker distributional restrictions than the changes-in-changes estimator. Callaway and Li (2019) propose a QTT that can be estimated if a parallel trends assumption holds in the entire distribution, as well as if the relationship between changes in potential outcomes for the treated group and initial levels of potential outcomes is stable over time. This latter assumption allows for the weakening of monotonicity in unobservable assumptions required in changes-in-changes, but adds the cost that at least three rather than two periods of data are required. The reason that a third wave of data is required is to first estimate the nature of distributional changes over time among the treated in the pre-treatment period, and then secondly this change in distributional structure can be scaled by the shift observed in the untreated group in the post-treatment period.

8.2.2.4 Regression discontinuity Finally, the estimation and inference for quantile treatment effects in a regression discontinuity design has been defined by Frandsen, Frölich, and Melly (2012). To do so they note that we can apply the formulae laid out in (8.8)–(8.9) to a fuzzy RDD if instead of taking expectations of the quantities in the numerator and denominator, we take limits of these expectations as approaching the discontinuity from above and from below. Frandsen, Frölich, and Melly (2012) show that under standard RD-style assumptions—namely the existence of a discontinuity, continuity of potential outcomes in quantiles around the cutoff, local monotonicity, and the existence of observations close to the cutoff—the same logic from Fuzzy RDD can be applied to estimate quantile treatment effects.

Extensions into the consideration of confidence bands covering all quantiles, the calculation of optimal bandwidths, and bias-corrected methods are discussed in Chiang, Hsu, and Sasaki (2019) and Qu, Yoon, and Perron (2024) for a number of sharp and fuzzy designs with and without covariates.

8.3 Relaxing SUTVA

One constant assumption we have maintained through the entirety of this book has been the SUTVA. This has allowed us to consider the assignment mechanism as essentially an individual-level problem and abstract away from any spillover effects, or network effects, of treatment. While we may believe SUTVA if individuals are diffuse or have relatively little space to directly interact, in other settings we will *not* believe SUTVA. One often-mentioned case is that of infectious disease where risks of exposure can compound in populations, and where treatments seek to avoid compounding rates of infection by achieving herd immunity cutting down transmission between members of a population (see, for example, discussion in Rosenbaum [2007]; Miguel and Kremer [2004]). In other cases, we may expect that treatments applied within groups such as classes, dormitories, or even small villages may spill over between peers in these groups (Manski 1993; Sacerdote 2001). What's more, if treatments are widespread or large enough to affect broader equilibrium in economies (Egger et al. 2022) or labor markets (Crépon et al. 2013), such general equilibrium effects may clearly spill over to any treated or untreated individuals in a complex way.

8.3.1 A Framework Without SUTVA

8.3.1.1 Potential outcomes Work to loosen the SUTVA has proceeded in a number of ways, and this is an area in which work is actively ongoing. While foundational work on spillovers existed earlier, such as Manski (1993) on the reflection problem in treatment effects,[3] early work mapping these considerations into a potential outcomes framework is laid out by Hudgens and Halloran (2008). A key implication in thinking about how to generalize *without* SUTVA is to note that it is no longer correct to think of two potential outcomes. Instead, potential outcomes depend upon the entire possible set of treatment assignments. If we write possible treatment assignment vectors as:

$$\mathbf{w} = (w_1, \ldots, w_N)',$$

where for simplicity we can assume that each w_i is a binary treatment assignment, we can now write potential outcomes for individual i as:

$$Y_i(\mathbf{w}). \tag{8.14}$$

Defining as $\mathbf{W}$ the specific realized treatment assignment, we will have a single observed potential outcome $Y_i(\mathbf{W})$. However, even with a binary treatment outcome, this is only one of the 2^N potential outcomes! The fact that there are now many potential outcomes makes even defining a treatment effect of interest a challenge, let alone considering how to identify such an effect in practice.

What is generally true is that in writing potential outcomes like (8.14), even though we now recognize that an individual's outcome can depend on all units' treatment assignment, including their own assignment W_i, we will generally view an individual's own treatment assignment as particularly relevant. For example, we would likely not expect in many settings that an individual who has multiple neighbors exposed to treatment and is also themselves exposed would have a similar effect if their same group of neighbors were treated but they were now unexposed. For this reason, in general when definining estimands we seek to explicity recognize an individual's treatment status while potentially simplifying the nature of spillovers.

There are a range of routes taken forward in the literature. One strand, including the early work of Hudgens and Halloran (2008), considers that spillovers may occur *within* some larger group, but not outside this group, a setting Sobel (2006) refers to as "partial interference." A related but potentially more general approach views spillovers as occurring through networks as "network interference." In this case, treatment spillovers can occur within networks in which individuals may be linked to other units, who may or may not be linked with each other.

A specific example of such a setting, and differences between partial interference and network interference, can be viewed in figure 8.3. In the top panel, a network in which partial interference may occur is graphed as individuals are grouped within three disjoint clusters (such as classrooms), within which each individual is linked. However, outside of these groups, no spillovers are assumed to occur. In the lower panel, we consider a case where individuals are viewed as linked in a more general fashion: For example while individuals A and D are not themselves joined, they are potentially linked by individual B, and so B's exposure may be relevant for both.

These cases can be described in adjacency matrices $\mathbf{D}$, which describe (direct) links between individuals as in (8.15). In the case where partial interference is assumed, $\mathbf{D}_{\text{PI}}$, this is simply a block matrix with 0s on the principal diagonal given that individuals are not linked with themselves, whereas in the case of network interference, $\mathbf{D}_{\text{NI}}$, no such regular structure is observed. Representing networks as adjacency matrices is common (see, e.g., Goldsmith-Pinkham and Imbens [2013]; Auerbach [2022]) and can be further generalized to allow for cases where distances can be represented as values instead of

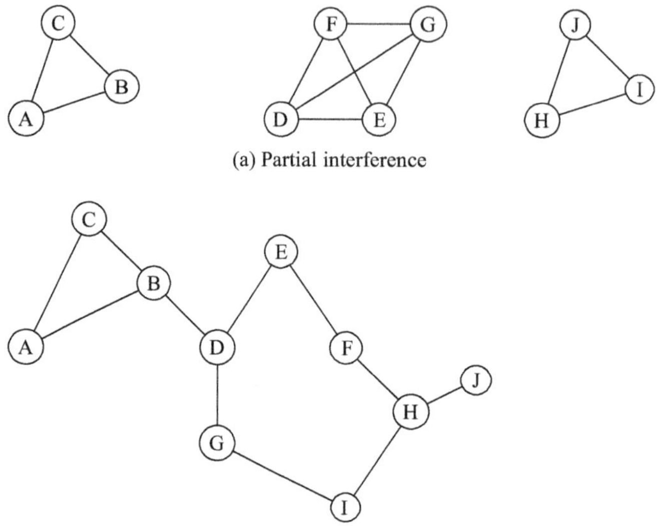

(a) Partial interference

(b) Network interference

Figure 8.3
Partial versus network interference.

binary outcomes, or where individuals need not be linked reciprocally (Auerbach and Tabord-Meehan 2023).

$$
\mathbf{D}_{\mathrm{PI}} = \begin{array}{c|cccccccccc}
 & A & B & C & D & E & F & G & H & I & J \\
\hline
A & 0 & 1 & 1 & 0 & 0 & 0 & 0 & 0 & 0 & 0 \\
B & 1 & 0 & 1 & 0 & 0 & 0 & 0 & 0 & 0 & 0 \\
C & 1 & 1 & 0 & 0 & 0 & 0 & 0 & 0 & 0 & 0 \\
D & 0 & 0 & 0 & 0 & 1 & 1 & 1 & 0 & 0 & 0 \\
E & 0 & 0 & 0 & 1 & 0 & 1 & 1 & 0 & 0 & 0 \\
F & 0 & 0 & 0 & 1 & 1 & 0 & 1 & 0 & 0 & 0 \\
G & 0 & 0 & 0 & 1 & 1 & 1 & 0 & 0 & 0 & 0 \\
H & 0 & 0 & 0 & 0 & 0 & 0 & 0 & 0 & 1 & 1 \\
I & 0 & 0 & 0 & 0 & 0 & 0 & 0 & 1 & 0 & 1 \\
J & 0 & 0 & 0 & 0 & 0 & 0 & 0 & 1 & 1 & 0
\end{array}
\qquad
\mathbf{D}_{\mathrm{NI}} = \begin{array}{c|cccccccccc}
 & A & B & C & D & E & F & G & H & I & J \\
\hline
A & 0 & 1 & 1 & 0 & 0 & 0 & 0 & 0 & 0 & 0 \\
B & 1 & 0 & 1 & 1 & 0 & 0 & 0 & 0 & 0 & 0 \\
C & 1 & 1 & 0 & 0 & 0 & 0 & 0 & 0 & 0 & 0 \\
D & 0 & 1 & 0 & 0 & 1 & 0 & 1 & 0 & 0 & 0 \\
E & 0 & 0 & 0 & 1 & 0 & 1 & 0 & 0 & 0 & 0 \\
F & 0 & 0 & 0 & 0 & 1 & 0 & 0 & 1 & 0 & 0 \\
G & 0 & 0 & 0 & 1 & 0 & 0 & 0 & 0 & 1 & 0 \\
H & 0 & 0 & 0 & 0 & 0 & 1 & 0 & 0 & 1 & 1 \\
I & 0 & 0 & 0 & 0 & 0 & 0 & 1 & 1 & 0 & 0 \\
J & 0 & 0 & 0 & 0 & 0 & 0 & 0 & 1 & 0 & 0
\end{array}
\tag{8.15}
$$

8.3.1.2 The assignment mechanism and exposure mappings What these approaches have in common is that they generally place some limits on how treatment can diffuse between individuals. One particularly flexible take proposed by Aronow and Samii (2017) refers to exposure mappings. Exposure mappings refer to the way in which a specific treatment assignment maps into a treatment *exposure*. They note that we can write an exposure mapping as follows:

$$f(\mathbf{W}, \theta_i), \tag{8.16}$$

which makes clear that an individual's treatment exposure can depend on the actual treatment assignment of all individuals $\mathbf{W}$, as well as potentially characteristics of the individual, θ_i. This allows for a broad range of treatment spillovers to be described, and treatment effects can then be defined based on specific exposures of interest. Indeed, within the framework of (8.16), we could easily model a case where SUTVA is viewed to hold, as this is equivalent to stating that $f(\mathbf{W}, \theta_i) = w_i$ for all i. We could also capture cases where spillovers exist *within* groups, as θ_i could be defined as an individual's group identifier, or model more complex dependencies up to cases where every single treatment assignment implies a different treatment exposure.

Such an idea is also embedded in Manski's (2013) definition of an effective treatment. An effective treatment, like the exposure mapping above, defines the potential different treatments an individual may be exposed to. This describes all possible treatments but notes that a large number of treatment assignments $\mathbf{w}$ may imply the same effective treatment. This may occur, for example, if an individual's effective treatment depends upon their own treatment status, as well as the treatment status of those in their network or group. In this case, changes in the treatment status of units *outside* of an individual's group would, all else constant, not result in changes to the effective treatment an individual was exposed to. Regardless of how this is conceptualized, what will be key for the estimation of treatment effects without a strict implementation of SUTVA is some framework to define both the exposure of interest, as well as the estimand or estimands of interest. We will discuss a number of strategies below that propose routes to identification in the absence of SUTVA.

8.3.2 Strategies for Estimation and Inference

8.3.2.1 Partial population and randomized saturation designs If we believe that spillovers are limited to only occurring within groups (i.e., partial interference), we may seek to learn about spillovers and treatment by varying both an individual's treatment status and their exposure to other treated individuals. Moffitt (2001) notes that if groups are randomized into treatment, and then within treated groups only certain individuals are treated, we can learn some limited treatment effect parameters related to the treatment effect itself (by comparing treated units in treated groups to units in untreated groups) as well as spillover effects (by comparing untreated units in treated groups to control units). Moffitt (2001) refers to these designs as "partial population experiments," and their properties have been further studied in, among other places, Hirano and Hahn (2010), who discuss optimal designs, and applied in many settings to examine direct and spillover effects. Highly cited cases include Duflo and Saez (2003) and Angelucci and De Giorgi (2009).

While these designs allow for one to learn about direct and indirect policy effects, they leave certain questions unstudied. Namely, we cannot say anything about whether treatment effects depend upon the number of other treated units, nor whether indirect effects depend on the number of treated units that spill over onto untreated units. For this reason, in an experimental setting, we may wish to vary both the exposure to treatment and the exposure to the treatment of others. This is the idea of randomized saturation designs. In randomized saturation designs, a two-stage randomization occurs. First, groups or clusters of observations are randomized into saturation levels, which refers to the proportion of other treated units in the group, which also includes a saturation level of zero implying completely untreated groups. And secondly, after a random assignment of a level of saturation, individuals within each cluster are randomly assigned treatment with a probability equal to the saturation level of their cluster.[4]

Such a two-stage design was discussed in Hudgens and Halloran (2008), in which groups were randomly assigned to differing levels of treatment. There are a range of ways in which this can be defined (see, for example, varying setups in Hudgens and Halloran [2008], Baird et al. [2018], and DiTraglia et al. [2023], with the notation here being closest to the latter). But in effect these designs are based on a series of saturations $\mathcal{S} \in \{s_1, s_2, \ldots s_J\}$ where each $s_j \in [0, 1]$, and a group of clusters or groups, denoted G. In a first stage, these saturations are then randomly assigned to clusters such that each cluster G is assigned a saturation level. In a second stage, individuals within each cluster are randomly assigned treatment with probability s_j.

Based on this design, and under the assumption of partial interference, we can write potential outcomes in terms of (only) an individual's treatment status as well as the treatment status of individuals within their own cluster. If we additionally assume that what is important for any spillovers is not who is treated, but rather the proportion of units in a given cluster that are treated, this means we can write potential outcomes as follows:

$$Y_{i,g}(W_i, \overline{W}_{i,g}), \tag{8.17}$$

where potential outcomes for individual i in group g depends on their own treatment status W_i as well as the average rate of treatment in their treatment cluster $\overline{W}_{i,g}$. This quantity is defined as the proportion of treated units *excluding* individual i so that it captures the proportion of other members in a groups that are exposed to treatment. Much of the simplification that allows us to rewrite potential outcomes from (8.14) as (8.17) comes from the assumption that what matters is the proportion of neighbors treated, rather than the precise identity of the neighbors treated. This is what Manski (2013) refers to as an anonymous interaction assumption.

In this setting, it is illustrative to note that even if only two levels of saturation are assigned in the first stage, we can learn a number of relevant parameters (Hudgens and Halloran 2008). First, we can learn about the causal effect of treatment given a specific group-level exposure. This is referred to as an average direct effect and is defined at each saturation level as the effect of receiving treatment. Secondly we can learn about the effect of differential group-level exposure holding fixed treatment exposure. And finally, we can learn about the effect of varying both treatment exposure and group-level exposure. However, with varying saturations, we consider quite a number of parameters of interest. If we use the naming of Baird et al. (2018), this includes the "treatment on the uniquely treated," defined as follows:

$$\tau_{\text{TUT}} \equiv \mathbb{E}[Y_{i,g}(1,0) - Y_{i,g}(0,0)]. \tag{8.18}$$

This is a logical estimand, which defines the effect of treatment in the absence of any spillovers by simply considering how an individual's potential outcomes would vary if they were the only treated unit in a cluster of all other untreated units, versus if they were untreated in a cluster with no treated units. However we can also consider spillover effects themselves, by defining a spillover on the treated (ST) and spillover on the nontreated (SNT) estimands. These are defined as follows:

$$\tau_{\text{ST}(\overline{W}_{i,g})} \equiv \mathbb{E}[Y_{i,g}(1,\overline{W}_{i,g}) - Y_{i,g}(1,0)] \tag{8.19}$$

$$\tau_{\text{SNT}(\overline{W}_{i,g})} \equiv \mathbb{E}[Y_{i,g}(0,\overline{W}_{i,g}) - Y_{i,g}(0,0)], \tag{8.20}$$

and compare treated and untreated units in specific treatment intensity clusters to similar individuals, in clusters, with no other treated observations. These latter quantities make clear that any spillovers will depend on the degree of saturation an individual is exposed to. For example, spillovers may be small where relatively few neighbors are treated and large where many neighbors are treated. This can be measured as the slope of spillovers on the treated:

$$\tau_{\text{DT}(\overline{W}_{i,g},\overline{W}'_{i,g})} \equiv \frac{\tau_{\text{ST}(\overline{W}'_{i,g})} - \tau_{\text{ST}(\overline{W}_{i,g})}}{\overline{W}'_{i,g} - \overline{W}_{i,g}}, \tag{8.21}$$

with analogous definitions for the slope of spillovers on the nontreated.

A key result here is that given that exposure to saturations and exposure to treatment is randomly assigned, all of the treatment effects above are defined and can be estimated by simple differences of means across judiciously chosen groups. These results have been formally documented in Hudgens and Halloran (2008), and variance estimators have been laid out by Hudgens and Halloran (2008), Liu and Hudgens (2014), and Tchetgen, J., and VanderWeele (2012). An example of such a design in highly cited empirical work is available in Crépon et al. (2013).

Instrumental variables Incorporating violations of SUTVA into IV methods can occur in much the same way as laid out above; however, further complexity is added given the endogenous nature of any treatment adoption decisions. Work in this line has been conducted in a number of papers, including Kang and Imbens (2016), Imai, Jiang, and Malani (2021), DiTraglia et al. (2023), and Vazquez-Bare (2023a). These papers take alternative approaches based on different assumptions resulting in different estimands. Kang and Imbens (2016) and Imai, Jiang, and Malani (2021) both consider two-stage randomizations and partial interference, and propose aggregate effects that capture effects of treatment *assignments* in a specific group. Imai, Jiang, and Malani (2021) define the complier average direct effect (or local average direct effect), which is similar to the LATE but, instead of quantifying the effect of treatment on compliers, quantifies the effect of being assigned a specific saturation level among all compliers in a cluster. In a similar vein, Kang and Imbens (2016) discuss the estimation of local direct effects (which abstract from any spillovers) and local peer effects (which consider spillovers). They show that these effects can be identified and estimated if selection into treatment only depends on an individual's own treatment status (not that of other members in their group) and in the case of local peer effects, if one-sided compliance holds (e.g., if individuals offered treatment can choose not to adopt treatment, but untreated individuals cannot access treatment).

In two more recent papers, DiTraglia et al. (2023) and Vazquez-Bare (2023a) show that if indeed one-sided noncompliance occurs, a richer set of treatment and spillover effects can be estimated that focus on treatment uptake decisions. DiTraglia et al. (2023) base their results on an assumption that they refer to as individualized offer response, which implies that an individual's treatment take-up *cannot* depend upon the treatment status of others in their group (as per the assumption in Kang and Imbens [2016]), while spillover effects do, of course, depend upon the treatment status of others. They additionally assume that spillovers do not depend upon the precise identity of others in the group who are treated but rather simply the saturation level in the group. They show that if this holds, and if a randomized saturation design is used, a rich set of parameters can be identified, effectively equivalent to the slope of spillovers on the treated and nontreated, as discussed above, and direct effects on the treated. A complementary approach is described in Vazquez-Bare (2023a) with a key feature being that spillovers can occur in both treatment adoption *and* in outcomes. In his principal layout, spillovers are permitted between pairs of people, and provided that a stricter monotonicity assumption is met,[5] he notes that two relevant treatment effects can be identified: both a direct effect among individuals whose partners are not treated as well as a spillover effect among untreated individuals whose partners are compliers.

Other settings Relatively more limited work exists on within-group spillovers in other designs discussed previously, including DD designs and RD designs. In the case of DD designs, while work of Chaisemartin and D'Haultfœuille (2017) exists that focuses on cases in which groups are exposed to varying levels of treatment (which the authors refer to as Fuzzy difference-in-differences), they are interested in a direct effect of treatment itself, rather than spillovers among treated and untreated units within groups. While this has some parallels with local average direct effects discussed above, the focus of the work is quite different, without a focus on interactions between units within treated groups. While additional work exists on spillovers between groups in difference-in-differences settings such as Clarke (2017) and Butts (2023), this focuses on cases where entire groups are treated, implying no spillovers *within* groups, while spatial or other spillovers are permitted of treatment *across* groups. Finally, in the case of regression discontinuity designs, some results have been documented by Aronow, Basta, and Halloran (2017) and Auerbach, Cai, and

Rafi (2024). Aronow, Basta, and Halloran (2017) consider a local randomization approach to RD, in which case—given its similarity to random experiment—spillovers may logically occur, and note that in this case, one can estimate a local average direct effect as in Hudgens and Halloran (2008). A more recent approach of Auerbach, Cai, and Rafi (2024) discusses a setting in spillovers may occur within limited bandwidths, leading to a number of potential estimands of interest, or, if spillovers wish to be avoided altogether, the implementation of a donut RD as discussed in section 6.4.3.

8.3.2.2 Estimation of treatment and spillover effects in network models In more generic forms of interactions, exposure to a treatment may spillover between individuals in ways that are clearly not consistent with partial interference. While in settings such as classes, villages, or local labor markets, we may be happy to assume that individuals are grouped in mutually exclusive groups, and not linked outside of that group, in other settings, individuals may be linked in more complex non-disjoint groups that prohibit such a concrete classification. For example, a treated individual may be linked to some group of friends or acquaintances who may themselves be treated or untreated, and who may or may not be friends with each other. Thus, a broader take on loosening SUTVA can be approached by considering estimation of treatment effects under "network interference" in which an individual's outcome may depend upon the treatment status of connected individuals within their network.

One considerable challenge in this case is that many possible treatment assignments may occur in a matrix, and even if limiting spillovers to only occur up to a given number of units, many potential outcomes exist. Given this, papers examining network effects can take a range of approaches, often quite specialized to a specific type of problem. Indeed, Athey and Imbens (2017) state that as "networks and peer effects can operate through many scenarios," this has "led to the literature becoming somewhat fractured and unwieldy." Nevertheless, there are some common themes that can be highlighted.

One line of research focuses on questions of the identification of peer effects themselves, often flowing from early work by Manski (1993) on the "reflection problem" and focusing on models that assume linear forms for peer effects (see, for example, Bramoullé, Djebbari, and Fortin 2009) but can be generalized beyond such linear models (Vazquez-Bare 2023b). Another line of work focuses on tests to rule out the existence of peer effects including randomization tests described in Athey, Eckles, and Imbens (2018) or inferential concerns in network models (Leung 2020). An alternative line of work examines network effects by randomly assigning networks (Basse et al. 2024) or breaking links in networks. Yet another line of work focuses on inferring the structure of networks themselves, via models of network formation (Goldsmith-Pinkham and Imbens 2013). While fully characterizing this literature would require substantial space, chapter-length reviews such as Bramoullé, Djebbari, and Fortin (2020) exist that can provide a far more broad handle on the nature of this work and a more complete coverage of canonical results and papers as well as an idea of key open areas.

8.4 Treatment Effects and External Validity

In section 2.5.3 of this book, we discussed the distinction between internal and external validity with regards to experimental methods in particular. Nevertheless, questions of internal versus external validity—namely whether estimates credibly hold for the population under study versus whether they can be extrapolated to other populations—in all contexts discussed to this point. While throughout this book we have focused our attention on questions of internal validity, it is important to ask what any specific finding may offer beyond the tightly defined setting in which it was estimated. Indeed, much of the focus of the literature on treatment effects places primacy on the internal validity of estimates given their fundamental importance in order to be able to say *something* with certainty (Campbell and Stanley 1963; Imbens 2010).[6] However, forceful arguments in favor of elevating the importance of external validity have been made by Deaton (2010) and Manski (2013) (among others), and the cost of generating any credibly defined causal estimate for even a *single* location (Angrist 2004), as well as the desire to map findings into policy (Muller 2015), makes the theoretical benefits of external validity abundantly clear.

8.4.1 Understanding External Validity

One reason why external validity is given less attention in most empirical literature is that it is inherently a very difficult question to answer even with very rich data and credible identification. The earliest work of Campbell and Stanley (1963) emphasizes that we cannot generalize beyond a specific setting without "mak[ing] guesses as to yet unproven laws." For this reason, a common lament of work on external validity is that knowing whether a result generalizes from a particular setting in which a parameter has been estimated to another setting in which a parameter has not been estimated would in fact require knowing this unknown parameter!

Generally work on external validity seeks to focus on assumptions under which identified parameters from one setting can be informative for another setting, or on how these parameters can be otherwise extrapolated to be informative more generally. It is useful to have a general idea of the problem before we discuss some proposals in a range of settings. An early framework was provided by Campbell and Stanley (1963) who note a number of factors that are key for the external validity of a result, including elements we are well-used to thinking about such as selection (into being a site of experimentation), treatments having time-specific impacts, and the existence of responses, or priming, to previously applied treatments if a treatment is reapplied.

While we will encounter a number of approaches below, one way to understand external validity is presented by Andrews and Oster (2019). Applied to the standard notation used throughout this book, Andrews and Oster (2019) consider a binary treatment W_i, outcome Y_i with potential outcomes $Y_i(0)$ and $Y_i(1)$. Some full population, or target population, P

exists, but treatment is only observed in a nonrandom subset of this population denoted P_S, where the binary indicator S_i is defined as equal to 1 if some individual i in the target population is part of the treated subset, and 0 if not. Assuming that we have some internally valid ATE in the trial population $\mathbb{E}_{P_S}[\tau_i] = \mathbb{E}_{P_S}[Y_i(1) - Y_i(0)]$, we can seek to understand what this may inform us about the more general effect of interest $\mathbb{E}_P[\tau_i]$.

In this framework, "external validity bias" is defined as:

$$\mathbb{E}_{P_S}[\tau_i] - \mathbb{E}_P[\tau_i], \tag{8.22}$$

and we would say that an estimate was externally valid if $\mathbb{E}_{P_S}[\tau_i] = \mathbb{E}_P[\tau_i]$. Treatment and outcome variables are not observed in general in the target beyond the sample $S_i = 1$, but some series of covariates X_i is observed in both the trial population, and knowledge of the mean value of these covariates $\mathbb{E}_P[X_i]$ is known for the target population.

Andrews and Oster (2019) propose a model whereby any selection into treatment can depend upon observable factors X_i and unobservable factors U_i. They write this as (firstly) a treatment effect heterogeneity function:

$$\tau_i = \alpha + X_i'\gamma + U_i'\delta + \varepsilon_i, \tag{8.23}$$

where $\mathbb{E}_P[\varepsilon_i | X_i, U_i] = 0$, and $\mathbb{C}\text{ov}(X_i, U_i) = 0$, and secondly, a selection into treatment function:

$$S_i = \mathbb{1}\left\{X_i'\kappa + U_i'\xi - \upsilon_i \geq 0\right\}. \tag{8.24}$$

These equations are relatively standard for models of selection allowing for treatment effects to depend arbitrarily on observable and unobservable factors that may differ across population and for selection into treatment to depend arbitrarily on observable and unobservable factors. By substituting (8.23) into (8.22), we can write the external validity bias as:

$$\mathbb{E}_{P_S}[\tau_i] - \mathbb{E}_P[\tau_i] = \left(\mathbb{E}_{P_S}[X_i] - \mathbb{E}_P[X_i]\right)'\gamma + \left(\mathbb{E}_{P_S}[U_i] - \mathbb{E}_P[U_i]\right)'\delta. \tag{8.25}$$

If unobservables are irrelevant in explaining treatment effects (i.e., $\delta = 0$), the above second term on the right-hand side of (8.25) disappears and we are left with a case where external validity bias depends only on differences in observables, as well as how observable factors affect treatment effects. In this case, external validity bias can be estimated and corrected, and we will discuss some strategies for this in section 8.4.3 below. However, in the more interesting case where unobservable factors are relevant in explaining treatment effects, Andrews and Oster (2019) note that *if* selection into treatment described in (8.24) is relatively small, this external validity bias term can be approximately expressed as follows:

$$\mathbb{E}_{P_S}[\tau_i] - \mathbb{E}_P[\tau_i] \approx \frac{\gamma'\Sigma_X\kappa + \delta'\Sigma_U\xi}{\gamma'\Sigma_C\kappa}\left(\mathbb{E}_{P_S}[X_i] - \mathbb{E}_P[X_i]\right)'\gamma_s, \tag{8.26}$$

where $\Sigma_X = \mathbb{V}_P(X_i)$ and $\Sigma_U = \mathbb{V}_P(U_i)$, and γ_s refers to the estimable treatment effect heterogeneity in the trial population. This casts the bias inherent in mapping one parameter estimate to another in terms of the difference between observable characteristics between the trial and target population, as well as an aggregate ratio that measures the importance of unobservable and observable treatment effect heterogeneity in explaining the (unobserved and observed) factors that drive selection.

While this is only one way to view external validity,[7] it provides a very useful representation, as it makes clear a number of key takeaways, which are generally addressed in studies on external validity and can help shape thinking about how treatment effects may generalize beyond a specific site. Firstly, any differences between characteristics across sites will be relevant for external validity bias if these factors explain treatment effect heterogeneity (the latter part of the above expression), which is an observable quantity. Second is an unknown term that the authors refer to as the selection ratio, which captures the relative importance of observed and unobserved drivers of selection in explaining treatment effect heterogeneity. The logic of this term is that if most of the correlation between selection and treatment effect heterogeneity owes to observables, the bias from observed variables will explain most of the true bias, whereas if selection and heterogeneity owe to unobservable components, this observed bias will understate the total bias. In section 8.4.3 we will consider some further illustrations of this point.

8.4.2 Extrapolating Local Treatment Effects Within a Specific Setting

An area in which quite concrete work exists is in thinking about how to map treatment effects that are local: namely effects like the LATE and estimates local to the cutoff in regression discontinuity designs, into quantities that are more global, such as the ATE. Work in this area can be viewed as seeking to address limits of particular designs and estimators, such as IV and RDD, in a particular setting, without explicitly seeking external validity beyond the specific context.

8.4.2.1 Instrumental variables Initial work focusing on the LATE, and what it can say about the ATE, was conducted by Angrist (2004) and presented in his very nicely written Sargan lecture. There, Angrist notes that if one wishes to generalize from a LATE—which is informative for compliers—to an ATE, which must also be informative for always-takers and never-takers, what is needed is knowledge of treatment effects for these latter two groups. However, as we have discussed at length in chapter 5, IV estimates cannot identify treatment effects for such groups, given that an IV does not generate any variation in treatment. Specifically, we write treatment effects for always-takers and never-takers as:

$$\mathbb{E}\left[Y_i(1) - Y_i(0)|D_i(1) = D_i(0) = 1\right] \qquad \mathbb{E}\left[Y_i(1) - Y_i(0)|D_i(1) = D_i(0) = 0\right].$$

While under the assumption of IV, treatment effects for compliers are identified, treatment effects for always-takers and never-takers are not. However, we do observe some of the information that makes up the above treatment effects. Namely, for the first treatment effect (always-takers), *we can* identify the quantity $\mathbb{E}\left[Y_i(1)|D_i(1)=D_i(0)=1\right]$, given that random assignment of the IV implies that

$$\mathbb{E}\left[Y_i(1)|D_i(1)=D_i(0)=1\right]=\mathbb{E}\left[Y_i(1)|D_i(1)=1\right]=\mathbb{E}\left[Y_i|D_i=1,Z_i=0\right]. \tag{8.27}$$

We cannot, however identify the expectation of $\mathbb{E}\left[Y_i(0)\right]$ for always-takers. Similarly, for the second quantity we can identify $\mathbb{E}\left[Y_i(0)|D_i(1)=D_i(0)=0\right]$ using the mean outcome of individuals assigned to treatment but who do not take up treatment. However, we cannot identify the quantity $\mathbb{E}\left[Y_i(1)\right]$ for never-takers.

Angrist (2004) then suggests that we can fully characterize potential outcomes as follows by writing the expectations for $Y_i(0)$ and $Y_i(1)$ as follows:

$$\mathbb{E}[Y_i(0)|D_i(0),D_i(1)]=\alpha_0+\beta_{00}D_i(0)+\beta_{01}D_i(1) \tag{8.28}$$

$$\mathbb{E}[Y_i(1)|D_i(0),D_i(1)]=\alpha_1+\beta_{10}D_i(0)+\beta_{11}D_i(1). \tag{8.29}$$

By substituting in values for $D_i(0)$ and $D_i(1)$ for always-takers, never-takers, and compliers, this allows for six potential outcomes to be written. The issue is that we cannot identify each of these six quantities given the variation generated from an instrument Z_i. For this reason, Angrist (2004) considers a range of restrictions that would allow for the quantities $\mathbb{E}[Y_i(0)]$ and $\mathbb{E}[Y_i(1)]$ to be estimated. The most realistic of these is what Angrist (2004) refers to as linearity, which is to assume that $\beta_{00}=\beta_{01}$ and $\beta_{10}=\beta_{11}$. This allows for (8.28)–(8.29) to be written as:

$$\mathbb{E}[Y_i(0)|D_i(0),D_i(1)]=\alpha_0+\beta_{01}[D_i(0)+D_i(1)] \tag{8.30}$$

$$\mathbb{E}[Y_i(1)|D_i(0),D_i(1)]=\alpha_1+\beta_{11}[D_i(0)+D_i(1)]. \tag{8.31}$$

This restriction still allows always-takers, never-takers, and compliers to have different treatment effects, but the assumption of linearity in treatment effects in $(D_i(0)+D_i(1))$ means that each separate treatment effect is estimable, and indeed, for compliers, always-takers and never-takers can be written as:

$$(\alpha_1+\beta_{11})-(\alpha_0+\beta_{01}), \qquad (\alpha_1+2\times\beta_{11})-(\alpha_0+2\times\beta_{01}), \qquad \alpha_1-\alpha_0.$$

Angrist (2004) shows that if such a restriction is imposed, it is easy to estimate both an ATE and an ATT (and also considers a number of further assumptions that permit extrapolation beyond the LATE). A related example of this is encountered in the Fuzzy RDD, as noted by Bertanha and Imbens (2020) and discussed in the following subsection.

This discussion makes clear that in an IV setting there will always be missing information if we wish to calculate an ATE. The approach in Angrist (2004) is to make some restrictions about treatment effect homogeneity, but there are also a range of other approaches that have been considered. One alternative is to seek to leverage information on covariates and make homogeneity assumptions about treatment effects *within* covariate groups. This is an approach taken by Angrist and Fernández-Val (2013) and Aronow and Carnegie (2013), who note that if for each specific covariate group the LATE is actually the ATE, we can arrive at an ATE (or other quantities such as an ATT) by reweighting such that the support of covariates in compliers matches that in the population. This, in effect, imposes the reasonably strong assumption that $\mathbb{E}\left[Y_i(1) - Y_i(0)|D_i(1) - D_i(0) = 1, X\right] = \mathbb{E}\left[Y_i(1) - Y_i(0)|X\right]$, and views the estimation of ATE as a reweighting problem given different distributions of covariates in the compliant and full population. An alternative take is provided by Oreopoulos (2006), who argues that we may view the LATE as informative of the ATE if multiple instruments are available, each of which shift different groups of the population, and LATEs for each case are similar. Somewhat similarly, if a larger portion of the population are compliers, LATEs will likely more closely approximate ATEs or other treatment effects of interest (see Ebenstein [2009] and Oreopoulos [2006] for empirical work in this line). Finally, below in section 8.5 we will consider a rich literature that goes well beyond LATE, noting that we can understand how the LATE is built up and seek to aggregate the "building blocks" of the LATE to construct other treatment effects of interest.

8.4.2.2 Regression discontinuity Considerations of external validity in regression discontinuity designs are particularly salient, because we know that any estimated effect is informative only for individuals local to the discontinuity. A number of procedures have been suggested to seek to provide greater generalization of effects beyond this very local point.

One approach to understand external validity in this setting is provided by Angrist and Rokkanen (2015). Angrist and Rokkanen leverage the fact that the reason why an RDD estimate is not informative away from the cutoff is because of the influence of the running variable on potential outcomes. They note that if we are willing to make a conditional independence assumption of the form:

$$\mathbb{E}[Y_i(0)|X_i, Z_i] = \mathbb{E}[Y_i(0)|X_i] \quad \text{and} \quad \mathbb{E}[Y_i(1)|X_i, Z_i] = \mathbb{E}[Y_i(1)|X_i], \tag{8.32}$$

where X_i are covariates, and Z_i the running variable, we can use this fact to estimate treatment effects away from the cutoff. The assumption in (8.32) implies that conditional on some set of covariates X_i we can fully capture the confounding that owes to the impact of the running variable. Thus, by conditioning on covariates X_i, we are indirectly capturing the impact of the running variable, and thus can extrapolate away from the cutoff. Based on this assumption, we can quite simply calculate quantities such as the ATT by comparing individuals with identical characteristics X_i above and below the cutoff, weighting based on the distribution of X_i among treated units. What's more, we can test whether the running variable is independent of outcomes conditional on some specific set of covariates by regressing outcomes on the running variable and covariates separately above and below the cutoff, and testing whether any significant relationship between outcomes and the running variable remain.

Bertanha and Imbens (2020) take a similar tack and ask how we may know if our estimated LATE is informative of an ATE in a Fuzzy RDD. They note that if compliance types are independent of potential outcomes at each point of the running variable (i.e., there is no selection into being a complier), then the LATE estimate from RD will be equal to the ATE. Apart from showing this formally, they note that tests exist about whether such an assumption may be reasonable. Specifically, noting that as in (8.27), for a Fuzzy regression discontinuity we can estimate the always-taker mean outcome just below the discontinuity giving $\mathbb{E}[Y_i(0)|G_i = A, Z_i = \kappa]$, and we can estimate the never-taker mean outcome just above the discontinuity, giving $\mathbb{E}[Y_i(1)|G_i = N, Z_i = \kappa]$. We can then compare these quantities to the complier means of $Y_i(0)$ and $Y_i(1)$ at the cutoff, which are also estimable. If compliance is independent of potential outcomes (and hence external validity holds), these quantities should be identical.

Finally, in the particular setting of regression discontinuity with *multiple* discontinuities, Cattaneo et al. (2021) show that we may be able to extrapolate treatment effects beyond areas local to discontinuities in a particularly convincing way. In this case, it is worth noting that we will have multiple treatment effects corresponding to separate cutoffs, as discussed in section 6.5.2 and (6.36). Cattaneo et al. (2021) propose extrapolating across cutoffs to infer treatment effects, as laid out in figure 8.4. Namely, if two local discontinuity estimates exist (indicated as ℓ and h, respectively), treatment effects can be extrapolated to points between these two estimates by approximating counterfactual outcomes for lower treated

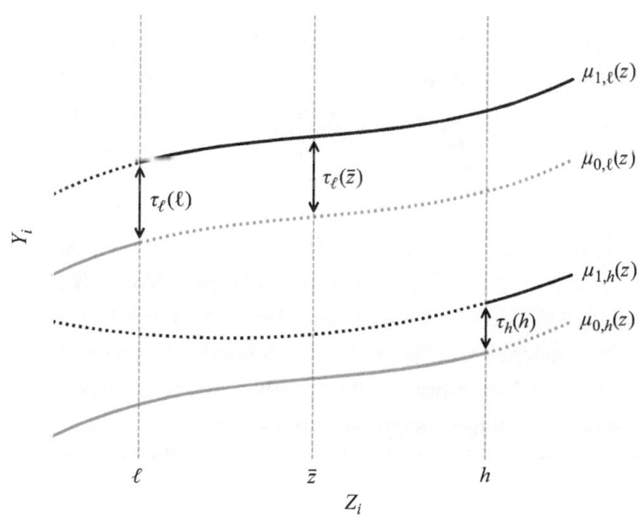

Figure 8.4
Extrapolating treatment effects in RDDs with multiple cutoffs.

units which are not observed beyond ℓ with trends among higher treated units (a parallel-trends assumption). In this way, the light dashed line in figure 8.4 is assumed to track the solid light line below, and hence $\tau_\ell(\bar{z})$ is inferred despite the lack of treatment discontinuity.

Code Callout 8.2: Extrapolating RDDs Away from the Cut-Off
We will consider the extrapolation of treatment effects away from the cut-off exploring data from Londoño-Vélez, Rodríguez, and Sánchez (2020). In this paper, the authors leverage eligibility scores for access to financial aid to determine the impact of aid receipt on college study. The fact that such scores vary by area means that treatment effect extrapolation is possible.

8.4.3 Extrapolating Out of Sample

While extrapolating from one estimate to another in a given setting requires homogeneity or other modeling assumptions, the case of seeking to map internally valid estimates from one context to another context entirely is arguably more challenging. One challenge in this setting is that it is exceedingly uncommon for the external validity of a finding to be observable given that estimates generally only exist in one setting. Nevertheless, there are a range of papers that have tackled the question of external validity across settings or populations, at times with multiple "experiments" to allow for a richer assessment of how and whether results generalize.

One such case is laid out in Hotz, Imbens, and Mortimer (2005), who seek to consider whether randomized evaluations of previous job training programs in the US can be informative for predicting the impacts of future programs. A nice element of this paper is that the authors have experimental evaluations of four training programs in separate areas. They lay out a basic framework in which a reference population (which here we will denote $R_i = 1$) is used to seek to infer treatment effects in some target population ($R_i = 0$). In the reference population, treatment assignment W_i, outcomes Y_i, and covariates X_i are observed, whereas in the target population no treatment or outcomes exist and simply covariates X_i are observed. Hotz, Imbens, and Mortimer note that if $R_i \perp\!\!\!\perp (Y_i(0), Y_i(1))|X_i$, this implies external validity of estimates. This assumption, which they refer to as "unconfounded location" or a "no macro-effects" assumption, implies that locations do not have systematically different potential outcomes, and hence treatment effects.

If this assumption is met, and provided that there is overlap in terms of characteristics X_i, this implies that the treatment effect for the target population $R_i = 0$ can be observed by simply reweighting such that the treatment effects from the reference population are representative of individuals for the target population.

$$\mathbb{E}\big[Y_i(1) - Y_i(0)\big|R_i = 0\big] = \mathbb{E}_X\Big[\mathbb{E}[Y_i\big|W_i = 1, R_i = 1, X_i] - \mathbb{E}\big[Y_i\big|W_i = 0, R_i = 1, X_i\big]\Big|R_i = 0\Big].$$

Of course if this no macro effects assumption is not met, such reweighting will not serve to extrapolate treatment effects, precisely because of the presence of these macro-effects. Such macro-effects can be viewed as factors that are fixed by area, but that affect the way a program generates effects in the population. In cases where *multiple* implementations of a program are observed, the presence of such macro-effects can be tested for and potentially adjusted for, but this, of course, requires multiple evaluations across multiple sites, which is a demanding requirement.

Quite unique work that seeks to consider both individual level covariates *and* macro effects is that of Dehejia, Pop-Eleches, and Samii (2021). They collect millions of observations of microdata from over 100 censuses in 61 countries and focus on a single natural experiment: that of the impact of births on parental labor supply. The novelty of this settings is that they observe many estimates of an identical relationship as well as both individual level covariates and macro-variables across settings. To study the relevance of each of these factors in understanding external validity they suggest writing an "external validity function," which asks how far an experiment run in a particular context may be from the mean effect in all locations. They find that in this setting, the effect of macro-level factors dominates the effect of individual level factors, and find that if extrapolating treatment effects based on individual-level covariates to a new context, this works well in areas that are "close" in terms of their macro-level variables but not well in areas with quite different macro-level contexts.

This presence of macro effects explains one circumstance in which we may expect external validity to be limited. There are, of course, other cases where we will not expect to see external validity given the nature of differences across sites. One case is discussed by Allcott (2015) as site selection bias. This refers to the case where programs are more likely to be located in areas that are particularly well-suited for the program to be successful, or where programs are more likely to be evaluated if they are successful. Allcott (2015) documents the existence of site-selection bias using data on over 100 RCTs of a specific program across different sites, and documents that predictions from the earliest evaluations suggest much larger effects than later evaluations. Another situation in which external validity will not hold by definition is if the contents of treatments are not identical across sites. This is discussed in theory in Hotz, Imbens, and Mortimer (2005). This is relevant as even if a program is in theory designed in an identical way, the implementation may occur differently across sites, and in these cases even if individuals and conditions in the two sites were identical, the results would not be. An illustration of this is provided by Bold et al. (2018) who document that identically defined treatment in schools in Kenya had vastly different impacts in NGO- and government-run schools, in line with quite different implementations of the intervention in each setting.

8.4.4 Related Points

There is a range of related work in this space considering how treatment effects vary across settings, and the key question of effect heterogeneity, which is often viewed as indicative of external validity (Meager 2019). If effects are highly heterogeneous across settings, the external validity of a specific study is likely to be limited, whereas if more limited heterogeneity is observed, effects from any specific setting will likely be more informative in other settings. Vivalt (2020) examines the question of how heterogeneous effects are observed to be across settings, as well as what explains heterogeneity in the effects of treatments. She documents substantial heterogeneity when examining estimated treatment effects from similar interventions across settings, documenting that smaller studies and those implemented by NGOs or academics generally documented larger effect sizes. Work from Meager (2019) considers aggregating information from across seven different analyses of microcredit, using *micro*-level data to conduct such aggregation, finding reasonably limited effect heterogeneity in this setting, with the majority of heterogeneity found to owe to sampling variation in individual estimates rather than heterogeneity of effects across settings. In a quite different setting, Snowberg and Yariv (2021) study the question of whether commonly used student samples behave in ways that are very different to representative samples. They find evidence of broad similarity of behavior in incentivized settings when compared to representative samples in the US, suggestive of external validity in this domain.

8.5 Sorting into Treatment and the Marginal Treatment Effects

When we spoke about the LATE, in Chapter 5 we first began to think about sorting. In the case of assignment to treatment and the LATE we allowed a certain type of sorting whereby individuals could choose whether to comply with a randomly assigned treatment status. However, more generally, sorting is a pervasive issue that we must deal with when considering economic and econometric models. Logically, in most cases, individuals make decisions based on what they perceive is best for them. Or in other words, when possible, individuals will "sort" themselves based on their potential outcomes, where possible sorting into treatment when they perceive that their $Y_i(1) > Y_i(0)$, or sorting into control when they perceive that their $Y_i(0) > Y_i(1)$.

Perhaps the most well known sorting model—at least in labor economics—is the so-called Roy model. This is a simple model where individuals choose their "treatment status" based on their outcomes under two scenarios. In an econometric sense, we can think of this as a decision made completely endogenously to the system under study. We will begin this section by briefly laying out the elements of the Roy model as a general framework to think about a broader class of sorting decisions, before turning to a particular model of thinking about treatment effects under endogenous decisions and sorting: the Marginal Treatment Effects framework.

8.5.1 The Roy Model

The classic Roy model is laid out in an expositional paper (Roy 1951), which describes all the details of the model without formalizing them mathematically. It sketches a clear picture of selection into (two) occupations based on the potential rewards each person faces in each occupation.[8] Specifically, the paper speaks of a village where individuals decide whether to fish or hunt rabbits, though abstractly the model applies to any cases where individuals seek to consider their well-being in both states of a decision when deciding between two options. In this sense, it is clear how it ties in with the potential outcomes framework: In this case, individuals will select into the treatment status that is most beneficial to them given their particular payoff. To the degree that an econometrician does not observe the payoffs an individual perceives to both states of the world, there will be challenges in identifying casual effects.

In the interests of space, we will not fully lay out the Roy model, though a concise formulation of the model is provided in Heckman and Taber (2010) and a more extensive formulation is available in Heckman and Honoré (1990). A key focus of the original Roy model is in determining if more efficient individuals will select into specific occupations, which in the treatment effect framework can be viewed as akin to asking whether individuals who gain the most from treatment—that is, those with the largest $Y_i(1)$ in the population will effectively select into treatment, while those who gain the most from control (those with the largest values of $Y_i(0)$ in the population) will select into control. It turns out that this depends entirely upon the nature of potential outcomes (returns to work in the Roy model) and in particular the returns to treatment and how potential outcomes correlate in the population.

The Roy model can, however, offer a number of concrete results. For example, suppose fishing is a more variable occupation than hunting—that is, the variance in fishing ability is higher than that in hunting. Then, positive selection into fishing must occur: Individuals with higher fishing ability will disproportionately select into that occupation. In contrast, selection into hunting (the lower-variance occupation) depends on the correlation between fishing and hunting skills. If skills are negatively correlated (those who are better at fishing tend to be poor hunters), we may observe positive selection into both occupations. If, however, skills are perfectly positively correlated, then individuals will select into the higher-variance occupation (fishing), and we may observe negative selection into hunting. For intermediate cases of imperfectly positive correlations, either positive or negative selection into hunting can arise, depending on the specific values of skill correlations and returns to work.

In sum, the Roy model illustrates that the pattern of selection across occupations (or treatments) hinges critically on the joint distribution of potential outcomes. This has implications for interpreting observed treatment effects: Observed differences may reflect not only causal effects but also sorting on gains or abilities.

This simplified model thus already gives some framework to think about selection and how a population of individuals will behave if they are seeking to maximize payoffs among choices. There are many extensions to these models as well as applications where it is used as a basis for estimation with real data (e.g., Taber and Vejlin 2020). However, here we lay out the Roy model as a precursor for thinking about heterogeneity, given its importance in thinking about marginal treatment effects, and the value for particular individuals of selecting into one or the treatment status. In the case laid out here, certain individuals may have a much higher wage in one of two occupations and, hence, have much to gain from choosing this, while others may have reasonably similar wages in both occupations, and thus less to gain from their occupational choice. This is something we turn to examine now.

8.5.2 "Marginal Treatment Effects" and Other Relevant Quantities

Abstracting, for now, from the Roy model in particular, the marginal treatment effects framework provides a particularly rich and flexible way to think about treatment effects, as well as, interestingly, a way to understand essentially all of the treatment effects we have viewed to this point. The marginal treatment effect, or MTE, was originally defined in Björklund and Moffitt (1987) and was taken forward in an influential series of papers and chapters by Heckman and Vytlacil (1999, 2005, 2007) (and others; Heckman [1997] is an important bridging work). The original conceptualization of the MTE of Björklund and Moffitt defined effects in terms of the cost of accessing treatment. Their version of marginal treatment effects is defined as the effect for individuals who are moved into treatment by a marginal change in the cost of treatment. The current conceptualization of marginal treatment effects follows this in close spirit, but is defined as the change in outcomes for individuals who are moved into treatment by a marginal change in the propensity score (Heckman and Vytlacil 1999). In this way, the effect exists at many margins. There is nothing that implies that a treatment effect for an individual who is shifted into treatment when the propensity score moves at a very low level (say from 0.01 to 0.05) should be the same as that for individuals who are shifted into treatment when the propensity score moves at a higher level (say from 0.9 to 0.95). Indeed, we likely believe these individuals will be quite different, given that the former individual is very open to receiving treatment: They are among the first to take it up when the propensity score moves, whereas the latter are quite resistant to take-up treatment.

8.5.2.1 Definition

The model It can be a challenge to get a hold of literature on the MTE because the model can be written in various ways. The most generalized formulation defines the model as follows (see, for example, Heckman and Vytlacil [2005, § 2]). We begin by noting that potential outcomes may be functions of observable factors, written as X_i, and unobservable factors, written as $U_i(0)$ and $U_i(1)$:

$$Y_i(0) = \mu_0(X_i, U_i(0)) \tag{8.33}$$

$$Y_i(1) = \mu_1(X_i, U_i(1)). \tag{8.34}$$

This is a very flexible way to write potential outcomes, and at times this is restricted to write unobservables as additively separable such that $Y_i(0) = \mu_0(X_i) + U_i(0)$, and similarly for $Y_i(1)$. Without yet defining anything further, we can write our treatment effects as standard as $\tau_i \equiv [Y_i(1) - Y_i(0)]$, though of course we still suffer from the fundamental problem of causal inference given that only one potential outcome will be observed.

Because we are interested in selection into treatment, a key element of the model is the selection decision itself, which is written as:

$$D_i^* = \mu_D(X_i, Z_i) - V_i \tag{8.35}$$

where

$$D_i = \mathbb{1}\{D_i^* \geq 0\}. \tag{8.36}$$

In this notation, D_i simply refers to an individual's treatment decision (1 if treated, 0 otherwise), and the variable D^* captures their net benefits of treatment. In (8.35) X_i and Z_i are observed factors (and we will return to discuss Z_i shortly), where μ_D is simply some function which describes how observable functions shape net benefits of treatment. Note that we are not saying anything about what enters into X_i or what this $\mu_D(\cdot)$ looks like yet, just that this is based on observed factors. Finally, there is an unobserved component V_i, which can be viewed as some unobserved propensity to not enter into treatment. Based on this, we can understand how an individual will make their choices—their D^* will be greater than or equal to 0, implying selection into treatment, if $\mu_D(Z,X) - V_i \geq 0$. The term on the left-hand side of this equation, $\mu_D(Z,X)$, is simply the observable net benefits for treatment for an individual with characteristics X and Z, while the term on the right-hand side is unobserved characteristics that affect their likelihood of opting into treatment. For a given observable level of benefits from treatment μ_D, an individual with a higher draw of V_i will be more likely to opt out of treatment, while a lower draw makes individuals more likely to opt into treatment.

The equations (8.33), (8.34) (potential outcomes), and (8.35) and (8.36) (treatment selection) define the model of interest here. Other conceptualizations exist (for example, this can be shown to be able to nest the Roy model as discussed below), but this is the minimum setup before making any assumptions about functional forms or the nature of observed and unobserved elements. However, in practice, it is often easier to write the selection equation in the following way:

$$D_i = \mathbb{1}\{D_i^* \geq 0\} \tag{8.37}$$

$$D_i = \mathbb{1}\{\mu_D(Z,X) - V_i \geq 0\} \tag{8.38}$$

$$D_i = \mathbb{1}\{\mu_D(Z,X) \geq V_i\} \tag{8.39}$$

$$D_i = \mathbb{1}\{F_V(\mu_D(Z,X)) \geq F_V(V_i)\}. \tag{8.40}$$

Steps (8.37)–(8.39) are trivial algebra, while (8.40) applies an identical transformation on each side of the equality, which is to take the cdf of V to each element. While notationally more cumbersome, the notation in (8.40) provides more convenient practical representations (on the right-hand side of the inequality) or has a more direct link to familiar quantities (on the left-hand side).

Specifically, the right-hand side transformation of (8.40) will mechanically transform V_i into a uniform distribution between 0 and 1 regardless of the distribution of V_i. This is a mechanical property that you can easily confirm if you simulate any variable with a known distribution, and then apply the cdf of this distribution to the simulated data.[9] This transformation maps the variable V_i into an identically ordered uniform variable, which at times is called $U_D \equiv F_V(V)$. This variable U_D then captures the centile of the aversion to treatment. What's more, the quantity on the left-hand side now also has a clearly understandable interpretation. It turns out that $F_V(\mu_D(Z,X))$ gives—by definition—the propensity score! While the quantity $F_V(\mu_D(Z,X))$ looks relatively complex, we can break it down to see that this is the case. To start, we know that F_V is simply the cdf of V. This is to say, F_V describes the portion of the distribution of V located below a point. Now what happens if we pass some other quantity to $F_V(\cdot)$, such as $\mu_D(Z_i,X_i)$? This simply tells us what portion of V_i is below the value $\mu_D(Z,X)$, or the probability that a draw from V falls below the value $\mu_D(Z_i,X_i)$. However, we can note from (8.35) that this is precisely the probability that an individual with $\mu_D(Z_i,X_i)$ will be treated. In questions 5(a) and (b) at the end of the chapter, you can work through this with simulated data. If we write the propensity score as $\Pr(Z) = \Pr(D_i = 1|X_i, Z_i)$, this allows us to rewrite the selection equation as:

$$D_i = \mathbb{1}\{\Pr(Z) \geq U_D\}.$$

Marginal treatment effects Having worked through the model (and, admittedly, a little bit of probability and algebra), we can now define the MTE and consider its identification and relevance. The marginal treatment effect is defined as

$$\tau_{\text{MTE}}(x, u_D) \equiv E\big(Y_i(1) - Y_i(0)\big|X = x, U_D = u_D\big), \tag{8.41}$$

or equivalently, $\tau_{\text{MTE}}(x, v) \equiv \mathbb{E}\big(Y_i(1) - Y_i(0)|X = x, V = v\big)$. The MTE is just a treatment effect at a specific point u_D. Remember that U_D is defined as the unobservable aversion to treatment. In reality, we may be interested in the variation in the MTE across the entire distribution of U_D. These MTEs have a clear interpretation given what we know about U_D. For points very low in the distribution of u_D, this is the effect of treatment for individuals with values of non-observables that make it very probable that they will participate in treatment. On the other hand, for very high values of u_D, the value of $\mu_D(X,Z)$ would need to be particularly large to convince individuals to participate.

Another way to understand the MTE is to note that, for a given X_i, individuals with a specific value of U_{Di} will be indifferent between adopting treatment or not if their propensity score is is equal to U_{Di}. For this reason we can also link the MTE with the propensity score, as laid out in (Heckman, Urzua, and Vytlacil 2006). Namely, the MTE also gives us the change in expected outcomes for a marginal change in the propensity score:

$$\tau_{\text{MTE}}(x, U_D = p) = \frac{\partial \mathbb{E}\big(Y_i|X_i = x, \Pr(Z_i) = p\big)}{\partial p}. \tag{8.42}$$

8.5.2.2 Identification and estimation We have not yet said anything about the elements of the selection equation, nor about whether these quantities can actually be estimated. You may have noted the use of Z_i in the definition of the propensity score, and the notation Z_i is not used casually. In fact, if Z_i is an instrument, this provides routes to identify these treatment effects. Specifically, we view Z_i as a shifter of the likelihood of entering treatment, which is excluded from the definition of potential outcomes themselves. If this factor Z_i is also independent of $U_i(1)$, $U_i(0)$, and U_D, we can take advantage of the fact that it provides exogenous variation in the likelihood of adopting treatment, effectively allowing us to potentially nail down marginal treatment effects. The precise conditions required for the MTE to be identified are laid out in Heckman and Vytlacil (2005, assumptions A.1–A.5) but are effectively the IV assumptions of relevance and independence, as well as overlap and some data regularity conditions.

If such an IV is available, this allows for MTEs to be identified, and in particular, these can be estimated with the local instrumental variables (LIV) approach described in Heckman (1997) and Heckman and Vytlacil (1999). The LIV estimand is defined as:

$$\tau^{\text{LIV}}(x,p) \equiv \frac{\partial \mathbb{E}(Y_i|X=x, \Pr(Z)=p)}{\partial p}. \tag{8.43}$$

The result that $\tau^{\text{LIV}}(x,p) = \tau_{\text{MTE}}(x,p)$ is discussed, for example in Heckman and Vytlacil (1999, 4731). One key point to note is that in implementing LIV estimators, a single binary instrument is not enough. This is perhaps unsurprising, given that we spent much of chapter 5 making clear that in cases with heterogeneity, IV identifies the LATE, and we will turn to this again shortly when thinking about how MTEs relate to other quantities of interest. Rather, to estimate LIV, we require instruments that generate variation effectively across the whole support of the propensity score. In practice, these methods proceed in two steps, first by modeling the propensity score in a flexible way and then by modeling outcomes Y_i in terms of the estimated propensity score. With this, derivatives in (8.43) can be estimated. Further details relating to the estimation of LIV can be found in Heckman and Vytlacil (1999, 2001a) as well as the review paper of Cornelissen et al. (2016). A range of applied papers, including Carneiro, Heckman, and E. Vytlacil (2010), which we review when working in code callout 8.3 below, or examples such as Doyle (2007) and Cornelissen et al. (2018), provide very useful illustrative examples of practical implementations.

8.5.2.3 Understanding the MTE and other estimands Heckman and Vytlacil (2005) state that "*the MTE is a choice-theoretic building block that unites the treatment effect, selection, and matching literatures.*" They refer to it as a "building block" because the MTE can be linked to many other treatment effects of interest, including the ATT, the ATE, the ATU, the LATE, and more. Specifically, these other treatment effects are (weighted) averages of the MTE at specific points of U_D. For example, we can simply enough write the ATE for a specific covariate group as the average of all MTEs:

$$\text{ATE}(x) = \int_0^1 \tau_{\text{MTE}}(x, U_D)dU_D.$$

What's more, we can view the ATT and ATU as weighted averages of MTEs, where weights refer to the likelihood of being treated or untreated at each point U_D:

$$\text{ATT}(x) = \int_0^1 \tau_{\text{MTE}} h_{\text{ATT}}(x, U_D)dU_D \quad \text{and} \quad \text{ATU}(x) = \int_0^1 \tau_{\text{MTE}} h_{\text{ATU}}(x, U_D)dU_D.$$

Above, the quantities h_{ATT} and h_{ATU} are nonnegative and integrate to one, and can be written as:

$$h_{\text{ATT}}(x, u_D) = \int_0^1 \left[\frac{\Pr(Z) > p}{\mathbb{E}[\Pr(Z)]}\right] dp \quad \text{and } h_{\text{ATU}}(x, u_D) = \int_0^1 \left[\frac{\Pr(Z) < p}{1 - \mathbb{E}[\Pr(Z)]}\right] dp.$$

A specific example of this is provided in figure 8.5 below. This is based on a specific simulation of MTEs and selection into treatment, as described in Heckman and Vytlacil (2005). The MTEs from this model are plotted as the thick solid line, while the weights assigned to each of these MTEs in estimates at the ATT, ATE, and ATU are plotted below as gray lines. Among individuals with a very low u_D, essentially all take up treatment, while among individuals with a very high u_D, few will have a probability of treatment that is high enough to overcome this draw, and hence nearly all will remain untreated. Thus, we observe

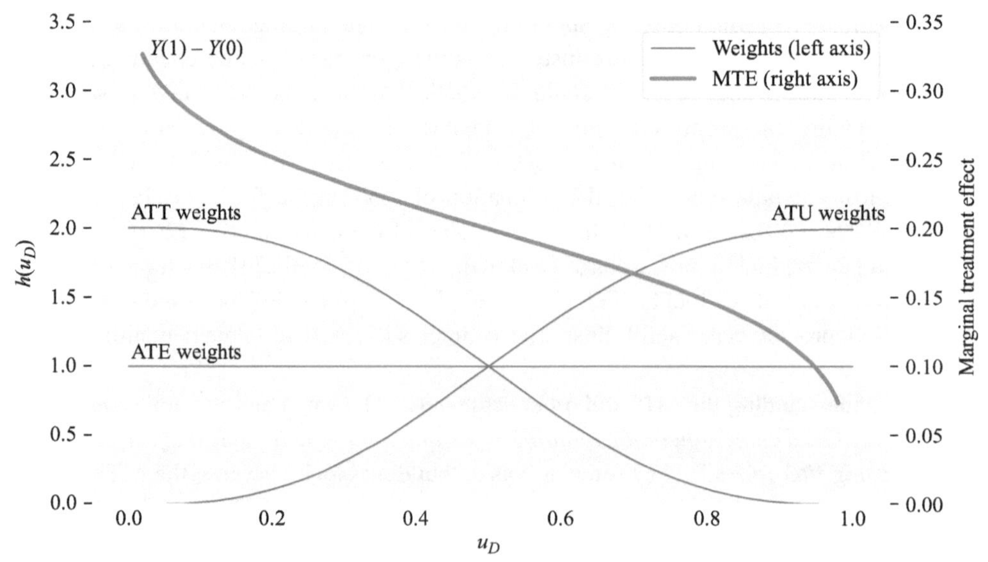

Figure 8.5
MTEs and estimand weights in a simulated setting (Heckman and Vytlacil 2005).

clear weightings whereby individuals with low draws of u_D are heavily represented in ATT estimands, and receive very low weights among ATUs. By construction, an ATE weights each unit equally. In this particular simulation (which we will explore in an end of chapter question), individuals with higher MTEs are more likely to be treated, as observed by the higher value of the red MTE curve for low draws of u_D. On the other hand, untreated units are those with relatively low MTEs.

MTE and LATE What's more, we can also understand the construction of *any* LATE estimate in terms of MTEs. This is because any instrument will shift a specific group of individuals into treatment: the compliers. If we consider an instrument that moves the proportion of treated units from $\Pr(z')$ to $\Pr(z)$, given monotonicity (and assuming the first stage is positive, rather than negative), we know that in this range either individuals will have only been shifted into treatment or not changed their treatment decision. And of the individuals who shifted their treatment decisions, these are precisely those individuals who would not participate when $P(Z) \leq P(z')$ but would participate when $P(z') < P(Z) \leq P(z)$. For this reason, the LATE can be written as the average MTE for the marginal changers moved by a particular instrument:

$$\tau_{\text{LATE}}(x, z', Z) = \frac{1}{u_D - u'_D}\left[\int_{u'_D}^{u_D} \tau_{\text{MTE}} du\right].$$

Policy-relevant treatment effects Note finally that, using this framework, there are many other treatment effects of interest one may wish to consider. Heckman and Vytlacil (2001b) and Carneiro, Heckman, and E. Vytlacil (2010) discuss the policy relevant treatment effect (PRTE), which comes from considering a variation in policy regimes that changes the costs of accessing treatment. A specific policy may move certain individuals from untreated to treated, and the PRTE is just the average MTE of those individuals who are convinced by a policy to move into treatment. This can be written as:

$$\tau_{\text{PRTE}} = \frac{E(Y_i|\text{Alternative Policy}) - E(Y_i|\text{Original Policy})}{E(D_i|\text{Alternative Policy}) - E(D_i|\text{Original Policy})},$$

and once again, as laid out in Heckman and Vytlacil (2005), this can be explicitly written as a weighted function of the relevant underlying MTEs. We will explore this further in code callout 8.3 below.

Code Callout 8.3: Marginal Treatment Effects

In code callout 8.3, we explore data from Carneiro, Lokshin, and Umapathi (2017). With these data on earnings and an individual's decision on whether to pursue a college degree, we discuss the implementation of local linear IV models, and we document MTEs and PRTEs discussed in Carneiro, Lokshin, and Umapathi (2017).

Relationship to the Roy model The marginal treatment effect (MTE) framework is very flexible and allows for settings such as those described in the Roy model. Above we have noted that the Roy model simply consists of potential outcomes and a selection equation. While this selection equation does not *have* to depend upon potential outcomes, it could. Specifically, if the selection equation depends upon individual returns such that the individuals who gain from the policy select into treatment, also referred to as selection on gains, or "essential heterogeneity" (Heckman and Urzúa 2010), we will be in the case of the Roy model.

Heckman and Vytlacil (2005) note that in this case, we can relate the MTE framework to a generalized Roy model, which augments the standard Roy model with a component capturing the cost of receiving treatment. We now define Z as observable costs of receiving treatment, such that an individual would select into treatment if their benefits of treatment exceed the benefits of not electing to receive treatment, net of any costs. The interest of this model is in allowing very flexibly for selection into treatment and considering which treatment effects can, and ideally should, be estimated. The decision of whether an individual should elect to receive treatment or not depends on their benefits with and without treatment ($Y_i(1)$ and $Y_i(0)$) as well as their costs to access treatment. These elements can be written as:

$$Y_i(0) = \mu_0(X_i) + U_i(0) \tag{8.44}$$

$$Y_i(1) = \mu_1(X_i) + U_i(1) \tag{8.45}$$

$$C_i = \mu_C(Z_i) + U_i(C). \tag{8.46}$$

Note that here potential outcomes with and without treatment can depend on observable factors (X), as well as unobserved error terms $U_i(0)$, $U_i(1)$, which are assumed to be mean 0. If we wish to capture the selection on gains feature of the Roy model we can now write our selection equation as $D = \mathbb{1}\{Y(1) - Y(0) - C > 0\}$, which along with the potential outcome functions in (8.44)–(8.45) defines our MTE model. The takeaway from this is that while the MTE framework is flexible enough to nest the Roy model—capturing selection on gains and essential heterogeneity—it also allows for richer forms of selection behavior, including cases where treatment decisions depend on observed costs, preferences, or other unobserved factors beyond potential outcomes. As such, it provides a unifying structure for understanding and identifying a wide range of treatment effect parameters across different empirical contexts.

Historical Context and Selected Further Reading

This chapter has touched on a number of themes that make clear that (a) there are of course limits to the methods laid out in previous chapters and that (b) some of these limits can be loosened or otherwise explored. There are a range of papers that highlight both the limits inherent in these methods and the importance of bringing to bear alternative methods, such as Deaton (2010), as well as those that highlight the importance of recognizing these limits, such as Leamer (2010), whose conclusion begins:

> Ignorance is a formidable foe, and to have hope of even modest victories, we economists need to use every resource and every weapon we can muster, including thought experiments (theory), and the analysis of data from nonexperiments, accidental experiments, and designed experiments. We should be celebrating the small genuine victories of the economists who use their tools most effectively, and we should dial back our adoration of those who can carry the biggest and brightest and least-understood weapons. We would benefit from some serious humility, and from burning our "Mission Accomplished" banners. It's never gonna happen (p.44).

The work in marginal treatment effects in particular has been highlighted as a bridging "reduced form" work, which seeks to estimate causal parameters with "structural" work, which seeks to link estimated parameters to optimizing behavior of economic agents. Useful initial readings in this line include Keane (2010) and Heckman (2010).

Exercises

1. In this question we will explore some of the mechanical details of quantile methods using data from the JTPA—a jobs training program from the United States—studied in Abadie, Angrist, and Imbens (2002). The data on the adult male sample studied by Abadie, Angrist, and Imbens (2002) are available as `Abadie_et_al_2002.csv`, which contains a measure of random treatment assignment (`assignment`), treatment take-up (`treatment`), and earnings over the thirty months following the evaluation (`earnings`).

   (a) Before using these data, let's explore the check function in (8.4). To do this, simulate one hundred observations from a uniform distribution between -1 and 1. Call these values u_i, where $i = 1, \ldots, 100$. For fixed quantiles $q \in \{0.1, 0.5, 0.9\}$, compute the check function value for each observation. Plot the points. Repeat this for each of the three values q and describe the differences in the shape of the function.

   (b) Use the data from Abadie, Angrist, and Imbens (2002). Your goal is to estimate the 25th percentile ($q = 0.25$) of the earnings distribution using the check function.

Define a candidate value $\mu = 2{,}000$, and compute the total loss function:

$$Q(\mu) = \sum_{i}^{N} \rho_{0.25}(Y_i - \mu).$$

Now vary the values you consider for μ and see how the quantity $Q(\mu)$ varies. Show that compared to many alternative values you calculate, $Q(\mu)$ is effectively minimized at the value of earnings from the 25th percentile in these data.

(c) Using the data from Abadie, Angrist, and Imbens (2002), estimate conditional quantile treatment effects at quantile 0.25, replicating results from panel A of their table II. Note that to do this, you will require the controls, which are all other variables included in the data that are not mentioned above.

(d) Estimate conditional quantile treatment effects at quantile 0.25, which corrects for potential endogenous treatment adoption by instrumenting treatment uptake with random assignment. Do this following the methods of Abadie, Angrist, and Imbens (2002) to replicate their results in table III. Note that this can be done with the reweighting estimator discussed in (8.11).

2. We will explore quantile treatment effects in a difference-in-differences setting using data from Callaway and Li (2019). These data consist of county-level unemployment rates (`unemprate1`) for 2,360 US counties (indexed `id`) between the years 2005 and 2007 (indexed `year`). Treated counties (`treat=1`) were exposed to an increase in the minimum wage between 2006 and 2007.

   (a) Estimate a simple difference-in-differences using a two-way fixed effects model where unemployment rates are regressed on treatment exposure along with county- and year-fixed effects. How can we interpret these results?

   (b) Estimate quantile DD following Callaway and Li (2019). Present these results at varying quantiles and discuss what insights they provide beyond what we can learn from the results in part (a).

   (c) Document cdfs of the county-level employment rate in treated and untreated counties in 2006 and in 2007 (i.e., plot 4 cds, as in figure 8.2).

   (d) Estimate Athey and Imbens's (2006) changes-in-changes method based on these data, documenting results at a number of quantiles. How do these line up with the distributions you documented in part (c)?

3. To explore local quantile treatment effects, we will explore the data and example laid out in Frölich and Melly (2013). These authors employ microdata from the US Census in which the impact of fertility on family income is examined, where fertility is instrumented by twin births. In data `Frolich_Melly_2013.csv` we generate an extract of Census data that seeks to mimic that described in the original paper.

(a) Estimate OLS and IV regressions in which family income (`faminc`) is regressed on fertility (`nbirth`), in the case of IV models, instrumenting with twins at first birth (`twin1`). Use all other controls included in the dataset.

(b) Estimate unconditional quantile treatment effects based on IV models using the formula of Frölich and Melly (2013) (8.11). Do this at a number of quantiles, and do so "manually" with weighting, also showing that this agrees with estimates from canned routines (if these exist in the language you are using).

(c) Generate a plot like figure 1 of Frölich and Melly (2013), which documents unconditional QTEs based on IV for a broad range of quantiles of data.

(d) Plot complier-specific quantile functions of family income assuming that the instrument holds unconditionally. This uses the results from Abadie (2002), which are laid out in (8.8)–(8.9).

4. We will examine extrapolation with an RDD by studying the setting from Melguizo, Sanchez, and Velasco (2016), and in particular the data used by Cattaneo et al. (2021), who lay out the theory in this setting. These data `Cattaneo_et_al_2021.csv` contain information on access to loans for higher education in Colombia as part of the ACCES program (`icfes_puesto`). This program provides loans to students, with eligibility depending on a test score that has changed over time, defined as `cutoff` in data. The data from Cattaneo et al. (2021) consider two particular cutoffs, rescaled to be at -850 (a low cutoff), and -571 (a high cutoff).

   (a) Generate regression discontinuity plots showing how the likelihood of college enrollment jumps at each cut-point based on data exposed to each cutoff. Do these patterns behave as you would expect?

   (b) Estimate the corresponding local linear regression discontinuity estimate based on the optimal bandwidth at each cutoff (-850 and -571).

   (c) If we wish to extrapolate this effect to a point in between this two cutoffs (-710), would it be a reasonable strategy to linearly interpolate our two RD estimates from part (b)? Why or why not?

   (d) Seek to generate a plot by hand along the lines of Cattaneo et al.'s (2021) figure 5(c). Namely, plot all data from the low cutoff and below cutoff data from the high cutoff, and seek to estimate the low cutoff untreated counterfactual from high cutoff data.

5. In this question we will simulate data to explore the estimation of MTEs. Specifically, we will follow simulations laid out in Heckman and Vytlacil (2005, 683), which generate data based on the following DGP:

$$\begin{aligned} Y_i(0) &= \alpha + \tau + u_i(0) \\ Y_i(1) &= \alpha + u_i(1) \end{aligned} \tag{8.47}$$

and

$$D_i = \mathbb{1}\{Z_i - V_i > 0\},$$

where $u_i(1) = \sigma_1 \varepsilon_i$, $u_i(0) = \sigma_0 \varepsilon_i$, and $V_i = \sigma_v \varepsilon_i$. Assume an instrument exists that is simulated as $Z \sim \mathcal{N}(-0.0026, 0.27)$ and $\varepsilon \sim \mathcal{N}(0, 1)$. Parameters are $(\alpha, \tau, \sigma_0, \sigma_1, \sigma_v) = (0.67, 0.2, 0.0012, -0.0050, -1)$. This implies that $U_D = \phi\left(\frac{V}{\sigma_v \sigma_\varepsilon}\right)$.

(a) Simulate one thousand realizations of data following this DGP. Calculate the unit-level treatment effect $\tau_i = Y_i(1) - Y_i(0)$ for each observation, as well as the aversion to treatment U_{Di}. Plot the treatment effect against U_{Di} (i.e., the MTE), and show that this replicates the values in figure 8.5.

(b) Model the propensity score using a nonlinear model such as a probit or logit, where D_i is regressed on Z_i. Do you observe overlap in terms of predicted propensity score $\widehat{\Pr(Z)}$? Generate histograms showing the propensity scores for treated and untreated individuals.

(c) Estimate a simple linear IV model in which Y_i is regressed on D_i, with Z_i as an instrument. What parameter does this estimate, and what is the value of this estimate? Does this make sense given the DGP laid out above?

(d) Seek to derive the weights that are implicit in the ATT and ATU and that are plotted as gray lines in figure 8.5. *Hint:* To do this, you may wish to refer to Heckman and Vytlacil (2005).

(e) Seek to estimate MTEs using a local IV approach by approximating the expectation of Y at distinct values of the propensity score and estimating $E(Y|\widehat{\Pr}(Z))$, and estimating the MTE as the derivative $\text{MTE}(u) = \frac{\partial E(Y)|\widehat{\Pr}(Z)}{\partial \widehat{\Pr}(Z)}$. Plot your estimated MTE against the value of the propensity score. *Hint:* There are a number of ways you may seek to do this. One option is to fit some sort of nonparametric relationship between the two variables and then take a numerical derivative.

9

Machine Learning

> "And now," cried Max, "let the wild rumpus start!"
> —Maurice Sendak, *Where the Wild Things Are*

As its name suggests, machine learning is about using a series of instructions that a machine can apply to learn something about a particular setting. The learning generally refers to prediction or classification: A "machine" wishes to "learn" about a context such that it can provide a reasonable prediction in cases it has not necessarily seen before, or in classifying an unseen case as belonging to some particular group of similar cases.

In our setting, the "learning" often refers to working out how to make the best prediction possible about a particular outcome—for example, a counterfactual state of the world. This can depend upon parameters that we estimate from a given dataset, but unlike the previous chapters where we have wished to estimate regression or other quantities to parameterize models, here learning can be a fair bit broader. We will see that two obvious extensions in the "learning" process is that firstly, learning can also be about which variables, or inputs, to include in models, and hence both the parameters *and* the variables to include can be part of the learning process. Secondly, the process of learning—or "training"—is often conducted on one dataset or partition of data, and the actual prediction can be conducted on another dataset or partition of the data. This process of training is conducted because when prediction is the end goal, if training and estimation were done on a single database, extremely good predictions could be made by including many variables in the model. However, many of these variables may be simply capturing noise that is specific to this particular sample, and hence the prediction would not generalize to other settings. This is a case of "overfitting," which machine learning wishes to avoid.

Machine learning (hereafter ML) has a wealth of applications and is an area of tremendous current development. However here we will focus on the application that is particularly relevant for our needs, which is in using ML methods to address questions of causality. In doing this, we will come across a range of new methods, and we will also see that at times, ML can be well-suited to extend models and methods we've discussed in previous chapters.

The general structure of this chapter will be twofold. Firstly, we will briefly lay out some general ideas and concepts about ML as well as discuss some tools that are frequently encountered in ML. Here, we will narrow our focus somewhat to the types of tools often found in causal applications, as this will be a basis for later models discussed in the chapter. This will be an overview, and the goal here is not delve into these tools at great depth, as there are entire textbooks dedicated just to this point. For example, a much broader background on these tools and general principals can be found in the textbook of Hastie, Tibshirani, and Friedman (2017).

Secondly, we will then discuss the application of these tools in microeconometrics, with a particular interest in methods that can be applied to seek to learn about causal relationships. Particularly nice overviews of this theme can be found in the review papers of Mullainathan and Spiess (2017), which is more general; Athey and Imbens (2019), which provides more specific examples of ML methods; as well as an earlier review of Varian (2014), which lays out a number of key considerations focused broadly on the growing use of big data in economics. Likely the canonical reference if you are seeking a textbook-length exposition of these themes in their own right is the recent work of Chernozhukov et al. (2024) (currently freely available online). This current chapter seeks to provide a focus that is particularly relevant for practitioners, focusing on key methods that are being applied with growing frequency in empirical work, linking to the methods we have already encountered throughout this book.

9.1 An Introduction

9.1.1 The Logic Behind Machine Learning

Most introductions to machine learning make clear that a key difference in ML compared with the econometrics we have encountered so far is its focus on prediction. Based on the common framework of OLS and the desire to causally estimate parameters of interest, which we generically call β, Mullainathan and Spiess (2017) state this as:

> Put succinctly, machine learning belongs in the part of the toolbox marked $\widehat{y}$ rather than in the more familiar $\widehat{\beta}$ compartment. (p. 88)

Probably not surprisingly, it turns out that this implies entirely different considerations and desires. While in econometrics, we would generally be concerned if we were estimating systematically biased parameters $\widehat{\beta}$ (or $\widehat{\tau}$ throughout this book), in ML we are not concerned with the parameters per se, but rather how these are used to generate good predictions from data. While these predictions $\widehat{Y}$ may be regression-based predictions of a continuous variable, they may also be predictions of some categorical outcome, in which case the prediction is a classification task and may be predicted in quite different ways—for example, while often based on observed information on Y, in certain circumstances information on Y may not be systematically observed.

Given that in ML, the goal is to predict outcomes, it will be important to have some way to measure good prediction. Generally, this is done by seeking to minimize some loss function, or error rate. This loss function can be written as $L(\widehat{Y}, Y)$, where a greater "loss" is associated with predictions of a given Y that are far away from its true value. However, rather than minimizing the loss associated with a particular observed dataset, which could be easily achieved by setting $\widehat{Y} = Y$, we wish to explain outcomes "out of sample," or with a new sample of data that we presume is drawn from the same distribution as the data we use to generate predictions. To consider one example, imagine that we have a vector of variables X that we believe are related to an outcome of interest Y, then we may define a loss function as: $L(\widehat{f}(X), Y)$. Our goal in machine learning will be to generate a function $\widehat{f}$ that will have low prediction error on new data points, which can be quantified using the expected prediction error:

$$\mathbb{E}_{y,x}[L(\widehat{f}(X), Y)],$$

where the expectation $\mathbb{E}_{y,x}$ seeks to emphasize the interest in considering data outside of original training data. Such criteria need not be very complicated. Common choices that one may seek to minimize are the squared error loss, or the absolute error, which, respectively imply defining the loss function as below:

$$L^{\text{squared error}}\left(\widehat{f}(X), y\right) = \left(y - \widehat{f}(X)\right)^2 \tag{9.1}$$

$$L^{\text{absoute error}}\left(\widehat{f}(X), y\right) = \left|y - \widehat{f}(X)\right|, \tag{9.2}$$

based on predicted outcomes $\widehat{f}(X)$ and observed outcomes y.

Some points on jargon There are a number of terms that are specific to this literature, despite having other more common labels in standard econometrics. A number of such terms are summarized in table 9.1.

There are a large number of ML-specific terms that are encountered in particular models, and we will discuss these in section 9.2 when encountering these models. There are also some other slightly less common terms that we may nevertheless come across, such as the idea of oracle models, which has some relationship to what we may commonly think of as knowing the true data generating process in econometrics. In certain settings our ML models or estimators will rely on predictions that we do not know, and we may wish to study properties of models under assumptions that these predictions are made correctly. In this case, we can refer to oracle estimators, which is somewhat related to cases where we study properties of estimators assuming a known data generating process in more standard econometric settings.

More broadly, machine learning techniques are often classified as either "supervised learning" or "unsupervised learning." The term supervised learning refers to cases where

Table 9.1
Some standard ML terms and their econometric counterparts

"Econometric" label	ML label	Notes
Estimation	Training	Process of fitting a model that will be applied for prediction with new data
Estimation sample	Training sample	A sample of data that will be used to generate a prediction, but not necessarily for final estimation
Covariates ($\boldsymbol{X}_i$)	Features/ attributes	Independent variables (in cases where these are used)
Regression parameters	Weights	Estimated coefficients on independent variables (in cases where these are used)
Observations	Instances/ examples	Data points available for analysis

both dependent variables X_i and outcome variables Y_i are observed, and hence prediction is "supervised" by the actual outcome we seek to predict. Unsupervised learning, on the other hand, refers to cases where we simply observe dependent variables or features of data, and we seek to classify observations in some useful way based on their features. In general, the vast majority of the applications of ML in causal methods are based on supervised learning given the central role of both outcomes and features. As such, most of our discussion here will center around supervised learning. However, we will very briefly touch on unsupervised learning when discussing some active areas of development at the end of this chapter.

9.1.2 Key Considerations for Application to Economics

The standard way we have thought in the book so far—and generally the standard way we think in econometrics—is that we wish to identify some causal parameter of interest. This is clearly different to the goals of ML, which is cast broadly as a prediction problem. Nevertheless, ML is finding a growing place in research in economics, and perhaps surprisingly this is particularly active in the literature interested in estimating treatment effects. Thus, while we are not necessarily always after prediction, it turns out the ML can be applied fruitfully. Of course, if prediction *is* the main aim of a model, for example, if we wish to predict a counterfactual outcome, ML tools will likely work even more directly to help us in our task.

A chapter from Athey (2018) makes a number of very nice points on the incorporation of ML in economics. In this chapter, Athey notes that ML can add considerable value when a goal of research is in estimating a low-dimensional parameter, but in settings where there are potentially quite high-dimensional nuisance parameters that complicate estimation. This would appear to be well-suited to many of the settings we have discussed up to this point in the book where we have a single (or few) treatment effects of interest and potentially many confounders where we need to "learn" functional forms or other relationships.

There are a number of problems in economics where the empirical challenge is actually focused on prediction. A discussion of these themes is provided in Kleinberg et al. (2015), who discuss "prediction policy problems" and note the importance of ML tools in providing the best-quality answers to questions being studied. They list a number of such problems such as predicting teacher value added in education, predicting unemployment length spells to support job seekers, optimally targeting regulation such as health inspections, predicting high-risk groups to receive social policy interventions, and assessing creditworthiness of potential borrowers. They additionally work through an illustrative example studying medical decisions of joint replacement surgery as well as patient characteristics and potential benefits from such surgeries. Additional examples are provided in Athey (2017), though she notes that while the application of "off-the-shelf" ML algorithms will often be simple, bridging the gap between making a prediction with ML and making an actual decision for policy will be much more challenging for a number of reasons, including interpretation of evidence, concerns for fairness and nondiscrimination, and data manipulation.

However, Athey (2018) suggests that beyond these pure prediction problems, many of the big applications of ML in economics may come directly in the treatment effects literature, where the tools of ML can be applied to causal inference. She notes that (at the time of writing) a movement was already under way in which tools from ML were applied to settings such as the estimation of treatment effects (and treatment effect heterogeneity) in randomized experiments, the consideration of conditional unconfoundedness, instrumental variable models, panel data settings including difference-in-difference style designs, and regression discontinuity models. Since the time of that article, this adoption has only increased, arguably at a much faster rate than we may have expected. Tools from ML can be applied to potentially generate a richer understanding of variation in data, correctly isolate causal effects, or consider optimal treatment assignment. In section 9.3 we will examine more specifically how ML can be used in a literature focused on the identification of causal effects, however first will focus on a number of general considerations when applying tools from ML, as well as a discussion of some of the main tools applied in economics.

9.1.3 New Points of Focus

Before turning to specific models or algorithms that are frequently used in machine learning and their implementations in economics, we will discuss a number of general principles that are central considerations in ML but not such prominent concerns in the econometric methods we've been using so far.

9.1.3.1 Model selection, evaluation, and tuning parameters In econometrics, model selection is often conceived as something that will be driven by economic theory, and, hence, estimation will proceed from a preconceived model. In ML, model selection is a key process in generating predictions. As laid out above, ML seeks to determine the model that best explains some particular outcome in unseen data, and as such, we will need to evaluate models in order to select that which best satisfies some criteria. These models are often based on decisions relating to tuning parameters, which are values on which models depend, but which need to be optimized, or "tuned," to a given empirical example. These tuning parameters may be things such as the number of splits of data that one may wish to consider, parameters that seek to determine how much to penalize the inclusion of additional variables in models to avoid models becoming overly complex, or simply fitting random noise in a given dataset, rather than more general patterns outside of a specific sample. This process of model selection and tuning is thus an integral part of ML.

Cross-validation One particular form to evaluate models, or evaluate tuning parameters in model selection, is through the use of cross-validation (for a comprehensive discussion of tuning parameter selection, see Chetverikov [2024]). The idea behind cross-validation is that if we seek to find models with the best out-of-sample fits, we can consider this out-of-sample fit by estimating models on one sample, and then testing their fit on other samples. Cross-validation does this by working with multiple selected samples of a given dataset. There are a number of ways to conduct cross-validation, including leave-one-out cross-validation (LOOCV) and K-fold cross-validation as particularly frequent examples.

To see how cross-validation (CV) works, we will discuss K-fold CV described in Geisser (1975), and imagine that we have a loss function that we seek to minimise—for example a squared-error loss as in (9.1), which depends on particular decisions related to the prediction function $\widehat{f}$. K-fold CV then proceeds in the following steps:

1. Randomly split the dataset in around K equal parts, each having approximately $N_k \approx \frac{N}{K}$ observations. We call each of these K segments of the data a "fold" and denote as I_k the observations in fold k.
2. For all folds in $k = 1, \dots, K$, conduct the following steps:
   (a) Remove fold k from the data, leaving the remaining $N - N_k$ observations.
   (b) Calculate the proposed estimator $\widehat{f}_{(-k)}$ using this data, where the subscript $-k$ makes clear that this prediction *does not* depend on the data in fold k.
   (c) Now apply this prediction function that was based off data excluding k to the fold of data in k. This calculates the predicted outcome as: $\widehat{Y} = \widehat{f}_{(-k)}(X_i)$ for all $i \in I_k$.
   (d) Calculate the mean squared error loss for fold k as: $MSE_k = \frac{1}{N_k} \sum_{i \in I_k} (y - \widehat{y})^2$.
3. The mean squared error loss can then be calculated summing the squared error loss for each fold: $MSE = \frac{1}{K} \sum_{k=1}^{K} MSE_k$.

Note here then that idea of cross-validation is simply to assess a model in its ability to predict outcomes for observations within a dataset but not used for model "training" based on the models determined from the rest of the data. In practice, given that ML algorithms depend on certain tuning parameters, one can conduct CV across many different values of the tuning parameter and then settle on the parameters that minimize the MSE found in CV. In practice, often ten folds are used for K-fold cross-validation, though there is no hard-and-fast rule used in all circumstances. Indeed, the variance of the quantity MSE will be minimized when a larger number of folds K is used, and the argument in favor of using five or ten folds is that gains from reduced variance are generally small after this point (Hastie, Tibshirani, and Friedman 2017). In the limit, if $K = N$, this is referred to as LOOCV, as in each fold a single observation is omitted in training, and then predictions are made for just this single observation. While in general LOOCV will be very computationally intensive, in certain models such as linear regression models, closed-form solutions exist for the MSE, and as such here LOOCV can be preferred to K-fold varieties.

9.1.3.2 Regularization and overfitting A common concern in prediction models is that of overfitting. When potentially many explanatory variables are present, and we wish to predict some outcome of interest, in our sample of data we can generate trivially good predictions by including many variables. Indeed, this is possibly something that you have seen when discussing the R^2 in standard regression models. In a sample of N observations, if an intercept and $N-1$ (non-colinear) variables are included, the R^2 will always be driven to 1. However, in ML the interest in generating a good prediction is not for in-sample prediction, but rather for predicting out-of-sample. While it may seem like the inclusion of irrelevant variables in a prediction should not matter, it turns out that it does, as if many irrelevant variables are included in predictions given that they have a good in-sample fit, when the model is applied out of sample, the irrelevant variables significantly increase the variance of predictions.

Thus, a challenge in ML is in seeking variables that truly explain the dependent variable of interest, and not those that simply pick up random noise. In practice, parsimony is often preferred, with more simple models doing a better job of explaining out-of-sample outcomes. For this reason, regularization is a common feature of ML algorithms. Regularization is a process by which complexity of a model is penalized. We will see particular examples of this in section 9.2 below, where often this will consist of adding a term to the loss function we desire to minimize, making it more "expensive" to include additional variables in predictions, favoring parsimony in prediction models. The way that these regularization terms are incorporated is often model-specific, via the definition of tuning parameters, with these tuning parameters determined by CV or other model selection criteria.

9.1.3.3 $k > N$ and sparsity Finally machine learning is often conducted in the domain of big data (for an early discussion of this, see Varian 2014). Growing availability of large datasets in economics makes this particularly useful, given that ML often has a focus on computational tractability of models even when datasets are very large. Here, it is not simply the case that large datasets refers to cases where the number of observations, N, is very large, but also cases where the number of variables (or features) k is very large. As one example, we can consider supermarket scanner data where many different purchases are observed (the N), with records of the number of purchases of a large number of products (the k).

A particularly nice feature of ML is that many algorithms can work with cases even where $k > N$. In models we work with in standard econometrics, this is generally not the case. For example, consider the OLS estimator $\widehat{\beta} = (X'X)^{-1}X'Y$. In cases where $k > N$, this quantity cannot be estimated, given that $X'X$ will not be of full rank, and hence cannot be inverted. In many ML algorithms, including the Lasso and Ridge regression discussed below, the fact that $k > N$ is not an issue, as models will be regularized, often leading to a more reduced set of variables to be included. In general, settings where the number of variables is large relative to the sample size are referred to as high-dimensional methods (Belloni, Chernozhukov, and Hansen 2014a).

A related point is that in many settings, even though k may be large, the underlying model may be approximately sparse, which implies that many of the potential explanatory variables actually are irrelevant in explaining the outcome of interest. In this case, an ML algorithm may seek both to determine which variables are relevant and to generate a prediction based on these (relevant) variables. These algorithms will determine which variables are relevant in prediction in a clearly defined way, and so are likely preferable to ad hoc assumptions made by researchers related to model selection (Athey and Imbens 2017). Of course, the assumption that the DGP is sparse—or at least approximately sparse—is itself a substantive modeling choice (Belloni, Chernozhukov, and Hansen 2014a; Chernozhukov, Wüthrich, and Zhu 2021). Certain ML-based econometric methods (some of which we will encounter below) explicitly rely on this assumption, which introduces important considerations and challenges for inference, as discussed in, among other sources, Belloni, Chernozhukov, and Hansen (2014a).

9.2 Some Key Methods

9.2.1 Regularized Regression and Related Methods

Regularized regression models are models that seek to explicitly penalize the inclusion of many variables. Such models are useful in cases where we seek to generate good predictions, as this can help to avoid overfitting. For example, if we seek to generate a prediction such as $\widehat{Y}$ using some sample of data and an underlying regression model, all variables will allow our prediction to explain more of the underlying Y, unless they are perfectly multi-colinear with other variables. However, if we then seek to use the coefficients estimated from this procedure to predict "out-of-sample," we may find that our prediction performs relatively poorly, as while a small number of variables included in our original model actually do have good predictive power for Y, many other coefficients were simply random noise, resulting in a clear case of overfitting.

By using regularization, we can seek to simplify our models, including variables in predictions only if they exceed specific thresholds or otherwise reducing the importance of variables in generating predictions. Regularization can also be useful in cases where the number of potential variables is large, in certain settings even where $k > N$, as it allows for a reduced number of variables to be selected for inclusion in a final model. Regularized regression models are frequently found in machine learning and in applications of ML in economics. Next we will consider two such regularized regression methods, the ridge and the lasso, which are particularly frequently encountered.

9.2.1.1 The Lasso A frequently used regularization-based estimator is the lasso (or LASSO), which stands for "least absolute shrinkage and selection operator." The "shrinkage" in the name of The Lasso refers to the fact that regularization occurs by shrinking parameters toward zero. Specifically, the lasso seeks to estimate parameters $\widehat{\beta}$ that resolve the following equation, where X_i refers to a $1 \times k$ a matrix of covariates, and a constant term:

$$\arg\min_{\beta} \sum_{i=1}^{N} (Y_i - X_i'\beta)^2 \quad \text{subject to} \quad \sum_{j=1}^{k} |\beta_j| \leq t. \tag{9.3}$$

Here the first term of this minimization is simply a residual sum of squares (as we know well from OLS), but the second term is new, and it controls the shrinkage in the model. As this shrinkage term requires all parameters to sum to no more than t, if progressively smaller values of t are imposed, this effectively shrinks the parameters toward zero, making certain parameters exactly zero or shrinking them away from their unconstrained values. This second term can be rewritten as $\|\beta\|_1$, or the ℓ^1 norm, following the standard definition of an ℓ^p norm as: $\|x\|_p = \left(\sum_{i=1}^{N} |x_i|^p\right)^{1/p}$. We will encounter other norms below.

To view this as a single optimization problem, the loss function for the lasso can be rewritten in Lagrangian form as follows:

$$\arg\min_{\beta} \left\{ \sum_{i=1}^{N} (Y_i - X'\beta)^2 + \lambda(\|\beta\|_1) \right\}, \tag{9.4}$$

where the Lagrangian form refers to the fact that we are optimizing subject to constraints. Note here that while the Lagrangian form of the Lasso in (9.4) is simply an alternative way to write the optimization problem we are seeking to resolve in (9.3), this does not imply that λ and t are identical. While λ and t *do* have a one to one correspondence in a given problem and dataset (Hastie, Tibshirani, and Friedman 2017), when the parameter t from (9.3) is smaller, this will imply shrinking parameters more toward zero, or setting more parameters at zero, while in the case of (9.4), a *larger* value for λ, implying that the imposed constraints bind more tightly, will imply shrinking parameters more toward zero. Typically, in computational implementations, one specifies λ (rather than t), which, as discussed below, can be optimally chosen through cross-validation.

One thing to note here is that, unlike in OLS, the scaling of variables in the Lasso is not innocuous. If a variable is multiplied by a constant, this will have implications for the parameter estimates and, hence, the estimation procedure in 9.4. For this reason, generally all variables are standardized prior to their inclusion in the lasso. This standardization is often to rescale each of the independent variables x_j such that $\sum_{i=1}^{N} x_{ij} = 1$. Alternative models have been proposed such as a lasso with "penalty loadings" in Belloni et al. (2012), which allows for estimation without rescaling independent variables. Specifically, Belloni et al. (2012) suggest estimating as follows:

$$\arg\min_{\beta} \left\{ \sum_{i=1}^{N} (Y_i - X'\beta)^2 + \lambda \sum_{j=1}^{k} \psi_j^2 |\beta_j| \right\}, \tag{9.5}$$

where the only difference between (9.5) and (9.4) is the existence of the "penalty loading" factor ψ_j. This allows, for example, unstandardized variables to be entered into the model and to set penalty loadings as $\psi_j = (\sum_{i=1}^{N} x_{ij}^2)^{-1/2}$, which is equivalent to a standard Lasso with the standardization noted above. This procedure also offers benefits in terms of rigorous theory for selecting tuning parameters discussed below in both homoscedastic and heteroscedastic settings.

The value of λ in the Lasso is a tuning parameter, and as such must be determined. This is generally conducted by K-fold CV, as discussed in section 9.1.3. In this case, the cross-validated mean squared error can be generated across a large range of different potential tuning parameters for λ, and the tuning parameter can be chosen that minimizes this MSE. Asymptotic consistency of the Lasso where λ has been chosen based on CV has been shown by Chetverikov, Liao, and Chernozhukov (2021), justifying this method of selecting λ. There are, however, alternative ways one can select λ including using a theoretically chosen plug-in parameter. This is shown in Belloni et al. (2012), who note that theoretically justified data-driven values can be chosen for both λ and ψ_j to ensure with a probability approaching one that variables will be correctly selected in the Lasso as data grows without limits. One nice thing about these theoretically chosen "plug-in" values is that they are calculated in an entirely data-driven way, and so can be quickly calculated, as well as theoretically supported.[1] Full formal details are provided in Belloni et al. (2012, §2.3), and a more applied discussion can be found in Ahrens, Hansen, and Schaffer (2020, §5.2).

9.2.1.2 Ridge regression The ridge regression predates the lasso, and is based on a similar logic. In the case of the ridge regression, instead of using an ℓ^1 norm for the regularization parameter, an ℓ^2 norm is used. Thus, the estimation procedure can be written analogously to 9.3 as:

$$\arg\min_{\beta} \sum_{i=1}^{N} (Y_i - X_i'\beta)^2 \quad \text{subject to} \quad \sum_{j=1}^{k} \beta_j^2 \leq t \tag{9.6}$$

or in Lagrangian form as:

$$\arg\min_{\beta}\left\{\sum_{i=1}^{N}(Y_i - X_i'\beta)^2 + \lambda\sum_{j=1}^{k}\beta_j^2\right\}. \tag{9.7}$$

Many of the details that hold for the lasso also hold for the ridge regression, including the use of standardized input variables, and λ as a tuning parameter that can be chosen by cross-validation. Unlike the Lasso, given its use of the ℓ^2 norm, the Ridge has a closed-form solution for β. By differentiating (9.6) we can see:

$$\widehat{\beta}^{\text{ridge}} = (X'X + \lambda I)^{-1}X'y.$$

The addition of a positive term λ to the principal diagonal of $X'X$ is why the Ridge offers a solution when $k > N$, as this makes the matrix invertible even if $X'X$ is not full rank.

One fundamental difference between Ridge regression and the Lasso is the nature of shrinkage in the estimated parameters. The Ridge, where regularization is based upon the same quadratic loss as that used to minimize squared errors effectively shrinks all parameters toward zero by a constant. The Lasso, which, on the other hand, is based on a linear regularization, acts to subtract a constant factor off each parameter truncating at zero. This implies that the Lasso both shrinks parameters and sets potentially many coefficients equal to precisely zero, while the Ridge regression simply shrinks parameters toward zero, never setting them exactly equal to zero. A visualization of how estimated parameters vary as the tuning parameter λ is increased is presented in figure 9.1. In these figures, estimates are defined using precisely the same (simulated) data, and we can observe the greater (linear) rate of shrinkage in the Lasso compared with slower shrinkage in the Ridge, with parameters never set exactly equal to zero. Considerably more discussion of the selection of tuning

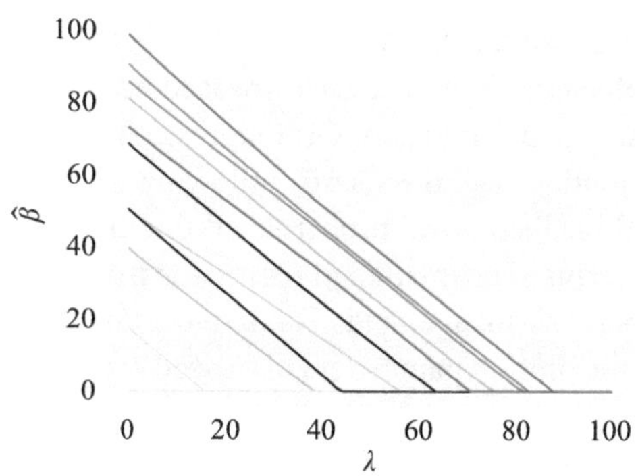

(a) Lasso

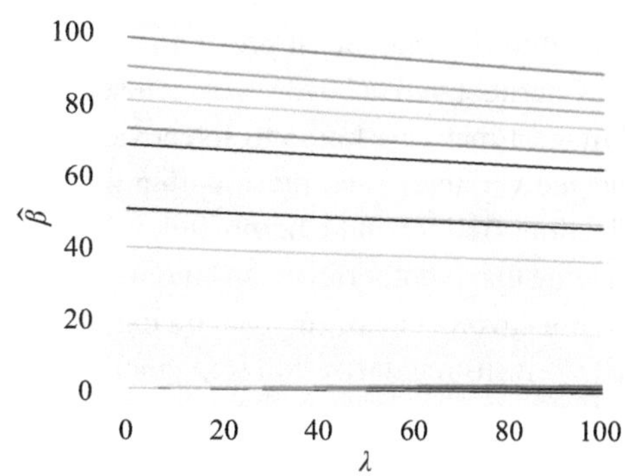

(b) Ridge

Figure 9.1
Shrinkage in the Lasso and ridge regression.

parameters, and how this varies between the Lasso, Ridge, and other regularized regression models, is provided in Abadie and Kasy (2019).

9.2.1.3 Elastic nets While both Lasso and Ridge regression offer benefits, an alternative that seeks to draw positive elements from both procedures is the elastic net. The elastic net is a hybrid model, which combines the Ridge and Lasso penalty, in the following way:

$$\underset{\beta}{\arg\min}\left\{\sum_{i=1}^{N}(Y_i - X_i'\beta)^2 + \lambda\left(\alpha\sum_{j=1}^{k}|\beta_j| + (1-\alpha)\sum_{j=1}^{k}\beta_j^2\right)\right\}. \tag{9.8}$$

If $\alpha = 1$, the elastic net collapses to the Lasso, whereas if $\alpha = 0$, it collapses to the Ridge regression. Intermediate values of α draw from both the Lasso penalty and the Ridge penalty. This offers benefits given that where correlated variables are included in the model, the Lasso is relatively indifferent to the variable chosen, whereas the Ridge generally shrinks the coefficients of correlated variables toward each other (Hastie, Tibshirani, and Friedman 2017, 662).

Code Callout 9.1: Exploring Regularized Regression Models
In code callout 6.1 we will explore the Lasso as a means of variable selection and see how it compares in terms of shrinkage with Ridge regression and the elastic net. To do so, we will follow Farrell (2015), who explores variable selection in observational models evaluating labor market training programs.

9.2.1.4 OLS post-Lasso In certain circumstances, we may wish to take advantage of the variable-selection properties of the Lasso without the shrinkage of (selected) coefficients implied in the estimation procedure. OLS post-Lasso, or the "post-Lasso," as per Belloni and Chernozhukov (2013), can be used in such cases. The post-Lasso procedure consists of first estimating a Lasso to select variables, and then running an OLS regression with the selected variables (i.e., those with a nonzero coefficient in the Lasso) following the Lasso selection. Belloni and Chernozhukov (2013) derive theoretical properties of this estimator, showing that it outperforms a standard Lasso in terms of estimation of regression parameters given its avoidance of the bias owing to parameter shrinkage, and also derive a theoretical (data-driven) regularization step, analogous to the plug-in parameters discussed previously.

9.2.1.5 Other variable selection methods The Lasso will likely be the most frequent type of variable-selection model we will encounter given its sparse solution and well-documented formal properties. However, there are a range of other variable selection methods we may encounter in practice. Some of these are Lasso-based such as the square root Lasso (Belloni, Chernozhukov, and Wang 2011) or the Adaptive Lasso (Zou 2006), which have been shown to offer benefits in terms of consistent model selection and the avoidance of the need to estimate auxiliary parameters. Others are similar to the Lasso in that they are based on ℓ^1 norms but take slightly different approaches such as the Dantzig selector (Candes and Tao 2007), which seeks to select variables while ensuring that the predictors are not overly correlated with the residuals, which can provide robustness to noise and multicollinearity. These methods, while sharing similarities with the Lasso, offer unique perspectives on balancing sparsity, model fit, and computational efficiency.

There are also other regularized regression models, which fall under the class of "subset selection models." These models simply seek to include a subset of variables in the final regression model, eliminating all other variables. This subset is based on a specific subset size that defines the number of variables to be included, and some criteria that are used to define how the best group of variables should be chosen. For example, "best-subset selection" for a specified subset of size chooses the specified number of variables that minimize the residual sum of squares in the regression model. In general, one drawback of subset selection models, which makes Lasso or Ridge a potentially more attractive option for estimating, is that the computational implementation of subset selection is more demanding, whereas Lasso and Ridge have efficient algorithms for estimation.

9.2.2 Regression Trees and Forests

9.2.2.1 Regression trees A regression tree is a procedure in which heterogeneity in data is uncovered by partitioning the sample based on a specific criteria. It is a particularly nonparametric style of analysis, based upon successive binary splits of the data in a manner that seeks to explain the data in the best way possible. Regression trees (or CART, for classification and regression trees) are composed of a series of branches, which successively partition the data into most alike groups. These branches are generated from binary splits of the data, based on potentially many underlying variables. The general nomenclature of regression trees refers to subsamples, or data splits, as "branches" and terminal branches as "leaves." Here, nodes refers to the points at which a branch splits into other branches.

Specifically, consider an independent (response) variable Y_i, and k dependent or input variables $X_{i1}, \ldots, X_{ik}$. The goal of a regression tree is to divide the data into M mutually exclusive regions, denoted $R_1, \ldots, R_M$, where within each region the dependent variable is simply modeled as a constant c_m. Thus, if we know the split points, the predicted outcome can be written as:

$$\widehat{Y} = \sum_{m=1}^{M} c_m \cdot \mathbb{1}\{X \in R_m\}.$$

An important question then is how to determine these splits, or nodes, in the data. As splits are binary, each node in the tree is based on a single variable. Thus, it may be the case that in a specific example, some variable X_1 is used to partition data at the first node, splitting at above and below a certain cut-point, but this need not imply that the same variable is used to split data at the second node. The criterion used to determine the nodes in regression trees is, fortunately, a criterion we know well: ordinary least squares. But here, OLS is conducted progressively at each node of the tree, giving rise to multiple branches that grow at each stage. Indeed, the process of estimation in a regression tree is termed "growing" a regression tree, and this is later refined via a process known as pruning. Consider the decision at a specific node, where we seek to split the data in two segments, estimating mean outcomes in each while minimizing the residual sum of squares. We wish to choose the variable X_j among all possible options $X_1, \ldots, X_k$ and split points s, such that the grouping provides a deterministic classification: $R_1 = \mathbb{1}\{X_j < s\}$ and $R_2 = \mathbb{1}\{X_j \geq s\}$. Specifically then, the regression tree algorithm considers all possible variables and all possible cut-points, minimizing the following quantity with the split at each node:

$$\min_{j,s}\left[\min_{c_1}\sum_{x_i \in R_1(j,s)}(y_i - c_1)^2 + \min_{c_2}\sum_{x_i \in R_2(j,s)}(y_i - c_2)^2\right]. \tag{9.9}$$

This is conducted sequentially, first creating one split leading to two branches, and then in each branch, creating another split, leading to another two branches. At each stage, the equation 9.9 is solved, providing a simple binary split of the remaining data.

To illustrate this method we can consider a quite simple example based on two independent variables (or features) and a dependent variable (response) Y. In figure 9.2 we lay out what a regression tree would do with a specific set of simulated data.[2] In panel (a) the regression tree is displayed. This regression tree has three levels, and at each level the split is conducted that minimizes the quadratic loss between the outcome Y and the means in each of the groups. For example, at the top level (or the "root" of the tree), the optimal split is found such that $X_2 < 0.541$, with observations below this point having an estimated mean of $\widehat{Y} = 13.116$, and observations above this point having an estimated mean of $\widehat{Y} = 28.381$. Similar such optimal splits are conducted to each of these groups, and to each of the resulting groups, resulting in a tress with eight leaves. The data on the features X_1 and X_2 is documented in panel (b), with the optimal partitions of the data being graphed in panel (c). Here it is apparent that at different levels, splits can occur optimally based on different variables. For example, at both the root and the first branch, optimal splits are observed to be generated by partitioning over X_2 (resulting in three horizontal lines in panel b). Thereafter, all optimal splits occur partitioning on X_1, resulting in four vertical lines. Finally the bottom panels document both the full set of tuples (X_1, X_2, Y), as panel (d) and the predictions generated from the model for all possible pairs of X_1 and X_2, giving the surface plot in panel (e) that can be described by the tuple $(X_1, X_2, \hat{y})$. Note that given that within each partition R_m, outcomes are simply modeled as c_m, giving rise to a step-like surface.

A tuning parameter in regression trees is the complexity of the model, with "deeper" trees consisting of more branches and leaves. As we wish to avoid overfitting, this tree depth can be calculated by including a penalty term in a loss function that we seek to minimize, which increases the cost of adding additional branches to the tree. The process of estimation

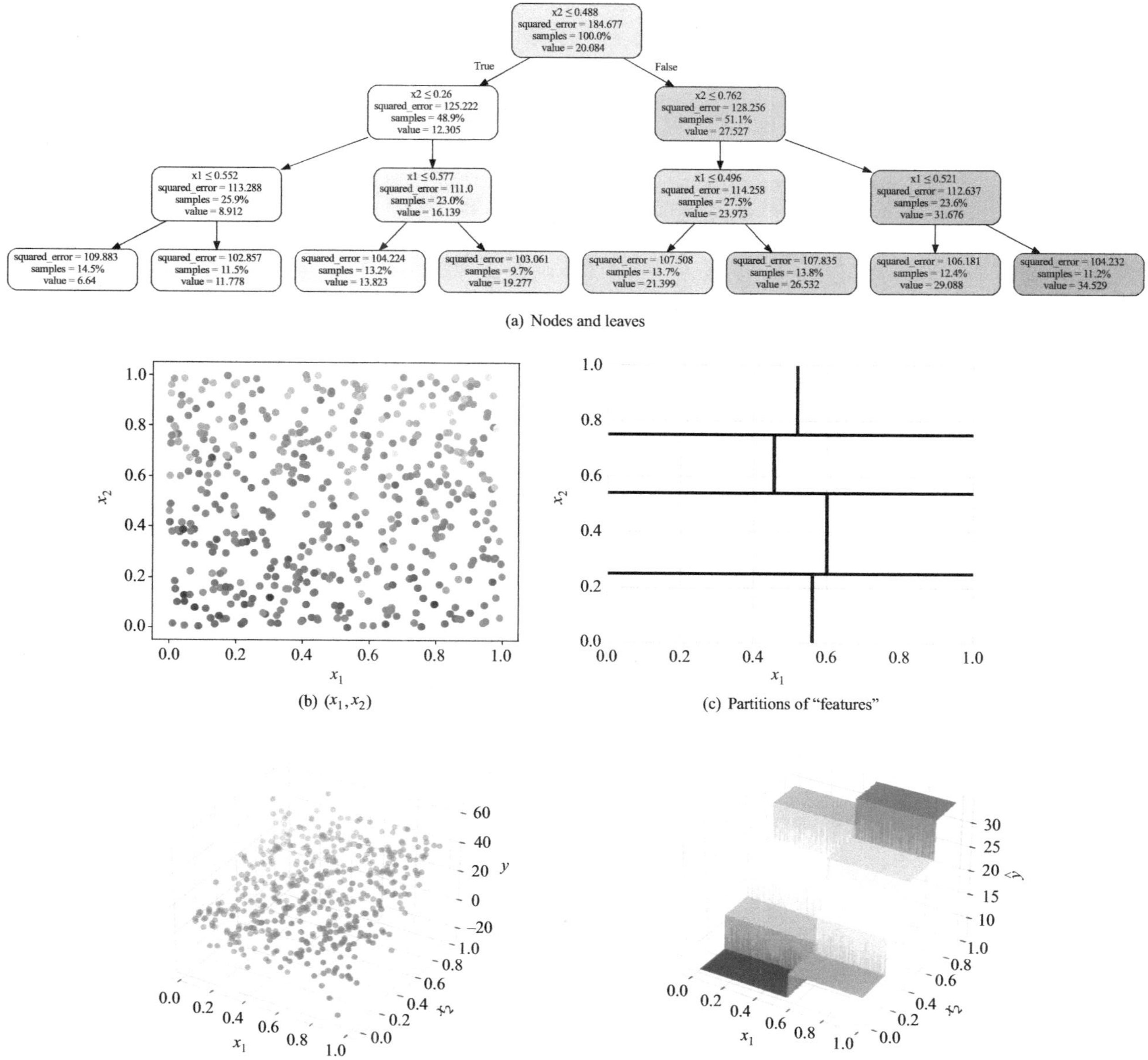

(a) Nodes and leaves

(b) (x_1, x_2)

(c) Partitions of "features"

(d) (x_1, x_2, y)

(e) Predictions from fitted CART

Figure 9.2
A regression tree with two dependent variables.

then consists of growing a regression tree based on some relatively large number of nodes and then pruning the tree back by progressively removing branches that add little to the explanatory power of the tree, until some optimal tree size is determined. This optimal size can be determined by cross-validation. If desired, formal discussions of this algorithm can be found in Hastie, Tibshirani, and Friedman (2017, §9.2.3) or Bruce Hansen (2022, §29.15). Note that this process of growing the tree to a large size and then pruning the tree back may seem unneccesarily costly, as the tree could just be grown to a smaller level and stopped originally, but it is important. This is because splits that seem to add relatively little to the explanatory power of a regression tree at a high level, may lead to splits lower in the tree that turn out to be very important.

9.2.2.2 Random forests Random forests, as their name suggests, are based on multiple estimations of regression trees. As laid out above, and as is particularly clear in the case of figure 9.2e, the use of regression trees leads to discontinuous jumps in predictions at points where branches occur, which is unlikely to reflect true features of the underlying data. The idea of random forests is that if instead of estimating a single regression tree, many regression trees are grown, and then averages are taken over regression trees, which results in greater smoothness in predicted outcomes.

The way that random forests grow many trees off of a particular single source of data is through the use of bootstrapping. Random bootstrap samples are generated from the underlying data, and within each bootstrap sample, a separate tree is grown. In ML, the process of averaging over bootstrap samples is referred to as "bagging" (for Bootstrap AGGregatING). However, unlike bagging, random forests introduce another innovation, and that is introducing more randomness into the predictions, which reduces the correlation between multiple regression trees, generating smoother predictions and improving the predictive power of the algorithm.

This additional randomness is introduced in random forests by—within each node of each tree—selecting at random only certain variables from among all possible explanatory variables to consider for generating sample splits. This process ensures that quite varying regression trees are produced, and a final prediction can be generated from the total set (or "ensemble") of all trees produced, as the simple average across regression trees. A full description of the random forest algorithm can be found in Hastie, Tibshirani, and Friedman (2017, §15.2).

9.2.2.3 Beyond regression trees and forests There are a range of other procedures that can be developed to "learn" heterogeneity. This at times leads to a slightly dizzying array of algorithms, though these are often based on deeper underlying principles, and at times the empirical performance of estimators we will discuss below will be documented under a number of alternative methods (see, e.g., Chernozhukov, Wüthrich, and Zhu [2021]; Athey et al. [2019]). One class of alternative methods is based on the idea of boosting, which uses the principle that relatively simple models can be fit, and to the degree that important residual heterogeneity remains, be fit again on the residuals. This can then build up a more complex prediction based on a series of iterative simple models. One such example of this is boosted trees, where in each step a regression tree with relatively few branches is fit to explain any residual unexplained variation. More elaborate algorithms such as neural nets or deep learning routines can also be applied in this setting, which seek to learn representations in multiple layers and based on transformations of underlying factors. These methods require a more elaborate setup to be described, though Athey and Imbens (2019, §3.3) provide a quite concise overview. Finally, at times, rather than seeking a single underlying procedure to make predictions, multiple methods are used, and averages or combinations of models are used to generate a final prediction. Such procedures are referred to as ensemble methods.

9.3 Machine Learning and Causality: Getting at Identification

Here, we will begin to consider how we can use methods from machine learning to help us in our goal of understanding (causal) treatment effects. As we will see, this will require some way to take advantage of tools that seek to predict while, at the same time, housing a structure for estimation of treatment effects. Some general principles, as well as specific examples related to this, are discussed in the review paper of Belloni, Chernozhukov, and Hansen (2014a). Below, we discuss a number of ways that this can be done, across quite a broad array of models, relating to estimation and inference goals we have discussed previously in this book.

9.3.1 An Illustration of the Idea: Post-Double-Selection Lasso

To see one setting in which ML can aid the identification of causal parameters, we can consider the double-selection Lasso, or post-double-selection estimator. The idea of this estimator is that there may be cases where we are willing to make conditional unconfoundedness assumptions like the ones we laid out in chapter 3, (i.e., assumption 2′), but we may not know precisely which variables we must condition on.

This problem is particularly challenging if we have a large group of variables that we think may be potentially relevant confounders, or if we are not sure of the correct functional form for control variables, perhaps requiring interaction terms between variables, or series expansions, splines, or dummy variable expansions to capture nonlinearities. Imagine, for example, that the dimension of controls X_i, which we are considering, denoted k, is large and potentially even substantially larger than the number of observations available, which we write as $k >> N$. This is clearly a problem for the methods we have discussed in chapter 3, as we will simply not have the degrees of freedom to estimate treatment effects with any of the methods discussed previously.

In cases such as this, even if we have some reasonable idea of the economic theory behind the relationship we wish to capture, we may need some help in learning about the precise way to control for confounding factors. Belloni, Chernozhukov, and Hansen (2014b) show that one reasonable way forward is to use a double-selection Lasso, effectively selecting variables (via a Lasso) from a larger set of variables if they are relevant in explaining the outcome of interest, *or* in treatment assignment. Specifically, considering an outcome of interest Y_i, treatment W_i, and controls X_i, the post-double-selection procedure consists of:

1. Estimating a Lasso to select the group of variables from X_i that are relevant for predicting treatment W_i.
2. Estimating a Lasso to select the group of variables from X_i that are useful for predicting outcome Y_i
3. Estimating the treatment effect of interest by simple linear regression of Y_i on W_i and the union of controls selected in step 1 and 2.

Thus, the double-selection Lasso refers to the selection of variables relevant in steps 1 and 2, and the "post" refers to estimation following this procedure. Belloni, Chernozhukov, and Hansen (2014b) show that this double-selection procedure results in valid inference for the treatment effect of interest provided that the DGP is sufficiently sparse, which will imply that the total number of selected variables in steps 1 and 2 should be relatively small compared to the total sample size, and approximation errors owing to variables not selected by the double-Lasso procedure are small compared to sampling error.

We will not lay out the precise details of the theory behind this procedure as they are laid out clearly in Belloni, Chernozhukov, and Hansen (2014b), and we will study a broader class of double-selection methods in the subsection below. However, understanding this procedure helps to illustrate the conditions in which ML can productively be used to infer causality, and the types of tweaks that may be required for these tools to be useful here. In this regard, it is illustrative to see that if a more standard implementation were considered based on a Lasso, this would actually *not* allow us to conduct valid inference on treatment effects. Consider, for example, if instead of the double-selection procedure described above, a single-step Lasso, was fit, but where the treatment of interest W_i was forced to remain in the model. In these cases, even though the Lasso would select variables that are relevant in explaining Y_i, this would likely not lead to a valid treatment effect estimate. This is precisely because the goal of the Lasso is in prediction and not in estimation of some particular parameter.

We can understand why this would be the case by thinking through econometric theory. Given that the Lasso seeks to predict outcomes Y_i, and given that W_i is obliged to remain in the model, the Lasso would generally not select variables that are highly correlated with treatment. But if we think about the types of omitted covariates that will bias treatment effects in a regression-based context, it is precisely those factors that are highly correlated with treatment. Indeed, thinking back to the standard omitted variable bias generally taught in early econometrics classes, we would have the information to note that failing to select variables that are highly correlated with W_i, *even if* they are relatively weakly correlated with Y_i, can be very problematic. For this reason we need our methods to be "aware of the context." In this sense, if we ever wish to learn about treatment effects τ we need to combine economic assumptions and models with processes that can be aided by ML. A nice high-level discussion of this is provided in Belloni, Chernozhukov, and Hansen (2014a), and we will see illustrations of this principle in a range of settings below where ML methods are used with the precise goal of causal inference.

9.3.2 Double/Debiased Machine Learning

A general theory for this style of methods is laid out by Chernozhukov et al. (2018). Their "Double/debiased machine learning," or DDML, procedure aims to estimate treatment effects where the nature of observable confounders is unknown, and potentially many confounders may be considered to be present. While based on a somewhat similar logic to post-double-selection methods, DDML seeks to provide a more flexible framework, extending beyond conditions where selection on observables is required, and permitting a far broader type of prediction models beyond Lasso.

Although these methods are suited to a broad range of settings—various of which we will discuss in this chapter—to get a good understanding of the key elements of their procedure we will start by imagining we're in a case where conditional unconfoundedness holds. In that case, we can write our setting of interest as a "partially linear model":

$$Y = \tau W + g_0(X) + \varepsilon, \qquad \mathbb{E}[\varepsilon|X, W] = 0 \tag{9.10}$$

$$D = m_0(X) + \nu, \qquad \mathbb{E}[\nu|X] = 0. \tag{9.11}$$

Here we are largely following original the notation of Chernozhukov et al. (2018), and can consider this as a case where we are interested in the effect of some treatment D on outcomes Y. This effect is indicated as τ in (9.10). We can see our conditional unconfoundedness assumption in (9.11), as apart from the influence of X on treatment receipt W, other elements have no systematic relation with treatment, written as $\mathbb{E}[\nu|X] = 0$. In this setting, if we knew the collection of relevant variables X and the functional form for their relationship with Y, we could estimate the parameter of interest τ very easily, as we have discussed in chapter 3.

The issue here is that we are not sure of two things. Firstly, we do not know the relationship between X and Y. We neither assume that it is linear (hence the general function $g_0(\cdot)$) nor that we know which of the variables from the potential k variables in the vector X are relevant. Secondly, we do not know the nature of the relationship between the potential confounding vectors X and the treatment variable of interest. This is summarized in equation 9.11, where $m_0(\cdot)$ is an unknown function, both in form and in variables. Additionally, it is not assumed that k is small relative to sample size—indeed the dimension of k may be large relative to the full sample size N.

Note here then that our main interest is in estimating the treatment effect τ, but this requires knowing some function $g_0(X)$, which is not directly of interest, apart from as a means to correctly isolate this effect. In other words, it is a series of "nuisance parameters" describing the relationship between Y and X. Here the utility of ML can start to be seen even in causal settings. We can seek to use ML to learn about these nuisance parameters, and, once this is done, isolate the causal effect of interest.

However, it is important to note that the solution is not just to learn $g_0(X)$ and plug this into equation 9.10. For example, imagine we use some ML procedure such as random forest or other procedures discussed above to learn $\widehat{g}_0$. Let's assume that we learn this in some training sample of the data to avoid overfitting. Then, imagine that we use this function in the estimation sample of data, below indicated I, to effectively residualize out, or account for the effect of X on Y in a highly flexible manner. We will follow the notation of Chernozhukov et al. (2018) in using $\check{Y}$ to refer to this residualization of Y, such that $\check{Y} \equiv Y - \widehat{g}_0(X)$. If we were now to seek to estimate the treatment effect by using an OLS estimate:

$$\widehat{\tau}^{\text{SML}} = \left(\frac{1}{N} \sum_{i \in I} W_i^2 \right)^{-1} \frac{1}{N} \sum_{i \in I} W_i \check{Y}_i, \tag{9.12}$$

Chernozhukov et al. (2018) show that this would *not* provide a consistent estimate of our quantity of interest τ. The reason why τ_{SML} (denoting single machine learning) will not generate a consistent estimate of τ is because there is a bias in the estimate $\widehat{g}_0$. This is, of course, inherent in ML procedures, as we seek to use regularization to reduce variance when making predictions (as discussed in the previous sections), but this by necessity builds in bias. This is what Chernozhukov et al. (2018) refer to as "regularisation bias," which is the bias in $\widehat{\tau}^{\text{SML}}$ that owes to the process of regularization when learning the nuisance parameters $g_0(\cdot)$.

Fortunately, they note that this can be overcome relatively simply, by using an additional learning process to effectively eliminate this bias (hence the "double" or "debiased" machine learning). This is done by learning and partialing out the effects of relevant X from the treatment variable W in a similar way to the process of learning about the impact of X on Y. Once again, however, we do not know the true relationship between W and X, so this can be inferred from some ML estimator. The suggestion is to obtain:

$$\hat{W} = W - \widehat{m}_0(x),$$

where $\widehat{m}_0$ is the ML estimator obtained using a "training" portion of the data. We can then arrive to a DDML estimate using the version of W with X partialed out as:

$$\widehat{\tau}^{\text{DDML}} = \left(\frac{1}{N} \sum_{i \in I} \check{W}_i W_i \right)^{-1} \frac{1}{N} \sum_{i \in I} \hat{W}_i \check{Y}_i. \tag{9.13}$$

This estimator has both (approximately) removed the influence of X from W and also removed the direct effect of confounding by subtracting $\widehat{g}_0$ from Y, which removes the regularization bias in equation 9.12. This can be understood given that, previously, regularization bias came from estimation errors of $\widehat{g}_0$, while, in this case, regularization bias will depend upon the interaction between estimation errors of $\widehat{g}_0$ and $\widehat{m}_0$, which will vanish at reasonably fast rates as sample size grows.

Provided that (a) the approximations $\widehat{g}_0$ and $\widehat{m}_0$ do a reasonable job in modeling g_0 and m_0, (b) there is sufficient variation in $\hat{W}$ after concentrating out m_0, and (c) a number of more technical regularity conditions hold (laid out in assumption 4.1 Chernozhukov et al. (2018)), then the estimator $\widehat{\tau}^{\text{DML}}$ will be approximately unbiased and normally distributed. Specifically, the assumption related to the quality of the ML prediction for $\widehat{g}_0$ and $\widehat{m}_0$ is that:

$$N^{1/4}\left(\|\widehat{g}_0 - g_0\|_2 + \|\widehat{m}_0 - m_0\|_2\right) \approx 0,$$

which also makes clear that any errors in modeling m_0 can be offset in improvements in modeling g_0, and vice versa. The key point of these quite technical results, however, is that provided conditional uncounfoundedness assumptions hold, causal parameters as well as their confidence intervals can be estimated quite simply by regression of the quantity $\check{Y}$ on $\hat{W}$.

It is important to note in the discussion above the importance of appropriately taking into account overfitting, as if one uses the full dataset to conduct both training and estimation, bias will remain due to overfitting. For this reason, the authors propose using a sample splitting procedure that allows for overfitting to be avoided and, at the same time, gains from using all data to conduct estimation. This procedure, which they call "cross-fitting," consists of splitting the sample into two approximately equal subsamples, and using one of the samples (say "sample A") to estimate $\widehat{g}_0$ and $\widehat{m}_0$ and the other sample ("sample B") to estimate $\widehat{\tau}^{\text{DDML}}$. Then, this procedure can be reversed, with sample B used to estimate the nuisance parameters and sample A used to estimate the $\widehat{\tau}^{\text{DDML}}$. The proposed DML estimate is then just an average of the estimates from each sample A and B. In practice, rather than using two samples, this can be done in K blocks, but the logic of the idea is identical.

This procedure is documented to work well in a range of settings. An illustrative example based on the partial linear model using a simulated example discussed by the authors is plotted in figure 9.3. In panel (a), the naive ML estimate with regularization bias is documented, while in panel (b), the DML estimate is conducted based on the full sample (leading to a small bias due to overfitting). In panel (c), DML is conducted with sample splitting, leading to approximately unbiased normally distributed estimates across many simulations of the particular data generating process considered.

It is worth highlighting a number of points about these methods that we have not discussed yet. The first is the clear relationship of these methods to the Frisch-Waugh-Lovell theorem on partialing out. We know that we can arrive at an unbiased estimate of some regression parameter on a variable X in a model with multiple variables if we "partial out" the other variable from both Y and X, and then regress the residuals on one another. The idea here is similar, but we have to actually learn what the other relevant variables are

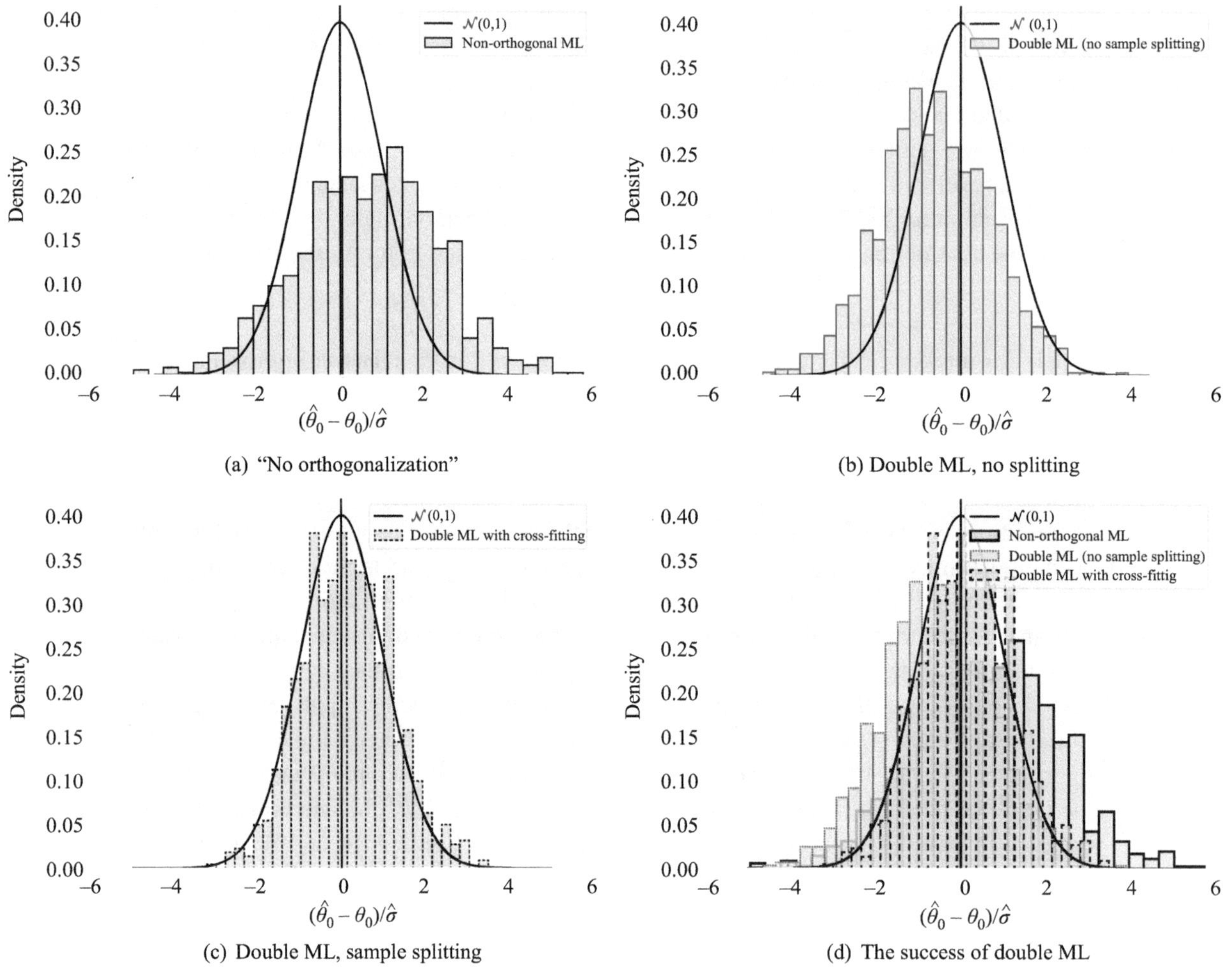

Figure 9.3
Simulated example of double/debiased machine learning.

using some technique from ML. This is key to the idea of applying ML to causality. It will not be enough to naively apply ML to learn some features of the data if we do not account for the fact that our goal here is estimation, not prediction. But, if we build prediction into some rigorous model of causal estimation, such as if we use ML to predict relevant variables for partialing out, these procedures can offer advantages over "standard" techniques.

A second point worth discussing is how this discussion of DDML with a partially linear model relates to post-double selection discussed above in section 9.3.1. Although the logic is similar, there are perhaps two key differences in which DDML varies, which adds richness to the framework of post-double selection. The first, simplest, differences is that in post-selection, controls were selected in two steps and then included in a post-section OLS model, while in DDML residualization was used in two steps, with residualized $\check{Y}$ then regressed on residualized $\hat{W}$. A second, more substantive difference is that DDML permits the use of a very broad class of ML models to learn about relationships between Y and W and control variables X, while post-double-selection is based only on the Lasso. It turns out that this also explains why in post-double-selection no sample splitting is required, while in DDML sample splitting is employed. In the case of post double selection, the Lasso is employed because a specific theoretically justified regularization parameter can be employed to limit overfitting. While this exists in the case of the Lasso, as defined in Belloni et al. (2012), it does not generally exist in other classes of ML models. Thus, in the case of DDML, expansions into other classes of ML models are permitted given the innovation in cross-splitting.

A further benefit of DDML is that it can be readily applied in other settings. Indeed, in their book, Chernozhukov et al. (2024) refer to DDML as "simply a practical meta-recipe." One specific example that is illustrative is to note that this can be pitched explicitly in terms of treatment effects such as the ATT and ATE in highly heterogeneous cases. This is laid out in a very efficient fashion in Chernozhukov et al. (2017). This allows us to consider the even more flexible model:

$$Y = g_0(X, W) + \varepsilon, \qquad \mathbb{E}[\varepsilon|X, W] = 0 \tag{9.14}$$

$$W = m_0(X) + \nu, \qquad \mathbb{E}[\nu|X] = 0. \tag{9.15}$$

The difference between (9.10) and (9.14) is considerable, as in (9.14) treatment effects are allowed to fully interact with covariates X, permitting very rich heterogeneity. In this setting, estimands of interest can be defined as:

$$\tau_{\text{ATE}}^{\text{DDML}} = \mathbb{E}\left[g_0(1,X) - g_0(0,X)\right] \tag{9.16}$$

$$\tau_{\text{ATT}}^{\text{DDML}} = \mathbb{E}\left[g_0(1,X) - g_0(0,X)|W = 1\right]. \tag{9.17}$$

In practice, Chernozhukov et al. (2017) and Chernozhukov et al. (2018) propose the use of doubly robust estimators for these quantities. In the case of the ATE this is:

$$\tau_{\text{DR,ATE}}^{\text{DDML}} = \mathbb{E}\left\{[g_0(1,X) - g_0(0,X)] + \left[\frac{W(Y - g_0(1,X))}{m_0(X)} - \frac{(1-W)(Y - g_0(0,X))}{1 - m_0(X)}\right]\right\}. \tag{9.18}$$

The first term in the parentheses models the treatment effect based on shifts across $g_0(W,X)$, while the second term builds in the model of predictors of treatment, much in the same way as we have observed with the doubly robust estimator discussed previously in section 3.5.2.

Indeed, you can note that this double-robust estimator precisely follows the notation of the augmented inverse propensity score estimator from (3.34), just with an ML-based estimator for the outcome regression and the propensity score!

Chernozhukov et al. (2017) discuss an estimation procedure based on sample splitting which proceeds in precisely the same fashion as before by first splitting the sample to estimate $\widehat{g}_0(1,X), \widehat{g}_0(0,X)$ and $\widehat{m}_0(X)$, and then estimating $\tau^{\text{DDML}}_{\text{DR,ATE}}$ in the remainder of the sample, and estimating across samples to arrive to an estimate $\widehat{\tau}^{\text{DDML}}_{\text{DR,ATE}}$. Estimates for ATTs are also provided, as is a discussion of variance estimation. Once again, provided that the approximations $\widehat{g}_0(W,X)$ and $\widehat{m}_0(X)$ are sufficiently good, these quantities are shown to be consistent and normally distributed.

Code Callout 9.2: Double-Debiased Machine Learning
In code callout 9.2 we will work with an example discussed in Belloni, Chernozhukov, and Hansen (2014b) which revisits a classic question of whether the passage of abortion laws in the US affected crime decades later when affected cohorts of children reached adulthood. We will see how to perform both post-double selection as well as DDML, and see how this improves performance compared to naive methods that do not conduct double selection or double/debiasing.

9.3.3 Difference-in-Differences and Related Settings

The DDML procedure described above has been shown to be extendable to other circumstances, such as difference-in-differences by Chang (2020). The use of double-debiased procedures are focused on cases where relevant covariates need to be learned, and so this application to DD with DDML is relevant for cases where conditional parallel trend assumptions are assumed to hold, as in assumption 4′, but the precise nature of controls is assumed to be unknown. For this reason, the DDML DD estimator is based on the Abadie (2005) estimator as in (4.14); however, it is generated using ML-based models for the propensity score as well as ML-based models for the outcome regression itself. In this sense, it is similar to the double-robust DD methods of Sant'Anna and Zhao (2020) discussed in section 4.2.2, while also leveraging the sample splitting procedures of Chernozhukov et al. (2018).

9.3.3.1 Matrix completion An alternative approach to this problem is provided by Athey et al. (2021). In this case, the challenge is not viewed as an issue of determining covariates, but rather optimally inferring counterfactuals themselves, somewhat in the spirit of synthetic control methods discussed in chapter 4.

They introduce the notion of "matrix completion," which is related to the imputation methods discussed when laying out estimators for difference-in-differences designs and synthetic methods. In general, in the panel data methods we've encountered, such as difference-in-differences and synthetic control and their many extensions, the challenge has been in inferring what would have happened to treated units had they not been treated. We saw this conceptualization of difference-in-differences estimators in section 4.3.3.2. The manner in which the standard estimators we've studied in this setting have "imputed" outcomes varies. For example, in DD, outcomes are "imputed" by using a parallel trends assumption: We assume that treated units would have followed the same trends as untreated units, based on a potentially different baseline level. Or in the case of synthetic control, outcomes are "imputed" by observing the mean of a group of untreated units that were estimated to be similar in pretreatment periods.

However, more generally, in a setting where outcomes $Y_{i,t}$ and treatment exposure $W_{i,t}$ vary over time, other ways could be sought to impute $Y_{i,t}(0)$ for all units i, t for which $W_{i,t} = 1$. This is a point taken up by Athey et al. (2021), who suggest the use of matrix completion methods. Matrix completion is a problem described in machine learning where "missing" elements of a matrix are sought to be filled in efficiently by inferring relationships between observed data in the matrix, and extrapolating these relationships to unobserved units. In the example studied by Athey et al. (2021), the matrix we wish to complete is precisely the matrix consisting of counterfactual outcomes $Y_{i,t}(0)$, which they refer to as $\mathbf{Y}(0)$, or for simplicity $\mathbf{Y}$. They use $\mathcal{O}$ to denote the units which are observed in $\mathbf{Y}(0)$—that is, units for whom $W_{i,t} = 0$. As they note, this matrix may be quite variable, depending on the context studied. Most generically, in a staggered adoption case where units adopt treatment at different points of time, or not at all, $\mathbf{Y}$ can be described as follows:

$$
\boldsymbol{Y}_{N\times T} = \begin{pmatrix}
t_1 & t_2 & t_3 & t_4 & t_5 & \dots & t_T & \\
\checkmark & \checkmark & \checkmark & \checkmark & \checkmark & \dots & \checkmark & \\
\vdots & \vdots & \vdots & \vdots & \vdots & \ddots & \vdots & \big\} \text{ Never Adopters} \\
\checkmark & \checkmark & \checkmark & \checkmark & \checkmark & \dots & \checkmark & \\
\checkmark & \checkmark & \checkmark & \checkmark & \checkmark & \dots & ? & \\
\vdots & \vdots & \vdots & \vdots & \vdots & \ddots & \vdots & \big\} \text{ Late Adopters} \\
\checkmark & \checkmark & \checkmark & \checkmark & \checkmark & \dots & ? & \\
\checkmark & \checkmark & \checkmark & ? & ? & \dots & ? & \\
\vdots & \vdots & \vdots & \vdots & \vdots & \ddots & \vdots & \big\} \text{ Medium Adopters} \\
\checkmark & \checkmark & \checkmark & ? & ? & \dots & ? & \\
\checkmark & ? & ? & ? & ? & \dots & ? & \\
\vdots & \vdots & \vdots & \vdots & \vdots & \ddots & \vdots & \big\} \text{ Early Adopters} \\
\checkmark & ? & ? & ? & ? & \dots & ? &
\end{pmatrix}
$$

Here, cells marked with a check are observed values (units in $\mathcal{O}$), while cells marked with a question mark are not observed, given that units are treated in these periods. Thus, if we could correctly impute values for the cells indicated with a question mark—in effect predicting the unobserved counterfactual—we could compare them with the outcomes actually observed when these units are treated, and calculate the ATT.

Athey et al. (2021) note that the challenge then is in completing the data matrix $\mathbf{Y}$, which they model as:

$$\mathbf{Y} = \mathbf{L}^* + \boldsymbol{\varepsilon}. \tag{9.19}$$

While this setup may feel nonstandard for a staggered adoption design, it is precisely what we are doing in other DD-style imputation estimators such as Borusyak, Jaravel, and Spiess (2024), just using some restrictive models for $\boldsymbol{Y}$ based on unit and time fixed effects (see, e.g., (4.33)). Athey et al.'s proposal is that we can use more flexible model for $\boldsymbol{Y}$, where relationships can be learned from the observed units of this matrix using a regularization-based approach. The key assumption in their method is:

Assumption 15. Independent $\boldsymbol{\varepsilon}$ with σ sub-Gaussian elements
$\boldsymbol{\varepsilon}$ is mean zero and independent of $\mathbf{L}^*$, $\mathbb{E}[\boldsymbol{\varepsilon}|\boldsymbol{L}^*] = \boldsymbol{0}$. Additionally, the elements of $\boldsymbol{\varepsilon}$ are σ-sub-Gaussian and independent of each other.

This is quite a technical assumption, and nests a number of features. In effect, it allows us to view $\mathbf{L}^*$ as some (unknown) systematic component of $\boldsymbol{Y}$, and $\boldsymbol{\varepsilon}$ as independent mean-zero noise, which can be viewed as measurement error. This implies that we can focus our attention on modeling $\mathbf{L}^*$. The second component of the assumption is that elements of $\boldsymbol{\varepsilon}$ are "σ-sub-Gaussian." This is not a term we have come across up to this point, though in effect it places limits on the nature of the noise in this proccss, specifically assuming that the tails of the distributions of elements of $\boldsymbol{\varepsilon}$ decay at least as fast as the tails of a normal distribution.[3]

While the independence of $\boldsymbol{\varepsilon}$ from $\boldsymbol{L}^*$ may feel like a strong assumption, the idea in matrix completion is that we can allow a very rich model for $\boldsymbol{L}^*$ to capture unit-fixed effects and time-fixed effects, but also elements that vary within units over time. Specifically, the proposal of Athey et al. (2021) is to estimate $\boldsymbol{L}^*$ as:

$$\boldsymbol{L}^* = \widehat{\boldsymbol{L}} + \widehat{\Gamma} + \widehat{\Delta}. \tag{9.20}$$

Here $\widehat{\Gamma}$ and $\widehat{\Delta}$ are unit- and time-fixed effects, respectively. The matrix $\widehat{\boldsymbol{L}}$ lets us infer information from potentially other units and time-periods that allow us to make a better predicted counterfactual outcome. This is where quite clear links to ML come in, as we need to choose this matrix $\widehat{\boldsymbol{L}}$ to minimize some loss function, though do not want to fall into a trap of overfitting by drawing in information from many other control units and time periods. In particular, what Athey et al. (2021) suggest is to use the data that are observed for $\boldsymbol{Y}$ to make the best possible prediction for $\boldsymbol{Y}$ by minimizing a loss function as follows:

$$(\widehat{\boldsymbol{L}}, \widehat{\Gamma}, \widehat{\Delta}) = \underset{\boldsymbol{L},\Gamma,\Delta}{\arg\min} \left\{ \frac{1}{|\mathcal{O}|} \|\boldsymbol{P}_{\mathcal{O}}(\boldsymbol{Y} - \boldsymbol{L} - \Gamma - \Delta)\|_F^2 + \lambda \|\boldsymbol{L}\|_* \right\}. \tag{9.21}$$

There are a number of relevant new elements here. One is the use of $|\mathcal{O}|$ in the denominator, which is simply used to define the cardinality of the set $\mathcal{O}$ (the number of untreated units). The matrix $\boldsymbol{P}_{\mathcal{O}}()$ is defined to take the value indicated in parentheses for units in $\mathcal{O}$, or simply 0 for units not contained in $\mathcal{O}$. The terms $||\cdot||_F$ and $||\cdot||_*$ in equation 9.21 are the Fröbenius norm and the Nuclear norm, respectively, which play a similar role to the ℓ^p norms used in regularized regression models, however based on matrices rather than vectors (refer to table 1 of Athey et al. [2021]).

The equation (9.21) provides the estimator that can be used to construct $\boldsymbol{L}^*$ in (9.20). Note here that the selection of $\boldsymbol{L}$ is regularized, much as we saw with the Lasso in section 9.2. We can also note that we are seeking to learn the relevant elements to construct $\boldsymbol{L}$ by evaluating within the observed set $\mathcal{O}$, while regularizing to avoid overfitting. Fixed effects Γ and Δ are always included, and so the regularization is used in the estimation of other (time- and unit-varying) elements $\boldsymbol{L}$. This implies that if a large enough value of λ is included as a penalization parameter, *only* the fixed effects will remain, and this matrix completion method will collapse to an imputation-based difference-in-differences estimator like Borusyak, Jaravel, and Spiess (2024). The regularization term above $\lambda\|\boldsymbol{L}\|_*$ is based on the Nuclear norm, which is important because it is computationally tractable and also ensures a relatively sparse (low-rank) solution for $\boldsymbol{L}$, unlike some other candidate norms considered. As in other regularization-based methods, the value of λ can be found by cross-validation.

In practice, the above equation (9.21) will estimate $\widehat{\boldsymbol{L}}, \widehat{\Gamma}, \widehat{\Delta}$ using untreated observations, but what we actually want is to use these estimates to predict outcomes $Y_{i,t}(0)$ for treated observations. To incorporate this, Athey et al. (2021) propose conducting an interactive procedure in which first an initial proposal for $\widehat{\boldsymbol{L}}$ in (9.21) is found using information on units in $\mathcal{O}$ only. Using the resulting estimate of $\widehat{\boldsymbol{L}}$ (which can be called $\widehat{\boldsymbol{L}}_1$) along with estimated time- and unit-fixed effects, $Y_{i,t}(0)$ can be predicted for treated units. Then, based on predicted $Y_{i,t}(0)$ for treated units along with true values $Y_{i,t}(0)$ among untreated units, a new proposal of $\widehat{\boldsymbol{L}}$ can be estimated ($\widehat{\boldsymbol{L}}_2$), which is now augmented to consider untreated units. This procedure continues iteratively up until the point that the estimated quantity $\widehat{\boldsymbol{L}}_{r+1} = \widehat{\boldsymbol{L}}_r$ where r simply refers to the iteration number.[4] This iterative process is ingenious because it allows for relationships between treated units to also flow into the prediction of counterfactuals for treated units.

A key result of Athey et al. (2021) is that under a number of conditions, errors in modeling $\widehat{\boldsymbol{L}}$ will converge to zero, and hence predicted outcomes will do a good job in modeling counterfactuals provided that N and T grow, provided that N is at least as large as T, and provided that there is a sufficiently large group of control units off of which to model counterfactuals (formal statements are provided in their theorem 2). While these results are shown for quite restrictive models, in practice Athey et al. (2021) show that these methods perform well—and better than synthetic control and DD procedures—in terms of prediction errors when working with real data and assuming placebo treatment dates. This is particularly so in cases of staggered adoption designs.

Code Callout 9.3: Matrix Completion and Other Imputation Methods
In code callout 9.3 we will work with an example discussed in Kumar and Liang (2024) that studies the impact of easier access to credit on labor market outcomes. We will examine the use of matrix completion methods and see how this compares to imputation-based DD estimators discussed in chapter 4.

9.3.4 ML with Instrumental Variables

There are a number of settings in which ML has been incorporated into routines based on instrumental variables. While related to the procedures laid out above that seek to learn about relevant covariates, there are also new ways that ML can be of use with IV, given that the *first stage* in IV is a prediction problem well suited to ML methods.

9.3.4.1 Selecting instruments Relatively early work integrating ML methods into the econometric toolbox was laid out in Belloni et al. (2012). There, Belloni et al. (2012) propose that if multiple potential instruments exist, selection of instruments using Lasso or post Lasso can result in IV estimates that are consistent and asymptotically efficient. Conceptually, this idea makes sense, because as noted in section 5.2.4.2, bias exists in models estimated via 2SLS precisely because of overfitting, and regularized models explicitly seek to guard against overfitting.

The setting of Belloni et al. (2012) is one in which many instruments Z_i exist, and the independence assumption is assumed to hold. While it may seem unlikely for such settings to be observed, there are a number of well-known examples where many IVs are employed. This includes judge fixed-effect designs where random assignment to judges of differing severity is used to instrument the effects of incarceration (Frandsen, Lefgren, and Leslie 2023), local fluctuations in weather which affect individual behavior (Gilchrist and Sands 2016), and the classic quarter of birth design from Angrist and Krueger (1991) where quarter of birth interacted with year and state of birth was proposed as an IV for educational attainment. The idea of Belloni et al. (2012) is that in this case, a Lasso can be used for selecting relevant variables in the first stage, and based on this first stage, a predicted quantity $\widehat{D}$ used in a second stage. Belloni et al. (2012) show that if either Lasso or Post Lasso is used to select variables and calculate $\widehat{D}$, provided that the setting is indeed sparse, then the resulting IV estimate based on this quantity:

$$\tau_{\text{IV}}^{2\text{SLS}} = \mathbb{E}[\widehat{D}_i D_i]^{-1}\mathbb{E}[\widehat{D}_i y_i]$$

is consistent and asymptotically as efficient as using the (unknown) true expectation of D_i based on all relevant instruments Z_i. Belloni et al. (2012) suggest the use of the data-driven tuning parameter for λ in the Lasso discussed in section 9.2.1.1, which allows for valid inference to be conducted as discussed in their theorem 3.

Chernozhukov, Hansen, and Spindler (2015) show extensions into cases where there are both multiple IVs *and* multiple exogenous controls. In this case they suggest that a post-Lasso procedure can be implemented in which Lasso is used to select relevant controls and instruments for endogenous (treatment) variables of interest, and these variables are then used to generate the predicted variable for use in IV. After this, a Lasso is used to select relevant exogenous regressors for inclusion if they are related to the outcome of interest, or the instrumented endogenous variable. A precise definition of this procedure is available in Chernozhukov, Hansen, and Spindler (2015, Algorithm 1).[5]

9.3.4.2 Selecting controls An alternative setting in which we may seek to combine ML methods with IV is in selecting exogenous controls when we only believe that exogeneity holds *conditional* on some larger set of controls. In particular, this is the case if we believe an IV may exist for which conditional independence holds (assumption 6′), but at the same time it is not clear what functional form the relationship between covariates X and outcomes Y takes, as well as what functional form the relationship between X and Z takes. In cases such as this, procedures from double/debiased machine learning can be employed. As a matter of fact, these results are developed by Chernozhukov et al. (2018) alongside the theory for the case of conditional unconfoundedness in the setting of ATE/ATT or in partially linear models, as laid out in section 9.3.2.

In much the same way as when we consider the estimation of the ATE or ATT, we can write this framework following Chernozhukov et al. (2018) as follows:

$$\begin{aligned} Y &= \mu_0(Z,X) + \upsilon \qquad & \mathbb{E}[\upsilon|X,Z] &= 0 \\ D &= m_0(Z,X) + \nu \qquad & \mathbb{E}[\nu|X,Z] &= 0 \\ Z &= p_0(X) + \zeta \qquad & \mathbb{E}[\zeta|X] &= 0. \end{aligned}$$

Here, outcomes Y depend flexibly upon a binary instrument Z and potentially high-dimensional covariates X. Similarly, treatment adoption D depends upon Z and X. Assume we are in a setting where we view Z as a valid instrument for the treatment variable D. This then implies that our LATE can be written as follows:

$$\tau_{\text{LATE}}^{\text{DDML}} = \frac{\mathbb{E}[\mu_0(1,X)] - \mathbb{E}[\mu_0(0,X)]}{\mathbb{E}[m_0(1,X)] - \mathbb{E}[m_0(0,X)]}. \tag{9.22}$$

Chernozhukov et al. (2018) propose that this LATE can be estimated as follows:

$$\tau_{\text{DR,LATE}}^{\text{DDML}} = \frac{\mathbb{E}\left\{[\mu_0(1,X) - \mu_0(0,X)] + \left[\frac{Z(Y-\mu_0(1,X))}{m_0(X)} - \frac{(1-Z)(Y-\mu_0(0,X))}{1-m_0(X)}\right]\right\}}{\mathbb{E}\left\{[m_0(1,X) - m_0(0,X)] + \left[\frac{Z(D-m_0(1,X))}{m_0(X)} - \frac{(1-Z)(D-m_0(0,X))}{1-m_0(X)}\right]\right\}}. \tag{9.23}$$

While this quantity looks quite elaborate, the key thing to note is that we are simply estimating a version of the double-robust ATE from (9.18) in both the numerator and the denominator. The numerator considers the reduced form, while the denominator considers the first stage. Chernozhukov et al. (2018) define the formal properties of this estimator as well as the conditions under which estimates of this quantity in (9.23) are consistent (for a formal definition, refer to their theorem 5.2).

A nice practical exploration of these themes is provided by Angrist and Frandsen (2022), and examples are also documented in Chernozhukov et al.'s original work. Angrist and Frandsen (2022) consider the selection of IVs in simulated data based on the well-known quarter of birth application of Angrist and Krueger (1991). They caution, however, that in this example, 2SLS estimation with a post-Lasso first stage does not necessarily outperform other estimation methods, pointing to potential breakdowns in sparsity assumptions with this many instrument case. Such an example highlights the importance of being clear on assumptions: While methods such as those discussed here can indeed work very well if assumptions are met and judicious choices are made (Fuhr, Berens, and Papies 2024), it is very important to be clear on these assumptions and consider cases why they may not be met.

9.4 Machine Learning and Causality: Understanding Heterogeneity

In the previously considered examples, we have seen how we can combine ML techniques and principles with the types of contexts we have studied in previous chapters of this book to assist us in finding average treatment effects. But this can also be used more generally to seek to understand the underlying heterogeneity in these treatment effects. A major area where learning-based approaches are used in microeconometric implementations is in "learning" about heterogeneous treatment effects with tools we have begun to discuss above.

Methods that seek to describe hetereogeneity in treatment effects generally start with the conditional average treatment effect (CATE) as a basic building block. The CATE, which we first defined in (1.9) as $\tau(x) \equiv \mathbb{E}[Y_i(1) - Y_i(0)|X_i = x]$, allows for heterogeneity over all dimensions of some covariate space. This implies that we view treatment effects as potentially varying in any way within the space of X_i, for example, permitting treatment effects to move in complex nonlinear ways across single variables, and to depend interactively on all covariates. Up to this point, when we've been working with the CATE we have generally used this implicitly to map conditional exogeneity assumptions into more aggregated average treatment effects—for example, as in (3.8) and (3.11). However, here we will explore more advanced techniques that have the explicit goal of estimating or describing CATEs themselves, which, it turns out, is a problem well-suited to ML-based techniques.

9.4.1 Causal Trees and Causal Forests

9.4.1.1 Causal trees An approach based on the tree logic we discussed in section 9.2.2 was developed in Athey and Imbens (2016). This paper seeks to consider the estimation of heterogeneous treatment effects assuming conditional unconfoundedness, as per assumption

2′. The interest of these methods is to estimate a series of CATEs based on partitions of the covariate space X, assuming that treatment effects are constant within partitions of X. You may note that this is similar to what a regression tree seeks to do, but here rather than seeking to predict a constant $\widehat{y}$ in leaves of the tree, the goal is to actually estimate a constant treatment effect in each leaf.

In effect, the goal of causal trees is to seek to group data in the most efficient way possible to estimate a series of parameters $\tau(x)$ that refer to the treatment effect in each leaf of the tree. If we consider a partition of data written as $L(x)$, which divides data into separate leaves L, we can define our treatment effects of interest as follows:

$$\widehat{\mu}(w,x) \equiv \frac{1}{\#(i: W_i = w, X_i \in L)} \sum_{i:W_i=w,X_i\in L} Y_i$$

$$\widehat{\tau}^{\text{causal tree}}_{\text{CATE}}(x) \equiv \widehat{\mu}(1,x) - \widehat{\mu}(0,x). \tag{9.24}$$

We can see here that the goal of this procedure is then one of building a tree to find the leaves L, and then estimate treatment effects as in (9.24). In the above, the notation $\#(\cdot)$ refers to the number of observations in a specific group, and hence $\#(i: W_i = 1, X_i \in L)$ simply refers to the number of treated observations in a specific leaf L.

The challenge of building the causal tree is in determining how to effectively split the data. While many of the mechanics of regression trees can be adopted in this procedure, there are also a number of substantive variations required to move from regression trees to causal trees. Perhaps the principal innovation required owes to the fact that regression trees are simply seeking to estimate $\widehat{Y}_i$, and underlying data Y_i is observed for each unit i. However, in the case of causal trees, the goal is to estimate $\widehat{\tau}_i$, a treatment effect, and the underlying treatment effect τ_i is not observed for each unit i. This is important, because in (9.9), we use data on Y_i to inform our splits of the regression tree, and clearly we cannot do the same thing with τ_i.

This requires some work, and Athey and Imbens (2016) propose an alternative criteria for assessing potential nodes of our trees: We should split data such that the expected mean squared error for treatment effects is minimized. Athey and Imbens (2016) show that we can write the expected mean squared error for some particular split of the data as follows:

$$EMSE = \mathbb{E}[\mathbb{V}(\widehat{\tau}^2(X_i))] - \mathbb{E}[\tau^2(X_i)], \tag{9.25}$$

where $\mathbb{V}(\widehat{\tau}^2(X_i))$ refers to the variance of the estimator and $\mathbb{E}[\cdot]$ refers to the expectation over all levels of X_i. The proposed procedure of Athey and Imbens (2016) consists of estimating this expected mean squared error term based on real data and selecting the split of data that minimizes this quantity. Athey and Imbens (2016) discuss how each term of (9.25) can be estimated. The $\tau^2(X_i)$ term can be estimated off of the underlying quantities resulting from (9.24) based on a specific data split, while they propose a variance term that accounts for within-leaf variance of outcomes and depends on the size of the estimation sample, and inversely on the proportion of treated and control units in each leaf, which guards against small samples of treated and control units in each resulting leaf of the tree.

A second key innovation of the causal tree algorithm is used to ensure that inference on estimated parameters can be conducted appropriately, and this is to use what they refer to as "honest" estimation. The process of honest estimation consists of randomly splitting the data into two equal parts. The first part is used as a training set of data to generate the partition of the tree based on treatment effect heterogeneity, and then the actual estimate of treatment effects based on this partition will be conducted with a the remaining half of the data (the estimation set). In practice, the causal tree algorithm consists of using the training data to determine nodes in data, at each step selecting nodes that lead to minimum values for the quantity in (9.25). Then, also using the training data, a cross-validation procedure can be used to prune the tree to a level that minimizes the overall estimated mean squared error. Finally, once this tree is in hand, the estimation sample is used, and treatment effects estimated based on the leaves defined by the training sample, and the quantity (9.24).

Athey and Imbens (2016) show that while there will be an efficiency loss in using only half of the data to estimate treatment effects following (9.24), the use of independent samples to train the tree and estimate parameters means that treatment effects will be unbiased in each leaf. Thus, the cost of increased variance comes at improvements in bias, and these methods thus perform relatively well in terms mean squared errors compared to a number of other alternatives considered.

9.4.1.2 Causal forests One drawback of the causal tree procedure is that it is somewhat noisy. Because data are randomly split into training and estimation samples, different random splits will result in different trees, and hence highlight different elements of heterogeneity in treatment effects. While both ways are valid ways to understand heterogeneity of treatment effects based on the specific training sample used, such variability may not be desired.

A logical way to avoid this is to move from trees to forests. Wager and Athey (2018) describe a process of causal forests that relate to causal trees in a way analogous to the relationship between regression trees and regression forests. Because this will be based on the estimation and averaging on many causal trees, this will also lead to a smoother function $\tau(x)$. The idea of causal forests is to simply estimate many causal trees, where each causal tree results in an estimate following (9.24). This can thus be viewed as an ensemble method, in which the ensemble consists of B such trees. If the resulting causal tree estimate for each tree in the ensemble is written as $\widehat{\tau}_{b,\text{CATE}}^{\text{causal tree}}(x)$, the causal forest estimator can be written as:

$$\widehat{\tau}_{\text{CATE}(x)}^{\text{causal forest}} \equiv \frac{1}{B}\sum_{b=1}^{B}\widehat{\tau}_{b,\text{CATE}}^{\text{causal tree}}(x). \tag{9.26}$$

Wager and Athey (2018) additionally demonstrate asymptotic normality of these causal forest estimators, implying that both estimation and inference can be conducted.

Code Callout 9.4: Causal Trees with an RCT
To see an example of causal forests in action, we will work with data from a large experiment conducted by Oreopoulos (2011). Here, using randomized characteristics on CVs and job call-back rates, Oreopoulos (2011) examines the impact of an individual's immigration status (native vs. immigrant) in determining application success. We use these data and consider heterogeneity in treatment effects based on a causal forest.

9.4.2 Meta-Learners

An alternative take on the challenge of estimating heterogeneous treatment effects and learning about CATEs is provided by a class of procedures known as meta-learners. Meta-learners seek to proceed in two steps. First, some sort of ML-based technique is employed to estimate conditional expectation functions in a rich way, and second, treatment effects are estimated as the difference between conditional expectation functions (CEFs) for treated units and untreated units, which are simply $\mathbb{E}[Y_i|X_i=x]$. In this way, we can zoom in on specific CATEs by considering differences in CEFs at specific values of X_i. This is clearly a problem well suited to ML, because the first step of approximating CEFs is a prediction problem. This first step is generally done with some of the ML tools we have explored in this chapter, or even prediction methods like simple regression functions, and is referred to as the base learner.

We can define a meta-learner as conditional expectation function, or "response function":

$$\mu(x, w) = \mathbb{E}[Y_i|X=x, W=w]. \tag{9.27}$$

This simply states that we will seek to model outcomes Y_i based on covariates X_i as well as treatment W_i. These can be modeled with a range of supervised learning methods such as regression trees, boosting, or neural nets. Different meta-learning algorithms vary somewhat in how they seek to estimate these functions, but perhaps the most simple is the S-learner, which estimates a single response function, resulting in a CATE estimator of the following type:

$$\widehat{\tau}^{\text{S-learner}}_{\text{CATE}(x)} = \widehat{\mu}(x, 1) - \widehat{\mu}(x, 0). \tag{9.28}$$

The S-learner is a very simple meta-learner, and in general we can do better than this. For one thing, as the base learners that generate (9.27) will likely use regularization, there is nothing that even ensures that W will enter $\mu(x, w)$, implying that all treatment effects in (9.28) would be zero.

One solution to this is to use a separate response function estimated for treated and untreated units, giving rise to the T-learner (Künzel et al. 2019). This simply estimates separate response function as:

$$\mu_0(x) = \mathbb{E}[Y_i|X_i = x, W_i = 0] \quad \text{and} \quad \mu_1(x) = \mathbb{E}[Y_i|X_i = x, W_i = 1]. \tag{9.29}$$

which has the effect of forcing treatment to explicitly enter the base learners by separately estimating a CEF for each group. A similar definition of CATEs can then be laid out as above, however now based on these separate response functions:

$$\widehat{\tau}^{\text{T-learner}}_{\text{CATE}(x)} = \widehat{\mu}_1(x) - \widehat{\mu}_0(x). \tag{9.30}$$

These CATE estimates are quite clear to see, and it is apparent in both cases that the final estimation step will depend on the quality of these response functions, which are, in effect nuisance parameters. What we actually care about is the function $\tau(X)$, but to estimate this we are estimating the underlying response function. For this reason, additional refinements have been proposed that seek to further optimize the resulting function $\tau(X)$ itself. These include the X-learner (or cross-learner) of Künzel et al. (2019), the R-learner (residualised learner) of Nie and Wager (2020), and the DR-learner (double-robust learner); see, for example, E. H. Kennedy (2023).

While full details can be found in the cited studies, these each have specific strengths. The X-learner of Künzel et al. (2019) seeks to learn about relationships between covariates and outcomes using separate functions for treated and control units as in the T-learner, but by also learning across groups, for example by accounting for covariate relationships in untreated units when predicting counterfacts for treated units. This is shown to be particularly useful when the size of each group is very different, especially when one group is small. The R-learner seeks to estimate flexible models of the propensity score and CEFs to residualize the effect of covariates from treatment and outcomes, and then finds treatment effects by estimating regression-based models based on these two residualized functions. The DR learner also models a propensity score as well as separate outcome regressions for treated and untreated units, and estimates treatment effects based on a doubly robust procedure.

As is the case of causal trees and causal forests, the meta-learners laid out above are based on unconfoundedness assumptions. The literature on meta-learners generally focuses on the expected mean squared error of resulting estimates, see for example the discussion of X-learners in Künzel et al. (2019) and more general discussion in Foster and Syrgkanis (2023). The flexibility of the meta-learner to incorporate a wide range of base-learners means that it is tricky to provide general results, though a number of recent papers have laid out some general procedures for inference in a range of settings (see, e.g., Jin, Ren, and Candès [2023]; Chernozhukov et al. [2025]).

9.5 Active Areas of Work and Other Themes

Recent developments in machine learning and artificial intelligence more generally mean that this area is actively growing and providing a full scope is well beyond the limits of a single chapter or single book. This chapter has focused on points particularly relevant for causal inference and machine learning, but even this area is growing incredibly rapidly. In closing, it is useful to note a number of areas within this space are being actively developed, and which may be of relevance, along with some key references should further details be sought.

Learning about optimal policies Building on work considering rich heterogeneous treatment effects is work that seeks to consider the assignment of policies or treatments themselves. Such policy learning or "prediction policy problems" (Kleinberg et al. 2015) asks about the optimal assignment of policies in settings where resource constraints imply that not all potentially productive uses of treatment can be assigned (Athey and Wager 2021), and as such the consideration of how to optimally assign treatments to individuals is important. There are a range of papers that take forward this challenge, including by Kitagawa and Tetenov (2018), who consider determining optimal treatment assignments by "empirical welfare maximisation," which seeks to find the treatment assignment set that maximizes total gains of a policy based on rich estimates of individual's propensity scores and predicted outcomes under cases where they are treated and untreated. This work is based on binary treatment and assumes exogenous treatment assignments (i.e., RCTs), and Athey and Wager (2021) extend these methods to consider the more general setting of potentially continuous treatments and endogenous treatment assignments, which require an IV. Both of these papers, and the broader literature on considering personalized returns to treatment gain considerably from ML-based methods given their need to predict individual-level policy returns.

Machine learning and novel data Another area that takes advantage of tools from ML and is central in certain areas of empirical work but not empirical specifications per se is the use of ML tools to generate data itself. A clear example of this is the use of both supervised and unsupervised machine learning tools in papers that seek to classify text into usable data. Just a few examples of this include measurements of slant in newspapers, analyzing sentiment from social media or search engines, mining personal essays to capture individual beliefs and attitudes, processing images to understand messages in culture, and seeking to understand communication in policy and financial communications. This draws on a very large area of work in natural language processing, which has been developed across other fields including in linguistics and computer science, and a very nice overview of key themes in this area is available in the survey of Gentzkow, Kelly, and Taddy (2019). More generally the use of deep neural networks and deep learning has been shown to have a multitude of uses in economics for work with digitization of data, linkages of records, and other classification of text and image at a scale that was previously infeasible (see, e.g., the recent survey of Dell [2024]).

Generative artificial intelligence Finally, it is worth noting that remarkable expansions in generative artificial intelligence tools including large language models (LLMs) has opened doors that are just starting to be explored. This is an area in which substantial advances are likely to be made, with early discussions highlighting the use of such AI tools in the generation of research hypotheses (Ludwig and Mullainathan 2023) as well as in generally aiding in the productivity of research and the automation of certain tasks (Korinek 2023). Of course, this area is a question of considerable importance more generally in the way labor markets are structured and the way AI is harnessed in economies, though such questions escape the scope of this book.

Historical Context and Selected Further Reading

In examining applied papers in economics at present, it is clear that ML is now a very much accepted and applied tool that is incorporated in researcher's tool kits. However, even ten years before the publication of this book, it was arguably not the majority view that ML clearly "fit in" to the econometrics canon. For this reason, many early texts and overview chapters focused on laying out how and why ML could be more widely adopted in econometric applications, and can be viewed as early proponents of a usefulness that is now taken as given today. Among other review papers in this line, Athey (2018) and Mullainathan and Spiess (2017) provide relevant reading.

However, the intellectual history of machine learning is considerably older, with roots in computer science, statistics, and optimization. Seminal work on neural networks, decision trees, and ensemble methods dates back several decades, and many of the algorithms now used, or updated for use, in empirical economics were originally developed in contexts far removed from causal inference or economic modeling. For readers interested in this broader history, standard ML texts such as Hastie, Tibshirani, and Friedman (2017) and Murphy (2012) provide useful technical and conceptual background.

Texts are now becoming available that bridge machine learning and econometrics, with the key reference being Chernozhukov et al. (2024). Some of the deeper formal details of ML algorithms discussed in section 9.2 are also available in Hansen's recently published econometrics textbook (Bruce Hansen 2022).

Exercises

1. In this question we will work with regularized regression models such as the Lasso, using data from Fryer and Levitt (2013). In their paper they study the emergence of test score gaps by race in the US, noting that differences are very small early in life (and null conditional on controls) but grow over time. The data `Fryer_Levitt_2013.csv` includes realizations of test scores from 30,002 black and white children along with a large number (78) of demographic controls.
   (a) Estimate a simple OLS regression where mental function aged eight to twelve months (`std_iq_9months`) is regressed on an indicator of a child's race, and repeat this analysis with mental function at the age of two (`std_iq_2years`).
   (b) How do these estimates vary if you now estimate a Lasso in which the full set of seventy-eight covariates are considered as potential controls?
   (c) Document, perhaps graphically, how the number of included features varies as the tuning parameter λ in the lasso varies.
   (d) Implement a post-double selection procedure in which selected variables are included if they are found to be relevant in predicting test scores, or vary substantially by race. Does this change the patterns documented in part (b) above?
   (e) How do results vary if rather than using a Lasso for estimation, ridge regression or elastic net are used?
2. To examine a case of selection of IVs, we will consider the study of Gilchrist and Sands (2016), who study the impact of social spillovers on the likelihood that individuals view films at the cinema. Specifically, they propose to instrument the intensity of movie consumption in an individual's local area with weather shocks selected from among fifty-two potential weather instruments. These data are available as `Gilchrist_Sands_2016.csv`. In order to respond to this question, you will need to read notes to Tables in Gilchrist and Sands (2016). There are many variables in the provided csv, and further information can be found in the file Gilchrist_Sands_2016.txt on the book website.
   (a) Seek to replicate the results from table 1 of Gilchrist and Sands (2016) in which the number of instruments in the first stage is limited to specific quantities, where instruments are selected by Lasso. Do selected instruments pass conventional weak instrument tests?
   (b) Estimate results from table 2, where selected instruments are used in a 2SLS strategy in which viewership in later weekends is regressed on opening day viewership instrumented by weather shocks.

(c) How do the results you document in part (b) vary by the quantity of instruments selected?

(d) Document the results using the procedures discussed in Belloni et al. (2012), where the Lasso is estimated with a theoretically driven plug-in parameter.

3. In this question we will explore the use of causal forests and other methods to explore the heterogeneity of treatment effects. We will do this with data from Riley (2024), who studies the impact of cash transfer receipts issued in either cash or a digital account. Data from this paper are available as `Riley_2024.csv`.

(a) Open these data and seek to estimate the main model where business earnings (`earn_business`) is regressed on indicators of whether the individual is granted access to a mobile account (`treatment2`) or has their loan distributed into a mobile account (`treatment3`).

(b) Seek to implement a random forest where the objective is simply to describe heterogeneity in savings at baseline (`much_saved_baseline`), using a range of covariates available in the data.

(c) Now seek to estimate a causal forest where similar characteristics used in part (b) are used to estimate heterogeneity in treatment effects themselves. For this, consider the treatment of mobile disbursement only, and document the variation in resulting treatment effects.

(d) Consider instead now the estimation of treatment effects via meta-learners. Implement the T-learner and S-learner "by hand" where you use a random forest to estimate the underlying response functions $\widehat{\mu}(x, D)$ or $\widehat{\mu}_D(x)$ for $D \in \{0, 1\}$. Document the CATE resulting from such procedures for a number of characteristics x.

(e) If such libraries are available for the computer language you are using, document how your procedures in part (d) compare to libraries that automate these procedures.

4. In this exercise, we will explore how different variable selection strategies affect the estimation of a treatment effect, and how the double-debiased machine learning (DDML) approach can help address these challenges. To do this, simulate a dataset with $N =$ 1,000 observations and $k = 100$ covariates $X = (X_1, \ldots, X_{100})$, where each $X_j \sim \mathcal{N}(0, 1)$ independently. Partition these covariates as follows: (1) S_T: 10 covariates strongly predictive of treatment but weakly related to the outcome; (2) S_Y: 10 covariates strongly predictive of outcome but weakly related to treatment; (3) S_{TY}: 10 covariates strongly predictive of both treatment and outcome; and (4) S_0: the remaining 70 covariates, which are unrelated to either treatment or outcome (pure noise).

Define the binary treatment W_i using a logistic model:

$$\Pr(W_i = 1 \mid X_i) = \Lambda\left(X_i'\beta_W\right),$$

where $\Lambda(z) = \frac{1}{1+e^{-z}}$ is the logistic function, and β_W is a sparse coefficient vector such that $\beta_{Wj} = 1$ for $j \in S_T$, $\beta_{Wj} = 1$ for $j \in S_{TY}$, $\beta_{Wj} = 0.1$ for $j \in S_Y$, and $\beta_{Wj} = 0$ otherwise. Finally, define the outcome as:

$$Y_i = \tau W_i + X_i' \beta_Y + \varepsilon_i, \quad \varepsilon_i \sim \mathcal{N}(0, 1),$$

where $\tau = 1$ and β_Y is also sparse and structured as: $\beta_{Yj} = 1$ for $j \in S_Y$, $\beta_{Yj} = 1$ for $j \in S_{TY}$, $\beta_{Yj} = 0.1$ for $j \in S_T$, and $\beta_{Yj} = 0$ otherwise.

(a) Use Lasso to select covariates that predict W. Then estimate τ by regressing Y on W and the selected covariates. How does this procedure perform in terms of the resulting estimated treatment effect?

(b) Now use Lasso to select covariates that predict Y. Estimate τ by regressing Y on W and the selected covariates. Compare the results to part (a).

(c) Estimate τ using OLS on Y with W and the combined set of selected covariates. Are these results surprising?

(d) Implement a "manual" version of the DDML procedure using twofold sample splitting. Namely, split the sample into two equal halves, in each fold, use Lasso on the other fold to predict W and Y. Obtain residuals $\hat{W}_i$ and $\hat{Y}_i$ from the prediction models, and estimate τ using OLS of residualized Y on residualized W. Does this perform as we may expect?

(e) Confirm that using some official version of DDML libraries results in a broadly similar result to that from part (d) for τ. Compare the estimate and confidence intervals from this approach to a model in which you include all of the one hundred covariates, and comment on your results.

Notes

Chapter 1

1. This discussion is indeed long-standing in the causal literature. For example, in 1975 Rubin noted that such questions are not generically defined and need further restrictions to logically fit in a causal framework:

> Any question that cannot be formulated in the above framework has no "causal" answer. For example, questions of the causal effect of sex or race as sometimes discussed are totally ambiguous with respect to what the treatment and its time of initiation mean. Do we mean at birth we "dye" the child's skin a different color, or at conception we "change" all Y chromosomes to be X chromosomes? The point is that we need well-defined treatments and times at which we are to initiate them before we can discuss their causal effects.
>
> Rubin (1975)

However, around ten years later, it is clear that this view suggests that the feasibility of the question simply requires some precise reformulation as in audit studies:

> which has many possible versions ranging from some hypothetical "at conception X to Y chromosome treatment" to replacing an "F" with an "M" on a job application form.
>
> Rubin (1986)

2. You may note that there is a slight abuse of notation here in that previously we have defined potential outcomes directly in terms of an individual's treatment status, i.e., we have already imposed that SUTVA holds. In Chapter 8 we will relax our definition of potential outcomes to also, possibly, depend upon the treatment status of other units.

3. These questions are far from simply academic endeavors. You may be familiar with the challenges and critiques that arose during the so called worm wars (see, e.g., Davey et al. 2015; Hicks, Kremer, and Miguel 2015). This was an example where SUTVA and particular violations of SUTVA, along with the consistent estimation of impacts of treatments, reached the popular press; see, for example, https://www.theguardian.com/global-development-professionals-network/2015/aug/05/explainer-wormwars-deworming-science-kenya.

4. Even more formally, if we use $\Pr_\tau$ to denote a family of probability distributions indexed by a parameter τ where τ represents the causal effect of interest, the parameter τ is identified if $\Pr_{\tau_1} = \Pr_{\tau_2} \Rightarrow \tau_1 = \tau_2$, which means that different values of the causal effect would generate different probability distributions of observable data, allowing us to distinguish between them given sufficient data.

5. References to identification are now ubiquitous in economic research. Currie, Kleven, and Zwiers (2020) note that only 4% of working papers published in the National Bureau of Economic Research (NBER) series in 1980 mentioned the word "identification," compared to around 50% today. A similar proportion of papers published in *The American Economic Review*, *The Quarterly Journal of Economics*, *The Review of Economic Studies*, *Econometrica*, and *The Journal of Political Economy* include references to identification.

Chapter 2

1. This comes from the properties of OLS regression.

2. For the sake of completion, the notation $\binom{N}{K}$ refers to "N choose K," or the number of ways that K units can be chosen from N units. The explicit formula for calculating $\binom{N}{K}$ is $\left({}^{N}_{K=}\frac{N!}{K!\times(N-K)!}\right)$, where $J!$ refers to $J \times (J-1) \times \cdots \times 1$.

3. Even with a quite moderate number of observations, the total number of possible combinations grows very quickly. For example, while 10 units with 5 randomly assigned treatments gives a reasonably manageable $\binom{10}{5} = 252$ possible combinations, this grows quickly, with 20 units and 10 treatments resulting in $\binom{20}{10} = 184,756$ possible combinations, and 30 units and 15 treatments a massive $\binom{30}{15}$=155,117,520 possible combinations.

4. This can be shown noting that with some algebra, the denominator in $\widehat{\mathbb{V}(\hat{\tau}_{\text{ATE}})}$ can be written as $= \frac{N_T \cdot N_C}{N}$, which becomes $\frac{N}{N_T N_C}$ when taken to the numerator, which can be written as $\frac{1}{N_C} + \frac{1}{N_T}$ given that $N = N_T + N_C$.

5. To see why effect heterogeneity implies heteroscedsaticity, note that from 2.7:

$$Y_i = \mu(0) + [\mu(1) - \mu(0)]W_i + [\varepsilon_i(0) + (\varepsilon_i(1) - \varepsilon_i(0))W_i].$$

Noting that $\varepsilon_i(1) = Y_i(1) - \mu(1)$ and $\varepsilon_i(0) = Y_i(0) - \mu(0)$, this can be rewritten as:

$$Y_i = \mu(0) + [\mu(1) - \mu(0)]W_i + \{Y_i(0) - \mu(0) + [(Y_i(1) - Y_i(0)) + (\mu(1) - \mu(0))]W_i\},$$

where the presence of $(Y_i(1) - Y_i(0))W_i$ in the error term implies that if $(Y_i(1) - Y_i(0))$ is not constant across i, the variance will differ when $W_i = 0$ and $W_i = 1$.

6. Several heteroscedasticity-consistent (HC) variance estimators exist to address small-sample bias, leading to variants of estimators referred to as HC0, HC1, HC2, and HC3 (among others). In brief, HC0 is the original White estimator, which is known to be biased downward in small samples. HC1 applies a small sample correction to variance estimates equivalent to $\frac{N}{N-1}$ to HC0. HC2 and HC3 estimators seek to adjust for observations that have particularly small variances with an observation-specific adjustment factor. The Bell-McCaffrey approach further refines these by implementing a "bias-reduced linearization" technique. Their recommended degrees-of-freedom adjustment is particularly useful when either treatment or control groups have few observations, addressing the Behrens-Fisher problem noted in the main text.

7. For completion, standard errors simply correspond to the square root of the variance estimate, while confidence intervals can be defined as:

$$CI^{95\%} = \left(\hat{\tau} - t_{0.975}^{N-2} \times \sqrt{\widehat{\mathbb{V}(\hat{\tau}_{\text{ATE}})}}, \hat{\tau} + t_{0.975}^{N-2} \times \sqrt{\widehat{\mathbb{V}(\hat{\tau}_{\text{ATE}})}}\right),$$

where $t_{0.975}^{N-2}$ is the 97.5th quantile of the t-distribution with $N - 2$ degrees of freedom.

8. Specifically, this special case refers to circumstances where covariates are all binary, and the model is written such that covariates are fully interacted to partition the population in groups. In this case, the conditional regression estimate of $\hat{\tau}_{\text{ATE}}$ is unbiased. For further discussion, see, for example, Athey and Imbens (2017, §5.2).

9. The logic of this is that standard errors based on clusters assume that treatment assignment is independent across clusters. However, if paired randomization occurs at the cluster level, the fact that one cluster receives treatment means that the other cluster will not receive treatment, and as such, treatment will be negatively correlated across clusters. However, if clustering occurs at the level of pairs, this accounts for this negative correlation, as treatment will be only correlated within pairs, not between pairs.

10. There has been quite interesting debate related to these discussions, which often focus on the idea that RCTs should be seen as a "gold standard." This has led to a range of critiques and responses; see, for example, the response from Imbens (2010) to the arguments raised in Deaton (2009) and the series of comments by Basu (2018), Imbens (2018), Drèze (2018), and Cook (2018) (among many others) in the same issue in which Deaton and Cartwright (2018) was published, both supporting and pushing back against some of the arguments raised by Deaton and Cartwright (2018).

Chapter 3

1. In the interests of completion, the law of iterated expectations states that for any two random variables Y and X, the expectation of Y can be written as $\mathbb{E}[Y] = \mathbb{E}_X[\mathbb{E}[Y|X]]$. In the context of (3.9), this means that

$$\mathbb{E}_{X_i|W_i=1}\left[\mathbb{E}(Y_i(1)|X_i, W_i = 1)\right] = \mathbb{E}(Y_i(1)|W_i = 1),$$

because we are averaging the conditional expectation of $Y_i(1)$ over the distribution of X_i within the treated population. This allows us to express expectations over potential outcomes using observable covariate distributions.

2. A norm is a function that assigns a nonnegative length or size to a vector. Common norms include the Euclidean norm (or ℓ_2-norm), defined as $||x||_2 = \sqrt{\sum_k x_k^2}$, and the Manhattan norm (or ℓ_1-norm, defined as $||x||_1 = \sum_k |x_k|$. More generally, an ℓ_p norm is defined as $||x||_p = \left(\sum_k |x_k|^p\right)^{1/p}$ for any $p \geq 1$. In the context of exact matching, any norm that equals zero only when $X_i = X_j$ component-wise suffices.

3. Methods exist that seek to approximate exact matching by grouping, or coarsening, continuous variables or high-dimensional spaces. For example Iacus, King, and Porro (2011) discuss coarsened exact matching, a procedure that consists of "coarsening" variables by grouping multiple levels or ranges of specific covariates, and then conducting exact matching.

4. The logit is a widely used nonlinear model that specifies the propensity score as $P(X) = \Pr(W = 1|X) = \frac{\exp(X'\beta)}{1+\exp(X'\beta)}$. In practice, other similar nonlinear estimation methods such as Probit models are equally valid (Imbens 2015).

5. Monte Carlo methods use repeated random sampling to simulate data and evaluate the performance of statistical procedures under a known data generating process. This allows researchers to assess how different matching approaches perform across many hypothetical datasets where there is no uncertainty about the true parameter to be estimated.

6. This implies that we can write $\sum_{i=1}^{N} W_i \widehat{\mu}_1(X_i)$ as $\sum_{i=1}^{N} W_i Y_i$, and similarly $\sum_{i=1}^{N}(1 - W_i)\widehat{\mu}_0(X_i) = \sum_{i=1}^{N}(1 - W_i)Y_i$.

Chapter 4

1. At times, you may see this written as some variation, such as $Treat_i \times Post_t$, where $Post_t$ refers to the period after which treatment has been switched on, as this makes explicit that $\mathbb{1}\{t = 2\}$ is relevant only in the sense that it indicates the treatment period.

2. It is worth noting that such assumptions are rarely made, as it, in effect, implies some type of treatment effect homogeneity that is unlikely to occur in practice. As such, by far the most common estimand in a DD design is the ATT.

3. If we have multiple groups and multiple time periods with a single transition, we could actually respecify our two-way FE model to be based on two groups (treated and untreated) and two time periods (pre and post), and then estimate following (4.11). Because there is a single transition, the point-estimate for τ in this model will be identical to that if we were to estimate the fully saturated model (4.10). However, standard errors would be different.

4. This formula may, at first glance, not seem so clearly linked to difference-in-differences methods, but note that when $D_i = 1$, the expectation in (4.14) is written as $E\left[\frac{Y_{i,2}-Y_{i,1}}{P(D_i=1)}\right]$. And when $D_i = 0$, the expectation is written as $E\left[-\frac{(Y_{i,2}-Y_{i,1})}{P(D_i=1)} \cdot \frac{P(D_i=1|X_i)}{1-P(D_i=1|X_i)}\right]$. These two terms make it slightly clearer that this is taking a difference among treated, and then subtracting the same difference among untreated units. This also makes clear that the weights for the untreated are $\frac{P(D_i=1|X_i)}{1-P(D_i=1|X_i)} = \frac{P(D_i=1|X_i)}{P(D_i=0|X_i)}$, which clearly provides *more* weight to untreated units whose covariates suggest they are more likely to be treated.

5. For completeness, this is $\omega_i = \frac{W_i}{\Pr(W_i=1)} - \frac{\frac{(1-W_i)P(X_i)}{1-P(X_i)}}{\mathbb{E}\left[\frac{(1-W_i)P(X_i)}{1-P(X_i)}\right]}$.

6. If we are primarily interested in the variance of the treatment effect estimate $\widehat{\tau}$, the CRVE can be written in a scalar form as:

$$\widehat{\mathbb{V}}_{\text{CR}}(\widehat{\tau}) = \frac{\frac{1}{N}\sum_{g=1}^{G}\left(\sum_{i\in g}\tilde{D}_i\tilde{\varepsilon}_i\right)^2}{\left(\frac{1}{N}\sum_{i=1}^{N}\tilde{D}_i^2\right)^2},$$

where $\tilde{\varepsilon}_i = \tilde{Y}_i - \widehat{\tau}\tilde{D}_i$, and $\tilde{Y}_i$ and $\tilde{D}_i$ denote the outcome and treatment variables after removing both group- and time-fixed effects (i.e., double-demeaned). See Abadie et al. (2023, equation 19) for further discussion.

7. This wild cluster bootstrap was extended to a heteroscedasticity-robust version in Liu (1988). The name "wild" bootstrap appears to have been given by Hardle and Mammen (1993).

8. This term appears to have been originally coined by Borusyak and Jaravel (2018), who pointed out these issues in a very early paper, and was later expanded in Borusyak, Jaravel, and Spiess (2024). They referred to "forbidden extrapolations" occurring in OLS.

9. In the interests of completion, a sketch of these results is laid out here. Chaisemartin and D'Haultfœuille (2020) note that for any group and time cell, an ATE could be defined as:

$$\tau_{g,t} = \frac{1}{N_{g,t}} \sum_{i=1}^{N_{g,t}} [Y_{i,g,t}(1) - Y_{i,g,t}(0)], \tag{9.31}$$

where $N_{g,t}$ refers to the number of observations in this group and the total quantity of observations is N. Based on this, a grouped estimand can be defined to capture an ATT. This is:

$$\tau_{\text{ATT}}^{\text{DCDH}} = \mathbb{E}\left[\sum_{g,t:W_{g,t}=1} \frac{N_{g,t}}{N_T} \tau_{g,t} \right]. \tag{9.32}$$

Chaisemartin and D'Haultfœuille (2020) show that under a series of quite standard assumptions often maintained in difference-in-differences settings, the regression parameter τ^{twfe} can be decomposed as follows. Specifically:

$$\tau^{\text{twfe}} = \mathbb{E}\left[\sum_{g,t:W_{g,t}=1} \frac{N_{g,t}}{N_T} \omega_{g,t} \tau_{g,t} \right], \tag{9.33}$$

where:

$$\omega_{g,t} = \frac{\varepsilon_{g,t}}{\sum_{g,t:W_{g,t}=1} \frac{N_{g,t}}{N_T} \varepsilon_{g,t}}, \tag{9.34}$$

and $\varepsilon_{s,t}$ is the residual from a regression of $W_{g,t}$ on state- and time-fixed effects. This is important, given that it implies that generally $\tau^{\text{twfe}} \neq \tau_{\text{ATT}}^{\text{DCDH}}$, or in other words, $\hat{\tau}^{\text{twfe}}$ is a biased estimator of the ATT. What's more, there is nothing that limits $\omega_{g,t}$ to even be positive, which explains how treatment effects could, in theory, all be positive but the two-way fixed effect estimate could be negative.

10. However, note that if simpler models hold for potential outcomes, synthetic control may be entirely unbiased. This is the case, for example, if potential outcomes are auto-regressive with time-varying coefficients (Abadie, Diamond, and Hainmueller 2010, 496).

Chapter 5

1. The focus on heterogeneity here is because it is a key element of both human behavior and microeconometric work; see, for example, the Nobel Lecture of Heckman (2001) and a summary of a number of recent papers in footnote 1 of Mogstad, Torgovitsky, and Walters (2021) and because it provides a more realistic and general version of the IV models of interest here. This chapter, however, generally focuses on particular types of average treatment effects. In chapter 8 we consider even more heterogeneity by moving away from simply *average* treatment effects to consider effects across their distribution.

2. A range of econometric texts begin with models assuming homogeneous treatment effects in which effects are assumed to be fixed in the population, and only then move on to models permitting heterogeneity (see, e.g., Bruce Hansen 2022; Angrist and Pischke 2009). If you are keen for a recap of IV methods assuming treatment effect homogeneity, these or other texts provide an excellent source.

3. The exposition in Angrist, Imbens, and Rubin (1996a) is actually more general, positing that an individual's treatment status may depend upon the entire random assignment vector for all individuals, and then only later is this limited to $D_i(Z_i)$ by a SUTVA. The idea to present $D_i(Z_i)$ in a potential outcomes framework was introduced in Imbens and Angrist (1994), and in a footnote of that paper, they suggest that this notation was suggested to them by Gary Chamberlain—a nice example of the collaborative nature of research.

4. Indeed, these can be simply combined into a single assumption that states that $(Y_i(1), Y_i(0), D_i(1), D_i(0)) \perp\!\!\!\perp Z_i$, where the definition of unconfoundedness is captured by the independence of Z_i, and the exclusion restriction is captured given that the definition of potential outcomes $Y_i(D_i)$ now explicitly omits (or *excludes*) Z_i, implying that

the exclusion restriction holds. Imbens and Rubin (1997a) actually note that exclusion restrictions can be written in weaker ways; however for our needs, it is nice to write a single exclusion restriction, and so we lay out our assumption as in (5.5).

5. The jargon of projection itself comes from the fact that we are projecting Z into the subspace of W in order to predict $\widehat{W}$. This uses the definition of the projection matrix $P_Z = Z(Z'Z)^{-1}Z'$, such that $P_Z X = \widehat{X}$.

6. Note also that even if we observe some value such as $F = 10$, this is not some magical cutoff; as in cases where $F = 10$, there will still be bias, but this bias will be considerably less than the OLS estimand. If instead we wish to reduce bias to 5% of the OLS parameter, this critical value jumps to near $F = 15$.

Chapter 6

1. A control function approach addresses endogeneity by modeling the relationship between an endogenous regressor and the outcome, then including this estimated relationship (the "control function") as an additional regressor. In the RD context, this means estimating the smooth part of the outcome model $m(Z_i)$ and controlling for it directly to isolate the discontinuity at the cutoff. This method hinges on correctly specifying $m(Z_i)$, which is often difficult in practice.

2. Specifying a second-order (quadratic) or third-order (cubic) polynomial is similarly easy. We just require incorporating additional higher-order relationships of the running variable, for example, as follows with a second order polynomial:

$$Y_i = \mu_0 + \beta_1^-(1 - W_i)(Z_i - \kappa) + \beta_2^-(1 - W_i)(Z_i - \kappa) + \beta_1^+ W_i(Z_i - \kappa) + \beta_2^+ W_i(Z_i - \kappa)^2 + \tau^{\text{SRD,global}} W_i + \varepsilon_i.$$

3. Incidentally, neither captures the true functional form, which is simulated as a slightly strange function that we will explore in end-of-chapter question 5.

4. More precisely, this is true in the case of kernels with compact support such as those typically employed for RDD (see section 6.3.2.6). If kernels with unbounded support (such as the Gaussian kernel) were used, all observations contribute to the estimation, though their influence declines rapidly with distance from the cutoff κ.

Chapter 7

1. The Neyman-Pearson framework refers to precisely the framework we are discussing here, which formalizes hypothesis testing by defining two types of errors—type I and type II—and emphasizing the trade-off between them. It introduced the idea of test size and power, arguing that, for a fixed size, the best test is the one with the greatest power.

2. Under an assumption of independent sampling and known variances, the difference in sample means $\bar{Y}_1 - \bar{Y}_0$ is normally distributed with mean τ and variance $\sigma_0^2/N_0 + \sigma_1^2/N_1$, by the central limit theorem, which justifies (7.8).

3. We should be quite careful in making sure that we understand the difference between a test where we are interested in knowing if there are various independent variables that may affect a single dependent variable, in which case all we need is an F-test, and one in which a single independent variable may impact various dependent variables. It is the latter that we are concerned with here.

4. This discussion, from p. 1487 of M. Anderson (2008) and related to assessing the impact of early childhood intervention programs, is reproduced here:

> FWER control limits the probability of making *any* type I error. It is thus well suited to cases in which the cost of a false rejection is high. In this research, for instance, incorrectly concluding that early interventions are effective could result in a large-scale misallocation of teaching resources. In exploratory analysis, we may be willing to tolerate some type I errors in exchange for greater power, however. For example, the effects of early intervention on specific outcomes may be of interest, and because overall conclusions about program efficacy will not be based on a single outcome, it seems reasonable to accept a few type I errors in exchange for greater power.

5. The precise details of the error rate limit in (7.15) rely on Boole's inequality for the first step. This notes that the union of a group of probabilities is, at most, the sum of each of the individual probabilities, given that $\Pr(A \cup B) = \Pr(A) + \Pr(B) - \Pr(A \cap B)$, and hence $\Pr(A \cup B) \geq \Pr(A) + \Pr(B)$.

6. Note that if the null is not 0, but rather some arbitrary value k, rather than centering the null statistic on 0, it should be centered on this value, which can be achieved by subtracting k from the denominator of (7.17).

7. Formally, this can be written as:

$$I_i^{\text{Anderson}} = (\mathbf{1}'\widehat{\boldsymbol{\Sigma}}^{-1}\mathbf{1})^{-1}\mathbf{1}'\widehat{\boldsymbol{\Sigma}}^{-1}\boldsymbol{Y},$$

where $\boldsymbol{Y}$ is an $S \times 1$ vector of outcomes for individual i, $\widehat{\boldsymbol{\Sigma}}$ is the sample variance-covariance matrix of these outcomes (typically estimated among control units), and $\boldsymbol{I}$ is an $S \times 1$ vector of ones.

8. PCA transforms a set of correlated variables $X_1, X_2, \ldots, X_p$ into a new set of uncorrelated variables called principal components. The first principal component (PC1) is given by

$$PC_1 = \alpha_1 X_1 + \alpha_2 X_2 + \cdots + \alpha_p X_p,$$

where the coefficients α_i are the elements of the eigenvector corresponding to the largest eigenvalue of the covariance matrix of X. This component is constructed to maximize the variance explained, meaning it captures the largest proportion of variability in the data, resulting in a single score PC_1 for each observation.

Chapter 8

1. In general in our definition of quantile treatment effects, we will seek to be systematic with the notation used throughout this book. Specifically, we will use τ to represent our treatment effects and q to represent quantiles of interest. In some settings (see, e.g., Firpo 2007), τ is used to represent quantiles, and treatment effects are denoted Δ_τ or $\Delta(\tau)$.

2. This contrasts with standard regression settings, where the law of iterated expectations allows for averaging over covariate groups. No such law holds for quantiles.

3. The reflection problem refers to the challenge of distinguishing between actual causal influence between individuals (spillover effects) and correlated behaviors due to similar characteristics or shared environments. In simple terms, when we observe similar behaviors in a group, it's difficult to determine if one person's actions are causing another's (i.e., spillover effects) or if both are simply responding to the same external factors.

4. Certain authors refer to both partial population experiments and randomized saturation designs simply as partial population experiments. However, it appears to be more common to give separate names to these two designs, and it allows for greater precision in nomenclature, and so it seems preferable to name the designs as laid out here. Specifically, we refer to partial population experiments as cases such as those laid out in Moffitt (2001) and Hirano and Hahn (2010), where the likelihood of treatment is fixed within treated clusters, whereas we denote as randomized saturated designs cases where the likelihood of treatment varies across treated clusters. Of course, these two desingns are very much related, and in this notation, a partial population design is simply a randomized saturation design with one level of saturation.

5. This monotonicity assumption disallows the existence of both never-takers and individuals who would adopt treatment if their partner were treated but not if they themselves were treated.

6. Campbell and Stanley (1963, 5) note that external validity is the sine qua non—or essential condition—in experimental and quasi-experimental design.

7. An alternative view of the problem proposed by Banerjee, Chassang, and Snowberg (2017) embraces the subjective nature of external validity, proposing a Bayesian framework in which external validity in the form of policy advice depends on an experimenter's (posterior) beliefs when accounting for an available estimate of a policy's effect in some other setting, as well as their prior beliefs about the impact of the policy in the environment of interest in which no evaluation is available.

8. The history of the adoption of the Roy model as a lens through which to understand selection and potential outcomes is fascinating in its own right. The statistician Andrew Gelman has a very widely read blog, and in a post in 2013 discussed the reasonably large jump between the original Roy model laid out in Roy (1951) and later implementations linked to the potential outcomes framework such as Heckman (1996b). Reading both this post as well as comments on the post by Guido Imbens and Judea Pearl provides very rich insight into how the generation of ideas is viewed both across and within fields.

9. This is worth doing if not clear and also works for any variable regardless of whether the distribution is known as it is simply a result of the definition of the cdf. Indeed, you can confirm this with any variable by estimating the empirical cdf of a variable and applying this to the variable itself.

Chapter 9

1. This parameter is $\lambda_{\text{homoscedastic}} = \frac{c\widehat{\sigma}}{\sqrt{N}}\Phi^{-1}\left(1-\frac{\gamma}{2k}\right)$ where c is some constant $c > 1$ (1.1 is suggested), $\widehat{\sigma}$ is an estimate of the variance, k is the number of potential covariates, and $\gamma = \frac{0.1}{\ln[\max(k,N)]}$. In the heteroscedastic case, a similar quantity is used, but adjustments are made for heteroscedasticity in penality loadings (Belloni et al. 2012).

2. This data is simulated quite simply, as 500 draws of a DGP with both X_1 and X_2 consisting of random draws of a uniform variable in the unit interval, with no correlation between the variables, and $Y = 10X_1 + 30X_2 + 0.5X_1X_2 + \varepsilon$, where ε is a mean zero normally distributed variable with standard deviation of 10. If you would like to explore regression trees at more length, you may wish to consider a richer simulation based on more variables or more complex functional forms, or explore some real data with considerably more complex (and presumably unknown) DGPs.

3. This implies that we are *not* assuming normality of the elements of $\boldsymbol{\varepsilon}$ but are limiting the importance of outliers. Formally, the definition of a σ-sub-Gaussian random variable ε is one for which $\mathbb{E}[\exp(t\varepsilon)] \leq \exp(\sigma^2 t^2/2)$ for all real numbers t.

4. While the precise details of this process can be found in Athey et al. (2021, §4.2), it essentially replicates the idea of (9.21), augmenting also with outcomes predicted for units not in $\mathcal{O}$. It does this using a regularized single-value decomposition considering outcome $Y_{i,t}(0)$ for units in $\mathcal{O}$, and predicted values based for $Y_{i,t}(0)$ for units not in $\mathcal{O}$.

5. More recently, extensions have also been defined for cases where there *also* many potential endogenous variables (see, e.g., Gold, Lederer, and Tao 2020; Belloni, Hansen, and Newey 2022), though this is potentially a more specialized case.

References

Abadie, Alberto. 2002. "Bootstrap Tests for Distributional Treatment Effects in Instrumental Variable Models." *Journal of the American Statistical Association* 97 (457): 284–292.

Abadie, Alberto. 2003. "Semiparametric Instrumental Variable Estimation of Treatment Response Models." *Journal of Econometrics* 113 (2): 231–263.

Abadie, Alberto. 2005. "Semiparametric Difference-in-Differences Estimators." *Review of Economic Studies* 72, no. 1 (January): 1–19.

Abadie, Alberto. 2020. "Statistical Nonsignificance in Empirical Economics." *American Economic Review: Insights* 2, no. 2 (June): 193–208.

Abadie, Alberto. 2021. "Using Synthetic Controls: Feasibility, Data Requirements, and Methodological Aspects." *Journal of Economic Literature* 59, no. 2 (June): 391–425.

Abadie, Alberto, Joshua Angrist, and Guido W. Imbens. 2002. "Instrumental Variables Estimates of the Effect of Subsidized Training on the Quantiles of Trainee Earnings." *Econometrica* 70 (1): 91–117.

Abadie, Alberto, Susan Athey, Guido W. Imbens, and Jeffrey M. Wooldridge. 2020. "Sampling-Based Versus Design-Based Uncertainty in Regression Analysis." *Econometrica* 88 (1): 265–296.

Abadie, Alberto, Susan Athey, Guido W. Imbens, and Jeffrey M. Wooldridge. 2023. "When Should You Adjust Standard Errors for Clustering?" *Quarterly Journal of Economics* 138, no. 1 (October): 1–35.

Abadie, Alberto, and Matias D. Cattaneo. 2018. "Econometric Methods for Program Evaluation." *Annual Review of Economics* 10:465–503.

Abadie, Alberto, and Matias D. Cattaneo. 2021. "Introduction to the Special Section on Synthetic Control Methods." *Journal of the American Statistical Association* 116 (536): 1713–1715.

Abadie, Alberto, Alexis Diamond, and Jens Hainmueller. 2010. "Synthetic Control Methods for Comparative Case Studies: Estimating the Effect of California's Tobacco Control Program." *Journal of the American Statistical Association* 105 (490): 493–505.

Abadie, Alberto, Alexis Diamond, and Jens Hainmueller. 2015. "Comparative Politics and the Synthetic Control Method." *American Journal of Political Science* 59 (2): 495–510.

Abadie, Alberto, and Javier Gardeazabal. 2003. "The Economic Costs of Conflict: A Case Study of the Basque Country." *American Economic Review* 93 (1): 113–132.

Abadie, Alberto, and Guido W. Imbens. 2006. "Large Sample Properties of Matching Estimators for Average Treatment Effects." *Econometrica* 74 (1): 235–267.

Abadie, Alberto, and Guido W. Imbens. 2008. "On the Failure of the Bootstrap for Matching Estimators." *Econometrica* 76 (6): 1537–1557.

Abadie, Alberto, and Guido W. Imbens. 2011. "Bias-Corrected Matching Estimators for Average Treatment Effects." *Journal of Business & Economic Statistics* 29 (1): 1–11.

Abadie, Alberto, and Guido W. Imbens. 2016. "Matching on the Estimated Propensity Score." *Econometrica* 84 (2): 781–807.

Abadie, Alberto, and Maximilian Kasy. 2019. "Choosing Among Regularized Estimators in Empirical Economics: The Risk of Machine Learning." *Review of Economics and Statistics* 101, no. 5 (December): 743–762.

Abadie, Alberto, and Jérémy L'Hour. 2021. "A Penalized Synthetic Control Estimator for Disaggregated Data." *Journal of the American Statistical Association* 116 (536): 1817–1834.

Abadie, Alberto, and Josep Vives-i-Bastida. 2026. "Synthetic Controls in Action." In *Advances in Economics and Econometrics: Twelfth World Congress,* edited by Victor Chernozhukov, Johannes Hörner, Eliana La Ferrara, and Iván Werning, 195–224. Cambridge: Cambridge University Press.

Abbring, Jaap H., and Gerard J. Van Den Berg. 2003. "The Nonparametric Identification of Treatment Effects in Duration Models." *Econometrica* 71 (5): 1491–1517.

Abel, Martin, Rulof Burger, and Patrizio Piraino. 2020. "The Value of Reference Letters: Experimental Evidence from South Africa." *American Economic Journal: Applied Economics* 12, no. 3 (July): 40–71.

Abramowicz, Michel, and Ariane Szafarz. 2020. "Ethics of RCTs: Should Economists Care About Equipoise?" In *Randomized Control Trials in the Field of Development: A Critical Perspective.* Oxford University Press, September.

Acemoglu, Daron, Simon Johnson, and James A. Robinson. 2001. "The Colonial Origins of Comparative Development: An Empirical Investigation." *American Economic Review* 91, no. 5 (December): 1369–1401.

Ahrens, Achim, Christian B. Hansen, and Mark E. Schaffer. 2020. "Lassopack: Model Selection and Prediction with Regularized Regression in Stata." *The Stata Journal* 20 (1): 176–235.

Alan, Sule, and Elif Kubilay. 2025. "Empowering Adolescents to Transform Schools: Lessons from a Behavioral Targeting." *American Economic Review* 115, no. 2 (February): 365–407.

Allcott, Hunt. 2015. "Site Selection Bias in Program Evaluation." *Quarterly Journal of Economics* 130, no. 3 (March): 1117–1165.

Almond, Douglas, Kenneth Y. Chay, and David S. Lee. 2005. "The Costs of Low Birth Weight." *Quarterly Journal of Economics* 120 (3): 1031–1083.

Anderson, Michael. 2008. "Multiple Inference and Gender Differences in the Effects of Early Intervention: A Reevaluation of the Abecedarian, Perry Preschool, and Early Training Projects." *Journal of the American Statistical Association* 103 (484): 1481–1495.

Anderson, T. W. 1951. "Estimating Linear Restrictions on Regression Coefficients for Multivariate Normal Distributions." *Annals of Mathematical Statistics* 22:327–351.

Anderson, T. W., and Herman Rubin. 1949. "Estimation of the Parameters of a Single Equation in a Complete System of Stochastic Equations." *Annals of Mathematical Statistics* 20 (1): 46–63.

Andrews, Isaiah, and Emily Oster. 2019. "A Simple Approximation for Evaluating External Validity Bias." *Economics Letters* 178:58–62.

Andrews, Isaiah, James H. Stock, and Liyang Sun. 2019. "Weak Instruments in Instrumental Variables Regression: Theory and Practice." *Annual Review of Economics* 11:727–753.

Angelucci, M., and V. Di Maro. 2016. "Programme Evaluation and Spillover Effects." *Journal of Development Effectiveness* 8 (1): 22–43.

Angelucci, Manuela, and Giacomo De Giorgi. 2009. "Indirect Effects of an Aid Program: How Do Cash Transfers Affect Ineligibles' Consumption?" *American Economic Review* 99, no. 1 (March): 486–508.

Angrist, Joshua, and Jinyong Hahn. 2004. "When to Control for Covariates? Panel Asymptotics for Estimates of Treatment Effects." *Review of Economics and Statistics* 86 (1): 58–72.

Angrist, Joshua, Victor Lavy, and Analia Schlosser. 2010. "Multiple Experiments for the Causal Link between the Quantity and Quality of Children." *Journal of Labor Economics* 28, no. 4 (October): 773–824.

Angrist, Joshua D. 1998. "Estimating the Labor Market Impact of Voluntary Military Service Using Social Security Data on Military Applicants." *Econometrica* 66 (2): 249–288.

Angrist, Joshua D. 2004. "Treatment Effect Heterogeneity in Theory and Practice." *The Economic Journal* 114 (494): C52–C83.

Angrist, Joshua D. 2022. "Empirical Strategies in Economics: Illuminating the Path from Cause to Effect." *Econometrica* 90 (6): 2509–2539.

Angrist, Joshua D., and William N. Evans. 1998. "Children and Their Parents' Labor Supply: Evidence from Exogenous Variation in Family Size." *The American Economic Review* 88 (3): 450–477.

Angrist, Joshua D., and Iván Fernández-Val. 2013. "ExtrapoLATE-ing: External Validity and Overidentification in the LATE Framework." In *Advances in Economics and Econometrics: Tenth World Congress,* edited by Daron Acemoglu, Manuel Arellano, and Eddie Dekel, 401–434. Econometric Society Monographs. Cambridge University Press.

Angrist, Joshua D., and Brigham Frandsen. 2022. "Machine Labor." *Journal of Labor Economics* 40 (S1): S97–S140.

Angrist, Joshua D., Kathryn Graddy, and Guido W. Imbens. 2000. "The Interpretation of Instrumental Variables Estimators in Simultaneous Equations Models with an Application to the Demand for Fish." *The Review of Economic Studies* 67 (3): 499–527.

Angrist, Joshua D., and Guido W. Imbens. 1991. *Sources of Identifying Information in Evaluation Models.* NBER Technical Working Papers 0117. National Bureau of Economic Research, December.

Angrist, Joshua D., and Guido W. Imbens. 1995. "Two-Stage Least Squares Estimation of Average Causal Effects in Models with Variable Treatment Intensity." *Journal of the American Statistical Association* 90 (430): 431–442.

Angrist, Joshua D., Guido W. Imbens, and Donald B. Rubin. 1996a. "Identification of Causal Effects Using Instrumental Variables." *Journal of the American Statistical Association* 91 (434): 444–455.

Angrist, Joshua D., Guido W. Imbens, and Donald B. Rubin. 1996b. "Rejoinder: Identification of Causal Effects Using Instrumental Variables." *Journal of the American Statistical Association* 91 (434): 468–472.

Angrist, Joshua D., and Alan B. Krueger. 1991. "Does Compulsory School Attendance Affect Schooling and Earnings?" *Quarterly Journal of Economics* 106, no. 4 (November): 979–1014.

Angrist, Joshua D., and Alan B. Krueger. 1999. "Empirical Strategies in Labor Economics." In *Handbook of Labor Economics,* edited by Orley C. Ashenfelter and David Card, 3:1277–1366. Elsevier.

Angrist, Joshua D., and Alan B. Krueger. 2001. "Instrumental Variables and the Search for Identification: From Supply and Demand to Natural Experiments." *Journal of Economic Perspectives* 15, no. 4 (December): 69–85.

Angrist, Joshua D., and Victor Lavy. 1999. "Using Maimonides' Rule to Estimate the Effect of Class Size on Scholastic Achievement." *Quarterly Journal of Economics* 114 (2): 533–575.

Angrist, Joshua D., and Jörn-Steffen Pischke. 2009. *Mostly Harmless Econometrics: An Empiricist's Companion.* Princeton University Press.

Angrist, Joshua D., and Miikka Rokkanen. 2015. "Wanna Get Away? Regression Discontinuity Estimation of Exam School Effects Away from the Cutoff." *Journal of the American Statistical Association* 110, no. 512 (December): 1331–1344.

Arai, Yoichi, Yu-Chin Hsu, Toru Kitagawa, Ismael Mourifié, and Yuanyuan Wan. 2022. "Testing Identifying Assumptions in Fuzzy Regression Discontinuity Designs." *Quantitative Economics* 13 (1): 1–28.

Arellano, M. 1987. "PRACTITIONERS' CORNER: Computing Robust Standard Errors for Within-groups Estimators." *Oxford Bulletin of Economics and Statistics* 49 (4): 431–434.

Arellano, Manuel. 2003. *Panel Data Econometrics.* Oxford University Press.

Arkhangelsky, Dmitry, Susan Athey, David A. Hirshberg, Guido W. Imbens, and Stefan Wager. 2021. "Synthetic Difference-in-Differences." *American Economic Review* 111, no. 12 (December): 4088–4118.

Arkhangelsky, Dmitry, and Guido W. Imbens. 2023. *Causal Models for Longitudinal and Panel Data: A Survey.* NBER Working Papers 31942. National Bureau of Economic Research, December.

Armstrong, Timothy B., and Michal Kolesár. 2020. "Simple and Honest Confidence Intervals in Nonparametric Regression." *Quantitative Economics* 11, no. 1 (January): 1–39.

Aronow, Peter M., Nicole E. Basta, and M. Elizabeth Halloran. 2017. "The Regression Discontinuity Design Under Interference: A Local Randomization-Based Approach." *Observational Studies* 3 (2): 129–133.

Aronow, Peter M., and Allison Carnegie. 2013. "Beyond LATE: Estimation of the Average Treatment Effect with an Instrumental Variable." *Political Analysis* 21 (4): 492–506.

Aronow, Peter M., and Cyrus Samii. 2017. "Estimating Average Causal Effects Under General Interference, with Application to a Social Network Experiment." *The Annals of Applied Statistics* 11 (4): 1912–1947.

Arpinon, T., and R. Espinosa. 2023. "A Practical Guide to Registered Reports for Economists." *Journal of the Economic Science Association* 9:90–122.

Ashenfelter, Orley. 1978. "Estimating the Effects of Training Programs on Earnings." *Review of Economics and Statistics* 60 (1): 47–57.

Askarov, Zohid, Anthony Doucouliagos, Hristos Doucouliagos, and T. D. Stanley. 2022. "The Significance of Data-Sharing Policy." Jvac053, *Journal of the European Economic Association* (September).

Athey, Susan. 2017. "Beyond Prediction: Using Big Data for Policy Problems." *Science* 355 (6324): 483–485.

Athey, Susan. 2018. "The Impact of Machine Learning on Economics." In *The Economics of Artificial Intelligence: An Agenda,* edited by Ajay Agrawal, Joshua Gans, and Avi Goldfarb, 507–547. University of Chicago Press, January.

Athey, Susan, Mohsen Bayati, Nikolay Doudchenko, Guido W. Imbens, and Khashayar Khosravi. 2021. "Matrix Completion Methods for Causal Panel Data Models." *Journal of the American Statistical Association* 116 (536): 1716–1730.

Athey, Susan, Mohsen Bayati, Guido W. Imbens, and Zhaonan Qu. 2019. "Ensemble Methods for Causal Effects in Panel Data Settings." *AEA Papers and Proceedings* 109 (May): 65–70.

Athey, Susan, Dean Eckles, and Guido W. Imbens. 2018. "Exact p-Values for Network Interference." *Journal of the American Statistical Association* 113 (521): 230–240.

Athey, Susan, and Guido W. Imbens. 2006. "Identification and Inference in Nonlinear Difference-in-Differences Models." *Econometrica* 74 (2): 431–497.

Athey, Susan, and Guido W. Imbens. 2016. "Recursive Partitioning for Heterogeneous Causal Effects." *Proceedings of the National Academy of Sciences* 113 (27): 7353–7360.

Athey, Susan, and Guido W. Imbens. 2017. "The Econometrics of Randomized Experiments." In *Handbook of Field Experiments,* edited by Abhijit Banerjee and Esther Duflo, 1:73–140. Handbook of Economic Field Experiments. North-Holland.

Athey, Susan, and Guido W. Imbens. 2019. "Machine Learning Methods That Economists Should Know About." *Annual Review of Economics* 11 (1): 685–725.

Athey, Susan, and Guido W. Imbens. 2022. "Design-Based Analysis in Difference-in-Differences Settings with Staggered Adoption." Annals Issue in Honor of Gary Chamberlain, *Journal of Econometrics* 226 (1): 62–79.

Athey, Susan, and Stefan Wager. 2021. "Policy Learning with Observational Data." *Econometrica* 89 (1): 133–161.

Attanasio, Orazio, Adriana Kugler, and Costas Meghir. 2011. "Subsidizing Vocational Training for Disadvantaged Youth in Colombia: Evidence from a Randomized Trial." *American Economic Journal: Applied Economics* 3, no. 3 (July): 188–220.

Auerbach, Eric. 2022. "Identification and Estimation of a Partially Linear Regression Model Using Network Data." *Econometrica* 90 (1): 347–365.

Auerbach, Eric, Yong Cai, and Ahnaf Rafi. 2024. *Regression Discontinuity Design with Spillovers.* arXiv: 2404 .06471.

Auerbach, Eric, and Max Tabord-Meehan. 2023. *The Local Approach to Causal Inference Under Network Interference.* arXiv: 2105.03810.

Baele, Stéphane. 2013. "The Ethics of New Development Economics: Is the Experimental Approach to Development Economics Morally Wrong?" *Journal of Philosophical Economics* 7 (1): 2–42.

Bai, Yuehao. 2022. "Optimality of Matched-Pair Designs in Randomized Controlled Trials." *American Economic Review* 112, no. 12 (December): 3911–3940.

Baird, Sarah, J. Aislinn Bohren, Craig McIntosh, and Berk Özler. 2018. "Optimal Design of Experiments in the Presence of Interference." *Review of Economics and Statistics* 100, no. 5 (December): 844–860.

Baird, Sarah, Joan Hamory Hicks, Edward Miguel, and Michael Kremer. 2016. "Worms at Work: Long-Run Impacts of a Child Health Investment." *Quarterly Journal of Economics* 131, no. 4 (July): 1637–1680.

Balke, Alexander, and Judea Pearl. 1993. *Nonparametric Bounds on Causal Effects from Partial Compliance Data.* Technical Report R-199. Computer Science Department, University of California Los Angeles.

Balke, Alexander, and Judea Pearl. 1997. "Bounds on Treatment Effects from Studies with Imperfect Compliance." *Journal of the American Statistical Association* 92 (439): 1171–1176.

Bandiera, Oriana, Iwan Barankay, and Imran Rasul. 2011. "Field Experiments with Firms." *Journal of Economic Perspectives* 25, no. 3 (September): 63–82.

Banerjee, A., S. Chassang, and E. Snowberg. 2017. "Chapter 4 - Decision Theoretic Approaches to Experiment Design and External Validity." In *Handbook of Economic Field Experiments,* edited by Abhijit Banerjee and Esther Duflo, 1:141–174. North-Holland.

Banerjee, Abhijit, Sylvain Chassang, Sergio Montero, and Erik Snowberg. 2020. "A Theory of Experimenters: Robustness, Randomization, and Balance." *American Economic Review* 110, no. 4 (April): 1206–1230.

Banerjee, Abhijit, Esther Duflo, Amy Finkelstein, Lawrence F. Katz, Benjamin A. Olken, and Anja Sautmann. 2020. *In Praise of Moderation: Suggestions for the Scope and Use of Pre-Analysis Plans for RCTs in Economics.* Working Paper 26993. National Bureau of Economic Research.

Banerjee, Abhijit V., and Esther Duflo, eds. 2017. *Handbook of Economic Field Experiments.* Vol. 1. Handbooks in Economics. North-Holland.

Baranov, Victoria, Sonia Bhalotra, Pietro Biroli, and Joanna Maselko. 2020. "Maternal Depression, Women's Empowerment, and Parental Investment: Evidence from a Randomized Controlled Trial." *American Economic Review* 110, no. 3 (March): 824–859.

Bari, Faisal, Kashif Malik, Muhammad Meki, and Simon Quinn. 2024. "Asset-Based Microfinance for Microenterprises: Evidence from Pakistan." *American Economic Review* 114, no. 2 (February): 534–574.

Barreca, Alan I., Melanie Guldi, Jason M. Lindo, and Glen R. Waddell. 2011. "Saving Babies? Revisiting the Effect of Very Low Birth Weight Classification*." *Quarterly Journal of Economics* 126, no. 4 (October): 2117–2123.

Basse, Guillaume, Peng Ding, Avi Feller, and Panos Toulis. 2024. "Randomization Tests for Peer Effects in Group Formation Experiments." *Econometrica* 92 (2): 567–590.

Basu, Kaushik. 2018. "The Trials of Randomized Control: Probability, Intuition and the Dinosaur Risk. A Commentary on Deaton and Cartwright." *Social Science & Medicine* 210:26–28.

Bédécarrats, Florent, Isabelle Guérin, and François Roubaud. 2020. "Editors' Introduction: Controversies Around RCT in Development: Epistemology, Ethics, and Politics." In *Randomized Control Trials in the Field of Development: A Critical Perspective.* Oxford University Press, September.

Bell, Robert M., and Daniel F. McCaffrey. 2002. "Bias Reduction in Standard Errors for Linear Regression with Multi-Stage Samples." *Survey Methodology* 28:169–181.

Bellégo, Christophe, David Benatia, and Vincent Dortet-Bernadet. 2024. "The Chained Difference-in-Differences." *Journal of Econometrics* 248:105783.

Belloni, A., D. Chen, V. Chernozhukov, and C. Hansen. 2012. "Sparse Models and Methods for Optimal Instruments with an Application to Eminent Domain." *Econometrica* 80 (6): 2369–2429.

Belloni, A., V. Chernozhukov, and L. Wang. 2011. "Square-Root Lasso: Pivotal Recovery of Sparse Signals via Conic Programming." *Biometrika* 98 (4): 791–806.

Belloni, Alexandre, and Victor Chernozhukov. 2013. "Least Squares After Model Selection in High-Dimensional Sparse Models." *Bernoulli* 19 (2): 521–547.

Belloni, Alexandre, Victor Chernozhukov, and Christian Hansen. 2014a. "High-Dimensional Methods and Inference on Structural and Treatment Effects." *Journal of Economic Perspectives* 28, no. 2 (May): 29–50.

Belloni, Alexandre, Victor Chernozhukov, and Christian Hansen. 2014b. "Inference on Treatment Effects After Selection Among High-Dimensional Controls." *The Review of Economic Studies* 81, no. 2 (November): 608–650.

Belloni, Alexandre, Christian Hansen, and Whitney Newey. 2022. "High-Dimensional Linear Models with Many Endogenous Variables." Annals Issue: In Honor of Ron Gallant, *Journal of Econometrics* 228 (1): 4–26.

Ben-Michael, Eli, Avi Feller, and Jesse Rothstein. 2021. "The Augmented Synthetic Control Method." *Journal of the American Statistical Association* 116 (536): 1789–1803.

Benjamin, Daniel J., James O. Berger, Magnus Johannesson, Brian A. Nosek, E.-J. Wagenmakers, Richard Berk, Kenneth A. Bollen, et al. 2018. "Redefine Statistical Significance." *Nature and Human Behaviour* 2:6–10.

Benjamini, Yoav, and Yosef Hochberg. 1995. "Controlling the False Discovery Rate: A Practical and Powerful Approach to Multiple Testing." *Journal of the Royal Statistical Society. Series B (Methodological)* 57 (1): 289–300.

Benjamini, Yoav, Abba M. Krieger, and Daniel Yekutieli. 2006. "Adaptive Linear Step-up Procedures That Control the False Discovery Rate." *Biometrika* 93 (3): 491–507.

Benjamini, Yoav, and Daniel Yekutieli. 2001. "The Control of the False Discovery Rate in Multiple Testing Under Dependency." *Annals of Statistics* 29 (4): 1165–1188.

Bertanha, Marinho. 2020. "Regression Discontinuity Design with Many Thresholds." *Journal of Econometrics* 218 (1): 216–241.

Bertanha, Marinho, and Guido W. Imbens. 2020. "External Validity in Fuzzy Regression Discontinuity Designs." *Journal of Business & Economic Statistics* 38 (3): 593–612.

Bertrand, Marianne, Esther Duflo, and Sendhil Mullainathan. 2004. "How Much Should We Trust Differences-In-Differences Estimates?" *Quarterly Journal of Economics* 119 (1): 249–275.

Bertrand, Marianne, and Sendhil Mullainathan. 2004. "Are Emily and Greg More Employable Than Lakisha and Jamal? A Field Experiment on Labor Market Discrimination." *American Economic Review* 94, no. 4 (September): 991–1013.

Besley, Timothy, and Anne Case. 2000. "Unnatural Experiments? Estimating the Incidence of Endogenous Policies." *The Economic Journal* 110 (467): 672–694.

Bhalotra, Sonia, and Damian Clarke. 2020. "The Twin Instrument: Fertility and Human Capital Investment." *Journal of the European Economic Association* 18 (6): 3090–3139.

Bhalotra, Sonia, Damian Clarke, Joseph Flavian Gomes, and Atheendar Venkataramani. 2023. "Maternal Mortality and Women's Political Power." Jvad012, *Journal of the European Economic Association* (February).

Bharadwaj, Prashant, Katrine Vellesen Løken, and Christophen Neilson. 2013. "Early Life Health Interventions and Academic Achievement." *American Economic Review* 103 (5): 1862–1891.

Bhatt, Monica P., Sara B. Heller, Max Kapustin, Marianne Bertrand, and Christopher Blattman. 2023. "Predicting and Preventing Gun Violence: An Experimental Evaluation of READI Chicago." *Quarterly Journal of Economics* 139, no. 1 (July): 1–56.

Björklund, Anders, and Robert Moffitt. 1987. "The Estimation of Wage Gains and Welfare Gains in Self-Selection Models." *Review of Economics and Statistics* 69 (1): 42–49.

Black, Bernard, Alex Hollingsworth, Letícia Nunes, and Kosali Simon. 2022. "Simulated Power Analyses for Observational Studies: An Application to the Affordable Care Act Medicaid Expansion." *Journal of Public Economics* 213:104713.

Blandhol, Christine, John Bonney, Magne Mogstad, and Alexander Torgovitsky. 2022. *When is TSLS Actually LATE?* Working Paper, Working Paper Series 29709. National Bureau of Economic Research, January.

Bloom, Howard S. 1984. "Accounting for No-Shows in Experimental Evaluation Designs." *Evaluation Review* 8 (2): 225–246.

Bodory, Hugo, Lorenzo Camponovo, Martin Huber, and Michael Lechner. 2020. "The Finite Sample Performance of Inference Methods for Propensity Score Matching and Weighting Estimators." *Journal of Business & Economic Statistics* 38, no. 1 (January): 183–200.

Bold, Tessa, Mwangi Kimenyi, Germano Mwabu, Alice Ng'ang'a, and Justin Sandefur. 2018. "Experimental Evidence on Scaling up Education Reforms in Kenya." *Journal of Public Economics* 168:1–20.

Bonferroni, C. E. 1935. "Il calcolo delle assicurazioni su gruppi di teste." In *Studi in Onore del Professore Salvatore Ortu Carboni,* 13–60. Rome.

Borusyak, Kirill, and Xavier Jaravel. 2018. *Revisiting Event Study Designs, with an Application to the Estimation of the Marginal Propensity to Consume.* Mimeo.

Borusyak, Kirill, Xavier Jaravel, and Jann Spiess. 2024. "Revisiting Event-Study Designs: Robust and Efficient Estimation." *Review of Economic Studies* (February): 3253–3285.

Bound, John, David A. Jaeger, and Regina M. Baker. 1995. "Problems with Instrumental Variables Estimation When the Correlation Between the Instruments and the Endogeneous Explanatory Variable Is Weak." *Journal of the American Statistical Association* 90 (430): 443–450.

Bramoullé, Yann, Habiba Djebbari, and Bernard Fortin. 2009. "Identification of Peer Effects Through Social Networks." *Journal of Econometrics* 150 (1): 41–55.

Bramoullé, Yann, Habiba Djebbari, and Bernard Fortin. 2020. "Peer Effects in Networks: A Survey." *Annual Review of Economics* 12:603–629.

Brodeur, Abel, Scott Carrell, David Figlio, and Lester Lusher. 2023. "Unpacking P-hacking and Publication Bias." *American Economic Review* 113, no. 11 (November): 2974–3002.

Brodeur, Abel, Nikolai Cook, and Anthony Heyes. 2020. "Methods Matter: p-Hacking and Publication Bias in Causal Analysis in Economics." *American Economic Review* 110, no. 11 (November): 3634–3660.

Brodeur, Abel, Nikolai M. Cook, Jonathan S. Hartley, and Anthony Heyes. 2024. "Do Preregistration and Preanalysis Plans Reduce p-Hacking and Publication Bias? Evidence from 15,992 Test Statistics and Suggestions for Improvement." *Journal of Political Economy Microeconomics* 2 (3): 527–561.

Brodeur, Abel, Derek Mikola, and Nikolai Cook. 2024. *Mass Reproducibility and Replicability: A New Hope.* IZA Discussion Paper 16912. Institute of Labor Economics (IZA), April.

Bruhn, Miriam, and David McKenzie. 2009. "In Pursuit of Balance: Randomization in Practice in Development Field Experiments." *American Economic Journal: Applied Economics* 1, no. 4 (October): 200–232.

Buckles, Kasey S., and Daniel M. Hungerman. 2013. "Season of Birth and Later Outcomes: Old Questions, New Answers." *The Review of Economics and Statistics* 95, no. 3 (July): 711–724.

Burgess, Stephen. 2014. "Sample Size and Power Calculations in Mendelian Randomization with a Single Instrumental Variable and a Binary Outcome." *International Journal of Epidemiology* 43, no. 3 (March): 922–929.

Burlig, Fiona. 2018. "Improving Transparency in Observational Social Science Research: A Pre-analysis Plan Approach." *Economics Letters* 168:56–60.

Burlig, Fiona, Louis Preonas, and Matt Woerman. 2020. "Panel Data and Experimental Design." *Journal of Development Economics* 144:102458.

Bursztyn, Leonardo, Thomas Fujiwara, and Amanda Pallais. 2017. "'Acting Wife': Marriage Market Incentives and Labor Market Investments." *American Economic Review* 107, no. 11 (November): 3288–3319.

Buse, A. 1992. "The Bias of Instrumental Variable Estimators." *Econometrica* 60 (1): 173–180.

Busso, Matias, John DiNardo, and Justin McCrary. 2014. "New Evidence on the Finite Sample Properties of Propensity Score Reweighting and Matching Estimators." *Review of Economics and Statistics* 96 (5): 885–897.

Butts, Kyle. 2023. *Difference-in-Differences Estimation with Spatial Spillovers.* arXiv: 2105.03737.

Caetano, Carolina, and Brantly Callaway. 2023. *Difference-in-Differences with Time-Varying Covariates in the Parallel Trends Assumption.* arXiv: 2202.02903.

Caliendo, Marco, and Sabine Kopeinig. 2008. "Some Practical Guidance for the Implementation of Propensity Score Matching." *Journal of Economic Surveys* 22 (1): 31–72.

Callaway, Brantly, Andrew Goodman-Bacon, and Pedro H. C. Sant'Anna. 2021. *Difference in Differences with a Continuous Treatment.* arXiv: 2107.02637.

Callaway, Brantly, and Tong Li. 2019. "Quantile Treatment Effects in Difference in Differences Models with Panel Data." *Quantitative Economics* 10 (4): 1579–1618.

Callaway, Brantly, and Pedro H. C. Sant'Anna. 2021. "Difference-in-Differences with multiple time periods." *Journal of Econometrics* 225 (2): 200–230.

Calonico, Sebastian, Matias D. Cattaneo, and Max H. Farrell. 2020. "Optimal Bandwidth Choice for Robust Bias Corrected Inference in Regression Discontinuity Designs." *Econometrics Journal* 23 (2): 192–210.

Calonico, Sebastian, Matias D. Cattaneo, Max H. Farrell, and Rocío Titiunik. 2019. "Regression Discontinuity Designs Using Covariates." *Review of Economics and Statistics* 101, no. 3 (July): 442–451.

Calonico, Sebastian, Matias D. Cattaneo, and Rocío Titiunik. 2014a. "Robust Nonparametric Confidence Intervals for Regression-Discontinuity Designs." *Econometrica* 82 (6): 2295–2326.

Calonico, Sebastian, Matias D. Cattaneo, and Rocío Titiunik. 2014b. "Supplement to 'Robust Nonparametric Confidence Intervals for Regression-Discontinuity Designs'." *Econometrica Supplemental Material* 82 (6): 1–101.

Calonico, Sebastian, Matias D. Cattaneo, and Rocío Titiunik. 2015. "Optimal Data-Driven Regression Discontinuity Plots." *Journal of the American Statistical Association* 110 (512): 1753–1769.

Cameron, A. Colin, Jonah B. Gelbach, and Douglas L. Miller. 2008. "Bootstrap-Based Improvements for Inference with Clustered Errors." *Review of Economics and Statistics* 90 (3): 414–427.

Cameron, A. Colin, and Douglas L. Miller. 2015. "A Practitioner's Guide to Cluster-Robust Inference." *Journal of Human Resources* 50 (2): 317–72.

Campbell, Donald T., and Julian C. Stanley. 1963. *Experimental and Quasi-Experimental Designs for Research.* Houghton Mifflin Company.

Candes, Emmanuel, and Terence Tao. 2007. "The Dantzig Selector: Statistical Estimation When P Is Much Larger than N." *The Annals of Statistics* 35 (6): 2313–2351.

Card, David. 1995. "Using Geographic Variation in College Proximity to Estimate the Return to Schooling." In *Aspects of Labour Market Behavior: Essays in Honour of John Vanderkamp,* edited by Linos Christophides, E. K. Grant, and Robert Swidinsky, 201–222. University of Toronto Press.

Card, David, Stefano DellaVigna, and Ulrike Malmendier. 2011. "The Role of Theory in Field Experiments." *Journal of Economic Perspectives* 25, no. 3 (September): 39–62.

Card, David, David S. Lee, Zhuan Pei, and Andrea Weber. 2015. "Inference on Causal Effects in a Generalized Regression Kink Design." *Econometrica* 83 (6): 2453–2483.

Carneiro, Pedro, James J. Heckman, and Edward E. Vytlacil. 2010. "Evaluating Marginal Policy Changes and the Average Effect of Treatment for Individuals at the Margin." *Econometrica* 78 (1): 377–394.

Carneiro, Pedro, Michael Lokshin, and Nithin Umapathi. 2017. "Average and Marginal Returns to Upper Secondary Schooling in Indonesia." *Journal of Applied Econometrics* 32:16–36.

Cattaneo, Matias D. 2018. "Multi-valued Treatment Effects." In *The New Palgrave Dictionary of Economics,* 9208–9210. Palgrave Macmillan UK.

Cattaneo, Matias D., Richard K. Crump, Max H. Farrell, and Yingjie Feng. 2024. "On Binscatter." *American Economic Review* 114, no. 5 (May): 1488–1514.

Cattaneo, Matias D., Yingjie Feng, and Rocío Titiunik. 2021. "Prediction Intervals for Synthetic Control Methods." *Journal of the American Statistical Association* 116 (536): 1865–1880.

Cattaneo, Matias D., Brigham R. Frandsen, and Rocío Titiunik. 2015. *Journal of Causal Inference* 3 (1): 1–24.

Cattaneo, Matias D., Nicolas Idrobo, and Rocío Titiunik. 2024. *A Practical Introduction to Regression Discontinuity Designs: Extensions.* Cambridge University Press, March.

Cattaneo, Matias D., Nicolás Idrobo, and Rocío Titiunik. 2020. *A Practical Introduction to Regression Discontinuity Designs: Foundations.* Elements in Quantitative and Computational Methods for the Social Sciences. Cambridge University Press.

Cattaneo, Matias D., Michael Jansson, and Xinwei Ma. 2018. "Manipulation Testing Based on Density Discontinuity." *The Stata Journal* 18 (1): 234–261.

Cattaneo, Matias D., Michael Jansson, and Xinwei Ma. 2020. "Simple Local Polynomial Density Estimators." *Journal of the American Statistical Association* 115, no. 531 (September): 1449–1455.

Cattaneo, Matias D., Luke Keele, and Rocío Titiunik. 2023. "Covariate Adjustment in Regression Discontinuity Designs." In *Handbook of Matching and Weighting Adjustments for Causal Inference,* 1st, edited by José R. Zubizarreta, Elizabeth A. Stuart, Dylan S. Small, and Paul R. Rosenbaum, 16. Chapman / Hall/CRC.

Cattaneo, Matias D., Luke Keele, Rocío Titiunik, and Gonzalo Vazquez-Bare. 2016. "Interpreting Regression Discontinuity Designs with Multiple Cutoffs." *Journal of Politics* 78 (4): 1229–1248.

Cattaneo, Matias D., Luke Keele, Rocío Titiunik, and Gonzalo Vazquez-Bare. 2021. "Extrapolating Treatment Effects in Multi-Cutoff Regression Discontinuity Designs." *Journal of the American Statistical Association* 116 (536): 1941–1952.

Cattaneo, Matias D., and Rocío Titiunik. 2022. "Regression Discontinuity Designs." *Annual Review of Economics* 14:1–48.

Cattaneo, Matias D., Rocío Titiunik, and Gonzalo Vazquez-Bare. 2016. "Inference in Regression Discontinuity Designs Under Local Randomization." *The Stata Journal* 16 (2): 331–367.

Cattaneo, Matias D., Rocío Titiunik, and Gonzalo Vazquez-Bare. 2017. "Comparing Inference Approaches for RD Designs: A Reexamination of the Effect of Head Start on Child Mortality." *Journal of Policy Analysis and Management* 36 (3): 643–681.

Cattaneo, Matias D., Rocío Titiunik, and Gonzalo Vazquez-Bare. 2019. "Power Calculations for Regression-Discontinuity Designs." *Stata Journal* 19 (1): 210–245.

Cattaneo, Matias D., Rocío Titiunik, and Gonzalo Vazquez-Bare. 2020. "Analysis of Regression-Discontinuity Designs with Multiple Cutoffs or Multiple Scores." *The Stata Journal* 20 (4): 866–891.

Cengiz, Doruk, Arindrajit Dube, Attila Lindner, and Ben Zipperer. 2019. "The Effect of Minimum Wages on Low-Wage Jobs." *Quarterly Journal of Economics* 134, no. 3 (May): 1405–1454.

Chaisemartin, Clément de. 2017. "Tolerating Defiance? Local Average Treatment Effects Without Monotonicity." *Quantitative Economics* 8 (2): 367–396.

Chaisemartin, Clément de, and Xavier D'Haultfœuille. 2017. "Fuzzy Differences-in-Differences." *Review of Economic Studies* 85, no. 2 (August): 999–1028.

Chaisemartin, Clément de, and Xavier D'Haultfœuille. 2020. "Two-Way Fixed Effects Estimators with Heterogeneous Treatment Effects." *American Economic Review* 110, no. 9 (September): 2964–2996.

Chaisemartin, Clément de, and Xavier D'Haultfœuille. 2022. "Two-Way Fixed Effects and Differences-in-Differences with Heterogeneous Treatment Effects: A Survey." *The Econometrics Journal* 26, no. 3 (June): C1–C30.

Chaisemartin, Clément de, and Xavier D'Haultfœuille. 2024. "Difference-in-Differences Estimators of Intertemporal Treatment Effects." *Review of Economics and Statistics* (February): 1–45.

Chaisemartin, Clément de, Xavier D'Haultfœuille, Félix Pasquier, Doulo Sow, and Gonzalo Vazquez-Bare. 2024. *Difference-in-Differences Estimators for Treatments Continuously Distributed at Every Period.* arXiv: 2201.06898.

Chaisemartin, Clément de, Xavier D'Haultfœuille, and Gonzalo Vazquez-Bare. 2024. "Difference-in-Difference Estimators with Continuous Treatments and No Stayers." *AEA Papers and Proceedings* 114 (May): 610–613.

Chaisemartin, Clément de, and Jaime Ramirez-Cuellar. 2024. "At What Level Should One Cluster Standard Errors in Paired and Small-Strata Experiments?" *American Economic Journal: Applied Economics* 16, no. 1 (January): 193–212.

Chang, Haoge, Joel A. Middleton, and P. M. Aronow. 2024. "Exact Bias Correction for Linear Adjustment of Randomized Controlled Trials." *Econometrica* 92 (5): 1503–1519.

Chang, Neng-Chieh. 2020. "Double/Debiased Machine Learning for Difference-in-Differences Models." *The Econometrics Journal* 23, no. 2 (February): 177–191.

Charness, G., and U. Gneezy. 2009. "Incentives to Exercise." *Econometrica* 77 (10): 909–931.

Chen, Jiafeng, and Jonathan Roth. 2023. "Logs with Zeros? Some Problems and Solutions." *Quarterly Journal of Economics* 139, no. 2 (December): 891–936.

Chernozhukov, Victor, Denis Chetverikov, Mert Demirer, Esther Duflo, Christian Hansen, and Whitney Newey. 2017. "Double/Debiased/Neyman Machine Learning of Treatment Effects." *American Economic Review* 107, no. 5 (May): 261–265.

Chernozhukov, Victor, Denis Chetverikov, Mert Demirer, Esther Duflo, Christian Hansen, Whitney Newey, and James Robins. 2018. "Double/Debiased Machine Learning for Treatment and Structural Parameters." *The Econometrics Journal* 21 (1): C1–C68.

Chernozhukov, Victor, Mert Demirer, Esther Duflo, and Iván Fernández-Val. 2025. "Fisher-Schultz Lecture: Generic Machine Learning Inference on Heterogenous Treatment Effects in Randomized Experiments, with an Application to Immunization in India." *Econometrica* 3:1121–1164.

Chernozhukov, Victor, and Christian Hansen. 2006. "Instrumental Quantile Regression Inference for Structural and Treatment Effect Models." *Journal of Econometrics* 132, no. 2 (June): 491–525.

Chernozhukov, Victor, and Christian Hansen. 2008. "The Reduced Form: A Simple Approach to Inference with Weak Instruments." *Economics Letters* 100 (1): 68–71.

Chernozhukov, Victor, Christian Hansen, Nathan Kallus, Martin Spindler, and Vasilis Syrgkanis. 2024. *Applied Causal Inference Powered by ML and AI.* arXiv: 2403.02467.

Chernozhukov, Victor, Christian Hansen, and Martin Spindler. 2015. "Valid Post-Selection and Post-Regularization Inference: An Elementary, General Approach." *Annual Review of Economics* 7:649–688.

Chernozhukov, Victor, Kaspar Wüthrich, and Yinchu Zhu. 2021. "An Exact and Robust Conformal Inference Method for Counterfactual and Synthetic Controls." *Journal of the American Statistical Association* 116 (536): 1849–1864.

Chetty, Raj, John N. Friedman, Nathaniel Hilger, Emmanuel Saez, Diane Whitmore Schanzenbach, and Danny Yagan. 2011. "How Does Your Kindergarten Classroom Affect Your Earnings? Evidence from Project Star." *Quarterly Journal of Economics* 126, no. 4 (November): 1593–1660.

Chetty, Raj, Nathaniel Hendren, and Lawrence F. Katz. 2016. "The Effects of Exposure to Better Neighborhoods on Children: New Evidence from the Moving to Opportunity Experiment." *American Economic Review* 106, no. 4 (April): 855–902.

Chetverikov, Denis. 2024. *Tuning parameter selection in econometrics.* arXiv: 2405.03021.

Chetverikov, Denis, Zhipeng Liao, and Victor Chernozhukov. 2021. "On Cross-Validated Lasso in High Dimensions." *Annals of Statistics* 49 (3): 1300–1317.

Chong, Alberto, Isabelle Cohen, Erica Field, Eduardo Nakasone, and Maximo Torero. 2016. "Iron Deficiency and Schooling Attainment in Peru." *American Economic Journal: Applied Economics* 8, no. 4 (October): 222–255.

Christensen, Garret, Jeremy Freese, and Edward Miguel. 2019. "Pre-analysis Plans." In *Transparent and Reproducible Social Science Research: How to Do Open Science,* 1st ed., 99–119. University of California Press.

Christensen, Garret S., and Edward Miguel. 2016. *Transparency, Reproducibility, and the Credibility of Economics Research.* Working Paper, Working Paper Series 22989. National Bureau of Economic Research, December.

Chyn, Eric, Brigham Frandsen, and Emily Leslie. Forthcoming. "Examiner and Judge Designs in Economics: A Practitioner's Guide." *Journal of Economic Literature* 10, no. 10 (January): 1–74.

Cilliers, Jacobus, Oeindrila Dube, and Bilal Siddiqi. 2015. "The White-Man Effect: How Foreigner Presence Affects Behavior in Experiments." Economic Experiments in Developing Countries, *Journal of Economic Behavior & Organization* 118:397–414.

Clarke, Damian. 2017. *Estimating Difference-in-Differences in the Presence of Spillovers.* MPRA Paper 81604. University Library of Munich, Germany, September.

Clarke, Damian, Nicolás Lillo Bustos, and Kathya Tapia-Schythe. 2026. "Estimating Intergenerational Returns to Medical Care: New Evidence from At-Risk Newborns." *Journal of Public Economics* 256:105597.

Clarke, Damian, Daniel Pailañir, Susan Athey, and Guido Imbens. 2024. "On Synthetic Difference-in-Differences and Related Estimation Methods in Stata." *Stata Journal: Promoting Communications on Statistics and Stata* 24 (4): 557–598.

Clarke, Damian, and Kathya Tapia Schythe. 2022. "Implementing the Panel Event Study." *The Stata Journal* 21 (4): 853–884.

Clarke, Paul S., and Frank Windmeijer. 2012. "Instrumental Variable Estimators for Binary Outcomes." *Journal of the American Statistical Association* 107 (500): 1638–1652.

Clingingsmith, David, Asim Ijaz Khwaja, and Michael Kremer. 2009. "Estimating the Impact of The Hajj: Religion and Tolerance in Islam's Global Gathering." *Quarterly Journal of Economics* 124, no. 3 (August): 1133–1170.

Cochran, William G., and Donald B. Rubin. 1973. "Controlling Bias in Observational Studies: A Review." *Sankhyā: The Indian Journal of Statistics, Series A (1961-2002)* 35 (4): 417–446.

Cohen, J. 1988. *Statistical Power Analysis for the Behavioral Sciences.* 2nd ed. Routledge.

Conley, Timothy G., and Christopher R. Taber. 2011. "Inference with "Difference in Differences" with a Small Number of Policy Changes." *Review of Economics and Statistics* 93 (1): 113–125.

Cook, Thomas D. 2018. "Twenty-Six Assumptions That Have to Be Met If Single Random Assignment Experiments Are to Warrant 'Gold Standard' Status: A Commentary on Deaton and Cartwright." Randomized Controlled Trials and Evidence-based Policy: A Multidisciplinary Dialogue, *Social Science & Medicine* 210:37–40.

Cornelissen, Thomas, Christian Dustmann, Anna Raute, and Uta Schönberg. 2016. "From LATE to MTE: Alternative Methods for the Evaluation of Policy Interventions." SOLE/EALE conference issue 2015, *Labour Economics* 41:47–60.

Cornelissen, Thomas, Christian Dustmann, Anna Raute, and Uta Schönberg. 2018. "Who Benefits from Universal Child Care? Estimating Marginal Returns to Early Child Care Attendance." *Journal of Political Economy* 126 (6): 2356–2409.

Cragg, John G., and Stephen G. Donald. 1993. "Testing Identifiability and Specification in Instrumental Variable Models." *Econometric Theory* 9 (2): 222–240.

Crépon, Bruno, Esther Duflo, Marc Gurgand, Roland Rathelot, and Philippe Zamora. 2013. "Do Labor Market Policies Have Displacement Effects? Evidence from a Clustered Randomized Experiment." *Quarterly Journal of Economics* 128, no. 2 (April): 531–580.

Crump, Richard K., V. Joseph Hotz, Guido W. Imbens, and Oscar A. Mitnik. 2009. "Dealing with Limited Overlap in Estimation of Average Treatment Effects." *Biometrika* 96 (1): 187–199.

Currie, Janet, Henrik Kleven, and Esmée Zwiers. 2020. "Technology and Big Data Are Changing Economics: Mining Text to Track Methods." *AEA Papers and Proceedings* 110 (May): 42–48.

Dahl, Gordon B., and Enrico Moretti. 2008. "The Demand for Sons." *Review of Economic Studies* 75, no. 4 (October): 1085–1120.

Davey, Calum, Alexander M. Aiken, Richard J. Hayes, and James R. Hargreaves. 2015. "Re-Analysis of Health and Educational Impacts of a School-Based Deworming Programme in Western Kenya: A Statistical Replication of a Cluster Quasi-Randomized Stepped-Wedge Trial." *International Journal of Epidemiology* 44, no. 5 (October): 1581–1592.

Davison, A. C., and D. V. Hinkley. 1997. *Bootstrap Methods and Their Application.* Cambridge University Press.

Dawid, P. 1979. "Conditional Independence in Statistical Theory." *Journal of the Royal Statistical Society. Series B (Methodological)* 41 (1): 1–31.

Deaton, Angus. 1985. "Panel Data from Time Series of Cross-Sections." *Journal of Econometrics* 30 (1): 109–126.

Deaton, Angus. 1997. *The Analysis of Household Surveys – A Microeconometric Approach to Development Policy.* Johns Hopkins University Press.

Deaton, Angus. 2009. *Instruments of Development: Randomization in the Tropics, and the Search for the Elusive Keys to Economic Development.* Working Paper, Working Paper Series 14690. National Bureau of Economic Research, January.

Deaton, Angus. 2010. "Instruments, Randomization, and Learning About Development." *Journal of Economic Literature* 48 (2): 424–455.

Deaton, Angus. 2020. "Randomization in the Tropics Revisited, a Theme and Eleven Variations." In *Randomized Control Trials in the Field of Development: A Critical Perspective,* edited by Florent Bédécarrats, Isabelle Guérin, and François Roubaud. (Oxford, 2020; online edn, Oxford Academic, 22 Oct. 2020). Oxford: Oxford University Press, September.

Deaton, Angus, and Nancy Cartwright. 2018. "Understanding and Misunderstanding Randomized Controlled Trials." Randomized Controlled Trials and Evidence-based Policy: A Multidisciplinary Dialogue, *Social Science & Medicine* 210:2–21.

Dehejia, Rajeev. 2005. "Practical Propensity Score Matching: A Reply to Smith and Todd." Experimental and Non-experimental Evaluation of Economic Policy and Models, *Journal of Econometrics* 125 (1): 355–364.

Dehejia, Rajeev, Cristian Pop-Eleches, and Cyrus Samii. 2021. "From Local to Global: External Validity in a Fertility Natural Experiment." *Journal of Business & Economic Statistics* 39 (1): 217–243.

Dehejia, Rajeev, and Sadek Wahba. 1999. "Causal Effects in Nonexperimental Studies: Reevaluating the Evaluation of Training Programs." *Journal of the American Statistical Association* 94 (448): 1053–1062.

Dehejia, Rajeev, and Sadek Wahba. 2002. "Propensity Score-Matching Methods for Nonexperimental Causal Studies." *Review of Economics and Statistics* 84, no. 1 (February): 151–161.

Dell, Melissa. 2010. "The Persistent Effects of Peru's Mining Mita." *Econometrica* 78 (6): 1863–1903.

Dell, Melissa. 2015. "Trafficking Networks and the Mexican Drug War." *American Economic Review* 105 (6): 1738–1779.

Dell, Melissa. 2024. *Deep Learning for Economists.* Working Paper, Working Paper Series 32768. National Bureau of Economic Research, August.

Deryugina, Tatyana. 2017. "The Fiscal Cost of Hurricanes: Disaster Aid Versus Social Insurance." *American Economic Journal: Economic Policy* 9, no. 3 (August): 168–198.

Diamond, Alexis, and Jasjeet S. Sekhon. 2013. "Genetic Matching for Estimating Causal Effects: A General Multivariate Matching Method for Achieving Balance in Observational Studies." *Review of Economics and Statistics* 95, no. 3 (July): 932–945.

Diaz, Juan Jose, and Sudhanshu Handa. 2006. "An Assessment of Propensity Score Matching as a Nonexperimental Impact Estimator: Evidence from Mexico's PROGRESA Program." *Journal of Human Resources* 41 (2): 319–345.

Díaz, Juan, Tomás Rau, and Jorge Rivera. 2015. "A Matching Estimator Based on a Bilevel Optimization Problem." *Review of Economics and Statistics* 97, no. 4 (October): 803–812.

DiTraglia, Francis J., Camilo García-Jimeno, Rossa O'Keeffe-O'Donovan, and Alejandro Sánchez-Becerra. 2023. "Identifying Causal Effects in Experiments with Spillovers and Non-compliance." *Journal of Econometrics* 235:1589–1624.

Djogbenou, Antoine A., James G. MacKinnon, and Morten Ørregaard Nielsen. 2019. "Asymptotic Theory and Wild Bootstrap Inference with Clustered Errors." *Journal of Econometrics* 212 (2): 393–412.

Dobbie, W. S., and R. G. Fryer. 2015. "The Medium-Term Impacts of High-Achieving Charter Schools." *Journal of Political Economy* 123 (5): 985–1037.

Dobbie, Will, Jacob Goldin, and Crystal S. Yang. 2018. "The Effects of Pretrial Detention on Conviction, Future Crime, and Employment: Evidence from Randomly Assigned Judges." *American Economic Review* 108, no. 2 (February): 201–240.

Doksum, K. 1974. "Empirical Probability Plots and Statistical Inference for Nonlinear Models in the Two-Sample Case." *Annals of Statistics* 2 (2): 267–277.

Donald, Stephen G, and Kevin Lang. 2007. "Inference with Difference-in-Differences and Other Panel Data." *Review of Economics and Statistics* 89, no. 2 (May): 221–233.

Dong, Yingying. 2015. "Regression Discontinuity Applications with Rounding Errors in the Running Variable." *Journal of Applied Econometrics* 30 (3): 422–446.

Dong, Yingying. 2018. "Alternative Assumptions to Identify LATE in Fuzzy Regression Discontinuity Designs." *Oxford Bulletin of Economics and Statistics* 80 (5): 1020–1027.

Dong, Yingying, and Arthur Lewbel. 2015. "Identifying the Effect of Changing the Policy Threshold in Regression Discontinuity Models." *Review of Economics and Statistics* 97, no. 5 (December): 1081–1092.

Donoho, David L. 1994. "Statistical Estimation and Optimal Recovery." *The Annals of Statistics* 22 (1): 238–270.

Doudchenko, Nikolay, and Guido W. Imbens. 2016. *Balancing, Regression, Difference-In-Differences and Synthetic Control Methods: A Synthesis.* Working Paper, Working Paper Series 22791. National Bureau of Economic Research, October.

Doyle, Joseph J. 2007. "Child Protection and Child Outcomes: Measuring the Effects of Foster Care." *The American Economic Review* 97 (5): 1583–1610.

Drèze, Jean. 2018. "Evidence, Policy and Politics: A Commentary on Deaton and Cartwright." Randomized Controlled Trials and Evidence-Based Policy: A Multidisciplinary Dialogue, *Social Science & Medicine* 210:45–47.

Duflo, Esther. 2006. "Field Experiments in Development Economics." In *Advances in Economics and Econometrics: Theory and Applications, Ninth World Congress,* edited by Richard Blundell, Whitney K. Newey, and Torsten Persson, 2:322–348. Econometric Society Monographs. Cambridge University Press.

Duflo, Esther. 2017. "The Economist as Plumber." *American Economic Review* 107, no. 5 (May): 1–26.

Duflo, Esther, Rachel Glennerster, and Michael Kremer. 2007. "Chapter 61 Using Randomization in Development Economics Research: A Toolkit." In *Handbook of Development Economics,* edited by T. Paul Schultz and John A. Strauss, 4:3895–3962. Handbook of Development Economics. Elsevier.

Duflo, Esther, and Emmanuel Saez. 2003. "The Role of Information and Social Interactions in Retirement Plan Decisions: Evidence from a Randomized Experiment." *Quarterly Journal of Economics* 118, no. 3 (August): 815–842.

Dupas, P., and E. Miguel. 2017. "Chapter 1 - Impacts and Determinants of Health Levels in Low-Income Countries." In *Handbook of Economic Field Experiments,* edited by Abhijit Banerjee and Esther Duflo, 2:3–93. Handbook of Economic Field Experiments. North-Holland.

Ebenstein, Avraham. 2009. "When Is the Local Average Treatment Close to the Average? Evidence from Fertility and Labor Supply." *Journal of Human Resources* 44 (4): 955–975.

Efron, B., and D. Feldman. 1991. "Compliance as an Explanatory Variable in Clinical Trials." *Journal of the American Statistical Association* 86 (413): 9–17.

Efron, Bradley. 1979. "Bootstrap Methods: Another Look at the Jackknife." *Annals of Statistics* 7 (1): 1–26.

Efron, Bradley, and Robert J. Tibshirani. 1986. "Bootstrap Methods for Standard Errors, Confidence Intervals, and Other Measures of Statistical Accuracy." *Statistical Science* 1 (1): 54–75.

Efron, Bradley, and Robert J. Tibshirani. 1993. *An Introduction to the Bootstrap.* Chapman & Hall.

Egger, Dennis, Johannes Haushofer, Edward Miguel, Paul Niehaus, and Michael Walker. 2022. "General Equilibrium Effects of Cash Transfers: Experimental Evidence from Kenya." *Econometrica* 90 (6): 2603–2643.

Eicker, Friedhelm. 1967. "Limit Theorems for Regressions with Unequal and Dependent Errors." Edited by Lucien M. Le Cam and Jerzy Neyman. *Berkeley Symposium on Mathematical Statistics and Probability* 5 (1): 59–82.

Fan, Jianqing. 1992. "Design-Adaptive Nonparametric Regression." *Journal of the American Statistical Association* 87 (420): 998–1004.

Fan, Jianqing, and Irene Gijbels. 1992. "Variable Bandwidth and Local Linear Regression Smoothers." *Annals of Statistics,* 2008–2036.

Fan, Jianqing, and Irene Gijbels. 1996. *Local Polynomial Modelling and Its Applications.* Vol. 66. Monographs on Statistics and Applied Probability. Chapman / Hall/CRC.

Farrell, Max H. 2015. "Robust Inference on Average Treatment Effects with Possibly More Covariates than Observations." *Journal of Econometrics* 189 (1): 1–23.

Fechner, G. T. 1860. *Element der Psychophysik.* Breitkopf / Härtel.

Ferman, Bruno, and Cristine Pinto. 2021. "Synthetic Controls with Imperfect Pretreatment Fit." *Quantitative Economics* 12 (4): 1197–1221.

Ferman, Bruno, Cristine Pinto, and Vitor Possebom. 2020. "Cherry Picking with Synthetic Controls." *Journal of Policy Analysis and Management* 39 (2): 510–532.

Filmer, Deon, and Lant H. Pritchett. 2001. "Estimating Wealth Effects Without Expenditure Data—Or Tears: An Application to Educational Enrollments in States of India." *Demography* 38 (1): 115–132.

Finkelstein, Amy, Sarah Taubman, Bill Wright, Mira Bernstein, Jonathan Gruber, Joseph P. Newhouse, Heidi Allen, Katherine Baicker, and Oregon Health Study Group. 2012. "The Oregon Health Insurance Experiment: Evidence from the First Year." *Quarterly Journal of Economics* 127, no. 3 (July): 1057–1106.

Firpo, Sergio. 2007. "Efficient Semiparametric Estimation of Quantile Treatment Effects." *Econometrica* 75, no. 1 (January): 259–276.

Fisher, R. A. 1925. *Statistical Methods for Research Workers.* Oliver & Boyd.

Fisher, R. A. 1926. "The Arrangement of Field Experiments." *Journal of the Ministry of Agriculture* 33:503–515.

Fisher, R. A. 1935. *The Design of Experiments.* Oliver & Boyd.

Foster, Dylan J., and Vasilis Syrgkanis. 2023. "Orthogonal Statistical Learning." *Annals of Statistics* 51 (3): 879–908.

Frandsen, Brigham, Lars Lefgren, and Emily Leslie. 2023. "Judging Judge Fixed Effects." *American Economic Review* 113, no. 1 (January): 253–277.

Frandsen, Brigham R. 2017. "Party Bias in Union Representation Elections: Testing for Manipulation in the Regression Discontinuity Design when the Running Variable is Discrete." In *Regression Discontinuity Designs,* 38:281–315. Advances in Econometrics. Leeds: Emerald Publishing Limited.

Frandsen, Brigham R., Markus Frölich, and Blaise Melly. 2012. "Quantile Treatment Effects in the Regression Discontinuity Design." *Journal of Econometrics* 168 (2): 382–395.

Freedman, D. A. 1981. "Bootstrapping Regression Models." *Annals of Statistics* 9 (6): 1218–1228.

Freedman, David A. 2008. "On Regression Adjustments to Experimental Data." *Advances in Applied Mathematics* 40 (2): 180–193.

Freyaldenhoven, Simon, Christian Hansen, and Jesse M. Shapiro. 2019. "Pre-event Trends in the Panel Event-Study Design." *American Economic Review* 109, no. 9 (September): 3307–3338.

Frölich, Markus. 2004. "Finite-Sample Properties of Propensity-Score Matching and Weighting Estimators." *Review of Economics and Statistics* 86 (1): 77–90.

Frölich, Markus, and Martin Huber. 2019. "Including Covariates in the Regression Discontinuity Design." *Journal of Business & Economic Statistics* 37 (4): 736–748.

Frölich, Markus, and Blaise Melly. 2013. "Unconditional Quantile Treatment Effects Under Endogeneity." *Journal of Business & Economic Statistics* 31 (3): 346–357.

Fryer, Jr., Roland G., and Steven D. Levitt. 2013. "Testing for Racial Differences in the Mental Ability of Young Children." *American Economic Review* 103, no. 2 (April): 981–1005.

Fuhr, Jonathan, Philipp Berens, and Dominik Papies. 2024. *Estimating Causal Effects with Double Machine Learning – A Method Evaluation.*

Gallego, Francisco A., Cristian Larroulet Philippi, and Andrea Repetto. 2024. "What's Behind Her Smile? Health, Looks, and Self-Esteem." *American Economic Journal: Applied Economics* 16, no. 2 (April): 359–388.

Ganong, Peter, and Simon Jäger. 2014. *A Permutation Test and Estimation Alternatives for the Regression Kink Design.* IZA Discussion Papers 8282. Institute for the Study of Labor (IZA), June.

Gardner, John. 2022. *Two-stage differences in differences.* arXiv: 2207.05943.

Geisser, S. 1975. "The Predictive Sample Reuse Method with Applications." *Journal of the American Statistical Association* 70 (350): 320–328.

Gelman, Andrew, and Guido W. Imbens. 2019. "Why High-Order Polynomials Should Not Be Used in Regression Discontinuity Designs." *Journal of Business & Economic Statistics* 37 (3): 447–456.

Gentzkow, Matthew, Bryan Kelly, and Matt Taddy. 2019. "Text as Data." *Journal of Economic Literature* 57, no. 3 (September): 535–574.

Gerber, Alan S., and Neil Malhotra. 2008. "Publication Bias in Empirical Sociological Research: Do Arbitrary Significance Levels Distort Published Results?" *Sociological Methods and Research* 37 (1): 3–30.

Gertler, P., James J. Heckman, R. Pinto, A. Zanolini, C. Vermeersch, S. Walker, S. M. Chang, and S. Grantham-McGregor. 2014. "Labor Market Returns to an Early Childhood Stimulation Intervention in Jamaica." *Science* 344 (6187): 998–1001.

Gilchrist, Duncan Sheppard, and Emily Glassberg Sands. 2016. "Something to Talk About: Social Spillovers in Movie Consumption." *Journal of Political Economy* 124 (5): 1339–1382.

Glennerster, R. 2017. "Chapter 5 - The Practicalities of Running Randomized Evaluations: Partnerships, Measurement, Ethics, and Transparency." In *Handbook of Field Experiments,* edited by Abhijit Banerjee and Esther Duflo, 1:175–243. Handbook of Economic Field Experiments. North-Holland.

Glennerster, Rachel, and Shawn Powers. 2014. "Balancing Risk and Benefit: Ethical Tradeoffs in Running Randomized Evaluations." In *Handbook of Professional Economic Ethics,* edited by George DeMartino. Oxford University Press.

Glennerster, Rachel, and Kudzai Takavarasha. 2013. *Running Randomized Evaluations: A Practical Guide.* Princeton University Press.

Gold, David, Johannes Lederer, and Jing Tao. 2020. "Inference for High-Dimensional Instrumental Variables Regression." *Journal of Econometrics* 217 (1): 79–111.

Goldsmith-Pinkham, Paul, and Guido W. Imbens. 2013. "Social Networks and the Identification of Peer Effects." *Journal of Business & Economic Statistics* 31, no. 3 (July): 253–264.

Goldsmith-Pinkham, Paul, Isaac Sorkin, and Henry Swift. 2020. "Bartik Instruments: What, When, Why, and How." *American Economic Review* 110, no. 8 (August): 2586–2624.

Goodman-Bacon, Andrew. 2021. "Difference-in-Differences with Variation in Treatment Timing." Themed Issue: Treatment Effect 1, *Journal of Econometrics* 225 (2): 254–277.

Gruber, Jonathan. 1994. "The Incidence of Mandated Maternity Benefits." *American Economic Review* 84 (3): 622–641.

Haaland, Ingar, Christopher Roth, and Johannes Wohlfart. 2023. "Designing Information Provision Experiments." *Journal of Economic Literature* 61, no. 1 (March): 3–40.

Hahn, Jinyong. 1998. "On the Role of the Propensity Score in Efficient Semiparametric Estimation of Average Treatment Effects." *Econometrica* 66 (2): 315–331.

Hahn, Jinyong, Petra Todd, and Wilbert Van der Klaauw. 2001. "Identification and Estimation of Treatment Effects with a Regression-Discontinuity Design." *Econometrica* 69 (1): 201–209.

Hamad, Rita, David F. Collin, and David H. Rehkopf. 2020. "Difference-in-Differences in the Time of Cholera: A Gentle Introduction for Social Epidemiologists." *Current Epidemiology Reports* 7 (4): 260–267.

Hansen, Ben B. 2004. "Full Matching in an Observational Study of Coaching for the SAT." *Journal of the American Statistical Association* 99 (467): 609–618.

Hansen, Benjamin. 2015. "Punishment and Deterrence: Evidence from Drunk Driving." *American Economic Review* 105, no. 4 (April): 1581–1617.

Hansen, Bruce. 2022. *Econometrics*. Princeton University Press.

Hardle, W., and E. Mammen. 1993. "Comparing Nonparametric Versus Parametric Regression Fits." *Annals of Statistics* 21 (4): 1926–1947.

Härdle, Wolfgang. 1990. *Applied Nonparametric Regression*. Econometric Society Monographs. Cambridge University Press.

Hastie, Trevor, Robert Tibshirani, and Jerome Friedman. 2017. *The Elements of Statistical Learning: Data Mining, Inference, and Prediction*. Springer Series in Statistics.

Heckman, James, and Rodrigo Pinto. 2024. "Econometric Causality: The Central Role of Thought Experiments." *Journal of Econometrics* 243 (1): 105719.

Heckman, James J. 1990. "Varieties of Selection Bias." *American Economic Review* 80 (2): 313–318.

Heckman, James J. 1996a. "Comment: Identification of Causal Effects Using Instrumental Variables." *Journal of the American Statistical Association* 91 (434): 459–462.

Heckman, James J. 1996b. "Randomization as an Instrumental Variable." *Review of Economics and Statistics* 78 (2): 336–341.

Heckman, James J. 1997. "Instrumental Variables: A Study of Implicit Behavioral Assumptions Used in Making Program Evaluations." *Journal of Human Resources* 32 (3): 441–462.

Heckman, James J. 2001. "Micro Data, Heterogeneity, and the Evaluation of Public Policy: Nobel Lecture." *Journal of Political Economy* 109 (4): 673–748.

Heckman, James J. 2010. "Building Bridges between Structural and Program Evaluation Approaches to Evaluating Policy." *Journal of Economic Literature* 48, no. 2 (June): 356–98.

Heckman, James J., and Bo E. Honoré. 1990. "The Empirical Content of the Roy Model." *Econometrica* 58 (5): 1121–1149.

Heckman, James J., Hidehiko Ichimura, Jeffrey Smith, and Petra Todd. 1998. "Characterizing Selection Bias Using Experimental Data." *Econometrica* 66 (5): 1017–1098.

Heckman, James J., Hidehiko Ichimura, and Petra Todd. 1997. "Matching as an Econometric Evaluation Estimator: Evidence from Evaluating a Job Training Programme." *Review of Economic Studies* 64 (4): 605–654.

Heckman, James J., Hidehiko Ichimura, and Petra Todd. 1998. "Matching as an Econometric Evaluation Estimator." *Review of Economic Studies* 65 (2): 261–294.

Heckman, James J., Robert J. Lalonde, and Jeffrey A. Smith. 1999. "Chapter 31 – The Economics and Econometrics of Active Labor Market Programs." In *Handbook of Labor Economics*, edited by Orley C. Ashenfelter and David Card, 3:1865–2097. Elsevier.

Heckman, James J., Lance Lochner, and Christopher Taber. 1998. "General-Equilibrium Treatment Effects: A Study of Tuition Policy." *American Economic Review* 88 (2): 381–386.

Heckman, James J., Jeffrey Smith, and Nancy Clements. 1997. "Making the Most Out of Programme Evaluations and Social Experiments: Accounting for Heterogeneity in Programme Impacts." *Review of Economic Studies* 64 (4): 487–535.

Heckman, James J., and Jeffrey A. Smith. 1999. "The Pre-programme Earnings Dip and the Determinants of Participation in a Social Programme. Implications for Simple Programme Evaluation Strategies." *The Economic Journal* 109 (457): 313–348.

Heckman, James J., and Christopher Taber. 2010. "Roy Model." In *Microeconometrics,* edited by Steven N. Durlauf and Lawrence E. Blume, 221–228. Palgrave Macmillan UK.

Heckman, James J., Sergio Urzua, and Edward J. Vytlacil. 2006. "Understanding Instrumental Variables in Models with Essential Heterogeneity." *Review of Economics and Statistics* 88 (3): 389–432.

Heckman, James J., and Sergio Urzúa. 2010. "Comparing IV with Structural Models: What Simple IV Can and Cannot Identify." *Journal of Econometrics* 156, no. 1 (May): 27–37.

Heckman, James J., and Edward J. Vytlacil. 1999. "Local Instrumental Variables and Latent Variable Models for Identifying and Bounding Treatment Effects." *Proceedings of the National Academy of Sciences* 96 (8): 4730–4734.

Heckman, James J., and Edward J. Vytlacil. 2001a. "Local instrumental variables." In *Nonlinear Statistical Modeling: Proceedings of the Thirteenth International Symposium in Economic Theory and Econometrics: Essays in Honor of Takeshi Amemiya,* edited by Cheng Hsiao, Kimio Morimune, and James L. Powell, 1–46. International Symposia in Economic Theory and Econometrics. Cambridge University Press.

Heckman, James J., and Edward J. Vytlacil. 2001b. "Policy-Relevant Treatment Effects." *American Economic Review* 91 (2): 107–111.

Heckman, James J., and Edward J. Vytlacil. 2005. "Structural Equations, Treatment Effects, and Econometric Policy Evaluation." *Econometrica* 73 (3): 669–738.

Heckman, James J., and Edward J. Vytlacil. 2007. "Chapter 71 Econometric Evaluation of Social Programs, Part II: Using the Marginal Treatment Effect to Organize Alternative Econometric Estimators to Evaluate Social Programs, and to Forecast their Effects in New Environments." In *Handbook of Econometrics,* edited by James J. Heckman and Edward E. Leamer, 6:4875–5143. Elsevier.

Hicks, Joan Hamory, Michael Kremer, and Edward Miguel. 2015. "Commentary: Deworming Externalities and Schooling Impacts in Kenya: A Comment on Aiken et al. (2015) and Davey et al. (2015)." *International Journal of Epidemiology* 44 (5): 1593–1596.

Hirano, Keisuke, and Jinyong Hahn. 2010. "Design of Randomized Experiments to Measure Social Interaction Effects." *Economics Letters* 106 (1): 51–53.

Hirano, Keisuke, and Guido W. Imbens. 2004. "The Propensity Score with Continuous Treatments." In *Applied Bayesian Modeling and Causal Inference from Incomplete-Data Perspectives,* Chap. 7, 73–84. John Wiley & Sons.

Hirano, Keisuke, Guido W. Imbens, and Geert Ridder. 2003. "Efficient Estimation of Average Treatment Effects Using the Estimated Propensity Score." *Econometrica* 71 (4): 1161–1189.

Holden, Kristian L. 2016. "Buy the Book? Evidence on the Effect of Textbook Funding on School-Level Achievement." *American Economic Journal: Applied Economics* 8, no. 4 (October): 100–127.

Holland, P. W. 1986. "Statistics and Causal Inference." *Journal of the American Statistical Association* 81 (396): 945–960.

Holm, Sture. 1979. "A Simple Sequentially Rejective Multiple Test Procedure." *Scandinavian Journal of Statistics* 6 (2): 65–70.

Horowitz, Joel L. 2001. "Chapter 52 – The Bootstrap." In *Handbook of Econometrics,* edited by James J. Heckman and Edward Leamer, 5:3159–3228. Elsevier.

Horowitz, Joel L. 2019. "Bootstrap Methods in Econometrics." *Annual Review of Economics* 11 (1): 193–224.

Horvitz, D. G., and D. J. Thompson. 1952. "A Generalization of Sampling Without Replacement from a Finite Universe." *Journal of the American Statistical Association* 47 (260): 663–685.

Hotz, V. Joseph, Guido W. Imbens, and Julie H. Mortimer. 2005. "Predicting the Efficacy of Future Training Programs Using Past Experiences at Other Locations." Experimental and non-experimental evaluation of economic policy and models, *Journal of Econometrics* 125 (1): 241–270.

Hsu, Louis. 1994. "Unbalanced Designs to Maximize Statistical Power in Psychotherapy Efficacy Studies." *Psychotherapy Research* 4 (2): 95–106.

Huber, Martin, Michael Lechner, and Conny Wunsch. 2013. "The Performance of Estimators Based on the Propensity Score." *Journal of Econometrics* 175 (1): 1–21.

Huber, Martin, and Giovanni Mellace. 2015. "Testing Instrument Validity for LATE Identification Based on Inequality Moment Constraints." *Review of Economics and Statistics* 97, no. 2 (May): 398–411.

Huber, Peter J. 1967. "The Behavior of Maximum Likelihood Estimates Under Nonstandard Conditions." Edited by Lucien M. Le Cam and Jerzy Neyman. *Berkeley Symposium on Mathematical Statistics and Probability* 5 (1): 221–233.

Hudgens, Michael G., and M. Elizabeth Halloran. 2008. "Toward Causal Inference with Interference." *Journal of the American Statistical Association* 103 (482): 832–842.

Hyytinen, Ari, Jaakko Meriläinen, Tuukka Saarimaa, Otto Toivanen, and Janne Tukiainen. 2018. "When Does Regression Discontinuity Design Work? Evidence from Random Election Outcomes." *Quantitative Economics* 9 (2): 1019–1051.

Iacus, Stefano M., Gary King, and Giuseppe Porro. 2011. "Multivariate Matching Methods That Are Monotonic Imbalance Bounding." *Journal of the American Statistical Association* 106 (493): 345–361.

Imai, Kosuke, Zhichao Jiang, and Anup Malani. 2021. "Causal Inference with Interference and Noncompliance in Two-Stage Randomized Experiments." *Journal of the American Statistical Association* 116 (534): 632–644.

Imai, Kosuke, and In Song Kim. 2021. "On the Use of Two-Way Fixed Effects Regression Models for Causal Inference with Panel Data." *Political Analysis* 29 (3): 405–415.

Imbens, Guido W. 2000. "The Role of the Propensity Score in Estimating Dose-Response Functions." *Biometrika* 87, no. 3 (September): 706–710.

Imbens, Guido W. 2004. "Nonparametric Estimation of Average Treatment Effects Under Exogeneity: A Review." *Review of Economics and Statistics* 86, no. 1 (February): 4–29.

Imbens, Guido W. 2010. "Better LATE Than Nothing: Some Comments on Deaton (2009) and Heckman and Urzua (2009)." *Journal of Economic Literature* 48 (2): 399–423.

Imbens, Guido W. 2015. "Matching Methods in Practice: Three Examples." *Journal of Human Resources* 50 (2): 373–419.

Imbens, Guido W. 2018. "Understanding and Misunderstanding Randomized Controlled Trials: A Commentary on Deaton and Cartwright." Randomized Controlled Trials and Evidence-Based Policy: A Multidisciplinary Dialogue, *Social Science & Medicine* 210:50–52.

Imbens, Guido W., and Joshua D. Angrist. 1994. "Identification and Estimation of Local Average Treatment Effects." *Econometrica* 62 (2): 467–475.

Imbens, Guido W., and Karthik Kalyanaraman. 2012. "Optimal Bandwidth Choice for the Regression Discontinuity Estimator." *Review of Economic Studies* 79 (3): 933–959.

Imbens, Guido W., and Michal Kolesár. 2016. "Robust Standard Errors in Small Samples: Some Practical Advice." *Review of Economics and Statistics* 98, no. 4 (October): 701–712.

Imbens, Guido W., and Donald B. Rubin. 1997a. "Bayesian Inference for Causal Effects in Randomized Experiments with Noncompliance." *Annals of Statistics* 25 (1): 305–327.

Imbens, Guido W., and Donald B. Rubin. 1997b. "Estimating Outcome Distributions for Compliers in Instrumental Variables Models." *Review of Economic Studies* 64 (4): 555–574.

Imbens, Guido W., and Donald B. Rubin. 2015. *Causal Inference for Statistics, Social, and Biomedical Sciences: An Introduction.* Cambridge University Press.

Imbens, Guido W., Donald B. Rubin, and Bruce I. Sacerdote. 2001. "Estimating the Effect of Unearned Income on Labor Earnings, Savings, and Consumption: Evidence from a Survey of Lottery Players." *American Economic Review* 91, no. 4 (September): 778–794.

Imbens, Guido W., and Stefan Wager. 2019. "Optimized Regression Discontinuity Designs." *Review of Economics and Statistics* 101, no. 2 (May): 264–278.

Imbens, Guido W., and Jeffrey M. Wooldridge. 2009. "Recent Developments in the Econometrics of Program Evaluation." *Journal of Economic Literature* 47 (1): 5–86.

Imbens, Guido W., and Tristan Zajonc. 2011. "Regression Discontinuity Designs with Multiple Forcing Variables." In *Essays on Causal Inference for Public Policy,* edited by Tristan Zajonc. Found in Chapter 2 of Doctoral dissertation, Harvard University. Permanent link: http://nrs.harvard.edu/urn-3:HUL.InstRepos:9368030. Harvard University.

Jacob, Brian A., and Lars Lefgren. 2004. "Remedial Education and Student Achievement: A Regression-Discontinuity Analysis." *Review of Economics and Statistics* 86 (1): 226–244.

Jiang, Liang, Xiaobin Liu, Peter C. B. Phillips, and Yichong Zhang. 2024. "Bootstrap Inference for Quantile Treatment Effects in Randomized Experiments with Matched Pairs." *Review of Economics and Statistics* 106, no. 2 (March): 542–556.

Jin, Ying, Zhimei Ren, and Emmanuel J. Candès. 2023. "Sensitivity Analysis of Individual Treatment Effects: A Robust Conformal Inference Approach." *Proceedings of the National Academy of Sciences* 120 (6): e2214889120.

Kahn-Lang, Ariella, and Kevin Lang. 2019. "The Promise and Pitfalls of Differences-in-Differences: Reflections on 16 and Pregnant and Other Applications." *Journal of Business & Economic Statistics* 0 (0): 1–14.

Kang, Hyunseung, and Guido W. Imbens. 2016. *Peer Encouragement Designs in Causal Inference with Partial Interference and Identification of Local Average Network Effects.* arXiv: 1609.04464.

Keane, Michael, and Timothy Neal. 2023. "Instrument Strength in IV Estimation and Inference: A Guide to Theory and Practice." *Journal of Econometrics* 235 (2): 1625–1653.

Keane, Michael P. 2010. "Structural vs. Atheoretic Approaches to Econometrics." Structural Models of Optimization Behavior in Labor, Aging, and Health, *Journal of Econometrics* 156 (1): 3–20.

Keele, Luke J., and Rocío Titiunik. 2015. "Geographic Boundaries as Regression Discontinuities." *Political Analysis* 23 (1): 127–155.

Kennedy, Edward H. 2023. "Towards Optimal Doubly Robust Estimation of Heterogeneous Causal Effects." *Electronic Journal of Statistics* 17 (2): 3008–3049.

Kennedy, Peter E. 2002. "Sinning in the Basement: What Are the Rules? The Ten Commandments of Applied Econometrics." *Journal of Economic Surveys* 16 (4): 569–589.

Kézdi, Gábor. 2004. "Robust Standard Error Estimation in Fixed-Effects Panel Models." *Hungarian Statistical Review,* Special number 9:95–116.

King, Gary, Emmanuela Gakidou, Nirmala Ravishankar, Ryan T. Moore, Jason Lakin, Manett Vargas, Martha María Téllez-Rojo, Juan Eugenio Hernández Ávila, Mauricio Hernández Ávila, and Héctor Hernández Llamas. 2007. "A 'Politically Robust' Experimental Design for Public Policy Evaluation, with Application to the Mexican Universal Health Insurance Program." *Journal of Policy Analysis and Management* 26:479–506.

Kitagawa, Toru. 2015. "A Test for Instrument Validity." *Econometrica* 83 (5): 2043–2063.

Kitagawa, Toru, and Aleksey Tetenov. 2018. "Who Should Be Treated? Empirical Welfare Maximization Methods for Treatment Choice." *Econometrica* 86 (2): 591–616.

Kleibergen, Frank. 2002. "Pivotal Statistics for Testing Structural Parameters in Instrumental Variables Regression." *Econometrica* 70 (5): 1781–1803.

Kleibergen, Frank, and Richard Paap. 2006. "Generalized Reduced Rank Tests Using the Singular Value Decomposition." *Journal of Econometrics* 133 (1): 97–126.

Kleinberg, Jon, Jens Ludwig, Sendhil Mullainathan, and Ziad Obermeyer. 2015. "Prediction Policy Problems." *American Economic Review* 105, no. 5 (May): 491–495.

Kleven, Henrik. 2016. "Bunching." *Annual Review of Economics* 8:435–464.

Kline, Patrick, and Christopher R. Walters. 2016. "Evaluating Public Programs with Close Substitutes: The Case of Head Start." *Quarterly Journal of Economics* 131, no. 4 (July): 1795–1848.

Koenker, Roger. 2005. *Quantile Regression.* Cambridge University Press.

Koenker, Roger, and Gilbert Bassett. 1978. "Regression Quantiles." *Econometrica* 46 (1): 33–50.

Korinek, Anton. 2023. "Generative AI for Economic Research: Use Cases and Implications for Economists." *Journal of Economic Literature* 61, no. 4 (January): 1281–1317.

Korting, Christina, Carl Lieberman, Jordan Matsudaira, Zhuan Pei, and Yi Shen. 2023. "Visual Inference and Graphical Representation in Regression Discontinuity Designs." *Quarterly Journal of Economics* 138, no. 3 (March): 1977–2019.

Kumar, Anil, and Che-Yuan Liang. 2024. "Labor Market Effects of Credit Constraints: Evidence from a Natural Experiment." *American Economic Journal: Economic Policy* 16, no. 3 (August): 1–26.

Künzel, S. R., J. S. Sekhon, P. J. Bickel, and B. Yu. 2019. "Metalearners for Estimating Heterogeneous Treatment Effects Using Machine Learning." *Proceedings of the National Academy of Sciences* 116 (10): 4156–4165.

Lai, Tze Leung, and Herbert Robbins. 1985. "Asymptotically Efficient Adaptive Allocation Rules." *Advances in Applied Mathematics* 6 (1): 4–22.

LaLonde, Robert J. 1986. "Evaluating the Econometric Evaluations of Training Programs with Experimental Data." *American Economic Review* 76 (4): 604–620.

Landais, Camille. 2015. "Assessing the Welfare Effects of Unemployment Benefits Using the Regression Kink Design." *American Economic Journal: Economic Policy* 7, no. 4 (November): 243–278.

Leamer, Edward E. 1978. *Specification Searches – Ad Hoc Inference with Nonexperimental Data.* John Wiley & Sons.

Leamer, Edward E. 1983. "Let's Take the Con Out of Econometrics." *American Economic Review* 73 (1): 31–43.

Leamer, Edward E. 2010. "Tantalus on the Road to Asymptopia." *Journal of Economic Perspectives* 24, no. 2 (June): 31–46.

Lechner, Michael. 2001. "Identification and Estimation of Causal Effects of Multiple Treatments Under the Conditional Independence Assumption." In *Econometric Evaluation of Labour Market Policies,* edited by Michael Lechner and Friedhelm Pfeiffer, 43–58. Physica-Verlag HD.

Lechner, Michael. 2002. "Some Practical Issues in the Evaluation of Heterogeneous Labour Market Programmes by Matching Methods." *Journal of the Royal Statistical Society. Series A (Statistics in Society)* 165 (1): 59–82.

Lechner, Michael. 2008. "A Note on the Common Support Problem in Applied Evaluation Studies." *Annales d'Économie et de Statistique,* nos. 91/92, 217–235.

Lee, David S. 2008. "Randomized Experiments from Non-random Selection in U.S. House Elections." The regression discontinuity design: Theory and applications, *Journal of Econometrics* 142 (2): 675–697.

Lee, David S., and David Card. 2008. "Regression Discontinuity Inference with Specification Error." The regression discontinuity design: Theory and applications, *Journal of Econometrics* 142 (2): 655–674.

Lee, David S., and Thomas Lemieux. 2010. "Regression Discontinuity Designs in Economics." *Journal of Economic Literature* 48 (2): 281–355.

Lee, David S., Justin McCrary, Marcelo J. Moreira, and Jack Porter. 2022. "Valid t-Ratio Inference for IV." *American Economic Review* 112, no. 10 (October): 3260–3290.

Lee, Myoung-Jae. 2008. *Micro-Econometrics for Policy, Program, and Treatment Effects.* Oxford University Press.

Lehmann, E. L. 1993. "The Fisher, Neyman-Pearson Theories of Testing Hypotheses: One Theory or Two?" *Journal of the American Statistical Association* 88 (424): 1242–1249.

Lehmann, E. L., and Joseph P. Romano. 2005. *Testing Statistical Hypotheses.* Springer.

Lehmann, Erich L. 1974. *Nonparametrics: Statistical Methods Based on Ranks.* Holden-Day.

Leung, Michael P. 2020. "Treatment and Spillover Effects Under Network Interference." *Review of Economics and Statistics* 102, no. 2 (May): 368–380.

Levitt, Steven D., and John A. List. 2009. "Field Experiments in Economics: The Past, the Present, and the Future." *European Economic Review* 53 (1): 1–18.

Levitt, Steven D., and John A. List. 2011. "Was There Really a Hawthorne Effect at the Hawthorne Plant? An Analysis of the Original Illumination Experiments." *American Economic Journal: Applied Economics* 3, no. 1 (January): 224–238.

Lewbel, Arthur. 2019. "The Identification Zoo: Meanings of Identification in Econometrics." *Journal of Economic Literature* 57, no. 4 (December): 835–903.

Li, Ker-Chau. 1989. "Honest Confidence Regions for Nonparametric Regression." *Annals of Statistics* 17 (3): 1001–1008.

Liang, Kung-Yee, and L. Zeger Scott. 1986. "Longitudinal Data Analysis Using Generalized Linear Models." *Biometrika* 73, no. 1 (April): 13–22.

Lin, Zhexiao, Peng Ding, and Fang Han. 2023. "Estimation Based on Nearest Neighbor Matching: From Density Ratio to Average Treatment Effect." *Econometrica* 91 (6): 2187–2217.

List, John A. 2011. "Why Economists Should Conduct Field Experiments and 14 Tips for Pulling One Off." *Journal of Economic Perspectives* 25, no. 3 (September): 3–16.

List, John A., and Imran Rasul. 2011. "Chapter 2 - Field Experiments in Labor Economics." In *Handbook of Labor Economics,* edited by Orley Ashenfelter and David Card, 4:103–228. Elsevier.

List, John A., Sally Sadoff, and Mathis Wagner. 2011. "So You Want to Run an Experiment, Now What? Some Simple Rules of Thumb for Optimal Experimental Design." *Experimental Economics* 14 (4): 439–457.

Liu, Lan, and Michael G. Hudgens. 2014. "Large Sample Randomization Inference of Causal Effects in the Presence of Interference." *Journal of the American Statistical Association* 109 (505): 288–301.

Liu, Licheng, Ye Wang, and Yiqing Xu. 2024. "A Practical Guide to Counterfactual Estimators for Causal Inference with Time-Series Cross-Sectional Data." *American Journal of Political Science* 68 (1): 160–176.

Liu, Regina Y. 1988. "Bootstrap Procedures Under Some Non-I.I.D. Models." *Annals of Statistics* 16 (4): 1696–1708.

Lochner, Lance, and Enrico Moretti. 2015. "Estimating and Testing Models with Many Treatment Levels and Limited Instruments." *Review of Economics and Statistics* 97, no. 2 (May): 387–397.

Ludwig, J., and D. L. Miller. 2000. "Does Head Start Improve Children's Life Chances? Evidence from a Regression Discontinuity Design." *Quarterly Journal of Economics* 122 (1): 159–208.

Ludwig, Jens, and Sendhil Mullainathan. 2023. *Machine Learning as a Tool for Hypothesis Generation.* Working Paper, Working Paper Series 31017. National Bureau of Economic Research, March.

Mackinnon, James, and Matthew Webb. 2017a. "Pitfalls When Estimating Treatment Effects Using Clustered Data." *Political Methodology* 24 (2): 20–31.

Mackinnon, James, and Matthew Webb. 2017b. "Wild Bootstrap Inference for Wildly Different Cluster Sizes." *Journal of Applied Econometrics* 32 (2): 233–254.

Mackinnon, James, and Matthew Webb. 2018. "The Wild Bootstrap for Few (Treated) Clusters." *The Econometrics Journal* 21 (2): 114–135.

MacKinnon, James G., Morten Ørregaard Nielsen, and Matthew D. Webb. 2022. "Cluster-Robust Inference: A Guide to Empirical Practice." *Journal of Econometrics* 232 (2): 272–299.

MacKinnon, James G., Morten Ørregaard Nielsen, and Matthew D. Webb. 2023. "Testing for the Appropriate Level of Clustering in Linear Regression Models." *Journal of Econometrics* 235 (2): 2027–2056.

MacKinnon, James G., and Matthew D. Webb. 2020. "Randomization Inference for Difference-Indifferences with Few Treated Clusters." *Journal of Econometrics* 218 (2): 435–450.

Maddala, G. S. 1983. *Limited-Dependent and Qualitative Variables in Econometrics.* Cambridge University Press.

Mammen, Enno. 1992. "Bootstrap, Wild Bootstrap, and Asymptotic Normality." *Probability Theory and Related Fields* 93 (4): 439–455.

Manning, Willard G., Joseph P. Newhouse, Naihua Duan, Emmett B. Keeler, and Arleen Leibowitz. 1987. "Health Insurance and the Demand for Medical Care: Evidence from a Randomized Experiment." *American Economic Review* 77 (3): 251–277.

Manski, Charles F. 1990. "Nonparametric Bounds on Treatment Effects." *American Economic Review* 80 (2): 319–323.

Manski, Charles F. 1993. "Identification of Endogenous Social Effects: The Reflection Problem." *The Review of Economic Studies* 60 (3): 531–542.

Manski, Charles F. 1994. "The Selection Problem." In *Advances in Econometrics: Sixth World Congress,* edited by Christopher A. Sims, 143–170. Econometric Society Monographs. Cambridge University Press.

Manski, Charles F. 2013. "Policy Analysis with Incredible Certitude." In *Public Policy in an Uncertain World,* 11–46. Harvard University Press.

Manski, Charles F., and John V. Pepper. 2018. "How Do Right-to-Carry Laws Affect Crime Rates? Coping with Ambiguity Using Bounded-Variation Assumptions." *Review of Economics and Statistics* 100, no. 2 (May): 232–244.

McCrary, Justin. 2008. "Manipulation of the Running Variable in the Regression Discontinuity Design: A Density Test." *Journal of Econometrics* 142, no. 2 (February): 698–714.

McKenzie, David. 2012. *A Pre-analysis Plan Checklist.* Accessed: 2025-03-08, October.

Meager, Rachael. 2019. "Understanding the Average Impact of Microcredit Expansions: A Bayesian Hierarchical Analysis of Seven Randomized Experiments." *American Economic Journal: Applied Economics* 11 (1): 57–91.

Melguizo, Tatiana, Fabio Sanchez, and Tatiana Velasco. 2016. "Credit for Low-Income Students and Access to and Academic Performance in Higher Education in Colombia: A Regression Discontinuity Approach." *World Development* 80:61–77.

Mellon, Jonathan. 2024. "Rain, Rain, Go Away: 194 Potential Exclusion-Restriction Violations for Studies Using Weather as an Instrumental Variable." *American Journal of Political Science* n/a (n/a): 1–18.

Melly, Blaise, and Kaspar Wüthrich. 2017. "Local Quantile Treatment Effects." In *Handbook of Quantile Regression,* 1st ed., edited by Roger Koenker, Victor Chernozhukov, Xuming He, and Limin Peng, 145–164. Chapman / Hall/CRC.

Mercatanti, Andrea, and Fan Li. 2014. "Do Debit Cards Increase Household Spending? Evidence from a Semiparametric Causal Analysis of a Survey." *Annals of Applied Statistics* 8 (4): 2485–2508.

Meyersson, Erik. 2014. "Islamic Rule and the Empowerment of the Poor and Pious." *Econometrica* 82 (1): 229–269.

Miguel, E., C. Camerer, K. Casey, J. Cohen, K. M. Esterling, A. Gerber, R. Glennerster, et al. 2014. "Promoting Transparency in Social Science Research." *Science* 343, no. 6166 (January): 30–31.

Miguel, Edward, and Michael Kremer. 2004. "Worms: Identifying Impacts on Education and Health in the Presence of Treatment Externalities." *Econometrica* 72, no. 1 (January): 159–217.

Miller, Douglas L. 2023. "An Introductory Guide to Event Study Models." *Journal of Economic Perspectives* 37, no. 2 (May): 203–230.

Miller, Grant. 2008. "Women's Suffrage, Political Responsiveness, and Child Survival in American History." *Quarterly Journal of Economics* 123 (3): 1287–1327.

Millimet, Daniel L., and Rusty Tchernis. 2009. "On the Specification of Propensity Scores, with Applications to the Analysis of Trade Policies." *Journal of Business & Economic Statistics* 27 (3): 397–415.

Moffitt, Robert A. 2001. "Policy Interventions, Low-Level Equilibria, and Social Interactions." In *Social Dynamics,* edited by H. Peyton Young Steven N. Durlauf. The MIT Press, April.

Mogstad, Magne, Alexander Torgovitsky, and Christopher R. Walters. 2021. "The Causal Interpretation of Two-Stage Least Squares with Multiple Instrumental Variables." *American Economic Review* 111, no. 11 (November): 3663–3698.

Montiel Olea, José Luis, and Carolin Pflueger. 2013. "A Robust Test for Weak Instruments." *Journal of Business & Economic Statistics* 31 (3): 358–369.

Morduch, Jonathan. 2020. "The Disruptive Power of RCTs." In *Randomized Control Trials in the Field of Development: A Critical Perspective.* Oxford University Press, September.

Moreira, Marcelo J. 2003. "A Conditional Likelihood Ratio Test for Structural Models." *Econometrica* 71 (4): 1027–1048.

Moulton, Brent. 1986. "Random Group Effects and the Precision of Regression Estimates." *Journal of Econometrics* 32 (3): 385–397.

Mourifié, Ismael, and Yuanyuan Wan. 2017. "Testing Local Average Treatment Effect Assumptions." *The Review of Economics and Statistics* 99, no. 2 (May): 305–313.

Mullainathan, Sendhil, and Jann Spiess. 2017. "Machine Learning: An Applied Econometric Approach." *Journal of Economic Perspectives* 31, no. 2 (May): 87–106.

Muller, Seán M. 2015. "Causal Interaction and External Validity: Obstacles to the Policy Relevance of Randomized Evaluations." *World Bank Economic Review* 29, no. $suppl_1$ (April): S217–S225.

Mundlak, Yair. 1978. "On the Pooling of Time Series and Cross Section Data." *Econometrica* 46 (1): 69–85.

Munroe, Russell. 2010. *SIGNIFICANT (xkcd).* https://xkcd.com/882/ Accessed February 3, 2017.

Muralidharan, Karthik, and Paul Niehaus. 2017. "Experimentation at Scale." *Journal of Economic Perspectives* 31, no. 4 (November): 103–124.

Muralidharan, Karthik, and Nishith Prakash. 2013. *Cycling to School: Increasing Secondary School Enrollment for Girls in India.* NBER Working Papers 19305. National Bureau of Economic Research, August.

Murphy, Kevin P. 2012. *Machine Learning: A Probabilistic Perspective.* MIT Press.

Murphy, Kevin R., Brett Myors, and Allan Wollach. 2014. *Statistical Power Analysis.* Routledge.

Nadaraya, E. A. 1964. "On Estimating Regression." *Theory of Probability and Its Applications* 9 (1): 141–142.

Nelson, Charles R., and Richard Startz. 1990a. "Some Further Results on the Exact Small Sample Properties of the Instrumental Variable Estimator." *Econometrica* 58 (4): 967–976.

Nelson, Charles R., and Richard Startz. 1990b. "The Distribution of the Instrumental Variables Estimator and Its t-Ratio When the Instrument Is a Poor One." *Journal of Business* 63 (1): S125–S140.

Neumark, David. 2018. "Experimental Research on Labor Market Discrimination." *Journal of Economic Literature* 56, no. 3 (September): 799–866.

Neyman, Jerzy, and Egon Sharpe Pearson. 1933. "Ix. On the Problem of the Most Efficient Tests of Statistical Hypotheses." *Philosophical Transactions of the Royal Society of London. Series A, Containing Papers of a Mathematical or Physical Character* 231 (694–706): 289–337.

Nie, Xinkun, and Stefan Wager. 2020. "Quasi-Oracle Estimation of Heterogeneous Treatment Effects." *Biometrika* 107 (4): 1101–1116.

Noack, Cladia, and Chistoph Rothe. 2023. *Donut Regression Discontinuity Designs.* arXiv: 2308.14464.

O'Brien, Peter C. 1984. "Procedures for Comparing Samples with Multiple Endpoints." *Biometrics* 40, no. 4 (December): 1079–1087.

Olden, Andreas, and Jarle Møen. 2022. "The Triple Difference Estimator." *The Econometrics Journal* (March).

Olken, Benjamin A. 2015. "Promises and Perils of Pre-analysis Plans." *Journal of Economic Perspectives* 29 (3): 61–80.

Oreopoulos, Philip. 2006. "Estimating Average and Local Average Treatment Effects of Education When Compulsory Schooling Laws Really Matter." *American Economic Review* 96, no. 1 (March): 152–175.

Oreopoulos, Philip. 2011. "Why Do Skilled Immigrants Struggle in the Labor Market? A Field Experiment with Thirteen Thousand Resumes." *American Economic Journal: Economic Policy* 3, no. 4 (November): 148–171.

Otsu, Taisuke, and Yoshiyasu Rai. 2017. "Bootstrap Inference of Matching Estimators for Average Treatment Effects." *Journal of the American Statistical Association* 112 (520): 1720 1732.

Ozier, Owen. 2018. "The Impact of Secondary Schooling in Kenya." *Journal of Human Resources* 53 (1): 157–188.

Papay, John P., John B. Willett, and Richard J. Murnane. 2011. "Extending the Regression-Discontinuity Approach to Multiple Assignment Variables." *Journal of Econometrics* 161 (2): 203–207.

Pearl, Judea. 2009. "Causality: Models, Reasoning and Inference," 2nd ed. Cambridge University Press.

Pei, Zhuan, David S. Lee, David Card, and Andrea Weber. 2021. "Local Polynomial Order in Regression Discontinuity Designs." *Journal of Business & Economic Statistics* 40 (3): 1259–1267.

Porter, Catherine, and Danila Serra. 2020. "Gender Differences in the Choice of Major: The Importance of Female Role Models." *American Economic Journal: Applied Economics* 12, no. 3 (July): 226–254.

Porter, Jack. 2003. *Estimation in the Regression Discontinuity Model.* Working Paper. University of Wisconsin.

Powell, David. 2021. *The Labor Supply Consequences of the Opioid Crisis.* RAND Corporation.

Quidt, Jonathan de, Johannes Haushofer, and Christopher Roth. 2018. "Measuring and Bounding Experimenter Demand." *American Economic Review* 108, no. 11 (November): 3266–3302.

Rambachan, Ashesh, and Jonathan Roth. 2023. "A More Credible Approach to Parallel Trends." Rdad018, *Review of Economic Studies* (February).

Ravallion, Martin. 2020. "Should the Randomistas (Continue to) Rule?" In *Randomized Control Trials in the Field of Development: A Critical Perspective.* Oxford University Press, September.

Riaño, Juan Felipe, and Felipe Valencia Caicedo. 2024. "Collateral Damage: The Legacy of the Secret War in Laos." *Economic Journal* 134, no. 661 (January): 2101–2140.

Riley, Emma. 2024. "Resisting Social Pressure in the Household Using Mobile Money: Experimental Evidence on Microenterprise Investment in Uganda." *American Economic Review* 114, no. 5 (May): 1415–1447.

Robins, James M., Andrea Rotnitzky, and Mark van der Laan. 2000. "On Profile Likelihood: Comment." *Journal of the American Statistical Association* 95 (450): 477–482.

Robins, James M., Andrea Rotnitzky, and Lue Ping Zhao. 1994. "Estimation of Regression Coefficients When Some Regressors Are Not Always Observed." *Journal of the American Statistical Association* 89 (427): 846–866.

Romano, J. P., and M. Wolf. 2005a. "Exact and Approximate Stepdown Methods for Multiple Hypothesis Testing." *Journal of the American Statistical Association* 100 (469): 94–108.

Romano, J. P., and M. Wolf. 2005b. "Stepwise Multiple Testing as Formalized Data Snooping." *Econometrica* 73 (4): 1237–1282.

Romano, J. P., and M. Wolf. 2016. "Efficient Computation of Adjusted P-Values for Resampling-Based Stepdown Multiple Testing." *Statistics and Probability Letters* 113:38–40.

Romano, Joseph P., Azeem M. Shaikh, and Michael Wolf. 2010. "Hypothesis Testing in Econometrics." *Annual Review of Economics* 2:75–104.

Roodman, David, Morten Ørregaard Nielsen, James G. MacKinnon, and Matthew D. Webb. 2019. "Fast and Wild: Bootstrap Inference in Stata Using Boottest." *Stata Journal* 19 (1): 4–60.

Rosenbaum, Paul R. 1984. "From Association to Causation in Observational Studies: The Role of Tests of Strongly Ignorable Treatment Assignment." *Journal of the American Statistical Association* 79 (385): 41–48.

Rosenbaum, Paul R. 1991. "A Characterization of Optimal Designs for Observational Studies." *Journal of the Royal Statistical Society. Series B (Methodological)* 53 (3): 597–610.

Rosenbaum, Paul R. 2007. "Interference Between Units in Randomized Experiments." *Journal of the American Statistical Association* 102 (477): 191–200.

Rosenbaum, Paul R., and Donald B. Rubin. 1983. "The Central Role of the Propensity Score in Observational Studies for Causal Effects." *Biometrika* 70 (1): 41–55.

Rosenbaum, Paul R., and Donald B. Rubin. 1984. "Reducing Bias in Observational Studies Using Subclassification on the Propensity Score." *Journal of the American Statistical Association* 79 (387): 516–524.

Rosenbaum, Paul R., and Donald B. Rubin. 1985. "Constructing a Control Group Using Multivariate Matched Sampling Methods That Incorporate the Propensity Score." *The American Statistician* 39 (1): 33–38.

Rosenthal, Robert. 1979. "The 'File Drawer Problem' and Tolerance for Null Results." *Psychological Bulletin* 86 (3): 638–641.

Rosenzweig, Mark, and Kenneth I. Wolpin. 1980. "Testing the Quantity-Quality Fertility Model: The Use of Twins as a Natural Experiment." *Econometrica* 48 (1): 227–240.

Ross, Heather. 1970. "An Experimental Study of the Negative Income Tax." *Child Welfare* 49 (10): 562–569.

Roth, Alvin E. 1986. "Laboratory Experimentation in Economics." *Economics & Philosophy* 2 (2): 245–273.

Roth, Jonathan. 2022. "Pretest with Caution: Event-Study Estimates After Testing for Parallel Trends." *American Economic Review: Insights* 4, no. 3 (September): 305–322.

Roth, Jonathan, Pedro H. C. Sant'Anna, Alyssa Bilinski, and John Poe. 2023. "What's Trending in Difference-in-Differences? A Synthesis of the Recent Econometrics Literature." *Journal of Econometrics* 235 (2): 2218–2244.

Rothe, Christoph, and Sergio Firpo. 2019. "Properties of Doubly Robust Estimators When Nuisance Functions Are Estimated Nonparametrically." *Econometric Theory* 35 (5): 1048–1087.

Roy, A. D. 1951. "Some Thoughts on the Distribution of Earnings." *Oxford Economic Papers* 3, no. 2 (June): 135–146.

Rubin, Donald B. 1974. "Estimating Causal Effects of Treatments in Randomized and Non-randomized Studies." *Journal of Educational Psychology* 66:688–701.

Rubin, Donald B. 1975. "Bayesian Inference for Causality: The Importance of Randomization." *Proceedings of the Social Statistics Section of the American Statistical Association,* 233–239.

Rubin, Donald B. 1977. "Assignment to Treatment Group on the Basis of a Covariate." *Journal of Educational Statistics* 2 (1): 1–26.

Rubin, Donald B. 1978. "Bayesian Inference for Causal Effects: The Role of Randomization." *Annals of Statistics* 6:34–58.

Rubin, Donald B. 1980a. "Bias Reduction Using Mahalanobis-Metric Matching." *Biometrics* 36 (2): 293–298.

Rubin, Donald B. 1980b. "Randomization Analysis of Experimental Data: The Fisher Randomization Test Comment." *Journal of the American Statistical Association* 75 (371): 591–593.

Rubin, Donald B. 1986. "Comment: Which Ifs Have Causal Answers." *Journal of the American Statistical Association* 81 (396): 961–962.

Sacerdote, Bruce. 2001. "Peer Effects with Random Assignment: Results for Dartmouth Roommates." *Quarterly Journal of Economics* 116 (2): 681–704.

Samii, Cyrus, and Peter M. Aronow. 2012. "On Equivalencies Between Design-Based and Regression-Based Variance Estimators for Randomized Experiments." *Statistics & Probability Letters* 82 (2): 365–370.

Sant'Anna, Pedro H. C., and Jun Zhao. 2020. "Doubly Robust Difference-in-Differences Estimators." *Journal of Econometrics* 219 (1): 101–122.

Saretsky, Gary. 1972. "The OEO P.C. Experiment and the John Henry Effect." *The Phi Delta Kappan* 53 (9): 579–581.

Sarsons, Heather. 2015. "Rainfall and Conflict: A Cautionary Tale." *Journal of Development Economics* 115:62–72.

Sawa, Takamitsu. 1969. "The Exact Sampling Distribution of Ordinary Least Squares and Two-Stage Least Squares Estimators." *Journal of the American Statistical Association* 64 (327): 923–937.

Schmidheiny, Kurt, and Sebastian Siegloch. 2019. *On Event Studies and Distributed-Lags in Two-Way Fixed Effects Models: Identification, Equivalence, and Generalization.* IZA Discussion Papers 12079. Institute of Labor Economics (IZA).

Schmidheiny, Kurt, and Sebastian Siegloch. 2023. "On Event Studies and Distributed-Lags in Two-Way Fixed Effects Models: Identification, Equivalence, and Generalization." *Journal of Applied Econometrics* 38 (5): 695–713.

Schultz, T. Paul. 2004. "School Subsidies for the Poor: Evaluating the Mexican Progresa Poverty Program." *Journal of Development Economics* 74 (1): 199–250.

Sekhon, J. S., and R. Titiunik. 2017. "On Interpreting the Regression Discontinuity Design as a Local Experiment." In *Regression Discontinuity Designs,* 38:1–28. Advances in Econometrics. Emerald Publishing Limited.

Sekhon, Jasjeet S. 2009. "Opiates for the Matches: Matching Methods for Causal Inference." *Annual Review of Political Science* 12 (1): 487–508.

Sergio, Firpo, and Possebom Vitor. 2018. "Synthetic Control Method: Inference, Sensitivity Analysis and Confidence Sets." *Journal of Causal Inference* 6, no. 2 (September): 1–26.

Shadish, William R., Thomas D. Cook, and Donald T. Campbell. 2002. *Experimental and Quasi-Experimental Designs for Generalized Causal Inference.* Houghton, Mifflin.

Shen, Dennis, Peng Ding, Jasjeet Sekhon, and Bin Yu. 2023. "Same Root Different Leaves: Time Series and Cross-Sectional Methods in Panel Data." *Econometrica* 91:2125–2154.

Simmons, Joseph P., Leif D. Nelson, and Uri Simonsohn. 2011. "False-Positive Psychology: Undisclosed Flexibility in Data Collection and Analysis Allows Presenting Anything as Significant." *Psychological Science* 22 (11): 1359–1366.

Simonsen, Marianne, Lars Skipper, and Niels Skipper. 2016. "Price Sensitivity of Demand for Prescription Drugs: Exploiting a Regression Kink Design." *Journal of Applied Econometrics* 31 (2): 320–337.

Słoczyński, Tymon. 2022. "Interpreting OLS Estimands When Treatment Effects Are Heterogeneous: Smaller Groups Get Larger Weights." *The Review of Economics and Statistics* 104, no. 3 (May): 501–509.

Smith, Jeffrey A., and Petra Todd. 2005. "Does Matching Overcome Lalonde's Critique of Nonexperimental Estimators?" Experimental and non-experimental evaluation of economic policy and models, *Journal of Econometrics* 125 (1): 305–353.

Snow, John. 1855. *On the Mode of Communication of Cholera.* 2nd ed. John Churchill.

Snowberg, Erik, and Leeat Yariv. 2021. "Testing the Waters: Behavior Across Participant Pools." *American Economic Review* 111 (2): 687–719.

Sobel, Michael E. 2006. "What Do Randomized Studies of Housing Mobility Demonstrate?" *Journal of the American Statistical Association* 101 (476): 1398–1407.

Sommer, Alfred, and Scott L. Zeger. 1991. "On Estimating Efficacy from Clinical Trials." *Statistics in Medicine* 10 (1): 45–52.

Splawa-Neyman, Jerzy. 1923,1990. "On the Application of Probability Theory to Agricultural Experiments. Essay on Principles. Section 9." Translated and edited by D. M. Dabrowska and T. P. Speed from the Polish original, which appeared in Roczniki Nauk Rolniczych Tom X (1923) 1–51 (Annals of Agricultural Sciences), *Statistical Science* 5, no. 4 (November): 465–472.

Staiger, Douglas, and James H. Stock. 1997. "Instrumental Variables Regression with Weak Instruments." *Econometrica* 65 (3): 557–586.

Stein, Charles. 1956. "Inadmissibility of the Usual Estimator for the Mean of a Multivariate Normal Distribution." In *Proceedings of the Third Berkeley Symposium on Mathematical Statistics and Probability,* 1:197–206. University of California Press.

Stevenson, Betsey, and Justin Wolfers. 2006. "Bargaining in the Shadow of the Law: Divorce Laws and Family Distress." *Quarterly Journal of Economics* 121 (1): 267–288.

Stock, James, and Motohiro Yogo. 2005. "Testing for Weak Instruments in Linear IV Regression." In *Identification and Inference for Econometric Models,* edited by Donald W. K. Andrews, 80–108. Cambridge University Press.

Stock, James H., and Francesco Trebbi. 2003. "Retrospectives: Who Invented Instrumental Variable Regression?" *Journal of Economic Perspectives* 17, no. 3 (September): 177–194.

Storey, John D. 2002. "A Direct Approach to False Discovery Rates." *Journal of the Royal Statistical Society: Series B (Statistical Methodology)* 64 (3): 479–498.

Stuart, Elizabeth A. 2010. "Matching Methods for Causal Inference: A Review and a Look Forward." *Statistical Science* 25 (1): 1–21.

Sun, Liyang, and Sarah Abraham. 2021. "Estimating Dynamic Treatment Effects in Event Studies with Heterogeneous Treatment Effects." Themed Issue: Treatment Effect 1, *Journal of Econometrics* 225 (2): 175–199.

Taber, Christopher, and Rune Vejlin. 2020. "Estimation of a Roy/Search/Compensating Differential Model of the Labor Market." *Econometrica* 88 (3): 1031–1069.

Tchetgen, Tchetgen, Eric J., and Tyler J. VanderWeele. 2012. "On Causal Inference in the Presence of Interference." *Statistical Methods in Medical Research* 21 (1): 55–75.

Teerenstra, Steven, Sandra Eldridge, Maud Graff, Esther de Hoop, and George F. Borm. 2012. "A Simple Sample Size Formula for Analysis of Covariance in Cluster Randomized Trials." *Statistics in Medicine* 31 (20): 2169–2178.

Thistlethwaite, Donald L., and Donald T. Campbell. 1960. "Regression-Discontinuity Analysis: An Alternative to the Ex Post Facto Experiment." *Journal of Educational Psychology* 51 (6): 309–317.

Thornton, Rebecca L. 2008. "The Demand for, and Impact of, Learning HIV Status." *American Economic Review* 98, no. 5 (December): 1829–1863.

Trochim, William. 1984. *Research Design for Program Evaluation: The Regression-Discontinuity Approach.* Sage Publications.

Tymon Słoczyński, S. Derya Uysal, and Jeffrey M. Wooldridge. 2025. "Abadie's Kappa and Weighting Estimators of the Local Average Treatment Effect." *Journal of Business & Economic Statistics* 43 (1): 164–177.

Urquiola, Miguel, and Eric Verhoogen. 2009. "Class-Size Caps, Sorting, and the Regression-Discontinuity Design." *American Economic Review* 99 (1): 179–215.

Van Der Klaauw, Wilbert. 2008. "Regression–Discontinuity Analysis: A Survey of Recent Developments in Economics." *LABOUR* 22 (2): 219–245.

Varian, Hal R. 2014. "Big Data: New Tricks for Econometrics." *Journal of Economic Perspectives* 28, no. 2 (May): 3–28.

Vazquez-Bare, Gonzalo. 2023a. "Causal Spillover Effects Using Instrumental Variables." *Journal of the American Statistical Association* 118 (543): 1911–1922.

Vazquez-Bare, Gonzalo. 2023b. "Identification and Estimation of Spillover Effects in Randomized Experiments." *Journal of Econometrics* 237 (1): 105237.

Vilhuber, Lars. 2020. "Reproducibility and Replicability in Economics." Https://hdsr.mitpress.mit.edu/pub/fgpmpj11. *Harvard Data Science Review* 2, no. 4 (December).

Vivalt, Eva. 2020. "How Much Can We Generalize from Impact Evaluations?" *Journal of the European Economic Association* 18, no. 6 (September): 3045–3089.

Viviano, Davide, Kaspar Wuthrich, and Paul Niehaus. 2025. *A Model of Multiple Hypothesis Testing.* arXiv: 2104.13367.

Wager, Stefan, and Susan Athey. 2018. "Estimation and Inference of Heterogeneous Treatment Effects Using Random Forests." *Journal of the American Statistical Association* 113 (523): 1228–1242.

Wald, Abraham. 1940. "The Fitting of Straight Lines If Both Variables Are Subject to Error." *Annals of Mathematical Statistics* 11 (3): 284–300.

Watson, G. S. 1964. "Smooth Regression Analysis." *Sankhyā: The Indian Journal of Statistics, Series A* 26 (4): 359–372.

Webb, Matthew D. 2023. "Reworking Wild Bootstrap-Based Inference for Clustered Errors." *Canadian Journal of Economics/Revue canadienne d'économique* 56 (3): 839–858.

Westfall, Peter H., and S. Stanley Young. 1993. *Resampling-Based Multiple Testing: Examples and Methods for p-Value Adjustment.* John Wiley & Sons.

White, Halbert. 1980. "A Heteroskedasticity-Consistent Covariance Matrix Estimator and a Direct Test for Heteroskedasticity." *Econometrica* 48 (4): 817–838.

Wong, Vivian C., Peter M. Steiner, and Thomas D. Cook. 2013. "Analyzing Regression-Discontinuity Designs with Multiple Assignment Variables: A Comparative Study of Four Estimation Methods." *Journal of Educational and Behavioral Statistics* 38 (2): 107–141.

Wooldridge, Jeffrey M. 2021. *Two-Way Fixed Effects, the Two-Way Mundlak Regression, and Difference-in-Differences Estimators.* Technical report https://dx.doi.org/10.2139/ssrn.3906345. Available at SSRN, August.

Wooldridge, Jeffrey M. 2023. "Simple Approaches to Nonlinear Difference-in-Differences with Panel Data." *The Econometrics Journal* 26, no. 3 (August): C31–C66.

Wright, Philip G. 1928. *The Tariff on Animal and Vegetable Oils.* Macmillan.

Wu, C. F. J. 1986. "Jackknife, Bootstrap and Other Resampling Methods in Regression Analysis." *Annals of Statistics* 14 (4): 1261–1295.

Young, Alwyn. 2019. "Channeling Fisher: Randomization Tests and the Statistical Insignificance of Seemingly Significant Experimental Results." *Quarterly Journal of Economics* 134, no. 2 (May): 557–598.

Zelen, Marvin. 1979. "A New Design for Randomized Clinical Trials." *New England Journal of Medicine* 300, no. 22 (May): 1242–1245.

Zhao, Zhong. 2004. "Using Matching to Estimate Treatment Effects: Data Requirements, Matching Metrics, and Monte Carlo Evidence." *Review of Economics and Statistics* 86 (1): 91–107.

Ziliak, Stephen T., and Deirdre N. McCloskey. 2008. *The Cult of Statistical Significance: How the Standard Error Costs Us Jobs, Justice, and Lives.* University of Michigan Press.

Zizzo, Daniel John. 2010. "Experimenter Demand Effects in Economic Experiments." *Experimental Economics* 13 (1): 75–98.

Zou, H. 2006. "The Adaptive Lasso and Its Oracle Properties." *Journal of the American Statistical Association* 101 (476): 1418–1429.

Zubizarreta, José R., Elizabeth A. Stuart, Dylan S. Small, and Paul R. Rosenbaum. 2023. *Handbook of Matching and Weighting Adjustments for Causal Inference.* 1st ed. CRC Press.

Index

Page numbers followed by an *f* denote a figure; *t* denotes a table.

Publisher contact:
The MIT Press
Massachusetts Institute of Technology
77 Massachusetts Avenue, Cambridge, MA 02139
mitpress.mit.edu

EU Authorised Representative:
Easy Access System Europe, Mustamäe tee 50,
10621 Tallinn, Estonia
gpsr.requests@easproject.com

Printed by Integrated Books International,
United States of America